Critical Medical Anthropology

Merrill Singer
Hispanic Health Council

and

Hans Baer
University of Arkansas at Little Rock

Critical Approaches in the Health Social Sciences Series
Series Editor: Ray H. Elling

Baywood Publishing Company, Inc.
AMITYVILLE, NEW YORK

AKS1795

Library of Congress Catalog Number 94-39810

ISBN: 0-89503-124-8 (Cloth)

Library of Congress Cataloging-in-Publication Data

Singer, Merrill.
    Critical medical anthropology / Merrill Singer and Hans Baer.
        p.   cm. - - (Critical approaches in the health social sciences series) (Political economy of health care series)
    Includes bibliographical references (p.   ) and index.
    ISBN 0-89503-124-8 (cloth). - - ISBN 0-89503-150-7 (paper)
    1. Medical anthropology.   I. Baer, Hans, 1944- . II. Title.
III. Series.   IV. Series: Political economy of health care series.
GN296.S56   1995
306.4'61- -dc20   94-39810
                                                                          CIP

Dedication

We dedicate this book to the students and colleagues with whom we share the vision that great progressive change is possible and probably closest at hand when it seems most distant.

Preface

This book, the culmination of over ten years of shared work by the authors, seeks to contribute to the effort to re-orient medical anthropology by means of a political economic contextualization of its field of study and application, and by way of a re-focus on power and inequality as central explanatory factors. In this volume, we have pulled together in one place many of the papers we have written as part of the effort to build a critical medical anthropology. All of these have been updated and in some cases considerably expanded. Through this effort we hope to offer a work that will clearly lay out the perspective and work of critical medical anthropology. While it is our hope that this book will be of interest to many anthropologists as well as other social scientists, health care providers, and public health professionals (including those who will find much to disagree with in it), we have written this book with a special concern that it be of use to undergraduate and graduate students. It is the interest of these students in becoming part of the effort to build a critical approach, especially students in medical anthropology programs around the country, that has offered the greatest gratification to us over the years. Some of these students we have gotten to know well, others we have met only briefly at conferences, forums, and campus lectures. When they tell us the impact critical medical anthropology has had on their lives and their careers, we feel that we already have achieved our objective.

Acknowledgments

We deeply wish to acknowledge the true support of our many anthropology colleagues who share with us the title of critical medical anthropologist, as well as those in other subfields of anthropology, in our health social sciences, and in health care and public health who see the world in a similar critical way. We greatly value our friendships and professional relations with these colleagues. Though titles may vary, the struggle is a common one. Especially, in this regard, we thank Ray Elling, editor of the book series in which this volume appears, for his many years of friendship and support. Most of us are uncertain if we ever make a difference in this world. Through his effort to always stay true to his principles, Ray Elling has made a difference. Also, we extend warm thanks to Bobbi Olszewski for her production work on the book and the entire crew at Baywood Publishing Company for the effort put into bringing out *Critical Medical Anthropology* in a timely fashion.

Several of the chapters to follow were written especially for this volume, others are expansions of a series of articles the authors have published on critical medical anthropology since the mid-1980s. For allowing us to include revised versions here, the authors gratefully acknowledge and thank the journals and books in which the following earlier versions of several of the chapters were first published:

Hans Baer, Prophets and Advisors in Black Spiritual Churches: Therapy, Palliative, or Opiate, *Culture, Medicine and Psychiatry, 5*:145-170, 1981.

Hans Baer, The Drive for Professionalization in British Osteopathy, *Social Science and Medicine, 19*:717-724, 1984.

Hans Baer, The American Dominative Medical System As a Reflection of Social Relations in the Larger Society, *Social Science and Medicine, 28*(11):1103-1112, 1989.

Hans Baer, Towards a Critical Medical Anthropology of Health-Related Issues in Socialist-Oriented Societies, *Medical Anthropology, 11*(2):181-194, 1989.

Hans Baer, Kerr-McGee and the NRC: From Indian Country to Silkwood to Gore, *Social Science and Medicine, 30*(2):237-248, 1990.

Hans Baer, How Critical Can Clinical Anthropology Be? *Medical Anthropology, 15*(3):299-317, 1993.

Merrill Singer, Cure, Care and Control: An Ectopic Encounter with Biomedical Obstetrics, in *Encounter with Biomedicine: Case Studies in Medical Anthropology,* Hans Baer (ed.), Gordon and Breach Science Publishers, pp. 249-265, 1987.

Merrill Singer, Lani Davison, and Gina Gerdes, Culture, Critical Theory, and Reproductive Illness Behavior in Haiti, *Medical Anthropology Quarterly, 2*:370-385, 1988.

Merrill Singer, Postmodernism and Medical Anthropology: Words of Caution, *Medical Anthropology, 12*(3):289-304, 1990.

Merrill Singer, Freddie Valentín, Hans Baer, and Zhongke Jia, Why Does Juan Garcia Have a Drinking Problem?: The Perspective of Critical Medical Anthropology, *Medical Anthropology, 14*(1):77-108, 1992.

Merrill Singer, AIDS and the Health Crisis of the U.S. Urban Poor: The Perspective of Critical Medical Anthropology, *Social Science and Medicine, 39*(7):931-948, 1994.

Merrill Singer, Beyond the Ivory Tower: Critical Praxis in Medical Anthropology, *Medical Anthropology Quarterly, 9*(1), 1995.

TABLE OF CONTENTS

SECTION A: Orientation 1

Introduction 3

Chapter 1
Medical Anthropology and its Transformation 11

Chapter 2
The Critical Gaze 59

Chapter 3
Postmodernism Medical Anthropology: A Critique 113

SECTION B: The Macro-Social Level 133

Chapter 4
Health-Related Issues in Socialist-Oriented Societies:
Ideals, Contradictions, and Realities 135

Chapter 5
Studying Up: The Political Economy of
Nuclear Regulation 157

SECTION C: The Intermediate-Social Level 179

Chapter 6
The American Dominative Medical System as a Reflection of
Social Relations in the Larger Society 181

Chapter 7
AIDS and the Health Crisis of the U.S. Urban Poor 203

Chapter 8
The Drive for Professionalization in British Osteopathy 235

SECTION D: The Micro-Social Level 251

Chapter 9
Medical Hegemony, Biomedical Magic, and Folk Medicine:
Reproductive Illness among Haitian Women 253

Chapter 10
Prophets and Advisors in African-American
Spiritual Churches: Therapy, Palliative, or Opiate? 277

SECTION E: The Individual Level 299

Chapter 11
Confronting Juan García's Drinking Problem:
The Demedicalization of Alcoholism 301

Chapter 12
Cure, Care and Control:
Agency and Structure in the Clinical Encounter 329

SECTION F: Directions 349

Chapter 13
How Critical Can Clinical Anthropology Be? 351

Chapter 14
Critical Praxis in Medical Anthropology 371

Topic Index 393

Name Index 396

Section A:

Orientation

Introduction

As an academic discipline, mode of discourse, and domain of action, medical anthropology is both young and old. From the beginning, anthropology has had an interest in health, sickness, and healing in local context, as these are issues and concerns that encompass the most poignant of human experiences and aspirations. Consequently, these topics were on the minds of participants in some of the earliest anthropological field expeditions dating to before the First World War. However, the actual emergence of medical anthropology as a distinct and labeled sector within the larger discipline is relatively recent. In a sense, contemporary medical anthropology can be traced to a lunch meeting at the Washington Hilton on December 2, 1967. Today, the Society for Medical Anthropology, a direct product of that meeting, is one of the largest sections within the American Anthropological Association, while health-related issues have become a major area of study among anthropologists in the United Kingdom, various countries on the European continent, Latin America, and elsewhere.

Anthropology has long maintained a relationship, varying in character and depth, with that most prominent and imposing brand of healing, the health care system we have come to call scientific or biomedicine. In Firth's evaluation, this perduring relationship has had many twists and turns, including occasional "periods of collaboration, cross fertilisation of ideas and common enthusiasms" [1, p. 237]. And this has been especially true of the branch of the discipline that claims health and healing as constituting its special domain of research, the field that has been inescapably marked by this relationship in its very title: medical anthropology.

For some, the often penetrating intimacy of the biomedicine/medical anthropology relationship is not especially problematic. Biomedicine has proven its metal in life and death issues as a science and praxis worthy of emulation, hence its social respectability, elite stature, and diffusion internationally. Indeed, anthropologists working in far flung corners of the globe report a demand for biomedical cure, even among peoples actively engaged in vital ethnomedical traditions. And even folk healers who daily enter into trance to query spirit beings, concoct all manner of magical potions, and construct curious looking protective talismans in ministering to their clients, have been quick to recognize the healing power of biomedicine and either attempt to usurp its imagery or refer patients to its practitioners for supplemental treatment. In the estimation of its advocates and admirers, scientific medicine can claim great gains in healing the sick, producing a broad decline in mortality in the Western world especially, and in eliminating infectious diseases that have caused pain and death from time immemorium. Consequently, for many anthropologists biomedicine has become "*the* reality through the lens of which the rest of the world's cultural versions are seen, compared, and judged" [2, p. 4]. Moreover,

> Despite the cultural relativism that is usually considered essential to anthropology, medical anthropologists generally have been reluctant to question the privileged epistemological position of scientific medicine [3 p. 115].

While some medical anthropologists continue to call for a deeper, more thoroughgoing integration with medicine, seeing it as setting the standard for relevance within the discipline, in recent years doubts have begun to surface. This apprehension has had various expressions and has been voiced by anthropologists who embrace differing perspectives. On the one hand, there has emerged a fear of the medicalization of medical anthropology, a discomfort with the expansion of medical jurisdiction over many aspects of social life and experience including social science. Kapferer laments that medical anthropology now "incorporates Western ideological medical assumptions in the routine of its practice," and as a result, the discipline "is oriented in its very work to give a medical significance to diverse human practices" [4, p. 429]. For example, there are medical anthropologists who study folk healers so as to judge the efficacy of their practice in biomedical terms [5]. Prominent medical anthropologists, like Carol Browner, Bernard Ortiz De Montellano, and Arthur Rubel [6], in fact, have devised a methodology for the cross-cultural study of ethnomedicine using scientific medicine to provide "universalistic units of measurement" to compare and contrast healing systems. These researchers argue,

> We do not idealize bioscience as the exclusive means by which understandings should be gained in the field of ethnomedicine, but we do want to demonstrate that *it offers productive anchoring referents* from which to launch cross-cultural comparative studies of human physiological processes and emic perceptions of them [6, p. 689, emphasis added].

Similarly, in a recent examination of folk medical illnesses, Ronald Simons and Charles Hughes commit themselves to the difficult task of fitting a host of so-called culture bound syndomes, like Latah (characterized by a vulgar and exaggerated reaction to surprise) from Malaysia and Indonesia and Koro (fear of the complete retraction of the penis into the body) from Asia, into the nosology of mental illnesses officially recognized by the American Psychiatric Association and codified in the (frequently revised) *Diagnostic and Statistical Manual of Mental Disorders,* [7]. In this undertaking, Latah is incorporated into the familiar realm of psychiatric discourse as a type of "Dissociative Disorder" of the "Atypical" subtype, a label used to include "individuals who appear to have a Dissociative Disorder but do not satisfy the criteria for a specific Dissociative Disorder" [quoted in 7, p. 112]. Koro, in this approach, is interpreted as a form of Conversion Disorder, although because of the tremendous fear it engenders in sufferers "it might also be appropriate to add Panic Disorder" or even Atypical Somatoform Disorder [7, p. 193].

The elevation of biomedical understanding to the status of objective reality implied in efforts of this sort has caused considerable debate in a discipline that prides itself on its cross-cultural awareness, sensitivity and relativity. One expression of discomfort in this regard is a growing concern with the medicalization of the discipline [8-10]. Often this anti-medicalism is expressed in the form of a radical phenomenology that seeks to eluciate sufferer experience independent of biomedical categorization or even diagnosis.

In addition to the anti-medicalization approach, a second critique of medical anthropology and its relationship with biomedicine has grown in recent years. Sharing aspects of the anti-medicalization perspective, and not always clearly distinguished from it by participants in and observers of the discipline, this other critique draws upon the insights of the political economy of health tradition from outside of anthropology. Unlike its radical phenomenological cousin, this approach understands biomedicine not *solely* as a powerful system with important social control functions in contemporary society, but more broadly in terms of its relationship with the capitalist world economic system. Since Marx and Gramsci, it has been recognized that dominant institutions and their understandings of reality tend to legitimize, rationalize, and reproduce the dominant relations of society. In adopting a supportive or subservient position vis-a-vis biomedicine, this other critique argues, medical anthropology becomes not only an instrument for the medicalization of social life and culture, but also, like biomedicine, an unintended agent of capitalist hegemony and a tag-along handmaiden of global imperialism.

The term critical medical anthropology has for several years been used by adherents of both oppositional approaches described above. These have hung together, fellow travelers with a shared passport, joined together by their common critique of medicalization, despite recognized differences and occasional sparring during anthropology conferences and in the anthropology literature. The authors of this book, coiners of the term critical medical anthropology, have been and remain strong advocates of the political economic approach within medical anthropology, although not, as the radical phenomenologists have suggested, a political economic approach that narrows the focus of its analysis to macro-systems to the neglect of micro-relationships or even sufferer experiences and struggles. Nor do we seek to construct, as some colleagues outside of critical medical anthropology sometimes suppose, a perspective that is unmindful of the complexities of biomedicine (e.g., its diverse expressions cross-culturally, its internal conflicts within a given society or across medical specialties, and its inclusion of individuals of diverse commitments and ideologies) or the non-political economic (e.g., cultural, social, ecological) mediations of health and healing.

The purpose of this book is to provide an introduction and overview of critical medical anthropology (CMA) as we see it. By this, we mean a critical medical anthropology that emphasizes the importance of political and economic forces, including the exercise of power, in shaping health, disease, illness experience, and health care. In our efforts to build a critical medical anthropology, we seek to move the subdiscipline away from its service sector subordination to biomedicine (which is not to say, away from collaboration with health care providers) toward a more holistic understanding of the causes of sickness, the classist, racist, and sexist characteristics of biomedicine as a hegemonic system, the interrelationship of medical systems with political structures, the contested character of provider patient relations, and the localization of suffer experience and action within their encompassing political-economic contexts. These aspects of the critical approach are explored here using data collected by the authors during field and applied work in various settings primarily in the United States but in England, Germany, and Haiti as well.

In light of recent reactionary efforts to "de-Vietnamize" anthropology (i.e., to shed the political conscientization that occurred as a result of the mass protests against the U.S. war in Viet Nam), it is important to note that CMA was born within the disquitude of the post-Vietnam War period. The lead author, Merrill Singer, began college in 1968 at the height of the anti-war movement, having already entered into progressive political activisim as a high school student. Singer's undergraduate education, at both a community college and a state university, consisted of an (at times) uneasy blend of anti-war marches, work as a sometimes full- sometimes part-time boycott organizer for the United Farm Workers Union, involvement as a co-founder of a community free clinic, cooperative living with a colorful band of fellow dissidents in both urban and rural communes, and studies initially in sociology but quickly giving way to anthropology because of its global orientation. Interest in medical anthropology began during graduate work at the University of Utah but was not consolidated until after graduation during a post-doctoral fellowship at the Center for Family Research, George Washington University Medical School. An institute of the Department of Psychiatry, at the time the Center focused on family factors in drinking and the transgenerational transmission of drinking problems. Working for a year in a medical school allowed Singer the chance to observe medical education at close range. The post-doctorate also afforded an opportunity to read extensively in the literatures of political economy of health, medical anthropology, and drinking behavior and to carry out a study of the treatment of alcohol-related problems among Christian Science practitioners. These experiences served to fix his identity as a medical anthropologist. During the next two years as a visiting assistant professor in the Department of Anthropology at American University, he taught various courses including medical anthropology and carried out a study among alcohol detoxification patients at Washington Hospital. He also directed a graduate student field school on research in medical anthropology that focused on sufferer experience of hypoglycemia. A second post-doctorate at the University of Connecticut Health Center beginning in 1982 added to his experience in a medical setting and provided the support for a study of the treatment of drinking-related problems at a Puerto Rican spiritist healing center.

As part of this post-graduate training, Singer carried out a community placement at the Hispanic Health Council, a Puerto Rican community based organization that combines social science of health research with community health education, the testing of culturally targeted intervention strategies, and advocacy on behalf of the health and social needs of the Puerto Rican population of Hartford. He has continued to work at the Hispanic Health Council for the last twelve years, serving over time as

Coordinator of the Substance Abuse Unit, Director of Research, and Deputy Director of the organization. During this period, he has directed several studies of folk healing, alcohol use, drug use, and AIDS knowledge and risk behaviors, and coordinated multiorganization consortium projects on substance abuse prevention for children and adolescents, drug treatment for pregnant women, and AIDS prevention for IV drug users, sexual partners of IV drug users, cocaine users, prostitutes, Latino gay men, and Latino women. He has worked in collaboration with physicians, nurses, health social workers, and other health care workers in drug treatment, diagnostic assessment and early intervention of children of substance using mothers, the development of culturally targeted genetics counseling, and needle exchange. A faculty member of the Department of Community Medicine of the University of Connecticut, he has sought to blend teaching with the practical testing of critically influenced health promotion and community development projects.

Singer has authored numerous publications in anthropology, social science, and health journals, and with Ralph Bolton is editor of *Rethinking AIDS Prevention: Cultural Approaches* (Gordon and Breach, 1992).

Hans Baer comes from a German immigrant family from the Pittsburgh area. Although his undergraduate education, like that of his father, was in engineering and he worked for several years as an engineer, Baer switched to anthropology when he returned to college to attend graduate school. He has taught at Kearney State College, George Peabody College for Teachers, St. John's University, the University of Southern Mississippi, University of California, Berkeley, and, as a Fulbright Lecturer, at Humboldt University in the former German Democratic Republic. Currently, he is a Professor of Anthropology at the University of Arkansas at Little Rock.

Baer has conducted research in several areas of anthropology. In the area of religion, he conducted ethnographic research on the Hutterites of South Dakota, the Levites of Utah (a Mormon sect), and African-American Spiritual churches. He also has conducted research on osteopathy, chiropractic, and naturopathy in both the United States and Britain. In addition, he has researched African-American religious healing practices. Over the last several years, he has initiated a study of various aspects of social life in East Germany before and after reunification.

Baer is the author of *The Black Spritual Movement* (University of Tennessee Press, 1984) and *Recreating Utopia in the Desert* (State University of New York Press, 1988). He is the editor of *Encounters with Biomedicine* (Gordon and Breach, 1987), and, with Yvonne Jones, *African Americans in the South* (University of Georgia Press, 1992).

Collaboration between Singer and Baer began during graduate school at the University of Utah. Both authors conducted studies of break away groups from the Mormon church (Church of Jesus Christ of Latter-day Saints) and attempted to understand both the origin of Mormonism and schisms from this established sect in terms of the wider political economy of U.S. society. Based on Baer's study of African-American Spiritualism and Singer's dissertation work on the Black Hebrew Israelite Nation, they co-authored a paper together in 1981 that analyzed religion among African Americans in terms of alternative responses to racism and class structure in American society. A jointly authored book on this same topic, *African American Religion in the Twentieth Century*, was published in 1992 by the University of Tennessee Press. During their experiences as post-doctoral fellows during the early 1980s, the authors began to formulate their perspective on medical anthropology and subsequently worked together in editing several collections of journal articles on critical medical anthropology. They have co-authored a number of articles on critical medical anthropology as well. This volume, like their early work together, is a product of intellectual collaboration and close and rewarding personal friendship. By interweaving studies carried out independently by the two authors, and using this opportunity to jointly revise in both large and small ways some of the papers they have written separately and together over the last several years, this book represents a consolidated statement on the nature, objectives, contributions, and insights of critical medical anthropology as an emergent perspective in the health social sciences. Through the many months spent in writing and rewriting this volume together, the authors have learned anew, in the words of children's poet Hilaire Belloc in "Dedicatory Odel":

> Fom quiet homes and first beginnings
>   Out to the undiscovered ends,
> There is nothing worth the wear of winning,
>   But laughter and the love of friends.

The book is divided into six sections. The first section includes three chapters that seek to locate the emergence of critical medical anthropology historically and theoretically, present its critique, define its perspective, and contrast its approach with contemporary alternatives within the discipline. The next four sections are organized around a model, first introduced in 1986 [11], for understanding various levels of complexity within the health/treatment domain, beginning with the macrosocial level in the second section and continuing through the intermediate-social, micro-social and individual levels in the subsequent three sections. Each of these sections includes several chapters based on specific field studies carried out by the authors. Building on the theoretical discussions in prior chapters, the final section moves to the arena of application. The objective of the two chapters included in this section is to illustrate the potential of medical anthropology to navigate the rough waters of cooptation and develop an effective and consequential praxis.

REFERENCES

1. R. Firth, Social Anthropology and Medicine—A Personal Perspective, *Social Science and Medicine, 12B,* pp. 237-245, 1978.
2. A. Gaines and R. Hahn, Among the Physicians: Encounter, Exchange and Transformation, in *Physicians of Western Medicine,* R. Hahn and A. Gaines (eds.), pp. 3-22, D. Reidel Publishing Co., Dordrecht, 1985.
3. S. Murray and K. Payne, The Social Classification of AIDS in American Epidemiology, *Medical Anthropology, 10:*2-3, pp. 115-128, 1989.
4. B. Kapferer, Gramsci's Body and a Critical Medical Anthropology, *Medical Anthropology Quarterly, 3,* pp. 426-432, 1988.
5. R. Anderson, The Efficacy of Ethnomedicine: Research Methods in Trouble, *Medical Anthropology, 13:*1-2, pp. 1-18, 1991.

6. C. Browner, B. Ortiz de Montellano, and A. Rubel, A Methodology for Cross-cultural Ethnomedical Research, *Current Anthropology, 29*:5, pp. 681-702, 1988.

7. R. Simons and C. Hughes, *The Culture-Bound Syndromes*, D. Reidel Publishing Co., Dordrecht, 1985.

8. N. Scheper-Hughes and A. Lovell, Breaking the Circuit of Social Control: Lessons in Public Psychiatry from Italy and Franco Basaglia, *Social Science and Medicine, 23*, pp. 159-178, 1986.

9. N. Scheper-Hughes and M. Lock, Speaking "Truth" to Illness: Metaphors, Reification, and a Pedagogy for Patients, *Medical Anthropology Quarterly, 17*, pp. 137-140, 1986.

10. N. Scheper-Hughes, Three Propositions for a Critically Applied Medical Anthropology, *Social Science and Medicine, 30*:2, pp. 189-197, 1990.

11. H. Baer, M. Singer, and J. Johnsen, Toward a Critical Medical Anthropology, *Social Science and Medicine, 23*, pp. 95-98, 1986.

CHAPTER 1

Medical Anthropology and its Transformation

How one thinks of biomedicine makes a difference in medical anthropology, influencing research, teaching, and one's orientation in one's own society.

Lorna Amarasingham Rhodes [1, p. 170]

Franz Boas, the man generally honored as the father of contemporary American anthropology, was, during the course of his distinguished career, the recipient of many honorary degrees and memberships in scholarly societies. But of all of these expressions of recognition of his contributions to the understanding of humanity, Boas is said especially to have treasured an honorary Doctorate of Medicine conferred by the University of Kiel on the fiftieth anniversary of his original doctorate in physics completed in 1881. The appreciation that Boas felt for this degree, while in part reflecting his lifelong emotional connection to his *alma mater*, can also be seen as symbolizing the prestige accorded medicine by anthropologists. While anthropologists have labored under a quiet stigma of professional marginalization—the field is popularly misunderstood and possesses limited recognition among policy—and decision-makers—medicine, by contrast, is the preeminent profession. As Friedson indicates,

> If we consider the profession of medicine today, it is clear that its major characteristic is preeminence. Such preeminence is not merely that of prestige but also that of expert authority. This is to say, medicine's knowledge . . . is considered to be authoritative and definitive [2, p. 5].

Anthropologists rarely have been granted such authority and this rebuke has colored their perspective. Even when, as in their involvement with issues of health and illness, they have attempted to have impact on practical affairs or on pressing human problems, their potential contribution often is overlooked. Writing of the formative years of anthropology under Boas' direction, Herskovits notes that the field "was regarded as something marked by exoticism and amateurishness, starved in the academic curriculum

11

and ignored by those concerned with policy-making and the direction of affairs in the secular world. . ." [3 p. 22]. Forty years after Boas' death, only a little has changed.

> Much of the literature in applied anthropology is neutral or negative reporting of the frustration of ignored or underutilized anthropological data—what 'might have been' if we could only get policymakers' attention [4, p. 1].

What gets their attention? According to Heggenhougen, "the anthropological point of view receives greater immediate credence with decision and policy makers when presented by a physician than by an anthropologist" [5 p. 131].

Through association with medicine, it can be argued, medical anthropology has sought to claim a degree of authority as a science and as a profession. As a result, being taken seriously by medicine is especially important in medical anthropology. This concern has been expressed repeatedly in the published literature of the field. For example, the well-known physician/anthropologist, Melvin Konner has cautioned his colleagues who study ethnomedicine to be sure not to even give the appearance of valuing its efficacy relative to biomedicine.

> if medical anthropologists allow themselves to be seen as insufficiently critical in their acceptance of primitive or heterodox medical treatments, they quickly lose all credibility with any but a small coterie of colleagues and students and risk the more serious censure that is associated with quackery. There seems to be a popular tendency, which medical anthropologists must strongly counter, to assume that a description of a non-Western medical practice is a defense of the practice, unless it is explicitly stated to be something else [6, p. 81].

Privileging biomedical treatment, by contrast, usually is not seen as problematic, although clearly all medical systems, including biomedicine, are cultural systems rooted in particular social traditions and socially constructed world views. While recent work in and beyond medical anthropology has begun to reveal the degree to which "[b]iomedical research is not the 'objective other' which it is often made out to be" [7, p. 139], and the same can be said of biomedical practice, explicitly and implicitly medical anthropology continues to hold up biomedicine "as the standard for judging the 'real' world of sickness" [8, p. 22].

The purpose of this chapter is to situate the relationship between biomedicine and anthropology in its historic and political contexts, tracing the many points of contact between the two fields that culminated, during the 1960s and 70s, in the appearance of medical anthropology as a distinct subfield of the larger discipline. This history reveals the extent to which biomedicine has shaped and often constrained anthropological thinking about health. This chapter is divided into three main sections. The first provides a critical framework for examining the significant periods of interaction between biomedicine and medical anthropology. The second offers a historic examination of the evolution of anthropological interest in health and the roles played by biomedicine and its practitioners in guiding this interest. The final section provides a history of the emergence of critical medical anthropology as an alternative vision for medical anthropology.

MEDICINE AND ANTHROPOLOY:
A TALE OF TWO ENCOUNTERS

The historic depth of the relationship between medicine and anthropology often is not fully appreciated. It stretches back before the turn of the nineteenth century, indeed to the beginnings of modern anthropology as a discipline. Along the way, two discernible periods of intensive interaction are identifiable. During the first, dating to the era Firth terms the pre-bacteriological days of nineteenth century medicine, "doctors often showed an interest in ancient or 'primitive' man" [9, p. 238]. Medicine at the time was still very much under the influence of religion and maintained a somewhat philosophical penchant, perhaps to compensate for its inability to account for or respond effectively to the infectious diseases and epidemics that claimed innumerable lives, especially among the poor and working classes. As Lieban indicates, "Interest in social and cultural dimensions of illness reached a peak in the West during the nineteenth century, stimulated by public health problems associated with the Industrial Revolution. . ." [10, p. 1031]. During this first period, anthropologists and physicians worked together closely, indeed a number of anthropological scholars were physicians, including some of the first to write about topics that would today be termed medical anthropology.

However, medicine turned away from a broader social understanding of health and disease in the early part of the twentieth century. This transition was "part of the broader conservative reply to the political theories of illness-causation developed by Virchow and other radical epidemiologists" [11, p. 185]. The focus of medicine switched to the identification and treatment of particular micro-organisms responsible for specific individual cases of disease. Biomedicine came to see "social factors only as clues to real causes of disease" [12, p. 59]. The effect on medicine's relationship with anthropology was profound: "With attention concentrated so heavily on direct, immediate causes of disease, such as the effect of microbes on body tissue, interest in the social and cultural context of medicine declined" [10, p. 1032]. While it is commonly assumed that the basis for this transformation of medicine was the discovery of micro-organisms and their role in disease causation, it also has been suggested that there was a significant political influence as well.

> It became clear to increasing numbers of physicians that the complete professionalization of medicine could come only when they developed an ideology and a practice that was consistent with the ideas and interests of socially and politically dominant groups in society. . . . The medical profession discovered an ideology that was compatible with the world view of, and politically and economically useful to, the capitalist class and the emerging managerial and professional stratum [13, p. 71].

The political utility of a biological understanding lay in the fact that disease would not be seen as "an outcome of specific power relations but rather a biologically individual phenomenon where the cause of disease was the immediately observable factor, the bacteria" [14, p. 166]. Thus, medicine initiated a process of depoliticizing its understandings, a characteristic it generally has retained ever since.

> In medicine it is basically believed that disease follows its own rules, neither those of kings or slaves. Disease is neither the fault of the individual nor of society. To be sure, different social classes become sick more than others, and this can be explained by differences in personal hygiene or "lifestyle." Disease is essentially an individual problem and is systematically abstracted from a social context [15, p. 28].

Like medicine, anthropology also turned away from a more holistic and macro-level orientation toward a microscopic focus at this time. In British functionalism and American historic particularism, anthropology struggled to find its own political utility. Notes Kuper, "From its very early days, British anthropology liked to present itself as a science which could be useful in colonial administration" [16, p. 100]. Ethnography, constructed narrowly as the field study "of 'living cultures,' of specified [autonomous] populations and their lifeways in locally delimited habitats" [17, p. 13], provided a vehicle for pursuing this objective. Argue Magubane and Faris, "The micro-investigation of cultural entities to emphasize their uniqueness provided a vital basis for the [colonial] policies of divide and rule" [18, p. 99].

To the degree that it was of interest to anthropologists during this period, the topic of health was reduced primarily to the study of ethnomedical beliefs and practices. Exemplary is Evans-Pritchard's first book *Witchcraft Oracles and Magic among the Azande*, which sought to demonstrate the "intellectual consistency" of Zande beliefs about the causation and healing of disease (and broader misfortune). At the time of his research, a period when "the colonial administration was undermining [the] authority structure" [19, p. xxiii] of the Azande, Evans-Pritchard was employed by the colonial Government of the Anglo-Egyptian Sudan. Although Evans-Pritchard later remarked that during the fifteen years that he worked in the Sudan he was "never once asked [his] advice on any question at all" by the colonial government [quoted in 16, p. 104], his studies with their functionalist bent contributed to the broader colonial era comprehension of the dominated Other. Generally, although with special reference to American anthropology, Wolf has characterized the anthropology of this period as "'political economy' turned inside out, all ideology and morality, and neither power nor economy" [20, p. 257]. The failure, as he indicates, was in coming to grips with the phenomenon of power.

The period of renewed engagement between biomedicine and anthropology began in the post-World War II period. Eight years after the war, Caudill commented:

> Recently anthropologists in the U.S.A. have been doing some very unusual things, participating with physicians on conferences on social medicine, working with public health services in Peru, studying the structure of hospitals and the flow of life on wards, interviewing patients undergoing plastic surgery, and doing psycho-therapy with Plains Indians. All of which indicates a tentative liaison between the social sciences and medicine, though as yet there has been little real communication [21, p. 771].

Nine years later, Polgar updated the extent of this liaison.

> The presence of anthropologists and other social scientists in medical settings is no longer as 'unusual' as it was when Caudill . . . reviewed applied anthropology.

> Rather, it would be unusual for a meeting of health workers or social scientists in the U.S. not to include some papers on topics of common interest [22, p. 159].

Though he spoke a bit hastily, an issue we return to in Chapter 7, Galdston recognized an important reason for the renewed contact between biomedicine and anthropology.

> The infectious diseases have been all but 'conquered.' Now there is emergent a new pathodemography. The disorders and diseases now dominant are due not to specific pathogens, but rather to economic, social, political, and cultural factors [23, p. 221].

Unable—if only temporarily, as the hunt for the genetic causes of non-infectious diseases suggests—to reduce the "Diseases of Civilization" to the microscopic organic level, biomedicine took a fresh look at behavioral and psychological factors, although from a depoliticized vantage. Thus, physicians like Donald Vickery became the darlings of the insurance industry by writing books like *Take Care of Yourself.* According to Vickery:

> What many people don't realize . . . is that medical care accounts for only about 10 percent of what influences health. Lifestyle decisions people make—smoking, drinking, exercise, and weight control—contribute more to good health than any other factors [quoted in 24, p. 1].

In this new intertwining of biomedicine and anthropology, the era of consolidation of medical anthropology as a field of work and study, the appointed task of anthropologists commonly has been "to get patients and healthy laymen to do things that medical practitioners consider to be good for them" [25, p. 65]. Medical anthropologists also found roles (and jobs!) in international health development, explaining "the health practices of peasants, tribal people, and lower class ethnic groups to physicians, nurses and health planners" [25, p. 65]. These circumstances reinforced and intensified the historic biomedical influences on the emergent field of medical anthropology. Also contributing to these strong biomedical effects on medical anthropology have been various clinicians, several of whom, it has been suggested, "have dominated the development of medical anthropology since its inception, both as theoreticians . . . , and as members of applied projects" [26, p. 1303]. The result has been a deepened biomedical structuring of anthropological understanding of health.

THE EMERGENCE OF MEDICAL ANTHROPOLOGY IN POLITICO-HISTORIC CONTEXT

The Pre-bacteriological Days: Medicine, Anthropology, and Racism

Firth, in her review of the relationship between anthropologists and the medical profession, reminds us that one of the earliest anthropological professional organizations was founded by a physician [9]. In 1862, James Hunt, a specialist in speech pathology and author of a book on the treatment of stuttering, founded the Anthropological Society of London. Firth does not mention, however, the ominous nature of this connection. In sharp contrast to Boas, an ardent opponent of racism whose writings on the topic were circulated by the anti-Nazi underground in Germany and burned by the Nazis, Hunt promoted the theory of polygenicism, the view that "the races of men were aboriginally distinct and permanently unequal species" [27, p. 75]. Haddon summarizes Hunt's 1863 address to the Society, entitled "The Negro's Place in Nature," as follows:

> After examining the evidence on the subject, he made several deductions, amongst which were: that the Negro is a different species from the European; that the analogies are far more numerous between the Negro and the ape than between the European and the ape; that the Negro is inferior intellectually to the European; that the Negro race can only be humanized and civilized by Europeans; that European civilization is not suited to the Negro's requirements or character. . . [28, pp. 44-45].

Useful as a rationale for the subordination of people of color, it is not surprising that "[s]ome of the most rabid defenders of slavery were doctrinal polygenists" [29, p. 89].

In the mid-1860s, and in no small way effected by the American Civil War, the intensity of the debate between the polygenists and the monogenists (those who believed that all humans shared a common ancestry) led to a fracturing of the Anthropological Society of London. To promote their views, the polygenists set up the journal *Anthropological Review*, in which Hunt published, among other things, an attack on John Stuart Mill for advocating extending suffrage to African Americans and women. In his attack, Hunt posed his differences with Mill as a nature/nurture debate. In so doing, he labeled Mill a 'materialist' who, unlike himself, accepted "the omnipotence of circumstances and the natal equality of mankind," while arguing that Mill's ideas were "but a far-off reverberation of Democritus and Epicurus" [30, pp. 115-116]. The leading materialists of Greek antiquity, Democritus and Epicurus embraced somewhat different understandings of the physical world, the subtleties of which were lost on Hunt but evident to Karl Marx. In his doctoral dissertation on the topic, Marx demonstrated that "Democritus, whose atoms moved in a straight line only, constructed a physical theory of strict determinism, whereas Epicurus, who allowed the atoms a slight deviation from the straight line, came to a much fuller world outlook that allowed freedom as well as determinism" [31, p. 14]. In championing Epicurus, Marx set the stage for rather different materialist conclusions than Mill, including conclusions, as we shall see, with significant implications for the study of health and illness.

The outcome of the Civil War having decided the fate of slavery once and for all, the warring factions in British anthropology were able to make their peace by the end of the decade and celebrated their reconciliation through the establishment of a unified Anthropological Institute, an organization which in its final reconstruction became the Royal Anthropological Institute.

To the degree that Hunt had any lasting impact on medical anthropology, it was through whatever influence he had on his nephew, W. H. R. Rivers, who also was trained and at times practiced as a physician. While Rivers is best known in anthropology for his contributions to the study of kinship and for initiating the rejection of early macro-level evolutionist thinking in the discipline, his work had a significant effect on medical anthropology as well. This influence stemmed from Rivers' participation, along with C. G. Seligman, also a physician, and Alfred Haddon, in the historic 1898 Cambridge Torres Straits expedition. Rivers used experiences gained during this and subsequent field work to promote the idea, still current in medical anthropology, that so called primitive ethnomedical practices "are not a medley of disconnected and meaningless customs" [32, p. 51], but instead reflect a coherent set of cultural beliefs about disease causation. Rivers' book on the topic of ethnomedicine, *Medicine, Magic and Religion,* which Landy has described as "the symbolic totem of medical anthropology" [33, p. 4], was first given as a series of lectures to the Royal College of Physicians and was originally published in the *Lancet.* Importantly, in this "epic-making study" [34, p. 5], Rivers imposes an impenetrable wall between indigenous and scientific medicine, much like the wall his uncle sought to erect between the peoples that produced the various healing traditions in question. Notes Wellin,

> Within Rivers' outlook, primitive and modern medicine constitute wholly separate universes of discourse. By focusing on world view and its linkages with belief and behavior, Rivers can find no way to accommodate magico-religious and naturalistic-scientific world views within the same domain of inquiry. As a result, Rivers' model precludes consideration of Western medicine and is limited to medicine among primitive groups [35, p. 50].

Press identifies the core ethnocentric premise linking Rivers to his uncle Hunt.

> In truth, the lumping of one, or perhaps several medical systems in contrast with all others is not unlike the lumping of human races into two categories: "caucasian" and "other." It focuses upon the characteristics—most usually a few selected characteristics—of *one* system as the typological bases for *all* systems. Lacking the characteristics of the type system—Western medicine, in this case—all other systems are largely indistinguishable from one another. "They all look alike" [36, pp. 45-46].

In this, we see a feature of the sustaining influence of biomedicine on anthropology (although medicine is hardly the only influence in this regard). Biomedicine does not present itself as *a* medical system (one healing tradition among many historically and ethnographically), but rather as *the* medical system, categorically different from all other pretenders to the title of medicine.

> It is presumed that traditional systems of ethnomedicine are circular in their reasoning; are consensual and complacent; rely little on experimentation; and entail no critical thinking. . . Biomedicine, in contrast, is presented as logical and self correcting through the deployment of standardized replicable procedures which test for the falsification of hypotheses [7, p. 139].

The broader separation of the West from the rest implied in this distinction, of Europe from the People Without History, to borrow Wolf's [17] apt phrase, has been a profound and troubling problem for medical anthropology.

Thus, a legacy of Rivers' approach has been the tendency to believe that ethnomedical healing activities can *only* be studied and understood in terms of religious and magical beliefs. In the estimation of Foster and Anderson, "This stereotype, uncritically accepted by a majority of anthropologists during the last half century, has severely limited us in our understanding of non-Western medical systems" [34, p. 6]. Additionally, Rivers' characterization of biomedicine as a wholly different phenomenon because of its acceptance of naturalistic causation long hindered the medical anthropological understanding of this form of healing as well.

> Anthropologists have failed to examine their own anthropological culture, including their common reliance on Biomedicine. They have not seen biomedicine as susceptible to the same sort of cultural analysis to which they readily subject other medical systems .... They have defined 'ethnomedicine' ... to exclude 'scientific' medicine ...; and medical anthropology texts ... have been divided into separate sections on biomedicine and 'ethnomedicines' [37, p. 4].

Not surprisingly, until recently, medical anthropologists have rarely recognized the degree to which their concepts perpetuate biomedicine's official image of itself as unique in its approach and wholly scientific in its practice (and the degree to which even science is cultural construction). Hughes, for example, employed a medico-centric understanding in his definition of ethnomedicine as indigenous healing practices "not explicitly derived from the conceptual framework of modern medicine" in his discussion of the topic in the *International Encyclopedia of the Social Sciences* [38, p. 87]. Nor has it always been clear to the discipline the extent to which biomedical elitism is rooted in social construction rather than demonstrated efficacy [39]. Murkier still is the historic relationship between the physician acting as authority with regard to the lived experience of the patient and the anthropologist speaking on behalf of dominated peoples.

It is worth noting, in examining the historic relations between medicine and anthropology, that the social context of the early ties in Britain was mirrored on the American side of the Atlantic. As Harris indicates, "the first distinctive school of anthropology to flourish in the United States," an approach that came to be known as the American School, "was founded by the Philadelphia physician of anatomy Samuel George Morton" [29, p. 90]. Like Hunt, Morton was a polygenist, a position he adopted based on his studies of several hundred human skulls sent to him by colleagues abroad. And like Hunt, Morton's anthropology was an anthropology of racial determinism. On both sides of the Atlantic, in other words, in the two countries that can fairly claim primary influence on the birth of anthropology, racialist thinking of the day was introduced to the disciple through its early biomedical founders. While this frame of mind was to falter under the burdening weight of relativist ethnographic investigation, it tended to be replaced, both within medicine and anthropology, by micro-level focus that, however much an advance in some regards, failed to fully confront and eliminate earlier tendencies.

Boas-Virchow-Ackerknecht-Marx: The German Connection

Franz Boas, himself no stranger to the measurement of heads, an activity he undertook to demonstrate social impact on human physiology, wrote *The Mind of*

Primitive Man with the expressed purpose of refuting and laying to rest the prejudicial and empirically unsound conclusions of Morton and his school. He ended this book, in the original version, by stating "all races have contributed in the past to cultural progress in one way or another, so they will be capable of advancing the interests of mankind if we are only willing to give them a fair opportunity " [40, p. 278], a bold rebuke of racial determinist thinking and a clear expression of the importance of politics in human affairs. Boas' early views on these matters went further still. In a letter to his fiancee dating to 1883, Boas wrote: "I believe one can be really happy only as a member of humanity as a whole, if one works with all one's energy together with the masses toward higher goals" [quoted in 41, p. 12].

The origins of Boas' perspective on these issues are of note because of the role he might have played in setting medical anthropology on a different course than the one actually taken. In accounting for Boas' politics, Lesser draws attention to the ideals of the German revolution of 1848, which Boas felt were a vital force in his homelife.

> Relatives and friends of the family [including Boas' father-in-law and uncle, both of whom were physicians] had been in the 1848 struggle in Germany and had left for the United States after its failure, some after getting out of jail. Drawn to the liberalism of his time, Boas was deeply troubled by Bismarck's Germany [41, p. 12].

Moreover, while still in Germany, Boas had developed a relationship with the physician, Rudolf Virchow, "upon whom his hopes for an appointment at the University of Berlin were pinned" [29, p. 265]. Virchow, a participant in the street battles of 1848, was among the earliest contributors to a political-economic understanding of the causes of disease and of the nature of medicine.

As a clinical pathologist at Charité Hospital in the late 1840s, Virchow early in his career became interested in the causes of epidemics.

> In late 1847 a typhus epidemic broke out in Upper Silesia, a chronically impoverished area of East Prussia with a large Polish-speaking minority. By the beginning of 1848, thousands were dying and famine complicated the problems. Virchow convinced his superiors to support a pathologically oriented investigation that would lead to recommendations about stopping the epidemic and preventing recurrences. He departed for a brief intensive field trip to Upper Silesia. Within days of his arrival, the horrors of the epidemic produced a profound emotional impact [42, p. 84].

In his subsequent writings, Virchow emphasized the ultimate political-economic causes of the epidemic, including unemployment, the failure of the government to provide food during a famine, and the poor quality of housing and extent of overcrowding in the region. Thus he wrote, "It is rather certain that hunger and typhus are not produced apart from each other but that the latter has spread so extensively only through hunger" [quoted 42, p. 84]. Also he noted the contribution of economic insecurity and political disenfranchisement. Virchow even discussed iatrogenic aspects of the epidemic, commenting in letters to his father about the failures of physicians for not taking care of the poor because of "love of money" and reluctance "to put bills aside," as well as noting the damaging effects of the linguistic differences between Prussian doctors and their Polish-speaking patients [quoted in

42, p. 84]. Consequently, he called for the creation of a public health service to respond effectively to medical emergencies, as well as for improved employment opportunities, better housing, the creation of agricultural cooperatives, a more progressive system of taxation, linguistic training for physicians, and autonomy in local decision-making. Virchow looked to medicine for a limited number of solutions, believing that the best approach to epidemics was to change the living and social conditions that allowed them to develop.

This precisely is what Virchow attempted to do, pistol in hand, when the revolution of 1848 broke out not long after his return to Berlin from Upper Silesia. His motivation in joining the struggle, as he wrote in a letter to his mother, came from the realization that "Improving the welfare of the poor, or, to say the same thing, the working class, was not possible . . . because the king's will alone was law and the working class had scarcely any means to make their advancement worthwhile" [quoted in 42, p. 85]. During the stage of active combat, Virchow busily documented cases of military brutality against working-class communities, in addition to active participation on the barricades that sprang up in many quarters. As the uprising began to peter out, Virchow founded a popular medical journal called *Die Medizinische Reform (Medical Reform)*, addressed to "those who form a medical (trained and practicing) proletariat" [quoted in 42, p. 85]. On the second page of the first issue of this journal, Virchow expressed his famous dictum: "Medicine is a social science, and politics is nothing more then medicine in larger scale" [quoted in 12, p. 31]. Additionally, it was his view that, only "Once medicine is established as anthropology, and once the interests of the privileged no longer determine the course of public events," should physicians become supporters rather than opponents of the existing social structure [quoted in 34, p. 3].

Although Virchow did not make reference at the time to the analyses of Marx and Engels, both of whom not only wrote extensively about the revolution but raised money to purchase weapons for the German working class combatants of the struggle, he considered himself a socialist. And while in later years Virchow adopted more reformist approaches, he never disavowed his early activism, despite considerable pressure to do so. Moreover, he continued to challenge Germany's ruling elite, both inside and outside of medicine, although never to a degree that might jeopardize his university position. In his epidemiological work, Virchow did make use of Engels' *Condition of the Working Class in England,* a seminal contribution to the political economy of health tradition. Notes Waitzkin,

> Virchow argued for a new 'materialism' in medicine that would replace dogma and spiritualism. . . . In his attempts to construct a dialectical materialist approach in biology, Virchow studied the early work of Engels. He cited with approval Engels's approach . . . and used some of Engels's data to demonstrate the relationships between poverty and illness. . . . He emphasized the concrete historical and material circumstances in which disease arose, the contradictory social forces that impeded prevention, and researchers' role in advocating reform. In the analysis of multifactorial etiology, Virchow claimed that the most important causative factors were material conditions of people's everyday lives [42, p. 87].

In Virchow's words, "The improvement of medicine would eventually prolong human life, but improvement of social conditions could achieve this result even more rapidly and successfully" [quoted in 42, p. 88].

One product of German working class struggle against the state was the implementation of the first compulsory national health insurance law in 1883. As early as 1849, Bismarck had drawn the conclusion that "The social insecurity of the worker is the real cause of their being a peril to the state" [quoted in 43, p. 376]. When he became chancellor of a united Germany, in an effort to undercut a new surge of social unrest, Bismarck pushed for the "Sickness Insurance Act," which mandated "medical care and sickness money in case of illness and also in case of accident during the first thirteen weeks; i.e., before accident insurance became effective, and in addition maternity and funeral benefits" [44, p. 147].

Although he authored "Rudolph Virchow's Anthropological Work" [45, p. 443], and in 1883 while studying among the Inuit of Baffin Island had his own opportunity to witness an epidemic at close range, Boas appears not to have been much influenced by "the cautious master" in either his concern with disease or its social causes. This is unfortunate because, acquainted as he was with Virchow's contributions and clearly in sympathy with his holistic orientation and strong empiricist bent, Boas might have played a role in setting medical anthropology on a different course than it took. Clearly in his attitude toward scholarship and the scholar's social responsibility, Boas was unabashedly Virchowian. For example, in 1919, despite the considerable controversy that it generated, Boas published in *The Nation* a sternly worded attack on anthropologists working as spies. As he stressed,

> A person ... who uses science as a cover for political spying, who demeans himself to pose before a foreign government as an investigator and asks assistance in his alleged researches in order to carry on, under this cloak, his political machinations, prostitutes science in an unpardonable way and forfeits the right to be classed as a scientist [quoted in 41, p. 16].

Earlier, Boas had hired two Russian revolutionaries living in political exile in Siberia as field workers on the Jesup North Pacific Expedition (1897-1902). When one of these men, Waldemar Borgoras, who after the Soviet revolution served as director of the Institute of the Peoples of the North, was arrested for political activism by Czarist agents, Boas attempted to organize support on his behalf [46]. Moreover, Boas took an activist stance in responding to racism, as we have seen, and to the rise of fascism in Germany, organizing the 11,000 strong Committee on Democracy and Intellectual Freedom in response to the latter (although, it is noteworthy that on other issues of which he also was keenly aware, such as the oppression of Native Americans or the colonial status of Puerto Rico, he was much less vocal or active). In fact, Boas used his address at the University of Kiel upon receipt of the honorary Doctorate of Medicine to discuss his views on the relationship between race and culture, only two years before Hitler assumed power.

This mention of Boas' political writings and activism is of note specifically because of the direction actually taken in medical anthropology in part under the influence of biomedicine's depoliticizing patronage. In criticizing recent writings in critical medical anthropology, for example, past-president of the Society for Medical Anthropology Susan Estroff argues,

> Situating an analysis of illness in time and space is a requirement of scholarship. Judging the worthiness, acceptability, and/or ideology of that context is not [47, p. 422].

Had he been focused on health as a research subject, it is very probable that Boas' would have disagreed. As he wrote in a letter to the *New York Times* in 1916:

> At the time of my arrival here, more than thirty years ago (1884), I was filled with admiration of American political ideals. . . . A rude awakening came in 1898, when the aggressive imperialism of that period showed that the ideal had been a dream. Well I remember the heated discussions which I had that year with friends when I maintained that control of colonies was opposed to the fundamental ideas of right held by the American people, and the profound disappointment that I felt when, at the end of the Spanish War, these ideals lay shattered. The America that had stood for right and right only, seemed dead; and in its place stood a young giant, eager to grow at the expense of others. . . [48, pp. 168-169].

Despite these views and although it is clear that Marx's political economic ideas form a link between Boas and 18th century environmental determinists, Boas, under neo-Kantian influence and naively optimistic that the mere advance of scientific knowledge would resolve social conflicts, ignored Marx and turned American anthropological theory down the cul-de-sac of historical particularism [29, 49]. Boasians generally were not focused on issues of health and disease, working as they did during the period of separation between anthropology and medicine. And despite Boas' deep respect for Virchow, as Foster and Anderson [34, p. 3] suggest, "Virchow really had nothing to do with the origin of the contemporary field," and, in fact, his potential contribution was largely ignored by medical anthropologists until the emergence of critical medical anthropology. Similarly, in Britain, the students of Rivers, Seligman, and Haddon, turned their attention away from issues related to health. In defining what came to be known as British social anthropology, Evans-Pritchard stressed that it is the application of sociology to primitive social life. In so doing, he differentiated the work of the early anthropological researchers from their descendents in Britain by emphasizing that the participants in the Torre Straits expedition "were interested in ethnological and psychological problems rather than in sociological ones" [50, p. 73]. Nonetheless, as we have seen, Evan-Pritchard's own contribution to what would become the pre-literature of medical anthropology "followed Rivers' line of analyzing thought processes in relation to disease and cure" [9, p. 238].

The primary link between the first and second periods of engagement with biomedicine is to be found in the work of Erwin Ackerknecht, especially during the 1940s. Although various papers and longer treatments on topics that would today be considered medical anthropology (e.g., folk nosology and healing) were published in both the medical and anthropology literatures during this era [e.g., 51-56], Ackerknecht was the most consistently committed to these issues and the most comprehensive in his efforts. Primarily a library and museum researcher concerned with comprehending the nature of indigenous healing, Ackerknecht, a physician, in fact is seen by some "as the 'father' of medical anthropology" [34, p. 52]. Wellin credits Ackerknecht with stimulating the rapid development of medical anthropology within the mainstream of socio-cultural anthropology after the Second World War [35].

Although the author of *Rudolf Virchow: Doctor, Statesman, Anthropologist,* Ackerknecht acknowledged and his work reveals that his primarily theoretical debt was to Boasian historical particularist and British social anthropology [57]. In a series of papers, primarily published in the *Bulletin of the History of Medicine,* but also in anthropology journals, Ackerknecht sought to develop a systematic cultural relativist and functionalist understanding of what he referred to as "primitive medicine." For example, in his analysis of shamanic healers, he took a relativist stance in arguing that a shaman's seemingly neurotic behavior must be viewed as cultural expression rather than individual psychopathology, and a functionalist approach in asserting the contribution of the shaman's role to the maintenance of the social group. In developing this perspective, Ackerknecht consistently stressed that indigenous healing practices cannot be understood except in relation to the wider culture of which they are an intimate and functionally interrelated part. Seen in this light, each primitive healing system has its own unique configuration dependant on its local cultural context. Additionally, while sometimes efficacious on empirical grounds (i.e., in the view of biomedicine), primitive medicine in Ackerknecht's view, is fundamentally rooted in magical beliefs and practices, and thus should be understood as forming a coherent system relative to the local culture [58].

A review of the titles of Ackerknecht's various articles reveals the source of his approach to making sense of indigenous healing practices.

> Ackerknecht . . . viewed non-Western cultures from an ethnocentric perspective based on the organizational structure professional medicine had evolved in the West. Thus, Ackerknecht wrote articles on "primitive surgery," "primitive psychotherapy," and "primitive prevention," [also primitive autopsy] in which he searched the ethnographic literature for cultural practices that he fit into these Procrustean categories [59, p. 29].

Furthermore, like Rivers before him, Ackerhnecht's ability to comprehend the social nature and social role of indigenous healing seemed to falter when his attention turned to biomedicine. In his view, "primitive medicine is primarily magico-religious, utilizing a few rational elements, while our medicine (i.e., biomedicine) is predominantly rational and scientific employing a few magic elements" [60, p. 467]. Also, he argued, unlike indigenous healing, biomedicine "has lost its 'sacred' character, its social control function, its subjective influence on society, its meaning in moral terms" [quoted in 61, p. 456]. Ackerknecht, for all his insight into the cultural patterning of healing beliefs and practices, and his realizations concerning the link between disease and the "general conditions . . . of the total society" [62, p. 120], was largely blind to the impact of biomedical categories on his understanding of indigenous healing, the cultural/political structuring of biomedicine, the social role of medicine in capitalist society, and the social production of contemporary pathology.

The Post Bellum Days: In the Field and In the Clinic

After the Second World War, there was a noticeable increase in the number of anthropologists concerned with health issues, especially of an applied nature, and a sizeable expansion in the anthropological literature on health-related topics. This development, which led to the concretization of medical anthropology as a distinct subfield within the discipline, occurred for several reasons.

> After the last war, Americans became involved with overseas health programmes on an even larger scale than those of the British colonial government between the wars. This was facilitated by expansion in staff and research funds of anthropology departments in the U.S.A., and the provision there for teaching across the disciplines [9, p. 239].

A primary task of anthropologists when they began to work in international health programs in the early 1950s was the promotion of biomedicine among indigenous peoples.

> The first significant anthropological research on problems of international health was begun simultaneously in several Latin American countries in 1951. I refer to the work of Institute of Social Anthropology staff members . . . , carried out under the auspices of the Institute of Inter-American Affairs (the ancestor of the U.S. Agency for International Development). . . . Quite uncritically the superiority of modern medicine and modern health care delivery was taken for granted, and the task was defined as the study of client groups to determine how modern medicine could be made most attractive to them, and how they could be led to patronize the newly-developing services of their countries [63, pp. 849-850].

Benjamin Paul, a leading figure in the promotion of this work, saw anthropologists as being "especially qualified by temperament and training. . . [for] the study of popular reactions to programs of public health carried out in foreign cultural settings" [64, p. 29]. Equally important, after the War many of them were in need of employment. As Hunter has argued, early international public health work among anthropologists "was motivated more by the availability of funding than theoretical interest" [26, p. 1300], a fact that probably led a number of reviewers of the literature of the 1950s and 1960s to conclude that much of the work from this period was "superficial, impressionistic, and nontheoretical" [12, p. 33].

Failing to see the highly political nature of international health aid, which he described as "generally uncontroversial," Paul [64, p. 31] felt that real problem facing anthropologists in international public health was in overcoming cultural resistance to new modes of behavior, as well as "the relatively low salience of health as a value among some groups" [64, p. 35]. For example, he notes the unexpected resistance of peasants in North Borneo to antimalarial spraying of DDT in their homes on several grounds including the allegedly unfounded complaint that their children and farm animals were being killed by the poison. Assuming that the nature of people's resistance to public health programs stems from culturally produced misunderstanding, rather than empirically sound observations among the recipients of aid, Paul urged anthropologists to find anthropologically creative ways and means of getting people to accept health programs. Because they were willing to perform this task, international health personnel . . . welcomed anthropologists with open arms. . . . The anthropological approach was acceptable to public health personnel, too, because it did not threaten them as professionals. They saw it as a safe approach, in that it defined the problems of resistance to change as lying largely with the recipient peoples [34, p. 8].

In retrospect, the writings of Paul and many of his contemporaries from this period seem unduly naive about the nature and function of U.S.-sponsored international health promotion. Based on work carried out at the peak of the Cold War, this literature is permeated with the official ideology of the West, including its medical ideology. As opposed to Paul's view of the uncontroversial nature of international health promotion, Brown argues that "medical 'modernization' programs . . . have had disastrous results for the health care of the majority populations of under-developed countries" [13, p. 585]. This has been so for several reasons. First, the primary motive for health development programs, like all government-sponsored aid, is not social development but the achievement of U.S. foreign policy objectives. Second, programs tend to benefit local, regional, and national elites more so than those most in need. Third, programs are used to dampen social unrest rather than to empower people to improve their lives [65-67]. Finally, health programs often focus on education, when the main problem "is not education or unwise allocation of resources but financial means" [68, p. 91]. In his study of U.S.-sponsored health care projects in the Cauca Valley of Colombia, for example, some of which date to the 1950s, Taussig found that projects were implemented shortly after peasants had attempted to reclaim land appropriated by expanding sugar plantations. A primary impact of the projects was increased food production, but this has been of little benefit to the majority of peasants. The basic cause of disease and malnutrition, social inequality in access to productive resources and power, was not addressed by the projects. Rather, the projects contributed to "forcing the previously independent small farmers into wage labor in the estates" [69, p. 102].

Work in international health development often has been frustrating for anthropologists. Called on to contribute in their particular arena of expertise (e.g., ethnographic study of the cultural basis of health-related behavior), they have found their proposals and conclusions ignored by biomedically oriented project administrators. For example, writing about the Mass Media and Health Practices Project in Honduras, Carl Kendall notes that despite the acclaim accorded the project for successfully using anthropological knowledge in a major health development effort, for the most part ethnographic findings were disregarded by the medical staff directing the project. Especially in instances where "anthropological evidence clashed with the viewpoint of medical authorities and with evidence collected from other sources" the contributions of anthropologists "were not considered to be of sufficient weight to change the implementation stategy" [70, p. 290]. Even the international public health movement, which was launched with the specific inten-tion of radically re-orienting international health development from a biomedical to a community health model, and solicited the contribution of many medical anthropologists to achieve this goal, often has come to serve traditional biomedical aims [71-74]. As Brigitte Jordan [75, p. 114] concludes, in many places primary health care has been "co-opted by planners who ignored the necessity for social and political reforms and instead concentrated on the extension of medical coverage to rural areas, thus laying the groundwork for the biomedical colonization of communities." Countries and regions where primary health care has achieved the original intention have tended to be places where political economic restructuring in the interest of the oppressed preceded public health development [76].

In addition to involvement in international health promotion projects, the postwar period also saw a movement of anthropologists into clinical settings as teachers, researchers, administrators, and as clinicians [77, 78]. The impact on the discipline of this development has been marked, because anthropologists in the clinical setting have had to adopt and, more tellingly, to extensively rationalize the adoption of, subservient roles relative to physicians.

> The anthropologist, to work in a hospital or medical school, must be accepted by the establishment. Access to these rich research areas is controlled by members of the establishment. Only if they feel that the anthropologist . . . will, in the course of research, be able to provide them with information they consider useful, or at least will upset no apple carts, will they be sympathetic to his [or her] presence [34, p. 207].

Clinically based anthropologists, who often toil under difficult conditions with a sincere commitment to finding ways anthropology might contribute to improving the quality of care patients receive, have provided instructions for gaining and maintaining access to clinical settings [8]. Polgar argued that for an anthropologist "to work effectively in a medical setting . . . it is essential that he should be in full sympathy with the ideals of the professional health actor . . ." [22, p. 179]. Kleinman encourages anthropologists to demonstrate their "respect [for] the therapeutic imperative" [79, p. 703], exhibit their usefulness to physicians, and patiently develop clinical credibility. Similarly, for anthropologists teaching in medical schools, the message has been, "the most effective way of introducing behavioral-science materials into medical curricula . . . is to adopt, adapt, and build on the clinical model, rather than trying to construct a different, competing tract" [77, p. 46]. While these comments are understandable given the location of power and decision-making in medical settings, it is not suprising that Hunter [26, p. 1302] concludes that to a large degree anthropologists working in hospitals, clinics, and medical schools have been "co-opted by the medical establishment."

Concommittant with the compromises often inherent in the clinical role is the risk of wholesale absorption of the biomedical worldview as "a kind of universal standard" [80, p. 305]. In response to her reading of the literature of clinically employed anthropologists, Scheper-Hughes comments,

> One has the image of the timid anthropologist—certainly out of his milieux—tiptoeing through the minefields of the modern clinic trying to mediate the worst and most potentially pathogenic interactions and miscommunications, trying to prevent the most extreme technomedical insensibilities from hurting vulnerable patients. All of which is necessary and praise-worthy. But, as with the early colonial anthropologists, what is not being called into question

is the inevitability . . . of the whole biomedical health enterprise itself. The oft-expressed professional concerns of clinically applied anthropologists with respect to 'establishing credibility' and 'legitimacy' within the powerful world of biomedicine and the fears of 'marginalization' or, even worse, 'irrelevancy' lead only to compromise and contradiction [81, p. 191].

Scheper-Hughes' point has been overlooked, it would appear, because of what Taussig has termed "the aura of benevolence" of biomedicine [22, p. 4]. Telling is Polgar's comment that, "It is certainly easier to share the value of improving health . . . than to aid the operations of a colonial administration [22, p. 179]. That there might be an underlying or even a direct relationship between the two within the context of biomedicine is not always appreciated [e.g., see 82], and when it is, medical anthropologists have been cautioned not to get "overwhelmed with the association between colonialism and Western medicine" [83, p. 400]. Nonetheless, as recent accounts of health and health care in colonial settings show, such association is of grave significance.

Packard, for example, writing of South Africa, notes that "white medical authorities had considerable influence on the development of popular thinking among whites about the status of Africans in South African society and in the development and persistence of . . . stereotypes" [84, p. 689], that legitimated oppressive policies against the African majority. Packard supports this argument with an examination of South African medical journals, conference reports, commission testimonies, and other medical records to show how tuberculosis and other diseases were construed in medical discourse as proof of the physiological susceptibility of Africans to life in white cities, supporting thereby the interests of the mining industry and the Bantusan policies of the apartheid system.

Inherently, the biomedical model lends itself to this type of use because it locates the causes of disease within the acts and organs of sufferers.

> A sick individual is regarded as a set of physical symptoms, rather than as a person who belongs to a social class in a particular society. This process turns our attention away from the political roots of disease, and conceals these roots by providing us with an alternative explanation. By and large, says this explanation, people are responsible for their own health. If they get sick it is a chance occurence, no-one is to blame, and it is their own fault. If people get cholera, it is because they do not use 'safe, chlorinated water.' If children are malnourished, their parents do not feed them properly, and they have more children than they can look after properly. Illness is seen as nature's revenge on people who live unhygienically and do not observe proper rules of cleanliness [85, p. 70].

Biomedicine, in this light, can be understood as a vital hegemonic force in the capitalist world-system, concepts to be examined in greater detail in the next chapter. As Waitzkin indicates, the hegemonic role of medicine has two expressions.

> The first concerns the health professional's therapeutic responsibilities and the tendency, within the therapeutic process, to reproduce oppressive social relations. Medical discourse narrows the scope of potential action to the individual level and to adjustments within existing institutions. The noncritical nature of medical

> discourse encourages clients' continued functioning in a social system that is
> often a major source of their personal problems. The second ... arises from
> medicine's tendency to depoliticize illness ... [86, p. 135].

This point is well captured in the words of a past president of the Rockefeller
Foundation (George Vincent) with reference to the Philippines.

> Dispensaries and physicians have of late been peacefully penetrating areas of the
> Phillippines Islands and demonstrating the fact that for purposes of placating
> primitive and suspicious peoples medicine has some advantages over machine
> guns [quoted in 13, p. 589].

The potential for biomedical co-optation of medical anthropology, that is, for the
incorporation of basic "Western ideological medical assumptions ... [that are] intrinsic both to structures of domination within Western contexts and to the controlling articulation of the West with non-Western peoples" [87, p. 429], in short, for
becoming "handmaidens of biomedicine" [88], is rooted in the role anthropologists
and other social scientists have been asked to play in the clinical setting. Riska and
Viten-Johansen contend,

> the medical profession has employed behavioral scientists to depoliticize issues
> in health politics. Political conflicts, actually reflecting different structural inter-
> ests in the health care system, are turned into 'social problems' to be solved
> apolitically by the intervention of experts [89, p. 594].

Clinical anthropologists, in particular, have become increasingly mindful of this
problem and have cautioned against "allowing system demands to determine their
roles" [90, p. 95]. The degree to which avoiding this eventuality is possible in many
settings and the extent to which biomedical thinking has shaped not just the roles but
the understanding of clinical anthropologists, including the questions they ask and
the answers they find salient, has, as we note in Chapter 13, received less atttention.

The Culmination: The Birth of Medical Anthropology

With the consolidation of the role of anthropologists in international public health
and in biomedical institutions, the sense emerged that a new subfield of anthropology
had come into being. As Landy indicates, "By the early 1960s, the term *medical
anthropology* had come to be used increasingly by anthropologists working in and
around problems in health and disease in human societies" [33, p. 9]. The term and
the field were further consolidated when Scotch selected "Medical Anthropology" as
the title for his review of the literature on the social dimensions of health and illness
published in the *Biennial Review of Anthropology*. In this paper, he notes,

> There are probably enough anthropologists now working either as researchers or
> teachers in medical settings so that it might be worth while to consider setting up
> a section of the American Anthropological Association analogous to the Medical
> Sociology section of the American Sociological Association [12, p. 59].

This happened in short order.

From [the meeting of the American Anthropological Association] 1967 in Washington, DC, through 1968 in Seattle, 1969 in New Orleans, and 1970 in San Diego, those with a special interest in an area called 'medical anthropology' moved from being a collectivity of interested persons to a Group for Medical Anthropology (GMA), and then to a Society for Medical Anthropology [91, p. 115].

Within the academy, institutionalization was no less thorough. In the early 1950s, anthropologists like Benjamin Paul and William Caudill began teaching a course at Harvard University entitled "Health and Illness in Cross-Cultural Perspective." Students trained at Harvard went on to offer their own courses in related topics at their respective universities. David Landy, for example, a student of Paul and Caudill, began offering courses in "Primitive and Folk Medicine" and "Social and Cultural Factors in Health and Disease" at the University of Pittsburgh in 1960. In time, graduate and undergraduate courses in medical anthropology were developed at many universities and specialized graduate tracks in medical anthropology were initiated across the United States and abroad [92]. The sociopolitical process of disciplinary construction, a process deeply marked by an enduring relationship with biomedicine, was nearing completion.

By 1977, Landy was cautiously prepared to say that "medical anthropology ha[d] begun to come of age" [33, p. 8], in one of the first collections of studies in medical anthropology [also see 93]. The first issue of a new journal entitled *Medical Anthropology* also rolled off the presses in 1977. The following year the first of several long awaited specially prepared medical anthropology textbooks appeared [34]. By 1980, a survey of U.S. medical schools showed that over eighty anthropologists had faculty appointments, while a comparison of employment among physical anthropologists employed in biomedical academic departments in 1984 and 1988, showed a proportionate growth of over 200 percent [77, 94]. By 1986, the Society for Medical Anthropology had over 2,000 members and was preparing to launch its own journal, creating a friendly rivalry with the existing journal in the field. The first number of the latter, entitled *Medical Anthropology Quarterly*, appeared in March, 1987. With the field now large enough to support two specialized professional journals, in addition playing signficiant roles in multidisciplinary journals like *Culture, Medicine and Psychiatry* and *Social Science and Medicine*, it was evident that medical anthropology had completed its coming of age process. However, no sooner was this so than the field's underlying premises became suspect, especially those absorbed from biomedicine.

MEDICAL ANTHROPOLOGY IN QUESTION

"I Perceive a Contradiction"

By its very nature as a social science concerned with socio-cultural phenomena, medical anthropology is a critical project that challenges, to some degree, the adequacy of the disease model of biomedicine. However, as is plain in its very title, medical anthropology (or, more , recently and more explicitly, "biomedical anthropology" [95, 96] has been marked by its long relationship with biomedicine. Consequently, until recently, its critique of biomedicine, while not insignificant, has been limited. As Young observes, "epistemological scrutiny is suspended for Western social science and Western medicine" [97, p. 260]. Similarly, at the end of his book length review of the subdiscipline, Landy added a concluding note in which he observed:

> I perceive a contradiction in medical anthropological writing in regard to the treatment of American society. . . . Our society, our culture is one among many. But very frequently in the pages of medical anthropological writings we find that the medical system of that society, or of a broader conception that we imprecisely label as "Western" or "Euroamerican" society, is accepted as an established baseline against which to measure the disease concepts, classifications, and systemic processes (diagnosis, prognosis, treatment, cure, etc.) of other peoples [80, pp. 304-305].

The recent uneasiness with medical anthropology's stance toward biomedicine has had varied expression, and has been voiced by anthropologists who embrace differing, although at some points, overlapping, perspectives. First, there are those, like Landy, who stress the view that, what ever else it is, biomedicine is culture. Gaines and Hahn for instance, emphasize that,

> Biomedicine is one among numerous alternative professional ethnomedicines. . . . All ethnomedicines share a basic epistemological quality: they are versions of reality, stocks of knowledge and modes of comprehension and action in reference to, but ontological distinct from, reality [37, p. 6].

The task of medical anthropology, therefore, is "to understand the worlds constructed by medical systems in radically diverse societies and from this perspective to criticize a narrowly biological reading of the work of culture in relation to mortality and human suffering" [98, p. 694]. This interpretive or constructivist orientation sees biomedicine as suffering from an overly narrow, biological understanding of reality. Medical anthropologists who adopt this perspective are especially critical of what they view as efforts to turn medical anthropology into a discipline whose primary mission is the "mapping of local cultural phenomena onto a biomedical grid" [98, p. 693].

The elevation of biomedicine's narrow and reductionist understanding to the status of objective reality is seen by interpretive anthropologists, and others, as a failure "to take into consideration the degree to which symptoms are grounded in the social and cultural realities of individual patients" [99, p. 166]. Rather than just a culturally colored version of one or another universal disease, so-called culture bound conditions, including those bound to Western culture (e.g., lower back pain, schizophrenia, obesity, hypoglycemia) are believed to be "associated with a typical set of personal stresses and social responses, to have specific links to basic social values of worth and well-being, and to provide a framework for individual episodes of illness" [99, p. 176]. Put simply, "disease cannot be perceived apart from a cultural context" [100, 198]. An objective of the interpretive approach is the collaboration with biomedicine in the construction of an expanded medical model sensitive to non-organic (i.e., cultural) antecedents to disease. This new model, sometimes called biopsychosocial medicine, understands health symptoms as not just patient experienced indications of organic malfuctioning, but also as expressions of cultural meaning.

> In attempting to free physicians from medicocentrism (a culture-bound model), [interpretive] anthropologists wish to convince physicians of the essential value of options, pluralistic ideas and practices, and understanding behavior and meaning in the cultural context [100, p. 198].

Part-and-parcel of this understanding is recognition that both the therapeutic process and therapeutic efficacy, including the unfolding of the treatment event and its "success" within biomedicine, have significant symbolic and metaphoric components [101]. While the representational aspects of folk or indigenous healing practices, such as the "laying on of hands," have been discussed for some time within medical anthropology [102], more recently the contribution of symbolism to biomedical practice and treatment outcome have gained attention [102-106]. Even the "laying on of steel" in surgery and the dispensing of pharmaceuticals, long portrayed as extremely objective and instrumental forms of biomedical treatment, have been shown to gain efficacy from their metaphoric aspects [107, 108]. Similarly, Emily Martin [109] in her discussion of "Science as a Cultural System," shows how dominant cultural metaphors of an economic origin (e.g., "production," "control") shape discussions of the human body in biomedical text books. Similarly she has argued that tropes of war and combat construct understandings of the immune system in biomedical education [110]. She speculates that one effect of such imagery "is to make violent destruction seem ordinary and part of the necessity of daily life" [110, p. 417]. Similary militarization characterizes biomedicine's approach to cancer, as seen the declaration of a "war on cancer" in the National Cancer Act of 1971. As Erwin observes, one consequence of medical militarization of this sort is that it encourages people to fight disease rather than to make the changes necessary to prevent it [111].

Taking things a bit further, a second critique of the influence of biomedicine on medical anthropology rests on a profound discomfort with the medicalization of medical anthropology on phenomenological and interpretive grounds. Scheper-Hughes and Lock lament the degree to which medical anthropology has fallen prey "to the biological fallacy and related assumptions that are paradigmatic to biomedicine" [112, p. 6]. In their view, this pattern of medicalization creates a tendency to transform the social into the biological. Rather than the global reification of the categories of mental disorder ensnared by history or culture within biomedical nosology, for example, some radical phenomenological medical anthropologists would reject psychiatric, and perhaps medical, nosology all together, even as applied to Western cases, and instead "allow madness (and other illness) to emerge from behind the medical mask that has concealed its most social properties: the cumulative effects of rejection, exclusion, and stigmatization" [113, p. 117]. The watchwords of this view are "freedom is therapy," and thus medical anthropologists should be less concerned with reforming biomedicine than with promoting modalities of "benevolent anarchy," alternative and empowering self-help approaches, or social acceptance and tolerance for the ill and suffering.

Also alarming to many medical anthropologists who hold this view is the medicalization of anthropological training. Over the last twenty years, several distinct graduate programs in medical anthropology have appeared that treat the discipline not as a social science, but as a technically oriented health science. Arguing for further development along these lines, Heggenhougen asserts, "Medical anthropologists should have more training in areas of public health, epidemiology, and even clinical medicine than has been the case" [5, p. 131]. Colby goes even further. In his view,

> students are required to take so many graduate courses in traditional anthropology that there is little time to go outside their departments to learn about immunology and other matters vital to medical anthropology. Social theory is important, but it doesn't have to be taught; it can be picked up through reading at any time. In contrast, biological understanding requires laboratory experience, and quantitative sophistication requires courses in math and statistics . . . [114, p. 691].

Opponents of this stance believe that in its effort to mimic biomedicine or the health sciences, medical anthropologists come to over-identify with medicine, a transference relationship that has perhaps contributed to the birth of clinical anthropology and related efforts to find a therapeutic role for anthropologists. As Scotch comments, "there are those anthropologists who, in working in a medical setting, like to get overinvolved; like to play the role of doctor or psychiatrist; prefer to play an active role rather than the role of the detached scientist" [12, p. 34].

Those who balk at the medicalization of medical anthropology routinely share an even deeper concern about the monopolistic medical control over an ever growing list of conditions, experiences, and roles in contemporary life. There is a fear of the potential "medical control of everything" [115, p. 77]. This discomfort aligns with Ivan Illich's view of biomedicine as social iatrogenesis [116]. Adds Taussig "[i]n the name of the noble cause of healing, the professionals have been able to appropriate . . . and in a very real sense exploit a social relationship in such a way that its power to heal is converted into the power to control" [69, p. 10]. Those whose critique of conventional medical anthropology is ultimately rooted in worries about the medical monopolization of modern life, are concerned that medical anthropology is moving toward a neglect of "the particular, the existential, the subjective content of illness, suffering, and healing as *lived* events and experiences" [117, p. 137]. In Mishler's apt summary, the view of these workers "might be read as a paraphrase of the well-known statement about wars and generals: Health is too serious an affair to be left to physicians" [118, p. 201]. Rather than closer ties with biomedicine, which is seen as an imposing and powerful structure, they support a turn to the phenomenology of suffering, toward an identification with the patient as actor, experiencer, feeler.

For example, conventional medical anthropologists have made much of the distinction between 'disease,' the clinical indication of biological abnormality, and 'illness,' the sufferer's subjective experience and understanding of his/her condition.

On the one hand, this distinction is nothing other than a replication of the biomedical separation of 'signs' and 'symptoms,' an act that defines "the physician as active knower and the patient as passively known" [119, p. 59]. On the other hand, this distinction serves to reify the allegedly scientific and objective (and thus culture-free, politically neutral) nature of medical categories, understandings, and treatments. But disease, understood as something natural rather than cultural, as inherent rather than constructed, is not seen as appropriate for anthropological investigation. This is why for so long biomedicine itself was assumed to be beyond the reach of anthropological analysis [120]. From the radical phenomenological perspective, it is time for medical anthropology to deconstruct its received biomedical foundations and recognize sickness as

> a form of communication—the language of the organs—through which nature, society, and culture speak simultaneously. The individual body should be seen as the most immediate, the proximate terrain where social truths and social contradictions are played out, as well as a locus of personal and social resistance, creativity, and struggle [112, p. 31].

Hence, the sufferer is said to use "her body (and its sufferings) to communicate with and influence her social world" [121, p. 80]. The task of the field, from this view, is "first to describe the variety of metaphorical conceptions (conscious and unconscious) about the body and associated narratives and then to show the social, political, and individual uses to which these conceptions are applied in practice" [122, pp. 49-50].

A Third Perspective: Critical Medical Anthropology

A third critique of medical anthropology and its relationship with biomedicine also has "come of age" [123, 124] in recent years. Sharing elements of the other two critiques, this approach, draws upon the insights of the political economy of health tradition from outside of anthropology [125]. Critical medical anthropology understands biomedicine not solely as a socially constructed system embedded in a wider cultural pattern, nor only as a mechanistic and depersonalizing structure with important social control functions in contemporary society, but more broadly in terms of its relationship with the truly global capitalist world economic system. Consequently, CMA opposes the biomedicalization of medical anthropology on that grounds that a "main but latent function of . . . . medicalization is the resolution of social conflict" [126, p. 1169] to the political and economic advantage of the dominant class. From the CMA perspective, in adopting a subservient position vis-a-vis biomedicine, medical anthropology gains credibility but at a painful cost. In Kapferer's assessment, medical anthropology, "largely directed and funded from within Western medical contexts" is "instrumental in a medical imperialism" [87, p. 429]. The emergence of critical medical anthropology reflects both the turn toward political-economic approaches in anthropology generally, as well as an effort to engage and extend the political economy of health approach [124, 127, 128].

Sometimes, this point, one which to a degree sets CMA off from the other critiques of conventional medical anthropology, has been misunderstood. Thomas Csordas, for example, remarks that "critical medical anthropologists .... often favor the term 'biomedical hegemony' as if biomedicine itself constituted the ruling class" [102, p. 417]. However, as Kenyon Stebbins' [129] study of transnational tobacco companies or Singer's [130] analysis of alcohol manufacturers and distributors demonstrate, CMA is quite aware of what Csordas accurately calls "the real ruling class," and that *it* "is the locus of hegemony, including hegemony over health and illness" [102, p. 420]. This is a point we develop further in our examination of the plutonium industry in Chapter 5. A central concern of CMA, as a result, is with the analysis of the dynamic relationship between biomedicine and the ruling class internationally, within the contexts of individual nation-states, and in local settings. As for the composition of the "real ruling class" and its relationship to biomedicine, while difficult to study because of the ability of this class to erect barriers to social science research, it has been documented in various papers published in the *International Journal of Health Services* [e.g., 131-133]. However, this is a source not regularly used by noncritical medical anthropologists, as suggested by its infrequent citation in medical anthropology journals.

The history of biomedicine's relationship with the ruling class is described in part by Brown [13]. As he makes clear, and as several papers by critical medical anthropologists underscore [e.g., 134], during the twentieth century

> Capitalists and corporate managers [came to believe] . . . that scientific medicine would improve the health of society's work force and thereby increase productivity. They also embraced scientific medicine as an ideological weapon in their struggle to formulate a new culture appropriate to and supportive of industrial capitalism. They were drawn to the professionals formulation of medical theory and practice that exonerated capitalism's vast inequities and its reckless practices that shortened the lives of members of the working class [13, pp. 10-11].

A cogent analysis of the mediating role of physicians and medicine is provided by Figlio in his discussion of the notion of "constitution" in nineteenth-century medicine.

> The history of the term shows the increasing emphasis upon the individual as industrialization took hold. Traditionally, it referred to the character of a locality at a certain time, including the people .... But during the 19th century the emphasis shifted away from depicting a total situation onto characterizing the general state of the individual. Constitutional weakness, stressed by an exciting cause, brought about disease . . . Disease was evidence that a predisposition existed .... Thus, constitution as the central presupposition in medical thinking carried the implicit personal responsibility for illness into the hard core of medical theory. The ideological structure of medicine, which concealed the working conditions organized by capitalism, combined with the individualistic ideology of personal responsibility to promote individualism, not only in the marketplace, but also in the sickbed [135, pp. 231-232].

While the terms have changed, the notion of constitution remains in late twentieth-century biomedicine. Roberts, for example, based on her interviews with British physicians, notes that "doctors tend to hold particular beliefs about the different 'nature' of men and women patients—beliefs that are largely rooted in social and cultural norms rather than biological givens;" as a result, "doctors frequently appear to distinguish between men and women patients along lines which are suggested by, and presumably not unwelcome to, the drug companies" [136, p. 57]. Similarly, medical textbooks, "which, as in any profession, express and preserve orthodoxies" [136, p. 43], conflate biological and politically conditioned social realities. Roberts cites as but one example Dennis Craddock's *A Short Textbook of General Practice* which informs medical students that "The Vast majority of women have a basic need to have a home and children of their own" [137, p. 116]. In their review of twenty-seven gynecological textbooks published since 1943, Scully and Bart found "a persistent bias towards greater concern with the patient's husband than with the patient herself [138, p. 1014]. Women are consistently described as anatomically destined to reproduce, nurture and keep their husbands happy." In like fashion, Hahn's review of the first seventeen editions of *Williams Obstetrics,* the central reference of the field, found a consistent "reduction of the personal experience and the interpersonal relations of childbearing to an operation on the body in which the childbearing woman and her women friends are deprecated and ignored" [139, p. 258]. Hysterectomy, one of the most commonly performed surgical procedures, also gives potent expression to the biomedical view of women, their social roles, and bodies. Historically, this view and the medicalization of women's bodies generally occurred simultaneous with the masculinization of the biomedical establishment [140]. Wright, in a widely noted article in the *American Journal of Obstetrics and Gynecology,* articulates the male-centered belief that helps account for the frequency of hysterectomy: "The uterus has but one function: reproduction. After the last planned pregnancy, the uterus becomes a useless, bleeding, symptom-producing, potentially cancer bearing organ and therefore should be removed" [141, p. 561]. In textbooks, clinical discourse, diagnoses, and medical procedures, the biomedical construction——and at times destruction—of women's bodies and temperments is not an independent process reflecting a uniquely medical or scientifically generated comprehension. Rather, biomedicine, in no small way, has absorbed its understanding of women from conventional ideology (and, in turn, butressed the power and sense of legitimacy of this ideology), the ultimate origin of which lies in the self-serving worldview of the dominant social class [109].

By promoting the status and authority of biomedicine, the ruling class, in short, was serving its own interests, as were biomedical professionals who accepted recognition, funds, and legitimacy from the ruling class. While physicians became agents of this social strata, the alliance hardly made them automatic members of the elite sector (although medicine certainly did attract some of the sons and daughters of ruling class families). As a group, physicians appear to conform to Gramsci's notion of "intellectuals of the urban type," in that they serve to articulate the relationship between the ruling and subordinate classes [142]. Indeed, as Howard Waitzkin argues, "professionals—especially doctors—are a primary interface between the capitalist class and the working class" [143, p. 603]. As such, biomedicine is contradictory and an arena of conflict. And some of that conflict is between the ruling class and biomedical professionals, who can have opposed as well as shared interests.

This last point is important, because the CMA critique of biomedicine has at times been labeled "doctor-bashing." Those who have issued this criticism of CMA have stressed the fact that doctors are individuals with differing personalities and commitments. Konner, for example, emphasizes that there are doctors who are "saddened and angered by poverty, world hunger, war and inequality" [6, p. 81]. Of this, there is no question. The issue for CMA, however, is not and has never been the personalities and convictions of individual physicians (although for the patients who are often our informants this can be very much the issue), but rather the nature of the structurally constituted relationships between physicians and patients as reflective of the relationship between biomedicine and the encompassing political economy. We are reminded of defenses we have read of both sociobiology and postmodernism against charges of inherent conservatism on the grounds that there are progressive thinkers among their respective ranks. The point, of course, as was made experimentally by the sociologist Philip Zimbardo, is that personalities are secondary to social roles in the conduct of institutional behavior [144]. As Zimbardo demonstrated in a now famous school-based experiment, individuals of relatively mild disposition can assume harsh and oppressive demeanors and practices given appropriate structural conditions. Those conditions, in this instance, include medical culture which "has a powerful system of socialization which exacts conformity as the price of participation" [109, p. 13]. Indeed, like others, Konner bases his allegation of doctor-bashing on the belief that "high-minded" critics lack "sympathy for the doctor's plight" [6, p. 81]. For him, this means trying to understand the forces that make physicians act the way they do. Ironically, the understanding of such forces is precisely one of the goals of CMA in its analysis of biomedicine, as seen in Chapter 12 in our description of a woman patient's protracted and continually stymied struggle to receive sensitive obstetric care. Whatever the condescension or aloofness that some physicians express in their treatment of some kinds of patients, we assume most physicians, like most critics of biomedicine, have honorable intentions. However, as Howard Waitzkin, a critical physician, suggests, "Wanting to help but unable personally to change the social structure, the health professional typically seeks a solution within the existing institutional context" [145, p. 343]. If this understanding constitutes doctor-bashing, it is of a curious sort indeed because it does not attempt to demonize the physician but instead localizes the biomedical practitioner and his/her ideology and action within channeling political-economic contexts and structures. Indeed, we would agree with Mull and Mull that "if anthropologists were all suddenly licensed to practice medicine, it is very possible that in short order the majority would behave rather like doctors" [146]. This recognition, in fact, motivates CMA concern about clinical anthropology as expressed in Chapter 13. It also bears mentioning that in their daily work, especially in the practical application of CMA to address health issues in society, there are a number of critical medical anthropologists who work closely with physicians or other health care professionals. As suggested in Chapter 14, it is evident that some physicians struggle to become what Rene Lorau [147] and Franco Basalia [148] referred to as "negative workers." By this term, they meant a "technicians of practical knowledge" who align with the oppressed rather than identifying with the bourgeois institution in which they are employed. Through their efforts, negative workers create "openings" in mainstream institutions that allow for critical medical anthropology practice.

Even if CMA should escape the doctor-bashing label, has it not stumbled in making so much of capitalism as a determinant force in biomedicine? Konner also raises this issue, suggesting that CMA views "bourgeois medicine" as a "capitalist plot" despite its evident appeal to doctors in socialist-oriented societies. While we recognize the rhetorical value of accusing your opponent of subscribing to a conspiracy theory, we believe the accusation plays rather poorly in this context. As many of the changes in the organization of biomedicine over the last 100 years are pretty much out in the open, including the increasing proletarianization of physicians, it must be something other than a plot that is under discussion in CMA texts. In fact, it is the social evolution of a medical system within the context of a particular political economy that is the focus of CMA analyses.

In using *bourgeois medicine* as an interchangeable term with biomedicine, adherents of CMA have something very different in mind than Konner apprehends. The term

> identifies a key attribute of the so-called Western or scientific health care system, namely its role in the promotion of the hegemony of capitalist society generally and the capitalist class specifically. *Capitalist medicine is not a 'thing' or a set of procedures and treatments so much as it is a particular set of social relationships and an ideology that legitimizes them* [149, p. 183, emphasis added].

The consequence of embracing a bourgeois approach to medicine in socialist-oriented countries has been discussed at some length by critical medical anthropologists and colleagues in the encompassing political economy of health [72, pp. 150-151]. Indeed, as we note in Chapter 4, although the Soviet Union emerged as the first nation-wide counter-hegemonic movement against the capitalist world system, the ideological hegemony of bourgeois medicine is so sweeping that Navarro [151] has applied this label to the Soviet medical paradigm. At any rate, the interest of physicians in socialist-oriented countries in biomedical procedures/technology says nothing about the class nature of biomedicine as constituted in capitalist nations. Further, CMA does not deny the efficacy of particular biomedical procedures (afterall we are patients on occasion too and some critical medical anthropologists are practicing physicians), but CMA does seek to understand the degree to which even efficacious approaches, to say nothing of questionable ones [152], are driven by nontherapeutic concerns.

Based on its critique of conventional medical anthropology and the nature of its relationship with biomedicine, adherents of CMA have attempted to forge a *new* medical anthropology that corrects the defects of earlier models within the field by incorporating what Elling termed the *progressive-holistic perspective.*

> Work from . . . [this] perspective understands societies as involving class conflict and sees the state apparatus and medical-health systems as mediating this conflict in favor of the ruling class in capitalist societies. The historical developments and political-economic conditions are viewed as primary, with value orientations and beliefs flowing from these fundamental conditions [153, p. 236].

In other words, as we show in Chapter 9, central to the CMA paradigm is a concern with the embeddedness of "webs of meaning" in "webs of power." CMA calls attention to the need for an alternative approach in which symbols and meanings are neither obscured nor unduly empowered and in which the analysis of the enactment of power is foregrounded and made pivotal to the project of medical anthropology and beyond [154].

The Development of Critical Medical Anthropology

The origin of CMA as an alternative trend within medical anthropology can be traced fairly directly to the symposium "Topias and Utopias in Health" at the IX International Congress for Anthropological and Ethnological Science, held in Chicago in 1973. This meeting was organized through the joint efforts of two medical social scientists at the University of Connecticut, Anthony E. Thomas, an anthropologist, and Stanley R. Ingman, a sociologist. At the time, Connecticut was a center of anti-Vietnam War sentiment and organizing, and a number of faculty and students in the department of anthropology began to adopt a critical orientation in their work. Interviews with several participants indicate that the radical "temper of the times," the prior research experience of the organizers, and concern about the atheoretical character of much work in medical anthropology were the dominant influences on the character of the symposium. Earlier, Thomas had conducted doctoral research in Kenya on Kamba response to the introduction of biomedicine, while Ingman, as a student of Ray Elling at the University of Pittsburgh, had examined the effects of class and professional dominance on rural health care delivery in Pennsylvania. Both felt the need to explore "change in both . . . health systems and in the larger nation-state systems within which health systems are embedded" [155, p. 2].

The title for the symposium reflected a basic idea of the critical health perspective still retained within CMA. The term "topia" (from the Greek word *Topos* for "a place") came into English usage through the writings of Karl Mannheim, a one-time progressive pioneer in the sociology of knowledge. The term itself was borrowed from Gustav Landaur, socialist leader of Bavaria and author of the book *Die Revolution*. In Mannheim's usage, penned before his move to England and subsequent embrace of more conservative politics, topia referred to an established and conventional social system. Utopia, by contrast taken by Mannheim from Thomas More's sixteenth-century fictious island paradise, was used to refer to efforts to challenge and replace the status quo. Using these terms, Thomas and Ingman conceptualized health care as an ongoing struggle beyond those who support existing social structures or who advocate only minimal reformation of them and those who seek radical restructing in an effort to achieve significant improvements in health and health care. Like CMA, their orientation and that of most of the participants in the symposium was toward the latter position.

The most significant product of the symposium was the book *Topias and Utopias in Health* [156] published in the World Anthropology book series. The volume consisted of twenty-seven papers, a number of which were written by authors who were not able to attend the conference. While not all of the contributors are anthropologists, the book included chapters on a variety of issues that remain of central concern to CMA, including the political character of health-related policies and practices, the structure of social relationships within health care, the effects of colonialism and neo-colonialism on health services in underdeveloped countries, environmental health, and the nature of socialist health. Several of these chapters were written by anthropologists (e.g. Brook Grundfest Schoepf and Sally Guttmacher) who remain active contributors to the literature of CMA.

In his review of the political economy of health literature, written a decade after the Chicago conference, Baer commented that "Topias . . . remains the only major book in the medical anthropological literature that includes political economic interpretations" [125, p. 16]. The volume, in fact, long remained a critical island in a swelling sea of microanalyses in medical anthropology, althrough it retained a small (and scattered) set of enthusiasts. Efforts to convene a follow up symposium to continue the thrust begun by Topias failed to achieve the intended results.

Several years later, however, Charles Leslie of the University of Delaware organized a small conference entitled "Theoretical Foundation for the Theoretical Study of Medical Systems" that did pick up some of the themes articulated in the Topias volume. Influenced early in his academic career by political economic analysis, Leslie later assisted in the publication of the first essay length set of papers under the title "Critical Medical Anthropology" through his position as senior editor for anthropology at the journal *Social Science and Medicine*. Held in Washington, D.C. following the 1976 American Anthropological Association meetings, the conference Leslie organized continued the pattern of bringing together critical scholars from several disciplines. Thomas was one of the anthropological participants, as were Ronald Frankenberg from Great Britain and Allan Young. Both of these scholars were to become strong influences on the CMA perspective. Also participating, from sociology, was Ray Elling, one of the important "discipline brokers" in the political economy of health tradition. A contributor to the Topias volume, Elling played an important role in encouraging the consolidation of CMA through his position in the Department of Community Medicine at the University of Connecticut, including publication of this volume.

Of the papers presented at the Washington conference, it is perhaps John Janzen's contribution that is still most often cited in the CMA literature as an early reminder of the importance of macro-level analysis within medical anthropology. Janzen urged medical anthropologists to move away from "handicapped micro-analysis by observing how power and authority are used in the conceptualization, structuring, and allocation of the resource which is healing" [157, p. 124]. Even more explicit calls for a political economic approach were uttered by other participants, especially Frankenberg.

An anthropologist with a long track record in militant labor circles in the UK, Frankenberg has contributed to a broad array of anthropological studies, including work on political systems, communities, the family, and play. In a letter to the lead author, he noted the early influences that helped to shape his theoretical direction in medical anthropology:

> I cannot remember a time when I was not aware of Marxism, since when at the
> age of eight I was asked to write a school essay on my favourite reading, I wrote

about a Key Books pamphlet by JBS Haldane lent tò me by my brother, . . . then secretary of the London Hospitals Socialist Society. The teacher was very surprised. I read the *Psychopathology of Everyday Life* when I was 11 or 12, my sister having bought the Penquin edition in mistake for a detective story. I was the only socialist at my Public (i.e., private) school and as a Cambridge medical student was much influenced by Julian Tudor Hart, who is now a famous left wing GP, the son of a Spanish War surgeon and hero; and to a lesser extent by the son of Wilhelm Reich's sister Ilse Reich-Ilendorff who worked at Neil's progressive school, Summerhill. The Cambridge anthropology department was really terrible in the years before the Forties, and so after graduating I joined Max [Gluckman] at Manchester, the only anthropologist in Britain at the time who was prepared to use not only Marx but Freud in his work. There I met Peter Worsley who was an influence in my remaining a Marxist.

Active in helping to set up a medical school in Zambia, Frankenberg went on to author one of the groundbreaking theoretical papers that helped to shape the perspective of CMA. In "Medical Anthropology and Development: A Theoretical Perspective," Frankenberg sought to present an orientation ("the making social of sickness") that incorporates the local, national, and international levels in social science of health and overcomes thereby the injury to understanding caused by the segregation of micro- and macrolevel processes [158]. In frank admission of the way in which disarticulation of levels is embodied both within the academy and in his own past work, he laments:

It is a criticism both of British sociology and anthropology as well as ourselves that on return from Luska, [Joyce] Leeson and I were constrained to produce two papers—one, Intermediate Technology and Medical Care, was correctly foreseen as interesting to sociologists, hardly mentioned traditional medicine, and discussed the emergence of Western medicine in the context of Zambian class relations, and world politics. The other . . . ignored this general context and concentrated on the nature of the Nganga's activity—social aspects of choice of healer . . . . Social anthropology is unwise (as is sociology) to confine itself in this way for it seems to me that it can potentially reveal the 'missing link' without which the analysis of major social change founders (for lack of an anchor chain); what effects are produced at the local level by national and international social processes; and what is coming from the local level in return [159, pp. 205-206].

By conducting what he termed "critical microanalysis," medical anthropology can avoid past shortcomings.

As he readily admits, Frankenberg's perspective in the above mentioned paper builds on the seminal work of Allan Young [159], especially his analysis of the cognitive and communicative roles of people's health beliefs and practices. In addition to his contributions to the analysis of religion and magic, traditional and Western medical systems, medical ideology, rationality, and, more recently, therapy and emotional disorder, Young too has played an influential role by introducing critical ideas into both the medical anthropology literature and the thinking of students through his position at Case Western Reserve University and more recently at McGill University.

Especially significant in Young's work has been his effort to call attention to the social determinants of scientific and medical knowledge. "Science produces facts, it does not uncover them" [160, p. 144], he argues; moreover this type of production and the commodity it creates are no less embedded in a particular social arrangement than any others. In failing to recognize its social origins, the producers and (ab)users of scientific and medical knowledge mystify social relations and participate thereby in the legitimation of existing social arrangements. Through such analyses, Young extends the profound understanding of "consciousness" developed by Marx and Engels, as expressed in *The German Ideology* and elsewhere, into the discourse of critical medical anthropology. Young also was influential in calling attention to the social determinants of health and healing. As he noted, "Social forces help to determine which people get sickness. . . Symbols of healing are simultaneously symbols of power . . .and medical practices are simultaneously ideological practices" [97, p. 270].

Despite the contributions of the workers discussed thus far, an explicit turn toward the political economy of health tradition awaited Soheir Morsy's "The Missing Link in Medical Anthropology: The Political Economy of Health" published in 1979 [161]. In this and a number of subsequent papers, Morsy advocated adoption of "a political economy perspective which undermines the idealist, reductionist and dualist approaches" [162, p. 159] characteristic of much medical anthropology. Drawing on the work of African anthropologist Omafume Onoge and Janzen, as well as her own research experience among peasants in her native Egypt, Morsy chided medical anthropologists, especially those working in the Middle East, for concentrating on supernatural etiology beliefs and folk healing, while ignoring even their informants' awareness of "social and asymmemtrical power relations as the *ultimate* causes of sickness" [162, p. 160]. In her analyses of health and illness in FatiHa village, Morsy situated the microlevel, including birthing practices, body concepts, and folk illness beliefs, within rural-urban, gender, and class relations.

> Indeed, medical care for the peasants of FatiHa, like that for the rural inhabitants of other parts of Egypt, cannot be divorced from the sociopolitical superordinate power relations which direct every facet of their lives. The peasants of FatiHa do not live an isolated, independent existence, they are part of a stratified sociopolitical entity. Their subservient power status within the nation state precludes independent planning of their lives in their own best interest and leaves them subject to the imposed planning of the requirements of their livelihood by the ruling power elite [163, p. 153].

Morsy's unambiguous call for attention to political economy helped spark the emergence of CMA as a distinct and named trend within medical anthropology .

As a postdoctoral fellow in the anthropology department at Michigan State University in the later 1970s, Morsy became an influence on Hans Baer, another MSU fellow with a long-time interest in macrolevel issues. A major turning point in the emergence of critical medical anthropology was Baer's subsequent review entitled "On the Political Economy of Health," which appeared in the widely read *Medical Anthropology Newsletter* [125]. Preparation of the review developed out of an increasing sense of frustration not only with the lack of attention within medical anthropology to the work of non-anthropological researchers like Vicente Navarro, Howard Waitzkin, Lesley Doyal, and Ray Elling but a seeming lack of awareness of their writings in many quarters of the subdiscipline.

A few weeks following the appearance of the review, we presented a jointly authored paper called "Why Not Have a Critical Medical Anthropology?" [164], that entitled the emergent perspective, at the annual meeting of the American Anthropological Association (AAA), and later utilized this material in a set of definitional articles. Adoption of the term *critical medical anthropology* was intended to reflect a two-sided approach involving: 1) criticism of conventional medical anthropology for the limitations in its perspective; and 2) social criticism, in the tradition of Marx, Mills, and other socially critical thinkers. These and subsequent efforts by the authors to promote a critical realignment in medical anthropology had their origin in discussions begun in graduate school at the University of Utah in the mid-1970s on the relevance of political economy for the understanding of religious revitalization movements [165, 166]. Soon after graduating, these concerns were extended to issues of health and medicine as a consequence of post-doctoral training and research experiences [131, 167, 168].

In addition to suggesting a critical redefinition of health ("access to and control over the basic material and non-material resources that sustain and promote life at a high level of satisfaction"), informal circulation of a long version of the AAA paper among colleagues was a factor in the coming together of a number of anthropologists, including several members of the Council on Marxist Anthropology, who shared its general concerns and orientation. These interactions led to a Society for Medical Anthropology invited symposium in 1983 at the AAA meetings entitled "Toward a Critical Medical Anthropology" organized by Hans Baer and John Johnsen. Importantly, a somewhat parallel session called "Beyond Medical Anthropology: A Political Economic Critique of Health" was organized independently by Stephen Graff and Athena McLean for the same meetings. The co-occurence of these sessions, the large audiences they attracted, and the presentation of a number of other like-minded papers in other sessions signaled a growing interest in critical approaches among medical anthropologists.

At the invitation of Charles Leslie, then the senior anthropology editor for *Social Science and Medicine,* papers from the two sessions and several additional papers were combined to form a special issue of the journal. Representing the first peer-reviewed published collection in critical medical anthropology, articles in the special issue addressed the social production of illness, the relationship between health care and political economy, and the shortcomings of some existing research instruments from a critical perspective. As these topics reflect, the collection attempted to draw attention to a variety of key questions that often go unexamined in mainstream medical anthropology. As we noted in the introductory paper in this set:

> It may seem presumptous to label our approach critical. After all, most medical anthropologists view their discipline as a critical endeavor that challenges the assumptions of the disease model in biomedicine. We contend, however, that this critical perspective is limited to lower levels of analysis and ignores the political economy. . . . [169, p. 1].

In order to continue the momentum begun in Chicago, a follow-up symposium was organized for the 1984 Northeastern Anthropological Association. Later that year,

Peter Kong-Ming New and John Donahue organized a symposium entitled "Strategies for Primary Health Care by the Year 2000: A Political Economic Perspective" with the intention of showing the necessity of going "beyond the internal configurations of the health system to achieve a degree of understanding of how health is influenced by the larger political economy" [170, p. 96]. Papers in this session, most of which were published as a set in *Human Organization,* used Segall's [171] discussion of Marxist epistemology as a guiding framework and Segall served as discussant for the symposium.

With the seeds of critical medical anthropology showing signs of germination, participants in the critical trend decided to broaden the issues under discussion and to enhance exchange with their colleagues outside anthropology. The vehicle for achieving these goals was a symposium called "Socialist Health/Capitalist Health: Is There a Difference?" at the 1985 AAA meetings. The session was inspired by Elling in a seminal paper in which he argued that the differences between the health systems in capitalist and socialist countries are sufficiently great that we should drop the term "international health" and instead "talk of capitalist world health and socialist world health" [67, p. 45]. Papers from the session were published in a special issue of *Medical Anthropology* in 1989. Continuing a tradition begun with *Topias,* this collection ignored disciplinary boundaries, underlining thereby the need for a unified medical social science.

Another significant symposium held at the 1985 AAA meetings was organized by Tony Whitehead and Nancy Scheper-Hughes, colleagues of Thomas when he taught at the University of North Carolina. Entitled "Topias and Utopias in Health Care: Papers in Memory of Anthony E. Thomas," the session marked both the untimely death in December 1984 of an initiator of critical thinking in medical anthropology as well the pioneering role of the volume he helped to produce. Papers by Scheper-Hughes (coauthored with Anne M. Lovell) and Lynn Morgen presented at this sesssion were included in the 1986 special issue of *Social Science and Medicine.*

Several other occurrences at the 1985 AAA meetings clearly revealed the growing influence of CMA. First, Scheper-Hughes received the 1985 Stirling Award for Contributions to Psychological Anthropology for her paper "Culture, Scarcity, and Maternal Thinking: Maternal Detachment and Infant Survival in a Brazilian Shantytown" [172]. Long a strong advocate for the rights of psychiatrically different individuals against the intrusions of medical "treatments," in her work in Northeast Brazil, Scheper-Hughes turned her attention to the effects of the relationship between the *macroparasitism* of class exploitation and the *microparasitism* of infectious diseases on the frailer and consequently neglected children of distraught mothers. Second, at the invitation of Tom Johnson, then the editor of the newsletter *Medical Anthropology Quarterly,* the authors began organizing a collection titled "Critical Approaches to Health and Healing in Sociology and Anthropology" [174]. Papers in this collection are concerned with defining CMA, suggesting directions to be taken in future work, and pointing to lessons to be learned from critical health sociology. Finally, the first formal organizational meeting of an interest group in critical medical anthropology was convened at the 1985 AAA meetings. While the advantages of such an organization had been under discussion for several years, participants in the critical trend hesitated because of concern over the potential fragmentation produced by the rapid proliferation of specialized interest groups within the Society for Medical Anthropology. At the suggestion of Donahue, however, the decision was made to organize so as to gain more formal recognition and representation within the subdiscipline, broaden the opportunities for open discussion of the goals and concerns of the trend, and regularize the formation of symposia at the annual meetings. Constituted ultimately as the Critical Anthropology of Health Interest Group (CAHIG), the first act of the new organization was to plan two events for the 1986 AAA meetings in Philadelphia.

In a number of ways, the active presence of critical ideas and their adherents at the AAA meetings in Philadelphia can be seen as representing the culmination of the first stage in the development of CMA. The approach emerged from the shadows as a major outlook within the subdiscipline with the *Social Science and Medicine, Medical Anthropology Quarterly,* and *Human Organization* collections all appearing in rapid succession just before the meetings. In Philadelphia, sessions devoted to the further articulation of CMA registered considerable attention among conferees; CAHIG, though still a fledgling organization, was more securely established; and a number of medical anthropologists not previously associated with CMA expressed their growing interest in the trend.

While the first phase in the development of critical medical anthropology had largely been devoted to establishing the legitimacy and vital importance of medical anthropologists addressing issues of macro-micro relationship, political economic aspects of health care and disease, and the nature of class, gender and race relations as they impact the health arena, concept clarifying debate among critical medical anthropologists with differing perspectives (e.g. radical phenomenology versus Marxist approaches) was emerging as the top agenda item for the next phase [175, 176]. Differences among critical medical anthropologists (from those who see political economy as *the* missing link versus those who see political economy as insensitive to local differences, inattentive to the role of struggle at the micro-level, and overly economic in its orientation) became increasingly evident. Nonetheless, by 1987, a shared sense had emerged that CMA had arrived as a core perspective within medical anthropology. For a while, as happens with new approaches, a band-wagon effect occurred in which presenters at anthropological meetings utilizing ethnomedical or phenomenological approaches applied the label of CMA to their analyses. At a more serious theoretical level, however, some came to see CMA as having split into two contending camps, the so-called political economy/world system theorists and the Foucaultian post-structuralists [174]. Scheper-Hughes and Lock, principal proponents of the latter "camp," while granting that the political economy of health perspective served a useful corrective to conventional medical anthropological studies, asserted that it has "tended to depersonalize the subject matter and the content of medical anthropology by focusing on the analysis of social systems and *things*, and by neglecting the particular, the existential, the subjective content of illness, suffering, and healing as *lived* events and experiences" [117, p. 137]. More recently, Scheper-Hughes argued for the creation of what she termed a

> third path between the individualizing, meaning-centered discourse of the symbolic, hermeneutic, phenomenologic medical anthropologists, on the one hand, and the collectivized, depersonalized, mechanistic abstractions of the medical

marxists, on the other .... To date much of what is called *critical* medical anthropology refers to ... the applications of marxist political economy to the social relations of sickness and health care delivery [81, p. 189, emphasis in original].

Scheper-Hughes refers to her approach as "critical, reflexive medical anthropology" [172, p. 536]. Ironically, in the same issue of *Medical Anthropology Quarterly* that Scheper-Hughes and Lock launched their critique of critical medical anthropology, one of the authors argued that "it has been the tendency of world systems and dependency theorists to focus their attention on the macrolevel" while giving insufficient attention to *local context factors,* "including the particular configuration of class, gender, and ethnic relationships, the availability of resources and technology, demographic and ecological factors, and historic and cultural patterns, that contribute to the short- and long-term effects of capitalist penetration of health care, as well as to any micropopulation's ability to resist the agents, agencies, and agendas of biomedicine" [173, p. 128]. Elsewhere, Singer argued that the examination of sufferer experience, situated in relation to "socially constituted categories of meaning and the political-economic forces that shape the contexts of daily life," is *central* to the project of critical medical anthropology [177, p. 184]. In short, as this volume is intended to reflect, it is our view that critical medical anthropology *itself* is the third path of which Scheper-Hughes wrote.

Contrasting views within the critical trend also found expression in the volume *Medical Anthropology: Contemporary Theory and Method* [178], which included a chapter on the approach by Lock and Scheper-Hughes [122] and a separate chapter on the political economic approach by Morsy [124]. While the dialogue continues between these troubled bedfellows, CMA also has engaged discussion with clinical [179], postmodern [180] and, perhaps most fruitfully thus far, ecologically oriented biological and cultural anthropologists [181].

In contrast with conventional biocultural approaches, during its initial years of development CMA focused only limited attention on ecological factors in health. This has changed increasingly in recent years. CMA has entered into debate with medical ecology, bioculturalism, and biological anthropology around three core issues: 1) the nature of nature; 2) the utility of the adaptationist perspective; and 3) the implications of ecological destruction. Effort to expand conventional anthropological understanding of nature have been central to the CMA engagement with issues of human/environment relationship. Raymond Williams, in his telling observation that "the idea of nature contains, though often unnoticed, an extraordinary amount of human history" [182, p. 6], captures a fundamental component of the CMA perspective. Further, in the CMA view, it is not only the *idea* of nature but, in addition, the actual physical shape of nature that has been profoundly influenced by the changing political economy of human society. This approach differs notably from the generally dominant Western worldview in which nature is seen as a constituting an autonomous reality that operates in terms of its own principles separate from human society, an understanding that traces to the project of Enlightenment thinkers to disengage from the spiritual ideology of the eighteenth century.

> Where once nature was seen as sacred, the reflection of a divine plan or the embodiment of Ideas . . . , the Enlightenment task was to 'disenchant' nature and see 'God's world' as a mechanism, composed of physical matter obeying natural mechanistic laws rather than spiritual ones. . . . In the naturalist view, the universe consists of discrete material essences . . . which are fixed and stable in their identity . . . [183, p. 24].

Moreover, processes "in nature" commonly are defined as standing apart from the workings of society. Nature, in fact, is seen as being "not only independent from culture but prior to it" [183, p. 27]. In common parlance, the term nature is used to refer to areas that allegedly are untarnished by human presence. Thereby, the world is divided into two discrete and contrasting realms, the natural world and the human order.

CMA, by contrast, in attempting to apprehend "the relation of people to their environment in all its complexity" [184, p. 48] seeks to treat political economy and political ecology as inseparable [185]. As Parson emphasizes, "economy is a matter of ecology" it has to do with the production and distribution of goods and services in the context of human society and nature [186, p. xii]. Crosby, who uses the term "ecological imperialism" to label the biological expansion of European life forms (from parasites to people) to all corners of the globe, has contributed an important concept for the exploration of the impact of political economy on *nature* [187]. Future theory development in CMA in this regard will benefit from current discussions among neo-Marxist scholars in the political economy of ecology like Andre Gorz [188] and Rudolf Bahro [189], and the debates unfolding in new journals like *Capitalism, Nature, and Socialism*. This discourse seeks to transcend the productivist ethic and inattention to the contradictory aspects of societal-nature interaction that have characterized much political economic analysis since Marx and Engels. Critical to this avenue of exploration is a reconsideration of human biology in light of political economy. In Duden's apt phrase, to fully appreciate human biology it is necessary to recognize that there is an entire "history beneath the skin" [190].

Another point of contention between CMA and bioculturalism revolves around the concept of adaptation and its use within the reigning adaptationist perspective. Darwinian adaptationism, as Levins and Lewontin note, is an clear cut expression of Cartesianism and its tendency to see the world as comprised of atomic units with intrinsic properties, as independent things-in-themselves, as smaller wholenesses merely lumped together as aggregates the way a group of individual potatoes when packaged together constitutes a sack to use a famous example from Marx [191]. From the adaptationist perspective, there are two primary parts, preformed ecological niches and the organisms fitted to them, with adaptation being the process by which organisms adjust biologically and behaviorally to external conditions. However, as Levins and Lewontin cogently argue:

> To maintain that organisms adapt to the environment is to maintain that such ecological niches exist in the absence of organisms and that evolution consists in filling these empty and preexistent niches . . . . But the external world can be divided up in an uncountable infinity of ways, so there is an uncountable infinity of ecological niches. Unless there is a preferred or correct way in which to partition the world, the idea of an ecological niche without an organism filling it

loses all meaning . . . . Adaptation cannot be a process of gradual fitting of an
organism to the environment if the specific environmental configuration, the
ecological niche, does not already exist. If organisms define their own niches,
then all species are already adapted, and evolution cannot be seen as the process
of *becoming* adapted [191, p. 68] (emphasis in original).

The whole notion of niches overlooks the shaping effects of "organisms" on the
"environment." When these effects are considered, it is clear that "the environment is
a product of the organism, just as the organism is a product of the environment" [191,
p. 69]. Neither of these so-called parts has a privileged existence, both are changing
and changing each other in the process. This understanding is grasped quickly in a
consideration of the relationship between predator and prey species, where a drop or
rise in the size of either group has immediate effects on the size of the other, raising
questions about which is to be treated as "organism" and which as "environment." Yet
the interrelationship is greater still. For example, "it is often forgotten that the seedling
is the 'environment' of the soil, in that the soil undergoes great and lasting evolutionary changes as a direct consequence of the activity of the plants growing in it, and these
changes in turn feed back on the organism' conditions of existence" [191, p. 134].
Indeed, the very oxygenation process that sustains life on Earth is a product of living
organisms, reflecting the "co-evolution of the biosphere and its inhabitants" [191,
p. 47].

From the CMA perspective, it is evident that holistic approach is needed, one that
includes political economy as a primary force underlying complex dialectical
relationships. Interestingly, advances in this orientation are proceeding most rapidly
among Andeanist anthropologists, a group of scholars who until recently tended to
construe their area of study as if it were an insulated, discrete, and natural category.

> More then the 'Oriental,' the 'Andean,' derived from a geological formation, has
> a concrete ring to it. Perhaps this aura of naturalness helps to explain the historical
> lack of reflexivity amongst Andeanists about the use of the label . . . .Central
> to many . . . projections is the imagery of the highlands as a region of 'remote,'
> 'isolated' mountain villages bracketed out of modernity. The same discourse that
> removes the peasants to a distant space also typically confines them to a primor-
> dial time of 'traditional,' 'premodern,' or 'ancient' folkways [192, p. 19].

The adaptationist perspective led Andeanists to focus on physical adaptation to high
altitude conditions, the topic still most likely to gain entry of Andean peoples in the
texts of biological and bio-cultural anthropology. While Andeanists recognized the
existence of poverty, their

> stress on ecological adaptations and sophisticated symbolism had as a conse-
> quence a tendency to minimize the full extent of economic suffering across the
> countryside. Ethnographers usually did little more than mention the terrible
> infant mortality, miniscule incomes, low life expectancy, inadequate diets, and
> abysmal health care that remained so routine [193, p. 168].

In response to the unexpected level of peasant involvement in insurgent movements like Shining Path, as well as engagement with the literature of CMA and
the political economy of health, adaptationist thinking among Andeanist
anthropologists is giving way to broader understandings. Carey, for example, has

attempted to synthesize medical ecology and CMA as a corrective to the Andeanist project [194]. His analysis of health among children in three communities of the Nuñoa District of Peru found an inverse relationship between altitude and morbidity, which is "directly opposite to what one would expect if physical stressors associated with altitude were the primary factors leading to poor health in the Nuñoa District population" [194, p. 285]. More significant in the health of the communities under study were social stressors. "Far from being the 'natural' order of things, these social stressors are created by social relations at the local level, which are shaped in turn by larger scale political-economic and sociocultural forces generated by the rest of Peru and beyond" [194, p. 272].

Unfortunately, in examining the ameliorative effects of interhousehold social support networks, Cary returns to the concept of adaptation. Use of this notion in medical anthropology, however, commonly fails to address the question of "adaptive for whom?" [123, p. 228]. In light of the foregoing discussion, CMA asserts that various practices that bioculturalist anthropologists have traditionally called "adaptations" might better be analyzed as social adjustments to the consequences of oppressive sociopolitical relationships. Alternative concepts of this sort are being explored by a number of other Andeanists like Brook Thomas and Tom Leatherman. A significant product of this re-thinking was the organization by Alan Goodman and Tom Leatherman in 1992 of the conference Political-Economic Perspectives in Biological Anthropology: Building a Biocultural Synthesis sponsored by the Wenner Gren Foundation for Anthropological Research, Inc.

Finally, CMA is attempting to more directly address the implications of ecological homogenization and out right destruction, as illustrated in Chapter 5. As Bodley notes, human societies have precipitated ecological crisis throughout their long history.

> Tribal hunters have contributed to the creation of grasslands; pastoral nomads have overgrazed their lands; peasant farmers have caused deforestation and erosion. From archeological evidence, it is clear that tribal cultures and early civilization at times faced their own local environmental crisis as imbalances occurred, and were forced to abandon certain regions or drastically alter their cultures [195, p. 27].

The dawn of agrarian states produced a far reaching transformation in society/environment relations. The dangers of ecological self-destruction that plagued archaic and feudal state societies, however, pale by comparison with those of industrial capitalism. As contrasted with the relatively limited environmental modification wrought by pre-state and ancient state societies, the capitalist world system, with its culture of consumption, "introduces completely new environmental pollutants that disrupt natural biochemical processes " [195, p. 49]. Capitalism, pushed by its inherent drive to reap greater profits, increase production, and capture new markets, historically has assumed that natural "resources" (i.e., those elements of the natural world valued by society at any point in time), not only minerals but water, fertile soil, trees and much more, exist in unlimited supply in nature's bountiful storehouse. While the emergence of a capitalist world-system contributed to the production of a plentiful (if not equitably distributed) food supply (including large quantities of nutritionally questionable foodstuffs), modern sanitation, and the powerful cures of biomedicine, these material benefits were obtained at the expense of the masses of people in the Third World and oppressed classes in the First World. Moreover, they were obtained often at the expense of perilous environmental damage. This destruction has significant implications for the health of many if not all human populations, including the potential well being of future generations.

As Barnet and Cavanagh stress, capitalist production threatens the environment at four distinct points: 1) at the point of production significant quantities of toxic substances are poured into the environment and "are being spread around the world to countries willing to exchange breathable air for jobs" [196, p. 289]; 2) packaging of products for market appeal consumes large quantities of natural resources; 3) the products themselves increasingly are high consumers of fuel; and 4) planned obsolescence and reduced durability of products drives new wasteful production. Significantly, countries at the core of the capitalist world-system have attempted to export pollutants to countries in the periphery, as exemplified by the case of the Khian Sea which set sail for Haiti in October 1987 with 13,000 tons of toxic incinerator ash from Philadelphia [197]. The ash was dumped on a Haitian beach, only to be shoveled back aboard ship (minus 2,000 tons left behind on shore) when Haitian officials discovered it was not the fertilizer that had been promised. The Khian Sea spent the next fourteen-months cruising the globe seeking a Third World country from Senegal to Sri Lanka willing to accept its toxic cargo. World attention frightened off would be takers and the ash was eventually dumped into the Indian Ocean.

Within the capitalist world-system, even post-revolutionary socialist-oriented countries have had a wretched environmental record. The former Soviet Union exhibited some of the worst historic occurrences of radioactive contamination, while the former Czechoslovakia and Poland had the highest levels of industrial pollution in Europe if not the world. Separation of these countries from their place in the world-system, a common strategy of those whose primary agenda is disparaging socialism, tends to disorder the origins of widespread pollution in socialist-oriented countries. As Yih notes, understanding the environmental record of these countries in part can be

> explained by the conditions under which socialist governments came into being —relative underdevelopment, external aggression, and, especially for the small dependent economies of the Third World, a disadvantaged position in the international market. The corresponding pressures to satisfy the material needs of the populations, ensure adequate defense, and continue producing and exporting cash crops and raw materials for foreign exchange, have led to an emphasis by socialist policy-makers on accumulation by the state, the uncritical adoption of many features of capitalist development, and a largely abysmal record vis-a-vis the environment (although there are exceptions, of course) [198, p. 22].

Full reincorporation of former socialist-oriented economies into the capitalist fold appears likely to exacerbate environmental problems rather than resolve them.

As the foregoing discussion suggests, CMA does not advocate a rejection of biology or a devaluing of the importance of the environment; that is to say, it does not heed the idealist or postmodern calls for shift away from a materialist perspective in science. Rather, CMA is oriented toward forging a socially informed view of these phenomena, while embracing a critical stance toward science predicated on the recognition that science and its concepts are culturally created and socially situated, and as a result cannot help but incorporate tenets of the dominant ideology.

The intent of all of these ongoing discussions between CMA and other perspectives within medical anthropology has been to achieve a more thorough-going re-synthesis of theory in medical anthropology and the emergence of an integrated critical medical anthropology that is equally sensitive to bio-environmental factors in health, the experience of suffering among those who are ill, and the primacy of political economy in shaping the impact of bio-environmental factors on disease, sufferer experience, and the character of the health care system deployed in response to disease and illness.

REFERENCES

1. L. Rhodes, Studying Biomedicine as a Cultural System, in *Medical Anthropology: Contemporary Theory and Method*, T. Johnson and C. Sargent (eds.), Praeger, New York, pp. 159-173, 1990.
2. E. Friedson, *Profession of Medicine,* Dodd, Mead and Co., New York, 1970.
3. H. Herskovits, *Franz Boas: The Science of Man in the Making,* Charles Scribner's Sons, New York, 1953.
4. R. Wulff and S. Fiske, Introduction, in *Anthropological Praxis: Translating Knowledge into Action,* R. Wulff and S. Fiske (eds.), Westview Press, Boulder, pp. 1-11, 1987.
5. H. Heggenhougen. The Future of Medical Anthropology, in *Training Manual in Medical Anthropology,* C. Hill (ed.), American Anthropological Association, Washington, D.C., pp. 130-136, 1985.
6. M. Konner, The Promise of Medical Anthropology: An Invited Commentary, *Medical Anthropology Quarterly, 5:*1, pp. 78-82, 1991.
7. M. Nichter, Ethnomedicine: Diverse Trends, Common Linkages, *Medical Anthropology, 13*:1-2, pp. 137-171, 1991.
8. N. Chrisman, and T. Maretzki, Anthropology in Health Science Settings, in *Clinically Applied Anthropology: Anthropologists in Health Science Settings,* N. Chrisman and T. Maretzki (eds.), D. Reidel Publishing Co., Boston, pp. 1-35, 1982.
9. R. Firth, Social Anthropology and Medicine—A Personal Perspective, *Social Science and Medicine, 12B*, pp. 237-245, 1978.
10. R. Lieban, Medical Anthropology, in *Handbook of Social and Cultural Anthropology*, J. J. Honigman (ed.), Rand McNally, Chicago, pp. 1031-1072, 1973.
11. E. Stark, A. Flitcraft, and W. Frazier, Medicine and Patriaechal Violence: The Social Construction of a "Private" Event, in *Women and Health: The Politics of Sex in Medicine*, E. Fee (ed.), Baywood Publishing Co., Amityville, New York, pp. 177-210, 1983.
12. N. Scott, Medical Anthropology, in *Biennial Review of Anthropology,* B. Siegel (ed.), Stanford University Press, Stanford, pp. 30-68, 1963.
13. R. Brown, *Rockefeller Medicine Men,* University of California Press, Berkeley, 1979.
14. V. Navarro, U.S. Marxist Scholarship in the Analysis of Health and Medicine, *International Journal of Health Services, 15*, pp. 525-545, 1985.
15. D. Gordon, Tenacious Assumptions in Western Medicine, in *Biomedicine Examined,* M. Lock and D. Gordon (eds.), Kluwer Academic Publishers, Dordrecht, The Netherlands, pp. 19-56, 1988.

16. A. Kuper, *Anthropology and Anthropologists: The Modern British School,* Routledge and Kegan Paul, London, 1983.
17. E. Wolf, *Europe and the People without History,* University of California Press, Berkeley, 1982.
18. B. Magubane and J. Faris, On the Political Relevance of Anthropology, *Dialectical Anthropology, 9,* pp. 91-104, 1985.
19. E. Gillies, Introduction, in *Witchcraft Oracles and Magic among the Azande,* by E. E. Evans-Pritchard, Oxford University Press, London, 1976.
21. W. Caudill, William, Applied Anthropology in Medicine, in *Anthropology Today: An Encyclopedic Inventory,* A. Kroeber (ed.), The University of Chicago Press, Chicago, pp. 771-806, 1953.
22. S. Polgar, Health and Human Behavior: Areas of Interest Common to the Social and Medical Sciences, *Current Anthropology, 3,* pp. 159-205, 1962.
23. I. Galston, Retrospect and Prospect, in *Man's Image in Medicine and Anthropology,* I. Galston (ed.), International Universities Press, New York, 1963.
24. The Travelers Bulletin, *Doctor Says Road to Health is Paved with Common Sense,* Corporate Communications Department, The Travelers Companies, Hartford, 1982.
25. C. Leslie, Introduction, *Social Science and Medicine, 12,* pp. 65-67, 1978.
26. S. Hunter, Historical Perspectives on the Development of Health Systems Modeling in Medical Anthropology, *Social Science and Medicine, 21,* pp. 1297-1305, 1985.
27. G. Stocking, *Race, Culture, and Evolution,* The Free Press, New York, 1968.
28. A. Haddon, *History of Anthropology,* Watts and Co., London, 1934.
29. M. Harris, *The Rise of Anthropological Theory,* Thomas Y. Crowell Co., New York, 1968.
30. J. Hunt, On the Application of the Principle of Natural Selection in Anthropology, *Anthropological Review, 4,* pp. 320-340, 1866.
31. D. Struik, Introduction, in *The Economic and Philosophic Manuscripts of 1844 by Karl Marx,* D. Struik (ed.), International Publishers, New York, pp. 9-56, 1964.
32. W. H. R. Rivers, *Medicine, Magic, and Religion,* Harcourt Brace, New York, 1924.
33. D. Landy, Introduction: Learning and Teaching Medical Anthropology, in *Culture, Disease, and Healing,* D. Landy (ed.), Macmillan Publishing Co., Inc., New York, pp. 1-9, 1977.
34. G. Foster and B. Anderson, *Medical Anthropology,* John Wiley and Sons, New York, 1978.
35. E. Wellin, Theoretical Orientations in Medical Anthropology: Continuity and Change Over the Past Half-Century, in *Culture, Disease, and Healing: Studies in Medical Anthropology,* D. Landy (ed.), Macmillan Publishing Co., New York, pp. 47-58, 1977.
36. I. Press, Problems in the Definition and Classification of Medical Systems, *Social Science and Medicine, 14B,* pp. 45-57, 1980.
37. A. Gaines and R. Hahn, Among the Physicians: Encounter, Exchange and Transformation, in *Physicians of Western Medicine,* R. Hahn and A. Gaines (eds.), D. Reidel Publishing Co, Dordrecht, pp. 3-22, 1985.
38. C. Hughes, Ethnomedicine, *International Encyclopedia of the Social Sciences, 10,* Macmillan Publishing Co., New York, pp. 87-92, 1986.
39. T. McKeown, A Historical Appraisal of the Medical Task, in *Medical History and Medical Care,* G. McLachlan and T. McKeown (eds.), Oxford University Press, New York, 1971.
40. F. Boas, *The Mind of Primitive Man,* Macmillan Publishing Co., New York, 1911.

41. A. Lesser and Franz Boas, in *Totems and Teachers: Perspectives on the History of Anthropology*, S. Silverman (ed.), Columbia University Press, New York, pp. 1-34, 1981.
42. H. Waitzkin, The Social Origins of Illness: A Neglected History, *International Journal of Health Services, 11*, pp. 77-103, 1981.
43. N. Sigerist, From Bismarck to Beveridge: Developments and Trends in Social Security Legislation, *Bulletin of the History of Medicine, 13*, pp. 365-388, 1943.
44. M. Kaser, *Health Care in the Soviet Union and Eastern Europe,* Croom Helm, London, 1976.
45. F. Boas, Rudolf Virchow's Anthropological Work, *Science, 16*, pp. 441-445, 1902.
46. S. Freed, R. Freed, and L. Williamson, Capitalist Philanthropy and Russian Revolutionaries: The Jesup North Pacific Expedition (1897-1902), *American Anthropologist, 90*:1, pp. 7-24, 1988.
47. S. Estroff, Whose Hegemony?: A Critical Commentary on Critical Medical Anthropology, *Medical Anthropology Quarterly, 2*, pp. 421-426, 1988.
48. F. Boas, *Race and Democratic Society,* J. J. Augustin Publisher, New York, 1945.
49. P. Rabinow, For Hire: Resolutely Late Modern, in *Recapturing Anthropology*, R. Fox (ed.), School of American Research Press, Sante Fe, pp. 59-71, 1991.
50. E. Evans- Pritchard, *Social Anthropology*, Routledge and Kegan Paul LTD, London, 1951.
51. W. Bradley, Medical Practices of the New England Aborigines, *Journal of the American Pharmaceutical Association, 25*, pp. 138-147, 1936.
52. F. Clements, Primitive Concepts of Disease, *University of California Publications* in *American Archaeology and Ethnology*, *32*, pp. 185-252, 1932.
53. A. Hrdlicka, Disease, Medicine and Surgery among the American Aborigines, *Journal of the American Medical Association, 99*, pp. 1661-1666, 1932.
54. W. La Barre, Folk Medicine and Folk Science, *Journal of American Folklore, 55,* pp. 197-203, 1942.
55. A. Leighton and D. Leighton, Elements of Psychotherapy in Navaho Religion, *Psychiatry, 4,* pp. 515-523, 1941.
56. M. Opler, Some Points of Comparison and Contrast between the Treatment of Functional Disorders by Apache Shamans and Modern Psychiatric Practice, *American Journal of Psychiatry, 92*, pp. 1371-1387, 1936.
57. E. Ackerknecht, *Rudolf Virchow: Doctor, Statesman, Anthropologist,* University of Wisconsin Press, Madison, 1953.
58. E. Ackerknecht, *Medicine and Ethnology: Selected Essays*, The Johns Hopkins Press, Baltimore, 1971.
59. A. Kleinman, *Patients and Healers in the Context of Culture*, University of California Press, Berkeley, 1980.
60. E. Ackerknecht, Natural Diseases and Rational Treatment in Primitive Medicine, *Bulletin of the History of Medicine, 19*, pp. 467-497, 1946.
61. A. Kiev, Implications for the Future, in *Magic, Faith and Healing,* A. Kiev (ed.), The Free Press, New York, pp. 454-466, 1964.
62. E. Ackerknecht, Paleopathology, in *Anthropology Today*, A. Kroeber (ed.), University of Chicago Press, Chicago, pp. 120-126, 1953.
63. G. Foster, Anthropological Research Perspectives on Health Problems in Development Countries, *Social Science and Medicine, 18*, pp. 847-854, 1980.
64. B. Paul, Anthropological Perspectives on Medicine and Public Health, in *The Cross-Cultural Approach to Health Behavior,* R. Lynch (ed.), Farleigh Dickinson University Press, pp. 26-42, 1969.

65. D. Goulet and M. Hudson, *The Myth of Aid,* IDOC, New York, 1971.
66. F. Lappe, J. Moore, J. Collins and D. Kinley, *AIDS as Obstacle*, Institute for Food and Development Policy, San Francisco, 1981.
67. R. Elling, The Capitalist World-system and International Health, *International Journal of Health Services, 11*, pp. 21-51, 1981.
68. K. Dewalt, and G. Pelto, Food Use and Household Ecology in a Mexican Community, in *Nutrition and Anthropology in Action*, T. Fitzgerald (ed.), van Gorcum, Assen, Amsterdam, pp. 79-93, 1977.
69. M. Taussig, The Social Origins of Illness: A Neglected History, *International Journal of Health Services. 11*, pp. 77-103, 1981.
70. C. Kendall, The Use and Non-Use of Anthropology: The Diarrheal Disease Control Program in Honduras, in *Making Ourselves Useful: Case Studies in the Utilization of Anthropological Knowledge*, J. van Willigen, B. Rylko-Bauer, and A. McElroy (eds.), Westerview Press, Boulder, pp. 283-303, 1989.
71. L. Crandon, Grass Roots, Herbs, Promotors and Preventions: A Re-Evaluation of Contemporary International Health Care Planning, The Bolivian Case, *Social Science and Medicine, 17*:17, pp. 1281-1289, 1983.
72. J. Donahue, *The Nicaraguan Revolution in Health: From Somoza to the Sandinistas,* Bergin and Garvey, South Hadley, Massachusetts, 1986.
73. L. Whiteford, A Question of Adequacy: Primary Health Care in the Dominican Republic, *Social Science and Medicine, 30*:2, pp. 221-226, 1990.
74. B. Turner, *Medical Power and Social Knowledge,* Sage, London, 1987.
75. B. Jordan, Technology and the Social Distribution of Knowledge: Issues for Primary Health Care in Developing Countries, in *Anthropology and Primary Health Care*, J. Coreil and J. D. Mull (eds.), Westview Press, Boulder, pp. 98-120, 1990.
76. J. D. Mull, The Primary Health Care Dialectic: History, Rhetoric, and Reality, in *Anthropology and Primary Health Care*, J. Coreil and J. D. Mull (eds.), Westview Press, Boulder, pp. 28-47, 1990.
77. H. Todd and M. Clark, Medical Anthropology and the Challenge of Medical Education, in Training Manual *in Medical Anthropology,* C. Hill (ed.), American Anthropological Association, Washington, D.C., pp. 40-57, 1985.
78. A. Gordon, Anthropologists in Hospitals, in *Training Manual in Medical Anthropology,* C. Hill (ed.), American Anthropological Association, Washington, D.C., pp. 70-83, 1985.
79. A. Kleinman, Interpreting Illness Experience and Clinical Meanings: How I See Clinically Applied Anthropology, *Medical Anthropology Quarterly, 16*, pp. 69-71, 1985.
80. D. Landy, Medical Anthropology: A Critical Appraisal, in *Advances in Medical Social Science,* J. Ruffini (ed.), Gordon and Breach Science Publishers, New York, pp. 185-314, 1983.
81. N. Scheper-Hughes, Three Propositions for a Critically Applied Medical Anthropology, *Social Science and Medicine, 30*:2, pp. 189-197, 1990.
82. J. O'Niell, The Cultural and Political Context of Patient Dissatisfaction in Cross-Cultural Clinical Encounters, *Medical Anthropology Quarterly, 3,* pp. 325-344, 1989.
83. P. Kundstadter, The Comparative Study of Medical Systems in Society, in *Culture and Healing in Asian Societies: Anthropological, Psychiatric and Public Health Studies,* A. Kleinman, P. Kunstadter, E. Russel Alexander, and J. Gate (eds.), Schenkman Publishing Co., Cambridge, Massachusetts, pp. 393-406, 1978.
84. R. Packard, The "Health Reserve" and the "Dressed Native": Discourses on Black Health and the Language of Legitimation in South Africa, *American Ethnologist, 16*:4, pp. 686-703, 1989.

85. C. de Beer, *The South African Disease,* African World Press, Inc, Trenton, 1986.
86. H. Waitzkin, Micropolitics of Medicine: Theoretical Issues, *Medical Anthropology Quarterly, 17,* pp. 134-136, 1986.
87. B. Kapferer, Gramsci's Body and a Critical Medical Anthropology, *Medical Anthropology Quarterly, 3,* pp. 426-432, 1988.
88. D. Greenwood, S. Lindenbaum, M. Lock, and A. Young, Introduction. Theme Issue: Medical Anthropology, *American Ethnologist, 15*:1, pp. l-3, 1988.
89. E. Riska and P. V. Johansen, The Involvement of the Behavioral Sciences in American Medicine: An Historical Perspective, *International Journal of Health Services, 11*:4, pp. 583-596, 1981.
90. N. Chrisman and T. Johnson, Clincally Applied Anthropology, in *Medical Anthropology: Contemporary Theory and Method,* T. Johnson and C. Sargent (eds.), Praeger, New York, pp. 93-113, 1990.
91. H. Weidman, On the Origins of the SMA, *Medical Anthropology Quarterly, 17*:5, pp. 115-124, 1986.
92. S. Hyland and S. Kirkpatrick, *Guide to Training Programs in the Applications of Anthropology,* Society for Applied Anthropology, Washington, D.C., 1989.
93. T. Weaver (ed.), Essays on Medical Anthropology, *Southern Anthropological Society Proceedings, 11,* University of Georgia Press, Athens, Georgia, 1968.
94. C. Wienker, Physical Anthropology in Multidisciplinary Biomedical Research, *Medical Anthropology, 3,* pp. 368-376, 1989.
95. C. Olsen, Applied Collaborative Biomedical Anthropology in a State Health Department Setting, *Medical Anthropology Quarterly, 3*:4, pp. 377-384, 1989.
96. L. Schell and A. Stark, Biomedical Anthropology in a Multidisciplinary, Multi-Institutional Research Project: The Albany Lead Study, *Medical Anthropology Quarterly, 3*:4, pp. 385-394, 1989.
97. A. Young, The Anthropologies of Illness and Sickness, *Annual Review of Anthropology, 11,* pp. 257-285, 1982.
98. B. Good, Comment on Browner et al. A Methodology for Cross-Cultural Ethnomedical Research, *Current Anthropology, 29,* pp. 693-694, 1988.
99. B. Good, and M-J. Good, The Meaning of Symptoms: A Cultural Hermeneutic Model for Clinical Practice, in *The Relevance of Social Science for Medicine,* L. Eisenberg and A. Kleinman (eds.), D. Reidel Publishing Co., Dordrecht, pp. 165-196, 1981.
100. J.-H. Pfifferling, A Cultural Prescription for Medicocentrism, in *The Relevance of Social Science for Medicine,* L. Eisenberg and A. Kleinman (eds.), D. Reidel Publishing Co, Dordrecht, pp. 197-222, 1981.
101. T. Cordes, and A. Kleinman, The Therapeutic Process, in *Medical Anthropology: Contemporary Theory and Method,* T. Johnson and C. Sargent (eds.), Praeger, New York, pp. 11-25, 1990.
102. T. Cordes, Elements of Charismatic Persuasion and Healing, *Medical Anthropology Quarterly, 2,* pp. 445-469, 1988.
103. J. Caster, Metaphor in Medicine, *Journal of the American Medical Association, 250*:14, pp. 1841-1844, 1983.
104. R. Davis-Floyd, The Role of Obstetrical Rituals in the Resolution of Cultural Anomaly, *Social Science and Medicine, 31*:2, pp. 175-189, 1990.
105. A. Millard, The Place of the Clock in Pediatric Advice: Rationales, Cultural Themes, and Impediments to Breastfeeding, *Social Science and Medicine, 31*:2, pp. 211-221, 1990.

106. R. Rapp, Chromosomes and Communication: The Discourse of Genetic Counseling, *Medical Anthropology Quarterly*, 2:2, pp. 143-157, 1988.
107. D. Moerman, Physiology and Symbols: The Anthropological Implications of the Placebo Effect, in *The Anthropology of Medicine: From Culture to Method*, L. Romanucci-Ross, D. Moerman, and L. Tandreci (eds.), Bergin and Garvey, South Hadley, Massachusetts, pp. 156-167, 1983.
108. S. van der Geest and S. Whyte, The Charm of Medicines: Metaphors and Metonyms, *Medical Anthropology Quarterly*, 3:4, pp. 325-344, 1989.
109. E. Martin, *The Woman in the Body: A Cultural Analysis of Reproduction*, Beacon Press, Boston, 1987.
110. E. Martin, Toward an Anthropology of Immunology: The Body as Nation State, *Medical Anthropology Quarterly*, 4:4, pp. 410-426, 1990.
111. D. Erwin, The Militarization of Cancer Treatment in American Society, in *Encounters with Biomedicine*, H. Baer (ed.), Gordon and Breach, New York, pp. 201-227, 1987.
112. N. Scheper-Hughes and M. Lock, The Mindful Body: A Prolegomenon to Future Work in Medial Anthropology, *Medical Anthropology Quarterly*, *1*, pp. 6-41, 1987.
113. N. Scheper-Hughes and A. Lovell, Breaking the Circuit of Social Control: Lessons in Public Psychiatry from Italy and Franco Basaglia, *Social Science and Medicine*, *23*, pp. 159-178, 1986.
114. B. Colby, Comment on A Methology for Cross-cultural Ethnomedical Research, *Current Anthropology*, *29*:5, p. 691, 1988.
115. P. Conrad and J. Scheider, *Deviance and Medicalization: From Badness to Sickness*, The C. V. Mosby Co, St. Louis, 1980.
116. I. Illich, *Medical Nemesis*, Pantheon Books, New York, 1976.
117. N. Scheper-Hughes and M. Lock, Speaking "Truth" to Illness: Metaphors, Reification, and a Pedagogy for Patients, *Medical Anthropology Quarterly*, *17*, pp. 137-140, 1986.
118. E. Mishler, The Health-Care System: Social Contexts and Consequences, in *Social Contexts of Health, Illness, and Patient Care*, E. Mishler et al. (eds.), Cambridge University Press, Cambridge, pp. 169-194, 1981.
119. L. Kirmayer, Mind and Body as Metaphors: Hidden Values in Biomedicine, in *Biomedicine Examined*, M. Lock and D. Gordon (eds.), Kluwer Academic Publishers, Dordrecht, pp. 57-94, 1988.
120. M. Lock, Introduction, in *Biomedicine Examined*, M. Lock and D. Gordon, (eds.), Kluwer Academic Publishers, Dordrecht, pp. 3-10, 1988.
121. P. Browdwin, Symptoms and Social Performances: The Case of Diane Reden, in *Pain as Human Experience: An Anthropological Perspective*, M-J Good, P. Brodwin, B. Good, and A. Kleinman (eds.), University of California Press, Berkeley, pp. 67-99, 1992.
122. M. Lock and N. Scheper-Hughes, A Critical-Interpretive Approach in Medical Anthropology: Rituals and Routines of Discipline and Dissent, in *Medical Anthropology: Contemporary Theory and Method*, T. Johnson and C. Sargent (eds.), Praeger, New York, pp. 47-72, 1990.
123. M. Singer, The Coming of Age of Critical Medical Anthropology, *Social Science and Medicine*, *28*, pp. 1193-1204, 1989.
124. S. Morsy, Political Economy in Medical Anthropology, in *Medical Anthropology: Contemporary Theory and Method*, T. Johnson and C. Sargent (eds.), Praeger, New York, pp. 26-46, 1990.
125. H. Baer, On the Political Economy of Health, *Medical Anthropology Newsletter*, *14*, pp. 1-2, 13-17, 1982.
126. A. de Swaan, The Reluctant Imperialism of the Medical Profession, *Social Science and Medicine*, *28*, pp. 1165-1170, 1989.

127. L. Morgan, International Politics and Primary Health Care in Costa Rica, *Social Science and Medicine, 30*:2, pp. 211-220, 1990.
128. M. Singer, The Limitations of Medical Ecology: The Concepts of Adaptation in the Context of Social Stratification and Social Transformation, *Medical Anthropology, 10,* pp. 223-234, 1989.
129. K. Stebbins, Transnational Tobacco Companies and Health in Underdeveloped Countries: Recommendations for Avoiding a Smoking Epidemic, *Social Science and Medicine, 30*:2, pp. 227-236, 1990.
130. M. Singer, Toward a Political Economy of Alcoholism: The Missing Link in the Anthropology of Drinking Behavior, *Social Science and Medicine, 23*:2, pp. 113-130, 1986.
131. V. Kemper, What's Blocking Health Care Reform?, *International Journal of Health Services, 23*:1, pp. 69-80, 1993.
132. M. Podhorzer, L. Discoll and E. Rothchild, Unhealth Money: The Growth in Health PACs' Congressional Contributions, *International Journal of Health Services, 23*:1, pp. 81-94, 1993.
133. J. Denny, V. Kemper, V. Novak, P. Overby, and A. Young, George Bush's Ruling Class, *International Journal of Health Services, 23*:1, pp. 95-132, 1993.
134. H. Baer, The Organizational Rejuvenation of Osteopathy: A Reflection of the Decline of Professional Dominance in Medicine, *Social Science and Medicine, 15A,* pp. 701-711, 1981.
135. K. Figlio, Chlorosis and Chronic Disease in 19th-century Britain: The Social Constitution of Somatic Illness in a Capitalist Society, in *Women and Health: The Politics of Sex in Medicine,* E. Fee (ed.), Baywood Publishing Company, Amityville, New York, pp. 213-241, 1983.
136. H. Roberts, *The Patient Patients: Women and Their Doctors,* Pandora Press, London, 1985.
137. D. Craddock, *A Short Textbook of General Practice,* H.K. Lewis and Co. Ltd., London, 1976.
138. D. Scully and P. Bart, A Funny Thing Happened to Me on the Way to the Orifice: Women in Gynaecological Textbooks, *American Journal of Sociology, 78*:4, pp. 1045-1049, 1973.
139. R. Hahn, Divisions of Labor: Obstetrician, Woman, and Society, in Williams Obstetrics, 1903-1985, *Medical Anthropology Quarterly, 1*:3, pp. 256-282, 1987.
140. S. Fisher, *In the Patient's Best Interest: Women and the Politics of Medical Decisions,* Rutgers University Press, New Brunswick, 1988.
141. R. Wright, Hysterectomy: Past, Present, and Future, *American Journal of Obstetrics and Gynecology, 33*:4, pp. 560-563, 1969.
142. A. Gramsci, *Selections from the Prison Notebooks,* International Publishers, New York, 1971.
143. H. Waitzkin, Medicine Superstructure and Micropolitics, *Social Science and Medicine, 13a,* pp. 601-609, 1979.
144. P. Zimbardo, Pathology by Imprisonment, *Society, 9,* pp. 4-8, 1972.
145. H. Waitzkin, The Micropolitics of Medicine: A Contexual Analysis, *International Journal of Health Services, 14*:3, pp. 339-379, 1984.
146. D. Mull and J. D. Mull, The Anthropologist and Primary Health Care, in *Anthropology and Primary Health Care,* J. Coreil and J. D. Mull (eds.), Westview Press, Boulder, pp. 302-322, 1990.
147. F. Basaglia, *Psychiatry Inside Out: Selected Writings of Franco Basaglia,* N. Scheper-Hughes and A. Lovell (eds.), Columbia University Press, New York, 1987.

148. R. Lorau, Lavoratori del Negatrivo, Unitevi!, in *Crimini di Pace*, F. Basaglia (ed.), Einaudi, Turin, pp. 191-212, 1975.
149. M. Singer, Rethinking Medical Anthropology: Toward a Critical Realignment, *Social Science and Medicine, 30*, pp. 179-187, 1990.
150. V. Navarro, *Social Security and Medicine in the USSR: A Marxist Critique,* Lexington Books, Lexington, 1977.
151. R. Sidel and V. Sidel, *The Health of China,* Beacon Press, Boston, 1982.
152. M. Bates, A Critical Perspective on Coronary Artery Disease and Coronary Bypass Surgery, *Social Science and Medicine, 30*:2, pp. 249-260, 1990.
153. R. Elling, *Cross-National Study of Health Systems*, Transaction Books, New Brunswick, 1980.
154. E. Wolf, Distinguished Lecture: Facing Power—Old Insights, New Questions, *American Anthropologist, 92*:3, pp. 586-596, 1990.
155. A. Thomas, Introductory Remarks, in *Topias and Utopias in Health*, S. Ingman and A. Thomas (eds.), Mouton, The Hague, pp. 1-3, 1975.
156. S. Ingman and A. Thomas, *Topias and Utopias in Health,* Mouton, The Hague, 1975.
157. J. Janzen, The Comparative Study of Medical Systems as Changing Social Systems, *Social Science and Medicine, 12*, pp. 121-129, 1978.
158. R. Frankenberg, Medical Anthropology and Development: A Theoretical Perspective, *Social Science and Medicine, 14B*, pp. 197-207, 1980.
159. A. Young, Some Implications of Medical Beliefs and Practices for Social Anthropology, *American Anthopologist, 78*, pp. 5-24, 1976.
160. A. Young, The Discourse on Stress and the Reproduction of Conventional Knowledge, *Social Science and Medicine, 14B*, pp. 133-146, 1980.
161. S. Morsy, The Missing Link in Medical Anthropology: The Political Economy of Health, *Reviews in Anthropology. 6*, pp. 349-363, 1979.
162. S. Morsy, Toward a Political Economy of Health: A Critical Note on the Medical Anthropology of the Middle East, *Social Science and Medicine, 15B*, pp. 159-161, 1981.
163. S. Morsy, Body Concepts and Health Care: Illustrations from an Egyptian Village, *Human Organization, 39*, pp. 92-96, 1980.
164. H. Baer, and M. Singer, *Why Not Have a Critical Medical Anthropology?*, presented at the American Anthropological Association, Washington, D.C., 1982.
165. H. Baer, and M. Singer, Toward a Typology of Black Sectarianism as a Response to Racial Stratification, *Anthropological Quarterly, 54*, pp. 1-14, 1981.
166. H. Baer and M. Singer, *African American Religion in the Twentieth Century,* University of Tenneessee Press, Knoxville, 1992.
167. H. Baer, Prophets and Advisors in Black Spiritual Churches: Therapy, Palliative, or Opiate, *Culture, Medicine and Psychiatry, 5*, pp. 145-170, 1981.
168. M. Singer, C. Arnold, M. Fitzgerald, L. Madden, and C. von Legat, Hypoglycemia: A Controversial Illness in U.S. Society, *Medical Anthropology, 8*, pp. 1-35, 1984.
169. H. Baer, M. Singer, and J. Johnsen, Toward a Critical Medical Anthropology, *Social Science and Medicine, 23*, pp. 95-98, 1986.
170. P. New and J. Donahue, Strategies for Primary Health Care by the Year 2000: A Political Economy of Health Perspective, *Human Organization, 45*, pp. 95-153, 1986.
171. M. Segall, On the Concept of a Socialist Health System: A Question in Marxist Epidemiology, *International Journal of Health Services, 13*, pp. 221-225, 1983.
172. N. Scheper-Hughes, Culture, Scarcity, and Maternal Thinking: Mother Detachment and Infant Survival in a Brazilian Shanty Town, *Ethos, 13*:4, pp. 291-317, 1984.
173. N. Scheper-Hughes, *Death Without Weeping,* University of California Press, Berkeley, 1992.

174. M. Singer, H. Baer, Hans, and R. Elling (eds.), Symposion: Critical Approaches in Medical Sociology and Medical Anthropology, *Medical Anthropology Quarterly, 17:5*, pp. 128-140, 1986.

175. L. Morgan, Dependency Theory in the Political Economy of Health: An Anthropological Critique, *Medical Anthropology Quarterly, 1:2*, pp. 131-155, 1987.

176. M. Singer, The Emergence of a Critical Medical Anthropology, *Medical Anthropology Quarterly, 17:5*, pp. 128-129, 1986.

177. M. Singer, The Limitations of Medical Ecology: The Concepts of Adaptation in the Context of Social Stratification and Social Transformation, *Medical Anthropology, 10*, pp. 223-234, 1989.

178. T. Johnson and C. Sargent, *Medical Anthropolopy: Contemporary Theory and Practice*, Praeger, New York, 1990.

179. B. Good, *Medicine, Rationality, and Experience*, Cambridge University Press, Cambridge, 1994.

180. M. Singer, Knowledge for Use: Anthropology and Community-Centered Substance Abuse Research, *Social Science and Medicine, 37:1*, pp. 15-26, 1993.

181. M. Blakey, Skull Doctors: Intrinsic Socal and Political Bias in the History of American Physical Anthropology with Special Reference to the Work of Ales Hrdlicka, *Critique of Anthropology, 7:2*, pp. 7-35, 1987.

182. R. Williams, *Problems in Materialism and Culture*, Verso, London, 1980.

183. D. Gordon, Clinical Science and Clinical Expertise: Changing Boundaries between Art and Science in Medicine, in *Biomedicine Examined*, M. Lock and D. Gordon (eds.), Kluwer Academic Publishers, Dordrecht, pp. 257-295, 1988.

184. M. Turshen, *The Politics of Public Health*, Rutgers University, New Brunswick, 1977.

185. J. O'Conner, The Political Economy of Ecology of Socialism and Capitalism, *Capitalism, Nature, Socialism, 3*, pp. 93-127, 1989.

186. H. Parson, *Marx and Engels on Ecology*, Greenwood, Westport, Connecticut, 1977.

187. A. Crosby, *Ecological Imperialism: The Biological Expansion of Europe, 900-1900*, Cambridge University, Cambridge, 1986.

188. A. Gorz, *Ecology as Politics*, South End Press, Boston, 1980.

189. R. Bahro, *Socialism and Survival*, Heretic Books, London, 1982.

190. B. Duden, *The Women Beneath the Skin*, Harvard University Press, Cambridge, 1991.

191. R. Levins and R. Lewontin, *The Dialectical Biologist*, Harvard, Cambridge, Massachusetts, 1985.

192. O. Starn, Rethinking the Politics of Anthropology: The Case of the Andes, *Current Anthropology, 35:1*, pp. 13-38, 1994.

193. O. Starn, Missing the Revolution: Anthropologists and the War in Peru, in *Rereading Cultural Anthropology*, G. Marcus (ed.), Duke University, Durham, North Carolina, pp. 152-180, 1992.

194. J. Carey, Social System Effects on Local Level Morbidity and Adaptation in the Peruvian Andes, *Medical Anthropology Quarterly, 4*, pp. 266-295, 1990.

195. J. Bodley, *Anthropology and Contemporary Human Problems*, Mayfield Publishing, Palo Alto, California, 1985.

196. R. Barnet and J. Cavanagh, *Global Dream: Imperial Corporations and the New World Order*, Simon and Schuster, 1994.

197. J. Vallette and H. Spaulding (eds.), *International Trade in Wastes*, (5th Edition), Greenpeace, Washington, D.C., 1990.

198. K. Yih, The Red and the Green, *Monthly Review, 42:5*, pp. 16-27, 1990.

CHAPTER 2

The Critical Gaze

INTRODUCTION

Eric Wolf, whose life-long concern with political economy contributed directly to a reorientation of anthropology away from studying individual communities as if they existed in isolation of a wider social world, has urged that we be "professionally suspicious of [reigning] categories and models; we should be aware of their historical and cultural contingencies" [1, p. 587]. Just as the hamlets, villages, and even whole societies of traditional anthropological interest must be studied in light of their location within an encompassing net of expansive, perhaps, global, social relationships (e.g., colonialism, the market system), so too the ideas and concepts that structure the anthropological worldview emerge from and are shaped by particular historic and social contexts. The historicity of conception was powerfully introduced into the social sciences by Marx and developed with great effect by the late French social historian and philosopher Michel Foucault. As Rabinow remarks, "For Foucault, there is no external position of certainty, no universal understanding that is beyond history and society" [2, p. 4]. In his archeology of biomedical understanding, for example, Foucault points out,

> At the beginning of the nineteenth century, doctors described what for centuries had remained below the threshold of the visible and the expressible, but this did not mean that, after over-indulging in speculation, they had begun to perceive once again, or that they listened to reason rather than imagination; it meant that the relationship between the visible and invisible—which is necessary to all concrete knowledge—changed its structure, revealing through gaze and language what had previously been below and beyond their domain. A new alliance was forged between words and things, enabling one *to see* and *to say* [3, p. xiii].

The emergence of this new "medical gaze," in other words, gave birth to a dramatic change in what was seeable, knowable, and speakable among physicians.

> Suddenly doctors were able to see and to describe what for centuries had been beneath the level of the visible. It was not so much that doctors suddenly opened

> their eyes; rather the old codes of knowledge had determined what was seen. . . A
> new way of seeing produced a new kind of knowledge. . . [4, p. 162].

Indeed, this is always the case with paradigmatic shifts; researchers "see new and different things when looking . . . in places they have looked before" [5, p. 110].

Critical medical anthropology is founded upon such a shift in perception. The goal of CMA is not to seek a rejection of traditional topics of medical anthropological regard, but rather, with undertaking a different reading of the nature of these issues, locations, and relations, a reading guided by a *critical gaze*. "Far from denying the importance of microanalytic studies of the existential particularities of sickness and healing—in essence, discarding the anthropological baby with the bath water" [6, p. 35], CMA promotes the situating of studies of sickness and healing, all sickness and all healing, within a broader frame than was traditionally brought to bear in medical anthropology.

Influenced by Marx's recognition that the dominant ideas and "common sense" understandings in each historic epoch disproportionately are those of the dominant social class or other preeminent social grouping, and Gramsci's analysis of hegemony, CMA seeks a re-examination of the guiding conceptions that have shaped the nature of understanding in medical anthropology. As suggested in the previous chapter, a driving concern of CMA is the recognition that the bedrock ideas upon which medical anthropology was founded and from which its praxis emerges, were shaped unduly by biomedicine. And further, that medical anthropology, in part through its relationship with this powerful medical system, absorbs the conventional understandings of the dominant social class in Western society.

> The problem is not a cadre of malevolent scientists [or physicians or medical anthropologists] who consciously buttress the status quo. Rather the pervasive climate of bourgeois ideology imperceptibly shapes the interests and concerns that guide research [in medicine and by extension in medical anthropology] [7, p. 1208].

The intent of adopting a critical gaze is the jettisoning of dominant conception in the interest of a deepened perception, an ongoing process that is never completed and demands constant referential reflexivity [8] for three reasons: 1) because, inavoidably, even critical understanding is historically and culturally rooted [9, 10]; 2) because of the "inevitable conservatism of settled positions" [11, p. 370]; and 3) because, without a fundamental reshaping of social relationships, even critical insight or action are subject to expropriation and co-optation in the interest of the dominant class.

Quite certainly, these comments raise a fundamental question. As posed by Radnitzky" If all anthropological knowledge is relative [to time, place, and social structure], how do we meaningfully choose between alternatives?" [12, p. 35]. On what basis can such choices be made? Growing from the long standing anthropological identification with the experience and striving of the oppressed, CMA asserts that its mission is consciously emancipatory and partisan: it aims not simply to understand but to change culturally inappropriate, oppressive and exploitive patterns in the health arena and beyond. *However, this does not imply a disregard for empirical research or an acceptance of the conscious shaping of research findings to meet preconceived political expectations.* Rather, it calls attention to the folly of so-called value-free social science. As Bellah points out:

> Many of us, frightened by Weber's contempt for those who use the lecture platform for political or religious prophecy, have forgotten that value neutrality had for Weber a very specific and a very confined meaning, namely the obligation not to let our value predilections dictate the results of our research, and that it was itself a moral norm, a tenet of scholarship. What is dangerous is not the presence of value judgements—they can be found in almost every line that Weber wrote—but only those judgements that remain beyond the reach of critical reflection and are not subject to revision in the light of experience [13, pp. xi-xii].

Gould adds that "fair and scrupulous procedures do not demand neutrality, but only strict adherence to the rules of the craft" [14, p. 17]. The aim of CMA, in this light, is to produce the most accurate data possible so that praxis (integrated theory and practice) emanating from its research can be useful in changing oppressive conditions or relieving suffering.

AN OVERVIEW OF THE THEORETICAL MODEL OF CRITICAL MEDICAL ANTHROPOLOGY

In this section, we lay out the theoretical perspective of critical medical anthropology by exploring its key concepts and some of its primary arenas of application, including:

- the examination of the social origins of disease and ill health;
- analysis of health policy, health resource allocation, and the role of the state in health and health care;
- exploration of the social relations among interacting medical traditions nationally and transnationally;
- analysis of the intertwining of medical systems with their political economic context; and
- location of sufferer experience within a framework of hegemony and resistance.

Additionally, following the argument developed in the last chapter, this discussion will extend the examination of biomedicine and its relationship to medical anthropology that is a central task of CMA.

Pivotal to the worldview of critical medical anthropology is recognition of class and related race and gender antagonisms as the defining characteristics of capitalist society and the reigning world-system. Classes have inherently conflicted social interests, in that, at its heart, capitalism is a system designed to promote the ability of one class to control and expropriate the labor of other classes. To maintain its dominance, the ruling class must keep conflict "on a terrain in which its legitimacy is not dangerously questioned" [15, p. 26]. According to Genovese, and as illustrated in several studies reported in subsequent chapters, "The success of a ruling class in establishing its hegemony depends entirely on its ability to convince the lower classes that its interests are those of society at large—that it defends the common sensibility and stands for a natural and proper social order" [quoted in 16, p. 259]. As summarized by Abercrombie, Hill, and Turner, ideology, the tool used to rationalize inequality or to minimize its visibility, is consequential because of its capacity to set the terms of discussion:

> In all societies based on class divisions there is a dominant class which enjoys control of both the means of material production and the means of mental production. Through its control of ideological production, the dominant class is able to supervise the construction of a set of coherent beliefs. These dominant beliefs of the dominant class are more powerful, dense, and coherent than those of subordinate classes. The dominant ideology penetrates and infects the consciousness of the working class, because the working class comes to see and to experience reality through the conceptual categories of the dominant class [17, p. 2].

This process of ideological domination constitutes class hegemony. Hegemony is achieved and maintained through the diffusion of self-interested values, attitudes, ideas, and norms from the dominant group to the rest of society. This process reinforces the ultimate social legitimacy of the existing structure of society, in that ruling class ideas and values tend to support and rationalize the status quo and to denigrate and demoralize subordinate strata. In this, biomedicine, as a core institution of capitalist society and as a system that reinforces dominance at the micro-social level, plays a vital function [18], a theme we will return to frequently throughout our discussion.

In response to the biomedical role in ruling class hegemony, CMA seeks to retrieve the lost threads of Virchow's and Engels' work in health-related anthropology. In so doing, its outlook is guided by questions like:

> (1) Who has power over the agencies of biomedicine? (2) How and in what form is this power *delegated*? (3) How is power expressed in the social relations within the health care system? (4) What are the economic, socio-political and ideological ends and consequences of the power relations that characterize biomedicine? and (5) What are the principal contradictions of biomedicine and arenas of struggle in the medical system? [19, pp. 95-96].

In other words, this perspective is committed to the "making social" and the "making political" of health and medicine and with the centering of this understanding in medical anthropology theory and praxis [20, 21]. In Morsy's apt phrase, CMA strives to shift "anthropological obsession with what is inside people's heads to a scrutiny of what is on their backs" [6, p. 31]. Further, high on the agenda of this approach is the exploration of the implications of all of these issues at the micro-level of individual experience and behavior; with the ways in which social conflict and oppressive experience is somatized or embodied in illness; and illness, in turn, becomes an arena for both resistance and political conscientization [22]. Argues Ellen Lazarus, a critical medical anthropologist whose research has focused on clinical interaction and structure, "[t]o ignore the meaning and variety of personal experiences and beliefs . . . is to dehumanize history and reduce human experience to abstract theory" [23, p. 54], shortcomings, in fact, of biomedicine.

As the foregoing discussion suggests, despite its assertion of the critical importance of ruling class hegemony and the contribution of biomedicine to the dissemination of ruling class ideology, CMA recognizes that "ideologies are not all-powerful in constraining those they potentially confine" [24, p. 183]. Social conflict at all levels produces alternative conception as well as both passive and more active resistance, in addition to, under certain conditions, open rebellion. While serving as an arena for the fortifications of hegemony, biomedicine thus generates considerable conflict and must be examined as a context in which resistance emerges and sometimes spreads to other arenas of social life. Conversely, because it is in no way isolated or insulated from the wider social environment, conflicts that emerge outside biomedicine find expression within its diverse settings and social relationships.

We have proposed that one way of conceptualizing these complex issues is in terms of a model of the levels of health care and health-related behavior (See Figure 1). As Figure 1 implies, we believe that discussions of the health arena profit from situating the topic under examination in terms of macro-micro levels of analysis. However, as Morsy points out, "[f]ar from exhibiting a fixed macro-micro 'ratio'" [6, p. 36], CMA analyses are concerned with issues at different levels, "from the consciousness of the patient . . . [25], to community organization . . . [26], regional political economy . . . [27], and international corporate power . . . [28]."

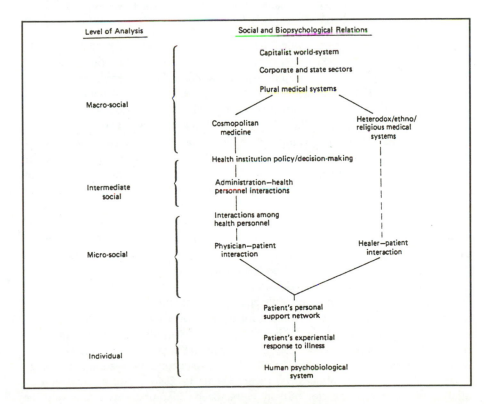

Figure 1. Levels of health care systems.

The Macro-Social Level

At the top-end, our model draws attention to the importance of locating health studies relative to the encompassing *capitalist world-system*. Expansion of capitalism as a world economic structure represents the most significant transcending social process in the contemporary historic epoch. Capitalism has progressively shaped and reshaped social life, bringing into being new social actors, new stages of dramatic enactment, and new scripts as it has developed and expanded its economic scope and hegemony over the last several centuries. As a discipline, anthropology lagged in its attention to the nature and transforming influence of capitalism until relatively recently. Nonetheless, the current discourse outside of anthropology on the nature of the capitalist world-system began in part with a recognition of important shortcomings of conventional anthropological descriptions of so-called traditional societies. As Immanuel Wallerstein, a major initiator of world-system theorizing recalls

> It was a false perspective to take a unit like a 'tribe' and seek to analyze its operations without reference to the fact that, in a colonial situation, the governing institutions of a 'tribe,' far from being 'sovereign,' were closely circumscribed by the laws (and customs) of a larger entity of which they were an indissociable part, the colony. Indeed this led me to the larger generalization that the study of social organization was by and large defective because of the widespread lack of consideration of the legal and political framework within which both organizations and their members operated [29, p. 5].

Ultimately, Wallerstein concluded that even nation-states were only partial systems. Nations have been linked since before the emergence of anthropology into a set of interconnected processes, the capitalist world-system. This system is not political, in the sense that it links local areas through a common governing structure, rather it is economic, tying diverse peoples together in a global system of production. As succinctly summarized by Marshall Sahlins: "History [has] been decided by economic power" [30, p. 2]. Location within the capitalist world-system, within what constitutes an international division of labor, Wallerstein argues, determines the character of a social organization. As he indicates, "the range of economic tasks is not evenly distributed throughout the world-system," enabling and legitimizing "the ability of some groups within the system to exploit the labor of others, that is, to receive a larger share of the surplus" [29, p. 349]. Core-states, the advantaged areas of the world-economy, are characterized by strong political structures and national cultures, developments that are, so to speak, "bought and paid for" by labor performed both in the core states as well as in more peripheral regions of the system. The peripheral areas tend to have weak and only partially autonomous state structures (hence their tendency to fall to periodic coups) and enfeebled economies, as well as national cultures that fail to create national unity. Mid-way between these two extremes is the semiperiphery, "middle areas [that] partially deflect the political pressure which groups primarily located in peripheral areas might otherwise direct against core-states" [29, p. 350]. The world capitalist economic system is not stagnant, its development continues. As recent events in Eastern European countries suggest, capitalist repenetration of their nationalized economies was extensive prior to the collapse of socialist-oriented regimes. How else to read the embrace of complete recapitalization as a solution to the failures of bureaucratic and non-democratic nationalization?

On ground cleared by Wallerstein, Andre Gunder Frank, and other analysts of global economic interconnection, Eric Wolf directs attention to the need for an alternative political economic perspective for anthropology.

> Concepts like 'nation,' 'society,' and 'culture' name bits and threaten to turn names into things. Only by understanding these names as bundles of relationships, and by placing them back into the field from which they were abstracted, can we hope to avoid misleading inferences and increase our share of understanding. . . . Yet the scholars to whom we turn in order to understand what we see largely persist in ignoring [global interconnections]. Historians, economists, and political scientists take separate nations as their basic framework of inquiry. Sociology continues to divide the world into separate societies. Even anthropology. . . divides its subject matter into distinctive cases: each society with its characteristic culture, conceived as an integrated and bounded system, set off against other equally bounded systems [31, pp. 3-4].

With the birth of ethnography early in this century and its elevation as the hallmark of anthropological research and purpose, anthropology turned its attention away from the study of evolutionarily conceived cultural forms to the detailed examination of "living cultures." Whole vistas opened to anthropological insight as a result. Anthropologists became engrossed in comprehending the configuration of behaviors and beliefs that constitute ethnographically studiable social segments. In short order, however, the sense of segmentation, the realization that the "bands," "tribes," "chiefdoms" and "states" that have been subject to anthropological inquiry are but pieces of a larger whole, the world-system, was forgotten. In a telling example of methodological determinism (one that should alert us to the fact that methods are not neutral tools that have no bearing on the theoretical nature of research outcomes), ethnography "was turned into a theoretical construct by assertion, a priori. The outcome was a series of analyses of wholly separate cases" [31, p. 14], a pattern duplicated for medical systems in conventional medical anthropology. Eclipsed in this approach to societies and their healing traditions is the role of power as a determinant of action and as a force that cross-cuts local groupings linking them to broader systems.

CMA seeks to cast light on this shaded arena through the re-insertion of cases back into the social field from which they are always abstracted. Cases "must be situated, placed in a context—historically, economically, politically. . ." [32, p. 161]. Consequently, CMA's understanding of health issues begins with analysis of the impact of political and economic forces that pattern human relationships, shape social behaviors, condition collective experiences, re-order local ecologies, and generate cultural meanings, including forces of institutional, national and global scale.

Beyond its hegemonic contribution, biomedicine serves other identifiable political-economic functions for the capitalist world-system, including profit-making [33]. As James Paul emphasizes, whatever its noted curative powers, biomedicine must be analyzed in terms of its function as an arena for "the voracious search for ever wider markets and profitable deals" [34, p. 272]. Indeed, one of the most significant forces shaping the nature of the health care scene in the contemporary period has been the rise of a *medical-industrial complex*. Paralleling the dual composition of the military-industrial-complex that President Eisenhower warned about in his famous January 17, 1961 farewell address to the nation, this other industrial complex consists of an immense biomedical health care establishment that is closely interconnected with a set of corporations with significant political and economic power. The latter include two groups of corporations. First, there are the insurance, pharmaceutical, medical equipment, and medical supply companies. Second, there is, what Relman has described as "a large and growing network of private corporations engaged in the business of supplying health care-services to patients for a profit—services heretofore provided by nonprofit institutions or individual practitioners" [35, p. 210].

As with the military industrial complex, it is evident that the state legitimizes the activities of the corporate sector in the health arena. Through its significant financial support of medical training and research, the state reinforces the reductionist framework of biomedicine. Corporate-controlled foundations augment the support of the state in these areas. In many core countries of the world-system, the state contracts with and subsidizes the involvement of the corporate sector in profit-making activities, such as health insurance. Conversely, the state tends to take responsibility for health services that are considered unprofitable by the corporate sector, e.g., services for the poor.

One obvious way in which health care has become a profit-making endeavor is in the pharmaceutical industry, an area, that has received growing interest in medical social science in recent years. While the anthropological literature largely has focused on the cultural and symbolic aspects of Western pharmaceuticals that contribute to their popularity among consumers in peripheral countries [e.g., 36, 37], other researchers have examined the marketing strategies of pharmaceutical corporations that contribute to the wide sale and use of drugs among individuals who are unaware of their specific purposes or side effects and the dumping of dangerous or banned drugs in peripheral markets. Of all Fortune 500 companies, U.S. pharmaceutical companies recorded the largest profits between 1960-1990, and since 1985 the gap in profits separating drugmakers from other big business has widened considerably. A primary reason for this notable boost in profits has been the lack of regulation on U.S. drug prices or pharmaceutical profits. During the 1980s, the average cost increase per prescription for established drugs was double the rate of inflation. Wholesale prices for 104 pharmaceuticals, which comprise 80 percent of industry revenue from drugs sold to the elderly, rose an average of 8.6 percent a year between 1981 and 1988, more than twice the consumer price index [38]. Because new drugs sell at wholesale prices that are from three to six times what it costs to research and produce them, pharmaceutical companies have large enough profits to pour enormous sums into aggressively advertising and marketing their products. Large pharmaceutical companies now have "armies of salesmen [to] march across the globe drumming up demand" [38, p. 50].

Other profitable activities in the health field include "hospital construction, development and outfitting, the supply of medical, surgical and diagnostic equipment, and numerous ancillary goods and services" [39, p. 270]. In this regard, Waitzkin has provided detailed analysis of the role of large profit-making corporations in the development, promotion, and proliferation of coronary care technology [40]. The Warner-Lambert Pharmaceutical Company, for example, played an active role in winning the acceptance of new coronary care technology among physicians and medical centers across the United States. Promotional material developed by the company, "contained the assumption, never proven, that the new technology was effective in reducing morbidity and mortality from heart disease" [40, p. 222]. Controlled studies of coronary care unit (CCU) efficacy, in fact, were delayed. Nonetheless, the costly new technology was readily adopted and CCUs became standard in larger urban and even community hospitals across the United States. Market saturation produced three profit-seeking responses from Warner-Lambert. First, the company expanded promotion and sales in foreign markets, both in core and semi-peripheral countries. Second, it developed new CCU products "whose intent was to open new markets or to create obsolescence in existing systems" [40, p. 223]. Finally, existing CCU technology was modified for use in other areas (e.g., early warning of heart rhythm disturbance in ambulatory patients). The tremendous expansion of CCU technology was supported by private foundations, such as the American Heart Association, which sponsored research that led to new monitoring systems and provided financial support to hospitals to acquire the expensive new technology. Waitzkin's analysis of the composition of foundation boards of directors and their historic ties to large industrial corporations helps explain their commitment to capital-intensive medicine. The W. R. Hewlett Foundation, founded by the CEO of Hewlett-Parkard Company (itself a major player in the CCU market), for example, was an important supporter of CCU growth. Similarly, agencies of the government played strategic roles in the promotion of CCUs, including encouraging CCU proliferation to smaller hospitals and providing market research information on foreign and domestic medical facilities (e.g., The Global Market Survey) that are prime candidates for the purchase of biomedical technology.

Waitzkin's general line of analysis has been applied by Bates [41] in a study of coronary bypass surgery with notably similar findings. Among the most costly of surgical procedures, coronary artery bypass graft (CABG) proliferated without evidence from controlled studies of its actual effectiveness. Not only has the rapid adoption of this procedure brought a secure economic boost to cardiac surgeons, assisting physicians, and hospitals, it is also a major source of corporate profit. Again, giants like Warner-Lambert and Hewlett-Packard are among the prime corporate promoters and profit-makers from CABG surgery.

The other arena of corporate growth noted above is the commodification of health care service delivery, reflected in the market gains of proprietary hospitals, nursing homes, home care services, laboratory services, and consumer diagnostic equipment. As Johnson comments, "[t]he huge success of proprietary (for profit) hospital corporations heralded the fact that health care had truly become big business" [42, p. 25]. Importantly, as Relman, points out:

> Physicians have direct financial interests in proprietary hospitals and nursing homes, diagnostic laboratories, dialysis units, and many small companies that provide health-care services of various kinds. Physicians are on the boards of

many major health-care corporations, and I think it is safe to assume that they are also well represented among the stockholders of these corporations [35, p. 215].

In Relman's liberal critique, if physicians are to represent their patient's health interests, "they should have no economic conflict of interest and therefore no pecuniary association with the medical-industrial complex" [35, p. 215]. In fact, the distinction between the nonprofilt and for-profit health care institution is increasingly a spurious one as the former become "holding companies for profit-making businesses" and as they acquire other enterprises including nursing homes, ambulatory care centers, health promotion programs and even hotels and shopping centers [43, p. 369]. In Gray's apt phrase, comparing the modern hospital to the traditional community hospital is "like comparing agri-business to the family farm" [44, p. 9]. All of these issues present significant arenas for CMA research and analysis.

At the next level, our model calls attention to the fact that the medical systems of complex societies are characterized by their plural character. These system are most accurately described as plural rather than pluralistic given the dominant position of biomedicine. The relationship between biomedicine and alternative medical systems, an issue examined in Chapter 6, has been characterized by processes of annihilation, restriction, absorption, and even collaboration. However, since certain strategic elites, members or representatives of the ruling class, ultimately shape health policy, the power of biomedicine over competing medical systems is delegated rather than absolute. The dominative status of biomedicine is legitimized by laws that afford it a monopoly over other medical systems in most contexts, while limiting or banning the practice of other types of health care.

Indeed, in differentiating the Western medical system that became dominant globally during this century from alternative systems, the vital feature may not be in the area of clinical efficacy but in political efficacy. Biomedicine achieved its dominant position in the West and beyond with the emergence of industrial capitalism and with abundant assistance from the industrial bourgeoisie whose inter-ests it commonly serves. As indicated in the last chapter, it is in this sense that CMA uses the term *bourgeois medicine* to refer to the medical system that promotes the hegemony of bourgeois society generally and the bourgeois class specifically, not only in the United States but elsewhere in the advanced capitalist and dependent capitalist worlds. While certain other professionalized medical systems, such as homeopathy, Ayurveda, Unani, and Chinese medicine, function in many parts of the world, bourgeois medicine constitutes the *world medical system* par excellence. Bourgeois medicine became the pre-eminent medical system in the world not simply because of its well known curative efficacy, but as a result of the expansion of the "capitalist world economy" generally.

The Intermediate Social Level

At the intermediate level in the model depicted in Figure 1, CMA is concerned with the study of relations among health care administrators and providers. The hospital, which varies in size from a sprawling medical center to a rural health clinic, has become the primary arena for the enactment of relations among players in the health sector. As the Sidel's indicate, "the modern U.S. hospital has come more and more to resemble a modern industrial plant with its elaborate division of labor and the increasing alienation of the hospital worker" [45, p. 182]. Navarro has examined the extensive control that members of the corporate and upper-middle classes have over both "reproductive institutions" (health foundations and private and state medical teaching facilities) and "delivery institutions" (primary voluntary hospitals) in the United States [46]. The power that hospital administrators and physicians enjoy at this level is an example of delegated power. As Freidson indicates, the professional dominance of medicine is "secured by the political and economic influence of the elite which sponsors it—an influence that drives competing occupations out of the same area of work, that discourages others by virtue of the competitive advantages conferred on the chosen occupation, and that requires still others to be subordinated to the profession" [47, p. 5]. While physicians exert a great deal of control over their work as a result of their monopoly over medical knowledge, it is especially in the hospital that they find themselves subject to bureaucratic demands. Mechanic captures this situation by referring to the physician as "increasingly an organizational man" [48, p. 49]. In addition to the growing number of physicians employed in public agencies, hospitals, medical schools, insurance companies, and health maintenance organizations, "even those primarily in office-based practice are dependent on their hospital affiliations to pursue their work, and increasingly face restrictions under the rules of the hospital as a social and legal entity" [48, p. 49]. In fact, some have suggested that because of the trend toward capital-intensive medicine, physicians are undergoing a process of "deprofessionalization" or "proletarianization." Derber, however, argues physicians are far from resembling the typical worker in that they "maintain significant power by capitalizing and keeping control of patient recruitment while ceding other market-mediation functions to third parties" [49, p. 591].

It is frequently argued that the modern hospital exhibits two lines of authority [50]. Although the ultimate authority over the hospital rests in the hands of the board of trustees, this group delegates the day-to-day management of the organization to the hospital administrator. Conversely, the medical staff controls matters concerning patient care and exercises substantial influence throughout the hospital organization. This dual authority lends itself readily not only to physician-administration conflict, but also to a confusion of roles among other health professionals, particularly nurses. One effect of the technological and organizational complexity of modern hospitals, government imposition of cost-controlling DRGs (diagnosis related groups), and hospital corporatization [43] is that an increasing degree of authority is being concentrated among administrators, who are less and less likely to be physicians [51, 52]. Despite strong efforts by physicians to resist administrative control, as Krause notes, "government intervention is putting more and more weapons into the hands of the administrator, as new laws require review teams composed of more than just physicians" [16, p. 67].

Traditionally physicians have enjoyed and continue to enjoy a position of professional dominance over an exploding array of health workers, including clinically applied medical anthropologists. Three levels of health workers comprise what might be called the professional class structure of biomedicine. The upper class is composed of physicians (who are disproportionately of upper middle class backgrounds).

The middle class is made up of subordinate professionals, including nurses, therapists, technologists and technicians (who tend to come from lower middle class families). The working class consists of auxiliary, ancillary and service personnel (who tend to come from the working class backgrounds). The typical structure is that of "a pyramid with the usually white, male physician on top, his orders carried out by middle level professionals who are generally women, and with the patients and the 'dirty work' left to low paid, frequently alienated, largely black female paraprofessionals at the boom of the pyramid" [45, p. 182]. In recent years, some changes have occurred in the biomedical pyramid. Enrollment of African Americans, Latinos, and Native Americans (who constitute about 16% of the total U.S. population) in medical school increased from 2.5 percent in 1968-69 to 8.2 percent by 1974-75, but leveled off at this percent [53]. Gains by women have been more impressive, rising from less than 10 percent to nearly 30 percent between 1970-1980 [54]. For the most part, changes brought about by the struggle for access to medical education among ethnic minorities and women were primarily individual rather than structural, and often served to pit one oppressed social group against another. Observes Rosengren:

> although we may pride ourselves on having open avenues of mobility through our occupational division of labor, medicine remains *primarily* a profession of the comfortable to well-to-do, white, male, urban, middle class, and especially in the case of those who have been favored in terms of having undergone preferential educational experiences at the collegiate level. In spite of the rigors of medical school application procedures, which *appear* to embody meritocratic criteria par excellence, evidences of 'sponsored' mobility far outweigh the evidence pointing to 'contest' mobility as the road to success in entering the portals of this choice profession [55, p. 132].

The Micro-Social Level

In their interactions with non-administrative layers of the medical hierarchy, physicians play the dominant role. Although the nurse is a relatively high-status subordinate, the medical construction of this role includes a marked degree of docility relative to physicians and the hospital bureaucracy. Early in *her* training, the nurse learns to play the "doctor-nurse game" in which she "must communicate her recommendations without appearing to be making a recommendation statement" [56, p. 699]. In response to professional subordination, nurse organizations have strongly pushed for an upgrading in the professional training and stature of nurses. Nursing education, as a result, became increasingly more university based with emphasis on graduate work. This, however, has in some ways only complicated the nurse's predicament.

> The dilemma which faces the profession as a result of this shift is that as the training becomes more technically and biologically grounded within scientific medicine, the limits imposed by physicians on nursing practice produce conflicts and contradictions for those newly educated nurses. They must confront occupational expectations that devalue, ignore, and even contradict what is now nursing's own expertise [57, p. 201].

Despite their stereotypic nurturant role, many registered nurses have been administratively removed (and as a bid for greater authority happy to move) from bedside care into the role of low-level managers (line supervisors of LPNs, nursing aides, ward clerks, and orderlies) who must carry out policies made at higher levels. As Reverby observes, "the more professional the nurse, the further removed she became from the patients and the more vulnerable she became to administrator's control" [58, p. 193]. The ironic twist is that the health care workers with the lowest status and least power are those who come into the most continuous and intimate contact with patients in hospitals.

The micro-social level in the model displayed in Figure 1 also incorporates physician-patient interaction, a relationship that is addressed in Chapters 9 and 12. Central to the CMA approach to this arena is Krause's reminder that "the gravest error of all is to assume that most definitions and decisions of who is ill or who needs help are unbiased and unmotivated by factors directly related to the broader social context which surrounds the patient and the physician" [16, p. 97]. As indicated in the discussion of key concepts in CMA that follows this section, our perspective seeks to draw attention to the non-medical functions of work-a-day biomedical practice in light of the relationship between biomedicine and the capitalist world-system. In examining the encounter between medical providers and patients, we seek to understand the play of power, as exercised both *during* (in the immediate structuring of provider-patient relations) and *through* the interaction (in the reinforcement of existing class, gender or racial relations). Also there is interest in the contradictions between the expressed purpose of medicine (patient well being) and the organization and routine of medicine [e.g., 59]. In other words, CMA attempts to transcend the common practice in medical anthropology of limiting analysis of patient satisfaction, patient compliance, and tensions in the clinical encounter to issues of provider-patient communication.

The importance of these points can be illustrated by examining O'Neil's analysis of dissatisfaction among Inuit people as patients of the Medical Services Branch of the Canadian Department of Health and Welfare [60]. As a medical anthropologist specializing in Inuit health culture at the Medical School at the University of Manitoba, O'Neil video-taped approximately 100 hours of health-care encounters between Inuit patients, Inuit medical interpreters, and non-Inuit nurse practitioners and doctors in three communities in the Keewatin region of the Canadian Northwest Territories. In addition, interviews were conducted with health care providers, administrators and interpreters; local and regional meetings on health were recorded; and an archival review of newspaper articles and public documents on Northwest health was conducted. Although primary health care is provided free of charge to the Inuit and at a higher per capita expenditure than is true for the rest of Canada, O'Niel cautions that the medical service "needs to be seen in the context of Northern political and economic history" [60]. He refers here to the colonial encounter and the forced incorporation of the Inuit people as colonial dependents, a process that radically transformed the indigenous way of life including Inuit health culture. One consequence of the sweeping changes visited upon the Inuit people has been the collapse of the traditional shamanistic healing complex and the biomedicalization of health care.

Analysis of the provider-patient interactions recorded by O'Niel's camera reveals a regular pattern of politically conditioned cross-cultural miscommunication. While interpreters might service as patient advocates in such instances, ensuring that the patient's point of view is made clear to the biomedical providers, in two-years of data collection this was rarely observed to happen. Instead, interpreters avoid the advocacy role or, in fact, attempt to support the view of the biomedical provider, reflecting their awareness of the clinician's control of the encounter and their hesitancy as low status individuals (in and out of the interpreter role) to directly challenge high status providers. The general tone of provider communications with patients is paternalistic, with providers seeing and treating Inuit patients as children (incapable of communicating without adult interpretation). Further, providers "trivialize aspects of patients' culture that are not easily understood" [60, p. 340]. Patient inability to fix a date for specific activities (e.g., onset of symptoms), for instance, is seen not as a reflection of cultural differences in temporal-spatial relationships but as an expression of low intelligence or lack of education. Finally, "care providers . . . tend to bracket out sociopolitical cues in patient discourse while they attend to cultural information" [60, p. 341]. Expressions of (what to non-Inuit health care providers are examples of) exotic behavior attract the curiosity of providers but little interest is evident in the noxious effects of colonial dominance.

These local patterns from the Canadian Northwest are exemplary of more general processes. For example, based on her study of prenatal care in a OB-GYN clinic of an inner city teaching hospital in the midwest, Lazarus identifies three major contradictions of day-to-day biomedical practice: 1) the asymmetrical relationship between doctors and patients (a relationship that replicates class, racial, and sexual hierarchies in society generally); 2) emphasis on the training of resident physicians rather than the provision of care to patients; and 3) a division of labor within the clinic that divides the patient into a poorly coordinated set of clinical functions bureaucratically delegated to an array of specialists (e.g., nurses, clerks, aides, physicians) [61]. Discrimination against women and minorities by health care providers is a fourth contradiction [62-64], one that is ingrained in medical education and ritual and shapes medical practice [65, 66]. For example, in their study of difference in access to coronary angiography, coronary artery bypass grafting, and coronary angioplasty in Massachusetts, relatively expensive cardiac procedures used to diagnose the extent of coronary artery disease and to relieve symptoms, Wenneker and Epstein found that

> whites underwent one third more coronary catheterizations and more than twice as many coronary artery bypass grafts and coronary angioplasties. These interracial inequalities were not merely a function of diminished physician contact and lower disease recognition for blacks. Rather, they were evident even among the cohort of individuals hospitalized for serious cardiovascular conditions [67, p. 255].

How are these contradictions experienced by patients, especially poor patients, minority patients, and women patients? Lazarus reports:

> Over the course of their pregnancies, the women in my study saw many different residents, nurses, aids, receptionists, nutritionists, and social workers. Few clinic personnel knew who they were. Women felt no one cared; no one could or would

give them needed social support. The message transmitted to them as they received it, was that they were unimportant and even resented. Unhappy and unappreciated, receptionists scolded them. Nurses were superfluous. Residents rushed them... Overwhelmed by the attitude permeating the clinic, pregnant women, often those most in need of professional attention, fell through the cracks of the system—not rescheduling appointments, not seeing the nurse, never learning danger signs requiring a trip to the emergency room [61, p. 275].

These examples, suggest the limitations of treating conflicts and dissatisfaction in doctor-patient interaction primarily as products of cross-cultural miscommunication. While there is much to be learned about the clinical encounter from a culturalist perspective and miscommunication is probably frighteningly common in this consequential setting, the relationship that is activated there is far more than a dyadic one between the doctor and the patient. Whole worlds come together in the clinical encounter. Indeed, the clinic is a major nexus between genders, classes, and races. Understanding the role of doctor-patient discourse in the maintenance of inequalities between social groups in terms of these three social axes is a major objective of CMA.

Beyond biomedicine, health-related patient/provider interactions unfold in a variety of settings, including within indigenous or alternative healing systems. Considerable work within medical anthropology has addressed the nature of these interactions and has led to some debate as to whether the nature of relations in these settings differs in any significant way from provider/patient relations in biomedicine. We address this issue in Chapter 10 with an examination of spiritist healing in the African American community.

The Individual Level

At the bottom-end of the macro-micro continuum exhibited in Figure 1, CMA seeks to elucidate the nature of sufferer experience, symptom expression, and behavior and the transformation of sufferer into a patient and the patient into the depersonalized site of an isolatable, treatable disease. In the view of CMA, the micro-level is embedded in the macro-level, while the macro-level is the embodiment of the micro-level but is *never reducible to it*. Empirically, of course, social life is not played out on different levels; there are only people enacting their lives in social relationship to others near and far. Rather, we use this language as a heuristic device in the effort to comprehend the vital linkage between unique configuration and general process, as seen in Chapter 11. The special contribution of anthropology, as we understand it, lies not only in its ability to explore first hand the immediate experiences, interpretive systems, motivations for action, behavioral repertoires, and ecological and social relations of local actors, but to investigate all of these aspects of human life in relation both to each other *and* to the broader and crosscutting set of political-economic relations that condition their very nature.

Elsewhere, Singer and co-workers have examined the nature of the individual level through the examination of sufferer experience of hypoglycemia [68, 69]. This condition was of special interest because it resides in the interstitial area between medically acknowledged disease and popularly recognized illness. While hypoglycemia or low blood sugar is seen as a relatively infrequent health problem by most mainstream physicians, a number of marginal private practice physicians as well as several suffer organizations and popular health publications view hypoglycemia as a major epidemic with multiple symptomatic expressions among patients. Consequently, individuals who believe they suffer from hypoglycemia undergo considerable frustration in their encounters with biomedicine. Similarly, sufferers express irritation that physicians commonly dismiss their symptoms—including fatigue, headaches, body pain, nervousness, dizziness, nausea, and bouts of mental confusion—as anxiety or depression without organic cause. Lacking biomedical legitimation for their illness, sufferers often fail to gain the benefits of the patient role, such as a temporary reduction in the number and kind of social demands they are expected to comply with. Consequently, these individuals commonly feel abandoned by society and the health care system. Through studies of this sort, CMA seeks to develop an insider's view of illness in order to expand health conception beyond what Pflanz has termed the "complex of values upheld by medicine" [70, p. 568], as well as to situate sufferer experience relative to structurally linked social values (e.g., the emphasis in U.S. society on individuation and personal responsibility) that are reinforced in the clinical encounter.

The ultimate goal of CMA is participation in the creation of a new social medicine oriented to fostering the conditions in and out of medicine that would accomplish "health for all." In other words, CMA seeks not only understanding but action. It is concerned more with the development of praxis (theory in action) than the generation of theory per se. This approach runs against the grain of prior understanding in medical anthropology. For example, Foster and Anderson, following a distinction made in medical sociology by Robert Straus, suggest a differentiation between the *anthropology of medicine,* which they conceive as the theoretical side of the subdiscipline, and *anthropology in medicine,* defined as the applied component of medical anthropology [71, p. 9]. This idea has been echoed by numerous other medical anthropologists. The perspective developed within this book, however, sees this distinction as not only creating a false dichotomy (because action and application always are guided and rationalized by theory, explicit or implicit), but more significantly, as a mystification of the biomedical source for the concepts that justify anthropology in medicine. Consequently, CMA rejects the dichotomy between "anthropology of medicine" and "anthropology in medicine." Rather, critical medical anthropologists seek to place their expertise at the disposal of labor unions, peace organizations, environmental groups, ethnic community agencies, women's health collectives, health consumer associations, self-help and self-care movements, alternative health efforts, national liberation struggles, and other bodies or initiatives that aim to liberate people from oppressive health and social conditions.

KEY CONCEPTS OF CRITICAL MEDICAL ANTHROPOLOGY

In its effort to introduce a more thorough-going critical perspective to the field, CMA has found it necessary to question in whole or in part the utility of some of the dominant conceptions within conventional medical anthropology (e.g., explanatory models, health as an expression of environmental adaptation, apolitical meaning-centered interpretation) [19, 21, 72, 73]. In addition, it has developed or borrowed alternative conceptions useful for the shift in perspective it proposes. Key concepts of the evolving CMA analytic arsenal include: *reification, privatization, depoliticalization of social issues, healthism, displacement of social etiology, medical hegemony, medicalization, medical social control, medical gatekeeping, micropolitics of medicine, compliance as ideology, comerciogenic disease and malnutrition, somatization*, and *health and medical social struggle*. Each of these are discussed in turn below and many are developed further in subsequent chapters.

In what is now considered a seminal paper in medical anthropology, Michael Taussig introduced the concept of *reification* to the field through the case of a forty-nine-year old white working class woman hospitalized for polymyositis—a progressive inflammation and deterioration of muscle tissue [25]. As a physician/anthropologist, Taussig interviewed this patient on five occasions to understand her view of her illness. In the process, it became clear that the women, like sick people generally, had been thrust "into a vortex of the most fundamental questions concerning life and death" [25, p. 4]. What the woman sought and could not find at the hands and technologies of biomedical practitioners were answers to basic existential questions: "Why me" "Why now?" Denied a satisfying answer to this quest for meaning, she developed her own understanding of her situation and its causes. Unlike biomedicine's, her explanation was social, relational, and moral. Her disease developed as a result of a life of poverty, malnourishment, over work, and exhaustion. In short, disease became an arch-metaphor for her enduring experience of oppression. But this conception was buffeted by the atomistic and mechanical "reality" presented to her by medical professionals, individuals whom she felt were the real authority and whom she trusted knew far more than she about her condition. The painful contradiction between pressing subjective experience and the "objective," authoritative view of biomedical professionals created consternation, which in Taussig's view was expressed behaviorally when the women began to complain of increased pain and an inability to urinate. Nurses responded by monitoring the patient's emotional status and by allowing her to "express her feelings." The possibility that she was experiencing greater pain was not addressed. The incident culminated in the patient throwing a cup of coffee on the floor, after which she was administered the powerful drugs Haloperidol to calm her down and amitriptiline for depression and anxiety.

On the morning of the coffee incident, but not connected to it in subsequent medical efforts to assess why the women had "acted out," she had been visited by a psychiatrist who woke her from sleep and began to ask her a series of questions. The women reported it was January when it was in fact December, she made three errors in subtracting various numbers from fifty, and the psychiatrist felt that she "demonstrated some looseness of associations" and "was difficult to follow as she jumped from topic to topic" [quoted in 25, p. 9]. At first, in his report the psychiatrist interpreted these "symptoms" as "evidence . . . strongly suggestive of an organic brain syndrome." By the end of the report, certainty emerged.

Having stated that the evidence was strongly *suggestive* of an organic brain syndrome (i.e., a physical disease of the brain) the psychiatrist in his recommendations wrote: 'Regarding the patient's organic brain syndrome. . .' In other words, what was initially put forward as a suggestion (and what a suggestion!) now becomes a real thing. The denial of authorship could not be more patent [25, p. 9].

The women was left crying and trembling following the psychiatrist's visit, unsettled by the psychiatric concern with her memory and mathematical ability, issues clearly irrelevant to her aching muscles and stormy life (especially since she had no difficulty whatsoever remembering or adding up the social causes of her progressively diseased body).

As used by Georg Lukac's in his landmark 1922 paper "Reification and the Consciousness of the Proletariat," reification refers to the mystification of properties of social relations as properties of physical objects. The concept builds on Marx's recognition that in capitalism commodities are treated as objective expressions of the performance of human labor upon nature, when, in fact, they also embody social relations (the domination of workers by their bosses), that governs the entire production process. In Taussig's application to medicine, reification, refers to the denial of human relationships embodied in symptoms, signs, and therapy. Disease is treated (literally) as constituting a physical reality, a natural entity separate from human consciousness. In the case presented above, the social relations (across the patient's life history including those with health care professionals) that were part and parcel of the her signs and symptoms were not seen in by the biomedical gaze. Rather, the active act of disease conception was transformed into the passive product of physician perception. Clinical constructions were seen "as really lying 'out-there—solid, substantial things-in-themselves" [25, p. 5] and the physician was empowered to act upon this fully "objective" reality, while the subjective experience of the patient was both denied and manipulated to ensure compliance. As Crawford observes, "[i]n the therapeutic relationship, the task of the patient is to understand the signs and symptoms of the problem as the physician reads them and thus to accept the medical definition of both problem and solution" [74, p. 373]. This definition focuses narrowly on the patient's problem, "transforming it into its most immediate property: the biological and physical manifestations of the individual, diseased, human body" [74, p. 373]. Even social relations within the clinical setting were obscured and their contribution to signs and symptoms ignored.

This case also reveals the process of *privatization* that is central to biomedical practice. Individual resistance to existing authority (medical or otherwise) commonly is diagnosed and diminished by transforming and treating complaint as individual pathology. Biomedical privatization, discussed more extensively in Chapter 12 within the context of another female patient struggling within the inner sanctum of clinical practice, becomes an important tool for social control in and beyond the clinic. With reference to the former setting, Zola reports the following case.

Recently, in a European country, I overheard the following conversation in a kidney dialysis unit. The chief was being questioned about whether or not there were self-help groups among his patients. 'No' he almost shouted 'that is the last thing we want. Already the patients are sharing too much knowledge while they sit in the waiting room, thus making our task increasingly difficult. We are now

working on a procedure to prevent them from even meeting with one another'
[75, p. 503].

More broadly, privatization directs attention toward some and away from other issues of potential relevance to illness. Rather than identifying or addressing the underlying social causes of much behavior that is seen as deviant, "the medical perspective focuses on the individual, diagnosing and treating the illness itself and generally ignoring the social situation" [76, p. 242]. Biomedicine through its theories of disease cause and location constructs "the individuality of sickness" [77, p. 56]. William Ryan coined the term "blaming the victim" to label this common activity (e.g., the frequent practice among emergency room physicians of labeling homeless people and other poor or elderly patients as "dirtballs" or "gomers") [78]. Perhaps the classic example is the disease drapetomania "discovered" by a prominent New Orleans physician, Samuel Cartwright, ten years before the Civil War. Drapetomania was quite easily diagnosed because it was only manifest among slaves and its primary symptom was attempting to escape slavery.

As this example suggests, privatization has as a primary function the *depoliticalization of social issues*. In Zola's phrase, "a Pandora's box would be opened if senility, drug addiction, alcoholism, poverty, the need for abortions, etc. were considered indicative of something wrong in the basic structure of society. . ." [79, p. 86]. In other words, were these and other issues not depoliticized and mystified by biomedicine and other institutions, the existing structure of society and the reigning configuration of class relations (arrangements that ruling class ideology seeks to portray as natural, inevitable, and pennant) might be called into serious question by large numbers of people. Zola, in effect, points up the seriousness of privitization and the potential consequences of politicizing health and disease. A significant example of privatization occurs during the practice of medicine in what Goffman called total institutions like the army or the prison [80, p. 1974], but also the company town as discussed below. Another is the process of medico-legalization, such as the development of workman's compensation laws and associated physical examinations and hearings to biomedically determine work-related compensable injury. By creating an aura of fairness in the settlement of worker/employer conflict, this structure "involves [a] process of neutralizing and containing politically volatile issues" by burying them beneath "a set of rules and a medico-legal discourse that often removes elements of oppressive social causation . . . from scrutiny" [81, p. 1119].

Critical to the privatization of illness is the biomedical *displacement of social etiology*. While for some physicians the social origins of illness are quite evident, if difficult to address effectively in a medical role, for others there appears to be clinical nonrecognition of social relations as significant or even possible sources of pathology. For the latter, the biomedical model is so dominant that alternative considerations, sometimes even including non-organic psychological explanation, are beyond the scope of consideration. This situation is institutionally promoted by several factors including fine grained medical specialization and the microscopic focus of medical education. Konner, based on his own experience as a medical student, points to another:

> Some interns and residents I met claimed they could be as thorough in an hour or two as I could in six, and at first I found their arguments convincing. But as I got closer to their stage of training, I could appreciate the corners they were cutting (which I would eventually have to cut as well). They focused more narrowly on the present illness, showed less concern for the patient's or, certainly, the family's general health; paid less attention to behavioral and social factors in the patient's illness; were more abrupt and brusque and less responsive to the patient as a human being [82, p. 33].

Even when psychological aspects are considered by physicians, they tend to be treated as individualistic problems stemming from stressful interpersonal relations or deep seated psychological wounds, rather than products of the determinant structure of social relations [e.g., see 83].

Yet such relations, locally, nationally, and internationally are the sources of much ill health. For example, critical medical anthropologists have begun to explore *comerciogenic disease and malnutrition*, health conditions that are the direct product of the international corporate marketing of health-impacting commodities, marketing that often is assisted with State funds and resources [84, 85]. The infant formula scandal probably is the best known example of this phenomenon. Similarly, Ferguson and others have studied the penetration of the multinational pharmaceutical industry into underdeveloped countries [28]. "Dumping," the sale in foreign markets of products banned (because of their harmfullness or uselessness) in core nations, is another expression of comerciogenesis. For example, the drug chloramphenicol produced by Parke-Davis was restricted in the United States to several life-threatening illnesses.

> But in Latin America, chloramphenicol was recommended to physicians for tonsillitis and bronchitis. No hazards were listed for the information of physicians in Colombia and Ecuador. Most importantly, with indiscriminate use, bacteria built up resistance. When an epidemic of typhoid fever broke out in Mexico in 1972-1973, some 100,000 people became ill. Doctors assumed they could use chloramphenicol, but it did not work. Some 20,000 people died of typhoid [86, p. 33].

Despite this beginning, comerciogenesis remains a noticeably understudied area in medical anthropology, a reflection of the discipline's participation in the nonrecognition of social etiology. A concern of CMA research, in this regard, is the manner in which social etiology is disattended within biomedicine and medical anthropology. This point is stressed by Mark Nichter and Elizabeth Cartwright in their discussion of U.S. involvement in fostering child survival and safe motherhood programs internationally. In a paper entitled, "Saving the Children for the Tobacco Industry," they note

> the disease focus of child survival programs, like the individual responsibility focus of antismoking campaigns, diverts attention away from the political and economic dimension of ill health. Saving children, the symbols of innocence, puts the United States in a favorable light in a turbulent world and competitive international marketplace, but it also deflects attention from other issues. One such issue is that families with young children represent a huge potential market for American products, such as tobacco, which undermine household health. While U.S. support of child survival programs received significant positive press

coverage, tobacco more quietly became the eighth largest souce of export for the United States in 1985-86 [87, p. 247].

Significantly, the U.S. government and its trade policy not only has protected but has directly supported the American tobacco industry, with various Third World countries being pressured by U.S. officials to open their doors to U.S. cigarettes and cigarette advertising or face sanctions. Consequently, tobacco exports reached $1.5 billion in 1991. This figure was boasted by $50 million through the efforts of the Commerce Department to help Philip Morris and RJR Nabisco to negotiate a deal with Soviet Union [88].

The tobacco industry defends its efforts by arguing that it does not promote the development of the habit among non-smokers but only pushes brand switching among existing smokers. The choice to smoke or not to smoke should be left to the individual to decide the industry emphasizes. This perspective is an expression of the ideology Robert Crawford calls *healthism,* the assignment of the lion's share of responsibility for maintaining health or becoming ill to the individual sufferer [74, 89]. For example, in his book *Who Shall Live? Health, Economics, and Social Choice,* Victor Fuchs, in language apparently selected to appeal to the American tradition of rugged individualism, argues that "[e]mphasizing social responsibility can increase security, but it may be the security of the 'zoo'—purchased at the expense of freedom" [90, p. 26]. Rather, it is individual responsibility that must be emphasized, in Fuchs' view, because "the greatest potential for reducing coronary disease, cancer, and other major killers still lies in altering personal behavior" [90, p. 46]. A similar chord is struck by the report of the Task Force on Health Promotion and Consumer Education of the National Institutes of Health and the American College of Preventive Medicine.

> In view of the overriding importance of individual behavior and lifestyle as major factors in the nation's unsatisfactory health status and ever-rising health care bill, CHE [consumer health education], with its emphasis on education and motivation of the individual and better individual use of the delivery system, must now be recognized as a top priority in the national commitment to health promotion [91, p. 40].

The ultimate extension of this line of thinking is individual blame. If you are responsible for your health, and you get sick, surely you have not acted in a responsible fashion: "We should not fool ourselves into thinking that disease is caused by an enemy from without. We are responsible for our disease" [92, p. 4]. This philosophy, of course, absolves others of responsibility. It is the patient's lack of will power and not the massive multi-media campaign to insinuate tobacco consumption into the core of cultural practice and personal identity that is ultimately responsible for an increase in cancer. It is a failure on the part of the worker to modulate job-related stress or get a more relaxing job that is primarily to blame for heart disease and stroke and not the worker's lack of control over the production process, the clock, or the job market. It is the individual inability to control one's eating habits rather than a food industry that makes it difficult *not* to be overweight that explains widespread obesity (at rates still equal to those recorded prior to the contemporary fitness craze).

While not necessarily the originator of healthism, biomedicine does adopt and promote its tenets as needed. Zola relates the following example:

> Many years ago my father . . . was diagnosed as having 'angina.' The doctor who transmitted this information to him was a specialist and recommended most strongly that he change jobs, preferably to one with less physical exertion, perhaps a desk job. My father thanked him dutifully as he left the office. The problem was that my father was a bluecollar worker, a dress-cutter in the garment industry with a less than high school education. He could no more get a desk job than he could climb Mt. Everest [93, p. 242].

In Stark's view, healthism (which, in its emphasis on individual responsibility, implies a withdrawal from reliance on biomedical expertise) is in contradiction with *medicalization*, the absorption of ever-widening social arenas and behaviors into the jurisdiction of biomedicine treatment through a constant extension of pathological nomenclature [94]. In fact, no contradiction need exist. Health clinics, HMOs, and other medical providers now offer classes on stress management, obesity control, overcoming sexual impotence, smoking cessation, child birth preparation, and a variety of other behaviors and conditions. Deficits in will-power, bodily control, life style management, and family relations are all diagnosed and treated along with cancer and the flu in biomedical institutions by "appropriate" specialists.

But medicalization reaches beyond consumer interest in overcoming troubling life experiences. The broader process is seen clearly in the case of homosexuality. The term homosexuality was invented in the mid-nineteenth century by Hungarian physician K. M. Benkert, who considered same-sex attraction to be a congenital condition. This view was introduced to the United States by the physicians J. C. Shaw and G.N. Ferris, whose 1881 article on the topic appeared in *The Journal of Nervous and Mental Disease*. The article relied in part on the work of the German physician Richard von Krafft-Ebing, a compiler of "sexual deviance" cases and a major contributor to medicalization of homosexuality. Krafft-Ebing argued that homosexuals should be treated medically rather than through the criminal justice system, their problem being a sickness and not an expression of criminality. On this foundation, during the twentieth century homosexuality has been variously defined in biomedicine as a disease of the endocrine system [95], an error in normal sexual ontogeny [96], and a mental disease characterized by oral regression, masochism, and (in males) irrational fear of women [97]. Efforts to pathologize homosexuality have been tied to a larger social attempt to control the behavior of gay men and lesbians [98]. As dramatically expressed by one gay activist, while disrupting a paper on aversion therapy for the treatment of homosexuality at the 1970 meeting of the American Psychiatric Association:

> You are the pigs who make it possible for the cops to beat homosexuals: they call us queer, you—so politely—call us sick. But it's the same thing. You make possible the beatings and rapes in prison, you are implicated in the tortuous cures perpetrated on desperate homosexuals [quoted in 99, p. 295].

Arguing that the labeling of homosexuality as a disease is little other than a self-serving exercise in social control, Thomas Szasz adds

> In stubbornly insisting that the homosexual is sick, the psychiatrist is merely
> pleading to be accepted as a physician . . . . psychiatric opinion about homosexuality
> is not a scientific proposition but a medical prejudice [100, pp. 173-174].

Ultimately, under growing pressure from an organized gay community, the medicalization of homosexualy (at least officially) collapsed and the term was deleted from the psychiatric nomenclature of the *Diagnostic and Statistical Manual,* [76]. Medicalization of other behaviors, developmental stages, and arenas of social life, from substance use to juvenile delinquency, from hyperkenesis to obesity, and from child rearing to menopause, however, has gone on unabbetted, especially but not solely in the United States. As Zola points out, medicalization reflects a tendency of biomedicine to generalize expertise beyond its range of effective intervention. In the process, like other social managers, physicians

> presume to tell society what is good and right for the individual and for society at
> large in some aspect of life [101]. Indeed they set the very terms in which people
> may think about this aspect of life [Hughes quoted in 101, p. 42].

One factor driving medicalization is the profit to be made from "discovering" new diseases in need of treatment and medicines.

> Medicalization can create new markets for products and services. This is true not
> only for medical practitioners but, perhaps more important, for entire industries.
> The pharmaceutical, health insurance, and medical technology corporations, as
> well as other medical industries, have achieved phenomenal growth . . . . [W]e
> contend that the profitability of medicine in American society has contributed in
> both specific and general ways to the medicalization of deviance [76, p. 265].

For example, Lock analyzes recent efforts to medicalize "menopausal syndrome" in Japan in light of the loss of revenue among private practice gynecologists because of the increase in hospital births and the use of contraception instead of abortion as a birth control mechanism [102]. There is, she notes "considerable incentive for gynecologists . . . to create new sources of income, and the promotion of the concept of menopausal syndrome and associated counseling for distressed women are recent innovations" [102, p. 56]. Beyond income, physicians are motivated by the established career structure of modern professions and the accepted markers of career success: "One of the greatest ambitions of the physician is to discover and describe a 'new' disease or syndrome and to be immortalized by having his name used to identify the disease" [47, p. 252]. Often these two motivations intertwine, as seen in the intensely acrimonious struggle between Robert Gallo of the National Cancer Institute in the United States and Luc Montagnier of the French Pasteur Institute over who should receive credit for discovering the human immunodeficiency virus. It was well known before the virus was identified that its discoverer would not only gain international fame and adulation but would be in a good position to gain lucrative patent rights for test kits designed to determine infection. The result has been a conflict of soap opera proportions.

As Stark stresses, "medicine is something more than the practice of medical care . . . ." [94, p. 420]. Underlying the medicalization of contemporary life is the broader phenomenon of medicine's role in *hegemony.* Anthropology has long been concerned with meaning in its social context, with the persuasive power of symbols to touch and motivate the individual and the group, with the complex process of socially situated signification. It is undisputed in anthropology, following Max Weber and Clifford Geertz, that we are suspended in webs of significance, webs composed of things that stand for other things so well that we live and die for them. But, we also know that

> Meanings are not imprinted into things by nature; they are developed and imposed by human beings. Several things follow from this. The ability to bestow means—to 'name' things, acts and ideas—is a source of power. Control of communication allows the *managers of ideology* to lay down the categories through which reality is to be perceived [31, p. 388; emphasis added].

The process that Wolf describes is critical to the smooth and orderly functioning of society, especially a society that is rift with internal contradictions, like being exploitive and oppressive across class, gender, racial or other lines. As noted earlier, hegemony labels the system by which the ruling class exerts control over the cognitive and intellectual life of society through non-coercive means. Within medicine, as explicated further in Chapter 9, hegemony in action can be seen in the doctor/patient encounter. Both parties to this interaction enter onto the social stage armed with socially constructed scripts about the nature of health and disease, about the world, and about the relation of the former to the latter. Kleinman, in a celebrated contribution to medical anthropological analysis, refers to these often dissimilar scripts as Explanatory Models (EMs) [103]. His concern is with the mediation of their differing content so as to facilitate effective and satisfying health care. However, the problem is not only one of cognition and communication, it is also one of hegemony. In a well-known critique of Kleinman, Taussig argues that:

> The patient's so-called model of illness differs most significantly from the clinician's not in terms of exotic symbolization but in terms of the anxiety to locate the social and moral meaning of disease. The clinician cannot allow this anxiety to gain either legitimacy or to include ever-widening spheres of social relationships, including that of the hospital and the clinician, for more often than not once this process of thought is given its head it may well condemn as much as accept the contemporary constitution of social relationship and society itself [25, pp. 12-13].

Illness, in other words, because it threatens to destroy all that is meaningful and cherished, disrupts normal every day suspension in hegemonic webs of significance spun by the managers of ideology (e.g., the media, schools, etc.). Susan DiGiacomo, based on her own citizenship in the kingdom of the sick, stresses that illness produces a form of culture shock.

> It is no mere literary turn of phrase to say that the seriously ill take up residence in another country for the duration. When emigration also means prolonged or periodic exile in the hospital, the sense of being a stranger in a strange land is further heightened [104, p. 315].

In its rupture of work-a-day complacency, illness, like culture shock generally (which itself has been interpreted as an illness of identity and a fear of symbolic death), has the capacity to awaken alternative perspectives and subject official realities to closer scrutiny. It forces the sufferer to think about what is important, what is essential, and what is real. As a result, illness is potentially dangerous (especially in light of the social origins of much disease). In her own illness, DiGiacomo, for example, was reminded of Jules Henry's anthropological critique of American society: "To think deeply in our culture is to grow angry and to anger others . . ." [105, p. 146]. In Taussig's view, treating this "disease" (i.e., dis-ease) is as critical to the functioning of biomedicine as the treating of physiological disruptions. In the clinical encounter, the doctor and patient

> are curing the threat posed to convention and to society, tranquilizing the distur-
> bance that sickness unleashes against normal thought . . . It is not the cultural
> construction of clinical reality that is here at issue, but the clinical construction
> and reconstruction of a commodotized reality that is at stake [25, p. 13].

By transforming person into depersonalized patient (cut off from normal social networks, settings, status symbols, abilities, in short, one's identity as a person), and then reducing and objectifying the patient as disjointed organ or disease ("the appendicitis in Room 104 or the rheumatoid arthritis down the hall" [93, p. 248]), or good "material" on which to practice surgical techniques [106, p. 220], biomedicine reproduces and thereby reinforces the hierarchical, mechanistic, standardized, alienated, privatized, and atomistic reality of capitalist production. Doctors, it must be stressed, are no less ensnared than patients in this hegemonic process. Observes Kirmayer, "[m]edical students are treated as disembodied intellects who can absorb endless amounts of detail with little attention to their own emotional and physical needs" [107, p. 81]. As bodies are cut off from self, emotion, and community in the clinic and in the medical academy, people are produced, doctors and patients, socialized to the dominant ideology. Potentially explosive moral and political issues produced by the processes of being sick and treating sickness are muted, pacified, controlled. Herein lies the value of biomedicine as a hegemonic institution.

Indeed, control (of knowledge, bodies, resistant individuals as well as disease) is central to biomedicine. Conrad and Schnieder define *medical social control* as "the ways in which medicine [all medicine, not just biomedicine] functions (wittingly or unwittingly) to secure adherence to social norms—specifically, by using medical means to minimize, eliminate, or normalize deviant behavior" [76, p. 242]. This action is tied to processes of medicalization because "for medical social control mechanisms to operate, deviance must be conceptualized in medical terms" [76, p. 159].

Medicine was first identified as an agent of social control by the sociologist Talcott Parsons in the early 1950s in his analysis of the physician and patient roles. As he noted in a now classic discussion, "[t]he sick role is . . . a mechanism which in the first instance channels deviance so that the two most dangerous potentialities, namely, group formation and successful establishment of the claim to legitimacy, are avoided" [108, p. 477]. Recognizing the inherently social nature of sickness, Parsons goes on to suggest that psychiatrically diagnosed diseases serve as political safety values by providing non-threatening social roles for problematic individuals. Psychotherapy, he notes, is oriented toward "'coping' successfully with the psychological consequence of the exposure of people to strain in social relationships" [108, p. 478]. In sum, Parsons early on revealed the degree to which the sick role bolsters the existing structure of society and the ways in which physicians, in the normal course of work providing health care treatment to patients, serve as instruments for achieving this goal.

These points have been supported through the seminal work of a number of other medical sociologists, including Irving Zola [75, 79], and Elliot Friedson [47]. In his analysis of the medical profession, for example, Friedson notes that

> insofar as illness is defined as something bad—to be eradicated or contained— medicine plays the role of what [Howard] Becker called the 'moral entrepreneur.' Medical activity leads to the creation of new rules defining deviance; medical practice seeks to enforce those rules by attracting and treating the newly defined deviant sick [47, p. 252].

Expansion of the sick role to new arenas of life, in short, is intimately tied to behavioral control.

Expansion of this sort, as Friedson recognized, is often carried out in conjunction with what he termed "special lay interest groups." Commonly, such groups (which may include individual physicians as patrons and promoters) lead the way while the medical establishment lags behind exhibiting what De Swaan calls "reluctant imperialism" [109]. In fact, a closer examination of all forms of imperialism, including that practiced by nation-states, reveals that empire-building is fraught with hesitancy and conflicted action, as the costs and benefits of expansion are tallied and weighed by various sectors comprising the dominant social stratum. Rarely does expansion not produce some debate between components of the ruling class, a group whose members have overlapping but not necessarily identical interests. While the ruling sector within society generally or within any of its major institutions, such as biomedicine, is sometimes described in monolithic terms, a more nuanced dialectical approach limits what Sayer has termed the violence of abstraction [110].

An important aspect of the social control function of physicians is performed through their management of patient emotions. Doctors "regularly deal with patients' anger, anxiety, unhappiness, social isolation, loneliness, and other emotional distress" [111, p. 344]. The sources of patient anger and distress are multiple. As seen in the case of the woman with polymyositis described above, one important source of patient upset is, in fact, the doctor-patient interaction. A common biomedical approach for controlling this problem is non-recognition: patient anger is denied legitimation as an issue worthy of recognition.

> There is collusion in every aspect of hospital routine to ignore patient mistrust and to undermine and cool out patient anger, for the direct expression of these feelings . . . is highly disruptive to the comfort, schedule and convenience of the medical staff. Patients and their families usually offer no resistance to this carefully engineered neutralization of doubt and anger . . . they fear (often with good reason) that unless they are uncritical and undemanding, they run the risk of receiving worse treatment from angry physicians and nurses [112, p. 182].

Beyond the clinical experience, patient anger may lie in stressful social or working conditions, acute or chronic economic difficulties, the anguish of unemployment, the painful insults and hidden injuries of class [113], or family conflict fueled by one or more of these other problems. For example, in their quasi-experimental study of auto workers, Hamilton et al. found that "[t]o be laid off meant worse mental health: more somatic complaints, more depression, higher anxiety . . . . For the low income, the less educated, and especially the less educated black worker [in other words, those with the least resources and alternatives] the mental health impact of layoff was profound" [114, pp. 135-136]. These findings have been supported by several other studies [115-117].

However, "eager to serve a client's needs," physicians commonly direct attention away from such hard to change social relations and conditions and instead provide "advice about ways to adjust to social stress" [11, p. 344]. Based on his ethnography of laid off rubber factory workers in Ohio, Pappas reports the following example:

> Betty Liston works as a cocktail waitress and earns enough to live on but has no health insurance. The burden of medical bills has increased steadily since she was told that she had an ulcer. Staying healthy is her preoccupation; as she put it, 'Well, I heard about stress. I suppose that could have something to do with my ulcer. My doctor tells me to worry less. Worrying won't pay the bills but not worrying doesn't pay them either' [118, p. 27].

As this case suggests, the enactment of social control in biomedicine takes place, in part, through

> the transmission of ideologic messages . . . These messages arise at the micro-level of professional-client interaction . . . . From a position of relative dominance, doctors can make ideological statements that convey the symbolic trappings of science. These messages reinforce the hegemonic ideology that emanates from other institutions in society . . . The . . . messages tend to direct clients' behavior into safe, acceptable, and non-disruptive channels [11, p. 342].

Waitzkin refers to this process of structurally supportive communication as the *micropolitics of medicine.* Integral to these micropolitics is the reproduction and reinforcement of hierarchical macrolevel political relations. In clinical interactions, for example, Crandon observes, "medical dialogue is a window through which we can see political and economic processes as they pertain to the nature of interethnic relations" [119, p. 464]. In the doctor-patient encounter the asymmetrical character of the interaction is emphasized in many ways from symbols of authority (e.g., white coat, stethoscope), degree of access to personal information about the Other or even about one's self (e.g., control of the patient's chart), right of access to areas of the body that are defined as private or emotionally charged, terms of address, and general demeanor. Asymmetry is magnified through dependence, expressed in the common belief that doctors know what is best for their patients. Clinical dependence provides a microcosm and a reinforcement for a broader pattern of subordination and trust in one's social "superiors." As DiGiacomo discovered, failure to assume one's proper role in the hierarchy leads to more overt efforts at social control.

> In the hospital, and later as an outpatient, I asked questions. I used the vocabulary of medicine to the extent that I knew it, and approached doctors as colleagues rather than as superiors. Generally, their first reaction was surprise at my failure

, to defer to them, then disapproval. Occasionally, when I persisted, conflict resulted [l04, p. 320].

Millman offers a similar example.

Upon entering his room on rounds one morning, the house officers came upon [a] patient as he was reading reprints from medical journals about his own particular disease. One of the residents grabbed the reprints from the patient's hands and demanded, 'Where did you get these' . . . The resident then lectured the patient about how it was 'dangerous' for non-medical people to read medical journals because they couldn't understand what they were reading and might reach the wrong conclusions about their illness. After the resident left with the reprints the intern added, 'You know, you could have asked us if you had any questions' [112, p. 189].

In addition to status-quo supporting verbal communication, social control is extended through the medicating of distress. Hills describes a typical Valium ad with its overt social control messages:

a middle-aged women in a rumpled housecoat and slippers is slouched in a chair surrounded by an ill-made bed, a broom, a pile of laundry. WEARINESS WITHOUT CAUSE the headline reads. The woman has 'psychic tension with depressive symptomatology'. . . .The text goes on: 'When the patient complains of a fatigue, and you can find no organic cause, you recognize that it may serve her as a means of *avoiding responsibility* or facing an emotional problem' [120, p. 119].

Getting women to fill the female domestic role, in this instance, can be achieved through the wonders of modern pharmacy. Lost in the process is any consideration of the role in question and the political economic and gender aspects of its construction or function.

Closely related to social control is the process of *medical gatekeeping,* an expression of biomedical capacity that stems from the fact that physicians are socially authorized by the State to regulate access to the sick role. This authorization empowers physicians to label one set of symptoms a legitimate organic disease and another as malingering or evidence of a stigmatized psychologistic condition. It further empowers them to regulate access to a variety of economic and social benefits to which the sick are entitled on the job and elsewhere in society. In part "because of the potentially disruptive effects of widespread adoption of the sick role, [physicians] restrict access according to unique criteria within each institutional setting" [80, p. 39]. In some institutions (e.g., the army), access to the sick role may be comparatively limited and narrow as medicine comes to serve institutional rather than patient needs. In all settings, however, it is easier for some people to get sick, or at least to be socially accepted as being sick, than others. Social class, for example, has been found to be a determinant of the character of doctor-patient interaction and sick role access [121, p. 1980]. In the army, it has been found that it is easier for soldiers who are resistant to military discipline to be diagnosed with disease than those who are compliant [122]. Diagnosis in this instance serves to withdraw non-compliance from public view, minimizing thereby the possibility of collective resistance to the authority of army brass.

Despite medical authority, doctors regularly encounter patients who refuse to accept noncertification, returning again and again with persistent complaints that challenge the medical diagnosis of nondisease or fuctional (non-organic) disorder. Labeled "crocks" or "turkeys" by doctors, these problem patients are a great source of frustration to biomedical providers, who, as one British doctor has suggested, "feel annoyed [at being] called upon to solve what are essentially social problems . . ." [quoted in 123, pp. 937-938]. That social factors can and often do play a major role in even established organic conditions tends to be overlooked in the medical discourse on the so-called "problem patient." Overall, the gatekeeper function spotlights a significant role biomedicine plays in supporting non-medical social institutions and the existing structure of society.

Discussion of the "problem patient" [124], raises a broader issue of expanding medical and medical social science concern, namely patient compliance with medical advice about taking medications, adhering to diets, or implementing other behavioral and lifestyle changes. It is estimated that patients do not follow between one third and one half of the instructions offered by physicians [125]. Yet the topic of noncompliance has not always been a major concern to medical providers. Trostle notes that fewer than twenty-five articles on compliance appeared in the literature before 1960, while over a thousand English-language research and review articles on the topic were listed in the *Index Medicus* bibliography during 1984 and 1985, reflecting a sizeable increase in the attention being paid to this topic [126]. A question is raised concerning the factors underlying the preoccupation with compliance in recent years. Have patients become less compliant? Has compliance become more important because biomedicine is now more efficious than it once was? Is the concern with patient compliance a reflection of a decline in physician control generally?

Trostle rejects explanations that involve increased non-compliance or enhanced medical capacity as insufficient and offers an alternative critical perspective based on the notion of ideology. As indicated above, ideology refers to the existence of a developed system of self-serving beliefs that legitimizes particular behavioral norms and wraps them in a cloak of factuality. Anthropologists have long recognized the ideological aspects of culture and adopted the notion of ethnocentrism to label a group's tendency to assume that its values are God-given, right and proper, or natural rather than a set of useful and situationally acquired preferences: this is *the way* to behave rather than this is *our way* of behaving (at this particular moment in time and space). Viewing *compliance as ideology* "transforms physicians' theories about the proper behavior of patients into a series of research strategies, research results, and potentially coercive interventions that appear appropriate, and that reinforce physicians' authority over health care" [126, p. 1300]. This ideology is promoted by several factors, including pharmaceutical companies that direct attention to compliance "as a promotional strategy to increase market share and product sales" [126, p. 1299]. In addition, we believe, the loss of physician autonomy and the weakening of patient trust produced by the institutionalization and depersonalization of medical care, expanded lay knowledge about the noxious side effects of many prescribed remedies, popular interest in natural health approaches and fitness, the expanded acceptance and legitimation of non-biomedical treatment (e.g., chiropractic), and the enhanced importance of non-infectious diseases (e.g., heart disease, cancer) that have no equivalent of a powerful antibiotic quick-fix, all contribute to intensified physician concern about patient compliance. As physician authority in society and even to a degree within the clinic becomes somewhat circumscribed and regulated by the changing character of the health care industry, physician anxiety about professional authority over the microcosm of patient behavior is magnified and finds expression in intensified uneasiness about compliance. In this sense, the escalating social science of health focus on patient compliance is a symptom of illness within the health care system.

The broader process of embodied expression of material conditions and social relations in illness has been referred to as *somatization*. As Kleinman [127, p. 56] indicates, under capitalism, somatization is "frequently an emblem of worker dissatisfaction, demoralization, and alienation." More broadly, he suggests, "persons who are at greatest risk for powerlessness and blocked access to local resources are most likely to somatize" [127, p. 174]. In short, this term labels "the physiologization of social and psychological problems" [128, p. 79]. In her study of airline flight attendants, for example, Hochschild describes the constant stress generated by the "emotional labor" these workers must perform (e.g., "service with a smile") to adequately adhere to the dictates of proper comportment as defined by their employers.

> My respondents often spoke of acts *upon* feelings: of *trying* to fall in love or *putting a damper on* love, of *trying to feel* grateful, of *trying not* to feel depressed, of *checking* their anger, of *letting* themselves feel sad. In short, they spoke of managed feelings [129, p. 13; emphasis in original].

In this context, emotion is a labor product that, in Marx's phrase, is an alien, hostile, powerful object that is independent of its producer, the worker. Somatization, in this sense and in this context is part of the human cost of alienated labor; it is the body's expression of self-estrangement produced by the experience of external control. Sensitivity to this form of embodied communication, avoids entrapment in both the biomedical conception of illness as individual and the narrow commonsense interpretation that the inner life of feelings and experiences are wholly unique, particular, and personal. When, as is the case under capitalism, even human feelings are transformed into commodities produced under alienated conditions for sale on the market, the individual can only be fully understood in the context of macrolevel relations and processes. Following C. Wright Mills, the starting point for comprehending "individual troubles," then, must be a careful analysis of "the structural transformations that usually lie behind them" [130, p. 1].

An example of the relationship between macrolevel processes and somatization can be found in the late nineteenth-century epidemic of invalidism among middle- and upperclass women in the United State and the United Kingdom. The condition, expressed variously as head or muscular ache, general fatigue and frailty, menstrual problems, indigestion, and depression, produced a host of diagnoses among physicians from neurasthenia to hyperesthesia and from cardiac inadequacy to hysteria. Physicians, concluding that the problem stemmed from the natural weakness of female anatomy (being burdened with a uterus and ovaries), prescribed extended bed rest and closer adherence to prevailing norms concerning proper feminine behavior. Review of women's diary entries from this period by Ehrenreich and English [131] provided hundreds of cases of women overcome by invalidism. As but one example, they cite the experience of Catherine Beecher, an educator who in 1871 undertook a trip to visit many of her friends, relatives and former students. In her journal, Beecher recorded case after case of illness among the female acquaintances she visited and concluded that a there had occurred a "terrible decay of female health all over the land." [quoted in 132, p. 165]. What was the cause of this widespread epidemic?

> During the late nineteenth century . . . many middle class women had started to question traditional roles. Conflicts between autonomy and dependence, sexual expression and repression, activity and passivity, may have been more intense than during earlier periods. Paradoxical impulses and wishes had actively surfaced . . . . Within the context of potentially increased independence both inside and outside the family and the possibility of greater sexual expression, many women developed emotional symptoms, became bedridden and then received the rest cure [133, pp. 147-148].

In short, women of certain social classes had began to experience considerable role conflict. On the one hand, their socially prescribed role as delicate ladies had come to seem devoid of meaning or purpose. Their primary responsibilities in this role were sexual reproduction and serving as an ornament to reflect the achievements of a successful husband. Fashions of the day seemed to express these features, emphasizing "wasp-like waists" and other elaborate embellishments designed to accentuate the female form rather than comfortable movement or any type of physical activity. On the other hand, there was a growing longing for alternative roles, but few were socially accessible to women and the social system and its dominant institutions, including medicine, issued redundant reinforcing messages about the naturalness and virtuousness of female idleness and dependency. Intensified gender role conflict appears to have found expression in somatization. Though treated as a series of independent, individual cases of disease or constitutional weakness by physicians, the epidemic appears to have been largely social in nature. Notably, African American women, who toiled long hours at hard physical labor were not seen as anatomically enfeebled and as a result were denied access by physicians to the female invalid role even when they expressed symptoms commonly associated with this condition.

Finally, there is the concept of *health and medical social struggle*. Within the context of biomedicine, the critical approach is directed toward locating the clinical relationship and the whole complex of medicine within its encompassing political-economic framework in order to remind us that physicians and patients alike are but two layers in a larger social dynamic characterized not only by inequality and dominance, but struggle as well. While it is recognized that physicians have the upper hand in the doctor-patient relationship and that this position of power is mobilized regularly in the service of self-interested and system-maintaining non-medical goals, the medical arena (or any other social field) cannot be thought of as comprised solely of dominating actors and dominated objects. Rather, the clinical encounter is an arena of considerable, although often subdued, social conflict. Consequently, it is problematic to assume, as some do, that because power is concentrated in macrolevel structures, the microlevel is mechanically determined from above. Lost in a mechanistic understanding of the construction of daily life is appreciation of the role played by conflict and struggle in all social relationship in and out of health care.

Struggle takes many forms, from passive resistance to outright rebellion. In the view of Ehrenreich and English the case of nineteenth-century women's somatization is an example of the former [131]. In the contradictory style that resistance often assumes (partly embracing the hated image thrust upon the self by the oppressor—if only to parody it by extending it to its natural limit—partly forthright in its avoidance of official rules or decrees), women's idleness expressed somatic resistance to dependency and social circumscription to reproductive capacity. While in some ways, somatization only reinforced the alleged feebleness of female anatomy, by latching onto the official characterization and magnifying its acute nature, somatization disrupted the ability of men to fully define women's role and function. In this sense, the resistance was quite direct: the birth rate of white middle and upper class Protestant women fell dramatically (by half between 1800 and 1900). Also, in their common (although not universal) failure to respond to the prescribed medical cure, women resisted definition by socially authorized male experts. Ultimatley, doctors found themselves locked in a power struggle with female patients. This struggle took full form in the case of "hysteria," a more active expression of female role conflict, to which doctors responded with increasingly more punitive "treatments" including ridicule, physical threats, beatings with wet towels, and even suffocation. Marked by episodic and unpredictable outbursts, loss of voice or appetite, uncontrollable screaming or crying, or constant sneezing or coughing, in hysteria women were both accepting their "inborn sickness" *as well as* defying assignment to an intolerable social role. Sickness, having become a gender-defined way of life, became an arena for struggle, as "medical treatment, which had always had strong overtones of coercion, revealed itself as frankly and brutally repressive" [131, p. 128]. Another example of gender-related medical struggle is presented in Chapter 12, while Chapter 5 presents a health-related clash of a different sort.

An example of fairly direct challenge to biomedical hegemony was launched by the women's health movement, which has raised a variety of issues in its engagement with biomedicine, including the physician monopolization of medical knowledge as private property (one that is paid for, ironically, with a healthy percentage of public funding), the dehumanizing reduction of living people into their medical parts during biomedical treatment, the overt mistreatment in the clinic of women and other oppressed groups, and the reproduction of male supremacy in the male doctor/female patient encounter. But the potential for cooptation and retrenchment is constant without fundamental restructuring. Indeed, it could be said that the price of struggle against the dominant ideology and the dominant class is eternal vigilance. Morgen, for example, analyzes the slow but thorough cooptation of a feminist health clinic as it moved from a voluntary group into a more formally funded, structured, administered, and monitored health care institution [134]. The gay health movement also has encountered renewed efforts at re-medicalization, especially in response to the AIDS crisis.

ARENAS OF CMA ANALYSIS

The Social Origins of Disease and Ill Health

As much as it is for biomedicine, a central question for medical anthropology is: what is disease? It is evident why this query is central to biomedicine. Its importance to medical anthropology is less clear and hence medical anthropologists have tended to avoid the question all together by defining "disease" (clinical manifestations) as the domain of medicine and "illness" (the sufferer's experience) as the appropriate arena of anthropological investigation. From the perspective of CMA, however, the bracketing of disease as outside the concern or expertise of anthropologists, at least cultural anthropologists, is a retreat from ground that is as much social as it is biological in nature.

CMA seeks to understand the social origin of disease, all disease. CMA work toward achieving this goal is guided by a conjunction of its political-economic reading of social constructionism and a political-economic understanding of vulnerability and risk. In other words, CMA is concerned both with the social causes of disease conception and disease manifestation in a social group.

First, there is a concern with the ways in which a disease comes to be "known" and used by medicine and society generally. The act of "discovering" a disease hinges on something more than an objective accumulation of scientific facts about the physical world and the micro-organisms or cellular tissues to be found there. The discovery of a disease, a process of abstraction from never identical individual cases and the imposition of a linguistic unification on physical diversity, is inavoidably as much an act of creation as it is one of detection. This view of disease does not imply a denial of biology, but instead expresses awareness that a difference exists between biology as a material fact (that is never knowable directly) and any particular cultural rendering of it (including the biomedical one); it is a recognition, in short, that disease (and not just illness) is as much social (and hence political) construction as physical reality. As Linder suggests with reference to biomedicine,

> Today in various nooks and crannies called consultation rooms, diagnosticians listen for the same elements and when they find them they do not say, I can put these things together and call them hysteria if I like (much as a little boy can sort his marbles now by size, now by colour, now by age); rather, the diagnostician, when he has competed his sort says: This patient is a hysteric! Here, then, is the creator denying authorship of his creation. Why? Because in turn he receives a greater prize: the reassurance that out there is a stable world; it is not all in his head [quoted in Taussig 25, p. 5].

What shapes this act of social construction? Why this disease from this set of symptoms? Why are there such glaring discontinuities in the discourse on disease? As Clatts and Mutchler remind us, "[s]cience and medicine do not exist in a social or

cultural vacuum" [135, p. 111]. Diseases come to be known (or forgotten) at particular times and places. They are products of identifiable historic epochs. Consequently, they are rooted in and embody specific social relations and modes of
production. And, like all social phenomena, they are colored by their social origins.

> Fatness, thinness, blood in one's urine, let alone blood per se, headache,
> nightmares, lassitude, coughing, blurred vision, dizziness, and so forth, acquire
> vastly different meanings and significance at different times in history, in dif-
> ferent classes of society, and so on [25, p. 5].

This discussion is clarified by turning to actual examples. The socio-political construction of *pédisyon* and *fibróm* in Haiti, conditions that would be called illnesses in
conventional medical anthropology (in that they are popularly experienced but not
validated by biomedicine), will be considered in Chapter 9. Because of its relatively
recent appearance, AIDS presents another especially observable case.

In Treichler's words, "AIDS is not merely an invented label, provided to us by
science and scientific naming practices, for a clear-cut disease entity caused by a
virus," rather "the very nature of AIDS is constructed through language and in
particular through the discourse of medicine and science . . ." [136, p. 263]. While the
human immunodeficiency virus (HIV) is indisputably a biological entity, representations of the disease (actually syndrome) "AIDS," by contrast, "are multiple and
discontinuous" and of a socio-political nature [137, p. 1]. This has been pointed out
with considerable effect with reference to the early inclusion of Haitians *en masse* as
a so-called "risk group" for AIDS [138]. As, Foucault, whose death is ample
evidence of the physicality of HIV, argued, social and political forces have always
structured "the conditions of possibility of medical experience" [3, p. xix]. Such
forces have molded the way HIV or any other disease entity is perceived and
interpreted by medicine and by society. Importantly, as Latour and Woolgar emphasize in their study of the construction of scientific facts, interpretations not only
*in*form they also *per*form, they serve to validate particular agendas or support particular worldviews [139].

Identified by biomedicine in 1981, AIDS was named and defined officially by the
U.S. Centers for Disease Control (CDC) the following year. The standard definition
became the combined state of exhibiting antibodies to HIV and the presence of one
or more specified degenerative or neoplastic diseases. However, the definition had to
be revised in 1987 to incorporate additional conditions (dementia and wasting
syndrome) that were only then accepted as demarcating development of AIDS.
However, even with these changes "many infected individuals who suffered from
clinical symptoms and laboratory abnormalities signaling the presence of HIV infection did not meet the CDC criteria for the disease" [140, p. 35]. Most notable in this
regard are opportunistic HIV-related conditions among women. As Anastos and
Marte indicate,

> the case definition of AIDS is centered in how the disease has manifested in men,
> and gynecologic conditions are not included as manifestations of HIV infection.
> If women's disease manifests with the same infections as it does in men, it may
> be recognized and reported as AIDS; if the infections, still HIV related, are
> different, the women are not considered to have AIDS [141, pp. 190-191].

Various infections, including pelvic inflammatory disease and yeast infection, as well as cervical cancer are more common, more severe, and less responsive to treatment among seropositive women, suggesting a diminished immune system capacity. However, these conditions were not defined or treated as manifestations of AIDS for many years. In cities at the epicenter of the epidemic like New York and Washington, D.C., there have been radical increases in deaths among younger women since the appearance of AIDS. However, these were not included as AIDS-related deaths because of the way AIDS was officially constructed as a disease [142]. Consequently, pressure from AIDS activists contributed to yet another redefinition of AIDS during 1992. This event underscores Treichler's larger argument that it is not sufficient just to be attentive to the cultural and biological dimensions of AIDS or any other disease, a common recommendation in conventional medical anthropology texts. As Treichler indicates,

> no clear line can be drawn between the facticity of scientific and nonscientific (mis)conceptions [about AIDS]. Ambiguity, homophobia, stereotyping, confusion, doublethink, them-versus-us, blame-the-victim, wishful thinking: none of these popular forms of semantic legerdemain about AIDS is absent from biomedical communication. But scientific and medical discourses have traditions through which the semantic epidemic as well as the biological one is controlled, and these may disguise contradiction and irrationality [136, p. 269].

Consequently, it is critical that we investigate the degree to which science and medicine are socio-politically constructed, an issue discussed further in Chapter 7.

Figlio's account of chlorosis also is pertinent to this discussion because like many others this is a disease that was discovered and discarded during particular epochs [143]. Chlorosis (the green sickness) was first described in the early eighteenth century and became common during the nineteenth century. It was said to be a discrete condition characterized by pallor, secondary anemia, perverted cravings, obstinate constipation, and nervousness. The disease most often was diagnosed among adolescent girls, particularly those from nöuveaurïche families. Chlorosis, in sum, "marked a new social group, the fashionable female adolescent, by physical illness" [143, p. 222]. Sigerist notes that "[w]ith the disappearence of this type [of young girl], the disease also disappeared" [cited in 143, p. 220]. In Figlio's interpretation, chlorosis medicalized lower middle class physician condemnation of the luxurious habits of the emergent idle rich. Discovery of the disease "expressed a class hostility—one which concealed aspiration to the same style" [143, p. 222] among nineteenth-century doctors. With the achievement of their upwardly mobile aspirations, through processes outlined in the last chapter, physician motivation for diagnosing chlorosis also disappeared. They were no longer, so to speak, seeing green with envy.

The biomedical handling of black lung disease (coal miner's pneumoconiosis) among Appalachian miners provides another angle on the social construction of disease (as well as its social production). Between the two world wars, the southern bituminous coal industry functioned almost like a Goffmanesque total institution for its workers [144]. Coal companies controlled public schools, police departments, churches, the monetary system, roads, housing, and doctors in mining towns. The company doctor, an example of what Daniels calls the "captured professional," was the only source of medical care for coal workers and their families [122]. Among company doctors, there was "a uniform tendency to ascribe accidents and disease to the fault of the miner—his carelessness and personal habits, such as alcoholism" [145, p. 53]. Overlooking the laundry list of health hazards, toxins, and unsafe working conditions confronting mine workers, an article written by one company doctor in the *Journal of Industrial Hygiene* concluded that

> Housing conditions, and hurtful forms of recreation, especially alcoholism, undoubtedly cause the major amount of sickness. The mine itself is not an unhealthful place to work [quoted in 145, p. 53].

The widespread breathlessness, chest congestion, and prolonged coughing spells among coal workers were termed "miner's asthma" by company doctors. The condition was seen as a normal part of miner's life rather than a disabling disease. Writing in another health journal, a company doctor noted

> As far as most of the men in this region are concerned, so called 'miner's asthma' is considered *an ordinary* condition that needs cause no worry and therefore the profession has not troubled itself about its finer pathological and associated clinical manifestations [quoted in 145, p. 53].

A radiologist in West Virginia reported that he regularly encountered chest X-rays done by company doctors that showed massive lung legions that were labeled "normal miner's chest" [146]. Miners who cited respiratory symptoms as a cause for missing work were diagnosed as malingerers or sufferers of "compensationitis." Those who persisted in these complaints often were referred to psychiatrists. Until the 1950s, the *Journal of the American Medical Association* printed articles [e.g., 147] on the psychological origin of miners' lung disease.

By contrast, *The Condition of the Working Class in England,* written by Frederick Engels in 1845 at the age of twenty-four, and without benefit of a medical education, provided a rather different view of the source of coal miner's respiratory complaints.

> In part from the bad, dust-filled atmosphere mixed with carbonic acid and hydrocarbon gas, . . . there arise numerous painful and dangerous affections of the lungs . . . . The peculiar disease of workers of this sort is 'black spittle', which arises from the saturation of the whole lung with coal particles, and manifests itself in general debility, headache, oppression of the chest, and thick, black mucous expectoration [148, p. 272].

Unlike Engels, biomedicine long failed to "see" miner's signs and symptoms as disease, revealing thereby the degree to which disease construction or nonconstruction is a political act conditioned not only by biological factors but by social relations of power and profit as well.

A similar story can be told in the case of "asbestosis," another workplace disease with a clear cut social origin [149]. Although the disease was known from ancient times, and Greek slaves who worked the asbestos mines were issued primitive respirators, it was not "re-discovered" in biomedicine until 1924. Clinical reports on asbestos-related lung cancer began to appear in the medical literature in the 1930s, including accounts of workplace exposure. Nonetheless, "millions of workers have been exposed knowingly in ship building, insulation work, automobile brake shoe manufacture, and numerous other industries" right up to the present [150, p. 1172]. Others have been exposed in schools and in their homes. But awareness of asbestos-related cancer, no more than recognition of cancer caused by exposure to hydrocarbons [151] or liver damage induced by polychlorinated biphenyls [152] etc., has not produced a re-orientation in standard biomedical emphasis on privatization and healthism, i.e., on the way the notion of "disease" is standardly constructed and conceived in biomedicine. "Even with all the epidemiological evidence laid before it," observes Stark, "medicine cannot see the social basis of disease . . ." [94, p. 430]. As a result, the bulk of biomedical resources mobilized in responding to conditions like cancer are devoted to "ex post radiation, chemotherapy, and surgical removal rather than environmental prevention" [153, p. 629].

While it is undeniable, as Konner contends, that disease has played a major role in the shaping of social reality, as these cases suggest, the reverse is no less true and possibly far more important [154]. In this light, the tendency, be it in biomedicine or in medical anthropology, to see disease as a given, as part of an immutable physical reality, can itself be understood as social construction with important political consequences. Disease deflects attention from social relations to assumed biological properties, achieving thereby a naturalization and privitization of sickness. The appearance and disappearance of diseases over time may be more a process of changes in social relations and related socio-linguistics than an expression of biological evolution, and hence disease no less than illness is a concern to CMA.

Second, CMA is concerned with the direct social production of ill health. To the degree that it is a physical entity, disease generally is much more than

> the straightforward outcome of an infectious agent or pathophysiological disturbance. Instead, a variety of problems—including malnutrition, economic insecurity, occupational risks, bad housing and lack of political power—create an underlying predisposition to disease and death [155, p. 98].

This insight suggests the importance of studying disease, including its manufacture and marketing, in terms of social structures [156, 157]. For example,

> an insulin reaction in a diabetic postal worker might be ascribed (in a reductionist mode) to an excessive dose of insulin causing an outpouring of adrenaline, a failure of the pancreas to respond with appropriate glucagon secretion etc. Alternatively, the cause might be sought in his having skipped breakfast because he was late for work; unaccustomed physical exertion demanded by a foreman; inability to break for a snack; or, at a deeper level, the constellation of class forces in U.S. society which assures capitalist domination of production and the moment to moment working lives of the proletariat [7, p. 1208].

The study of the social origins of disease in this sense has a convoluted history in the health and social sciences. It is a field, Waitzkin concludes, that began with Frederick Engels in the work cited previously but has "been largely forgotten and then rediscovered with each succeeding generation" [155, p. 77]. Within medical anthropology, it is a subject that attracted negligible attention until the emergence of CMA. In the last several years, critical medical anthropologists attempted to correct this shortcoming through studies of the social causes of malnutrition, environmental and occupational ill-health, homelessness, substance abuse, infant mortality, infectious disease, emotional conflicts and disorders, and other health and societal problems that contribute to human suffering malnutrition. Commonly, in our studies, causation is found to be situated in terms of the structural contradictions of capitalist production and the for-profit character of capitalist distribution.

Consider the issue of malnutrition. In an article deemed sufficiently enlightening to be reproduced in one of the most widely read early collections of medical anthropology papers, Newman argues the following about its causes:

> On a gross world basis the American Geographical Society (1953) maps show that the areas of undernutrition and malnutrition closely coincide with the tropical and warmer temperate regions of backward food producing technologies . . . . To a considerable extent the nutritional deficiency diseases are distributed by climate zones, are often worse at certain seasons, and are sometimes related to specific food crops. When these deficiency diseases reach epidemic proportions, they appear to represent the worst lags in man's adaptation to his nutritional environment [158, p. 322].

By contrast, in his study of Cauca Valley in the tropical country of Columbia, where 50 percent of the children are malnourished, Taussig found it necessary to consider the effects of a burgeoning agribusiness sector, the World Bank, U.S. multinational corporations, USAID, the Rockefeller Foundation, U.S.-based private consulting firms, U.S. and Columbian university staff and the like [159]. Except by examining the role of powerful national and international forces with vested interests in the production or protection of profit, Taussig found it impossible to understand malnutrition in a fertile region that exports cash crops to the United States. Similarly, Davison argues that efforts to account for hunger in Haiti, the tropical breadbasket of the French empire in the eighteenth century, only in terns of ecological or cultural factors, eliminates from consideration the effects of several hundred years of colonial and neocolonial extraction from the island [160]. Perhaps most telling is a report that was issued by the British Royal Institute of International Affairs in 1932. The report notes:

> Two generations ago the banana was a luxury; oranges were a seasonal fruit only; the use of tobacco was for the rich alone, and cocoa unknown. Today bananas, oranges all the year, tea, coffee and cocoa figure in the humblest domestic budget in North America and Great Britain . . . . Man and beast are fed increasingly from tropical countries [quoted in 39, p. 106].

CMA studies, such as those cited above, demonstrate the necessity of placing the examination of ill health within the "wider field of force" [31], i.e., the global social relations (often implemented by multinational corporations, facilitated by international lending institutions, and supported by "development" agencies) that determine what is produced, how it is produced, and who benefits (or suffers) from production [161]. As Scheper-Hughes shows in her work in yet another tropical setting, Northeast Brazil, conventional perspectives that interpret the extremely high rates of death and disease ... in the developing world as the almost inevitable consequences of largely impersonal ecological, climactic or demographic conditions.... obscure ... the role of economic relations in the social production of morbidity and mortality ... [162, p. 535].

Several other studies done in Brazil indicate that it is social class that most significantly determines morbidity and mortality patterns [163, 164], a pattern that is found throughout the world [165], rather than ecology per se. In sum,

malnutrition is the result of the unequal distribution of world income and not the result of an insufficient availability of food. *It is clearly a poverty problem and not a food problem* [166, emphasis in original].

Biomedicine, of course, rarely limits its discussion of causation solely to microorganisms. But the social context to which it tends to draw attention is of a much more circumscribed nature than that of CMA. Consider, the following discussion from a text on the psychosocial basis of medical practice.

Two levels of pathological process must usually be considered simultaneously: the disease and the illness. Pneumococcal pneumonia of the lower lobe of the lung is a specific *disease*. The pathological process can be understood in technical, impersonal terms, and it involves a specific etiological agent, *Diplococcus pneumoniae*. But the physician does not treat that disease in vacuo. Rather, he treats a person with an illness; pneumonia. This means that he needs to evaluate all of the factors which may have played a role in the development of the illness ... In the case of pneumonia, this may include such considerations as other diseases which predispose to infection, the patient's age, the physical care he gave himself and the risks to which he exposed himself, his alcoholic drinking pattern, the adequacy of heating in his home and his willingness to acknowledge and seek medical care for significant distress [167, pp. 11-12].

While the factors listed by Bowden and Burstein may play a role in the development of pneumonia, they are hardly *all* of the potentially relevant factors. Notably missing from this discussion is any mention of the political-economic factors cited above by Waitzkin, such as malnutrition, economic insecurity, occupational risks, bad housing and lack of political power.

Consequently, in the view of CMA, medical anthropology must strive, in McNeill's terms, to understand the relationship between microparasitism (the organisms, malfunctions, and individuals behaviors that are the agents or proximate causes of disease) and macroparasitism (the social relations that are the ultimate cause of much disease) [168]. As Farmer emphasizes, "[i]t is inexcusable to limit our horizons to the ideally circumscribed village, culture, or case history and ignore the social origins of much— if not most—illness and distress" [128, p. 80]. Failure to consider this wider frame constitutes an abdication of anthropology's holistic legacy.

Health Policy, Health Resource Allocation, and The Role of The State in Health

The re-insertion of societal cases back into the world economic system for understanding also is evidenced in CMA studies of the relationship between the State, health policy, and resource allocation. For many of the cases of traditional interest to anthropology, this means an examination of contemporary health policy and practice in relation to the legacy of colonialism and the development of underdevelopment on the one hand and the emergence of neocolonialism and the functioning of a comprador elite on the other.

A primary health effect of colonialism was the spread of infectious disease. For example, largely due to introduced disease and its interference with normal social processes, within fifty years of Cortez's arrival the American Indian population of central Mexico "had shrunk ... to about one tenth of what had been there when Cortez landed" [168, p. 180]. Starting in the sixteenth century, European imperial expansion triggered a series of similar epidemiological disasters across the world. These epidemics "helped to destroy the economic and social foundations of indigenous communities and the resulting disintegration and impoverishment greatly facilitated the establishment of colonial hegemony" [161, p. 102]. This process also was accelerated by colonial food policies. These were designed to transform local production for consumption or symmetrical trade into commodity production for provisioning Europe and profitable sale on the world market. For the colonies, however, these policies contributed to malnutrition and a further decline in the health status of indigenous peoples. Even colonial policies designed to prevent famine, such as compulsory cultivation of maize and cassava in Africa, may have contributed to an overall lowering of nutritional levels as crops with higher nutrient content like sorghum and millet could not be planted. Finally, labor policies, implemented to extract cheap labor from colonized peoples, moved large numbers of workers from their traditional areas, concentrated them in work camps with unhealthy living and working conditions, fed them inexpensive diets that were high in bulk and low in vitamins and nutrients, offered them alcohol as an escape from loneliness and frustration, worked them long hours at hard physical toil, and exposed them to a host of new diseases. Based on data from East Africa, Turshen indicates that the "emiseration of the population in labour supply areas was reflected in persistent high rates of maternal, infant and child mortality, in widespread malnutrition and in high levels of morbidity" [169, p. 308]. With reference to Africa as a whole, Doyal concludes, "[t]here is little doubt that for the vast majority of Africans, participation in wage labour meant a marked deterioration" [161, p. 111], in living and health standards.

Several critical medical anthropologists have examined the medical policies of colonial regimes [170-172]. These accounts parallel Lasker's description of the role of health services in the Ivory Coast.

> Study of the Ivory Coast reveals that many ways in which French colonizers, clearly the dominant group until independence, relied on the Western health system to further their economic and political aims. As the goals of colonial rule changed over time, so did the nature of medical care organizations. The result has been a highly unequal allocation of services, benefiting primarily the French and those Africans who were considered important for the maintenance of a productive economy and of political stability. Although many individuals who worked in the health services in the colonies were motivated by humanitarian concerns

and many positive results were achieved in improving health, it should nevertheless be . . . clear . . . that the health system was developed primarily to promote
French interests [173, p. 278].

Ultimately, colonialism commonly gave way to a pseudo-independence in
which the class structure created by the colonial regime served as a foundation for
maintaining the metropolis-satellite relationship, and in which the health care sector
remained shackled to the colonial past and the neocolonial present. As Whiteford
reveals in her research in the Dominican Republic, under pressure or persuasion from
without, Third World countries adopt health care policies and programs designed to
maintain ties with the capitalist core rather than improve the health of the masses
[174]. Features of the medical sector identified by critical medical anthropologists in
dependent capitalist countries include: 1) provision of a costly and centralized
biomedicine to the national bourgeoisie (and the military) that is woefully ill-suited
to the health care needs of an underdeveloped country; 2) maintenance of a highly
centralized and rigidly organized health system with decision-making power concentrated at the top; 3) production of medical specialists that rapidly are drained into
the lower echelons of the health systems of core countries; 4) creation of a market for
imported pharmaceuticals and other medical commodities; and 5) emergence (or
continuation in ever changing form) of a lower tier of health workers and folk healers
who treat the masses.

On the whole, as McDermott shows in her study of health policy in Hong Kong,
State intervention "has done little more than further implant and solidify
biomedicine" [175, p. 198]. A more general conclusion of CMA, is illustrated
by Stebbins in his work on Mexican health policy, namely that State intervention
in health care without a significant reallocation of resources "addresses
symptoms rather than causes of disease and is not likely to significantly improve the
health status of the people who are most in need of such assistance" [176, p. 139].
State intervention, in fact, most commonly serves not to challenge but to reproduce
inegalitarian social relations.

The Social Relations among Interacting Medical Traditions Nationally and Transnationally

Wherever it has been transported, biomedicine has encountered other medical
systems, some of recent and others of far older vintage. The result has been the
creation in diverse settings of complex webs of healing systems, perhaps hostile at the
level of the provider but unified in treatment at the level of the patient. The rich
tapestry of medical pluralism described in numerous medical anthropology reports
does not float in the rarified air of symbolic meanings and explanatory models as has
sometimes been suggested in conventional analyses, but, as Frankenberg insists,
[177, p. 198] is anchored to class divisions, as illustrated for diverse settings in
Chapters 8, 9, and 10 .

An important aspect of medical pluralism is the role of the State. In the Third
World, State support for folk medicine appeals to popular anti-imperialist sentiment
but is often shallow; "Members of the ruling class whose ailments require deeper

penetration look to injections, drugs or surgical intervention from the West" [177, p. 198]. Even in situations where explicit financial or legal support for traditional medicine is lacking, governments "like to keep traditional medicine alive, because it is recognized that traditional physicians take some of the strain off Western doctors in dealing with self-limiting disease" [178, p. 265]. More broadly, it has been argued that traditional medicine is allowed and even fostered by the State as a means of handling the potentially disruptive "human fallout" associated with capitalist development (including market penetration, proletarianization, urban migration, and poverty) that is not easily fitted to the diagnostic categories and treatment modalities of biomedicine [179]. Thus, in Chapter 10 an African American folk medical system is shown to be compensatory and accommodative rather than corrective. In sum, as indicated in Chapter 8, the success of folk and heterodox healing systems [e.g., 180] in capitalist countries is contingent upon gaining the acceptance of strategic elites who are seeking solutions to the contradictions of capitalist medicine medicine and of patients who demand forms of treatment neglected by the dominant medical system.

The attention accorded folk medicine by conventional medical anthropology is another issue of concern to critical medical anthropologists. While some have interpreted this as further expression of anthropology's preoccupation with anything purportedly traditional to the neglect of everything transformed, Harrison contends a more explicitly political function.

> Traditional healers became fashionable for anthropologists and other social sciences because [such research] gave former colonial nations access to the local population's thought patterns and medicines .... As a result, colonial powers . . . are able to maintain a presence in these countries . . . under the guise of helping them develop new local level low cost health care delivery systems [181, p. 131].

The Intertwining of Medical Systems with Their Political Economic Context

As Krause observed

> Throughout history, to a marked degree, health services have reflected in miniature the achievement of the societies in which they have existed. Otherwise put, the place to understand the functioning of the health care system is primarily outside of its narrowly conceived boundaries. One can gain some understanding of Nazi Germany, for example, by studying relations between guards and inmates within concentration camps, but no one would assert that the primary social and political explanation for this phenomenon lay there, or, for that matter, the primary explanation of the quality of guard-inmate relations [16, p. 2].

And yet, this exact type of analysis and explanation is common in anthropology and sociology of health studies. Medical systems, or parts thereof, are extracted from the political economy that sets the conditions under which they develop and explanation is sought in terms of individual or micro-social level phenomena. The doctor-patient relationship, for example, as Schoepf indicates, is not, as it has sometimes been treated, "an internally balanced and self-maintained dyadic social system" [182, p. 112]. Rather, as we have attempted to show, the character of doctor-patient interaction is structured by a wider field of class and other relations embedded within, but not always directly visible from, the clinical setting. Failure to locate personal ties, face-to-face interactions, social networks, social support systems, and other bonds of a similar order within the encompassing and ultimately determinant set of social relations has been a significant weakness of mainstream medical anthropology. The CMA approach, by contrast, is to consider individual health care systems or parts of such systems in light of their relationship to the world economic-system, local class structure, and gender, racial or other social relations that shape access to resources, health, and power.

Sufferer Experience, Cultural Hegemony and Resistance

Sufferer experience, an arena long neglected in the social science of health, increasingly has become an area of research interest [183, 184]. From the perspective of CMA, sufferer experience is a social product, one that is constructed and reconstructed in the action arena between socially constituted categories of meaning and the political-economic forces that shape the contexts of daily life. Recognizing the powerful role of such forces, however, does not imply that individuals are passive, only that they respond to the material conditions that they face in terms of the set of possibilities created by the existing configuration of social relations and as a result of the effect of potent influencers.

While the newfound interest in sufferer experience is to be welcomed, there is a danger in exploring this arena of life without a theoretical framework that incorporates the macro-level. In the absence of such a framework, Western "common sense" (i.e., socially constructed) understandings about the nature of the individual steer research efforts. The inherent problem is that Western culture views "the fundamental unit of social life . . .[as] the concrete human interactant, and . . . the atomic unit of social organization [as] the social act" [185, p. 160]. In other words, stemming from an economic system predicated on the social rootlessness of the individual worker (who lacks traditional rights of access to the means of production and is therefore "free" to sale his/her labor on the open labor market), Western ideology has long de-emphasized social relations and the collectivity in favor of an enthronement of the individual as an independent actor. On the strength of his/her personal agency, will power, and labor alone, the individual succeeds or fails in free and fair economic and social competition. Hidden by this de-socialized conceptualization of the individual is the fact that

> society is no more just a collection of individual human beings than a house is just a conglomeration of lumber, bricks and nails . . .[A] house is defined in terms of its organizations, not its components [186, p. 17].

In approaches that place undue emphasis on the individual, both the actor and social interaction come to be thought of as "not merely as autonomous but as causal in their own right, apart from their economic, political, or ideological context" [31, p. 9]. Each individual is thought of as "moving in response to an inner clockwork" [31, p. 9] and explanation is phrased in terms of inner-dwelling psychological forces, self-contained meaning-systems, or microlevel decision-making processes, while the social structures that condition ego-development, the empowerment of symbols, and cost/benefits calculations used in reaching decisions are mystified and fade from view.

Clearly, a variety of factors influence sufferer experience, including individual psychobiology, social support networks and therapy management groups, the nature of the pathogenic agent/body interaction, and folk constructions of illness, pain, and symptom expression. In addition, macro- and intermediate-social factors play a significant role, including helping to shape all of the above mentioned influence factors. This is evident, for instance, in sufferer experience of diseases like AIDS. As discussed in Chapter 7, early in the AIDS epidemic, epidemiologists and policy makers promoted the idea of risk groups, including gay men and IV drug users, which could be said to be responsible for their own illness because of their participation in socially "deviant" behaviors. The mass media played up this aspect of the epidemic with articles in the mainstream press that made it seem "as if AIDS [was] something you got for being gay" [187, p. 6]. The incurability of AIDS may have contributed to the blame-the-victim quality that is now central to the social construction of this disease in society generally and within biomedicine. As Murray and Payne note

> American doctors prefer to deal with acute disease amenable to capital-intensive, high-tech remedies involving considerable control over patients. No such remedies are available for AIDS. A disease that kills previously healthy men in their twenties and thirties is both personally and professionally distressing. It is even a threat to the reputation of medicine in American society. We believe there is a need felt to explain AIDS away as 'their own fault,'—quite apart from pre-existing hostility to homosexuality—not that doctors are free of homophobia . . . [188, p. 123].

As a stigmatized disease—one that is erroneously attached to oppressed pariah groups—AIDS magnifies rather than reduces the sufferer's level of personal responsibility. As a result, the sufferer's experience is shaped in notable ways. For example, when seventeen-year-old AIDS patient Henry Nicols was asked what worried him the most about his disease, he responded,

> I was afraid of what people might think if they found out. What they might do. We had seen what happened to Ryan White and some other hemophiliac boys with AIDS who went public. We told no one outside of the immediate family [quoted in 189, p. 4].

The fear of ostracism or physical harm expressed by this AIDS patient is not secondary to his experience of AIDS, it is central to it. Indeed, it is what he worries about *most*.

Physician expectation, in fact, can play a powerful role in shaping illness expression. Describing Charcot's classic study of hysteria, for example, Eisenberg states, "the patients were ill before they saw Charcot; what changed was the patterning of symptoms . . . He expected what they produced; they came to produce what he expected" [190, p. 12]. If to some degree people learn to be ill in ways that conform to physician expectation—expectation communicated through past clinical encounters, mass media presentations of various kinds, or experience with third party payment plans—the social origins of these expectations warrant investigation. If, as Taussig asserts, physicians attempt to "modulate and mold the patient's self-awareness" [25, p. 9], the impact of physician-patient interactions on subsequent illness and popular conception cannot be ignored. And, as a result, the individual sufferer cannot be treated as leading an autonomous existence free of the same forces and interests predominant at other levels of the health care system. Individual experience and behavior are extensively molded by prevailing cultural patterns and these in turn are conditioned by the prevailing structure of social relations within and outside of the health care system.

These points are graphically illustrated by Nancy Scheper-Hughes' analysis of poor people's conception of organ transplant in Northeast Brazil [191]. She reports that beginning in 1987 a terrifying rumor began to circulate among shantytown residents outside the city of Recife and beyond. The rumor had it that poor people, especially children, were being abducted to serve as involuntary organ donors for wealthy transplant patients at home and abroad. Large blue and yellow vans, conspicuously driven by North Americans and Japanese, were said to be patrolling poor neighborhoods hunting for likely victims, who would then be grabbed off the street and mutilated for their desired organs. Dismembered bodies were reported to be discarded by the side of the road or in hospital dumpsters. These fears were so palpably real for shantytown residents that they began to lock their children in-doors all day long for fear of having them fall victim to the greedy demands of the wealthy in their quest to avoid old age and death. The poor, as a powerless group, were ideal targets to serve the needs of upper class vanity. As one older women told Scheper-Hughes, "So many of the rich are having plastic surgery and organ transplants, . . . we really don't know whose body we are talking to anymore" [191, p. 59].

How are we to understand this folk belief? As one source of the rumors, Scheper-Hughes points to a real theft of bodies that goes on daily in Brazil, the export of as many as 3,000 Brazilian children a year by the international adoption industry. Some of these children are abandoned or put up for adoption because their parents are so poor that they believe their children will have a better life with adoptive parents in the United States or in Europe. Others, are bullied into turning their children over to orphanages by patrons or orphanage workers. Still others are tricked into losing their children. The end result is the same, poor parents of Brazil produce children for comparatively wealthy would-be parents in core nations of the world-system. From the export of living bodies to that of living organs is not a very great leap of the imagination. In addition, Scheper-Hughes argues that the organ transplant rumors appear to express,

> poor people's perceptions grounded in a social and in a biotechnomedical reality, that their bodies and those of their children might be worth more dead than alive to the rich and powerful. These perceptions are generated within the context of sometimes macabre performances of doctor-patient relations in public clinics and teaching hospitals where the body parts of the rural and working poor are often viewed as 'dispensable' [191, p. 58].

She relates the case of Seu Antonio, a rural sugar cane cutter who went to his local clinic following a series of small strokes that damaged the vision in his left eye.

Without bothering to examine the impaired eye, the clinic doctor concluded, "Well, it's not worth anything, let's just have it removed" [quoted in 191, p. 58].

Finally, it is not unreasonable to suggest, although Scheper-Hughes does not extend her discussion to this point, that the rumors serve as a trope for concretely expressing the searing experience of exploitation and resultant suffering that are the twin pillars of daily existence among Northeast Brazil's impoverished masses. Just as their body's labor is daily extracted only to disappear into the marketplace as commodities that enrich the lives of the middle and wealthy classes of the world, in their collective imagination their very bodies are experienced as being similarly at risk of being transformed into commodities for others well being. In the organ theft metaphor, a graphically telling image of capitalist domination (in which even the individual body is broken down into autonomous organs free to be sold on the organ market), biomedicine is revealed as the servant of the dominant social classes. Folk conception, in short, and the sufferer experience that it helps to shape it, are tied directly and powerfully to political economy.

Inherent in the organ theft metaphor is a bold exposure and biting critique of the vulnerability that comprises the daily experience of the poor. At the same time, the metaphor is an expression by the poor of their rejection of ruling class benevolence and of biomedicine as a humane institution. Martin labels this form of alternative consciousness to ruling class hegemony as *lament*: "A focus of grief, pain, or unhappiness, with or without perception of structural factors outside of the individual's control" [24, p. 184]. Other forms of oppositional thinking and acting that she identifies include *nonaction* (avoiding interactions with dominant institutions and settings), *sabotage* (the conscious interference with official policies and processes), *resistance* (rejection of official definitions or instructions), and *rebellion* (attempting to force change of social relations and their expression in policies and procedures). As we indicate in the following chapters, these forms of defiance and struggle are in evidence as much within as outside the domain of biomedicine. As a form of alternative consciousness or counter-hegemony, critical medical anthropology is itself an expression of resistance, which through its praxis seeks to contribute to popular struggles for change.

REFERENCES

1. E. Wolf, Distinguished Lecture: Facing Power—Old Insights, New Questions, *American Anthropologist, 92*:3, pp. 586-596, 1990.
2. P. Rabinow, *The Foucault Reader,* Pantheon Books, New York, 1984.
3. M. Foucault, *The Birth of the Clinic*, Vintage Books, New York, 1975.
4. L. Rhodes, Studying Biomedicine as a Cultural System, in *Medical Anthropology: Contemporary Theory and Method*, T. Johnson and C. Sargent (eds.), Praeger, New York, pp. 149-158, 1990.
5. T. Kuhn, *The Structure of Scientific Revolutions,* Unviersity of Chicago Press, Chicago 1962.
6. S. Morsy, Political Economy in Medical Anthropology, in *Medical Anthropology: Contemporary Theory and Method,* T. Johnson and C. Sargent (eds.), Praeger, New York, pp. 26-46, 1990.

7. S. Woolhandler and D. Himmelstein, Ideology in Medical Science: Class in the Clinic, *Social Science and Medicine, 28*, pp. 1205-1209, 1989.
8. S. Woolgar, (ed.), *Knowledge and Reflexivity: New Frontiers in the Sociology of Knowledge,* Sage Publications, London, 1988.
9. B. Scholte, Toward a Reflexive and Critical Anthropology, in *Reinventing Anthropology,* D. Hymes (ed.), Vintage Books, New York, pp. 431-457, 1974.
10. J. Derrida, Structure, Sign and Play in the Discourse of the Human Sciences, in *The Languages of Criticism and the Sciences of Man,* R. Macksy and E. Donato (eds.), John Hopkins University Press, Baltimore, pp. 247-272, 1970.
11. M. Pollner, Left of Ethnomethodology: The Rise and Decline of Radical Reflexivity, *American Sociological Review, 56,* pp. 370-380, 1991.
12. G. Radnitzky, *Continenal Schools of Meta-Science,* Akademiforlaget, Göteborg, 1968.
13. R. Bellah, Foreword, in *Reflections on Fieldwork in Morocco,* by P. Rabinow, University of California Press, Berkeley, California, 1977.
14. S. Gould, The Chain of Reason vs. the Chain of Thumbs, *Natural History, 7,* pp. 12-21, 1989.
15. E. Genovese, *Roll, Jordan, Roll,* Vintage Books, New York, 1974.
16. E. Krause, *Power and Illness: The Political Sociology of Health and Medical Care,* Elsevier North-Holland, New York, 1977.
17. N. Abercrombie, S. Hill, and B. Tumer, *The Dominant Ideology,* George Allen and Unwin Ltd, London, 1980.
18. H. Waitzkin, *The Politics of Medical Encounters,* Yale University Press, New Haven, 1991.
19. H. Baer, M. Singer, and J. Johnsen, Toward a Critical Medical Anthropology, *Social Science and Medicine, 23,* pp. 95-98, 1986.
20. R. Frankenberg, Sickness as Cultural Performance: Drama, Trajectory, and Pilgrimage. Root Metaphors and the Making Social of Disease, *International Journal of Health Services, 16,* pp. 603-626, 1986.
21. M. Singer, The Limitations of Medical Ecology: The Concepts of Adaptation in the Context of Social Stratification and Social Transformation, *Medical Anthropology, 10,* pp. 223-234, 1989.
22. C. Flores, L. Davison, I. Rey, M. Rivera, and M. Serrano, La mujer Puertorriqueña, su cuerpo y la lucha por la vida: Experience with Empowerment in Hartford, Connecticut, in *Fighting for Our Lives: Defending Abortion Rights,* M. Gerber Freed (ed.), Southend Press, Boston, 1990.
23. E. Lazarus, Theoretical Considerations for the Study of the Doctor-Patient Relationship: Implications of a Perinatal Study, *Medical Anthropology, 2,* pp. 34-58, 1988.
24. E. Martin, *The Woman in the Body: A Cultural Analysis of Reproduction,* Beacon Press, Boston, 1987.
25. M. Taussig, Reification and the Consciousness of the Patient, *Social Science and Medicine, 14B,* pp. 3-13, 1980.
26. I. Susser, Union Carbide and the Community Surrounding It: The Case of a Community in Puerto Rico, *International Journal of Health Services, 15*:4, pp. 561-583, 1985.
27. S. Morsy, Islamic Clinics in Egypt: The Cultural Elaboration of Biomedical Hegmony, *Medical Anthropology Quarterly, 2*:4, pp. 355-367, 1988.
28. A. Ferguson, Commercial Pharmaceutical Medicine and Medicalization: A Case Study from El Salvador, *Culture, Medicine, and Psychiatry, 5,* pp. 105-133, 1981.
29. E. Wallerstein, *The Modern World-System Vol. 1,* Academic Press, New York, 1974.
30. M. Sahlins, *Tribesmen,* Prentice Hall, Inc., Englewood Cliffs, New Jersey, 1968.

31. E. Wolf, *Europe and the People without History,* University of California Press, Berkeley, 1982.
32. R. Keesing, Anthropology as Interpretive Quest, *Current Anthropology, 28,* pp. 161-176, 1987.
33. S. Ungar, Get Away With What You Can, in *In The Name of Profit,* R. Heilbroner, M. Mintz, C. McCarthy, S. Ungar, V. Sanford, S. Friedman, and J. Boyd, (eds.), Doubleday, Garden City, New York, pp. 106-127, 1972.
34. J. Paul, Medicine and Imperialism, in *The Cultural Crisis of Modern Medicine,* J. Ehrenreich (ed.), Monthly Review Press, New York, pp. 271-286, 1978.
35. A. Relman, The New Medical-Industrial Complex, in *The Sociology of Health and Illness: Critical Perspectives,* P. Conrad and R. Kern (eds.), St. Martin's Press, New York, pp. 210-218, 1986.
36. S. van der Geest and S. Reynolds Whyte, *The Context of Medicines in Developing Countries: Studies in Pharmaceutical Anthropology,* Kluwer, Dordrecht, 1988.
37. S. van der Geest and S. Reynolds Whyte, The Charm of Medicines: Metaphors and Metonyms, *Medical Anthropology Quarterly, 3*:4, pp. 325-344, 1989.
38. B. O'Reilly, Drumakers Under Attack, *Fortune, 124*:3, pp. 48-63, 1991.
39. L. Doyal, *The Political Economy of Health,* South End Press Boston, 1979.
40. H. Waitzkin, Micropolitics of Medicine: Theoretical Issues, *Medical Anthropology Quarterly, 17,* pp. 134-136, 1986.
41. M. Bates, A Critical Perspective on Coronary Artery Disease and Coronary Bypass Surgery, *Social Science and Medicine, 30*:2, pp. 249-260, 1990.
42. T. Johnson, Physician Impairment: Social Origins of a Medical Concern, *Medical Anthropology Quarterly, 2*:1, pp. 17-33, 1988.
43. S. Poirier-Bures and A. Bures, Doctor-Hospital Relations: An Old Partnership Reconsidered, in *Dominant Issues in Medical Sociology,* H. Schwartz (ed.), Random House, New York, pp. 366-374, 1987.
44. B. Gray, *The New Health Care for Profit Doctors and Hospitals in a Competitive Environment,* National Academy Press, Washington, D.C., 1983.
45. V. Sidel and R. Sidel, Health Care and Medical Care in the United States, in *The Sociology of Health and Illness,* P. Congrad and R. Kern, (eds.), St. Martins Press, New York, 1986.
46. V. Navarro, *Medicine Under Capitalism,* Prodist, New York, 1976.
47. E. Friedson, *Profession of Medicine,* Dodd, Mead and Co., New York, 1970.
48. D. Mechanic, *The Growth of Bureaucratic Medicine,* John Wiley and Sons, New York, 1976.
49. C. Derber, Sponsorship and the Control of Physicians, *Theory and Society, 12,* pp. 561-601, 1983.
50. H. Smith, Two Lines of Authority Are One Too Many, *Modern Hospital, 85,* pp. 48-52, 1955.
51. G. Denton, *Medical Sociology,* Houghton Mifflin, Boston, 1983.
52. A. Birenbaum, *Health and Society,* Osman, Allanheld, Montclair, New Jersey, 1981.
53. H. Rodriquéz-Trias, The Women's Movement: Women Take Power, in *Reforming Medicine,* V. Sidel and R. Sidel (eds.), Pantheon, New York, pp. 107-126, 1984.
54. H. Strelnick and R. Younge, Affirmative Action in Medicine: Money Becomes the Admissions Criterion on the 1980s, in *Reforming Medicine,* V. Sidel and R. Sidel (eds.), Pantheon, New York, pp. 150-175, 1984.
55. W. Rosengren, *Sociology of Medicine,* Harper, New York, 1980.
56. L. Stein, Male and Female: The Doctor-Nurse Game, *Archives of General Psychiatry, 16,* pp. 699-703, 1967.

57. N. Aries and L. Kennedy, The Health Labor Force: The Effects of Change, in *The Sociology of Health and Illness,* P. Conrad and R. Kern (eds.), St. Martin's Press, New York, pp. 196-207, 1986.

58. S. Reverby, Re-forming the Hospital Nurse: The Management of American Nursing, in *The Sociology of Health and Illness,* P. Conrad and R. Kern (eds.), St. Martin's Press, New York, pp. 187-195, 1986.

59. P. Katz, How Surgeons Make Decisions, in *Physicians of Western Medicine,* R. Hahn and A. Gaines (eds.), D. Reidel Publishing Co., Dordrecht, pp. 155-175, 1985.

60. J. O'Niell, The Cultural and Political Context of Patient Dissatisfaction in Cross-Cultural Clinical Encounters, *Medical Anthropology Quarterly, 3,* pp. 325-344, 1989.

61. E. Lazarus, Falling Through the Cracks: Contradictions and Barriers to Care in a Prenatal Clinic, *Medical Anthropology, 12,* pp. 269-287, 1990.

62. J. Weaver and S. Garret, Sexism and Racism in the American Health Care Industry: A Comparative Analysis, *International Journal of Health Services, 8,* pp. 677-702, 1978.

63. P. Wilson, J. Griffith, and P. Tedeschi, Does Race Affect Hospital Use?, *American Journal of Public Health, 75,* pp. 263-269, 1985.

64. R. Gillum, Coronary Artery Bypass Surgery and Cornonary Angiography in the United States, 1979-1983, *American Heart Journal, 113,* pp. 1255-1260, 1987.

65. D. Segal, Playing Doctor, Seriously: Graduation Follies at an American Medical School, *International Journal of the Health Services, 14*:3, pp. 379-396, 1984.

66. H. Roberts, *The Patient Patients: Women and their Doctors,* Pandora Press, London, 1985.

67. M. Wenneker and A. Epstein, Racial Inequalities in the Use of Procedures for Patients with Ischemic Heart Disease in Massachusetts, *Journal of the American Medical Association, 261*:2, pp. 253-257, 1989.

68. M. Singer, C. Arnold, M. Fitzgerald, L. Madden, and C. von Legat, Hypoglycemia: A Controversial Illness in U. S. Society, *Medical Anthropology, 8,* pp. 1-35, 1984.

69. M. Singer, M. Fitzgerald, L. Madden, C. Arnold, and C. Voight von Legat, The Sufferer's Experience of Hypoglycemia, in *Research in the Sociology of Health Care Volume 6. The Experience of Sick People and their Significant Others*, P. Conrad and J. Roth (eds.), JAI Press, Greenwich, Connecticut, pp. 147-176, 1988.

70. M. Pflantz, A Critique of Anglo-American Medical Sociology, *International Journal of Health Services, 4,* pp. 565-574, 1974.

71. G. Foster and B. Anderson, *Medical Anthropology,* John Wiley and Sons, New York, 1978.

72. M. Singer, The Coming of Age of Critical Medical Anthropology, *Social Science and Medicine, 28,* pp. 1193-1204, 1989.

73. M. Singer, Postmodernism and Medical Anthropology: Words of Caution, *Medical Anthropology, 12*:3, pp. 289-304, 1990.

74. R. Crawford, Healthism and the Medicalization of Everyday Life, *International Journal of Health Services, 10*:3, pp. 365-388, 1980.

75. I. Zola, Medicine as an Institution of Social Control, *Sociological Review, 20,* pp. 487-504, 1972.

76. P. Conrad and J. Scheider, *Deviance and Medicalization: From Badness to Sickness*, The C. V. Mosby Co., St. Louis, 1980.

77. B. Turner, *Medical Power and Social Knowledge,* Sage Publications, London, 1987.

78. W. Ryan, *Blaming the Victim,* Vintage Books, New York, 1971.

79. I. Zola, In The Name of Health and Illness: On Some Socio-political Conseq Medical Influence, *Social Science and Medicine, 9,* pp. 83-87, 1975.

80. H. Waitzkin and B. Waterman, *The Exploitation of Illness in Capitalism,* Bobbs-Merrill Educational Publishing, Indianapolis, 1974.
81. A. Bale, Medicine in the Industrial Battle: Early Worker's Compensation, *Social Science and Medicine, 28*:11, pp. 1113-1120, 1989.
82. M. Konnor, *Becoming a Doctor: A Journey of Initiation in Medical School,* Viking, New York, 1987.
83. D. Dross, The Problem Patient: Evaluation and Care of Medical Patients with Psychosocial Disturbances, *Annals of Internal Medicine, 88*, pp. 366-372, 1978.
84. M. Singer, Toward a Political-Economy of Alcoholism: The Missing Link in the Anthropology of Drinking, *Social Science and Medicine, 23*, pp. 113-130, 1986.
85. K. Stebbins, Tobacco or Health in the Third World: A Political Economic Perspective with Emphasis on Mexico, *International Journal of the Health Services, 17*:3, pp. 521-536, 1987.
86. R. Elling, The Capitalist World-system and International Health, *International Journal of Health Services, 11*, pp. 21-51, 1981.
87. M. Nichter and E. Carwright, Saving the Children for the Tobacco Industry, *Medical Anthropology Quarterly, 5*:3, pp. 236-225, 1991.
88. J. Denny, V. Kemper, V. Novak, P. Overby, and A. Young, George Bush's Ruling Class, *International Journal of Health Services, 23*:1, pp. 95-132, 1993.
89. R. Crawford, You Are Dangerous to Your Health: The Ideology and Politics of Victim Blaming, *International Journal of Health Services, 7*:4, pp. 663-680, 1977.
90. V. Fuchs, *Who Shall Live? Health, Economics, and Social Choice,* Basic Books, New York, 1974.
91. Task Force on Health Promotion and Consumer Health Education, *Preventive Medicine USA,* Prodist, New York, 1976.
92. N. Muramoto, *Healing Ourselves,* Avon Books, New York, 1973.
93. I. Zola, Structural Constraints in the Doctor-Patient Relationship: The Case of Non-Compliance, in *The Relevance of Social Science for Medicine,* L. Eisenberg and A. Kleinman (eds.), D. Reidel Publishing Co., Dordrecht, pp. 241-252, 1981.
94. E. Stark, Doctors in Spite of Themselves: The Limits of Radical Health Criticism, *International Journal of Health Services, 12*:3, pp. 419-457, 1982.
95. M. Margolese, Homosexuality: A New Endocrine Correlate, *Hormones and Behavior, 1*, pp. 151-155, 1970.
96. M. Diamond, A Critical Evaluation of the Ontogeny of Human Sexual Behavior, *Quarterly Journal of Biology, 40*, pp. 147-175, 1965.
97. E. Bergler, *Homosexuality: Disease or a Way of Life?,* Hill and Wang, New York, 1956.
98. V. Bullough, *Sexual Variance in Society and History,* John Wiley and Sons, Inc, New York, 1976.
99. D. Teal, *The Gay Miltants,* Stein and Day Publishers, New York, 1971.
100. T. Szasz, *The Manufacture of Madness,* Harper and Row, Publishers, Inc., New York, 1970.
101. I. Zola, Healthism and Disabling Medicalization, in *Disabling Professions,* I. Illich (ed.), Marion Boyars, London, 1977.
102. M. Lock, Introduction, in *Biomedicine Examined,* M. Lock and D. Gordon (eds.), Kluwer Academic Publishers, Dordrecht, pp. 3-10, 1988.
103. A. Kleinman, *Patients and Healers in the Context of Culture,* University of California Press, Berkeley, 1988.
104. S. DiGiacomo, Biomedicine as a Cultural System: An Anthropologist in the Kingdom of the Sick, in *Encounters with Biomedicine: Case Studies in Medical Anthropology,* Hans Baer (ed.), Gordon and Breach Science Publishers, New York, pp. 315-346, 1987.

105. J. Henry, *Culture Against Man*, Vintage, New York, 1965.
106. D. Scully, *Men Who Control Women's Health*, Houghton Mifflin Co., New York, 1980.
107. L. Kilmayer, Mind and Body as Metaphors: Hidden Values in Biomedicine, in *Biomedicine Examined*, M. Lock and D. Gordon (eds.), Kluwer Academic Publishers, Dordrecht, pp. 57-94, 1988.
108. T. Parsons, *The Social System*, The Free Press, New York, 1951.
109. A. de Swaan, The Reluctant Imperialism of the Medical Profession, *Social Science and Medicine, 28,* pp. 1165-1170, 1989.
110. D. Sayer, *The Violence of Abstraction: The Analytic Foundations of Historical Materialism,* Basil Blackwell, Oxford, 1987.
111. H. Waitzkin, The Micropoltics of Medicine: A Contexual Analysis, *International Journal of Health Services, 14*:3, pp. 339-379, 1984.
112. M. Millman, The Enactment of Trust: The Case of Cardiac Patients, in *Dominant Issues in Medical Sociology,* H. Schwartz (ed.), Random House, New York, pp. 182-190, 1987.
113. R. Sennett and J. Cobb, *The Hidden Injuries of Class,* Vintage Books, New York, 1973.
114. V. Hamilton, V. Lee, C. Broman, W. Hoffman, and D. Renner, Hard Times and Vulnerable People: Initial Effects of Plant Closing on Autoworkers' Mental Health, *Journal of Health and Social Behavior, 31*, pp. 123-140, 1990.
115. R. Kessler, J. Turner, and J. House, Effeces of Unemployment in a Community Survey: Main, Modifying, and Mediating Effects, *Journal of Social Issues, 44*, pp. 69-85, 1988.
116. R. Liem and J. Liem, Psychological Effects of Unemployment, *Journal of Social Issues, 44*, pp. 87-105, 1988.
117. P. Ulbrich, G. Warheit, and R. Zimmerman, Race, Socioeconomic Status, and Psychological Distress: An Examination of Differential Vulnerability, *Journal of Health and Social Behavior, 30*, pp. 131-146, 1989.
118. G. Pappas, *The Magic City: Unemployment in a Working Class Community,* Cornell University Press, Ithaca, 1989.
119. L. Crandon, Medical Dialogue and the Political Economy of Medical Pluralism: A Case from Rural Highland Bolivia, *American Ethnologist, 13*:3, pp. 463-476, 1986.
120. S. Hills, *Demystifying Social Deviance*, McGraw-Hill Book Co., New York, 1980.
121. D. Pendleton and S. Bochner, The Communication of Medical Information in General Practice Consultations as a Function of Patients' Social Class, *Social Science and Medicine, 14A*, pp. 669-673, 1980.
122. A. Daniels, The Captive Professional: Bureaucratic Limitations on the Practice of Military Psychiatry, *Journal of Health and Social Behavior, 10*, pp. 255-265, 1969.
123. J. Crutcher and M. Bass, The Difficult Patient and the Troubled Physician, *The Journal of Family Practice, 11*:6, pp. 933-938, 1989.
124. J. Lorber, Good Patients and Problem Patients: Conformity and Deviance in a General Hospital, *Journal of Health and Social Behavior, 16*, pp. 213-225, 1975.
125. R. Haynes, R. Taylor, and D. Sackett, *Compliance and Health Care,* Johns Hopkins University Press, Baltimore, 1979.
126. J. Trostle, Medical Compliance as Ideology, *Social Science and Medicine, 27*:12, pp. 1299-1308, 1988.
127. A. Kleinman, *The Social Origins of Distress and Disease*, Yale University Press, New Haven, 1986.
128. P. Farmer, Bad Blood, Spoiled Milk: Bodily Fluids as Moral Barometers in Rural Haiti, *American Ethnologist, 15*:1, pp. 62-83, 1988.
129. A. Hochsschild and A. Russell, *The Managed Heart: Commercialization of Human Feelings,* University of California Press, Berkeley, 1983.
130. C. W. Mills, *The Sociological Imagination*, Grove Press, New York, 1959.

131. B. Ehrenreich and D. English, *For Her Own Good*, Doubleday, New York, 1978.
132. G. Parker, *The Oven Birds: American Women on Womanhood*, Doubleday, New York, 1972.
133. E. Bassuk, The Rest Cure: Repetition or Resolution of Victorian Women's Conflicts, in *The Female Body in Western Culture*, S. Suleiman (ed.), Harvard University Press, Cambridge, Massachusetts, pp. 139-151, 1986.
134. S. Morgen, The Dynamics of Cooptation in a Feminist Health Clinic, *Social Science and Medicine, 23*:2, pp. 201-210, 1986.
135. M. Clatts and K. Mutchler, AIDS and the Dangerous Other: Metaphors of Sex and Deviance in the Representation of Diseased, *Medical Anthropology, 10*:2-3, pp. 105-114, 1989.
136. P. Treichler, AIDS, Homophobia, and Biomedical Discourse: An Epidemic of Signification, *Cultural Studies, 1*:3, pp. 263-305, 1987.
137. C. Patton, *Inventing AIDS*, Routledge, New York, 1990.
138. P. Farmer, *AIDS and Accusation*, University of California Press, Berkeley, 1992.
139. B. Latour and S. Woolgar, *Laboratory Life: The Construction of Scientific Facts*, Cambridge University Press, Cambridge, 1985.
140. National Academy of Sciences, *Confronting AIDS: Update 1988*, National Academy of Sciences Press, Washington, D.C., 1988.
141. K. Anastos and C. Marte, Women The Missing Persons in the AIDS Epidemic, in *The AIDS Reader*, N. McKenzie (ed.), Meridian Books, New York, pp. 190-199, 1991.
142. C. Norwood, Women and the 'Hidden' AIDS Epidemic, *Network News*, pp. 1, 6, November 1988.
143. K. Figlio, Chlorosis and Chronic Disease in 19th-century Britain: The Social Constitution of Somatic Illness in a Capitalist Society, in *Women and Health: The Politics of Sex in Medicine*, E. Fee (ed.), Baywood Publishing Company, Amityville, New York, pp. 213-241, 1983.
144. E. Goffman, *Asylums*, Doubleday Anchor, New York, 1961.
145. B. Smith, Black Lung: The Social Production of Disease, in *The Sociology of Health and Illness*, P. Conrad and R. Kern (eds.), St. Martin's Press, New York, pp. 50-63, 1986.
146. B. Aronson, Black Lung: Tragedy of Appalachia, *New South, 26*:4, p. 54, 1971.
147. W. Ross, Emotional Aspects of Respiratory Disorders among Coal Miners, *Journal of the American Medical Association, 156*:4, pp. 484-487, 1954.
148. F. Engels, *The Conditions of the Working Class in England*, Granada, London, 1969.
149. P. Epstein, *The Politics of Cancer*, Anchor Books, New York, 1979.
150. R. Elling, The Political Economy of Workers' Health and Safety, *Social Science and Medicine, 28*:11, pp. 1171-1183, 1989.
151. J. Wagoner, Occupational Carcinogenesis: The Two Hundred Years Since Percival Post, *New York Academy of Science, 271*, pp. 1-3, 1976.
152. J. Nash and M. Kirsch, Polychlorinated Biphenyls in the Electrical Machinery Industry: An Ethnological Study of Community Action and Corporate Responsibility, *Social Science and Medicine, 23*:2, pp. 131-138, 1986.
153. S. Kelman, The Social Nature of the Definition Problem in Health, *International Journal of Health Services, 5*:4, pp. 625-642, 1975.
154. M. Konner, The Promise of Medical Anthropology: An Invited Commentary, *Medical Anthropology Quarterly, 5*:1, pp. 78-82, 1991.
155. H. Waitzkin, The Social Origins of Illness: A Neglected History, *International Journal of Health Services, 11*, pp. 77-103, 1981.

156. J. McKinlay, A Case for Refocusing Upstream: The Political Economy of Illness, in *The Sociology of Health and Illness: Critical Perspectives*, P. Conrad and R. Kern (eds.), St. Martin's Press, New York, pp. 484-498, 1986.

157. B. Maxwell and M. Jacobson, *Marketing Disease to Hispanics*, Center for Science in the Public Interest, Washington, D.C., 1989.

158. M. Newman, Ecology and Nutritional Stress, in *Culture, Disease and Healing*, D. Landy (ed.), Macmillan, New York, pp. 319-326, 1977.

159. M. Taussig, Nutrition, Development, and Foreign Aid: A Case Study of U.S.-Directed Health Care in a Columbian Plantation Zone, *International Journal of Health Services*, 8, pp. 101-119, 1978.

160. L. Davision, *Malnutrition in Haiti: A World-system Perspective*, presented at the 82nd. Anual meeting of the American Anthropological Association, Chicago, 1983.

161. R. Elling, *Cross-National Study of Health Systems*, Transaction Books, New Brunswick, 1980.

162. N. Scheper-Hughes, Culture, Scarcity, and Maternal Thinking: Mother Detachment and Infant Survival in a Brazilian Shanty Town, *Ethos, 13*:4, pp. 291-317, 1984.

163. J. de Cavallo and C. Wood, Mortality, Income Distribution, and Rural-Urban Residence in Brazil, *Population Development Review, 4*, pp. 405-415, 1978.

164. T. Merrick, The Effect of Piped Water on Early Childhood Mortality in Urban Brazil, *World Bank Staff Working Paper No. 594*, World Bank, Washington, D.C., 1983.

165. S. A. Zaidi, Poverty and Disease: Need for Structural Change, *Social Science and Medicine, 27*:2, pp. 119-127, 1988.

166. World Bank, The Economic Dimension of Malnutntion in Young Children, *World Bank Staff Working Paper No. 294*, Washington, D.C, 1978.

167. C. Bowden and A. Burstein, *Psychosocial Basis of Medical Practice*, The Williams and Wilkins Company, Baltimore, 1979.

168. W. McNeill, *Plagues and Peoples*, Anchor Books, Garden City, New Jersey, 1976.

169. M. Turshen, *The Political Economy of Health*, Ph.D. Thesis, University of Sussex, 1975.

170. J. Leeson, Social Science and Health Policy in Preindustrial Society, *International Journal of Health Services, 4*, pp. 429-440, 1974.

171. T. Aidoo, Rural Health Under Colonialism and Neocolonialism: A Survey of the Ghanaian Experience, *International Journal of Health Services, 12*:4 pp. 637-657, 1982.

172. E. Gruenbaum, Medical Anthropology, Health Policy and the State: A Case Study in Puerto Rico, *Policy Studies Review, 1*, pp. 47-65, 1981.

173. J. Lasker, The Role of Health Service in Colonial Rule: The Case of the Ivory Coast, *Culture, Medicine and Psychiatry, 1*, pp. 277-297, 1977.

174. L. Whiteford, A Question of Adequacy: Primary Health Care in the Dominican Republic, *Social Science and Medicine, 30*:2, pp. 221-226, 1990.

175. K. McDermott, Community Health and Reform in Hong Kong, *Social Science and Medicine, 23*, pp. 191-200, 1986.

176. K. Stebbins, Curative Medicine, Preventive Medicine and Health Status: The Influence of Politics on Health Status in a Rural Mexican Village, *Social Science and Medicine*, pp. 139-148, 1986.

177. R. Frankenberg, Medical Anthropology and Development: A Theoretical Perspective, *Social Science and Medicine, 14B*, pp. 197-207, 1978.

178. M. Topley, Chinese and Western Medicine in Hong Kong: Some Social and Cultural Determinants of Variation, Interaction, and Change, in *Culture and Healing in Asian Societies*, A. Kleinman (ed.), Schenkman, Cambridge, Massachusetts, 1978.

179. M. Singer and M. Borrero, Indigenous Treatment for Alcoholism: The Case for Puerto Rican Spiritism, *Medical Anthropology, 8*:4, pp. 246-272, 1984.

180. M. McGuire, *Ritual Healing in Suburban America,* Rutgers University Press, New Brunswick, 1988.
181. I. Harrison, Colonialism, Health Care Systems, and Traditional Healers, *ABA Occasional Papers No. 5,* 1984.
182. B. Schoepf, Human Relations versus Social Relations in Medical Care, in *Topias and Utopias in Health,* S. Ingman and A. Thomas (eds.), Mouton, The Hague, pp. 99-120, 1975.
183. J. Roth and P. Conrad, (eds.), *The Experience and Managment of Chronic Illness,* JAI Press, Inc, Greenwich, Connecticut, 1987.
184. E. Cassell, *The Nature of Suffering,* Oxford University Press, Oxford, 1991.
185. R. Straus, Religious Conversion as a Personal and Collective Accomplishment, *Sociology Annual, 40,* pp. 158-165, 1971.
186. T. Lewellen, *Political Anthropology,* Bergin and Garvey, South Hadley, Massachusetts, 1983.
187. C. Patton, *Sex and Germs: The Politics of AIDS,* Southend Press, Boston, 1985.
188. S. Murray and K. Payne, The Social Classification of AIDS in American Epidemiology, *Medical Anthropology, 10*:2-3, pp. 115-128, 1989.
189. L. Minton, Fresh Voices: What a Teenager with AIDS Wants You to Know, *Parade Magazine,* pp. 4-7, July 7, 1991.
190. L. Eisenberg, Disease and Illness: Distinctions between Professional and Popular Ideas of Sickness, *Culture, Medicine and Psychiatry, 1,* pp. 9-23, 1977.
191. N. Scheper-Hughes, Theft of Life, *Society, 27*:6, pp. 57-62, 1990.

CHAPTER 3

Postmodernism Medical Anthropology: A Critique

Once we lift our eyes from their texts we see, not 'post-industrial' society', but an all-too recognizable capitalism, authentically global for the first time in its history, palpably in deep crisis, yet rapidly transforming itself . . .

Alex Callinicos [1, p. 99]

Our efforts to develop a critical perspective in medical anthropology coincide with other developments within the discipline as well as changes beyond its boundaries that seep in and seem to demand anthropological attention. In particular, an interrelated set of postmodern debates have dominated cultural and academic discourse in recent years. Beginning among artists and art critics in New York during the 1960s, adopted especially by French (e.g., Lyotard) but also other European philosophers and theorists the following decade, by the 1980s postmodernism had become a global phenomenon permeating many spheres of life and discourse [2].

In aesthetic and cultural theory, polemics emerged over whether modernism in the arts was or was not dead and what sort of postmodern art was succeeding it. In philosophy, debates erupted concerning whether or not the tradition of modern philosophy had ended, and many began celebrating a new postmodern philosophy associated with Nietzsche, Heidegger, Derrida, Rorty, Lyotard, and others. Eventually, the postmodern assault produced new social and political theories, as well as theoretical attempts to define the multifaceted aspects of the postmodern phenomenon itself [3, p. 1].

Beyond the cultural and academic intelligentsia, postmodernism "has even penetrated mass culture with frequent articles on such disparate topics as the postmodern presidency, postmodern love, postmodern management, postmodern theology, the postmodern mind, and postmodern television shows like MTV or Max Headroom" [3, p. 28].

In anthropology, "the postmodern assault" has come across what some have seen as our ill-attended borderland with cultural studies. Whatever its route, the assault has been swift and far reaching. At every turn now, we are told that it is time for "a break with the past" because the world we now inhabit "demands changes in practices of questioning and representation" [4, p. ix]. At conferences and in journals, in classrooms and hallway discussions, the ideas of postmodernism and the special language used to convey them are "in the air" [5, p. ix]. As Strathern confirms, "Whether we are or are not entering a postmodern phase in social anthropology, enough people seem to be speaking as though we were for the idea to be of interest" [6, p. 263]. Just as Marxism not so long ago was mined, often by non-Marxist "metaphysical materialists and dialectical idealistsl" [7], for poignant phrases and timely configurations, now the postmodern lexicon, e.g., deconstruction, discourse, dialogue, textuality, defamiliarization, voice, poetics, decenteredness, is providing fresh fodder for "AnthropologySpeak" and for "AnthropologyThought" as well. Indeed, we have reached the stage in the evolution of postmodernism as an in vogue approach that failure to be "up on" postmodernism is cause for worry and professional insecurity.

Of course, the postmodern trend amounts to more than a new rhetorical style, especially in anthropology, "because unlike most other disciplines affected, the debate in anthropology has occupied a central focus of attention in which the identity of the discipline itself is at stake for its practitioners" [4, p. viii]. Anthropology, we are told, is in a predicament, a crisis of representation, a time of reassessment. Culture and hence cultural analysis have become "deeply compromised" notions [8, p. 10]. Moreover, the present is depicted as a period lacking in "riveting theoretical debates or fashions" [4, p. 5]; the authority of grand theory "seems to be suspended" [5, p. 8], while the postmodern imagination has come to question "the value of any universalizing formulation" [9, p. 6]. Instead, anthropology is now described in postmodern texts as reviewing its methods, experimenting with new styles for representing the ethnographic Other, rethinking its role in the postmodern world, indeed, reconstructing itself from the ethnographic bottom up. In the interim, it would appear, theory building, or as the postmodernists would have it, the fabrication of totalizing paradigms, is to be put on hold so that conceptual risk-taking, innovative questioning of implicit conventions, and the development of a jeweler's-eye view of cultural experience can commence. The specific nature of the change involved is referred to as a "radical break" from modernist appeal to "grand narrative" to a postmodern focus on "little narratives" [10].

With all of these changes said to be occurring in anthropology, it seems prudent to consider the implications for medical anthropology generally and for the development of critical medical anthropology in particular. Already, the language of postmodernism appears in medical anthropology texts. From analyses of the immune system as an "unambiguously . . . postmodern object—symbolically, technically, and politically" [11, p. 207] to calls for new, image-conscious approaches to folk medicine that move beyond "the trivialized sense with which a medical anthropology has now buried this object of scrutiny" [12, p. 8], the voice of postmodernism can be heard within our domain of study. Like others, but perhaps for different reasons, much that we read and hear in self-styled postmodern texts and discussions leaves us uneasy. Our discomfort with postmodernism as a set of new social and political theories stems not from the heartfelt postmodern concern with the basis of ethnographic authority or with questioning appropriate approaches for "writing culture," nor even from the mystification of the postmodern "will to power" [13] or the careerist decisions of postmodern writers [14]. Rather, primarily, it is with the implications for medical anthropology of the postmodern eschewal of so-called grand theory, while, in our view, *smuggling in a theory of their own*, that we wish to take issue.

In short, our aim in this chapter is not to oppose a "good" modernism with a "bad" postmodernism, as some critics like Habermas have done, and even less do we intend to "declare war" on postmodernism and attempt to banish it from the anthropological kingdom, as have others. In fact, to the degree that its project is focused on the decolonization of anthropology, as it to some degree is, we are in sympathy with the postmodernist "school." Our goal, however, is to bring to the fore problematic underpinnings of postmodernism in its anthropological incarnation and the relevance of these limitations for the emergent critical direction in medical anthropology.

Before embarking on this endeavor, it is important to emphasize that, as in any tradition, there is both variation and marked differences of approach and view among writers seen as adhering to a postmodern perspective, including explicit internal critiques of fellow travelers. For example, within anthropological postmodernism, there is Stephen Tyler "who valorizes the oral and the aural at the expense of the visual (especially, as domesticated in writing)," while, by contrast, Michael Taussig "exalts mimesis, performance, and the strongly emotive and physical power of images" [4, p. x]. Similarly, as Crapanzano stresses

> Many definitions of 'postmodernism' have been advanced, and, for the most part, as even the most superficial reading reveals, they are vague, over-generalizing, and contradictory. . . . Some stress epistemological skepticism, hyper-reflexivity, and the artifice of all accounts including those which articulate a perduing self. Others emphasize play, language games, the 'logical operations of cultural terms' within a structure that seems independent of its medium of expression, indeed of reality itself. And still others point out the arbitrariness, the conventionality, of those temporal connections that give us the illusion of history and continuity and take ironic delight in a sort of promiscuous quotationalism that subverts history, continuity and memory [15, p. 88].

To the extent that sharp disagreements or alternative understandings exist, it might be more appropriate to talk of postmodernisms were this not a cumbersome convention. And, as also is commonly the case with historically grouped schools of thought, there are those seen by others but not themselves as belonging to the fold. Finally, we recognize that many people in and out of anthropology are unhappy with the term postmodernism and are in disagreement about whether it labels a style of knowledge or a condition of society, or is conceptualized as an extension or repudiation of modernism. To minimize these entanglements in a chapter that is not intended to be a thoroughgoing critique of postmodernism, we use frequent quotations from particular writers, clarifying thereby the source of the specific ideas we attribute to the postmodern trend.

THE POSTMODERN PERSPECTIVE

As the name implies, the postmodern perspective is said to have emerged in response to something that happened in the "real" world, rather than a demi-decadal rethinking reflecting changing fads and fashions in academic culture [16]. Interestingly, the changes in the world that produced changes in anthropology (and beyond) are said to have occurred at the macro-level.

> This trend may have much to do with the unfavorable shift in the relative position of American power and influence in the world, and with the widespread perception of the dissolution of the ruling postwar model of the liberal welfare state at home [5, p. 9].

With greater specificity, Huyssen adds:

> In the years of Watergate and the drawn-out agony of the Vietnam War, of the oil-shock and the dire predictions of the Club of Rome, it was indeed difficult to maintain the confidence and exuberance of the 1960s [17, p. 196].

Impinging macro-level events like these produced a *crise de conscience* marked by an insecure national mood and a loss of faith in the existing array of order-affirming theories. Suspicion was raised concerning "the ability of encompassing paradigms to ask the right questions, let alone provide answers, about the variety of local responses to the operation of global systems, which are not understood as certainly as they were once thought to be under the regime of 'grand theory' styles" [5, p. 9]. Further, in the view of some practitioners, with postmodernism the "transcendent authorization of interpretation is lost, and with it the ontology grounding of 'Western' epistemology" [11, p. 153].

In addition, and with special relevance to anthropology, the ethnographic Other changed. Illustrative is Meyers' [18] account of the impact of acrylic painting among Australian Aborigines. Painting with acrylics is a new form for Aborigines. It was initiated in 1971 as commodity production to meet tourist demand rather than for indigenous ritual or practical use. The paintings, incorporating "traditional" designs, have found their market and become highly sought after by art collectors in cosmopolitan cities in distant lands. As a consequence, "the people whom the *Guiness Book of Records* inscribed as having the simplest material culture of any people on earth . . . , representatives of a people regarded disparagingly by the dominant white majority in Australia, are now accorded international appreciation as producers of 'high art,' an appreciation rarely granted to Australia's white art producers" [18, p. 320]. Elevated from isolation on a local stage to an upstage role on an international one, Aboriginal painters have used their "art" as means to "add their voices to the cultural discourses of the world" [18, p. 322]. Film and video have been used for a similar purpose elsewhere in Australia. Comprising a hybrid product, a bricolage of borrowed and indigenous elements, indigenous media has blossomed "in the altered environment that Aborigines live in today" [19, p. 370].

Literacy, in particular, has been central to the transformation of the Other. Notes James Clifford, who has stressed this point in various works, "a very widespread, empowering distinction has been eroded: the division of the globe into literate and nonliterate peoples" [20, p. 117]. As a result, "the silence of the ethnographic workshop has been broken—by insistent, heteroglot voices, by the scratching of other pens" [21, p. 121].

> After 1950 peoples long spoken for by Western ethnographers, administrators, and missionaries began to speak for and act more powerfully for themselves on a global scale. It was increasingly difficult to keep them in their (traditional) places. Distinct ways of life once destined to merge into 'the modern world' reasserted their difference, in novel ways [21, p. 6].

The effect of these developments on anthropology, on what anthropologists can get away with, and hence on what anthropology can and should now be is telling postmodernists believe.

> If the ethnographer reads culture over the native's shoulder, the native also reads over the ethnographer's shoulder as he or she writes each cultural description. Fieldworkers are increasingly constrained in what they publish by the reactions of those previously classified as nonliterate [20, p. 119].

In sum, the conventional expectation of world homogenization in the image of the West, a world in which all peoples are one people, fully modern, developed or at least developing along a common urban industrial pathway, speaking a variously accented but clearly understandable English, and fulfilling their obligations as producers and consumers in the "global village" has gone sour. Within the medical domain, modernism even has come to be defined as an important cause of disease and untimely death [22]. So too, there is a blossoming realization that non-Western cultures "must be met by means other than conquest or domination, as Paul Ricoeur put it more than twenty years ago, and that the erotic and aesthetic fascination with the 'Orient' and the 'primitive'—so prominent in Western culture—including modernism—is deeply problematic" [17, p. 220]. In disillusionment with modernism, during "disassembled and dissembling times" [11, p. 186], the postmodern world and the postmodern perspective are born.

The watchwords of postmodern understanding are contingency, partiality, juxtaposition, reflexivity, poetics, surrealism, fragmentation, multivocality, and irony. The flavor of disarrangement and off-centeredness, or what Jencks [23] calls "plural coding," said to be at the heart of the postmodern experience is well captured in Clifford's account of the creation and format of his text, *The Predicament of Culture*.

> This book is a spliced ethnographic object, an incomplete collection . . . . Written from within a 'West' whose authority to represent unified human history is now widely challenged and whose very spatial identity is increasingly problematic, the explorations gathered here cannot—should not—add up to a seamless vision. Their partiality is apparent. The chapters vary in form and style, reflecting diverse conjunctures and specific occasions of composition. I have not tried to rewrite those already published to produce a consistent veneer. Moreover, I have included texts that actively break up the book's prevailing tone, hoping in this way to manifest the rhetoric of my accounts. I prefer sharply focused pictures, composed in ways that show the frame or lens [8, p. 13].

This pastiche, characteristic of experimental expression, is applauded as "a form well suited to a time such as the present, when paradigms are in disarray, problems intractable, and phenomena only partly understood" [24, p. 191]. Jameson thus stresses pastiche as one of the defining features of the postmodern style, not in the sense of a random hodge podge, but closer to the French *hochepot,* or stew [25]. Unlike Clifford, who would seem to favor the creation of ethnographic albums filled with numerous "sharply focused pictures," Jameson sees the postmodernist pastiche as creating a blurring of differences, a blending that flattens temporal and spatial diversity (which, in fact, is what happens before long to all of us while scanning other people's snapshots of foreign lands). One consequence of such blurring of difference is nostalgia.

> Postmodern culture is a wave we ride in the disorganizing and all pervasive economy of late capitalism. Awash in a sea of faces, we look back nostalgically to the shore in a sudden memory of a ground already lost. Once, where there was a time and a place for everything, there was also a time and a place for nostalgia. But now, threatened with a deadening pluralism that makes us all just an 'other' among others . . . , in which differences erase into an utter indifference . . . , and where the self is a pastiche of styles glued to a surface, nostalgia becomes the very lighthouse waving us back to shore—the one point on the landscape that gives hope of direction [26, pp. 253-254].

Hand-in-glove with pluralism is multivocality, which is claimed as the appropriate voice for the postmodern text. With time and place merged, attention turns to words and to voice [25]. Says Clifford, "Paradigms of experience and interpretation are yielding to paradigms of discourse, of dialogue and polyphony" [21, p. 133]. Because of their concern with the ways ethnographic texts are constructed through anthropologist/informant exchange or the juxtaposition of their respective voices, studies like Marjorie Shostack's *Nisa: The Life and Words of a !Kung Woman,* Vincent Crapanzano's *Tuhami: Portrait of a Moroccan,* Kevin Dwyer's *Moroccan Dialogues,* and Michael Taussig's *Shamanism, Colonialism and the Wild Man* are held in high regard by postmodernist anthropologists. Concern with dialogue, according to Clifford [27, p. 15], reminds us that culture "is always relational, an inscription of communicative processes that exist, historically, *between* subjects in relation to power" (emphasis in original).

In this vein, Stephen Tyler, a picture of whom "writing ethnography" graces the cover and frontispiece of the important postmodern collection *Writing Culture,* argues that the form of ethnographic texts

> should emerge out of the joint work of the ethnographer and his narrative partners. The emphasis is on the emergent character of textualization, textualization being just the initial interpretative move that provides a negotiated text for the reader to interpret [28, p. 127].

It is after this sort of bargained/constructed reality that postmodern ethnography strives "by means of a participatory text in which no one has the exclusive right of synoptic transcendence" [28, p. 129].

Achievement of postmodernism's idealized text comes not through representational strategies—such as those employed in more traditionally interpretive writing—but rather through evocation. Asserts Tyler:

> To represent means to have a magical power over appearances, to be able to bring into presence what is absent . . . The true historical significance of writing is that it has increased our capacity to create totalist illusion with which to have power over things or over others as if they were things [28, p. 131].

Evocation, by contrast, eliminates "the inappropriate mode of scientific rhetoric that entails 'objects,' 'facts,' 'descriptions,' 'inductions,' 'generalizations,' 'verifications,' 'experiment,' 'truth,' and like concepts," that to Tyler, "have no parallels either in the experience of ethnographic fieldwork or in the writing of ethnographies" [28, p. 130]. And while nothing is to be explained, described, represented, or interpreted by the postmodern ethnography, what is to be evoked? According to Tyler, it is the fractured anthropological experience of a disjointed postmodern world.

> A post-modern ethnography is fragmentary because it cannot be otherwise. Life in the field itself is fragmentary, not at all organized around familiar ethnological categories . . . We confirm in our ethnographies our consciousness of the fragmentary nature of the post-modern world, for nothing so well defines our world as the absence of synthesizing allegory [28, pp. 131-132].

Similarly, Clifford states

> Reality is no longer a given, a natural familiar environment. The self, cut loose from its attachments, must discover meaning where it may—a predicament, evoked at its most nihilistic, that underlies both surrealism and modern ethnography [8, p. 119].

Thus Marcus [24, p. 191] praises Theodor Adorno for his "refusal to impose order through writing on a world whose essence is its fragmentary character." Postmodernism, he maintains, avoids representing the world, social systems, or human events in an orderly fashion. Orderliness was a construction of modernism, and with its passing so too its product. As Baudrillard asserts

> All that remains to be done is to play with the pieces. Playing with the pieces— that is post-modern [29, p. 24].

Thus, postmodernism, like surrealism and much poetry, "legitimates fragmentation, rough edges, and the self-conscious aim of achieving an effect that disturbs the reader" [24, p. 191]. But disturb with what intent, in whose interest, with what lasting effect or motivation to action? These questions dangle unanswered at the margins of the postmodern essay.

As the foregoing demonstrates, postmodernists are especially concerned about the *writing of ethnography,* believing, as they do, that, ethnography "is always writing" [27, p. 26]. Indeed they complain that the discipline has been lackadaisical in its attention to this defining feature of the field. Writing has been reduced to a matter of method: "keeping good field notes, making accurate maps, 'writing up' results" [27, p. 2]. Little attention has been given to the *determinants* of eth- nographic production. Clifford notes six: 1) context (the milieu of the writer influen- ces what is written); 2) rhetorical style (there is reliance on literary nuance); 3) institutional (writing addresses particular audiences and is grounded in particular traditions); 4) generic (ethnography is a special kind of writing with its own stand- ards); 5) political (ethnographic writing assumes a foundation of authority upon which to write about the Other); and 6) historic (all of the above determinants change over time) [27]. For postmodernists, the effect of all of these constraints and conven- tions is to see ethnographies not as windows upon social facts but as kaleidoscopes depicting constructed fictions. The ethnographer writes with hidden agendas: to assert the authority of experience ("I was there, I know what I'm talking about") and to mask the preliminary and partial nature of ethnographic understanding [e.g., see 30].

> The ethnographer conventionally acknowledges the provisional nature of his interpretations. Yet he assumes a final interpretation—a definitive reading . . . . He resents the literary critic's assertion that there is never a final reading. He simply has not got to it yet [31, p. 51].

Further, there is the question of the ethnographer's relationship not just to those under study or to what is being written about them, but to the encompassing social totality that unites all of these. Asserts Taussig,

> To take social determination seriously means that one has to see oneself and one's shared modes of understanding and communication included in that deter- mining. To claim otherwise, to claim the rhetoric of systematicity's determinisms and yet to except oneself, is an authoritarian deceit, a magical wonder . . . . As far as I'm concerned, . . . this puts writing on a completely different plane than hitherto conceived. It calls for understanding of the representation as contiguous with that being represented and not as suspended above and distant from the represented—what Adorno referred to as Hegel's programmatic idea—that knowing is giving oneself over to a phenomenon rather than thinking about it from above [12, p. 10].

An end result, as it often is in the academic milieu, has been the creation of a new journal, *Cultural Anthropology,* used during its early years to create a meeting place and a spawning ground for all of the concerns of postmodernism and related trends, a place from which "cultural anthropology's revitalization might occur" [4, p. viii].

REREADING POSTMODERN ANTHROPOLOGY: A CRITICAL GAZE

As many of the articles in *Cultural Anthropology* indicate, for all the questioning of authority and representation, all the doubting of convention and canon, postmodern ethnographers continue to write, to produce ethnographies, and to assert the primacy of ethnography within anthropology in the contemporary moment. Herein begins our nervousness with postmodernism and motivates our sense that ethnography of the postmodern bustle is itself a worthy task.

Our effort, however, does not begin with the sense that text is all. That type of "literary myopia" [32, p. 3] snobbishly ignores much of anthropology. Applied anthropologists, for example, who may not view the writing of ethnography as the paramount "work" of the discipline, have felt called on to respond as best they can to diverse social problems and health crises knowing their opus may amount to little more than the reports and evaluation documents known as "grey literature." As Kotarba suggests with reference to AIDS, although well aware of the issues raised in the postmodern debates ethnographers studying the pandemic

> have had to suspend or ignore the academic issues surrounding their method in order to respond quickly to a pressing public health problem. Thus the issue of whether ethnography can arrive at the 'truth' about people's everyday ways of life . . . has largely been waived in favor of the practical goal of achieving the particular kinds of truths needed to establish programs to save people's lives [33, p. 260].

Gudeman and Rivera register protest from a different angle:

> We take issue with this view that would pass over the special anthropological practice of listening to the other voices and evade consideration of the many skills anthropologists have developed and learned, used and refined, in their research. Curiously the 'postmodernists' argument would deny that anthropology itself has a history of learning and change, for the new view seems to consign the imaginative and hard work of learning about others' lives to a passing moment on the way to text production; and it disregards the complex, evolving relationship between practice and inscription [34, p. 268].

That is to say, in our view, the postmodern view itself is partial, incomplete, and potentially static. Whence comes this partiality? In part, we suggest, from the source. The roots of the postmodern perspective lie not only in the changing world, changing popular sentiment, and changing anthropological ethics, they are planted as well in particular schools of academic predilection. In anthropology, these sources clearly are various overlapping interpretive/hermeneutic, semiotic, and phenomenologic paradigms, thus the postmodernist concentration on symbols, meanings, and mentality, as well as personhood, selfhood, and emotions. It is for this reason that the postmodern worldview finds sharpest expression in "the writings of those who, as graduate students during the 1960s and 1970s, were trained in the new developments in interpretive anthropology . . . " [5, p. 33], i.e., individuals whose postgraduate writings continue to follow "naturally in the wake of Geertz's interpretive turn" [14, p. 242].

While not rejecting the claimed insights of interpretive anthropology, most postmodernists see their work as a revision or extension of this tradition. On the one hand, this revision is said to involve an expanded sensitivity to issues of historic context and political economy, and on the other, to postwar reflections on the epistemology of fieldwork. While the impact of the latter on the postmodern vista is unarguable, the perspective's stance toward political economy and history are problematic. In a curious passage, Marcus and Fischer state:

For its part, interpretive anthropology clearly has not paid as much attention to issues of political economy and historical process in fieldwork and the writing of ethnography *as it should have, and as many of its practitioners would have liked* [5, pp. 84-85, emphasis added].

Just what prohibited or inhibited interpretive anthropologists from addressing political economy and history (against their will!) is left unspecified, and thus the effect of the passage is to excuse interpretive myopia. Political economists within anthropology, by contrast, are not let off so easy. The work of Eric Wolf, Sidney Mintz, June Nash, and Eleanor Leacock is faulted because it

tended to *isolate itself* from cultural anthropology's concurrent development of a *more sophisticated* ethnographic practice on interpretive lines. It *retreated* into the *typical* Marxist relegation of culture to an epiphenomenal structure, dismissing much of cultural anthropology itself as idealist [5, p. 84, emphasis added].

Even Wolf's *Europe and the People Without History,* a powerful critique of non-anthropological political economy for failing to come to terms with the very real and very important issue of culture, is rejected (surprisingly) because "attention to culture is systematically elided" [5, p. 85].

In the end, all their questioning of the role of theory in the contemporary moment notwithstanding, the postmodernists appear as partisans. Thus they tell us:

The time now seems ripe for a thorough integration of an ethnographic practice that remains markedly interpretive and interested in problems of meaning with political economy and historic *implications* of any of its projects of research [5, p. 85, emphasis added].

This unambiguous statement of side-taking in a theoretical debate is rationalized on the grounds that texts written in the interpretive mode are self-consciously concerned with resolving the micro-macro dilemma in anthropology, while "those from the tradition of political economy research appear mostly to devalue cultural analysis or are satisfied with its present state, and thus perhaps perceive no dilemma to be resolved" [5, p. 86], points that are hotly contested by political economic anthropologists [35, 36].

In short, according to prominent postmodern thinkers, the issues of research in anthropology should be those valorized by interpretive anthropology; the discipline's understanding of culture should be the one appropriated by that perspective; and the role of political economy and history are contextual, they provide backgrounding but do not raise questions or define key issues for examination [see 13, pp. 413 and 417]. Herein lies the heart of our concern about the implications of postmodernism for medical anthropology in the contemporary period.

Before examining this concern in more detail, it is important to stress that critical medical anthropology shares some common ground with postmodernism. In pursing its goal of exploring the micro/marco nexus as a means of constructing an integrated paradigm, analyses in critical medical anthropology have benefited from several aspects of postmodernism, including the attention it has drawn to social determinants of textual production, its understanding of culture as alterable and contestable, its appreciation of the inseparability of language and politics, and its questioning of the foundation of ethnographic authority.

Turning greater attention to the forces and forms shaping critical medical anthropology texts has enabled adherents of this perspective to begin achieving a valued objective: unmasking bourgeois ideology embraced as conventional insight. Critical thought demands reflexive vigilance because of the seeming naturalness and self evident quality of official truths, products of their redundancy in diverse sectors of socio-cultural systems. Exploring the contestable nature of culture provides a route for understanding the role of power and social struggle in shaping various features of the health domain, including the "identification" of disease, the practice patterns of providers, and the popularity of treatments, that are assumed to be dictated by science rather than created by culture. Examining the relation of health and medical language to power is a natural extension of this activity. For too long, language and communication processes have been avoided (as idealist) by those with a critical perspective. But, this is a grave error, argues Irvine, because

> linguistic forms have relevance for the social scientist not only as part of a world of ideas, but also as part of a world of objects, economic transactions, and political interests. The verbal sign . . . relates to a political economy in many ways: by denoting it; by indexing parts of it; by depicting it . . .; and by taking part in it as an object of exchange [37, p. 263].

Indeed, part of what a patient pays for (and often the part s/he is least satisfied with) is verbal exchange with a provider. And part of what is transfered in such exchanges are messages of power [38]. Finally, reflexive consideration of the ground of our authority offers a check upon the anthropological tendency to speak for rather than with ethnographic Others. Because a central goal of critical medical anthropology is to leave the trail leading medical anthropology toward a replication of the structures and organizations of biomedicine, we must also avoid reproducing biomedical authority patterns in the ways we develop, express, and use the body of knowledge unique to our discipline.

Sympathy with these concerns and with contemporary Third and Fourth world critique of the social sciences flows naturally from critical awareness of the social production of medical knowledge, the contribution of hegemonic ideology to the maintenance and reproduction of structures of oppression, the functions of medicine in social control and the appropriation of power, the role of anthropology as sometime handmaiden to dominating powers in and beyond medicine, and the importance of consciousness and agency in health-related social action. Indeed, critical medical anthropology has its deepest roots in Third World criticism of conservatism within the subdiscipline [39-43].

Unlike postmodernism, however, critical medical anthropology's concern with ethnographic authority is not motivated by a desire to evoke a fragmented world or conflicted experience (even though it recognizes the role of capitalism in the fracturing of lifeways and the magnification of alienation), but rather by a *commitment* to solidarization with Third World efforts to understand the nature of oppressive systems and relations so as to abrogate them. As Onoge [43, p. 221] concludes, the deficiency of modernism is not its reification of an orderly social world, but its "mystification of contemporary reality" through its failure "to name the concrete social formations that now exist." While critical medical anthropology recognizes, welcomes, and is a product of the "scratching of other pens" (and the tapping of other computer keyboards), it does not hold that the rise of literacy in the Third World nor the arrival of "quieter . . . times in academia" [5, p. xii], free anthropologists for playful retreat into the analysis of textual construction, unless that analysis seeks to produce more accurate, more useful ethnographies of concrete social relations.

Instead, critical medical anthropology struggles to free itself from the cocoon of uncertainty and disrupted confidence that at times appears almost to smother postmodernism's ability to conclude anything at all. Indeed, it seeks to resurrect an activist spirit in an age of somnolence. Not surprisingly, critical medical anthropology's explicit commitments have been cause for concern among its critics. Wiley, for one, in contrasting CMA with a bioculturalist approach, writes:

> An important difference between 'critical' medical anthropology and biocultural medical anthropology is the motivation driving the research and conclusions. The workers in the latter domain neither research nor write with an explicit advocacy of political activism or social transformation. Their work is presented as scientific documentation . . . . Bioculturalists view themselves first as scientists trying to build models of reality with an attempted objective stance [44, p. 225].

Yet, like other critical approaches (e.g., feminism), CMA views the notion of pure, apolitical scholarship as a phantasm; the production and use of knowledge always occurs in relationship to power. The vital questions remain "knowledge for what, knowledge in whose interest?" And, unless we are to write improving health and health care and reducing the sum of human misery off as ultimate objectives of medical anthropology, judgment (informed by the weight of anthropological sensitivity, understanding, experience, and method) is unavoidable and appropriate. As Stephen Jay Gould remarks with reference to critical scientists of another era, "fair and scrupulous procedures do not demand neutrality, but only strict adherence to the rules of the craft" [45, p. 17].

By contrast, the commitments of postmodern writers often are opaque. On the one hand, they express a laudable concern with liberating the voice of the Third World ethnographic Other (or at least adding that voice to the cacophony of speakers that comprise human discourse), and with re-assessing the proper role and ground of authority of anthropology in a changed world. On the other, the final ends of the postmodern project and the ultimate purpose served by its texts are open to question. It may be that in its concern with multivocality and fragmentation postmodern writing erases

> difference, implying that all stories are really about one experience: the decentering and fragmentation that is the current experience of Western white males [46, p. 29].

This "masking and empowering of Western bias" [46, p. 30] and Western ethnocentricism is a common product of "new" approaches and visions with muddled commitments.

The suggestion also has been raised that postmodernism is less a state of the world than it is a condition of intellectuals in the contemporary period. Featherstone, for example, interprets the postmodern mood as an expression of "powerlessness and retreat into skepticism" [2, p. 213], produced by a loss in social stature and mission among the denizens of academia. There has been, as Bauman labels it, an "implosion of intellectual vision" [46, p. 28], borne of self-awareness and the sense of out-of-placessness. Beneath this loss of confidence and purpose lies "the advanced erosion of that global structure of domination, which—at the time modern intellectuals were born—supplied the 'evidence of reality' of which the self-confidence of the West and its spokesmen has been built" [47, pp. 219-220]. While producing an awareness of self as rooted in a particular social location, global change appears not to have generated a parallel awareness of the particularness of intellectual experience relative to other experiences.

> As a rule . . . intellectuals tend to articulate their own societal situation and the problems it creates as a situation of the society at large, and its, systemic or social, problems. The way in which the passage from 'modernity' to 'postmodernity' has been articulated is not an exception [47, p. 225].

Intellectuals, even in—and perhaps especially in—the postmodern vogue, look to themselves and, at themselves, as a source of global knowledge. Indeed, the postmodern anthropological text commonly "finds the ethnographer more interesting than the natives" and the ethnography an item of greater curiosity than the social behavior it purports to illuminate [48, p. 334].

Herein may lie the source of the peculiarly complex voice of the postmodern text, with its openly expressed "discontent with plain style" [49, p. 51]. In Murphy's interpretation, most of the practitioners of what he calls postmodern "thick writing" are scholarly men "who seem to be engaged in a curiously competitive game in which obscure literary allusions and baroque rhetorical forms are weapons, a kind of egghead rap-talk" [48, p. 332] (and, in Spain, at least, neo-baroque is a term used to refer to postmodernism). Consider the following example, an excerpt from Taussig's writing after observing folk healing rituals in Western Colombia.

> What I was being invited to do in those hallucinatory curing sessions of magical practicality on the frontier where Indians cured colonists was to rethink the mode of work in which I was involved as work better approached from the tension involved in the disconcerting experiments in representation tried out by European and (as I later learnt to appreciate, early Soviet) Modernism—e.g. Joyce, Cubism, Woolf, Myerhold, Zurich, Dada, Berlin Dada, Constructionism, Brecht, Eisenstein, and Benjamin moving from allegory to the shock of montage and the liberating (messianic) mimetic snapshot of the 'dialectial image' [12, p. 7].

Whatever the intended purpose, the postmodern text, with its "involuted puzzle boxes of imbedded clauses" [48, p. 332] seems designed to shore up intellectual uncertainty about the value and uniqueness as well as the potency and artistry of intellectualism itself. Who else can write like that? Who else can read it? Critical medical anthropology, by contrast, while obviously an intellectual practice, is intended to construct a space for demystifying hegemony as ruling class ideology, that is, for challenging rather than reinforcing hierarchy and class domination.

Consequently, whatever commonalties may exist between critical medical anthropology and postmodern anthropology in areas like the operation of power in relationship and communication, there can be found few avenues for rapprochement between these perspectives in the domains of epistemology and theory. Belief that "the post-modern world is a post-scientific world" [28, p. 135] and consequent postmodern proscriptions for a suspension of theory (as if ethnography were possible without a point of view and a framework of interpretation) can only lead to the infiltration and reinscription of self evident or commonsense (i.e., hegemonic) paradigms. As Sangren reminds us:

> It is not the divide between ideas and real that characterizes bourgeois mystifica-tion but the idea that the real is exhausted by individual experience. Asserting the latter leads to the kind of phenomenological/existential relativism characteristic of much postmodernism with the effect that bourgeois individualism is legitimated by appropriating the authority of its own demystification [13, p. 418].

The ultimate extension of bourgeois individualism is the Thatcherian denial of society in the interest of the richest segment thereof [50]. The co-ascendency of Thatcherian politics and postmodernist thinking has been seen by some as something more than guilt by temporal association. Habermas [51], for example, links postmodernism to neoconservatism and the effort to quash both progressive aspects of modernism as well as leftist culture of the 1960s, while Owens sees business-asusual sexism in postmodern texts:

> The absence of discussions of sexual difference in writings about postmodernism, as well as the fact that few women have engaged in the modernism/postmodernism debate, suggests that postmodernism may be another masculine invention to exclude women [52, p. 61]

In the eyes of Mascia-Lees and co-authors [47] this is a double injustice as much that postmodernists claim as new and exciting in their reappraisal of the discipline is old hat in feminist literature.

Moreover, as Tess argues:

> The denial of depth to the self, the refusal of firm and legitimate grounding to claims of any kind, the contempt for reason, and the preoccupation with appearance—themes that have become the hallmark of the postmodern attitude—should serve as ready evidence that, ultimately this philosophical orientation will not produce the deep understanding that . . . [we] want and need . . . . Without the possibility of stable meaning, insight and self understanding becomes trivial, irrelevant. There is nothing worth understanding . . . . Without the primacy of reason and intelligence, injustice can flourish unrestrained [53, p. 196].

Which is to say: "There is no logical reason why we cannot apprehend the order in human affairs" [54, p. 66] and there is plenty of reason for trying.

In making sense of their perspective, postmodern anthropologists recognize the causal importance of macrolevel factors, factors that produced a changed world in which old certainties are thrown into question and old relations subject to re-negotiation, especially from below. This lesson would seem to be lost, however, when attention shifts to the ethnographic workshop. Suddenly, issues of personhood or emotion are foregrounded and heretofore causal factors like politics, economics, history become "implications." The observation by postmodernists that "ideological radicals" abound in their ranks [15] is irrelevant and only "deflects attention from the possibility that the approach itself may embody and reproduce a conservative ideology, whatever the political intentions of the practitioners" [13, p. 417]. The source of that conservativeness, we suggest, is the same as for conventional medical anthropology.

> The problem is not a cadre of malevolent scientists who consciously buttress the status quo. Rather, the pervasive climate of bourgeois ideology imperceptibly shapes the interests and concepts that guide research [55, p. 1208].

Telling is the observation by Fife and Black that conservatism among contemporary anthropology graduate students is in part a reaction to feeling "afloat" in the postmodern "experiment" [56].

This raises clearly the question of postmodernism's politics. Herein CMA's inherent differences with postmodernism are most clearly revealed. As Lyotard makes plain, attempts at social transformation are ill conceived for any sought after alternative to the status quo "would end up resembling the system it was meant to replace" [10, p. 66]. All that remains for the postmodern body—while the postmodern mind constructs and deconstructs texts—is some form of resistance to domination without organized efforts to overturn it. As Callincos argues, this postmodern strategy

> presupposes a theory of power whose fundamental assumption, that domination is omnipresent, either makes of resistance a mystery or collapses into Nietzschean metaphysics. Either way, post-modernist politics saves the radical intellectual's honour by identifying the cultural avant-garde with resistance to the status-quo, while freeing him or her from the political obligation of participating in any collective project whose call is what Marx called 'human emancipation.' 'Resistance' can only too easily become an aesthetic or moral stance rather than a genuinely political matter [1, p. 99].

At the very moment when medical anthropology has embarked on a quest to develop ways and means of situating its understandings of health, illness experience, the origin of disease, patient-provider relations, medical pluralism, treatment strategies and the like within a political economic framework, a full turn toward the perspective of postmodernism could lead the subdiscipline back down the dark tunnel of depoliticalization, rejection of which sparked the creation of critical medical anthropology in the first place. Such an historic twist would truly, if tragically, confirm Strathern's keen observation that:

> If there is one word which summarizes the anthropological recognition of a postmodern mood, it is *irony* (emphasis in original) [6, p. 265].

There is in critical medical anthropology, a recognition of the importance of the postmodern critique of traditional ethnographic authority and an acceptance that "ethnographic truth" is "a complex, negotiated, historically contingent truth specific to certain relations" of fieldwork [57, p. 125]. Further, there is acknowledgement of the importance of Clifford's most trenchant historic observation about the discipline.

> Anthropology, a science and an aesthetic that functioned rather comfortably within the imperial context, can no longer ignore that its 'data'—the human objects of its study and affection—have often been exploited, sometimes dying, individuals and cultures. As a response to this unhappy circumstance, a tone of elegiac regret is no longer sufficient [58, pp. 124-125].

Indeed, regret is far from sufficient, for anthropology continues to operate in imperial contexts, if now with considerable uneasiness and with a renewed understanding of power and responsibility to the exploited [59]. Importantly, in part because of postmodern writers, these issues are being "discussed in the open, rather than covered over with a professional mystique" [30, p. 138]. However, from the CMA perspective, the answer to our dilemma does not lie in the creation of a new mystique or in waiting for the salvationary "new age of writing" dreamed of by some postmodernists [49]. In the end, there is no getting around "the un-get-roundable fact that all ethnographical description are homemade, that they are the describer's descriptions, not those of the described" [30, pp. 144-145]. And yet, ethnography and anthropology generally retain merit. As we seek to demonstrate in the following pages by addressing a range of specific issues within the domain of health, it little more than "a gratuitous indulgence merely to debate epistemological niceties, or to argue [endlessly] over the impossibility of making 'objective' statements about the world" [60, p. xiv], while systems that are injurious to health reign, while even the clinical encounter serves to sustain hegemonic control, while the experience of the suffer goes unnoticed. With all its limitations and potential to serve rather than resist oppression, anthropology is worth doing if it struggles constantly to assess its social role and its commitments while bringing to light and responding to, however imperfectly, the social relations and understandings, the contexts and environments, the conflicts and suffering of diverse peoples.

REFERENCES

1. A. Callinicos, Postmodernism, Post-structuralism, Post-Marxism?, *Theory, Culture, and Society,* 2:3, pp. 85-101, 1985.
2. M. Featherstone, In Pursuit of the Postmodern: An Introduction, *Theory, Culture, and Society,* 5:2-3, pp. 195-217, 1988.
3. S. Best and D. Kellner, *Postmodern Theory,* The Guilford Press, New York, 1991.
4. G. Marcus, Introduction, in *Rereading Cultural Anthropology,* G. Marcus (ed.), Duke University Press, Durham, pp. vii-xiv, 1992.
5. G. Marcus and M. Fischer, *Anthropology as Cultural Critique,* The University of Chicago Press, Chicago, 1986.
6. M. Strathern, Out of Context: The Persuasive Fictions of Anthropology, *Current Anthropology,* 28, pp. 251-281, 1987.

7. D. Hakken and H. Lessinger, *Perspectives in U.S. Marxist Anthropology*, Westview Press, Boulder, 1987.
8. J. Clifford, *The Predicament of Culture*, Harvard University Press, Cambridge, Massachusetts, 1988.
9. S. Trachenberg, *The Postmodern Moment*, Greenwood Press, Westport, Connecticut, 1985.
10. J-F. Lyotard, *The Postmodern Condition*, University of Minneapolis Press, Minneapolis, 1984.
11. D. Haraway, *Simians, Cyborgs, and Women*, Routledge, New York, 1991.
12. M. Taussig, *The Nervous System*, Routledge, New York, 1992.
13. P. S. Sangren, Rhetoric and the Authority of Ethnography: "Postmodernism" and the Social Reproduction of Texts, *Current Anthropology, 29*:3, pp. 405-435, 1988.
14. P. Rabinow, Representations are Social Facts: Modernity and Post-modernity in Anthropology, in *Writing Culture: The Poetics and Politics of Ethnography*, J. Clifford and G. Marcus (eds.), University of California, Berkeley, pp. 234-261, 1986.
15. V. Crapanzano, The Postmodern Crisis: Discourse, Parody, Memory, in *Rereading Cultural Anthropology*, G. Marcus (ed.), Duke University Press, Durham, pp. 87-102, 1992.
16. P. Salzman, Fads and Fashions in Anthropology, *Anthropology Newsletter, 29*:5, pp. 1 and 32-33, 1988.
17. A. Huyssen, *After the Great Divide*, University of Indiana Press, Bloomington, 1986.
18. F. Myers, Representing Culture: The Production of Discourse(s) for Aboriginal Acrylic Painting, in *Rereading Cultural Anthropology*, G. Marcus (ed.), Duke University Press, Durham, pp. 319-355, 1992.
19. F. Ginsburg, Indigenous Media: Faustian Contract or Global Village?, in *Rereading Cultural Anthropology*, G. Marcus (ed.), Duke University Press, Durham, pp. 356-376, 1992.
20. J. Clifford, On Ethnographic Allegory, in *Writing Culture: The Poetics and Politics of Ethnography*, J. Clifford and G. Marcus (eds.), University of California, Berkeley, pp. 98-121, 1986.
21. J. Clifford, On Ethnographic Authority, *Representations, 1*, pp. 118-146, 1983.
22. J. Eyer, Hypertension as a Disease of Modern Society, *International Journal of Health Studies, 5*, pp. 539-585, 1975.
23. C. Jencks, *The Language of Post-Modern Architecture*, Rozzoli, New York, 1977.
24. G. Marcus, Contemporary Problems of Ethnography in the Modern World System, in *Writing Culture*, J. Clifford and G. Marcus (eds.), University of California Press, Berkeley, pp. 165-193, 1986.
25. E. Jameson, Postmodernism and Consumer Society, in *The Anti-Aesthic Essays on Postmodern Culture*, H. Foster (ed.), Bay Press, Port Townsend, Washington, pp. 111-125, 1983.
26. K. Steward, Nostalgia—A Polemic, in *Rereading Cultural Anthropology*, G. Marcus (ed.), Duke University Press, Durham, pp. 252-266, 1992.
27. J. Clifford, Introduction: Partial Truths, in *Writing Culture: The Poetics and Politics of Ethnography*, J. Clifford and G. Marcus (eds.), University of California, Berkeley, pp. 1-26, 1986.
28. S. Tyler, Post-Modern Ethnography: From Document of the Occult to Occult Document, in *Writing Culture: The Poetics and Politics of Ethnography*, J. Clifford and G. Marcus (eds.), University of California, Berkeley, pp. 122-140, 1986.
29. J. Baudrillard, On Nihilism, *On the Beach, 6*, pp. 38-39, 1984.

30. C. Geertz, *Works and Lives: The Anthropologist as Author*, University of California Press, Stanford, 1988.
31. V. Crapanzano, Hermes' Dilemma: The Masking of Subversion in Ethnographic Description, in *Writing Culture: The Poetics and Politics of Ethnography*, J. Clifford and G. Marcus (eds.), University of California, Berkeley, pp. 51-76, 1986.
32. D. Tomas, From Gesture to Activity: Dislocating the Anthropological Scriptorium, *Cultural Studies, 6*:1, pp. 1-27, 1992.
33. J. Kotarba, Ethnography and AIDS, *Journal of Contemporary Ethnography, 19*:3, pp. 259-270, 1990.
34. S. Gudeman and A. Rivera, Colombian Conversations: The Strength of the Earth, *Current Anthropology, 30*:3, pp. 267-281, 1989.
35. W. Roseberry, *Anthropologies and Histories,* Rutgers University Press, New Brunswick, New Jersey, 1989.
36. H. Rebel, Cultural Hegemony and Class Experience, *American Ethnologist, 16*:1, pp. 117-136, 1989.
37. J. Irving, When Talk Isn't Cheap: Language and Political Economy, *American Ethnologist, 16*, pp. 248-267, 1989.
37. H. Waitzkin, The Micropolitics of Medicine: A Contexual Analysis, *International Journal of Health Services, 14*, pp. 339-378, 1984.
39. S. Morsy, The Missing Link in Medical Anthropology: The Political Economy of Health, *Reviews in Anthropology, 6,* pp. 349-363, 1979.
40. G. Bonfil Batalla, Conservative Thought in Applied Anthropology: A Critique, *Human Organization, 25*, pp. 85-92, 1966.
41. D. Banerji, The Political Economy of Western Medicine in Third World Countries, in *Issues in the Political Economy of Health Care,* J. McKinlay (ed.), Tavistock, New York, pp. 257-282, 1984.
42. T. Aidoo, Rural Health Under Colonialism and Neocolonialism: A Survey of the Ghanaian Experience, *International Journal of Health Services, 12:4*, pp. 637-657, 1982.
43. O. Onoge, Capitalism and Public Health. A Neglected Theme in the Medical Anthropology of Africa, in *Topias and Utopias in Health,* S. Ingman and A. Thomas (eds.), Mouton, The Hague, pp. 219-232, 1975.
44. A. Wiley, Adaptation and the Biocultural Paradigm in Medical Anthropology: A Critical Review, *Medical Anthropology Quarterly, 6*:3, pp. 216-236, 1992.
45. S. J. Gould, The Chain of Reason vs. the Chain of Thumbs, *Natural History, 7,* pp. 12-21, 1989.
46. Z. Bauman, Is there a Postmodern Sociology, *Theory, Culture, and Society, 5*:2-3, pp. 217-238, 1988.
47. F. Mascia-Lees, P. Sharpe, and C. Cohen, The Postmodernist Turn in Anthropology: Cautions from a Feminist Perspective, *Signs, 15*:1, 1989.
48. R. Murphy, The Dialectics of Deeds and Words: Or Anti- the Antis (and the Anti-Antis), *Cultural Anthropology, 5*:3, pp. 331-338, 1990.
49. S. Tyler, On Being Out of Words, in *Rereading Cultural Anthropology,* G. Marcus (ed.), Duke University Press, Durham, pp. 8-14, 1992.
50. R. Frankenberg, Gramsci, Culture, and Medical Anthropology: Kundry and Parsifal? or Rat's Tail to Sea Serpent?, *Medical Anthropology Quarterly, 2*:4, pp. 324-337, 1988.
51. J. Habermas, Modernity versus Postmodernity, *New German Critique, 22*, pp. 3-14, 1981.
52. C. Owens, The Discourse of Others: Feminists and Postmodernism, in *The Anti-Aetheic Essays on Postmodern Culture*, H. Foster (ed.), Bay Press, Port Townsend, Washington, pp. 57-82, 1983.

53. D. Tess and D. McGowan, Comment on Flax's "Postmodernism and Gender Relations in Feminist Theory," *Signs, 14*, pp. 196-208, 1988.
54. J. Lett, *The Human Enterprise,* Westview Press, Boulder, 1987.
55. S. Woolhandler and D. Himmelstein, Ideology in Medical Science: Class in the Clinic, *Social Science and Medicine, 28*:11, pp. 1205-1209, 1989.
56. W. Fife and D. Black, A Conservative Generation of Students? Comments on "Anthropology's Other Press," *Current Anthrogology, 29*:3, pp. 491-492, 1988.
57. J. Clifford, Power and Dialogue in Ethnography: Marcel Griaule's Initiation, in *Observers Observed: Essays on Ethnographic Fieldwork*, G. Stocking, Jr. (ed.), The University of Wisconsin Press, Madison, pp. 121-156, 1983.
58. J. Clifford, *Person and Myth: Maurice Leenhardt in the Melanesian World,* University of California Press, Berkeley, 1982.
59. T. Swendenburg, Occupational Hazards: Palestine Ethnography, in *Rereading Cultural Anthropology*, G. Marcus (ed.), Duke University Press, Durham, pp. 68-76, 1992.
60. J. Comaroff and J. Comaroff, *Of Revelation and Revolution,* University of Chicago Press, Chicago, 1991.

Section B:

The Macro-Social Level

CHAPTER 4

Health-Related Issues in Socialist-Oriented Societies: Ideals, Contradictions, and Realities

To date, most research in critical medical anthropology has focused on health-related issues in developed and underdeveloped capitalist societies [1, 2]. However, critical medical anthropology also seeks to understand the nature of health concepts and practices in post-capitalist, post-revolutionary societies, or what we term in this chapter socialist-oriented societies. In this chapter, we sketch the outlines for a critical analysis of such matters in societies that made an effort to embark upon the path of socialism. The recent collapse of the Soviet Union and the Soviet-bloc raises serious questions as to the nature and future of socialist-oriented societies and the concept of a socialist health. As Krause argues, "[t]hroughout history, to a marked degree health services have reflected in miniature the achievements and failures of the societies in which they have existed" [3, p. 2]. Because health care systems tend to reproduce the structure of relations in the larger society [4], including class relations, relations among the sexes, and relations between ethnic groups, certain notable differences appear in the nature of health care in capitalist and socialist-oriented countries.

A meaningful discussion of socialist health is ultimately grounded in our ability to make analytical distinctions between capitalism and socialism. A satisfactory definition of socialist health is ultimately related to our ability to define socialism itself. As Segall argues, "the concept of socialism is of no use to people seeking solutions within capitalism, but it is essential for those interested to see that system transcended" [5, p. 222]. Given that a social formation acts as a major determinant in the production and the treatment of disease and illness, any definition should address the question of the extent to which post-revolutionary societies have or had, prior to recent changes, achieved socialism. With these thoughts in mind, the first part of this chapter reviews the essential dimensions of socialism and theories on the nature of

135

post-revolutionary or socialist-oriented societies. The second part of this chapter critically examines health care and health problems in societies established, at least initially, upon socialist ideals.

Despite the growing trend in anthropology to study aspects of complex societies, a perusal of general textbooks in our discipline reveals a general neglect of post-revolutionary societies. Indeed, it would appear that more interest has focused on the collapse of socialist-oriented systems than on their construction. Nevertheless, perhaps more so than ever, anthropologists assert that they are engaged in the holistic study of people and their sociocultural systems. Most general textbooks that make fleeting comments on post-revolutionary societies, such as the Soviet Union, China, and Cuba, accept them as "socialist" or "communist" at face value, apparently due to the large degree of state control over production and distribution in these societies. Even Roger Keesing, who explicitly espouses a "neo-Marxist" approach, devotes only a short subsection and a few sentences here and there to what he loosely terms "socialist states" in his textbook [6]. Inasmuch as textbooks mirror the general concerns and state of the art of a discipline, it is obvious that most anthropologists exhibit a superficial understanding of a category of societies that have encompassed approximately one-third of humanity.

THE ESSENTIAL DIMENSIONS OF SOCIALISM

Although we eschew a ritualistic reading of Marx and Engels as ultimate authorities on questions under dispute in political economic studies, unavoidably consideration of the nature of socialism must begin with an examination of what socialism meant to these seminal thinkers. In fact, Marx and Engels refrained from drawing up a detailed blueprint of what form or forms socialism and communism would take. Yet, here and there in their writings, they delineated the essential dimensions of "the lower phase of communism" (socialism) and "the higher phase of communism" (communism per se). Socialism, as Navarro observers,

> is not a mode of production: it is a social formation in transition from the capitalist mode of production to the communist mode of production. . . . Socialism as a social formation has several modes of production, including capitalist and communist modes [7, p. 85].

A perusal of Marx and Engels' writings indicates that they believed that socialism would exhibit four basic components: 1) public ownership of the means of production, 2) increasing social equality, 3) proletarian democracy, and 4) developed productive forces. Public ownership of the means of production by the state or other collective bodies would be a necessary condition for achieving an economic system in which production is oriented toward meeting social needs rather than the creation of profit that enriches a small ruling class. As opposed to communism, which would be guided by the dictum "from each according to his ability, to each according to his needs," income under socialism would be calculated according to the work performed because of the persistence of bourgeois values. Since a select few could no longer derive income from the private ownership of property, income differentials would diminish greatly. The distinction between manual and intellectual labor would continue under socialism but would be abolished under communism.

Marx, who was committed to the ideal of direct democracy from his earliest writings, referred to his conception of socialist democracy as the "dictatorship of the proletariat." The term "dictatorship" did not refer to an authoritarian government, but to the domination of a class over productive forces and the institutions of society. Just as the capitalist state, despite the presence of voting rights and parliaments, is governed by a "democracy of all factions of the capitalist class, but a dictatorship over the working class, [Marx] expected a democracy of the working class to exert a dictatorship over their former masters, the capitalists, until the capitalists would disappear completely" [8, p. 292]. Although he never explicitly described how collective decision-making might occur under socialist democracy, Marx believed that various features of the Paris Commune of 1871, referred to in *The Civil War in France,* foreshadowed the proletarian state:

> The Commune was formed of the municipal councillors, chosen by universal suffrage in various wards of the towns, responsible and revocable at short terms. The majority of its members were naturally working men, or acknowledged representatives of the working class. The Commune was to be a working, not a parliamentary body, executive and legislative at the same time. . . . From the members of the Commune downwards, the public service had to be done at workmen's wages. The vested interests and the representation allowances of the high dignitaries of State disappeared along with the high dignitaries themselves. Public functions ceased to be the private property of the tools of the Central Government . . . [quoted in 9, p. 632].

It is important to add that Marx extended his concept of democracy to include workers' control over the forces of production. For example, in *Capital,* he referred to "associations of working-men" who will freely regulate their own labor and determine the terms of their intercourse with nature. Many modern Marxist scholars concur that socialism implies economic and political democracy. For Navarro, the "key criterion in defining a social formation as socialist is whether there is control by the working class and its allied forces of the political instance in that formation" [7, p. 80].

Marx argues that the attainment of socialism would occur after capitalism had "exhausted" its potential for developing the productive forces. In the *Preface to a Contribution to the Critique of Political Economy,* he stated that

> [n]o social order ever perishes before all the productive forces for which there is room in it have developed; and new, higher relations of production never appear before the material conditions of their existence have matured in the womb of the old society itself [quoted in 9, p. 5].

In later years, however, both Marx and Engels relaxed the strict determinism of this statement by conceding that revolution in certain underdeveloped countries, particularly Russia, might provide the impetus for proletarian revolution in Western Europe. In 1882, in the Preface to the Russian edition of *The Communist Manifesto,* they concluded: "If the Russian revolution becomes the signal for a proletarian revolution in the West, so that both complement each other, the present Russian common ownership of land may serve as the starting point of a communist development" [quoted in 9, p. 472].

INTERPRETATIONS OF THE NATURE OF THE POST-REVOLUTIONARY SOCIETIES

The historical reality that successful socialist-inspired revolutions occurred in semi-peripheral and peripheral capitalist nations rather than in core capitalist nations has contributed to a considerable amount of debate among Western Marxist scholars on the nature of post-revolutionary societies. Characterization of societies, such as the former Soviet Union and other Eastern European states, China, North Korea, Vietnam, Cuba, and Mozambique, tend to fall into one of the following categories: 1) socialism; 2) transitional forms between capitalism and socialism; 3) state capitalist; and 4) new class societies or social formations [10, 11].

Some scholars contend that post-revolutionary societies are basically socialist in nature, despite their ongoing contradictions [8, 18, 19]. Szymanski provides perhaps the most systematic attempt to demonstrate that post-revolutionary societies are socialist. In this view,

> [t]he immediate producers may or may not make the day-to-day production decisions. As long as they authentically determine the fundamental decisions— such as the nature of the product, the basic structure of the production process, the fundamental distribution of the product, etc.—they are socialist [20, p. 22].

Szymanski develops a typology of socialist systems, which is illustrated in Figure 1. According to Szymanski,

> state socialism, where the initiative as well as day-to-day operational decision making is in the hand of state officials, is just as much a socialist society as decentralized socialism, where initiative and day-to-day decision making are in the hands of the producing classes themselves. Whether or not a society is in fact socialist . . . must be determined . . . on the basis of whether or not decisions made are in the interests of the producing classes [20, pp. 24-25].

He argues, further, that socialism may evolve from one form into another. For example, whereas, in his assessment, the Soviet Union was a charismatic state socialist form between the 1920s and early 1950s, it became a technocratic socialist one following the death of Stalin. Following Szymanski, the communal socialism of China during the Cultural Revolution evolved into bureaucratic state socialism following the demise of the so-called "Gang of Four." He also states that the bureaucratic state socialism can regress into state capitalism as state and party officials acquire an increasing number of privileges, and market socialism can develop over time into market capitalism.

Most Western Marxists do not share Szymanski's belief that workers exerted considerable input, either directly or indirectly, in economic and political decision-making in the former Soviet Union and most other post-revolutionary societies. Perhaps the most common alternative interpretation of these societies is that they

A. State Socialism

    1. Charismatic socialism: predominant role of leaders
    2. Bureaucratic socialism: predominant role of bureaucracy
    3. State market socialism: predominant role of markets
    4. Technocratic socialism: predominant role of technocrats

B. Decentralized Socialism

    1. Decentralized market socialism: predominant role of markets with decision-making by producers' collectives
    2. Communal socialism: predominant role of collective decision-making without reliance on markets

Forms of socialist-oriented systems (Adapted from [20, p. 17].)

Figure 1. A typology of socialist systems.

constitute transitional forms between capitalism and socialism. Mandel, for example, asserts that

> [s]tate ownership of all important industrial, transportation, and financial (i.e., of the means of production and circulation), combined with legal (constitutional) suppression of the right to their private appropriation, centralized economic planning and state monopoly of foreign trade, imply the absence of generalized commodity production and of the rule of value (and thus value) in the U.S.S.R. [21, p. 35].

Conversely, the survival of partial commodity production due to several factors, including the pressure of the world market and the underdevelopment of the forces of production, prevented the achievement of socialism in the Soviet Union. Instead, a privileged bureaucratic stratum of working class came to control, but did not own, the means of production. While Mandel admits that the nature of the Chinese workers' state differs from that of the Soviet Union and the Eastern European countries, he maintains that the

> the fundamental character of Soviet society as a society in transition from capitalism to socialism, halted in that transition by the usurpation of power by a privileged bureaucracy that can be removed only through an anti-bureaucratic political revolution, is also essentially applicable to China [22, p. 159].

Wallerstein has developed a more recent version of the transition model. In his view, "socialist" countries are largely semi-peripheral units in the capitalist world economy, although the Soviet Union was, at least until recently, emerging as a core power; "the October Revolution changed the face of world politics and undermined, just by having occurred, a major pillar of the political stability of the world capitalist system" [23, p. 234]. Nevertheless, Wallerstein believes that the transition from capitalism to a socialist world government would be a protracted (and by no means an inevitable) one, which would take another 100 to 150 years to complete. During this interim period,

> several state machineries (and others will) have come under the control of socialist parties which are both seeking to bring about this worldwide transition and seeking to prefigure within their state boundaries some aspects of a socialist mode of production (such as collective ownership of the means of production, the institution of non-material incentives for productivity, etc.) [24, p. 56].

While the notion that the Soviet Union prior to its collapse had already been transformed into a capitalist formation, albeit of a state capitalist variety, has been in circulation for some time [25]. Bettelheim is the most prominent Western Marxist scholar who was an early advocate of this interpretation [26, 27]. He argues that programs, such as the New Economic Policy, restored capitalism in the Soviet Union during the 1920s and 1930s. In Bettelheim's view,

> [w]hat was supposed to give rise to increasingly socialist relations has instead produced relations that are essentially capitalist, so that behind the screen of 'economic plans,' it is the laws of capitalist accumulation, and so of profit, that decide how the means of production are utilized [26, p. 44].

A "bureaucratic state bourgeoisie" consisting of party and state bosses came to control, but did not own, the means of production. State enterprises in Soviet-type societies, he argued, reproduced capitalist relations of production in two ways: 1) by separating workers from control and ownership of the means of production and 2) through a system of commodity exchange between state enterprises. In addition to collectively appropriating surplus value or profit from the workers, the state bourgeoisie imposed its hegemony by means of a highly centralized, undemocratic party apparatus.

Whereas few Marxist theorists would go so far as to refer to all post-revolutionary societies as state capitalist, many assert that they are in fact manifestations of a new social formation. Amin contends that "so-called socialist societies are not socialist but constitute a new group of class societies based on the state mode of production" [28, pp. 218-219]. For Bahro, "actually existing socialism" in the Soviet Union and Eastern Europe served as a non-capitalist road to industrialization [29]. He argues that actually existing socialism resembles the Asiatic mode of production in that its form of domination is based on state control rather than on private property. Political domination in these societies was due to the low level of their productive forces. Sweezy arrives at a somewhat similar conclusion:

> [T]he most important difference between capitalism and post-revolutionary society is that this overwhelming dominance of capital has been broken and replaced by the direct rule of a new ruling class which derives its power and privileges not from ownership and/or control of capital but from the unmediated control of the state and its multiform apparatuses of coercion. This means that the utilization of society's surplus product—which, as under capitalism and some forms of precapitalist society, is produced by a propertyless working class—is no longer governed by the laws of value and capital accumulation but instead becomes the center of a political process and of course of political struggles, including (but not exclusively) class struggles. In this respect post-revolutionary

societies are unlike capitalism but similar to precapitalist societies which lack an autonomous economic foundation [30, p. 147].

Our review of theories on the nature of post-revolutionary societies is intended primarily to dispel any misconceptions that all Marxist scholars agree on this matter. However, we do not attempt to fully settle this complex debate within the confines of this chapter. Our general view, nonetheless, is presented below. Following Elling [31], we, along with John Johnsen referred to post-revolutionary formations as "socialist-oriented" societies in an earlier work [32]. These societies were established on the basis of socialist ideals and were guided by them, despite their bureaucratization, hierarchical relations, and the contradictory policies of their governments on various issues, for an extended period of time. In light of the collapse of the Soviet bloc, the degree to which they presently are guided by them varies considerably from country to country. As Gouldner observes, "socialist ideology fosters expectations and tensions subversive of those structures of domination characteristic of 'socialist' nations today" [33, p. 292]. Socialist-oriented societies implemented many of the requisites (especially economic ones) of socialism. According to Lane, "the forms of political participation developed in the USSR [were] not completely meaningless and contained some genuine forms of public involvement" [34, p. 42]. Similarly, Navarro refers to recent development of popular participation in Cuba [35]. In contrast, the existence of multi-party systems in advanced capitalist nations does not guarantee meaningful popular input into political decision-making. In the case of the United States, it may be argued that the Republican and Democratic parties constitute representative factions of the ruling party—namely the capitalist class [36, 37]. Even challenges to the two party system, such as the independent candidacy of Ross Perot during the 1992 presidential election, can be seen as intra-class conflict within the economically and politically dominant ruling class.

As Gorz observes, "[i]t is the historical circumstances of socialist accumulation and the ethics of productivity they determined which account for many of the shortcomings of present-day socialist society . . ." [38, p. 188]. The contradictions of socialist-oriented societies have been shaped by both internal and external forces. Marx and Engels argued that socialism would have to emerge within capitalist societies with highly developed productive forces. Sherman and Wood maintain that "political dictatorship in the Soviet Union resulted from the Russian autocratic tradition, the underground political tradition, civil war, foreign wars (and encirclement), and from economic backwardness. It was *not* caused by socialism, but arose in spite of socialism" [39, p. 261]. In a somewhat similar vein, Schwartz maintains that "[i]n an isolated and relatively backward country, lacking strong democratic traditions, and where a militant but extremely small working class had been decimated by civil war, the bureaucracy was able to impose Stalinism as a noncapitalist crash modernization programme" [40, p. 68]. Post-revolutionary societies created the human resource, which was provided with a relatively high level subsistence and social services (including health care), that was essential for economic development in underdeveloped societies. At the same time, this program of development entailed great human suffering, pain, and death, especially in the collectivization of agriculture and political repression. Conversely, it is important to point out that the impersonal market forces of capitalist development probably produced an even greater extent of tragedy over the long run and on a global scale. Furthermore, socialist-oriented societies have been besieged since their inception by hostile forces including the Western Allies and Japan immediately following the Bolshevik Revolution, Nazi Germany during World War II, and the United States and other NATO powers following World War II. As the cases of Grenada, Nicaragua, and Eastern Europe reveal, the ultimate goal of besiegement has been the complete re-incorporation within the capitalist world-system.

In response to such threats, a bureaucratic administrative structure emerged on top of a socialist-oriented base consisting of nationalized property, formal public owner-ship of the means of production and centralized planning. The former Soviet Union was never able to develop a peace-time economy. While internal contradictions, including an inefficient command structure contributed to the collapse of the Soviet Union, the arms race that was stepped up by the Reagan administration during the 1980s certainly played a significant role in creating economic difficulties for a nation that was forced to play catch-up in a strategy designed to cripple it. In a desperate effort to save a stagnating social system, Gorbachev implemented *glasnost* and *perestroika* and called off the Cold War and the arms race. Soviet withdrawal of support for satellite regimes in Eastern Europe led to the "revolutions" of 1989. Although Gorbachev initially intended to create some sort of democratic socialist system in the Soviet Union, *perestroika* offered an unsystematic program that created even more economic difficulties while planting the seeds for the possible restoration of capitalism.

Of the Soviet-bloc countries, the German Democratic Republic was fully incor-porated into the welfare capitalist economy of the Federal Republic of Germany, although as a sort of periphery of its larger and richer neighbor. It is evident from Baer's research in the German Democratic Republic that the reform of socialism rather than reincorporation with capitalism was the preferred goal of many East Germans who opposed the Honecker regime [41]. According to Cox, former Soviet-type societies may follow one of the following scenarios:

(1) "a combination of political authoritarianism with economic liberalization leading towards market capitalism and the integration of the national economy into the global capitalist economy" (e.g., Poland) [42, p. 186];

(2) "political authoritarianism together with a command-administrative economic centre incorporating some subordinate market features and some bureaucratic reform" (e.g., the People's Republic of China) [42, pp. 186-187]; and

(3) "democratization plus socialist reform" involving either producer self-management, or a democratization of the central planning process, or some combination of the two [42, p. 187].

Only time will tell which of these three options will appear in the Commonwealth of Independent States, as the former Soviet Union minus the Baltic republics and Armenia is currently called. Although many reform-minded members of the former *nomenklatura* or party elite, such as Boris Yeltsin, as well as of the intelligentsia favor the restoration of some form of capitalism in the new commonwealth, despite their lack of a strong sense of collective identity, most workers want to retain job security and social benefits (including access to nationalized health care) and exhibit skepticism toward unregulated markets. While the prospects of the emergence of a global socialist system seem remote in the foreseeable future, the collapse of the Soviet bloc may over the long run provide space for the eventual development of such a system. As Chomsky observes,

> With Bolshevism disintegrating, [laissez faire] capitalism long abandoned and state capitalist democracy in decline, there are prospects for the revival of libertarian socialist and radical democratic ideals that had languished, including popular control of the workplace and investment decisions, and, correspondingly, the entrenchment of political democracy as constraints imposed by private power are reduced. These and other emerging possibilities are still remote, but are no less exciting than the dramatic events unfolding in Eastern Europe [43, p. 133].

HEALTH CARE AND HEALTH STATUS IN SOCIALIST-ORIENTED SOCIETIES

The most commonly used criterion in defining the concept of socialist health system is public ownership of health services. As a result, there has been a tendency to refer to various nationalized health systems as examples of "socialized medicine" [44, 45]. Furthermore, social scientists often refer to countries, such as Britain, France, Israel, India, and New Zealand, as "socialist" because certain industries and social services, including health care, have been nationalized. Although the United States continues to be the only major industrial society without a nationalized health service, Marvin Harris characterizes its political economy as a mixture of "state socialism" and capitalism [46, pp. 288-289]. In that the means of production continue to reside largely in private hands in these countries, it is surprising to say the least that they are designated in this fashion.

Any attempt to distinguish health care in welfare capitalist societies from health care in socialist societies must be based upon a distinction between "nationalization" and "socialization." As Markus observes,

> Marx's theory does not imply . . . a clear distinction between nationalization as a legal-political act giving a public character to property, and socialization as the effective transformation of economic relations, establishing a collective-social property based on the real power of immediate producers to determine the conditions and products of their labour. . . . And Marx did warn against the possibility that the central economic organ of society could transform itself into the despotic rule of production and trustee (Verwalterin) of disposition and counterposed it to socialism where it can be nothing more than a board which keeps the books and counts for a society producing in common" [13, p. 30].

The function of the state in advanced capitalist societies is to resolve the contradictions which develop in a market economy and to reduce social tensions which may threaten existing social relations [47]. Advanced capitalist societies are characterized by various combinations of involvement by the private and state sectors in health care, with the United States at one end and perhaps Great Britain at the other end of this continuum. While the benefits for the average patient in Britain are far greater than those deriving from the state sector in the United States, Doyal argues that the National Health Service constitutes a form of "nationalized medicine" rather than "socialized medicine" in that it is an integral part of the British political economy [48]. For example, consultants can treat private patients in National Health Service hospitals and the Service purchases drugs and equipment from private corporations.

Whether or not health care systems are socialized ultimately depends on the extent to which post-revolutionary societies have achieved socialism. Sidel and Sidel argue that the former Soviet Union had developed a "centralized, socialized medical-care system" in that:

> 1) It provides health care totally free of charge at the need of its entire population; 2) it is a government operated, centrally planned system which functions as an integral part of a planned economy; 3) it has trained vast numbers of physicians (70% of whom are women) and other health workers, and consequently has the highest ratio of health workers to population of any country in the world; 4) it has given high priority to services for special problems, such as the prevention of infectious disease and the care of people with medical emergencies; and 5) it has given high priority to services for special groups such as mothers and children and industrial workers, services which in the United States are particularly fragmented and weak [49, pp. 176-177].

The polyclinic served as the core of former Soviet primary medical care in urban areas and was sometimes situated alongside a hospital [50, p. 491]. Specialized polyclinics were created for adults, women, children, and industrial workers. The polyclinic generally served several *uchastocks* (residential areas), each of which was catered to by a physician who worked at the polyclinic in the morning and made house calls in the afternoon. Rural health care was provided in a feldsher-midwife post based in a village or collective farm which was periodically visited by a physician. Both polyclinics and feldsher-midwife posts referred patients onto a hierarchy of local, district, regional, and specialized hospitals. The former Soviet hospital system had 12.1 beds per 1,000 people, which exceeded similar figures for most industrialized societies, except for Norway, Sweden, and Finland [50, p. 497].

Although the Soviet health care system had greatly diminished inter-republic differences in the availability of health resources, it was still fraught with many problems. The primacy of heavy industry relegated health care to a supportive role in the development of the Soviet Union and other Eastern European countries. As Navarro noted prior to the collapse of the Soviet Union, "medicine in today's Soviet Union represents clear signs of alienation, undemocratic control and inequitable distribution of resources, a bourgeois and individualist interpretation, and hierarchicalization and discrimination in the health sector" [51, p. xvii]. The Soviet medical paradigm was described as "mechanistic," "Flexnerian," and curative with an orientation toward specialized hospital care. Further, he maintained that nationalization rather than socialization had occurred in the Soviet Union and that "socialist development will not take place automatically, but rather will go through an evolutionary process which takes the time of generations" [51, p. 111]. *Perestroika* with its emphasis on market mechanisms, however, contributed to an expansion of fee-for-service polyclinics [52, p. 327]. In 1988 and 1989, the number of medical cooperatives rose from nearly none to 3,289, with a total of 61,000 employees [53, p. 225]. The new Commonwealth of Independent States passed a law to be implemented in 1993 that calls for "employer-based health insurance and decentralized competitive bidding for hospital and speciality care" [54, p. 7].

Economic stagnation in the former Soviet Union and other Eastern European countries contributed to cuts in the decreasing proportion that health services received from total national expenditures. In 1987, of the entire state budget, expenditures for health care took 4.5 percent in the Soviet Union, 5.8 percent in Bulgaria, 7.1 percent in Hungary, 8.7 percent in Czechoslovakia, and 10.8 percent in Poland [55, p. 835]. The former Soviet health care system has faced chronic shortages in the provisions of medical services (crowded waiting rooms, cramped work spaces for staff), medical equipment and instruments, and medicines. According to Davis, "Relative to international standards the Soviet Union has low levels of technology" [56, p. 253]. Shortages and deficiencies encouraged the emergence of a "second economy" in health care under which physicians expect "gifts" of a modest nature for providing routine treatment and specialists receive higher payments for their services. Many physicians supplemented their low salaries by writing work- and draft-deferments for patients who "tipped" in cash [53, p. 194].

> Medicines often were illegally acquired by black marketeers through thefts from factories, warehouses, importing agencies, and pharmacies. These goods were then sold through informal networks to hospital and polyclinic patients. In other cases speculators or pharmacy personnel legally purchased at full price, large quantities of desirable goods and thereby contributed to shortages. After a suitable period these medicines were re-sold to consumers. A third practice was for pharmacy personnel to keep medicines in high demand 'under the counter' for sale to acquaintances at official prices or to others who paid a premium [56, p. 252].

In her comparative study of professionalism among British and Soviet physicians, Haug found that, like in the West, Soviet physicians played a gatekeeper role by controlling access to various non-medical benefits, such as valued jobs and vacation privileges [57]. Although some evidence was found that professional authority, largely due to the increasing role of technology and bureaucratization in medicine, was eroding, many of the polyclinic physicians interviewed found the possibility of having their expertise being challenged as incomprehensible.

In other Eastern European countries, such as Poland, the specialist care sector, particularly hospital care, absorbed a disproportionate share of health resources, and the notion that primary care was unrewarding permeated the medical academies [58]. According to Sokolowska and Rychards, alternatives in health care, including medical cooperatives, private medical practices, health organizations and facilities affiliated with the Catholic church, and self-help groups and healers developed in Poland as a result of inefficiencies in the state health system [59]. In former Yugoslavia, where one byproduct of the decentralization of health and financing had been accentuated, differences in access to health between rural and urban areas as well as between communes, health professionals retained considerable control of health institutions, despite the existence of workers' councils, and "patients continue[d] to defer to the 'professional mystique' of physicians" [60, p. 1392].

As opposed to the "centralized-concerted" structure of the Soviet Union and various Eastern-bloc countries, Elling categorizes the organization of authority in China and Cuba (as well as Sweden) as "decentralized-pluralistic"—a pattern which he maintains is "likely to be most supportive of the regionalized and otherwise ideal health and medical care system" [31, p. 10]. In keeping with the principle of "democratic centralism," plans tend to originate at the top and flow to lower levels for comment. While final decisions are made by the central leadership, implementation was left largely in the hands of local leaders and health bodies.

The degree of centralization and decentralization in the Chinese health system has in reality varied over time and has reflected changes in political and economic policies. Whereas a health care system based on the Soviet Model was adopted following the 1949 Revolution, the Great Leap Forward starting in 1958 emphasized decentralization. Gradual return to a more professionalized and centralized organization of health care was followed by the Cultural Revolution beginning in 1966. According to Sidel and Sidel, "in sum, the emphasis in health during the early seventies was on deprofessionalization, demystification, decentralization, popular participation, providing care for those who formerly had the least, and on 'serving the people' " [61, p. 7]. During this period, the Chinese health system came closest to approximating Elling's decentralized-pluralistic type. Although the widely acclaimed "barefoot doctor" concept is rooted in the Great Leap Forward, it took its most elaborate and legitimized form during the Cultural Revolution. Mao announced in June 1965 that the barefoot doctor program would address the continuing shortage of physicians in the countryside, but also served to undercut the Ministry of Health's professional control of medical work [62]. Another hallmark of the Cultural Revolution was an attempt to integrate Chinese and Western medicine so as to create a medical form that was both effective and appropriate nationally. As Crozier observes, however, "popularized Chinese medicine in vogue today differs considerably from traditional Chinese medicine" [63, p. 353].

The modernization policies of the current political leadership shifted administrative control of most health services from the neighborhood committees, which were abolished in 1979, back to the district level [61]. Although the barefoot doctor program has not been dismantled, additional training requirements led to a significant decrease of barefoot doctors. Furthermore, with the strengthened position of the medical profession, barefoot doctors now find themselves in a more restricted role and under greater medical supervision. Despite the continued use of traditional medical techniques for various health problems, its overall status has declined. While Sidel and Sidel attempt to be optimistic about China's future, their assessment of the impact of modernization on health care is generally negative:

> Rapid economic modernization may . . . result in a slowdown in the unfinished agenda for rural areas and widen rural-urban gaps in medical care. The 'raising of standards' and the increased 'professionalization' may lead to less assignment of urban medical workers to the countryside, to the building of larger, more

decentralized primary and secondary care facilities, and to reduction in local management of health care facilities. The general trend toward clinical specialization is likely to increase the wage differentials among professionals and lead to their greater emphasis on treatment rather than prevention. The training of personnel in other countries is likely to lead to wider gaps in their ability to deal with poor people in their own society, to concern themselves with high-technology care or with basic research rather than its applications, and to the demand for even greater centralization of sources [61, p. 189].

Health insurance in China has been less comprehensive, coordinated, and readily available than in the former Soviet Union and Eastern European societies. China spends only about 2.5 percent of its national income on health care and Chinese hospitals are always crowded due to the population to hospital bed ratio of around 500 [64]. In the early 1980s, three types of health insurance coverage were available:

> 1) public expense medical insurance for state cadres and students (about 2% of the population); 2) labor medical insurance for workers or staff members in factories and state firms; and 3) cooperative medical insurance that was promoted in 1966 as a voluntary program at the commune level in rural areas [64, p. 141].

Despite the dismantlement of the collective system and the implementation of the production responsibility program in China, the national government has not given up its control over public health programs. Conversely, the policy of financial self-help in rural health care adopted in the 1970s has reportedly created a marked disparity in terms of access to health services between rich and poor brigade clinic in Lin Village (pseudonym) established in 1969 broke up in 1984 into three private practices subsidized by standard fees charged to patients and modest financial support from the new village administration and township government (the former commune administration) [65]. The Chinese government has decided that care of the elderly should continue to be primarily a family responsibility [66].

Various other developing socialist-oriented societies, such as Cuba and Nicaragua under the Sandinistas, intensified accessibility to and popular control over health services [35, 67, 68]. In 1985 Cuba implemented a family doctor program in which a physician was to live and work directly with 120 families [69, p. 94]. At the same time, Cuba began to devote increased attention and resources to sophisticated technological tertiary care and research. The post-independence government in Zimbabwe developed a health care program based upon the primary health care approach which brought about a significant drop in infant and young child mortality despite drought, recession, and economic stabilization programs [70]. Unfortunately,

> economic recession and stabilisation attempts [imposed in large measure by pressure from the International Monetary Fund] have reduced real incomes for large numbers of rural and urban households since the immediate post-independence boom. This reflects itself in discrepantly high levels of childhood undernutrition which seem to have remained static or improved only very slightly despite the health care drive. This apparent inconsistently expresses a funda-mental shortcoming in what is becoming known as the 'selective health care

approach,' where targeted technical interventions can rapidly reduce mortality but more basic causes of undernutrition are not addressed [70, p. 731].

Whereas Zimbabwe has experienced external economic constraints in the development of its health care system, Nicaragua encountered a U.S.-funded *contra* offensive as well as an economic embargo that made it difficult to obtain needed medicines. Despite these difficulties, Nicaragua illustrated the potential of primary health care programs in socialist-oriented Third World countries. Immediately following the revolution in Nicaragua, the Sandinistas established a "National Strategy for Health" emphasizing health care for all, community participation, technological development, and increase in the number of health workers and facilities.

Whereas in 1977 there were 172 health centers, there are now 446. . . . Parental care now reaches 82% of all pregnancy women. Well-baby visits have tripled since 1981. The number of doctor visits per person doubled between 1977 and 1982, with 70% of the population having regular contact with medical care as of 1982, as compared with 28% in 1979 [71, p. 2].

According to Donahue, despite the Sandinista government's efforts to strengthen the popular health care sector, professionals tended to view the *brigadistas* as an extension of the medical staff in area health clinics [72].

Nicaraguan health care received international recognition when the World Health Organization and UNICEF chose it as a model primary health system. A U.S.-backed military offensive, however, not only limited funds available for health care but forced the Nicaraguan people to choose between an increasingly brutal and debilitating counter-insurgency and voting the Sandinistas out of power, further indicating the importance of examining health issues within the wider field of social forces. Nonetheless, the Sandinistas retain an important influence in that they hold about 40 percent of the seats in the National Assembly, are well represented in the judicial system, and have strong representation in popular organizations, especially labor unions.

While disease is bound to occur under any mode of production in that people will continue to be subject to certain hazards and infectious diseases in the natural environment and the physiological degeneration that inevitably accompanies aging, in socialist and eventually in communist society it should be possible to resolve the basic tension between providing for human material and social psychological needs and preserving the health of people. The partial achievement of this goal is illustrated by comparing health statistics in capitalist and socialist-oriented countries. Table 1 classifies the nations of the world into high-income, middle-income, and lower-income categories based on their per capita incomes in 1976.

Although the three Asian countries of the fourteen socialist-oriented countries (China, North Korea, Albania, Cuba, Mongolia, Rumania, Yugoslavia, Hungary, Bulgaria, Soviet Union, Poland, Czechoslovakia, and East Germany) were among the poorest countries in the world prior to their revolutions, by the 1980s none of them were in the bottom category. In contrast, "[f]orty-one countries (34 percent of the population of the world) have lower per capita income than the poorest socialist country" [73, p. 20].

Table 1. Classification of countries by Income Level
(GNP per capita)*

	Capitalist countries	N	Socialist-oriented countries	N
Low-income	$100-390	(41)		
Middle-income	$410-4,250	(49)	$410-4,220	(13)
High-income	$4,480-15,480	(17)		

*Adapted from [72, p. 14].

Table 2 indicates that the worst health statistics are concentrated in the low-income capitalist countries. The health statistics of the middle-income socialist-oriented countries are not only significantly better than those of the middle-income capitalist countries, but also approach those in the high-income capitalist countries.

The AIDS epidemic not withstanding, to a notable degree, infectious diseases in industrial countries, whether capitalist or socialist-oriented, have been brought under control. Conversely, the prevalence of chronic diseases, many of which are ultimately related to industrial pollution and hazards and stresses in the workplace, and at least in capitalist societies, from the fear of unemployment and abject poverty, are remarkably similar in both types of societies [74]. The former Soviet Union tended to lag behind most Eastern European countries on most health statistics.

Also, the former Soviet Union exhibited considerable regional variation in mortality rates and life expectancy. Whereas the overall life expectancy at birth in 1985-1986 was 73.3 years in Armenia, it was only 64.8 in Turkmenistan [75, p. 874].

> In the period from 1965 to 1984, mortality indices revealed some unfavourable tendencies. The rate of general mortality increased as a result of population 'aging', i.e. there was an increase in the proportion of elderly people and hence in the crude rate of mortality. Simultaneously, there was a marked increase in the mortality rates of the working-age population, especially of male deaths which might be resulting from cardiovascular disease and from accidents. Since 1985, due to efficient measures to combat alcoholism, deaths due to alcoholism have fallen substantially. As a result, life-expectancy increased to 69.8 years in 1987. However, the U.S.S.R. still lags 5-8 years behind such countries as Great Britain, the Federal Republic of Germany, U.S.A., France, and Japan [75, p. 867].

Whereas the infant mortality rate was 9.0 per 1,000 births in Great Britain in 1987 and 10.4 per 1,000 birth in the United States in 1987, it was 25.1 per 1,000 births in the former Soviet Union [54, p. 7].

In Soviet-bloc countries, the high-paced drive for industrialization and an elaborate division of labor, which were rooted in the threat posed by the capitalist

Table 2. Selected Health Statistic in Capitalist and Socialist-Oriented Societies*

	Low-income	Middle-income	High-income
Life expectancy at birth (mid-1970s)			
Capitalist	45	60	69
Socialist		68	
Infant mortality rate (mid-1970s)			
Capitalist	149	78	31
Socialist		41	
Population/physician (1974)	22,589	3,426	1,053
Capitalist		1,385	
Socialist			

*Adapted from [72, p. 27]

world-system, produced not only considerable alienation among workers, often manifested by high rates of alcoholism, but also in serious environmental pollution. Automobiles are not as prevalent in the former Soviet Union as in the United States, Western Europe, or Japan. Nevertheless, "[t]he USSR, with one-tenth the number of [private automobiles] and with truck freight one-half of the U.S. volume, still managed to produce about two-thirds as much as atmospheric poison from automobile exhausts" [53, p. 96]. The managerial objective of producing maximum output at minimum cost resulted in the dumping of sewage and industrial wastes into rivers and lakes, a lack of safety precautions in industrial plants, and crop-dusting with dangerous pesticides [8, pp. 257-258; 53]. The disposal of nuclear waste materials, most of which come from meeting the threat of the superior nuclear arms build-up of the capitalist countries, particularly the United States, also became a serious problem. The former Soviet Union had exhibited the worse instances of radioactive contamination, the most spectacular being that of the Chernobyl nuclear plant. Czechoslovakia and Poland had the highest levels of industrial pollution in Europe and perhaps in the world [76, pp. 219-220]. Industrial pollution also con- stituted a serious problem in the former German Democratic Republic, particularly in the vicinity of cities such as Bitterfeld, Halle, Leipzig, and Karl Marx Stadt. The weak development of democratic institutions in socialist-oriented societies and bureaucratic suppression of information about the environmental impact of agricul- tural and industrial practices had until recently inhibited the emergence of an inde- pendent environment movement. Although *glasnost* had permitted the emergence of a small Green movement in the former Soviet Union, the official policy of *perestroika* under Gorbachev and the ongoing emphasis on a productivist ethic and market mechanisms under the new Commonwealth of Independent States may serve as impediments to the implementation of strict environmental protection standards in the foreseeable future.

Further contradictions exist in the type of consumer products that the former Soviet bureaucracy produces. According to Cooper and Schatzkin, "despite progressive anti-smoking laws, the government continues to produce more cigarettes each year and has not acted decisively to reduce their consumption. As with alcohol, large profits accrue from the sale of tobacco products" [74, p. 474].

Some less developed socialist-oriented societies had in a remarkably short period of time improved the general health status of their populations, often to the point that the health profiles of these societies begin to approach those of highly industrialized societies. Life expectancy in China has increased from thirty-four years in 1931 to sixty-nine years in 1981 [77, p. 481]. Unfortunately, underdeveloped socialist-oriented societies also exhibit some of the same contradictions that exist in their more developed counterparts [31, 78]. In the case of China, "modernization" has increased industrial pollution [61, pp. 72-79]. While efforts to control this pollution are being stepped up, large amounts of industrial waste are being discharged, without treatment, into rivers, lakes, and seas. Air pollution from factories, coal-burning furnaces, and an increasing number of motor vehicles, particularly trucks and buses, are growing rapidly. Despite the fact that China's factories are not as hazardous as those in other industrializing countries, modernization has resulted in an increase in occupation injuries and illnesses. As a society embarked upon a program of rapid industrialization (somewhat moderated in recent years) with limited capital resources, "the additional cost of providing for industrial pollution control and safety is apparently often resisted" [61, p. 77]. According to Yang, Lin, and Lawson,

> Despite knowledge of the smoking-cancer relationship, China's cigarette consumption nearly doubled between 1979 and 1986. It is estimated that during the last ten years, half of the new smokers in the world were from China. Furthermore, it is projected that by the year 2025, 2 million Chinese may die each year from chronic diseases associated with smoking [77, p. 488].

ACHIEVEMENTS AND LIMITATIONS OF HEALTH CARE IN SOCIALIST-ORIENTED SOCIETIES

Our review of health care and health problems in socialist-oriented societies suggests the following observations:

1. External threats contributed to the emergence of a centralized structure in a number of socialist-oriented societies. In an effort to escape the vulnerability of underdeveloped, these defensive bureaucratic structures commonly adopted the path of least resistance and least cost, with resulting health consequences for the population.
2. In a similar manner, changes within the health care field in early socialist-oriented countries have been directed primarily at developing and modernizing the existing bourgeois medical care institutions while extending access to the broad masses.

3. In later socialist-oriented countries, those that emerged under the protective umbrella of an already existing political bloc, great attention has been devoted to experimentation with alternative, more participatory models, while still emphasizing broad accessibility and improved health.

These observations further underline the critical importance of examining questions of health and health care in terms of a macro-level framework that understands local and even national phenomena within their broader context within and beyond the medical arena. Ultimately, any attempt to create a socialist health system and socialism per se must not, as Wright so aptly asserts, focus "simply on the provision of various services by the state and various regulations of capital (as is the case under welfare capitalism), but also on the democratization of the forms of delivery of such services of administration of such regulations" [79, p. 124]. Hopefully, the demise of Stalinism and the ongoing crisis of the capitalist world system will serve to illustrate this argument. In this process, critical medical anthropology has an important role to play in providing careful analysis of health care systems in social context and in contributing to the direct application of this information in improving the quality of health care, accessibility of services, and popular empowerment within the health care domain.

REFERENCES

1. H. A. Baer, M. Singer, and J. Johnson (eds.), *Toward a Critical Medical Anthropology,* Special Issue of *Social Science and Medicine, 23*:2, 1986.
2. M. Singer, H. A. Baer, and E. Lazarus (eds.), *Critical Medical Anthropology: Theory and Method,* Special Issue of *Social Science and Medicine, 30*:2, 1990.
3. E. Krause, *Power and Illness: The Political Sociology of Health and Medical Care,* Elsevier, New York, 1977.
4. H. Waitzkin, *The Second Sickness: Contradictions of Capitalist Health Care,* MacMillan, New York, 1983.
5. M. Segall, On the Concept of a Socialist Health System: A Question of Marxist Epidemiology, *International Journal of Health Services, 13,* pp. 221-225, 1983.
6. R. Keesing, *Cultural Anthropology: A Contemporary Perspective* (2nd Edition), Holt, Rinehart and Winston, New York, 1981.
7. V. Navarro, The Limits of the World System Theory in Defining Capitalist and Socialist Formations, *Science and Society, 46,* pp. 77-90, 1982.
8. H. Sherman, *Radical Political Economy,* Basic Books, New York, 1972.
9. R. Tucker (ed.), *The Marx-Engels Reader* (2nd Edition), W. W. Norton, New York, 1978.
10. D. Lane, *Politics and Society in the USSR,* New York University Press, New York, 1978.
11. T. Long, On the Class Nature of Soviet-Type Societies: Two Perspectives from Eastern Europe, *Berkeley Journal of Sociology, 26,* pp. 157-188, 1981.
12. P. Clawson et al., Introduction to a Special Issue on the Soviet Union, *Review of Radical Political Economics, 13*:1, pp. iii-viii, 1981.
13. G. Markus, Western Marxism and Eastern Societies, *Dialectical Anthropology, 6,* pp. 291-318, 1982.
14. C. K. Chase-Dunn, Socialist States in the Capitalist World-Economy, in *Socialist States in the World-System,* C. K. Chase-Dunn (ed.), Sage, Beverly Hills, California, pp. 21-55, 1982.

15. R. Miliband, L. Panitch, and J. Saville (eds.), *Revolution Today: Aspirations & Realities— Socialist Register 1989,* Merlin Press, London, 1989.

16. W. K. Tabb (ed.), *The Future of Socialism: Perspectives from the Left,* Monthly Review Press, 1990.

17. R. Miliband and L. Panitch (eds.), *Communist Regimes: The Aftermath—Socialist Register 1991,* Merlin Press, London, 1991.

18. G. Silver and G. Tarpinian, Marxism and Socialism: A Response to Paul Sweezy and Ernest Mandel, *Review of Radical Political Economics, 13*:1, pp. 11-21, 1981.

19. K. N. Cameron, *Marxism: The Science of Society,* Bergin and Garvey, South Hadley, Massachusetts, 1985.

20. A. Szymanski, *Is the Red Flag Flying? The Political Economy of the Soviet Union Today,* Zed, London, 1979.

21. E. Mandel, The Laws of Motion in the Soviet Economy, *Review of Radical Political Economics, 13*:1, pp. 35-39, 1981.

22. E. Mandel, *Revolutionary Marxism Today,* New Left Books, London, 1979.

23. I. Wallerstein, *The Capitalist World-Economy,* Cambridge University Press, Cambridge, 1979.

24. I. Wallerstein, *The Politics of the World-Economy: The States, the Movements and the Civilizations,* Cambridge University Press, Cambridge, 1984.

25. T. Cliff, *State Capitalism in Russia,* Pluto, London, 1974.

26. C. Bettelheim, *Class Struggles in the USSR, First Period: 1917-1923,* Monthly Review Press, New York, 1976.

27. C. Bettelheim, *Class Struggles in the USSR: Second Period: 1923-1930,* Monthly Review Press, New York, 1978.

28. S. Amin, *Class and Nation: Historically and in the Current Crisis,* Monthly Review Press, New York, 1980.

29. R. Bahro, *The Alternative in Eastern Europe,* Verso, London, 1978.

30. P. M. Sweezy, *Post-Revolutionary Society,* Monthly Review Press, 1980.

31. R. H. Elling, *Cross-National Study of Health Systems,* Transaction, New Brunswick, New Jersey, 1980.

32. H. A. Baer, M. Singer, and J. Johnsen, Toward a Critical Medical Anthropology, *Social Science and Medicine, 23*:2, pp. 95-98, 1986.

33. A. Gouldner, *The Dialectic of Ideology and Technology: The Origins, Grammar, and Future of Ideology,* Seabury Press, New York, 1976.

34. D. Lane, *The Socialist Industrial State,* George Allen & Unwin, London, 1976.

35. V. Navarro, Workers' and Community Participation and Democratic Control in Cuba, *International Journal of Health Services, 10,* pp. 197-216, 1980.

36. M. Parenti, *Power and the Powerless,* St. Martin's Press, New York, 1978.

37. G. W. Domhoff, *Who Rules America Now? A View for the 80s,* Prentice-Hall, Englewood Cliffs, New Jersey, 1983.

38. A. Gorz, *Socialism and Revolution,* Anchor/Doubleday, Garden City, New York, 1973.

39. H. J. Sherman and J. L. Wood, *Sociology: Traditional and Radical Perspectives,* Harper & Row, New York, 1979.

40. J. Schwartz, A Future for Socialism, in *Communist Regimes: The Aftermath—The Socialist Register 1991,* Ralph Miliband and Leo Panitch (eds.), Merlin Press, London, pp. 67-94, 1991.

41. H. A. Baer, The Legitimation Crisis in the German Democratic Republic Before the Opening of the Wall: Views from Below, *Dialectical Anthropology, 17,* pp. 319-337, 1992.

42. R. Cox, "Real Socialism" in Historical Perspective, in *Communist Regimes: The Aftermath—The Socialist Register 1991,* Ralph Miliband and Leo Panitch (eds.), Merlin Press, London, pp. 169-193, 1991.
43. N. Chomsky, The Dawn, So Far, Is in the East, *The Nation,* January 29, 1990.
44. H. E. Siegrist, Socialized Medicine, in *National Health Care: Issues and Problems in Socialized Medicine,* R. Elling (ed.), Aldine-Atherton, Chicago, pp. 21-37, 1971.
45. W. A. Glaser, "Socialized Medicine" in Practice, in *National Health Care: Issues and Problems in Socialized Medicine,* R. Elling (ed.), Aldine-Atherton, Chicago, pp. 38-59, 1971.
46. M. Harris, *Cultural Anthropology,* Harper & Row, New York, 1983.
47. R. Miliband, *The State in Capitalist Society,* Basic Books, New York, 1969.
48. L. Doyal with I. Pennell, *The Political Economy of Health,* South End Press, Boston, 1979.
49. V. W. Sidel and R. Sidel, *A Healthy State: An International Perspective on the Crisis in United States Medical Care* (rev. ed.), Pantheon, New York, 1983.
50. N. K. Raffel, Health Services in the Union of Soviet Socialist Republic, in *Comparative Health Systems: Descriptive analyses of Fourteen National Health Systems,* M. W. Raffel (ed.), Pennsylvania State University, University Park, pp. 488-513, 1984.
51. V. Navarro, *Social Security and Medicine in the U.S.S.R.,* Lexington, Lexington, Massachusetts, 1977.
52. D. Lane, *Soviet Society Under Perestroika,* Unwin Hyman, Boston, 1990.
53. M. Feshbach and A. Friendly, Jr., *Ecocide in the USSR: Health and Nature Under Seige,* Basic Books, New York, 1992.
54. D. W. Light, Perestroika for Russian Health Care? *Footnotes* (American Sociological Association), *20:*3, p. 7, March 1992.
55. E. Wnuk-Lipinski and R. Illsley, Introduction to Symposium on Non-Market Economies in Health, *Social Science and Medicine, 31:*8, pp. 833-836, 1990.
56. C. M. Davis, The Soviet Health System: A National Health Care Service in a Socialist Society, in *Success and Crisis in National Health Systems: A Comparative Approach,* M. G. Field (ed.), Routledge, London, pp. 233-262, 1989.
57. M. R. Haug, The Erosion of Professional Authority: A Cross-Cultural Inquiry in the Case of the Physician, *Health and Society, 54,* pp. 83-106, 1976.
58. L. F. Millard, Health in Poland: From Crisis to Crisis, *International Journal of Health Services, 12,* pp. 497-515, 1982.
59. M. Sokolowska and A. Rychards, Alternatives in the Health Area: Poland in Comparative Perspective, in *Cross-National Research in Sociology,* L. Kohn (ed.), Sage, Beverly Hills, California, pp. 263-278, 1989.
60. D. E. Parmeless, G. Henderson, and M. S. Cohen, Medicine Under Socialism: Some Observations on Yugoslavia and China, *Social Science and Medicine, 16,* pp. 1389-1396, 1982.
61. V. W. Sidel and R. Sidel, *The Health of China,* Beacon, Boston, 1982.
62. M. M. Rosenthal and J. R. Greiner, The Barefoot Doctors of China, From Political Creation to Professionalization, *Human Organization, 41,* pp. 330-341, 1982.
63. R. C. Crozier, The Ideology of Medical Revivalism in Modern China, in *Asian Medical Systems,* C. Leslie (ed.), University of California Press, Berkeley, pp. 341-355, 1976.
64. T. Hu, Health Resources in the People's Republic of China, in *Comparative Health Systems: Descriptive Analyses of Fourteen National Health Systems,* Pennsylvania University Press, University Park, pp. 133-147, 1984.
65. S. Huang, Transforming China's Collective Health Care system: A Village Study, *Social Science and Medicine, 27,* pp. 879-888, 1988.

66. C. Inkels, Aging and Disability in China: Cultural Issues in Measurement and Interpretation, *Social Science and Medicine, 32,* pp. 649-665, 1991.
67. J. C. Escudero, Starting from Year One: The Politics of Health in Nicaragua, *International Journal of Health Services, 10,* pp. 647-656, 1980.
68. J. Donahue, The Politics of Health Care in Nicaragua Before and After the Revolution of 1979, *Human Organization, 42,* pp. 264-272, 1983.
69. J. Stubbs, *Cuba: The Test of Time,* Latin American Bureau, London, 1989.
70. D. Sanders and R. Davies, The Economy, the Health Sector and Child Care in Zimbabwe since Independence, *Social Science and Medicine, 7,* pp. 723-731, 1988.
71. R. Gould, Statement of Nicaragua's Health System, *Comparative Health Systems Newsletter, 4*:3, 1983.
72. J. M. Donahue, *The Nicaraguan Revolution in Health: From Somoza to the Sandinistas,* Bergin & Garvey, South Hadley, Massachusetts, 1986.
73. S. Cereseto, Socialism, Capitalism, and Inequality, *Insurgent Sociologist, 11*:2, pp. 5-29, 1982.
74. R. Cooper and A. Schatzkin, The Pattern of Mass Disease in the U.S.S.R.: A Product of Socialist or Capitalist Development?, *International Journal of Health Services, 12,* pp. 459-480, 1982.
75. E. Mensentseva and N. Rimachevskaya, The Soviet Country Profile: Health of the U.S.S.R. Population in the 70s and 80s—An Approach to a Comprehensible Analysis, *Social Science and Medicine, 31,* pp. 867-877, 1990.
76. B. Commoner, *Making Peace with the Planet,* Pantheon Books, New York, 1990.
77. P. Yang, V. Lin, and J. Lawson, Health Policy Reform in the People's Republic of China, *International Journal of Health Services, 32,* pp. 481-491, 1991.
78. J. A. Valdes-Brito and J. A. Henriquez, Health Status of the Cuban Population, *International Journal of Health Services, 13,* pp. 479-486, 1983.
79. E. O. Wright, Capitalism's Future, *Socialist Review, 13*:2, pp. 77-126, 1983.

CHAPTER 5

Studying Up:
The Political Economy
of Nuclear Regulation

As part of the larger endeavor of "reinventing anthropology" or developing a critical anthropology, Laura Nader urged anthropologists to "study up" [1]. More recently, John McKinlay argued that medical social scientists need to refocus their "attention away from those individuals and groups who are mistakenly held to be responsible for their condition, toward a range of broader upstream political and economic forces [2, p. 485]. In responding to Nader and McKinlays' recommendations, this chapter examines the political economy of state regulation of hazardous industries by considering the relationship between the Nuclear Regulatory Commission (NRC) and the Kerr-McGee Corporation, an energy conglomerate engaged in the mining, milling, and processing of radioactive materials. We view such case studies as part of critical anthropology's endeavor to make linkages between, on the one hand, transnational corporations, governments, foundations, and think tanks, and, on the other hand, the masses of both industrial and underdeveloped nations. Along with other critical anthropologists, including those specializing in medical anthropology, we seek to return to "one Enlightenment inheritance that we [anthropologists] have lost; the theoretical, instrumental unity of thought and action" [3, p. 435]. This does not mean, however, that we should simply go the way of conventional applied anthropology, which often serves as the handmaiden of the powers that be, but rather that we must make our knowledge available to those peoples who have been the traditional objects of our studies. As Marx so aptly observed, "The philosophers have only *interpreted* the world in various ways; the point, however, is to *change* it" [4, p. 245].

An overview of the voluminous literature on the role of the state in advanced capitalist societies indicates that it facilitates the process of capital accumulation and legitimates this activity in a variety of ways, including the creation of regulatory agencies ostensibly designed to protect public health but which actually serve to pacify its concerns. With respect to the nuclear industry, both of these functions were carried out under the aegis of the Atomic Energy Commission (AEC) until 1974. As an agency of the state, the AEC assumed the role of coordinating a highly complex nuclear fuel cycle which could be called into question at a number of points, including those of mining, milling, processing, and reprocessing of radioactive materials, reactor safety, and waste storage, transportation and disposal.

Because in time various grass-roots organizations began to question the merger of promotional and regulatory activities within the AEC, Congress passed legislation that created separate structures under the guise that these processes were now independent from each other. Yet, regulatory agencies, including the Nuclear Regulatory Commission, are arenas which permit little public input. As Szymanski observes,

> Although the regulatory commissions . . . are legally administrative agencies of the U.S. government, they function largely as parts of the industries they regulate. The private corporations dominate them by controlling appointments to the commission and providing staff, through official advisory committees and intensive lobbying, and promises of jobs for retiring commissioners and leading staff people. The governmental commissions reinforce and strengthen the private associations of corporations in each economic sector. They grant them legal powers to supervise, levy taxes, maintain internal courts, and impose sanctions, as well as the power to compel membership [5, p. 205].

This chapter traces Kerr-McGee's safety record from its uranium mining and milling operations in the Four Corners area to the Cimarron plutonium facility, where Karen Silkwood (a union activist who died mysteriously) was employed, to its uranium processing plant near Gore, Oklahoma. Despite a long history of safety and environmental accidents and violations, Kerr-McGee was permitted by the NRC to continue and to expand its operations. Drawing upon the Kerr-McGee–NRC connections and a detailed account of events prior to and after the rupture of a cylinder containing uranium hexafluoride on January 4, 1986, at the Gore facility, it is argued that the government regulatory system attempts to legitimate the activities of the nuclear industry rather than to protect workers and the public from the hazards associated with its operations.

In keeping with the commitment of critical medical anthropology to the empowerment of people in their struggle against hegemonic institutions, we do not purport to be conducting a "value-free" investigation of the relationship between the NRC and Kerr-McGee. Baer has been a member of the Arkansas Peace Center for nearly a decade and served on its board between 1986 and 1988 and again since 1990. His presence at various meetings and demonstrations reported in this chapter constituted a form of "partisan participation" as contrasted with traditional "participant observation" research [6]. As Singer states,

> advocacy, in the broad sense of putting knowledge to use for the purpose of social change, is the explicit aim of the anthropological endeavor. . . . The practical use of knowledge allows scholarship of a particular kind (based on an understanding of social life as a dialectical relationship between culture and history) while embracing commitment as a defining feature of anthropology [7, p. 548].

In conducting his research, Baer relied heavily upon various archival materials, including NRC reports which were readily available to him because the Arkansas

Peace Center was one of several intervenor groups that opposed various operations at Kerr-McGee's Sequoyah facility. As Nader argues, personal, public relations and internal organizational documents "may substitute for anthropological participation in some areas of culture that take long years of participation to really understand" [1, p. 307].

REGULATION OF THE NUCLEAR INDUSTRY: FROM THE AEC TO THE NRC

The American nuclear program emerged as an integral component of the military-industrial complex. The principal actors in this development were "the armed services, private industry and finance, the legislative and executive organs of government, intelligence organizations and to a lesser extent the emerging atomic bureaucracy, sections of the scientific and technological community and even elements of the trade union movement" [8, p. 5]. The Atomic Energy Act of 1946 established the Atomic Energy Commission (AEC) and charged it with the responsibility of promoting and regulating the new industry as well as establishing health and safety standards for nuclear operations. The AEC was to consist of five members appointed by the President for staggered five-year terms. The 1946 Act created the Congressional Joint Committee on Atomic Energy (JCAE) to oversee the activities of the AEC and to deal with proposals for nuclear-related legislation.

The linkages between the AEC and private industry were defined early on when in October 1947 the AEC created an Industrial Advisory Group for the purpose of exploring areas in which industry could participate in nuclear energy development. The Atomic Energy Act of 1954 loosened security precautions and permitted private ownership of nuclear facilities. While most of the early nuclear projects focused on military endeavors, beginning in the mid-1950s the AEC embarked upon a major public relations campaign to promote nuclear energy under the Atoms for Peace program. "In the 1960's, when utilities began to order nuclear power plants, the AEC assisted the utilities in easing public concern" [9, p. 70].

Despite such promotional efforts, a few groups challenged the safety of nuclear facilities. The International Union of Electric, Radio and Machine Workers formally contested in 1956 the construction of the Fermi fast breeder reactor near Detroit, arguing that the AEC should not have granted a provisional construction permit prior to a guarantee of adequate protection for the health and safety of the public [10]. For the most part, however, opposition to the rapidly growing nuclear industry remained muted prior to the late 1960s. Perhaps spurred on in part by a general disenchantment with American society expressed in the nuclear disarmament, civil rights, anti-Vietnam War, and environmental movements, an increasing number of Americans did become concerned with the environmental implications of nuclear development. However,

> The AEC ridiculed citizens who dared to question the safety of nuclear power even as it suppressed internal reports documenting nuclear's enormous potential health risks. It ignored such serious problems as waste disposal while it spent hundreds of millions of dollars developing the next generation of reactor

technology, the fast breeder. Perhaps most important of all, it approved construction and operation of nuclear power stations without first researching, establishing, and enforcing a system of rigorous safety standards [11, pp. 257-258].

In responding to charges about the incompatibility of promotional and regulatory functions within the same agency, the AEC in 1963 physically separated its promotional offices from its regulatory offices. Growing pressure from environmental groups and the passage of the National Environmental Policy Act of 1969, which received heavy labor union backing, forced the AEC to incorporate wider environmental standards. The Energy Reorganization Act of 1974 abolished the AEC and created the Energy Research and Development Administration (ERDA), which was assigned the task of developing nuclear weapons and nuclear power, and the Nuclear Regulatory Commission, which was authorized to regulate commercial nuclear power. In 1977 Congress dissolved the JCAE and dispersed its duties to various committees. Despite a purported separation of promotional and regulatory functions, the new NRC was "mostly staffed by those who staffed the AEC during its last years" [12, p. 81].

THE DISMAL SAFETY RECORD OF KERR-McGEE

While not as large as some of the twenty-four corporations (e.g., Westinghouse, General Electric, Exxon) that dominate the nuclear industry, as a result of key political connections Kerr-McGee headquartered in Oklahoma City grew into a major actor in the "Atomic Brotherhood" [11]. The Kerr-McGee Corporation had its roots in the Anderson & Kerr Drilling Company, started in 1929 by James L. Anderson and Robert S. Kerr [13]. Under the astute leadership of Dean A. McGee, who joined the growing oil company in the early 1940s, Kerr-McGee grew into an energy conglomerate. At the same time, Robert S. Kerr, first as Governor of Oklahoma and later as one of the most influential Senators in Washington, D.C. until his death in 1963, provided the political connections necessary to sustain this growth. With revenues of over 3.5 billion dollars, Kerr-McGee operations include petroleum drilling, coal mining, chemical production, timber cutting, and uranium mining and processing. By 1970 Kerr-McGee had become the largest uranium producer in the United States [14, p. 44] and with Gulf, controlled over half of the uranium reserves in the country [15, p. 268].

Kerr-McGee in Indian Country

Kerr-McGee entered the nuclear industry when in 1952 it purchased the Mesa Mine located in the Lukachukai Mountains section of the Navajo Reservation in New Mexico. Two years later, it opened a $3 million uranium mill near Shiprock, thirty-five miles east of the mine. In return for a lease to extract uranium on the reservation, Kerr-McGee hired 100 Navajo miners. According to Churchill and LaDuke,

> Wages for these non-union Navajo miners were low, averaging $1.60 per hour or approximately two-thirds of the then-prevailing off-reservation rate. The corporation cut operating costs significantly by lax enforcement of worker-safety regulations. In 1952, consequently, a federal mine inspector found that the

ventilation units in the mine's primary shaft were not in operation. Two years later the ventilation system was still not functioning properly. When the inspector returned in 1955, the ventilation blower ran out of gas during his visit. One report, from 1959, noted radiation levels in the Kerr-McGee shaft were ninety times the 'permissible' limit [16, p. 102].

Contrary to a provision in its lease to provide for the health of the miners, Kerr-McGee, as well as the Bureau of Indian Affairs and the AEC, failed to inform the Navajos that the uranium mining and milling could cause lung cancer. Although the International Commission of Radiological Protection had been tightening mining standards almost every year since 1925, the AEC asserted that its responsibility began once uranium ore was extracted from the ground, and displaced jurisdiction over miner safety to state governments, the Department of Interior's Bureaus of Mines and Indian Affairs, the Department of Health, Education and Welfare, or the Department of Labor [14].

The Mesa mines had been shut down by the time federal regulations were established for uranium mining in 1968, but other Kerr-McGee operations, such as the mining and milling facility at Ambrosia Lake near Grants, New Mexico, continued to spew uranium dust. After Kerr-McGee abandoned the Shiprock facility in the early 1970s, it left some seventy-one acres of uranium tailings behind. Since the pile lies next to the San Juan River, it seriously contaminated the water supply of several downstream communities. Furthermore, some of the uranium tailings left behind by Kerr-McGee and the Vanadium Corporation of America were mixed into building materials for new Navajo dwelling units [17, p. 155-156].

> Of the hundred-fifty-odd Navajo miners who worked underground at the Shiprock facility, eighteen had died of radiation-induced lung cancer by 1975. By 1980, twenty more were dead, and another ninety-five had contracted respiratory ailments and cancers. Birth defects such as cleft palate, leukemia, and other diseases commonly linked to increased radiation exposure have risen dramatically both at Shiprock and in the downstream communities [16, p. 103].

American taxpayers paid $12 million to cover the uranium tailings left by Kerr-McGee on the bank of the San Juan River [18].

Although Kerr-McGee closed the last of its uranium operations in New Mexico in January 1985, its Churchrock mine near Tuba City, Arizona, discharged some 80,000 gallons of radioactive water per day into local and downstream water supplies during the late 1980s.

Kerr-McGee and Karen Silkwood

To complement its mining and milling activities in the Four Corners area, Kerr-McGee undertook several additional processing operations associated with the uranium fuel cycle. In 1968 the company opened a facility on the Cimarron River near Crescent, Oklahoma, that converted uranium hexafluoride into nuclear fuel rod pellets. Two years later the firm constructed a facility next door for fabricating fuel pins. The AEC had licensed Kerr-McGee to keep up to 700 pounds of plutonium from spent nuclear fuel rods at the Cimarron plant. In August 1972, Karen Silkwood, a young woman of part Cherokee ancestry, began working as a laboratory assistant assigned to polish plutonium rod welds. When in November 1972, the Oil, Chemical and Atomic Workers (OCAW) local went on strike against Kerr-McGee for higher wages, better training and improved health and safety programs, Silkwood took her turn on the picket line.

Kerr-McGee provided its workers with minimal training in the handling of plutonium and routinely failed to inform them about its health hazards. Safety standards at the Cimarron facility were so marginal that Silkwood was exposed to high levels of radiation on three occasions within her first two years of employment there. She became increasingly alarmed about the company's poor health and safety practices when Kerr-McGee's stepped-up production, in the spring of 1973, translated into long work shifts, spills and contaminations [14, p. 14].

These events spurred Silkwood to run for the three-person steering committee of the OCAW local. When Silkwood and the other two committee members visited the Washington headquarters of the OCAW, Anthony Mazzochi, the union's head, arranged for them to report thirty-nine allegations of violations (20 of which the AEC later at least partially verified, including failure to reject cracked and chipped pellets) at the plutonium plant. After she discovered in November 1974 that she and her apartment, including food in the refrigerator, had been contaminated by high levels of plutonium, Silkwood began to systematically document safety abuses for the OCAW. On the evening of November 13, 1974, she was killed while driving to deliver additional evidence of safety violations to a New York Times reporter and an OCAW official.

> Although the police report indicated that she had fallen asleep at the wheel, a private investigation firm hired by the union found evidence that she had been struck from behind by another vehicle. The safety abuse documents were missing. The Federal Bureau of Investigation collaborated in the police report but did not release its own report [19, pp. 155-156].

After five employees were contaminated on December 17, 1974, "Kerr-McGee quietly announced that it would shut down its plutonium plant because it had completed its contract with ERDA and had no more buyers for plutonium fuel rods" [15, p. 72].

In April 1976, the House Small Business Committee's Subcommittee on Energy and Environment conducted a hearing on the Cimarron plutonium facility. In contrast to Karl Z. Morgan, a Professor at the Georgia Institute of Technology, who testified that the facility exhibited inadequate radiation protection and that Kerr-McGee's management had demonstrated "little concern" over long-term cancer risks, an NRC spokesperson responded, "We said there were no serious violations, but we did feel the company needed considerable improvement" [13, pp. 448-449].

The NRC released three major reports related to the Silkwood affair. In the first of these, although the NRC concluded that Silkwood and her apartment had been deliberately contaminated, it made no effort to determine the source of these contaminations. In the second report, the AEC downplayed the significance of its finding that indeed violations of quality assurance procedures for cracks and chips in sample pellets had occurred. While the third report confirmed in whole or in part twenty of the thirty-nine allegations made by the OCAW steering committee, "The AEC hastened to add, however, that only three of these were violations of AEC rules . . . [and] that these violations did not threaten the health and safety of the workers" [14, p. 108].

In May 1979 an Oklahoma City jury ordered Kerr-McGee to pay 10.5 million in punitive damages to the Silkwood estate for exposing Karen Silkwood to plutonium contamination and harassing her for union-related activities. Due to the company's appeal of the decision, the case lingered in the courts until August 1986 when Kerr-McGee paid a settlement of $1.38 million to the Silkwood estate.

Radioactive Waste Disposal at the Sequoyah Fuels Corporation

In 1970 Kerr-McGee opened a $20 million plant, called the Sequoyah facility which became Sequoyah Fuels Corporation in 1983, near the confluence of the Illinois and Arkansas Rivers in the Gore-Vian area of eastern Oklahoma. The Sequoyah plant is one of two facilities (the other being the Allied Chemical Corporation facility in Metropolis, Illinois) that convert "yellowcake" uranium oxide concentrate to uranium hexafluoride. Upon becoming liquefied, the uranium hexafluoride is drained into cylinders, where it solidifies before shipment to a Department of Energy (DOE) facility for uranium-235 enrichment in preparation for fabricating nuclear weapons, fuel, and medicine.

The principal waste by-product of the conversion process at the Sequoyah facility is a radioactive liquid substance called *raffinate* which contains traces of uranium-238, thorium-234, thorium-230 and radium-234. In conjunction with its application of September 23, 1969, for a license to carry out the conversion process, Kerr-McGee requested permission to dispose untreated raffinate by deep-well injection into the Arbuckle Formation, a dense to porous dolomite/limestone sediment containing salt water. Although the AEC granted a license for the conversion process, it rejected additional applications for the deep-well injection scheme in October 1970, September 1972, and January 1974 on the grounds that, contrary to Kerr-McGee's contention, the raffinate might not be contained by faults on four sides. The agency argued that the hydrological structure of the Arbuckle Formation could result in the flow of the radioactive liquid waste to fresh aquifers and even to the land surface.

Kerr-McGee did obtain permission to discharge the raffinite into two storage ponds with a combined capacity of 25,000,000 gallons. The Sequoyah facility first discharged waste into Pond No. 1 in January 1971 and Pond No. 2 in November of the same year. Liquid raffinate waste and sludge had been leaking since at least May 1974, when a nearby monitor indicated a 350-fold increase in uranium concentration. The leakage produced at least five areas of dead vegetation in the vicinity of Pond No. 2 between October 1976 and March 1984, when the NRC finally decided that the excess liquid should be removed to reduce seepage into the groundwater [20, p. 24]. Contrary to its own regulations, which required an empty pond in the possible event of a leak in ponds carrying raffinate, the NRC has permitted storage of waste in the reserve pond as well.

Instead of constructing additional ponds to store its rapidly growing raffinate waste, Kerr-McGee reapplied in 1982 to the NRC for a permit to utilize the deep-well injection method of disposal. By justifying approval of a previously rejected plan, the NRC authorized disposal of five million gallons of treated raffinate waste by deep-well injection in 1983, with "the possibility of increasing to twenty-five million gallons over the next five years" [20, p. 30]. The NRC accepted the plan on the grounds that the treated raffinate exhibits a drastically reduced radioisotope content than untreated raffinate. Expressing his enthusiasm about the treated raffinate, the manager of the Sequoyah facility boasted that the solution was safe to drink, despite the fact that Kerr-McGee's reported total Curie content of 31.14pCi/l was more than twice the Environmental Protection Agency's 15pCi/l limit for drinking water. In line with the Reagan administration's policy of transferring governmental responsibilities from the federal level to the state and local levels, the NRC turned jurisdiction of the injection well issue over to the Oklahoma Department of Health [21]. As we will see in greater detail in the next section of this chapter, approval of the deep-well injection served as the focus for the formation of what evolved into an environmental/peace coalition, protesting not only Kerr-McGee's current activities but also its proposal to produce nuclear materials for conventional armaments.

In the interim, between the earlier denial of the injection proposal and its acceptance, Kerr-McGee investigated alternative methods for disposing its radioactive wastes. In 1974, with NRC approval, the company initiated an experimental program in which it fertilized crops, such as Bermuda grass, rye and fescue, with treated raffinate. In 1979 the NRC permitted Kerr-McGee to graze twelve head of cattle on Bermuda grass on a 160-acre test plot near the Sequoyah facility [22, pp. 43-44]. Given expensive distribution and marketing costs and possible customer resistance to the notion of purchasing fertilizer with even traces of radioactive materials, Kerr-McGee allegedly considered the possibility of giving the treated raffinate away to local farmers. As an integral part of its effort to dispose of the treated raffinate, Kerr-McGee began purchasing large plots of land in surrounding counties. Between June 1980 and April 1982, the NRC granted the Sequoyah Fuels Corporation several license amendments allowing Kerr-McGee to use treated raffinate on its lands on a permanent basis and to release its crops publicly, including for cattle consumption, on the provision that they are not used directly as human food [23, p. 6].

The NRC allowed Kerr-McGee to routinely discharge about 5000 kg of uranium per year into a natural drainage ditch which flows into the Illinois River, the only federally-designated scenic waterway in the state of Oklahoma. In March 1984, the NRC finally asked Kerr-McGee to develop a better method, such as a discharge pipe or a black-topped ditch, for transferring wastes from the Sequoyah facility to the river. Sequoyah Fuels Corporation justified its disposal of uranium into the Illinois-Arkansas river system by asserting, without providing documentation, that "the natural flow in the Illinois River amounts to nearly 11,000 kilograms of uranium per year and the natural flow in the Arkansas River is approximately 250,000 kilograms of uranium per year" [24, p. 44].

Numerous spills of radioactive materials occurred at the Sequoyah facility prior to the national publicized rupture of a cylinder containing uranium fluoride gas [20]. In the spring of 1971, liquid raffinate from a settling basin overflowed its retention dike.

In September 1976, 100 pounds of UF6 were released inside the plant; 1450 pounds of uranyl nitrate hexadyrate spilled into a drainage stream flowing into the Illinois River in December 1978. In February 1982, a ruptured pipeline released an estimated 3000 gallons of liquid raffinate into a drainage ditch.

THE EMERGENCE OF THE
ENVIRONMENTAL/PEACE COALITION

Organized opposition to Kerr-McGee's waste disposal program was initiated by Native Americans for a Clean Environment (NACE), a group of Cherokees and associate non-Indian members whose mission is to educate people in eastern Oklahoma about the dangers of toxic wastes, particularly those emanating from the Sequoyah Fuels Corporation. Jessie Deer in Water, who resided at the time near Vian, decided to establish NACE due to her growing concern about environmental pollution from the Sequoyah facility. When a small notice appeared in the Sallisaw (Oklahoma) newspaper announcing that Kerr-McGee had applied to the Oklahoma Department of Health for a permanent permit, in lieu of its temporary permit, to deep-well inject treated raffinate, William Deer in Water brought it to his wife's attention. Shortly thereafter at a public meeting attended by about 200 people, a state health official defended the Sequoyah facility manager's contention that opponents could not stop Kerr-McGee from injecting its wastes into a deep well. An uproar ensued and the health officials quickly adjourned the meeting with the promise that another meeting would be convened in two weeks. When Deer in Water learned that Kerr-McGee was dumping waste into the Illinois River, she decided to establish NACE, which was formed in May 1985. As part of an informal health survey conducted by NACE, Deer in Water, who worked at the time as a beautician, began to query her patrons about local residents who had died of cancer in the past decade, resulting in her being laid off.

Of immediate concern to NACE was Kerr-McGee's plans to open a second facility at the Gore site which would convert depleted uranium hexafluoride into enriched uranium (UF4). The company applied on January 24, 1985, to the NRC for authorization to open such a facility. Kerr-McGee's application received support in a letter from Major General Peter Burbules dated May 14, 1985, stating that the military had been using UF4 in the fabrication of "penetrator munitions" (e.g., armor-piercing shells and shielding for military vehicles) from the DOE stockpile but felt that it was now "imperative" that private industry convert UF6 into UF4. NACE and Citizens Action for Safe Environment, a group of people residing within a fifty mile radius of the Sequoyah facility and concerned about arms proliferation and the environment, petitioned the NRC for a hearing on Kerr-McGee's proposed UF6-UF4 conversion operation. On July 25, 1985, the NRC ruled that

> the hearing requests do not give cause to exercise our discretion and grant a formal hearing under the 'public interest' standard . . . or to find due process concerns require that a formal hearing need be convened. Therefore, only an informal hearing need be instituted at this time [25].

In August 1985 NACE called for a demonstration by concerned groups and individuals. The demonstration, which was co-sponsored with the Arkansas Peace Center (APC) headquartered in Little Rock, drew more than 150 people to assemble at the front gates of the Sequoyah facility. In contrast to the white middle-class composition of most peace and environmental demonstrations, the event on September 21 included a substantial representation of Native Americans, African Americans, and Hispanics as well. Wilma Mankiller, the Vice-Chief of the Cherokee Nation and soon thereafter the first female chief of the tribe, and Winona LaDuke, a nationally-renowned Chippewa activist and the Director of Anishinable Akkeng (People's Land Organization), as well as others, spoke on behalf of NACE's demands. Prior to the demonstration, Mankiller had received a $150 check from Kerr-McGee with no explanatory letter, which she returned to the sender.

On September 20, 1985, the NRC renewed the Sequoyah Fuel Corporation's operating license, which had expired in October 1982. The Sequoyah facility operated for almost three years on a legal technicality that allowed a plant to continue production if it had applied for a license renewal. The report, which served as the basis for renewing the Sequoyah facility's license, noted that the fifteen recorded violations since the last renewal were excessive, and the presence of repeated problems indicated a lack of management oversight for operations [26]. Despite admission that compliance with regulations and license conditions at the Sequoyah facility was marginal, the evaluation team concluded that operations at the Sequoyah Fuels Operation "will not constitute an undue risk to the health and safety of the public" [26, p. 41]. Furthermore, in November, NRC staff recommended that the NRC grant Kerr-McGee a license for operating a UF6-UF4 conversion facility [27].

The Arkansas Peace Center and the National Water Center (headquartered in Eureka Springs, Arkansas) joined NACE and CASE as intervenors in the informal hearing which was initially slated to convene on December 17-18, 1985, but which was rescheduled for January 7-8, 1986. In addition to dealing with the proposed UF6-UF4 conversion facility, the intervenors hoped that the hearing, despite its informal designation, would provide them with an opportunity to address a wide array of peace and environmental issues and, more specifically, those relating to the hazards that the Sequoyah facility posed to Oklahomans and Arkansans. John Fry III, the NRC judge appointed to conduct the hearing, issued an order ruling on three categories of concerns raised by the intervenors [26]. On the grounds that they did not relate directly to the proposed UF6-UF4 conversion facility, he ruled that deep-well injection of effluents, determination of a safe level of radiation, creation of a nuclear waste dump, disposition of wet sludge in Pond No. 2, as well as several other items constituted "matters outside the scope of this proceeding." Some items, including critical accidents, decommissioning costs, transportation of UF6 to the plant of UF4 from the plant, and site suitability, were deemed to be "matters within the scope of proceeding but which require no further consideration." The intervenors were to direct their remarks at the hearing to selected items, such as the fact that Kerr-McGee had already begun construction of the UF6-UF4 conversion-facility without formal NRC authorization, the qualifications of plant personnel, and Kerr-McGee's environmental and accidental analyses. While the intervenors were far from satisfied with the limits placed on their rights to speak at the scheduled hearing, they hoped that the meeting would serve as a forum for communicating their concerns, if not to the NRC, at least to the general public. At any rate, the intervenors did achieve one small victory when Kerr-McGee abandoned its plan to pump wastes into a deep injection well, and the Oklahoma Department of Health sealed the well.

THE CYLINDER RUPTURE AND ITS AFTERMATH

The Accident of January 4, 1986

Three days before the NRC hearing scheduled to be convened in Fort Smith, Arkansas, about forty miles east of the Sequoyah facility, an unexpected but not entirely unforeseen tragedy, that vindicated the intervenor's concerns, occurred. At about 11:30 a.m. on January 4, 1986, an overfilled UF4 cylinder ruptured while it was being heated in a steam chest outside of the Sequoyah plant because the UF6 expanded as it changed from its solid to liquid phase. James Neil (Chief) Harrison, a twenty-six-year-old worker of African-American and Cherokee ancestry who was standing on a structure about twenty feet above and to the side of the steam, was enveloped suddenly by UF6 gas. Virginia Callison helped Harrison out of the dense cloud and, with several other workers, placed him in a car. Because they could not find one in the plant,

> The workers drove eight miles away to pick up a cannister of oxygen at a nursing home in Vian before taking Harrison to Sequoyah Memorial Hospital some eleven miles away in Sallisaw. Kerr-McGee had established no prior emergency plans with Memorial. Harrison was sent off to a larger hospital, Sparks Regional Medical Center in Fort Smith, Arkansas, twenty-one miles away, where he was pronounced dead soon after arrival [28].

A spokesperson at the hospital stated that Harrison died of toxic chemical exposure with hydrofluoric acid burns to the face and lungs [29].

Although the rupture occured outdoors, UF6 filtered into the lunchroom, where several workers were eating, through the facility's air conditioning and ventilation systems. Because Kerr-McGee had failed to make virtually any contingency plans for such an emergency, workers chaotically evacuated the plant and lined up against the compound fence gasping for air. The released gas separated in the thirty-five to forty mile/hour southward-blowing wind into uranyl flouride, a white, heavy, radioactive material which rapidly fell to the groud at the plant site, and highly corrosive hydrofluoric acid gas, which created a three square mile fog south of the plant. As the cloud dissipated, it drifted southward for at least eighteen miles. Over 100 workers and residents were taken to the hospitals in Sallisaw and Fort Smith, and twenty-nine of them were admitted for observation and treatment of exposure to the gas.

In the aftermath of the accident, officials at the Sequoyah facility and Kerr-McKee headquarters in Oklahoma City attempted to blame the workers for the accident.

> Richard Perles, director of corporate communications for Kerr-McGee, declared at a press briefing that the procedure being used by the workers at the time of the lethal release was contrary to company guidelines . . . But according to officials of the company and the U.S. Nuclear Regulatory Commission (NRC), the

workers had permission from shift supervisor Bill Bradley to heat the overfilled cylinder. Dearl Anderson, the maintenance mechanic, who has worked at the uranium processing plant for the last eleven years, says the heating procedure to remove an overload of uranium hexaflouride was frequently used at the plant [28, p. 23].

Reactions by the NRC and the Intervenors to the Accident

Jessie Deer in Water of NACE called on NRC Judge Frye to postpone the scheduled hearing for Kerr-McGee's request to process UF6 into UF4 until an investigation of the accident and environmental impact was made [29]. Bob Bland, an APC spokesperson, observed that "the very thing they [Kerr-McGee] said was not credible because of their safety devices happened right under their noses" [30].

The report, which served as the rationale for renewal of the Sequoyah Fuel Corporation's operating license just about three months prior to the accident, states, "The staff has identified the rupture of a hot cylinder containg liquid UF6, resulting in the release of UF6 to the main processing building and the environment, as the most likely scenario having potentially severe consequences for health and safety, and the environmet" [31, p. 20]. As a requirement for license renewal, the NRC asked Kerr-McGee to submit within six months, reports outlining handling procedures for cylinders containing UF6 and a detailed plan for mitigating the effects of UF6 release. After the accident, some NRC officials pointed to this requirement as proof that the agency was concerned about hazardous conditions at the Sequoyah facility. Commissioner Aselstine stated, "It [the required safety evaluation report] focuses on exactly what happened," and Commissioner Zech added, "It's just that it's a little late. It's very unfortunate that we didn't have it a little earlier" [quoted in 32]. Conversely, in the aftermath of the accident, NRC regional director Robert Martin dismissed the safety evaluation report as having been prepared by "low-level staff members" and being "stronger than need to be" [quoted in 33]. The NRC also gave the Sequoyah Fuels Corporation high marks for its safety record and the director of radiation protection at the Oklahoma Department of Health saw no reason to criticize the alarm procedure used by Kerr-McGee following the accident.

Two days after the accident, an NRC team supervised removal of topsoil and scrubbing of roads to remove uranium particles spilled by the cylinder rupture. An NRC spokesperson asserted that radiation levels resulting from the accident were very low [34, p. 3A]. The head of the NRC clean-up team noted that the cylinder ruptured while it was being heated by employees attempting to reduce its contents from 29,500 pounds to its rated capacity of 27,500 pounds, and explained that the cylinder was overfilled because it was "not positioned squarely on the scale so they weren't getting a true reading" [quoted in 34, p. 3A]. He did admit that several plant employees had been exposed to high levels of radiation. For the most part, however, NRC and Kerr-McGee officials emphasized the chemical rather than the nuclear nature of the accident, despite the fact that urine samples of residents in nearby towns indicated significant traces of uranium. Commissioner Frederick J. Bernthal argued, "To say we are responsible when we don't have the in-house expertise doesn't cut it" [quoted in 28, p. 23], but confessed that no other state or federal agency was monitoring chemical processing at the Sequoyah facility.

In lieu of the originally scheduled NRC hearing, NACE and the APC held a "citizens hearing" at the Sallisaw civic center on January 7. James Ikard, NACE's lawyer and one of the Silkwood lawyers, told the audience that the NRC essentially allows nuclear facilities to regulate themselves, does not conduct "surprise inspections," and rarely regards violations as serious enough to warrant fines. At the same time as the citizens' hearing, Kerr-McGee and NRC officials held a joint press conference at the Sequoyah facility. A cameraman who had filmed the press conference for a national television network commented on the apparently cozy relationship that he perceived between the NRC and Kerr-McGee officials to several people at the citizen's hearing [35, personal communication].

Investigation of the Accident

The NRC formed an Augmented Investigation team consisting of representatives from various federal and state government agencies to investigate the incident. Concerning the causes of the rupture, the team concluded that

(1) the physical equipment and facilities used for filling and weighing UF6 cylinders were inappropriate for safe use with 14-ton cylinders and (2) The training of workers in operating procedures and ensuring the implementation of these procedures were not carried out effectively [36, p. 4].

On March 13, 1986, James G. Randolph, the President of the Sequoyah Fuels Corporation, delivered a prepared statement before a closed NRC hearing. Although he lamented Harrison's death and expressed the company's intention to prevent a similar mishap in the future, he shifted some of the blame for the accident of January 4th to the workers, noting that "subsequent investigation has revealed that the filling procedures were not fully understood by some employees, and that, in some instances, those procedures were not uniformly followed" [quoted in 37, pp. 1, 3]. Randolph outlined changes in operating procedures, including expansion of the facility's emergency preparedness program, that Kerr-McGee intended to implement and assured the NRC that the Sequoyah facility would be safe for both employees and the public [37, p. 12].

In June 1986, the NRC released the report of the Lessons-Learned Group which was formed to prevent mishaps similar to the one of January 4 [38]. In addition to making numerous recommendations for improving the regulation of nuclear processing facilities, the report of the group sheds further light on various violations by Kerr-McGee and the failure of the NRC to carry out its stated role. Both the Sequoyah facility and the Allied Chemical facility routinely overfilled cylinders with UF6 gas and lacked instrumentation to measure pressure in a cylinder while it was being heated. Despite their commercial availability, both facilities did not use monitors for detecting UF6 releases. Although an emergency plan had been prepared by the parent company, its implementation remained unstated [38, p. 51]. The company failed to inform personnel about the specifics of its contingency plan. When corporate officials notified the NRC of the accident, they contacted the wrong office and did not report that the accident fell into the "general emergency" classification, nor did the NRC ask them whether it did. Finally, the contingency plan did not provide for training of support personnel, such as police, hospital workers, ambulance drivers, and state and county health officials.

Despite the fact that emergency response procedures for an event such as the cylinder rupture call for notification of other relevant agencies, the NRC failed to contact directly most of these, including the EPA, the Center for Disease Control and the Oklahoma Department of Health. In the weeks after the accident, the NRC and EPA argued that each of them did not possess jurisdiction for investigating the accident, apparently because the former defined it as a chemical event while the latter regarded it as a nuclear event. Although under the Clean Water Act Kerr-McGee should have reported the cylinder rupture to the EPA's National Response Center, the "criminal penalty provision is ambiguous with respect to a situation like the Sequoyah incident, where the licensee did not report to the National Response Center, but did report to the NRC" [39, p. 26].

In the months following the rupture of January 4, several additional groups and individuals joined NACE, the Arkansas Peace Center, and the National Water Center as intervenors against Kerr-McGee. The Carlile Area Resident Association, which confined its membership to individuals residing within a 2.5 mile radius of the Sequoyah facility, argued that the odorous fumes, danger from the facility, and the proposed waste site do or will adversely affect their property values. Environmental Action expressed alarm about the contamination of groundwater and the Illinois River. Barbara Synar, an aunt of U.S. Representative Michael Synar, requested that she be made party to the UF6-UF4 hearing on the grounds that the proposed facility would impair her health and devalue her property. People's Action for a Safe Environment, an organization based in Fayetteville, Arkansas, and the Cherokee nation also entered the case as intervenors.

Since the intervenors had every intention of referring to the conditions contributing to the accident on the January 4, Sequoyah Fuels attempted to counter their position by arguing that further discussion of the incident would be unnecessary because it "has been fully investigated by the NRC and numerous federal and state agencies and relevant Congressional committees" [39, p. 1]. The company added that it had fulfilled the commitments made at the NRC's hearing of March 13 by devising multiple precautions against the possibility of overfilling cylinders, implementing a comprehensive program of safety education, adding well-qualified managerial personnel to the faculty, clarifying the facility's operating procedures, and developing a new contingency plan and offsite emergency response plan.

Public Meetings Related to the Proposed Reopening of the Facility

Upon the initiation of Michael Synar, the representative from the Congressional District in which the Sequoyah facility is located, and following an inspection of the facility in early June, the NRC scheduled a "public meeting" in Gore, Oklahoma, on July 8-9 ostensibly to solicit comments concerning Kerr-McGee's request to resume UF6 production. The agency ruled that discussion of Kerr-McGee's waste disposal plan and the UF6-UF4 conversion process were matters outside the scope of the proceedings, but could be addressed in later proceedings. The NRC stated that individuals or organizations wishing to speak at the meetings should sign the "speakers' list" which would be made available one hour before the meeting. Organizations were allotted six minutes of speaking time, which could be divided up among individual members, and individuals or "concerned citizens" were allotted three minutes. The NRC also accepted written statements from interested parties.

Several hundred Sequoyah Fuels Corporation employees, their families, relatives, and business associates crowded into the high school auditorium in Gore equipped with company signs, badges and other paraphernalia. According to one of the intervenors, their presence "turned the meeting into an SFC pep rally and caused many citizens to leave in disgust after listening to hours of SFC employees giving testimony of loyalty" [40]. As an NRC representative admitted during the meeting when pressured by Bob Bland of the Arkansas Peace Center, the NRC sent a letter to all employees at the Sequoyah facility inviting them to present their concerns. Conversely, none of the intervenors received such a letter of invitation. Jessie Deer in Water first learned of the scheduled meeting when she read the legally required notice announcing it in the Sallisaw newspaper. NRC officials justified their differential treatment by arguing that Kerr-McGee employees would be the ones most affected by the opening or closing of the facility. When Kerr-McGee employees asked how they should represent themselves on the speakers' list, NRC officials, according to a member of the Arkansas Peace Center present at the proceedings, instructed them to identify themselves as "concerned citizens." When a second APC member registered on behalf of her organization, she was eliminated from the speakers' list. It was only after the intervenors objected that she was permitted to speak as a "concerned citizen."

Additionally, NRC officials rearranged the speakers' list so that pro-Kerr-McGee forces could express their views while the media was present. Jessie Deer in Water, who was among the first fifty or so to register to speak, was not able to do so until around 10:45 p.m. of the first day, well after the media had left. Pat Costner called for a "point of order" on the rearrangement of speakers, but NRC officials dismissed her complaint on the grounds that they were conducting a "meeting" rather than a "hearing." Bob Bland, the APC spokesperson, noted a point of order when again NRC officials began to rearrange the speakers' list on the second day of the proceedings. They replied that the media people were free to stay as long as they wished.

Kerr-McGee supporters asserted repeatedly that they needed the jobs provided by the plant, that all pre-existing hazards there had been eliminated, and that the plant's presence provided tax revenue for local schools and prosperity for local businesses. A Sequoyah facility engineer argued that birds would not nest at the plant site if it were not safe. When the intervenors or local critics of Kerr-McGee finished their allotted speaking time, Kerr-McGee supporters chanted that "time is up." When Jessie Deer in Water finally was permitted to speak, Kerr-McGee loyalists shouted "send her back to Berkeley," despite the fact that she had never been there. Wilma Mankiller spoke on behalf of the Cherokee Nation against Kerr-McGee. As a general rule, Kerr-McGee accused the intervenors as being "outside agitators."

Apparently wishing to avoid a confrontation, the NRC scheduled a hearing for September 10 in Washington, D.C., in order to decide on whether the Sequoyah facility should be reopened. When the intervenors, who had not been asked for input, learned of the hearing and objected, the NRC postponed it. On October 16, however, the NRC held a hearing in Washington, following which it summarily approved the reopening of the Sequoyah facility for the production of uranium hexafluoride. The NRC did make a few concessions to the intervenors by fining the Sequoyah Fuels Corporation its maximum limit of $310,000 and requiring the company to employ an "independent" monitoring firm to oversee the safety of its operations, with the provision that findings would be reported directly to the NRC. Despite these concessions, the intervenors felt they had won a few skirmishes but lost the war since the NRC approved Kerr-McGee's application for operating a UF6-UF4 conversion facility in early 1987. In late 1987 Kerr-McGee sold its Sequoyah facility to G.A. Technology, Inc., of San Diego, formerly named General Atomics, a partnership of Gulf Corporation and Shell [41].

THE POLITICAL ECONOMY OF NUCLEAR REGULATION

Initial state monopoly of nuclear materials, production and energy was a direct consequence of the U.S. military program during World War II and the ensuing Cold War era. David Lilienthal, the first chairperson of the AEC, emphasized that the commission intended to move away from the existing government monopoly by creating new profit-making opportunities for private industry. In December 1948 the Industrial Advisory Group recommended that the government provide industry with relevant information about atomic energy, promote direct personal contacts between civil servants and industrialists, enhance the effectiveness of industrial committees, and strengthen the contract system [8, p. 23].

While the corporate sector welcomed the opportunity for new avenues of profit-making, it demanded that the state cover the risks associated with the nuclear enterprise by sponsoring basic research, ensuring a minimal profit margin, and carrying the financial burden to potential nuclear mishaps. At the same time, the AEC faced from its beginning a serious problem of legitimacy and in large measure addressed this by emphasizing the purportedly peaceful dimensions of nuclear power. As Camilleri observes,

> [i]t was the function of the state to reassure the public that the cycle could be safely and effectively closed and to ensure that technical failures or political bottlenecks at any point in the cycle did not lead to the paralysis of the entire project [8].

The "revolving door" syndrome in which there is an interchange of personnel between state regulatory agencies and the private enterprises that they purportedly regulate well describes the relationship between the NRC and the nuclear industry. One study found that the four major federal agencies dealing with energy matters, namely the Energy Research and Development Administration, the Federal Energy Administration, the Nuclear Regulatory Commission and the Department of Interior, were "being run, to a substantial degree, by officials who used to work with private energy companies or organizations that have close dealing with the agencies" [42, p. 15].

In the case of the NRC, the study also revealed that: 71.5% (or 307) of the 429 NRC senior personnel have been employed by private enterprises active in the energy field; 90% (or 279) of these 307 employees came from private enterprises holding licenses, permits, or contracts from NRC. This represents 65% of NRC's top 429 personnel (Common Cause, 42, p. 15].

In keeping with this pattern, "The key nuclear-power policy positions within the Reagan administration were without exception filled with men either drawn directly from the nuclear industry or very sympathetic to its plight" [11, p. 212].

The historical record of the Kerr-McGee–NRC connection presented in this chapter indicates that, despite a consistent record of violations and nuclear mishaps by Kerr-McGee, the NRC has permitted the energy conglomerate essentially to monitor its own activities and to operate in a virtually unhampered manner. When NRC reports revealed some hazardous procedures, such as the potential for the rupture of a cylinder containing UF6 at the Sequoyah facility, upper-echelon officials tended to dismiss these as resulting from overzealous efforts on the part of rank-and-staff members. For the most part, such internal reports, while theoretically available to the public, are not readily accessible, are not consulted by the mainstream media, and are difficult for most people to interpret. In contrast to the lives that have been endangered by Kerr-McGee's dismal nuclear safety record, the contamination of the air and water by its waste disposal practices and accidents, and the millions of dollars that some of these practices have cost American taxpayers, the NRC has generally refrained from fining the company, preferring instead to admonish it periodically. Even the fine of $310,000 that the NRC imposed upon Kerr-McGee for the cylinder rupture on January 4, 1986, did not have a significant impact on the company's profit earnings.

In attempting to evade its regulatory functions, the NRC, as did its predecessor, has consistently displaced its responsibilities onto other agencies. Throughout its existence, the AEC "asserted that where there already were federal, state, or regional environmental standards it would not assess the environmental effect of the plant" [12, p. 81]. On matters relating to the thermal pollutants generated by nuclear power plants, the AEC insisted "that its purview was limited to radiological characteristics and that it had no jurisdiction over the thermal qualities of reactor effluent" [12, p. 45]. Eventually intervenors were successful in forcing the AEC to meet the requirements of the National Environmental Policy Act of 1969 concerning thermal and effluent standards. In the chaotic aftermath of the cylinder rupture at the Sequoyah facility on January 4, 1986, the NRC argued that since the accident was a chemical, rather than nuclear, it fell under the jurisdiction of the EPA. The Reagan administration's polities of deregulation and transferring regulatory functions from the federal government to state and local governments (another form of deregulation in the view of some) also relieved the NRC of jurisdiction over the disposal of radioactive wastes by Kerr-McGee into the Illinois River. This responsibility theoretically was to be undertaken by the Oklahoma Water Resources Board. Although Robert S. Kerr, Jr., serves as one of the members of the latter, he denies any conflict of interest on the grounds that he does not vote on matters affecting Kerr-McGee.

The NRC routinely grants construction permits for nuclear facilities on the basis of preliminary design information. In the case of Kerr-McGee's proposed design for a conversion facility, the NRC claimed that the licensing of the completed facility was not guaranteed [43]. Yet, as Ebbin and Kasper note,

> once an application for a permit to construct a power plant comes up for hearing, considerable capital expenditures have already been made and others arranged for, a site has been acquired, the staff of the AEC [and later the NRC], the applicant and the vendor have worked out the details of construction, and the Preliminary Safety Analysis Report (PSAR) has been submitted. Not until this point, after a significantly large allocation of both financial and manpower resources has already been made, do citizens privy to the plan [10, p. 6].

NRC (and earlier AEC) hearings and other public meetings constitute the most explicit mechanisms for legitimizing nuclear projects and defusing public controversy. According to Ebbin and Kasper, "the hearing process was originally designed to provide a mechanisms to inform the local citizenry of the benefits of a nuclear power generating plant" [10, p. 5]. Ironically, what the AEC intended to use as a promotional device altered with the advent of contested proceedings. As Rolph observes, "the rather unusual openness of the AEC's licensing process attracted opponents" [12, p. 42].

The NRC and its predecessor countered the growing strength of the anti-nuclear movement by developing a variety of strategies for limiting intervenor input into the hearings. During James Schlesinger's term as AEC chairperson, the agency instituted a prehearing conference which delineated the issues which could be considered at a hearing [13, p. 6]. As seen in NRC Administrative Judge Fyre's decision to categorize intervenor's petitions against the Sequoyah Fuel Corporation's operations into matters outside the scope of the scheduled proceeding, those within its scope but not warranting further consideration, and a few that actually could be addressed at the "informal" as opposed to "formal" hearing, the NRC's immediate response, "with rare exceptions, is to find some justification for opposing the intervenor's positions on all substantive and procedural issues, a stance that continues during the entire hearing process" [44, p. 68]. If intervenors raise general safety problems which are common to many nuclear reactors or plant systems, the NRC often label such issues as "generic" ones which allegedly will be addressed at a larger proceeding. In reality, "the NRC has left some of the most serious safety problems unresolved for years—in some instances longer than a decade" [44, p. 8]. Removal of generic issues from hearings seriously limits the ability of intervenors to argue their position.

According to the Union of Concerned Scientists, the NRC's antipathy "toward the public is demonstrated by the behavior of the staff and hearing boards, by specific Commission actions unfavorable to public participants, and in attempts to 'reform' the licensing process by restricting public participation" [44, p. 67]. NRC staff exhibited such an attitude at the "public meeting" of July 7-8, 1986, in Gore, Oklahoma, when they consistently attempted to restrict the intervenor's input and their access to media coverage. The NRC's decision to conduct the hearing dealing with the proposed reopening of the Sequoyah facility in Washington rather than at a more accessible local site also illustrate a general pattern of hampering public involvement in hearings.

To a large extent, the relationship involving the interconnection between the nuclear corporations and their governmental sponsors and intervenors constitutes a form of class conflict. The regulating process serves to contain and reproduce "class conflict within the state" [45, p. 65]. In contrast to the nuclear industry, intervenor groups have access to limited financial resources and scientific and technological expertise. Despite this, as Ebbin and Kasper state,

> It follows that the burden of raising issues and proving shortcomings in safety, environmental, and quality assurance programs lies with the intervenors, the Agency having been satisfied earlier in the application process that such matters had already been sufficiently provided for [10, p. 7].

The intervenors who opposed Kerr-McGee's operations at the Sequoyah facility for the most part educated themselves on issues relating to the case. Furthermore, the intervenors often must rely upon reports and documents that the company and the NRC are willing to release to them. In essence, intervenors must challenge both the applicant and the NRC at licensing or other hearings. Nevertheless, intervenor pressure sometimes does force nuclear industries to alter their practices, as occurred when the Sequoyah Fuels Corporation plugged, at least temporarily, its deep-injection well. In other instances, such as the NRC's recent requirement that Kerr-McGee pay for "independent" monitoring of its Sequoyah facility, it takes a life-threatening accident to bring about stricter regulation. Still,

> Against the tremendous obstacles erected to meaningful public participation, intervenors have had some significant successes. Safety improvements have resulted from intervenors or individual members of the public raising issues on their own, or with the aid of whistleblowers. In some cases, of their verdicts on issues raised in the hearings; in others, boards issue requirements based on agreements negotiated between the utilities and intervenors. Improvements have also resulted from public participation in rule making and other decision making processes [42, p. 78].

On the whole, the NRC does not function as a neutral arbiter of class conflict but as an ally of the nuclear industry. As Szymanski observes, "[S]tate-sanctioned self regulation gives the illusion of popular control over the corporations, thereby 'cooling out' popular hostility" [5, p. 204]. At the same time, it is mandatory that a single actor, such as Kerr-McGee, not endanger the larger nuclear enterprise by overstepping the social boundaries which protect capital accumulation and property relations. To prevent such a scenario, the state must impose sanctions, monetary or symbolic, to redefine the ground rules by which individual corporations must comply in order to preserve the legitimacy of the capitalist system. In the end, even the maximum monetary sanctions, such as the $310,000 fine received by Kerr-McGee for the cylinder rupture at the Sequoyah facility, that state regulatory agencies impose on corporations tend to be more symbolic than financially punitive given the profits reaped by ignoring health and safety issues.

CONCLUSION

This chapter examines the relationship between the Kerr-McGee Corporation and the Nuclear Regulatory Commission in order to shed further light upon the political economy of nuclear regulation. The Atomic Energy Act of 1946 specified that private possession of fissionable materials would be conditional on the licensee observing certain safety standards.

> Nuclear law was . . . designed to protect against radiation hazards connected with the civilian application of nuclear energy and radioactive substances, and to prevent the non-peaceful uses of nuclear energy by means of a safe-guards system. Nuclear law thus required to set health and safety standards for radio-logical protection, to regulate the licensing and supervision of nuclear activities, and to provide for sanctions for offenses against nuclear regulations. Its primary function was to inspire public confidence in nuclear energy at a time of mounting public anxiety [8, p. 69].

As our examination of Kerr-McGee's safety record from Indian Country to Silkwood to Gore reveals, both the NRC and the AEC have historically overlooked or minimized a consistent pattern of hazardous procedures, accidents, and violations by the energy conglomerate, and have thus failed to carry out their stated regulatory functions. As the contradictory merger of promotional and regulatory activities within the same agency became increasingly apparent to the public, the state dismantled the AEC and created the NRC as a purportedly autonomous regulatory agency. In reality, the NRC continued to function as an integral part of the state's legitimation role. Its hearings continued to serve as pro forma events designed to depoliticize popular opposition not only to specific nuclear facilities but also to the larger nuclear enterprise. At the same time, the NRC in order to give at least token recognition to public concern was forced to make some concessions to the intervenors. While at times the NRC had demanded that nuclear industries implement improved procedures, it has tended to not fully enforce these demands.

While Kerr-McGee's nuclear activities have tended to be confined to the nuclear reactor fuel cycle, its application for a license to convert depleted $UF6$ into enriched $UF4$ to be used in conventional armaments serves to remind us of the military nature of the nuclear enterprise. Civilian nuclear power grew directly out of the military program and can be easily altered to sustain new military projects. It seems likely that as American capitalism finds itself threatened by counterhegemonic movements around the world, the existing relationship between nuclear energy and nuclear arms production will become increasingly apparent, despite the end of the Cold War. Furthermore, this case study of the relationship between Kerr-McGee and the NRC illustrates one more example of how the state functions not only as a guarantor of corporate profit-making but also as a regulator of working class resistance to dangerous technical projects. As Levine observes, the state channels "working-class struggles within parameters compatible with capitalist social relations of production, thereby short-circuiting independent working-class political organization" [46, p. 104]. Critical anthropologists engaged in partisan observation can provide insights to counter-hegemonic groups that hopefully will avert the success of such tactics.

REFERENCES

1. L. Nader, Up the Anthropologist—Perspectives Gained From Studying Up, in *Reinventing Anthropology,* D. Hymes (ed.), Random House, New York, pp. 284-311, 1972.
2. J. McKinlay, A Case for Refocusing Upstream: The Political Economy of Illness, in *The Sociology of Health and Illness: Critical Perspectives,* P. Conrad and R. Kern (eds.), St. Martin's Press, New York, 1985.
3. S. Diamond, A Revolutionary Discipline, *Current Anthropology, 5,* pp. 432-436, 1964.
4. K. Marx, Theses on Feuerbach, in *Marx and Engels: Basic Writings on Politics and Philosophy,* Lewis S. Feuer (ed.), Doubleday/Anchor, Garden City, New York, pp. 243-245, 159, 1959.
5. A. Szymanski, *The Capitalist State and the Politics of Class,* Winthrop, Cambridge, Massachusetts, 1978.
6. M. D. Caufield, Participant Observation or Partisan Participation?, in *The Politics of Anthropology: From Colonialism and Sexism Toward a View From Below,* G. Huizer and B. Mannheim (eds.), Mouton, The Hague, pp. 182-212, 1979.
7. M. Singer, Another Perspective on Advocacy, *Current Anthropology, 31,* pp. 548-550, 1990.
8. J. Camilleri, *The State and Nuclear Power: Conflict and Control in the Western World,* University of Washington Press, Seattle, 1984.
9. S. Hiltgartner, R. Bell, and R. O'Connor, *Nukespeak: The Selling of Nuclear Technology in America,* Penguin, New York, 1982.
10. S. Ebbin and R. Kasper, *Citizen Groups and the Nuclear Power Controversy: Uses of Scientific and Technological Information,* MIT Press, Cambridge, Massachusetts, 1976.
11. M. Hertsgaard, *Nuclear, Inc.: The Men and Money Behind Nuclear Energy,* Pantheon, New York, 1983.
12. E. Rolph, *Regulation of Nuclear Power: The Case of the Light Weight Reactor,* Rand, Santa Monica, California, 1977.
13. J. Ezell, *Innovations in Energy: The Men and Money Behind Nuclear Energy,* University of Oklahoma Press, Norman, 1979.
14. R. Raskhe, *The Killing of Karen Silkwood: The Story Behind the Kerr-McGee Plutonium Case,* Penguin, New York, 1981.
15. R. Nader and J. Abbotts, *The Menace of Atomic Energy,* Nortoon, New York, 1977.
16. W. Churchill and W. LaDuke, Radioactive Colonization and Native Americans, *Socialist Review, 81,* pp. 95-119, 1985.
17. R. Weyler, *Blood of the Land: The Government and Corporate War Against the American Indian Movement,* Random House, New York, 1982.
18. *APC Agenda,* October 1985.
19. J. Price, *The Antinuclear Movement,* Twayne, Boston, 1982.
20. R. Phillips, *The Kerr-McGee Uranium Processing Facility Near Gore, Oklahoma: A Case Study in Radioactive Waste Management, Revised and Updated Version,* unpublished manuscript, July 8, 1985.
21. *N.A.C.E. Fact Sheet,* n.d.
22. Uranium Waste as Fertilizer, *Chemical Week,* October 24, pp. 3-4, 1979.
23. P. Costner, *Motion to Reconsider: Memorandum to the NRC, National Water Center,* Eureka Springs, Arkansas, June 13, 1986.
24. Response to Sequoyah Fuels Corporation to Petitions Concerning the Proposed UF6-UF4 Conversion Facility, *Sequoyah Fuels Corporation,* 1986.
25. Nuclear Regulatory Commission, *Memorandum and Order in the Matter of Sequoyah Fuels Corporation,* November 5, 1985.

26. Nuclear Regulatory Commission, *Safety Evaluation Report by the Division of Fuel Cycle and Material Safety Related to the NRC Source Material License Renewal for Sequoyah Fuels Corporation UF6 Conversion Plant,* September 20, 1985.
27. D. Cool, *Safety Evaluation Report by the Director of Fuel Cycle and Material Safety Related to the NRC Source Material License Amendment for Sequoyah Fuels Corporation Depleted UF6-UF4 Conversion Facility,* Gore, Oklahoma, November 11, 1985.
28. D. Bernstein and C. Blitt, Lethal Dose: The Untold Story at Kerr-McGee, *The Progressive, 50,* 1986.
29. *Arkansas Gazette,* p. 3A, January 6, 1986.
30. *Southwest Times Recorder,* Fort Smith, Arkansas, January 5, 1986.
31. Nuclear Regulatory Commission, *Safety Evaluation Report,* September 20, 1985.
32. *Southwest Times Recorder,* January 11, 1986.
33. *Guardian,* January 22, 1986.
34. *Arkansas Gazette,* p. 3A, January 7, 1986.
35. Personal communication with Hans Baer.
36. Nuclear Regulatory Commission, *Rupture of Model 48Y UF6 Cylinder and Release of Uranium Hexafluoride: Sequoyah Fuels Facility, 4 January, 1986,* Nuclear Regulatory Commission, Region IV, Denver, February 1986.
37. J. Randolph, *Statement Before Nuclear Commission Concerning Sequoyah Facility Incident of 4 January, 1986,* Sequoyah Fuels Corporation, March 13, 1986.
38. Nuclear Regulatory Commission, *Release of UF6 From a Ruptured Model 48Y Cylinder at Sequoyah Fuels Corporation Facility: Lessons-Learned Report,* June 1986.
39. *Sequoyah Fuels Corporation,* Memorandum, July 1986.
40. E. Lammers, CARA's Response to the Presiding Officer's Memorandum Recommending That the Commission Institute Additional Procedures: Memorandum Before NRC, July 31, 1986.
41. *N.A.C.E. Newsletter,* December 1987.
42. Common Cause, *Serving Two Masters: A Common Cause Study of Conflicts of Interest in the Executive Branch,* Common Cause, Washington, D.C., 1976.
43. *N.A.C.E. Newsletter,* August 1986.
44. Union of Concerned Scientists, *Safety Second: A Critical Evaluation of the NRC's First Decade,* Union of Concerned Scientists, Washington, D.C., February 1985.
45. P. Freitag, Class Conflict and the Rise of Government Regulation, *Insurgent Sociologist, 12:*4, pp. 51-65, 1985.
46. R. F. Levine, Bringing Classes Back In: State Theory and Theories of the States, in *Recapturing Marxism: An Appraisal of Recent Trends in Sociological Theory,* R. F. Levine and J. Lembcke (eds.), Praeger, New York, pp. 96-116, 1987.

Section C:

The Intermediate-Social Level

CHAPTER 6

The American Dominative Medical System as a Reflection of Social Relations in the Larger Society

In keeping with Navarro's assertion that classes as well as races and sexes within capitalist societies "have different ideologies which also appear in different forms of culture" [1, p. 171], it may be argued that these social categories also construct different medical systems to coincide with their respective views of reality. In contrast to a fair number of medical anthropologists, who observe that complex societies, including the United States, exhibit a pattern of medical pluralism— multiple, often antagonistic medical systems in the same society, many neo-Marxian health social scientists confine their attention to the dominant capital-intensive system of medicine and ignore or at best give fleeting attention to alternative medical systems [2-6]. Critical medical anthropology, which builds on the work of the political economic tradition in health research, attempts to overcome these shortcomings.

CMA recognizes that medicine has served as an arena of class struggle in advanced capitalist societies. Although bourgeois medicine is presently the dominant medical paradigm in advanced capitalist societies, it is not the only existing medical system nor has its hegemony always been so pervasive. The medical systems of complex societies are characterized by pluralism. However, these systems are hierarchical rather than adjacent in that bourgeois medicine enjoys a dominant status over heterodox and ethnomedical practices. This dominative status is legitimized in many advanced capitalist countries by laws that give bourgeois medicine a monopoly over certain medical practices, and limit or prohibit the practice of other types of healers. Various heterodox medical systems, such as Ayurveda in India, natural medicine (*Naturheilhunde*) in Germany, and chiropractic in the United States, Canada, Australia, and New Zealand, may have their own professional associations, schools, hospitals, and clinics and thus replicate the social organization of bourgeois medicine. Conversely, in much folk and popular culture medicine is practiced and learned outside of bureaucratic settings.

This chapter attempts to provide a corrective to the paucity of neo-Marxian analyses of medical pluralism by viewing the American medical system as a reflection of class, racial/ethnic, and gender relations in the larger society. It traces the evolution of the American medical system from a relatively pluralistic one in which no single medical system was clearly dominant to a dominative one in which bourgeois medicine achieved dominance over competing systems. In addition to replicating social divisions in the larger society, it is argued that the American dominative medical system constitutes an arena of struggle among these social divisions.

As American capitalism evolved from a competitive to a monopoly form, the bourgeoisie found it necessary to exert control over an increasingly restless populace. Along with the state and education, medicine became yet another powerful hegemonic vehicle by which the corporate class came to indirectly legitimate capital accumulation and to filter its view of reality down to the masses. With its emphasis upon pathogens as the external cause of disease, "scientific medicine" or "biomedicine" provided the capitalist class with a paradigm that neglected the social roots of illness, but yet could in at least some instances restore workers back to a level of functional health essential to capital accumulation. This paradigm, in the form of the germ theory, focused on discrete, specific and external agents of disease and diverted attention from the social origins of illness.

Given its professional dominance, the relationship between bourgeois medicine and alternative medical systems has been characterized by processes of annihilation, restriction, absorption, and even collaboration. In order to survive, some heterodox medical systems, as manifested in intraprofessional struggles between "purists" and "mixers," incorporated more and more philosophical and therapeutic dimensions of bourgeois medicine. However, since certain strategic elites ultimately shape health policy, the power of bourgeois medicine over competing medical systems is delegated rather than absolute. As Navarro observes, "[t]he medical profession is a stratum of trustworthy representatives to whom the bourgeoisie delegates some of its authority to run the house of medicine" [1, p. 27]. Yet, the state increasingly has come to act as an arena of class struggle and to assume the role of pacifying social dissent and resolving the contradictions of a capitalist society, including those in the health sector. Therefore, it periodically must make concessions to alternative health practitioners and their clients, who often belong to lower-middle, working and even lower social classes. Corporate and government elites involved in health policy decision-making may partially or completely legitimate a particular alternative medical system by licensing its practitioners, certifying its educational institutions, and providing subsidies for patient care and medical research.

Consequently, some alternative practitioners, even in Western society (e.g., osteopaths, chiropractors, Christian Science practitioners, folk healers), have been able to override opposition by bourgeois medicine to their licensing or even provision of services in bourgeois medical settings. Furthermore, the corporate class and its state sponsors may provide support of one sort or other to alternative medical systems if they feel that these systems serve certain functions for them or are cheaper than bourgeois medicine. Conversely, patterns of legitimation and even professionalization of various alternatives may illustrate, on the one hand, that indeed the dominance of organized bourgeois medicine is limited, while on the other, reflect the growing accommodation by alternative practitioners to a reductionist disease theory, which is compatible with capitalist ideology, and to the bourgeois medical model of organization and social control.

THE EVOLUTION OF AMERICAN MEDICINE:
FROM A PLURALISTIC TO A DOMINATIVE SYSTEM

The evolution of the American medical system from a relatively pluralistic to a dominative form occurred in the wake of the transition of the American political economy from competitive capitalism to monopoly capitalism. Over the course of the nineteenth century, the American medical system came increasingly to reflect the great cultural, regional, class, racial/ethnic and gender diversities of this era. The first part of the nineteenth century witnessed the emergence of three major heterodox medical systems, namely Thomsonanism, eclecticism, and homeopathy. Whereas as the latter appealed largely to the affluent social strata, the former two become popular among more ordinary people, particularly in rural areas and small towns. Many middle-class people were attracted to the health reform movement of which Grahamism and hydropathy became the overt and institutionalized expressions. Beginning in 1860s, Christian Science as a religious healing system began to gain popularity among certain segments, particularly women, of the urban middle-class. During the final decades of the nineteenth century, osteopathy and chiropractic found appeal among farmers and working class people in small towns. Various forms of Euro-American heterodox medicine as well as African-American ethnomedicine drew upon Native American medicine in their creation of eclectic modes of therapy.

Berliner maintains that two "medical modes of production" coexisted in early nineteenth-century American society—a "domestic mode" in which medical care was produced and performed as a use value, generally within the family, and a "petty commodity mode" in which medical care assumed exchange value [7]. The domestic mode actually consisted of a variety of folk medical systems, including Euro-American ethnomedicine, African-American ethnomedicine, Native American ethnomedicine, bonesetting, and cure-all potion sellers. On the American frontier, these folk systems often liberally borrowed from one another and to some degree coalesced into a syncretic amalgam. According to Berliner,

> Medications tended to be botanic and herbal, reflecting the agrarian life of the population. The beginning of the rural to urban migration and the associated demise of the extended family and the generational community led to the need for a new mode of health care and health-care delivery—one more suited to the increasingly urban environment. For the majority of people in the United States, the notion of paying a healer for medical systems was both novel and frowned upon [7, p. 164].

Despite the emergence of a Popular Health Movement that protested the new petty commodity mode of medicine, most regular as well as heterodox physicians practiced within it.

The Emergence of Professionalized Heterodox Medical Systems

Regular or allopathic medicine and homeopathic medicine constituted the two principal species of the petty commodity mode of medical production in that they were performed by trained physicians who charged a fee for their services. While allopathy with its heroic procedures, such as bleeding, leeching, and strong drugs, functioned as virtually the sole form of professionalized medicine during the eighteenth century, homeopathy as an "extremely minimalist medicine" imported from Europe in the mid 1820s found a niche in the competitive medical market-place of the new American republic [7]. Homeopathy initially appealed to some lower-class people, but its professional orientation quickly transformed it into a fashionable form of medicine for the wealthy.

As a professionalized heterodox medical system, homeopathy posed a threat to regular physicians and prompted them to establish the American Medical Association in 1847 [8]. Nonetheless, homeopathic physicians maintained therapeutic links with regular medicine. Samuel Hahnemann, the founder of homeopathy, was a German physician who was disturbed by the tendency of allopathic physicians to fight disease with heavy doses of several drugs taken in combination. According to Rothstein, "the early American homeopaths were all well educated and cultured physicians" [8, p. 160]. Homeopathy continued to attract regular physicians to its ranks as late as the final decades of the nineteenth century. In 1845 the American Institute of Homeopathy (AIH) restricted membership only to physicians who had received a regular medical education [9]. Like other emerging heterodox medical systems, homeopaths quickly divided into various shades of "purists" and "mixers." The purists or "high" homeopaths subscribed to the belief that a very diluted dosage acts as the most potent drug, whereas the mixers or "lows" not only administered low potency homeopathic drugs but also allopathic ones as well. Since homeopaths were barred from regular medical societies, hospitals, college faculties, and consultations with regular physicians, they established their own hospitals and medical schools. As Rothstein observes,

> [t]he wealth and influence of their clientele enabled homeopaths to amass an impressive number of institutions during the last decades of the century. In 1898, homeopaths had 9 national societies, 33 state societies, 85 local societies and 39 other local organizations, 66 general homeopathic hospitals, 74 speciality homeopathic hospitals, 57 homeopathic dispensaries, 20 homeopathic medical colleges, and 31 homeopathic medical journals [8, p. 236].

In contrast to homeopathy, other variants of the petty mode of medical production appealed to frontier people, farmers, and the growing urban proletariat. Samuel Thomson, a botanic practitioner reared on a New Hampshire farm, systematized the principles of the most popular variant of these petty modes by combining the use of over sixty botanicals with steam baths and the theory that disease resulted from the loss of body heat. Thomsonianism became an integral part of the "Popular Health Movement, a loose populist movement of lay healers, herbal practitioners, artisans, farmers, and working people who fought to remove the legal sanctions that protected the privileged position of physicians" [10, p. 63].

Contrary to its initial emphasis on self-care, Thomsonianism underwent an institutionalization and professionalization of its own, and became supplanted by eclecticism after 1850. Wooster Beach, a regular medical school graduate, dubbed himself an "eclectic" because he blended allopathy with the techniques of Thomsonians, "Indian doctors," herbalists, and others. Although the eclectics initially used botanical drugs as their major therapeutic modality, most of them eventually incorporated allopathic drugs and procedures into their regimen of treatment. As Rothstein observes,

> the eclectics' small town practices probably enhanced their influence and political power, because eclectic physicians were often the only physicians in their communities. This gave them the enthusiastic support of the local residents in any state-wide battle with the regular physicians [8, p. 170].

Christian Science, Osteopathy, and Chiropractic

At the same time that the allopaths were beginning to consolidate their position by lobbying for licensing laws, and the homeopaths and eclectics were incorporating more and more aspects of regular medicine into their respective regimens of treatment, several new alternative medical systems appeared in the last decades of the nineteenth century. In 1866 Mary Baker Eddy, the founder of Christian Science, announced that God revealed to her the "key" by which to heal herself of an injury from a fall that physicians had declared incurable. She was influenced by the teachings of Phineas Parkhurst Quimbey, a mesmeric healer who cured her [11, pp. 58-60]. Viewing material reality, including disease and illness, as illusory, Eddy asserted that "mental healing" restores health by eradicating this misconception. Christian Science healing is predicated on the patient realizing "that it is impossible to be sick. The practitioner's task in large part is to assist the patient in achieving this realization" [12, p. 3]. It took homeopathy's administration of infinitesimal dosages to its ultimate extension by eliminating drugs altogether. In large measure, Christian Science initially functioned as a protest movement on the part of upper and middle-class women who rejected the restrictive lifestyle that male physicians prescribed for them. During a period when the allopathic profession placed tremendous barriers upon the admission of women into its ranks, the fact that 90 percent of some 3,156 Christian Science practitioners in 1901 were female strongly suggests that Christian Science provided an alternative avenue for obtaining the prestige that healing in all societies commands [13, p. 139]. Since Christian Scientists did not administer drugs, perform surgery, manipulate or touch the patient, although they do charge for their services [12], it appears that regular physicians did not regard them as serious an economic threat as other heterodox practitioners.

Whereas Christian Science found its greatest appeal among certain segments of New England petite-bourgeois society, osteopathy and chiropractic, the other two major heterodox medical systems of late nineteenth-century America, reflected the aspirations of Midwestern populism. As systems of manipulative therapy, they both posited common sense, mechanical, and unitary etiologies that were congruent with the pragmatic value orientation of rural America [14]. Andrew Taylor Still, a regular physician who became disenchanted with the inability of allopathic medicine to prevent the death of his wife and three of his children, concluded upon detailed anatomical investigations that many, if not all, diseases are due to faulty articulations or *lesions* in various parts of the musculoskeletal system. Along with William Smith, a graduate of the University of Edinburgh medical school, Still established in September 1892 the American School of Osteopathy in Kirksville, Missouri. Osteopathy appealed to thousands of ordinary rural and small town people, particularly those who were suffering from chronic spinal or joint dysfunctions.

> Dr. Still took pride in making osteopathy available to everyone including the uneducated under classes. . . . During its early years, osteopathy welcomed even patients who could not pay, as they provided osteopaths with opportunities to demonstrate the movement's altruism and to "Spread the Word." Thus, osteopathy extended to those unable to secure a medical education or treatment elsewhere a medical alternative which was available and eager to have them [15, p. 82].

The opening of an additional seventeen osteopathic schools between 1895 and 1900 offered many individuals of humble origins the hope of becoming medical practitioners [16, p. 74]. Despite the opposition of regular physicians, who often aligned themselves with homeopathic and eclectic physicians on the matter, osteopaths, with the support of satisfied patients and patrons, quickly acquired at least limited practice rights and occasionally full practice rights in most states during the 1890s and the first decade of the twentieth century.

Daniel David Palmer, the "discover" of chiropractic, administered his first "spinal adjustment" in Davenport, Iowa, in September 1895, when he cured a black janitor of a seventeen-year deafness. He began to offer instruction at the Palmer Infirmary and Chiropractic Institute in 1898. Under the astute management of B. J. Palmer, D.D.'s flamboyant son, the Palmer School grew into "one of the largest institutions that trained health practitioners in the United States, graduating its first *One Thousand Class* in 1921" [17, p. 215]. Although the Palmer School became the recognized "Fountainhead" of chiropractic, several hundred chiropractic schools of one sort or the other have functioned for varying periods during the turbulent history of this heterodox medical system [18]. Even more so than osteopathy, chiropractic served as a vehicle by which thousands of lower-middle and working-class individuals, who were denied access to a career in regular medicine, became health practitioners.

Rothstein estimates that "in 1900, there about 110,000 regular physicians, 10,000 homeopaths, 5,000 eclectics, and over 5,000 other practitioners" in the United States [8, p. 345]. In that same year, 126 allopathic schools, twenty-two homeopathic schools, and nine eclectic schools were training physicians. Concurrently, osteopathy was in process of institutionalizing and professionalizing itself, and chiropractic was emerging as yet another alternative medical system. Although beginning in the 1870s organized bourgeois medicine initiated a drive to consolidate its position by lobbying state legislators to pass licensure laws, allopaths, contrary to the ethical guidelines of the AMA, were legally forced to accept the presence of homeopaths and eclectics on medical examining boards. As Burrow observes, "The growth of the osteopathic and chiropractic movements caused orthodox leaders to increase their agitation for single boards from which representatives would be excluded, but they conceded representation of homeopaths and eclectics as a price for their support" [19, p. 58].

The Rise of Bourgeois Medicine

In addition to the competition posed by heterodox practitioners, allopaths faced considerable competition within their own ranks. Due to the proliferation of proprietary medical schools following the Civil War that attempted to attract unemployed war veterans, individuals of relatively humble origins could become regular physicians following several months to a year or two of medical education. In keeping with the rise of industrial capitalism during the late nineteenth century, regular medicine was transformed into a commodity in the fullest sense of the term and medical practitioners attempted to legitimize themselves by claiming to be "scientific" [7]. Bourgeois medicine in the guise of "scientific medicine" held itself to be above sectarianism—a contention which many medical historians and social scientists accept [8, p. 170]. In recognizing that alternative medical systems, including non-Western ones, may also be scientific in that they also engage in the systematic search for cause-and-effect relationships, many medical anthropologists have come to refer to the dominant medical paradigm in Western societies as "biomedicine." As such, biomedicine focuses on human biology, or more accurately, on physiology, even pathophysiology [20, 21] and thus tends to divert attention from the social origins of illness. Given the increasing labor unrest in the cities, populist sentiments among farmers and small town people, and the emergence of social medicine which recognized that many of the new illnesses had occupational and environmental underpinnings, it is notable that the new mode of medical production focused on pathogens as the cause of disease. As Brown asserts, the regular medical profession "discovered an ideology that was compatible with the world view of, and politically and economically useful to, the capitalist class and the emerging managerial and professional stratum" [10, p. 71].

Consequently, the emerging alliance around the turn of the century between the AMA, which consisted primarily of elite practitioners and medical researchers based in prestigious universities, and the industrial capitalist class ultimately permitted biomedicine to establish political, economic and ideological dominance over rival medical systems.

While, as Waitzkin [22, p. 140] observes, Gramsci did not consider medicine as a hegemonic agency, these developments suggest that it indeed functions as a vehicle by which the bourgeoisie came to exert indirect control over social reality [23, pp. 258-259; 24]. Navarro asserts that the bourgeoisie came to support a version of medicine in which:

... disease was not an outcome of specific power relations but rather a biological individual phenomenon where the cause of disease was the immediately observable factor, the bacteria. In this redefinition, clinical medicine became the branch of scientific medicine to study the biological individual phenomena and social medicine became that other branch of medicine which would study the distribution of disease as the aggregate of individual phenomenon. Both branches shared the vision of disease as an alteration, a pathological change in the human body (perceived as a machine), caused by an outside agent (unicausality) or several agents (multicausality) or several agents (multicausality) [1, p. 166].

According to Berliner, the AMA's decision to grant licensure only to graduates of schools deemed acceptable by American Council of Medical Education in 1906 "proved to be the beginning of the end of the pluralistic system of medical care in the United States" [25, p. 583]. The hegemony of bourgeois medicine was even further advanced by the Flexner Report of 1910, which was sponsored by the corporate-based Carnegie Foundation upon a recommendation by the AMA that a comprehensive survey of the quality of medical education be made. While the Flexner Report may have in some ways contributed to improving the quality of medical education in the United States, it also drastically altered the socio-economic composition of the regular medical profession. Following the Flexner Report, there was a rapid decline in the number of medical schools in the United States from 162 in 1906 to ninety-five in 1916 to seventy in 1924. Whereas, in 1900 there were 173 physicians for every 100,000 Americans, by 1920 there were only 137 and by 1930 only 125 [26, p. 56]. Furthermore, whereas in 1910 there were eight medical schools that educated African Americans and a substantial number that educated primarily women, the Flexner Report contributed to the closing of all but two of the African-American medical schools and all except one of the women's medical schools. In the shadow of the medical educational reforms of the early twentieth century, the bourgeois medical profession emerged as largely a white upper and upper-middle class male preserve.

The decision of the corporate-sponsored philanthropies, particularly the Rockefeller Foundation, to only fund the allopathic schools defined as inferior by the Flexner Report, but also the heterodox medical schools in part spelled the demise of homeopathy and eclecticism. Corporate-sponsored foundations were willing only to fund bourgeois medical schools that conducted supposedly non-sectarian, "scientific" research in elaborate laboratories. According to Kaufman,

Moreover, with the development of unified examining boards, homeopathic courses were relegated to a minor role in the curriculum. The instruction in homeopathy was given short shrift in favor of the subjects required for licensure. Obviously, the homeopathic colleges could not compete with colleges having large endowments and enough resources to pay high salaries and purchase the latest instruments [27, p. 175].

The number of homeopathic schools declined from twenty-two in 1900 to twelve in 1910 to five in 1920; the number of eclectic schools declined from nine in 1900 to eight in 1910 to five in 1920 [8, p. 287]. Most homeopathic physicians resigned themselves to assimilation into bourgeois medicine.

In order to pass AMA-dominated state licensing examinations and later basic science examinations, the osteopathic schools and even the chiropractic schools increasingly oriented their curricula to those of the biomedical schools. The early history of osteopathy saw a debate between the "lesion" osteopaths, who desired to focus on osteopathic manipulation therapy (OMT), and the "broad" osteopaths, who wished to incorporate many aspects of bourgeois medicine and, for a while, even naturopathy [28, pp. 61-74]. While Andrew Still never accepted the germ theory, many of his followers redefined the osteopathic paradigm to incorporate it and reintroduce the materia medica that the "Lightening Bonesetter" so vehemently rejected. New suggests that as early as 1902, except for the inclusion of OMT, the curriculum of osteopathic schools "was probably not too different from most standard medical schools" [29, p. 41]. In responding to Flexner's negative comments on eight osteopathic schools, the American Osteopathic Association lengthened the courses of study in osteopathic schools to four years and forced many schools to shut their doors [30]. By 1926, only six osteopathic schools remained in operation, and in 1940 the Massachusetts College of Osteopathy also closed. In time most osteopaths came to regard OMT as an adjunct to bourgeois medicine, consider themselves as "osteopathic physicians," and to refer to their practice as "osteopathic medicine." Lacking the resources provided by corporate-sponsored foundations to regular medical schools, the osteopathic profession concentrated on the training of primary-care providers rather than on medical research, and treated a clientele ignored by bourgeois medicine as it increasingly became a highly specialized form of treatment. Nonetheless, most of the specialities found in bourgeois medicine eventually were reproduced in the structure of osteopathic medicine.

While osteopathy obtained full practice rights in most states by the 1950s and evolved into a medical system parallel to and intertwined with bourgeois medicine, chiropractic continued to function as a distinct heterodox medical system. As opposed to the "straights," who regarded spinal adjustment as an all-purpose therapeutic technique, chiropractic "mixers" incorporated a wide variety of naturopathic modalities, including physiotherapy, dietetics, vitamin therapy, exercise, and colonic irrigation. While dozens of chiropractic schools with widely varying admission requirements, periods of study, and facilities sprang up around the country, the Depression forced many of these schools to close. In preparing their students to pass basic science examinations and meet licensing requirements, the curricula of the chiropractic schools also began to resemble those of bourgeois medical schools. Chiropractic also eventually incorporated the disease theory of bourgeois medicine.

In short, as the foregoing discussion suggests, after the turn of the century, the American medical system underwent a rapid transformation from a relatively pluralistic form to a dominative one. During the last decades of the nineteenth century, as Brown notes, "[w]ith the convergence in practice and education of homeopaths, eclectics, and regular physicians, it was possible to assure the dominance of scientific training and politically necessary to ignore, for the moment, the sectarian separations" [10, p. 89]. Once, with the backing of corporate-sponsored foundations, organized bourgeois medicine achieved hegemony over its rivals, it quickly proceeded to co-opt most homeopaths and eclectics by admitting them into state medical societies. Given the refusal of the private foundations to fund heterodox medical schools and the departure of many homeopaths and eclectic physicians from their respective professional associations, homeopathic and eclectic schools either closed or converted into bourgeois medical schools. In 1936 the New York Homeopathic College, the last of the homeopathic schools, renamed itself the New York Medical College [27, p. 175]. The Eclectic Medical Institute, the last of the eclectic schools, offered its final course in 1938-1939 [9, p. 93]. While osteopathy and chiropractic remained organizationally separate from bourgeois medicine (except for the merger of the California Osteopathic Association with the California Medical Association in 1961), they were forced to accommodate their training programs to the bourgeois medical paradigm and to accept, for the most part, niches in the medical market-place that had been either ignored or vacated by regular physicians.

THE AMERICAN DOMINATIVE MEDICAL SYSTEM UNDER CORPORATE CAPITALISM

Navarro contends that the class structure of American society is "reflected in the composition of the different elements that participate in the health sector, either as owners, controllers, or producers of services" [31, p. 138]. Members of the upper class and, to a lesser degree, the upper-middle class predominate on the boards of foundations involved in health policy decision-making, private and state medical schools, and voluntary hospitals. The remaining social classes are distributed in positions of differential power within the bourgeois medical division of labor. Most regular physicians are white upper-middle class males. Paraprofessionals (e.g., nurses, therapists, technologists, and technicians) fall into the lower-middle class. Most of them are female and about 9 percent are African American. Finally, "the working class per se of the health sector, the auxiliary, ancillary, and service personnel represent 54.2 per cent of the labor force, who are predominantly women (84.1 per cent) and who include an overrepresentation of blacks (30 per cent)" [1, p. 138]. The 1980 U.S. Census reported that only 2.8 percent of diagnostic practitioners (MDs, DOs, and DDSs) were African Americans and only 11.7 percent were female [32].

Navarro's description of the American health sectors refers primarily or exclusively to its bourgeois medical component. In this section, we will present a rank order of the medical systems in the American dominative medical system, and will attempt to demonstrate that the American dominative medical system tends to replicate class, racial/ethnic, and gender division in the larger society. While to a certain degree the multiplicity of medical systems that existed during the nineteenth century reflected these social divisions as well, regular physicians at the time were drawn from a wider spectrum of social classes than is the case today. Conversely, most homeopathic physicians enjoyed a higher socio-economic status than the great bulk of their allopathic counterparts. Figure 1 illustrates in rank order the major components of the dominative medical system.

Due to its perceived contribution to personnel well-being and functional health, which is essential to the maintenance of a productive work-force, entree into the role of health care provider in capitalist societies has historically been seen as a ready vehicle for improving one's socio-economic status. When individuals from lower social strata are denied entree into the dominant medical profession, they sometimes turn to alternative healing groups, some of which endeavor to professionalize themselves. Theoretically, emerging health occupations seeking to advance their interests may embark upon one of two strategies, namely professionalization or unionization. Krause asserts,

> In general, professionalization appeals to a social consensus model; it aims to gain acceptance by all other occupational groups in the field and by the general public, of the new higher value of the striving occupation and the legitimacy of its requests for more rewards, power, status, and so forth. Unionization, in contrast, is a conflict-based process: the individuals and the occupations band together to force from the power structure and the society what it will not give up without such a struggle [23, p. 76].

Although health occupational groups (e.g., nurses, medical technologists and technicians, etc.), which find themselves subordinate to administrators and physicians in the bourgeois medical division of labor, occasionally adopt the unionization approach, alternative medical practitioners, who often exhibit marked petty-bourgeois ambitions, almost invariably adopt professionalization as a strategy of collective social mobility. In reality, professionalization acts as a subtle, but highly effective, hegemonic process by which alternative practitioners internalize some, if not many, of the philosophical premises, therapeutic approaches, and organizational structures of bourgeois medicine. As Larson observes, "The persistence of profession as a category of social practice suggests that the model constituted by the first movements of professionalization has become an ideology—not only an image which consciously obscures real social structures and relations" [33, p. xviii]. In a similar vein, Willis argues that the "ideology of professionalism" reproduces

A. Bourgeois Medicine
B. Osteopathic Medicine as a Parallel Medical System Focusing on Primary Care
C. Professionalized Heterodox Medical Systems
   1. Chiropractic
   2. Naturopathy
D. Partially Professionalized or Lay Heterodox Medical Systems (e.g., homeopathy, acupuncture, Rolfing, reflexology, etc.)
E. Anglo-American Religious Healing Systems (e.g., Christian Science, Seventh Day Adventism, evangelical faith healing)
F. Ethnomedical Systems (e.g., African American ethnomedicine, *curanderismo, espiritismo, santeria*, Chinese medicine, Native American healing systems)

Figure 1. The American Dominative Medical System

"aspects of the dominant ideology and thus promoting ideological hegemony which as Gramsci argues, provides the basis for bourgeois rule in monopoly capitalism" [34, p. 16].

As professionalized heterodox medical systems, osteopathy, chiropractic, and, to a lesser degree, probably naturopathy held out the promise of improved social mobility for thousands of lower-middle class working-class individuals as well as members of other social categories, who were denied access to a career in bourgeois medicine due to the structural barriers erected in the wake of the Flexner Report.

Osteopathic Medicine

Although initially osteopathy attracted regular physicians and other individuals who wanted to practice a less interventive form of therapy than allopathy, eventually many, if not most, of those who entered the profession did so because they wanted to become physicians, but found admission to bourgeois medical school closed to them for various structural reasons. During the mid-1950s, Peter New, based on interviews with 103 students at four of the six then-existing osteopathic schools, found that the social profile of osteopathic students differed considerably from that of bourgeois medical students [29]. Most of the students had entered osteopathy as second choice, and some of them had discovered it when they discovered that they would have no opportunity to be admitted to a bourgeois medical school. Only thirty-four out of the 103 interviewees had not applied previously to a bourgeois medical school. Forty-four students went directly into an osteopathic school after their undergraduate school [29, p. 90].

The average age of both juniors and seniors was twenty-eight years. Of the students reporting their father's occupations, "36 students reported that their father was in clerical or small business types of profession, 27 students mentioned farmer or blue-collar work as their father's profession, and 16 students' fathers were in professional work" [29, p. 90]. For most of the students, osteopathy clearly represented a means of upward social mobility. New also found that eighteen of the students in his sample were Jewish. Given that many bourgeois medical schools during the period 1920-1960 maintained implicit or explicit quotas on the number of Jews admitted, osteopathic schools apparently provided an alternative avenue by which academically qualified Jewish students could become physicians [15, p. 111; 29, pp. 89-90]. Ironically, while osteopathy initially was relatively open to women, in later years "the decline in female enrollment was significantly more severe in osteopathic medical schools than in allopathic ones" [15, p. 113].

By the mid-1970s the osteopathic profession had obtained full practice rights in all states and received charters to establish several state-affiliated medical schools. Nevertheless, some evidence indicates that osteopathy continues to function as a second choice career [35, 36].

As bourgeois medicine became an increasingly capital-intensive, specialized, urban-based endeavor, the osteopathic profession convinced health policy makers in various areas of the country that it could address the growing shortage of primary-care physicians, particularly in rural areas and smaller communities [37]. In keeping with the growing concern about rising health costs, legislators have obviously been impressed that "osteopaths earn 25 percent less than traditional doctors in general practice and 15 percent less in speciality work" [16, p. 191].

Because the osteopathic profession developed its hospital system relatively late and had limited funds for education and research, it has been far slower in specializing than bourgeois medicine. "In 1967-68, 29 percent of traditional physicians and 90 percent of osteopaths were in general practice. By 1978 only 18 percent of the allopaths were in general practice whereas 88 percent of the osteopaths remained in general practice" [16, p. 191]. Despite efforts in the early 1960s by organized bourgeois medicine to absorb osteopathy, the Michigan legislature's decision in 1970 to convert a new private osteopathic school into the Michigan State University College of Osteopathic Medicine marked the organizational rejuvenation of osteopathy [37]. Of an additional nine osteopathic colleges established since that date, six are state-supported institutions. In April 1992, 32,207 osteopathic physicians accounted for over 4 percent of the total physician population [38].

While osteopathy, despite the opposition of organized bourgeois medicine, has obviously achieved a considerable degree of legitimacy, it continues to find itself ranked below bourgeois medicine. Osteopathy occupies this position partly for the same reasons that primary-care physicians find themselves at the bottom of the bourgeois medical profession's hierarchy, but also because its practitioners are drawn from lower strata in the American class system than are regular physicians. Osteopathic medicine continues to suffer from an identity crisis, evidenced by the facts that the general public tends to have no or a vague idea of what it is and that many osteopathic physicians present themselves publicly merely as "doctors" or "physicians." As Gevitz observes, fiscal constraints also constitute another dilemma for the osteopathic profession.

> The daily census of hospitals has shrunk in recent years because of tighter governmental and insurance company oversight and control over admissions criteria and length of patient stays. As a result, a large number of institutions have had to close wings or have been forced to shut down entirely. This trend poses a real threat to the osteopathic profession, both in the continuation of its postdoctoral training programs and in the autonomy of osteopathic practice. Increasingly, osteopathic physicians have been given staff privileges in M.D. hospitals so that the latter institutions can expand their potential pool of patients. To assure adequate patient census levels, osteopathic hospitals must be able to retain their current physician staff as well as to secure new D.O.s [39, p. 153].

Chiropractic

Even more so than osteopathic students, various studies have attested to the relatively humble social origins of chiropractic students. The Stanford Research Institute [40] study reports that most Californian chiropractors "come from families of modest means," and that 65 percent of them worked twenty hours or more per week while attending chiropractic school (comparable figures for osteopathic and biomedical students were 17% and 1% respectively). Less than 10 percent of the chiropractors had earned a bachelor's degree. In his study of students at New York's Columbian Institute of Chiropractic (CIC), Sternberg found that most of them came from working-class families, and that the "American Dream value pattern seems very dominant in CIC's subcultural definition of the practice of chiropractic" [41, p. 268]. Whereas the median annual income at the time for chiropractors who had been practicing for ten to fifteen years was $28,400, the students anticipated earning a median income of $52,000. Based upon a questionnaire completed by thirty chiropractors in three Ohio counties, White and Skipper report that their respondents typically "were white, Protestant, male, and from lower-class origins in the midwestern section of the country" and enjoyed a "more comfortable existence than that to which the chiropractors were accustomed while growing up" [42, p. 304]. In contrast to the WASPish composition of the Ohio sample, Sternberg found that the CIC students, who were "not ethnically nor religiously typical of chiropractic" but were "much more heavily Jewish or Italian" [41, p. 52]. Despite the appreciable representation of "white ethnic" chiropractors in certain regions of the country, African Americans and other minorities "make up only one percent of the nation's chiropractors and students" [43, p. 53].

A relatively recent study of 149 students at a southern California chiropractic school presents the following social profile of chiropractic student:

> The typical chiropractic student is male, although 25 percent are female. He is between the ages of twenty-eight and thirty, although ages range from eighteen to fifty-six, single (47 percent) or married but with only one or two children. . . . Women are becoming increasingly attracted to chiropractic arts, in part as a result of the recruiting of women by the profession and the schools, but more commonly younger women attend chiropractic school. . . . In obvious contrast to medical students, chiropractic students are from primarily working- and middle-class backgrounds: 40 percent of the fathers were skilled laborers, 15 percent small business owners, 14 percent managers or executives, 19 percent professionals (which included chiropractors, medical doctors, teachers, engineers), 9 percent sales men or clerical workers and 4 percent farmers [44, pp. 36-36].

Despite vigorous opposition from organized bourgeois medicine, chiropractic has undergone considerable legitimation in the past two decades. As osteopathic physicians filled the vacuum left by regular physicians in primary care, they in turn left the treatment of musculoskeletal complications almost totally in the hands of chiropractors. The process by which chiropractic obtained support from government agencies and private parties awaits further exploration. The generally lower costs of both chiropractic education and care when compared to bourgeois medical education and care undoubtedly have played a role in this process [45, 46]. Rather than treating primarily working-class and farm people as they once did, chiropractors now serve a broader clientele, which includes substantial numbers of affluent professionals [47-51].

Naturopathy

While medical historians and social scientists have written a fair amount on heterodox medical systems such as botanic medicine, homeopathy, chiropractic, and osteopathy, little is known about naturopathy. According to Reed, American naturopathy attained importance "contemporaneous with the development of 'mixing' in chiropractic" [52, p. 63]. Registration as naturopaths allowed chiropractors in some states to engage in a wide scope of practice without danger of legal repercusions [53, p. 137]. The decline of American naturopathy during the 1940s appears to have been closely related to the evolution of chiropractic from a form of drugless general practice to a neuromuscular-skeletal speciality [54, p. 161]. Despite its weakened position by mid-century, naturopathy found a last ditch stronghold of sorts in the Pacific Northwest, a region that has provided a sanctuary for maverick social movements and alternative medical systems [55]. In responding to the plans of the Western States College of Chiropractic to drop its ND program, three individuals established the National College of Naturopathic Medicine (NCNM) in Portland, Oregon, in 1956. NCNM operated a campus in Seattle from 1959-1976. In 1978 three NCNM graduates established the John Bastyr College of Naturopathic Medicine (JCBNM) in Seattle. In Spring 1988, JBCNM had 130 students in its ND program and twenty-nine in its nutrition program, which grants a BS and a MS. The American Association of Naturopathic Physicians has sixteen state associations (Arizona, California, Colorado, Connecticut, Florida, Hawaii, Idaho, Kansas, Massachusetts, Minnesota, Nevada, North Carolina, Oregon, Texas, Utah, and Washington). Naturopathy appears to be undergoing what may be the beginnings of a rejuvenation a process that is occurring within the context of the larger holistic health movement [56].

Other Alternative Medical Systems

Limitations of space do not permit an extensive discussion of non-professionalized medical systems—namely lay heterodox medical systems, religious healing systems, and ethnomedical systems. Yet, even these medical systems reflect social divisions within the larger society. While the roots for many lay heterodox medical systems (e.g., herbalism and acupuncture) are quite old, they along with, to some extent, osteopathic manipulation therapy, chiropractic, and naturopathy, have been subsumed under the diffuse umbrella of the holistic health movement. For the most part this movement, which emerged largely as "an outgrowth of the counterculture and human potential movements of the late 1960s and early 1970s," constitutes a middle-class protest against the bureaucratic and iatrogenic dimensions of bourgeois medicine as well as its high costs [46]. In that lay heterodox practitioners often exhibit strong entrepreneurial aspirations, fees for their services may be out of the reach of many working- and lower-class people.

Just as religious denominations and sects reflect class, racial/ethnic, and gender relations in the larger society, the same can be said of religious healing systems. As in the nineteenth century, Christian Science continues to appeal to the "urban middle classes" [57, p. 179]. While apparently few Christian Science practitioners (about 80% of whom are women in the United States) earn substantial incomes from their mental therapeutic activities, this pattern is mitigated by "the fact most of the women practitioners are married, and are, therefore, not reliant on their earnings to maintain themselves" [58, p. 50]. Anglo-American Spiritualism, which focuses heavily on metaphysical healing, caters primarily to lower-middle class people, and provides many women an opportunity to function as healers [59-61]. Finally, evangelical faith healing with its roots in the Holiness and Pentecostal movements has historically served the needs of working- and lower-class whites and African Americans [62].

Whereas practitioners of bourgeois medicine and professionalized heterodox medical systems tend to be drawn from the so-called WASP majority group and, to a lesser extent, Jewish and non-Hispanic Catholic ethnic groups, the practitioners and clients of ethnomedical systems, such as rootwork, *curanderismo, espiritimo, santeria,* peyotism, and herbalism are largely concentrated among African Americans, Hispanics, Native Americans and poor rural whites. Unfortunately, despite an abundance of anthropological studies on ethnomedical systems in American society, only a few of these have attempted to view the persistence of ethnomedicine as a response to the racist and class features of the American dominative medical system [37, 63-66].

DISCUSSION

In keeping with the transformation of the American political economy from competitive to monopoly capitalism, its associated medical system evolved from a relatively, although never completely, pluralistic form to a dominative one. In this process, allopathy, the predominant but not the clearly dominant medical system during the nineteenth century, evolved into what many medical anthropologists term "biomedicine" and what we term "bourgeois medicine." Given its emphasis on pathogens as the purported cause of disease and its neglect of the social origins of illness, bourgeois medicine appealed to the capitalist class which recognized it as a ready vehicle for ameliorating social dissent. As a result of the financial backing of corporate-sponsored foundations for its research activities, bourgeois medicine asserted scientific superiority and clearly established hegemony over alternative medical systems. Nonetheless, bourgeois medicine's dominance over rival medical systems has never been absolute. The state, which primarily serves the interests of the bourgeoisie, must periodically make concessions to subordinate social groups in the interests of maintaining social order and the capitalist mode. As a result, certain heterodox practitioners, with the backing of clients and particularly influential patrons, were able to obtain legitimation in the form of full practice rights (e.g., osteopathic physicians) or limited rights (e.g., osteopathic physicians) or limited rights (e.g., chiropractors and naturopaths). Lower social classes, racial and ethnic minorities, and women have often utilized medicine as a forum for challenging not only bourgeois medical dominance but also, to a degree, the hegemony of the capitalist class.

Organized osteopathy, despite seemingly insurmountable odds, has engaged in vigorous efforts for public acceptance since the 1890s. The astute lobbying activities of the osteopathic profession eventually resulted in it obtaining full practice rights in all fifty states. As early as 1910, osteopathic physicians obtained separate licensing boards in seventeen states [19]. Osteopathy has tended to be the strongest in states, such as California (prior to 1961 when the California Medical Association absorbed the California Osteopathic Association), Michigan, and Pennsylvania, in which it has its own licensing boards as opposed to those states, such as New York, Wisconsin, and Indiana, in which osteopathic physicians are licensed by composite boards (or, in some cases, boards consisting entirely of regular physicians). The American Osteopathic Association maintains an office in Washington, D.C., which attempts to obtain inclusion of osteopathic physicians in health bills. Many state osteopathic associations employ osteopathic physicians and lay people to lobby for the passage of legislation favorable to the interest of the profession. In its early drive for licensure, osteopaths often treated legislators as a way of demonstrating the merits of their treatment procedures.

Chiropractors themselves, with the backing they solicited in many cases from patients, lobbied heavily for reimbursement from Workmen's Compensation programs, Medicare, and Medicaid. "Various unions (e.g., the steelworkers, postal employees) also pressured insurers to pay benefits for chiropractic services. Legislatures were lobbied to pass *insurance equality laws* measuring inclusion of chiropractors in all health insurance policies" [17, p. 227].

Because their resources are much more limited than those of organized osteopathy and chiropractic, lay heterodox practitioners, with the exception of Christian Scientists, have achieved relatively little success in directly challenging the professional dominance of bourgeois medicine. Nevertheless, their popularity among various segments of the American populace attests to their potential as a counter-hegemonic force. Conversely, while licensing laws and other forms of state recognition have legitimated, at least in part, certain alternative medical systems, particularly osteopathy and chiropractic, these measures have forced them to adapt their training programs and therapeutic procedures to the bourgeois medical model.

As we have seen, medical pluralism in American society tends to replicate class, racial/ethnic, and gender relations. Individuals often assume the healer role in order to improve their social status. In attempting to enter the medical market-place, as Larkin observes, "innovatory groups in medical science often commence with low status, particularly through their involvement in activities previously regarded as outside of a physician's or surgeon's role" [67, p. 5]. As the new medical system grows, it accumulates

> more and more members who are interested in making a good living and in raising their status in the outer world. In the health sphere, this means that they become more concerned with obtaining respectable (or at least respectable-looking) credentials, providing services that more clearly follow the medical model, and eventually even developing working relationships with the orthodox medical world [68, pp. 40-41].

In their effort to professionalize themselves, homeopathic physicians underwent this process and eventually were absorbed by organized bourgeois medicine. Conversely, osteopathy and chiropractic, although in large measure accepting the bourgeois medical model, have remained to varying degrees organizationally separate. Although osteopathic medicine has achieved considerable legitimacy due to its ability to address certain structural dilemmas emanating from capital-intensive, specialized medicine, its status within the American dominative medical system falls a notch below that of bourgeois medicine. While chiropractic initially aspired to function as a drugless medical system, most of its practitioners, both straight and mixer, have resigned themselves to function as musculoskeletal specialists and aspire now to be accepted as such within the contexts of regular and osteopathic hospitals. If one acknowledges that it is no longer appropriate to refer to osteopathic medicine as a professionalized heterodox medical system, naturopathy probably now constitutes the most comprehensive professionalized heterodox medical system in the United States [56].

Under the rubric of the holistic movement, a wide array of lay heterodox medical systems (e.g., acupuncture, homeopathy, irridignosis) as well as metaphysical systems (e.g., yoga, transcendental meditation) have achieved popularity during the past two decades or so. Although cognizant that the holistic health movement poses a potential challenge to the hegemony of biomedicine, Berliner and Salmon also observe that it exhibits

> many of the same organizational and social patterns that predominate in the present health care system: solo, fee-for-service entrepreneurial practice; knowledge or skill sold to consumers in commodity forms; elitist and sexist behavior on the part of practitioners; a concentration of availability of services to middle-class, white people able to pay; and clear separation between practitioners and those who are served. Most practices also tend to be focused on the individual, as in scientific medicine, and lack virtually any focus on the larger social grouping [6, p. 143].

Given these tendencies, bourgeois medicine may easily be able to co-opt the techniques of specific heterodox medical systems, such as acupuncture [69, 70], while discarding their theoretical or metaphysical premises. Already studies on acupuncture treatment for substance abuse—a problem that has not been well addressed by bourgeois medicine—is being supported by federal research institutes. In addition, some regular and osteopathic physicians are now turning to "holistic medicine" as a strategy for attracting patients in an increasing competitive medical market-place that has developed in the more affluent sections of large cities [71]. Finally, in light of "the fact that the major portion of health expenditures flows out of the corporate sector and State into the hands of professionals and hospitals," various health policy decision-makers in these sectors are considering "holistic medicine as a strategy for reducing medical costs and stressing individuals responsibility in health maintenance" [46, p. 41].

While various alternative medical systems have achieved a certain degree of legitimacy and the professional dominance of regular physicians has declined in recent decades, we should not view these developments as signaling the end of the hegemony of the reductionist bourgeois medical model per se and the beginning of a truly pluralistic medical system. As long as the corporate class and its state sponsors dictate health policy, the American medical system will remain a dominative one and continue to reflect social relations in the larger society. Attention to the influence of the dominant social structure on the structure of medicine has largely been ignored in conventional, non-critical medical anthropology. Critical medical anthropology, by contrast, seeks to identify the importance of broader social relations on the character of health and health care policy, and the health of subpopulations. This work, we assert, is a significant contribution of the critical perspective to expanding the scope of medical anthropological understanding.

REFERENCES

1. V. Navarro, *Crisis, Health and Medicine: A Social Critique,* Tavistock, New York, 1986.
2. C. Leslie (ed.), *Asian Medical Systems: A Comparative Study,* University of California Press, Berkeley, 1976.
3. J. Janzen, *The Question for Therapy: Medical Pluralisms in Lower Zaire,* University of California Press, Berkeley, 1978.
4. L. Crandon-Malamud, *From the Fat of Souls: Social Change, Political Process, and Medical Pluralism in Bolivia,* University of California Press, 1991.
5. R. Frankenberg, Allopathic Medicine, Profession, and Capitalist Ideology in India, *Social Science and Medicine, 15A,* pp. 115-125, 1981.
6. J. Salmon (ed.), *Alternative Medicines: Popular and Policy Perspectives,* Tavistock, New York, 1984.
7. H. Berliner, Medical Modes of Production, in *The Problem of Medical Knowledge,* A. Treacher and P. Wright (eds.), Edinburgh University Press, Edinburgh, 1982.
8. W. Rothstein, *American Physicians in the Nineteenth Century,* Johns Hopkins University Press, Baltimore, 1972.
9. H. Coulter, *Divided Legacy: A History of Schism in Medical Thought,* Wehawken, Washington, D.C., 1973.
10. E. R. Brown, *Rockefeller Medicine Men: Medicine and Capitalism in America,* University of California, Berkeley, 1979.
11. R. C. Fuller, *Alternative Medicine and American Religious Life,* Oxford University Press, New York, 1989.
12. M. Singer, Christian Science Healing and Alcoholism: An Anthropological Perspective, *Journal of Operational Psychiatry, 13*:1, pp. 2-12, 1982.
13. J. Haller, *American Medicine in Transition, 1840-1910,* University of Illinois Press, Urbana, 1981.
14. T. McCorkle, Chiropractic: A Deviant Theory of Disease, *Human Organization, 20,* pp. 20-23, 1961.
15. M. Cohen, *Medical Social Movements in the United States (1820-1982),* PhD dissertation, University of California, San Diego, 1983.
16. G. Albrecht and J. Levy, The Professionalization of Osteopathy: Adaptation in the Medical Marketplace, in *Research in the Sociology of Health Care: Changing Structure of Health Services,* J. A. Roth (ed.), JAI Press, Greenwich, Connecticut, pp. 161-206, 1982.
17. W. Wardwell, Chiropractors: Challengers of Medical Domination, in *Research in the Sociology of Health Care: Changing Structure of Health Services,* J. A. Roth (ed.), JAI Press, Greenwich, Connecticut, pp. 207-250, 1982.
18. G. Wiese and A. Ferguson, Historical Directory of Chiropractic Schools and Colleges, *Research Forum, 1*:3, pp. 79-94, 1985.
19. J. Burrow, *Organized Medicine in the Progressive Era: The Move Toward Monopoly,* Johns Hopkins University Press, Baltimore, 1977.

20. R. Hahn and A. Kleinman, Biomedical Practice and Anthropological Theory: Frameworks and Directions, in *Annual Review of Anthropology, Vol. 12*, B. Siegal (ed.), Annual Editions, Palo Alto, California, pp. 305-333, 1983.
21. M. Lock and D. Gordon (eds.), *Biomedicine Examined*, Kluwer Academic Publishers, Dordrecht, 1988.
22. H. Waitzkin, *The Second Sickness: Contradictions of Capitalist Health Care*, Macmillan, New York, 1983.
23. E. Krause, *Power and Illness: The Political Sociology of Health and Medical Care*, Elsevier, New York, 1977.
24. R. Elling, The Political Economy, Cultural Hegemony, and Mixes of Traditional and Modern Medicine, *Social Science and Medicine, 15A*, pp. 89-99, 1981.
25. H. Berliner, A Larger Perspective on the Flexner, *International Journal of Health Services, 5*, pp. 573-592, 1975.
26. B. Ehrenreich and J. Ehrenreich, Medicine and Social Control, in *The Cultural Crisis of Modern Medicine*, J. Ehrenreich (ed.), Monthly Review Press, New York, pp. 39-79, 1978.
27. M. Kaufman, *Homeopathy in America: The Rise and Fall of a Medical Heresy*, Johns Hopkins University Press, Baltimore, 1971.
28. N. Gevitz, *The D.O.s: Osteopathic Medicine in America*, Johns Hopkins University Press, Baltimore, 1982.
29. P. New, *The Application of the Osteopathic Student*, PhD dissertation, University of Missouri, 1960.
30. A. Flexner, *Medical Education in the United States and Canada*, Bulletin No. 4, Carnegie Foundation for Advancement of Teaching, New York, 1910.
31. V. Navarro, *Medicine Under Capitalism*, Prodist, New York, 1976.
32. *1980 United States Census*, United States Department of Commerce, 1984.
33. M. Larson, *The Rise of Professionalism: A Sociological Analysis*, University of California Press, Berkeley, 1977.
34. E. Willis, *Medical Dominance: The Division of Labour in Australian Health Care*, George Allen & Unwin, Sydney, 1983.
35. S. Sharma and P. Dressel, *Interim Report of an Exploratory Study of Michigan State University College of Osteopathic Medicine Training Program*, Office of Institutional Research, Michigan State University, East Lansing, Michigan, 1975.
36. D. L. Eckberg, The Dilemma of Osteopathic Physicians and the Rationalization of Medical Practice, *Social Science and Medicine, 25*, pp. 1111-1120, 1987.
37. H. Baer, The Organizational Rejuvenation of Osteopathy: A Reflection of the Decline of Professional Dominance in Medicine, *Social Science and Medicine, 15A*, pp. 701-711, 1981.
38. Fact Sheet provided by the American Osteopathic Association, April 1992.
39. N. Gevitz, Osteopathic Medicine: From Development to Acceptance, in *Other Healers: Unorthodox Medicine in America*, N. Gevitz (ed.), Johns Hopkins University Press, Baltimore, pp. 124-156, 1988.
40. Stanford Research Institute, *Chiropractic in California*, Haynes Foundation, Los Angeles, 1960.
41. D. Sternberg, *Boys in Plight: A Case Study of Chiropractic Students Confronting a Medically-Oriented Society*, PhD dissertation, University of Buffalo, 1969.
42. M. White and J. Skipper, The Chiropractic Physician: A Study of Career Contingencies, *Journal of Health and Social Behavior, 12*, pp. 300-306, 1971.
43. B. Westbrooks, The Troubled Legacy of Harvey Lillard: The Black Experience in Chiropractic, *Chiropractic History, 2*:1, pp. 47-53, 1982.

44. P. Wild, Social Origins and Ideology of Chiropractors: An Empirical Study of the Socialization of the Chiropractic Student, *Sociological Symposium, 22,* pp. 33-54, 1978.
45. *Chiropractic Health Care, Volume 1,* Foundation for the Advancement of Chiropractic Tenets and Science, 1980.
46. H. Berliner and J. Salmon, The Holistic Alternative to Scientific Medicine: History and Analysis, *International Journal of Health Services, 10,* pp. 133-147, 1980.
47. E. Koos, *The Health of Regionville,* Columbia University Press, New York, 1954.
48. M. Schmitt, The Utilization of Chiropractors, *Sociological Symposium, 22,* pp. 55-86, 1978.
49. M. Kelner, O. Hall, and I. Coulter, *Chiropractors: Do They Help?,* Fitzhenry & Whiteside, Toronto, 1980.
50. D. Coburn and L. Biggs, Limits to Medical Dominance: The Case of Chiropractic, *Social Science and Medicine, 22,* pp. 1035-1046, 1986.
51. W. I. Wardwell, *Chiropractic: History and the Evolution of a New Profession,* Mosby, St. Louis, 1992.
52. L. Reed, *The Healing Cults,* University of Chicago Press, Chicago, 1932.
53. W. I. Wardwell, *Social Strain and Social Adjustment in the Marginal Role of the Chiropractor,* PhD dissertation, Harvard University, 1951.
54. H. Baer, A Comparative View of a Heterodox Health System, *Medical Anthropology, 8,* pp. 151-168, 1984.
55. J. Whorton, Drugless Healing in the 1920s: The Therapeutic Cult of Sanapractic, *Pharmacy in History, 28,* pp. 14-25, 1986.
56. H. Baer, The Potential Rejuvenation of American Naturopathy as an Aftermath of the Holistic Health Movement, *Medical Anthropology, 13,* pp. 369-383, 1991.
57. W. I. Wardwell, Christian Science Healing, *Journal for the Scientific Study of Religion, 4,* pp. 175-181, 1965.
58. B. Wilson, The Religious Teachings and Organization of Christian Science, in *Medical Care: Readings in the Sociology of Medicine,* H. Scott and E. Volkart (eds.), Wiley, New York, pp. 41-67, 1966.
59. R. Fishman, Spiritualism in Western New York, *Medical Anthropology, 3,* pp. 1-22, 1979.
60. M. McGuire and D. Kantor, *Ritual Healing in Suburban America,* Rutgers University Press, New Brunswick, New Jersey, 1988.
61. C. Shepherd McClain (ed.), *Women as Healers: Cross-Cultural Perspectives,* Rutgers University Press, New Brunswick, New Jersey, 1989.
62. L. Snow, The Religious Component in Southern Folk Medicine, in *Traditional Healing,* P. Singer (ed.), Conch, New York, pp. 26-51, 1977.
63. J. Roebuck and R. Quan, Health-Care Practices in the American Deep South, in *Marginal Medicine,* R. Wallis (ed.), Free Press, New York, pp. 141-161, 1976.
64. M. Singer, Indigenous Treatment for Alcoholism: The Case of Puerto Rican Spiritism, *Medical Anthropology, 8,* pp. 249-273, 1984.
65. M. Singer and M. Borrero, Indigenous Treatment for Alcoholism: The Case of Puerto Rican Spiritism, *Medical Anthropology, 8,* pp. 246-272, 1984.
66. M. Singer and R. Garcia, Becoming a Puerto Rican Espirista: Life History of a Female Healer, in *Women as Healers: Cross-Cultural Perspectives,* C. Shepherd McClain (ed.), Rutgers University Press, New Brunswick, New Jersey, pp. 157-185, 1989.
67. G. Larkin, *Occupational Monopoly and Modern Medicine,* Tavistock, New York, 1983.
68. J. A. Roth, *Health Purifiers and Their Enemies,* Prodist, New York, 1976.
69. J. Kotarba, Social Control Function of Holistic Medicine in Bureaucratic Settings: The Case of Space Medicine, *Journal of Health and Social Behavior, 24,* pp. 275-288, 1983.

70. P. Wolpe, The Maintenance of Professional Autonomy: Acupuncture and the American Physician, *Social Problems, 32,* pp. 409-424, 1985.
71. M. Goldstein et al., Holistic Doctors: Becoming a Non-Traditional Medical Practitioner, *Urban Life, 14,* pp. 317-344, 1985.

CHAPTER 7

AIDS and the Health Crisis of the U.S. Urban Poor

In some ways it is reasonable and useful to describe the United States as constituting (at least) two separate if intertwined societies: people of the inner city and everyone else. While poverty is by no means confined to the inner city, and neither are all oppressed ethnic minorities or people of color, the intersection of urban poverty and socially devalued ethnicity (especially being African American and Latino, and in some parts of the country, Native American and Asian as well) have proven to be a particularly unhealthy combination. Not only does it often appear as though the United States has more-or-less turned its back on the inner city [1]—a lesson brought home with furious intensity in the Spring of 1992 in the Los Angeles inner city uprising—but the consequences of such abandonment are seemingly uncontainable. One of these consequences is the rampant spread of AIDS in many U.S. inner city areas. Almost half of people in the United States who have been diagnosed as having AIDS are African Americans and Latino from impoverished urban neighborhoods. This chapter examines AIDS within the context of health and social issues facing the urban poor and attempts to locate this crisis in terms of the class, ethnic, and gender relations that define American society. To this task, the chapter brings an understanding of AIDS as both a health crisis and a cultural crisis, both of which are rooted ultimately in social conditions and social relations. While the chapter analyzes the way AIDS in the inner city has been constructed as a public health concern, a larger goal is to move beyond both Geertzian interpretation of cultural construction and epidemiological analysis of disease toward the political economic contextualization of AIDS.

We begin with the presentation of a framework for grounding political economic analysis in medical anthropology by reflecting on a parallel but earlier development in cultural anthropology. This discussion suggests the importance of re-inserting AIDS into the encompassing inner city landscape of health and social conditions from which it was extracted for purposes of public health intervention, an analysis carried out in the next section. The conceptual categories constructed and mobilized in this intervention process are then re-examined in light of ethnographic findings by anthropologists recruited to the fight against AIDS. Reconsideration of AIDS in terms of its social dimensions allows the development, in the final section of the chapter, of an alternative political economic perspective on inner city AIDS.

A CONCEPTUAL FRAMEWORK FOR THE ANTHROPOLOGY OF AIDS AMONG THE URBAN POOR

Anthropological involvement in health research among the inner city poor has been growing steadily in recent years and it has been an important part of the work of both authors of this volume [2, 3]. This research effort is emblematic of a significant re-direction in anthropological focus in recent years. This shift in research attention is reflective of a broader turn toward to the study of American society by North American anthropologists. Having overcome the traditional anthropological "suspicion ... of trying to understand one's own society" [4, p. 3], medical anthropologists have encountered a problem that has beset the discipline at several critical junctures in its history. As they move into the study of new social fields characterized by patterns of social relationship unseen in previous research, anthropologists' conceptual tools have been stretched beyond utility, producing intellectual turmoil and leading, in time, to a reconceptualization of basic frames of explanation.

An understanding of this process can be seen by examining briefly an earlier and by no means unrelated conceptual shift that occurred among cultural anthropologists as they moved from the study of small scale, subsistence communities to the investigation of peasant populations. As Roseberry comments,

> We can see in this ... literature the recognition of a crisis of anthropological theory and method, a recognition that the methods for the study of primitives did not serve those studying peasants in 'complex societies'. . . Peasants were, quite simply, not isolated from wider historical process ... How were we to understand these anthropological subjects in terms of the world-historical process through which they emerged or by means of which they maintained themselves without simplistically reducing the dynamics of their communities to the dynamics of world history? What did the anthropological perspective mean when the assumptions of holism were so clearly inadequate? [5, pp. 146-147].

One of the most successful early efforts to directly confront and address these issues in peasant research was the book *The People of Puerto Rico* [6]. Based on a series of local community studies carried out in different regions of the Island by Julian Steward's students, the book attempted to describe and analyze each local community, fit these communities together by examining the larger economic and historical processes that shaped their development, and, finally, locate social developments in Puerto Rico in terms of "processes of proletarianization as these have developed throughout the world" [6, p. 505]. The end result of this early effort was a significant rethinking of peasant communities, which, through the ongoing work of some of the participants in the Puerto Rico project [e.g., 7, 8], has led to fundamental changes in anthropological thinking generally, including the emergence of a political economic orientation in anthropology and a reconceptualization of all ethnographic cases in light of intertwined political and economic "processes that transcend separable cases, moving through and beyond them and transforming them as they proceed" [7, p. 17]. Remarks Appadurai,

> As we drop our anthropological blinders, and as we sharpen our ethnohistorical tools, we are discovering that pristine Punan of the interior of Borneo were probably a specialized adaptation of the larger Dayak communities, serving a specialized function in the world trade in Borneo forest products . . .; that the San of South Africa have been involved in a complex symbiosis with other groups for a very long time . . .; that groups in Melanesia have been trading goods across very long distances for a long time, trade that reflects complex regional relations of supply and demand . . .; that African 'tribes' have been reconstituting and deconstructing essential structural principles at their 'interior frontiers' for a very long time . . . [9, p. 17].

As medical anthropologists address health conditions in the inner city, they too experience a crisis of theory and method, and increasingly, feel the need to develop new conceptual tools [9, p. 37]. This crisis has been magnified by the sudden appearance of HIV/AIDS as a serious health problem among the U.S. inner city poor. Although first described and still a major cause of suffering and death among middle class, white gay men, AIDS has come to be recognized as a world health problem and a special problem among the urban poor. The special features of AIDS in the inner city are suggested in the following passage:

> In kindergarten this year, my six year old son has been learning the Pledge of Allegiance. Recently, as he proudly recited it at the dinner table, the thought came to mind to insert the words 'and AIDS' after liberty and justice in the final sentence. But the truth is that just as liberty and justice are not equally distributed to all, neither is AIDS. For those who have the least liberty and justice have the most AIDS and vice versa. And it is no coincidence that this is so . . . . As Ira Harrison has quipped: 'AIDS—poverty strikes again'. And behind poverty in this country, behind the unequal distribution of liberty and justice lies the issue of race. And behind the issue of race, as W. E. B. Du Bois [10. p. v], the renown Black sociologist and author of *The Souls of Black Folk* so forcefully wrote, 'lies a greater problem which both obscures and implements it: and that is the fact that so many civilized persons are willing to live in comfort even if the price of this is poverty, ignorance and disease of the majority of their fellowmen' [11, p. 89].

This comment suggests the importance of examining the U.S. AIDS crisis in terms of social class and ethnic relations, and, as indicated below, in terms of gender politics as well. Yet, as Ortner, argues, "The first thing that strikes an anthropologist reading the ethnographic literature on America, written by both sociologists and anthropologists, is the centrality of 'class' in sociological research and its marginality in anthropological studies" [12, p. 164]. Moreover, she reports that anthropological ethnographies of America society focus on "the minutiae of everyday life" while exhibiting a "tendency to avoid almost any kind of macrosociological analysis, let alone making class a central category of research" [12, p. 166]. Indeed, as she suggests, the chronic tendency of urban ethnography has been "to 'ethnicize' the groups under study, to treat them as so many isolated and exotic tribes," rather than to recognize their interconnections in light of transcendant processes and overarching structures [12, p. 166].

Reversing this more general trend in anthropology generally was one of the driving forces in the writing of *Europe and the People Without History*, Eric Wolf's seminal account of the broad historical patterns of political economic relationship between so-called core and peripheral areas of the world economic system. As Wolf has argued, the adoption of ethnography—the observation of social processes in natural contexts—as the defining hallmark of anthropological research had both beneficial and problematic consequences. While revealing "hitherto unsuspected connections among sets of social activities and cultural forms," it nonetheless "lulled its users into a false confidence" about the nature of social behavior [7, p. 13]. Increasingly, human groupings came to be seen and understood as concrete, independent wholes when they were in fact, like peasants, part-and-parcel of larger social units brought into being and shaped continually by wider fields of power. Unfortunately, these wider fields are not always clearly observable "on the ground," especially not by anthropologists who have been trained to avoid seeing them because they were defined as being beyond the pale of anthropological concern. Indeed, as Wolf noted in his Distinguished Lecture to the 88th meeting of the American Anthropological Association, the very term power tends to make anthropologists uncomfortable [13].

It is in light of Wolf's challenge to avoid exoticizing the people anthropologists study by focusing on relationships of power and broader nets of interconnection that we turn to an examination of the issue of AIDS in the inner city. Without doubt, the study of AIDS has taken anthropologists into a new domain of human biocultural experience. Consequently, Herdt stresses, AIDS "is not only affecting how we live and organize society but how we in anthropology and the social sciences must analyze that reality" [14, p. 3]. These changes warrant a careful consideration of the concepts we employ as we study the AIDS crisis. As Wolf indicated in the lecture mentioned above, "We need to be professionally suspicious of our categories and models; we should be aware of their historical and cultural contingencies . . ." [13, p. 587]. Among the inner city poor, the beginning point for re-examining the concepts mobilized by the public health system in responding to AIDS lies in situating this disease in terms of the broader configuration of health and social conditions that structures the epidemic.

CONTEXTUALIZING INNER CITY AIDS: FROM EPIDEMIC TO SYNDEMIC

AIDS was a profoundly unexpected disease, "a startling discontinuity with the past" [15, p. 1]. As McCombie suggests, global public health efforts that predate the beginning of the AIDS epidemic, such as the smallpox eradication program, "reinforced the notion that mortality from infectious disease was a thing of the past" [16, p. 10]. Consequently, whatever the actual health needs of the heterogeneous U.S.

population, the primary concerns of the health care system were the so-called Western diseases, that is chronic health problems, such as cancer and cerebrovascular problems, of a developed nation with an aging population [17]. Comments Brandt:

> The United States has relatively little recent experience dealing with health crises .... We had come to believe that the problem of infectious, epidemic diseases had passed—a topic of concern only to the developing world and historians [18, p. 367].

However, as a result of AIDS and widespread drug use as well, the term epidemic has re-entered popular vocabulary in recent years. It is evident that low-income, marginalized areas of American cities have been rocked by an explosive chain-reaction of interconnected epidemics.

Many definitions of the term epidemic exist. Marks and Beatty, in their history of the subject, adopt a broad approach and include both communicable and noncommunicable diseases that affect many persons at one time [19]. Epidemics (from *epi* or "in" and *demos* "the people") are conceptually linked to other terms in the "demic" family, including "endemics" (from *en* or "on"), which are non-explosive, entrenched diseases of everyday life in particular communities, and "pandemics" (from *pan* or "all of"), which are epidemics on an enlarged, perhaps, global scale.

None of these concepts, however, quite captures the contemporary inner city health crisis, which is characterized by a set of closely interrelated endemic and epidemic conditions, all of which are strongly influenced by a broader set of political-economic and social factors, including high rates of unemployment, poverty, homelessness and residential overcrowding, substandard nutrition, environmental toxins and related environmental health risks, infrastructural deterioration and loss of quality housing stock, family breakup and disruption of social support networks, youth gang and drug-related violence, and health care inequality [1, 20]. As a result, as McCord and Freeman have observed, men in Bangladesh have a higher probability of survival after age thirty-five than men in Harlem [21]. More generally, "the death rate in blacks is higher than that in whites, and for many causes of death mortality differentials are increasing rather than decreasing" [22, p. 1238]. However, these differences cannot be understood only in terms of racial inequalities, there are significant class factors involved as well. The vast majority of urban-dwelling African Americans, as well as Latinos, "are members of the low paid, poorly educated working class that have higher morbidity and mortality rates than high-earning, better educated people" [22, p. 1240]. Indeed, these mortality differentials are directly tied to the widening wealth and income differentials between the upper and lower classes.

Consequently, rather than treating AIDS in isolation as a new epidemic with unique features, this chapter understands AIDS in terms of the broader inner-city health crisis. Singer has suggested the term *syndemic* to refer to the set of synergistic or intertwined and mutual enhancing health and social problems facing the urban poor [23]. Developing this concept necessitates a closer examination of health in the Inner City.

A Profile of the Syndemic

Urban minority populations suffer from disproportionately high rates of preventable infant mortality and low birthweight, diabetes, hypertention, cirrhosis, tuberculosis, substance abuse, human immuno-deficiency disease, and sexually transmitted diseases [24-26]. For many health indicators, these differences are striking. Infant mortality, which is often used as a general reflection of the health of a population, provides a disturbing example. Infant mortality among inner city African Americans and Puerto Ricans has been called America's shameful little secret [27]. In 1987, the Children's Defense Fund announced that a child born in Costa Rica had a better chance of surviving beyond its first birthday than an African American child born in Washington, D.C. [28]. This pattern is not limited to the nation's capitol. Overall,

> .... African American children are twice as likely to be born prematurely, die during the first year of life, suffer low birthweight, have mothers who receive late or no prenatal care, be born to a teenage or unmarried parent, be unemployed as teenagers, have unemployed parents, and live in substandard housing. Furthermore, African-American children are three times more likely than whites to be poor, have their mothers die in childbirth, live in a female-headed family, be in foster care, and be placed in an educable mentally-retarded class [29, p. 153].

In some inner city neighborhoods of Hartford, where Singer has been involved in health research for the last ten years, the rate of infant mortality has been found to be between twenty-nine to thirty-one per 1,000 live births, more than three times the state average [30]. Similarly, in 1985 Boston experienced a 32 percent increase in infant mortality, with African American infants dying at two and a half times the rate of white infants. Rising infant mortality in Boston as elsewhere has been linked to a sharp increase in the percentage of low birth-weight babies, which in turn is seen as a product of "worsening housing conditions, nutrition and access to medical care" among inner city ethnic minorities [31, p. 1]. Although these "contributing variables act additively or synergistically," household income stands as the single best indicator of an infant's vulnerability, with poor families having infant mortality rates that are one and a half to three times higher than wealthier families [32, p. 374].

Class disparities in mortality rates are not limited to infancy, substantial differences also have been found among older children. For example, children from inner city poor families are more likely to die from respiratory diseases or in fires, than children from wealthier suburban families. Inadequately heated and ventilated apartments also contribute to death at an early age for poor urban children. Hunger and poor nutrition are additional factors. As Fitchen indicates

> That malnutrition and hunger exist in the contemporary United States seems unbelievable to people in other nations who assume that Americans can have whatever they want in life. Even within the United States, most people are not aware of domestic hunger or else believe that government programs and volunteer efforts must surely be taking care of hunger that does exist here [33, p. 309].

However, several studies have shown that a significant link exists between hunger, malnutrition, and inner city poverty, especially among ethnic minorities. A study by the Hispanic Health Council of 315 primarily minority households (39% African American, 56% Latino) with elementary school age children in eight Hartford neighborhoods found that 41.3 percent reported experiencing hunger during the previous twelve months (based on having positive answers to at least 5 of 8 questions on a hunger scale) and an additional 35.4 percent experienced food shortages that put them at risk of hunger (based on having a positive answer to at least one question on the hunger scale) [34]. It should be noted that the 1990 census (as did the 1980 census) found Hartford to be among among the 10 poorest cities (of over 100,000 population) in the country (as measured by percentage of people living in poverty). Over 27 percent of the city's residents fall below the federal poverty line, compared to a Connecticut statewide rate of just under 7 percent, according to the census [35]. Hartford, however, is not unique. Research conducted through the Harvard School of Public Health found that federal cuts in food assistance programs has contributed to significant drops in the number of children receiving free and reduced-price school lunches, producing growing reports of hunger and malnutrition from pediatricians in cities around the country [36]. The study, for example, found reports of marasmus (protein-calorie deficiency) and kwashiorkor (protein deficiency) in Chicago.

Cardiovacular disease commonly has been portrayed as primarily a consequence of either genetic predisposition or "life-style choice," including such factors as personal eating or exercise habits. As Crawford suggests, "Americans have . . . been exposed to a virtual media and professional blitz for a particular model of health promotion: one that emphasizes lifestyle change and individual responsibility" [37, p. 75]. Often these portrayals have had the ring of victim-blaming, implying that individuals personally select their "lifestyle" from a range of equally accessible options [38]. As a consequence, even at the popular level, health comes to be defined "in terms of self-control and a set of related concepts that include self-discipline, self-denial, and will power" [37, p. 66]. Research by David Barker and his colleagues on cardiovascular disease suggests the folly in this line of thinking. These researchers show that the lower the birthweight of a newborn or body weight of a one-year old infant, the greater the level of risk for developing heart disease or stroke in adulthood. Low birthweight babies, they report, have higher blood pressure and higher concentrations of the clotting factors fibrinogen and factor VII and low-density-liproprotein (LDL) cholesterol as adults, factors that are associated with susceptibility for cardiovascular disease. Numerous attempts have been made to explain excessive levels of premature morbidity and mortality from cardiovascular diseases, especially heart diseases, stroke, and hypertension. Some have attempted to explain this pattern in terms of racial-genetic predisposition. Research by Barker and others, however, reveals the relationship of these diseases to the larger syndemic health crisis [e.g., 39].

Alcohol-related problems have been found to be especially common among Latinos, particularly Mexican-American and Puerto Rican men. A study in the San Francisco Bay area, for example, found that 35 percent of Latino men reported at least one alcohol-related health or social problem compared to 26 percent of white men [40]. A study of drinking patterns among Puerto Rican men in Hartford found that, compared to a national sample of men, they were much more likely to report health problems associated with drinking, acting belligerently under the influence, having a friend or spouse complain about their drinking, having alcohol-related problems with the police, and engaging in binge-drinking [41]. Similarly, studies of inner city African Americans have found they experience higher than average rates of physiological complications, such as esophageal cancer and cirrhosis mortality, related to long-term heavy alcohol consumption [42-45]. While both Latino and African American cultures include strong proscriptions on alcohol consumption (in certain contexts, for certain social subgroups, or in relationship to particular religious belief systems), while inner city areas are populated by people who embrace a range of values and social practices related to drinking [43, 46, 47], and while abstinence is notably high among particular social groupings in the inner city, drinking-related problems are comparatively high for both ethnic populations. As Herd indicates with specifilc reference to African Americans,

> Medical problems associated with heavy drinking have increased very dramatically in the black population. Rates of acute and chronic alcohol-related diseases among blacks, which were formerly lower than or similar to whites, have in the post war years increased to almost epidemic proportions. Currently, blacks are at extremely high risk for morbidity and mortality for acute and chronic alcohol-related diseases such as alcohol fatty liver, hepatitis, liver cirrhosis, and esophageal cancer [48, p. 309].

The association between drug use and deteriorated inner city areas has been discussed in the social science literature since the days of the Chicago School of Sociology [49, 50]. More recently, several large- and small-scale epidemiological studies have collected data on drug-related incidence, prevalence, morbidity and morality among inner city ethnic minorities. The findings of these studies have been summarized by Andrea Kopstein and Patrice Roth in a report for the National Institute on Drug Abuse (NIDA). These researchers note that while the National Household Survey on Drug Abuse indicates a decline in current illicit drug use nationally, "Minorities, particularly blacks and Hispanics, are more likely to reside in central city areas and may therefore be *more at risk* for drug abuse and ultimately more at risk for the negative social and health consequence associated with drug abuse" than the general U.S. population [51, pp. 1-2]. Specifically, the National Household Survey shows that among adults over thirty-five years of age, African American men are the population subgroup most likely to report illicit drug use at least once in their lives, in the past year, and in the past month. Thirty-seven percent of African American men in this age group report lifetime use, compared to 25 percent of white men. For example, the prevalence of drug use in the month prior to the interview was 2 percent for white men compared to 5 percent for African American men. An examination of individual drug prevalence patterns also confirms the high level of risk among ethnic minority groups. For cocaine use, Hispanic youth aged twelve to seventeen have higher prevalence rates than African American or white youth, while African Americans have the highest cocaine prevalence rates among adults over thirty-five years of age. Regarding heroin use, 2.3 percent of African Americans, 1. 1 percent of Hispanics, and 0.8 percent of whites have ever been users. Data from NIDA's Drug Abuse Warning Network (DAWN), a national system for monitoring the medical consequences of drug abuse as reported by participating hospital emergency rooms and medical examiner offices, show a similar pattern. According to the 1989 data reported by the DAWN system, African American patients were the most likely group to mention use of an illicit drug in conjunction with their emergency room visit. All of these data suggest that directly and indirectly drug abuse disproportionately affects inner-city ethnic minority populations. Importantly, despite this fact, Kopstein and Roth, note that "blacks presenting with a drug abuse problem at the emergency rooms in the DAWN system were more likely than whites to be treated and released. Whites, on the other hand were more likely to be admitted to the hospital" [51, p. 51].

Additionally, both African Americans and Latinos have been found to be over-represented among the large number of injection drug users (IDUs) in U.S. urban areas [52]. David Musto, whose book *The American Disease* is a classic in the drug field, has assembled data to suggest a steady rise in the number of IDUs from the 1970s on [53]. He estimates that the number of heroin injectors soared from 50,000 to at least a half-million between 1960 and 1970. By 1987, the National Association of State Alcohol and Drug Abuse Directors, Inc. (NASADAD) concluded that there were about 1.5 million IDUs in the United States based on aggregated data from state alcohol and drug agencies [reported in 26]. The level of minority involvement in injection drug use is seen by examining New York City data, in that New York is a national center of drug injection and has the highest number of IDUs in the country. Friedman et al., using New York State Division of Substance Abuse Services admissions data, estimate that the ethnic composition of injection drug users in New York City is 38 percent African American, 38 percent Latino, and 23 percent white, while the city as a whole is 52 percent white, 24 percent African American, and 20 percent Latino [54].

These data suggest that under conditions of discrimination, poverty, deprivation, unemployment, and frustrated expectations, mood altering drugs found an open market in inner city areas [1]. As Hanson comments

> Many of the minority newcomers [to urban areas] became victims of unemployment, poverty, and racial discrimination . . . . Is it surprising that they sometimes coped with this situation by turning to drugs? [55, p. 3].

This response to oppressive conditions was facilitated by the ready availability of drugs in ghetto and barrio neighborhoods, a consequence of Mafia targeting of these areas for drug distribution. As Waldorf observes, "Heroin is seemingly everywhere in Black and Puerto Rican ghettos and young people are aware of it from an early age" [56]. To these youth, drugs offer insulation from the outside world allowing users to

> feel that their harsh and hostile environment cannot penetrate their lives. They escape from their problems, other people, and feel better [57, p. 89].

For inner city residents, drug involvement can come to seem like the only available path, a natural life development, as expressed by a twenty-two year-old addict from Miami:

> You grow up in a place where everything is a real mess. Your father's a thief, your mother's a whore, your kid sister gets herself some new clothes by fucking the landlord's son, your brother's in the joint, your boyfriend gets shot trying to pull down a store, and everybody else around you is either smokin' dope, shooting stuff, taking pills, stealing with both hands, or working on their backs, or all of the above. All of a sudden you find that you're sweet sixteen and you're doing the same things . . . . It all came on kind of naturally [quoted in 58, p. 162].

In this way, drug use and drug injection became widespread among urban minority youth in the 1950s and has continued its prevalence ever since [59, 60].

The transmission of AIDS, of course, has been closely linked to drug injection [61-66]. Among drug injectors with AIDS nationally, 79.2 percent are African American or Latino [67]. In New York City, there was a threefold increase in overall mortality and morbidity among IDUs in treatment between 1984 and 1987. While rates of hospitalization in this population rose by 40 percent for AIDS between 1986 and 1987, they rose by over 300 percent for tuberculosis and 100 percent for endocarditis [68]. Among women, 51 percent of all U.S. AIDS cases are African American, and another 20 percent are Latina [67]. Among children, over 75 percent of AIDS cases are among ethnic minorities. The incidence of heterosexually acquired AIDS is almost ten times greater for African Americans and four times greater for Latinos than for whites [69]. Similarly, "[a] disproportionate share of the burden of adolescent AIDS cases is borne by minority youth" [70, p. 160].

To date, there have about 250,000 diagnosed cases of AIDS in the United States. Of these, 30 percent are African Americans and 17 percent are Latinos [71]. While these two ethnic groups comprise about 28 percent of the U.S. population, they account for 47 percent of AIDS cases. Importantly, the median survival time of individuals diagnosed with AIDS varies by ethnicity. In Connecticut, for example, the median survival in months is 11.2 for Whites compared to 7.7 for African Americans and 10.2 for Latinos [72], reflecting the broader differences in the general health and access to health services of these populations.

Since the mid-1980s, there has been a dramatic rise in the incidence of syphilis in the United States, "attributable to a very steep rise in infection among black men and women" [69, p. 63]. While rates of infection dropped below 5,000 cases per 100,000 population for white men in 1985 and continued to decline through 1988, for African American men the rate began climbing in 1985 and by 1988 was about 17,000 cases per 100,000 population. Among women, in 1988 there were about 2,000 and 13,000 cases per 100,000 for white and African American women respectively. By 1991, 85 percent of primary and secondary syphilis cases recorded in the United States were among African Americans [73]. In part, this sharp increase has been linked to sex for drugs or money exchanges associated with cocaine use. Blood test data show that low income, urban residence, and lack of education are all associated with positive blood results for syphilis. Rates of gonorrhea infection also show marked racial differences, and these differences have noticeably widened since 1984 when the incidence among African Americans began a sizeable increase. By 1991, of the 544,057 cases of gonorrhea reported to the Centers for Disease Control, 82 percent were among African Africans [73]. Beginning in 1984, another sexually transmitted disease, chancroid, which produces open lesions and has been associated with HIV transmission in parts of Africa, began to appear in a number of U.S. inner cities. The total number of chancroid cases reported in the United States rose from 665 in 1984 to 4,714 by 1989 [69]. Similarly, African American women report 1.8 times the rate of pelvic inflammatory disease as do white women, while herpes simplex virus type 2 is 3.4 times higher in African Americans, hepatitis B is 4.6 times higher, and cervical cancer with a suspected STD etiology is 2.3 times more common among African Americans than whites [74].

As this epidemiologic overview suggests, the diseases and conditions that comprise the inner city syndemic are closely intertwined. Poverty contributes to poor nutrition and susceptibility to infection. Poor nutrition, chronic stress, and prior disease contribute to a compromised immune system, increasing susceptibility to new infection. A range of socio-economic problems and stressors increase the likelihood of substance abuse and exposure to HIV. Substance abuse contributes to increased risk for exposure to an STD, which can, in turn, be a co-factor in HIV infection. HIV further damages the immune system, increasing susceptibility to a host of other diseases. In this way, HIV increases susceptibility to tuberculosis, however, there is growing evidence that the tuberculosis bacterium, in turn, can activate latent HIV.

An overview of the grave nature of the health crisis of the inner city poor suggests that problem-specific, short-term health projects, the kind that time-limited, soft-money funding commonly are designed to launch, are short-sighted and ill conceived. Rather, there is a critical need for longer-term, more comprehensive, systemic public health efforts that address the root causes of the crisis, causes that lie in the oppressive structuring of class, ethnic, and gender relations in U.S. society. Additionally, locating and reconceptualizing AIDS within the broader syndemic that plagues the inner city poor, helps to demystify the rapid spread of the disease in marginalized populations. In this context, *AIDS, itself emerges as an opportunistic disease*, a disease of compromised health and social conditions, a disease of poverty. It is for this reason, that it is important to examine the social origins of disease and ill health, whatever the immediate causes (e.g., particular pathogens) of specific health problems. In the case of AIDS, conceptually isolating this disease from its wider health environment has resulted in the epidemiological construction of "risk groups" and "risk behaviors" which, rather than unhealthy living and working conditions, discrimination, racism, homophobia and related issues, have become the primary focus of public health efforts. Lost in this effort, is an understanding of AIDS as a disease that is spreading under particular historic and political conditions [75]. Instead, an approach has been adopted that has "skewed the choice of models and hypotheses, determined which data were excluded from consideration . . ., and offered scientific justification for popular prejudice . . ." [76, p. 50].

FUZZY CONCEPTUAL CATEGORIES IN THE AIDS FIELD

The conceptual skewing alluded to by Oppenheimer has its roots in the fact that epidemiologists, like other scientists, are "cultural actors, prone to the blind spots and folk theories of their own society" [76, p. 7]. Because the first few cases of AIDS in New York and Los Angeles were among self-identified gay men, the initial etiological questions generated by the public health system had to do with whether there was something peculiar about the biology or social behavior of gay men that was causing this new disease. Soon other kinds of people were found to be contracting the disease, leading to the creation of the risk group *4 H Club*: homosexuals, hemophiliacs, Haitians, and heroin users. As this heterogeneous listing suggests, from the beginning of the epidemic, there has been an effort to divide people into distinct social categories. While the idea of risk group has been strongly challenged, and the emphasis in recent years has been on risk behaviors, there remains the sense that discrete and bounded categories of people exist that are at special risk and in need of special prevention efforts, including, if necessary, isolation from the "mainstream" population. Indeed, the language of prevention often has implied that the primary motivation for prevention among high risk groups is to avoid spread of AIDS into the "mainstream" (i.e., white, heterosexuals who are neither prostitutes or injection drug users).

The primary constructed categories of AIDS risk and transmission in the United States, which show up in the regular Centers for Disease Control and Prevention surveillance reports on the epidemic, and the reports of city and state health departments around the country, include:

homosexual/bisexual

intravenous drug use

sex partner of an IV drug user

While, from a distance, these terms seem to be meaningful and to label real types of people or at least types of behavior, a closer examination shows the fuzziness and constructed character of these epidemiological categories. Often, epidemiologically constructed "risk groups" have little correspondence with the active social identities and social locations of those at risk for HIV infection. As Kane and Mason note, "The static and fragmented sense of the social dimension of HIV risk conveyed by risk group categories is inevitably challenged by ethnography" [77, p. 220]. Ethnography also reveals the problem of attempting to use these categories as the basis for directing prevention efforts.

Firstly, what is a homosexual? Do homosexual constitute a group? A subculture? In what sense is this a discrete entity or natural category? For example, in much of Latin America and among Latinos in the United States a differentiation is made between *activos* and *pasivos*, the former being men who insert during anal intercourse and the latter being those who receive [78, 79]. Unlike among white gay men in the United States, these appear to be somewhat distinct and enduring sexual identities rather than interchangeable sexual positions. Importantly, activos do not consider themselves to be homosexuals but they do consider pasivos to be homosexuals. Writing of Mexico, Carrier notes that males who play the insertive role

are not stigmatized as 'homosexual' .... The masculine self-image of Mexican males is thus not threatened by their homosexual behavior as long as the appropriate role is played and they also have sexual relations with women. Males playing this role are referred to as *mayates*; and may be called *chichifo* if they habitually do so for money. Although involved in bisexual behavior, they consider themselves to be heterosexual [80, p. 134].

Unlike in the United States generally, the key defining issue in homosexuality is not who you do it with but what you do with them. Additionally, Carrier maintains that

> at any given age, more sexually active single males in Mexico have had sexual intercourse with both genders than have Anglo-American males. The Kinsey . . . data suggest that about 15 percent of single sexually active Anglo-American males between 15 and 25 have mixed sexual histories. The percentage of Mexican males with mixed histories may be as high as 30 or more for the same age group [80, p. 135].

These patterns are not limited to Mexico, but are found as well in the barrio neighborhoods of the U.S. inner city. A study of Mexican Americans in California thus reports that "even though immigrant Mexican male patterns of sexual behavior are somewhat modified by new and quite different sociocultural factors, their homosexual behaviors in California continue to be mainly patterned on their prior sexual experiences in Mexico. As a result of selective acculturation by individuals of Mexican origin to mainstream Anglo American patterns of sexual behavior, however, considerable behavior variations exist among Mexican American males involved in homosexual behavior" [81, p. 252].

Singer and his colleagues have encountered this same "problem" of diversity at the Hispanic Health Council in developing AIDS prevention targeted to the inner city gay Latino population of Hartford, Connecticut. In recruiting an outreach worker for the Latino Gay Men's Health Project, they found that it was difficult to identify a Latino gay or bisexual man with any prior experience in AIDS prevention, reflecting the failure of training programs to reach this population. The individual who ultimately was hired to fill this position brought a substantial background in AIDS outreach. However, it soon became evident that as a transvestite his primary outreach contacts were confined to one sector of the gay/bisexual community and it was difficult for him to recruit from other sectors of the complex and diverse Latino gay/bisexual population. Activities and approaches that were acceptable for one sector of this multifarious "group" were inappropriate and uncomfortable for another. Some participants, for example, complained about the lack of a "serious attitude" toward AIDS prevention among those they identified as the "drag queens" in the group.

Consequently, despite being lumped together by the homophobia of the dominant society, it is evident that men who have sex with men do not constitute one or even two distinct social groups, rather they comprise a broad range of individuals and include those organized into several different (in part overlapping, in part mutually exclusive) activity/identity oriented subgroups and those who do not identify with any specific subgroup or embrace a homosexual identity. Failure to recognize this diversity stems from the historic biomedical construction of homosexuality as a fixed inverted behavioral pattern rooted in genetic make-up, hormonal malfunctions, or specific developmental psychodynamics and family patterns. In AIDS research and prevention, this essentialist view of homosexuality often has "blinded researchers [and providers] to the diversity of behavioral patterns within the gay community" [82, p. 193].

IV drug user is another problematic epidemiological category for several reasons. First, not all people who inject illicit drugs, inject them into their veins, that is, not all drug injectors are IV drug injectors. Consequently, despite its wide use in the literature, the label IV drug user increasingly is being replaced by the term injection drug user (IDU). Even the drugs that people inject vary considerably. For example, some individuals have been found to be alcohol injectors. This practice, though apparently limited, is legal, although it is no less risky in terms of HIV transmission than illicit drug injection. Second, to what degree are drug injectors a discrete group? To a large degree, the construction of drug injectors as a distinct, coherent, and social isolated group has been achieved through a professional discourse on the drug subculture. A broad literature on this "subculture" existed prior to the 1980s and it has been expanded considerably since then because of AIDS. For example, Fiddle comments: "addicts share a . . . culture with its own language," [83, p. 4] while Freudenberg writes that "[d]rug using behavior is deeply rooted in the drug subculture" [84, p. 1128]. On the positive side, the subculture perspective has been offered as an alternative to psychologistic understandings of injection drug user behavior. Note Friedman and his coworkers,

> In contrast to views that see IV drug use as simply a matter of individual pathol-
> ogy, it is more fruitful to describe IV drug users as constituting a "subculture" as
> this term has been used within sociological and anthropological research. . . .
> This calls our attention to the structured sets of values, roles, and status alloca-
> tions that exists among IV drug users . . . From the perspective of it members,
> participating in the subculture is a meaningful activity that provides desired
> rewards, rather than psychopathology, an "escape from reality," or an "illness"
> [85, p. 385].

Although contributors to the drug subculture literature recognize that there are regional and ethnic variations, they often write as though it is nonetheless possible to analyze IDUs as constituting a single subculture. The existence of a distinct subculture among IDUs has been dated to the 1930s and is attributed, at least by some researchers, to the passage of the Harrison Act in 1914, which began the process of criminalizing drug use in the United States. As a result, subcultural drug users came to "perceive themselves as culturally and socially detached from the life style and everyday preoccupations of members of the conventional world" [86, p. 128] and to associate more-or-less exclusively with other IDUs [87].

Drug users' vernacular is said to perform several significant functions in maintaining the subculture, including setting its social boundaries, labeling in-group experiences so that they might serve as bonding mechanisms, shaping members' identities, and allowing access to drugs and protection from the police. Argues Iglehart, a shared drug-related language is used in "informational exchanges . . . and as a manipulative tool to insulate and protect the users within his world and from the larger society outside" [88, p. 111].

Beyond discussions of drug language, the substance abuse subculture literature includes descriptions of group rituals for drug injection (e.g., "booting," the process of drawing blood into the needle while shooting up), behavioral expectations in several socially constructed subcultural scenes (e.g., rules for appropriate behavior in shooting galleries and drug copping areas), subculturally patterned social interaction and recognized social roles (e.g., social control activities by the houseman at a shooting gallery), life coping strategies (e.g., pooling resources to purchase drugs, diverse hustling schemes, techniques for hiding drugs to avoid police detection), and group-specific values (e.g., respect shown to long time drug injectors), in short, an authentic cultural florescence. Pivotal to this subcultural system, needle sharing has been described as a core rite of intensification, "a symbol of social bonding among people who otherwise have little occasion to trust one another" as Conviser and Rutledge put it, [89, p. 45] while "tracks" (evidence of needle-inflicted damage to veins) are described as proud badges of group membership.

Further, Inciardi argues that violence is an integral component of the drug subculture and one that does not necessarily stem from the fact that drug possession and use are illegal [58]. He cites a number of contexts in the subculture in which violence is prescribed: "territorial disputes between rival drug dealers; assaults and homicides committed within dealing and trafficking hierarchies as means of enforcing normative codes; robberies of drug dealers, often followed by unusually violent relataliations; elimination of informers; punishment for selling adulterated, phony, or otherwise 'bad' drugs; punishment for failing to pay one's debts; and general disputes over drugs or drug paraphernalia" [58, pp. 137-138]. AIDS and the fear of using infected needles, he asserts, has added a new context for the expression of violence among drug users.

A major implication of the drug subculture literature is the belief that injection drug users are so marginalized and estranged from the mainstream world that ethnic identity or other social roles are of minimal salience to them and, by extension, may not be of particular relevance to AIDS prevention efforts developed in the inner city for hardcore drug users. From this view, what matters most to the IDU is his/her next "fix" and hence the cultural mechanisms that facilitate access to drugs are more meaningful and valued than ethnic heritage or other cultural identities such a kinship.

However, there are reasons to be cautious in adopting a subcultural model for understanding IDUs [90]. First, it is far from clear that they possess an enduring, homogeneous, or well developed subculture that exists in any significant degree of isolation from broader cultural traditions. According to Page, injection drug use has a relatively short history; group lore is fairly limited; injection vernacular, though real and important, is characterized by considerable geographic variability; orthodoxy in shooting practices is unlikely given geographic variation in drugs of choice; and drug use patterns are subject to rapid shifts, including adoption of non-injection patterns of drug consumption when injectable drugs are in short supply, available drugs are of particularly poor quality, or in response to health education efforts [91]. A comparison between injection drug users in Miami and Hartford, in fact, shows that there exists considerable variation in drug use practices, drugs of choice, needle practices, injection locations, level of sexual risk, and sociodemographic characteristics of drug injectors [92]. For example, while 76 percent of the IDUs recruited through inner city street outreach in Hartford reported at least daily drug injection, in Miami only 33 percent reported this level of injection frequency. Frequency of heroin use was found to be particularly important in differentiating Hartford and Miami injectors. Thus, while 69 percent of Hartford IDUs reported daily injection of heroin, this was true for only 19.5 percent of their Miami counterparts. Even within ethnic groups, diversity is considerable across geographic areas. An analysis of drug use and AIDS risk among Puerto Rican IDUs in eight U.S. cities found that crack was used in much greater frequency in Miami and Harlem than in the other six cities; while the inhalation of heroin was fairly common among Puerto Rican IDUs in Newark, this practice was rare in some other cities, especially Miami; speedball (a mixture of heroin and cocaine) was quite commonly injected in Hartford but unusual in Chicago; and while injected cocaine was the drug of choice in Philadelphia, and injected heroin filled this bill in Jersey City, in Hartford, both drugs injected alone and in combination, was found to be the norm [92]. This inter-city variation in drug use patterns reflects even wider behavioral differences associated with the routes of consumption and biochemical effects of specific drugs as well as the cultural construction of these effects. Considerable variation also exists within individual cities. In a survey using a random sample of persons with AIDS in New Jersey, IDUs were found to have varied life styles, rather than to be participants in a single subculture [93].

Additionally, Bovelle and Taylor point out that while IDUs make use of a *drug argot,* many users express their "connection with mainstream culture by their ability to shift easily in and out of standard English when expediency demanded . . ." [94, p. 178]. In fact, drug users, for the most part, have not developed a unique idiom. Rather, much of what has been identified as drug language has its origin in working class Black English. As Inglehart recognizes, the "[t]erminology and metaphorical imagery used by addicts are often drawn from Black slang, and reflect Afro-American cultural values as expressed in dynamic, performance-oriented speech" [88, p. 112]. While Latino drug users in U.S. inner city areas have been heavily influenced by African American cultural and linguistic patterns as well, they tend also to draw on their Latino subculture as a linguistic and cultural source. Additionally, the language of both African American and Latino drug users has been heavily influenced by the drug treatment "subculture" especially the 12-Step self-help movement but other treatment modalities as well.

Further, closer investigation has shown that the primary reason that most injection drug users share needles is not ritual expression or social bonding but survival-oriented pragmaticism [95]. For example, in his study of male prostitute injection drug users in San Francisco, Waldorf found that the primary reason for sharing was lack of needles rather than a symbolic importance placed on the act of sharing [96]. Additionally, many drug injectors have been found to try hard to avoid developing tracks so that they will not be identifiable as a drug user [76]. "Passing" as a non-user, by painstakingly avoiding fitting any of the reigning drug user appearance or behavioral stereotypes is a survival strategy adopted by some IDUs. This gambit involves limiting participation in drug-oriented social scenes to the minimum necessary to secure drugs, a behavioral pattern that constrains the development of a drug subculture.

In sum, while it is not incorrect to talk of a drug subculture, in doing so, we believe, it is important to avoid reifying and exoticizing this phenomenon while undervaluing

other identities and cultural influences on IDUs, including the pull of ethnic identification, attachment to local communities, and involvement in kin networks. The
Heroin Lifestyle Study of African American IDU men, for instance, identified many
"long-time, serious heroin users" who nonetheless were "still active in their communities."

> A common 'bond' among these men was minority group status in a society
> perceived by many to be racist. This ingroup experience of being Black and poor
> was reflected repeatedly in the comments of study participants. For example, in
> response to the question, how do you spend your day, one man responded: 'I
> listen to records . . . things like that, watch T.V. I enjoy doing what anybody else
> would do. No different, I'm Black and I'm poor [55, p. 6].

Also, existing research points to important differences among IDUs across ethnic
groups. In terms of life experience, psychological impairment, and drug use course a
number of differences have been noted [97]. For example, a comparison of Chicano
and Anglo IDUs by Anglin and co-workers [98] found that the former tend to traverse
a shorter road to drug injection that includes consumption of a narrower variety of
drugs than the latter.

Moreover, the notion of a subculture of injection drug use can be problematic if it
suggests that subcultural norms and values independently generate and sustain risk
behavior [76]. As indicated, needle sharing tends to be produced by lack of access to
needles not subcultural values about the social bonding achieved by sharing. The critical
issue is the social location of injection drug users as social outcasts (and hence the federal
ban on use of federal funds for needle exchange) and not IDU subculture per se.

Finally, there is the category, sex partner of an injection drug user. As Glick
Schiller points out, unlike members of the dominant society, IDUs commonly are
"described as having 'sex partners' rather than lovers or spouses" [99, p. 243]. One of
the common conceptual leaps that occurs with this term is the assumption that it
refers to women who are partners of male drug users with little thought given to the
possibility of men who do not use drugs being in relationships with women who do.
Also, as Kane has emphasized, sex partner of a drug injector is not a natural category,
it is not a social group, nor is it necessary a part of an individual's identity [100].
Indeed, many people are sex partners of injection drug users and do not know it.
Others may suspect but fear knowing the full truth. Needless to say, this makes
prevention efforts targeted to individual at risk in this way very difficult. As Herdt
has written: "Though the notion of sexual partner may seem obvious, it varies across
cultures and is probably the source of significant error in research design. Whether a
partnership is sexual and/or social, culturally approved or disapproved, voluntary or
coercive, is of real import . . . ." [14, p. 13].

In sum then, we see the degree to which epidemiology, in responding to AIDS, has
constructed rather than discovered relevant social categories and the extent to which
there is a "lack of correspondence between . . . categories and the social reality to
which these categories are meant to refer" [100, p. 1049]. As Stone emphasizes

> risk factors and designations of high-risk groups do not grow immediately and
> automatically out of epidemiological research. They are created in a social

context that involves judgement, persuasion, bargaining and political maneuvering [101, pp. 91-92].

Unfortunately, one of the primary consequences of the association in the public's mind of these so-called risk groups with AIDS is that most people have been allowed to feel that they are not at risk, when in fact they are. Observes Glick Schiller,

In 1989 the Presidential Commission on the Human Immunodeficiency Virus Epidemic recommended that 'people who fall into any (high risk) categories should seek testing and counseling services from their physician or public health agency, regardless of presence or absence of symptoms. The logical result of such advice was that if you did not see yourself as gay, as an IV drug user, or as a sex partner of an IV drug user, you did not think of yourself as being at risk for AIDS [99, p. 245].

A number of serious consequences flow from the social and epidemiological construction of AIDS risk groups. These include: 1) perpetuating popular misunderstanding of who is at risk for AIDS and how they are at risk; 2) mistargeting of health education efforts; 3) spreading of the disease because people miscalculate their personal level of risk; 4) stigmatizing, silencing, and abusing individuals with AIDS; 5) dividing communities and thereby reducing their ability to participate collectively in building unified and effective responses to the epidemic; 6) reinforcing social divisions that block politically conscious class formation among the poor and working classes, 7) increasing the mistreatment of socially stigmatized groups; and 8) concentrating public health resources specifically on AIDS while comparatively ignoring the syndemic and social nature of AIDS in the inner city [99].

From the perspective of critical medical anthropology, avoiding these problems requires a reconsideration in light of three important *social dimensions* of AIDS, its: *social construction, social transmission,* and *social location.*

THE SOCIAL DIMENSIONS OF AIDS

Like nineteenth-century cholera, AIDS is accurately described as a disease of society in the most profound sense [102]. This is true because of three social dimensions of AIDS that have helped to shape the character of the disease and the challenge it presents for carrying out useful work in medical anthropology in the inner city.

AIDS as a Social Construction

AIDS is socially constructed, in the sense that its impact as an arena of focused human experience is shaped by social definitions, social values, and social relationships. For example, there has been the protracted discussion at the Centers for Disease Control and Prevention over the definition of AIDS: should AIDS be defined in terms of a blood test showing the presence of HIV antibodies (i.e., immune system response to infection with the virus) combined with the development at least one so-called opportunistic disease (proving a deterioration of bodily functioning) from an approved list of identified AIDS-related diseases, or should it be defined in terms of blood test results plus a specified rate of a special type of white blood cell (CD4 type leukocytes) per unit of blood, given the tendency of the virus to target, penetrate, and progressively destroy these cells. While the latter option has won out, either way, of course, the AIDS diagnosis is a socially constructed label. AIDS is present only when those with authority to define disease say so. As Treichler [103] has suggested, the situation is reminiscent of a apocryphal story from baseball: Three empires are talking. The first empire says: I call 'em as I sees 'em. The second empire says: I calls 'em as they are. And the third empire, they one who perhaps best understands the social nature of the game, says: They ain't nothin till I calls 'em. In AIDS, the latter condition reigns but not without challenge.

For example, at the beginning of the epidemic, AIDS, or GRID (gay-related immunodeficiency) as it was then called, was biomedically constructed exclusively as a disease of gay men. Consequently, the appearance of AIDS-like symptoms ("gay cancer," "gay pneumonia") among inner-city children did not lead to a diagnosis of AIDS. In December 1981, when Arye Rubinstein, chief of Albert Einstein's Medical College Division of Allergy and Immunology submitted a paper to the annual conference of the American Academy of Pediatrics suggesting that the African American children that he was treating in the Bronx were suffering from the same disease as immunodeficiency gay men, he was rebuffed.

> Such thinking ... was simply too farfetched for a scientific community that, when it thought about gay cancer and gay pneumonia at all, was quite happy to keep the problem just that: gay. The academy would not accept Rubinstein's abstract for presentation at the conference, and among immunologists, word quietly circulated that [Rubinstein] had gone a little batty [104, p. 104].

The same pattern occurred among inner city drug injectors who presented immunodeficiency disorders in the early 1980s. Consistently, health officials "reported them as being homosexual, being strangely reluctant to shed the notion that this was a gay disease; all these junkies would somehow turn out to be gay in the end, they said" [104, p. 106].

Similarly, even since AIDS came to be seen as a disease transmitted through the "sharing" of drug injection equipment, there are indications that many people in the inner city had died of HIV-related causes even though they were never diagnosed as having AIDS. For example, while Commissioner of Health for New York City, Joseph, reported:

> During the last five years, we have seen a dramatic increase in the numbers of deaths of IV drug abusers ... They have been dying from TB, pneumonia, and other conditions that could very well be complications of AIDS- related immunosuppression *not identified as CDC-defined AIDS* .... If we adjust our surveillance for this increase in deaths among IV drug addicts, the absolute number of AIDS-related ... deaths in the City would be as much *as 50% higher than is currently reported* (emphasis added) [105, p. 163].

Indeed, the redefinition of AIDS that has recently occurred followed on the heels of a protracted debate about the failure of the CDC-definition to include opportunistic vaginal and pelvic infections that are peculiar to women, and are disproportionately common among inner city women who have died in increasing numbers from immunodeficiency conditions in recent years.

Understanding the social construction of AIDS, in short, is critical to fighting AIDS in the inner city. However, because it "accords social class (in the form of class-linked power differentials) a central role in the study of social relations of sickness and healing" [106, p. 29], it is sometimes assumed that critical medical anthropology is only concerned with macrolevel phenomena and overlooks the importance of culture as a signifying system used by people to construct a meaningful social world. Following the approach of Roseberry [107], however, it is possible to sidestep the traditional materialist/idealist antinomy in anthropological theory build-ing by viewing social construction itself as a material social process. The objective of this approach is to understand cultural categories "not simply as socially constituted but as socially constituting" [107, p. 28], that is, not just as products or fixed metaphoric, symbolic, or evaluative expressions of a given culture (i.e., cultural texts to be read or interpreted) but as part of the flow of ongoing politically and economi-cally influenced cultural production. This emphasis on creation draws attention to the context of cultural production, including raising questions about who is involved in the productive process, who controls or shapes the direction of cultural production, and who benefits thereof, as well as what is the historic and socio-political location of this process. In Mintz's apt phrase, "Where does the locus of meaning reside?" [8, p. 157] In other words,

> If culture is text, it is not everyone's text. Beyond the obvious fact that it means different things to different people or different sorts of people, we must ask who is (or are) doing the writing [107, p. 24].

This discussion focuses attention on the ways in which the construction of AIDS as a meaningful cultural category proceeds within social fields of power. Whether it be the development of disease definitions, creation of AIDS-related knowledge about the immune system, the construction of "risk groups," the defining of risky settings (e.g., gay bath houses, ghettos, shooting galleries), the labeling of risk behavior (e.g., promiscuity, prostitution), or the setting of parameters on AIDS education (e.g., federal ban on portraying homosexuality in a positive light in AIDS projects sup-ported with federal dollars), the social construction of AIDS occurs in a world of contested interests and hierarchical relations.

Further, attention is drawn to the historic impact of particular meaningful con-structs as they gain acceptance and are transmitted socially as the lens through which aspects of the world are known and experienced. Once a social construction like AIDS becomes established (i.e., becomes part of either the dominant/hegemonic culture or a sub-/counterhegemonic culture), it acts as a material force in shaping subsequent social behavior and relationship, including helping to set the parameters of latter social contestation. The rise to prominence of particular configurations and their influences on social action can only be understood therefore by linking cultural construction to the structure of social relationship. For, in addition to endowing the world with meaning and order, culture "perpetuates and legitimates power" [108, p. 166].

We would like to stress that this does not mean that the social understandings packed into AIDS as a cultural concept are products of social forces alone. As a materialist perspective, CMA begins with the assumption that HIV has an independent physical existence (that is, independent of its meaningful construction in one or another cultural system, including that of immunology or biomedicine generally), and that characteristics and organic effects of the virus impose themselves on human experience. Experience of the virus, in short, is shaped, in part, by its biotic qualities. Treichler has identified a continuum of approaches to understanding the relationship between culture and biology in AIDS:

> First, the virus is a stable, discoverable entity in nature whose reality is certified and accurately represented by scientific research; a high degree of correspondence is assumed between reality and biomedical models. Second, the virus is a stable, discoverable entity in nature but is assigned different names and meanings within the signifying systems of different cultures; all are equally valid though not all are equally correct. Third, our knowledge of the virus and other natural phenomena is inevitably mediated through our symbolic construction of them; biomedicine is only one among many, but one that currently has privileged status [103, p. 67] .

At either end of this epistemological and ontological continuum are two additional approaches. The *mechanical materialist* view understands HIV as a discrete and knowable part of physical reality that cultures merely label, while the *radical idealist* approach portrays HIV as a fully human construction, an abstraction from a whirling buzzing world that is not directly knowable but must be responded to by an encultured being. In Treichler's view, conventional medical anthropologists have tended to opt for the middle ground: "Most seem more comfortable with the notion of a single, stable, underlying biological reality to which different cultures assign different meanings than with the view that everything we know about reality is ultimately a cultural construction" [103, p. 68].

The CMA perspective differs from the conventional view in medical anthropology because it argues that even if it is assumed that HIV is a part of nature, it need not be seen as having an existence that is necessarily independent from human activity and culture, including political economy, because nature need not be understood from an ahistoric naturalistic perspective. From this standpoint, it is readily seen that nature is shaped by society no less than society is shaped by its encounter with nature [108]. In our encounter with nature we confront ourselves through the imprint of past human interactions with the physical world. For example, it has been suggested that both the evolution of HIV from a simian virus into a species adapted to human hosts as well as the initial spread of the virus among people in Africa were consequences of the polio vaccination campaign conducted in the Congo during the 1950s (on the grounds that oral polio vaccine was prepared from the kidneys of African green monkeys). While this particular connection has been disputed by vaccine researchers [109], it suggests one of the many ways human actions historically have played a significiant role in shaping the physical world including human biology. Writes Crosby,

> On the pampa, Iberian horses and cattle have driven back the guanaco and rhea; in North America, speakers of Indo-European languages have overwhelmed speakers of Algonkin and Muskhogean and other Amerindian languages; in the antipodes, the dandelions and house cats of the Old World have marched forward, and kangaroo grass and kiwis have retreated [110, p. 7].

These changes, components of European colonial expansion, Crosby labels *ecological imperialism*. In examples like this one, we see that nature is not as "natural" as we sometimes like to imagine. Rather, to a considerable degree, it is product of human labor, although often not the intended or desired product.

The development of malaria as a major source of human morbidity and mortality worldwide presents another example well known to anthropologists. The Anopheles mosquito that serves as vector for the parasite that causes malaria was greatly influenced by human environmental reshaping for purposes of food cultivation, a development that reflected and expressed significant changes in the human social relationships and polity associated with production of a surplus and food storage. Cultivation created sunlit pools of stagnant water favored by Anopheles mosquitos for breeding while storage of a food surplus allowed the concentration of a large number of human victims in settled villages. During this process, there is little doubt that the mosquito changed to facilitate more effective exploitation of human created environments for breeding and humans as a major source of the blood needed for reproduction. As this example suggests, nature does not exist apriori to and separate from humans, nor, by extension, does HIV. If, as is now widely believed by virologists, HIV-1 and HIV-2 had their origins as benign simian retroviruses (SIV_{cpz} and SIV_{Smm} respectively), the successful cross-species transmission and subsequent worldwide spread in the new human host undoubtedly was significantly influenced by human social activity, ways of life, and patterns of interrelationship, including, again, powerful forces of a political economic nature.

This argument can be made most clearly if we move beyond the U.S. inner city to consideration of AIDS in Africa, given that Africa commonly is proposed as the site of origin of HIV and simultaneously, as the "dark continent" of European imagination, has long served the West as a trope for nature, at once wild, unexplored and threatening [111, 112]. Whatever the origin of HIV, an issue mired in controversy because under conditions of oppression "the question of origin becomes confused with the idea of responsibility" [16, p. 15], AIDS is widely spread in several parts of Africa. Some would see this as a consequence of the virus having existed longer in Africa than elsewhere. And yet, understanding the distribution of AIDS on the African continent requires a consideration of political economic factors, including colonial and post-colonial factors. For example, writing of Southern Africa, Baldo and Cabral argue:

> The most important historical structural processes concerning HIV in Southern Africa are the LIW [Low Intensity Wars] and the disruption of the economy, particularly the rural economy. Various population groups are forced into continuous movements, including displacement flight from the war affected areas, regular armies and groups of bandits, rural populations moving to towns (joining

the poverty and marginality circle including prostitution and street children) and rural populations moving near army barracks for trading [113, p. 40].

In this instance, the effort by South Africa to maintain its internal system of exploitation through Apartheid and its regional dominance by promoting low intensity wars of destablization against its neighboring countries produced social conditions that contribute significantly to the opportunities for human infection. Other, yet related, political economic factors have been discussed with reference to the spread of AIDS elsewhere. With reference to Zaire, for example, Schoepf comments:

> Disease epidemics generally erupt in times of crisis, and AIDS is no exception. Zaire, like most other sub-Saharan nations and much of the Third World, is in the throes of economic turmoil. Propelled by declining terms of trade and burdensome debt service, the contradictions of distorted neocolonial economies with rapid class formation have created what appears to be a permanent, deepening crisis .... In Zaire, as elsewhere in the region, economc crisis and the structure of employment inherited from the colonial period shape the current configuration, contributing to the feminization of poverty and consequently to the spread of AIDS (e.g., through prostitution or multiple partner sexual relationships associated with smuggling networks developed to contend with the worsening economic conditions) [114, p. 262].

As these two examples show, while the human immunodeficiency virus has a material existence independent of social factors, its role and importance as a source of morbidity and mortality among humans cannot be understood in isolation from political economy. Contrary to the arguments of some critiques of CMA [e.g., 115], placing emphasis on the social origins of disease does not constitute a denial of the biotic aspects of pathogens, hosts, and environments. Rather, it is an affirmation of the critical importance of adopting a holistic biosocial approach to health.

Social Transmission of AIDS

A second way in which AIDS is a social disease is that it is spread through social behaviors, especially intimate behaviors like sexual contact and injection drug use. For this reason, it is tempting to think of AIDS as an easily preventable disease: people need merely avoid identified risk behaviors and no one will become infected. This simplistic line of thinking about human behavior leads easily to victim-blaming, because individuals who become infected can be said to be responsible for putting themselves at risk. Importantly, the ability of individuals to adopt known AIDS prevention strategies is to no small measure socially determined. Research on AIDS risk, for example, unveils its close connection to issues of power in interpersonal relations. Illustrative of this point are the following comments of inner city Puerto Rican women participants in a community focus group discussion on AIDS conducted by the Hispanic Health Council. Discussing the issue of encouraging a partner to use a condom, one women stated:

> If he's a violent guy, she's exposing herself to violence, because she is implying that he's cheating on her or because she's implying that she might have gone out with somebody. Or he might reject having any sexual activity. Some of them

would just walk away. They would just get up and walk away. Either they'd try to persuade her not to use condoms and if she insists, he'd walk away [78, p. 96].

Commenting on her own situation, another focus group participant noted,

> I know that the first time I was so afraid I said you'd better use them. He was kind of upset, you know, because of the fact that I did not believe him, but I had to think about myself. He used them in the beginning, but afterward he just didn't. I was kind of worried, and now the fact that I find out that he's still using drugs and things like that, it scares me, and I think, you know, should I go for a test or what should I do [78, p. 96].

As both of these examples indicate, sexual politics can be a significant determinant of AIDS risk [116, 117, but also see 118]. Notes Sibthrope, "Safer sex is unsafe if it has the potential to challenge a relationship with a significant partner . . ." [119, p. 208]. Moreover, prevention education (e.g., emphasis on monogamy and condom use) can overlook the fact that under certain circumstances, especially those where limited options prevail and individuals must make the best of what is available, it is possible for "the benefits of taking . . . risk [to] outweigh the advantages to avoiding it" [120, p. 597]. This applies not only to gender relations, but to other types of emotionally and materially supportive social relations as well. While known to be highly risky, injecting drugs in a shooting gallery, for example confers definite benefits (e.g., access to needles, access to water, protection from police surveillance, help in case of a drug overdose, potential access to drugs). Similarly, sharing drug injection equipment can be seen as a form of "life insurance" among people with scarce resources if it helps to maintain a relationship with someone who can be called on in time of need [120]. Consequently, the social transmission of AIDS must be understood in light of the cultural and political economic nature of specific social relationships among the urban poor. No less than cultural concepts, even intimate social relations are generated, enacted, and revised in contexts of social inequality.

The Social Location of AIDS

Finally, AIDS is a disease of society in the sense that the disease spreads, as Bateson and Goldsby [121] suggest, along the fault lines of society. In the United States especially, AIDS is disproportionately a disease of the dispossessed, a disease of the socially condemned and denegrated, a disease of social outcasts. In this sense, the epidemic is a social mirror reflecting back the seams that divide society and divide off some groups and individuals for critical social labeling and physical suffering. Central to the epidemiological picture of AIDS in the United States has been the high prevalence of infection in so-called "hidden populations" [122], that is, groups that are not well known because their social activities generally are staged outside the view of mainstream institutions and agencies of social control. Indeed, some have noted that AIDS is simultaneously two epidemics in one, a health epidemic and an epidemic of accusation and condemnation against the afflicted. Hence the slogan of AIDS activists: Fight AIDS not those with AIDS.

Moreover, class plays no small role in determining exposure to HIV. Summarizing data on HIV seroprevalence for newborns in New York City, Novick et al. notes that the areas of the city with the highest levels of infection are poor inner city neighborhoods, where low income ethnic minorities constitute a substantial portion of the population [123, p. 1749]. These are the same neighborhoods that have suffered the highest rates of AIDS-related deaths. Yadira Davila, a drug addict from the lower East Side of New York describes the impact of the AIDS epidemic on her neighborhood in the following words

> Everybody is dead. The lower East Side is almost entirely empty. The only people left are the crackheads. Everybody at the Essex Street market are gone. Before we would pass by and it would be crowded. Everybody selling this and that. Now everything is empty [124, p. 46].

Roderick Wallace has analyzed the social distribution of AIDS in New York in terms of the social disorganization of poor neighborhoods caused by changes in social policy, such a withdrawal of essential municipal services like fire protection, implemented with the intention of lowing population densities and achieving planned population shrinkage in targeted areas [1]. After service withdrawal by the City Planning Commission and other agencies, Wallace has documented a mass migration of refugees from burning areas into nearby neighborhoods, which themselves become overcrowded and are targeted for service reduction and subsequent burnout and migration. In these areas undergoing urban desertification, social networks and other forms of support are severely disrupted. These changes are associated with heightened rates of substance use and HIV infection. At the heart of one of the most devastated urban zones studied by Wallace, the Morrisiania section of the South-central Bronx, 25 percent of emergency room patients in the local hospital now test positive for HIV infection. Wallace concludes that social policies, which are fairly direct expressions of social relations among contending social groups, propelled the urban environmental changes that resulted in skyrocketing HIV infection and death [1, p. 811].

Following Arras, it is useful to differentiate "democratic" from "undemocratic" diseases [125]. In the former (e.g., influenza), disease is transmitted easily and widely across class, racial, and ethnic lines, making it difficult to stigmatize and lay blame for illness on less empowered groups. In undemocratic diseases, marginalized groups are disproportionately affected. As the foregoing discussion makes clear, the "undemocratic nature of the AIDS epidemic is not the inevitable result of an encounter with infectious disease" [126, p. 324], rather it is the unfortunately but inevitable result of encounter with morbid social conditions and oppressive social relations.

CONCLUSION

In this chapter, we have tried to illustrate some of the ways in which AIDS, as part of the inner city syndemic, has acutely challenged research in medical anthropology. Further we have suggested a framework that is conscious of the political economic construction, transmission, and location of AIDS as a way to respond to this challenge. An even larger challenge facing the field lies in translating our research findings, rapidly and usefully, into AIDS prevention, support and intervention. Our primary task lies in designing research that matters, research that makes a difference. We must be as concerned about the applications of our research as we are about the elegance or creativity of our design, as sure that what we find may help save lives or give comfort as it will lead to any publications or presentations. Over ten years into the AIDS crisis, we are in much need of taking stock of just how useful our work in AIDS has been. If, as Socrates suggested, a life unexamined is not worth living, then research that is not very relevant to furthering life in a time of crisis is surely not worth doing.

REFERENCES

1. R. Wallace, Urban Desertification, Public Health and Public Order: 'Planned Shrinkage,' Violent Death, Substance Abuse and AIDS in the Bronx, *Social Science and Medicine, 31*:7, pp. 801-813, 1990.
2. M. Singer, Organizational Culture in A Community-based Health Organization: The Hispanic Health Council, *Anthropology of Work Review, 11*:3, pp. 7-12, 1990.
3. H. Baer and Y. Jones, (eds.), *African Americans in the South,* The University of Georgia Press, Athens, Georgia, 1992.
4. E. Martin, *The Woman in the Body*, Beacon, Boston, 1987.
5. W. Roseberry, Anthropologies and Histories, Rutgers University Press, New Brunswick, 1991.
6. J. Steward, R. Manners, E. Wolf, E. Padilla, S. Mintz, and R. Scheele, *The People of Puerto Rico*, University of Illinois Press, Urbana, 1956.
7. E. Wolf, Distinguished Lecture: Facing Power—Old Insights, New Questions, *American Anthropologist, 92*:3, pp. 586-596, 1990.
8. S. Mintz, *Sweetness and Power: The Place of Sugar in Modern History*, Viking, New York, 1985.
9. A. Appadurai, Putting Hierarchy in Its Place, in *Rereading Cultural Anthropology,* G. Marcus (ed.), Duke University Press, Durham, pp. 34-47, 1992.
10. W. E. B. DuBois, *The Souls of Black Folk,* Fawcett, Greenwich, Connecticut, 1961.
11. M. Singer, AIDS and U.S. Ethnic Minorities: The Crisis and Alternative Anthropological Responses, *Human Organization , 51*:1, pp. 89-95, 1992.
12. S. Ortner, Reading America: Preliminary Notes on Class and Culture, in *Recapturing Anthropology: Working in the Present*, R. Fox (ed.), School for American Research, Sante Fe, pp. 163-189, 1991.
13. E. Wolf, Distinguished Lecture: Facing Power—Old Insights, New Questions, *American Anthropologist, 92*:3, pp. 586-596, 1990.
14. G. Herdt, Introduction, in *The Time of AIDS,* G. Herdt and S. Lindenbaum, (eds.), Sage Publications, Newbury Park, California, pp. 3-26, 1990.
15. E. Fee and D. Fox, Introduction: The Contemporary Historiography of AIDS, in *AIDS: The Making of a Chronic Disease,* E. Fee and D. Fox (eds.), University of California Press, Berkeley, pp. 1-19, 1992.
16. S. McCombie, AIDS in Cultural, Historic, and Epidemiologic Context, in *Culture and AIDS,* D. Feldman (ed.), Praeger, New York, pp. 9-28, 1990.
17. D. Barker, Rise and Fall of Western Disease, *Nature, 338,* pp. 371-372, 1989.

18. A. Brandt, AIDS in Historical Perspective: Four Lessons from the History of Sexually Transmitted Disease, *American Journal of Public Health, 78*:40, pp. 367-371, 1989.
19. G. Marks and W. Beatty, *Epidemics*, Charles Scribners Sons, New York, 1976.
20. D. Wallace, Roots of Increased Health Care Inequality in New York, *Social Science and Medicine, 31*:11, pp. 1219-1227, 1990.
21. C. McCord and H. Freedman, Excess Mortality in Harlem, *New England Journal of Medicine, 322*, pp. 173-175, 1990.
22. V. Navarro, Race or Class versus Race and Class: Mortality Differentials in the United States, *The Lancet, 336*, pp. 1238-1240, 1990.
23. M. Singer and C. Snipes, Generations of Suffering: Experiences of a Pregnancy and Substance Abuse Treatment Program, *Journal of Health Care for the Poor and Medically Underserved, 3*:1, pp. 325-239, 1992.
24. Council on Scientific Affairs, Hispanic Health in the United States, *Journal of the American Medical Association, 265*:20, pp. 248-252, 1991.
25. Secretary's Task Force on Black and Minority Health, *in Crosscutting Issues in Minority Health, Vol. 2*, U.S. Department of Health and Human Services, Washington, D.C., 1985.
26. C. Turner, H. Miller, L. Moses, *AIDS: Sexual Behavior and Intravenous Drug Use*, National Academy Press, Washington, D.C., 1989.
27. D. Jackson, America's Shameful Little Secret, *Boston Globe,* p. 20, December 24, 1989.
28. M. Edelman, *Families in Peril: An Agenda for Social Change,* Harvard University Press, Cambridge, Massachusetts, 1987.
29. K. Hope, Child Survival and Health Care among Low-income African American Families in the United States, *Health Transition Review, 2*:2, pp. 151-164, 1992.
30. North Central Health Systems of Connecticut, *Review and Analysis of Medically Underserved areas of Hartford,* document on file at the Hispanic Health Council, Hartford, Connecticut, 1981.
31. R. Knox, Hub Infant Deaths Up 32%, *Boston Globe,* p. 1 and p. 5, February 9, 1987.
32. W. Nersesian, Infant Mortality in Socially Vulnerable Populations, *Annual Review of Public Health, 9*, pp. 361-377, 1988.
33. J. Fitchen, Hunger, Malnutrition, and Poverty in the Contemporary United States: Some Observations on their Social and Cultural Context, *Food and Foodways, 2*, pp. 309-333, 1988.
34. G. Damio and L. Cohen, *Policy Report of the Hartford Community Hunger Identification Project,* Hispanic Health Council, Hartford, Connecticut, 1990.
35. E. Lipton, Hartford Still among 10 Poorest Cities in Census Report, *Hartford Courant,* pp. C-1 and C 11, December 16, 1992.
36. Physician Task Force on Hunger in America, *Hunger in America: The Growing Epidemic,* Harvard University School of Public Health, Boston, 1985.
37. R. Crawford, A Cultural Account of "Health": Control, Release, and the Social Body, in *Issues in the Political Economy of Health Care,* J. McKinlay (ed.), Tavistock Publications, New York, pp. 60-103, 1984.
38. R. Crawford, You are Dangerous to Your Health: The Ideology and Politics of Victim Blaming, *International Journal of Health Services, 7,* pp. 663-680, 1977.
39. W. Dressler, Social Class, Skin Color, and Arterial Blood Pressure in Two Societies, *Ethnicity and Disease, 1*:1, pp. 60-77, 1991.
40. R. Caetano, *Drinking Patterns and Alcohol Problems in a National Sample of U.S. Hispanics,* paper presented at the National Institute on Alcohol Abuse and Alcoholism Conference, Epidemiology of Alcohol Use and Abuse among U.S. Ethnic Minorities, Bethesda, Maryland, 1985.

41. M. Singer, F. Valentin, H. Baer, and Z. Jia, Why Does Juan García Have a Drinking Problem?: The Perspective of Critical Medical Anthropology, *Medical Anthropology, 51*:1, pp. 89-95, 1992.

42. D. Herd, Ambiguity In Black Drinking Norms: An Ethnohistorical Interpretation, in *The American Experience with Alcohol: Contrasting Cultural Perspectives,* L. Bennett and G. Ames (eds.), Plenum Press, New York, pp. 149-170, 1985.

43. D. Herd, Migration, Cultural Transformation, and the Rise of Black Liver Cirrhosis Mortality, *British Journal of Addictions, 82*, pp. 1101-1110, 1985.

44. E. Rogers, L. Goldkind, and S. Goldkind, Increasing Frequency of Esophageal Cancer among Black Americans, *Cancer, 49*, pp. 610-617, 1982.

45. J. Marlin, C. Kaelber, C. Sorenson, C. Dadovrian, and N. Munch, Trends of Cirrhosis of Liver Mortality, *U.S. Alcohol Reference Manual,* National Institute on Alcohol Abuse and Alcoholism, Rockville, Maryland, 1980.

46. U. Hannerz, *Soulside: Inquiries into Ghetto Culture,* Columbia University Press, New York, 1969.

47. A. Gaines, Alcohol: Cultural Conceptions and Social Behavior among Urban Blacks, in *The American Experience with Alcohol: Contrasting Cultural Perspectives,* L. Bennett and G. Ames (eds.), Plenum Press, New York, pp. 1171-1197, 1985.

48. D. Herd, Drinking Patterns in the Black Population, in *Alcohol in America: Drinking Patterns and Problems*, W. Clark and M. Hilton (eds.), State University of New York Press, Albany, 1991.

49. N. Anderson, *The Hobo: The Sociology of the Homeless Man,* University of Chicago Press, Chicago, 1923.

50. H. Zorbaugh, *The Gold Coast and the Slum,* University of Chicago Press, Chicago, 1923.

51. A. Kopstein and P. Roth, *Drug Use among Ethnic Minorities,* National Institute on Drug Abuse, Rockville, Maryland, 1990.

52. S. Friedman, B. Stepherson, J. Woods, D. Des Jarlais, and T. Ward, Society, Drug Injectors, and AIDS, *Journal of Health Care for the Poor and Underserved, 3*:1, pp. 73-89, 1990.

53. D. Musto, *The American Disease: Origins of Narcotic Control*, Oxford University Press, 1987.

54. S. Friedman, A. Sotheran, B. Abdul-Quader, B. Primm, D. Des Jarlais, A. Kleinman, C. Mauge, D. Goldsmith, W. El-Sadr and R. Maslansky, The AIDS Epidemic among Blacks and Hispanics, *The Milbank Memorial Fund Quarterly, 65*:2, pp. 455-499, 1987.

55. B. Hanson, Introduction, in *Life With Heroin: Voices From the Inner City,* B. Hanson, G. Beschner, J. Walters, and E. Bovelle (eds.), Lexington Books, Lexington, Massachusetts, pp. 1-16, 1985.

56. D. Waldorf, *Careers in Dope,* Prentice-Hall, Englewood Cliffs, New Jersey, 1973.

57. G. Beschner and E. Bovelle, Life with Heroin: Voices of Experiences, in *Life With Heroin: Voices from the Inner City*, B. Hanson, G. Beschner, J. Walters, and E. Bovelle (eds.), Lexington Books, Lexington, Massachusetts, pp. 75-107, 1985.

58. J. Inciardi, *The War On Drugs,* Mayfield Publishing Company, Mountain View, California, 1986.

59. I. Chein, D. Gerard, R, Lees, and E. Rosenfeld, *The Road to H,* Basic Books, New York, 1964.

60. R. Glick, Dealing, Demoralization and Addiction: Heroin in the Chicago Puerto Rican Community, *Journal of Psychoactive Drugs, 15*, pp. 281-292, 1983.

61. R. Battles and and R. Pickens, *Needle Sharing among Intravenous Drug Abusers: National and International Perspectives*, U.S. Department of Health and Human Services, Washington, D.C., 1988.

62. I. Inciardi, AIDS and Intravenous Drug Use, *American Behavioral Scientists, 33*:4, pp. 395-502, 1990.
63. J. Inciardi, AIDS and Intravenous Drug Use, *Journal of Drug Issues, 20*:2, pp. 179-347, 1990.
64. J. Strang and G. Stimson, *AIDS and Drug Misuse,* Routledge, London, 1990.
65. S. Friedman and D. Lipton, *Cocaine, AIDS, and Intravenous Drug Use*, Harrington Park Press, New York, 1991.
66. J. Sorenson, L. Wermuth, D. Gibson, K-H. Choi, J. Guydish, Joseph, and S. Batki, *Preventing AIDS in Drug Users and Their Sexual Partners,* The Guilford Press, New York, 1991.
67. Centers for Disease Control, *HIV/AIDS Surveillance: U.S. AIDS Cases Reported through July 1990,* 1990.
68. P. Selwyn, D. Hartel, W. Wasserman, and E. Drucker, Impact of the AIDS Epidemic on Morbidity and Mortality among Intravenous Drug Users in a New York City Methadone Maintenance Probram, *American Journal of Public Health, 79*:10, pp. 1358-1362, 1989.
69. S. Aral, Sevgi and K. Holmes, Sexually Transmitted Diseases in the AIDS Era, *Scientific American, 264*:2, pp. 62-69, 1989.
70. H. Miller, C. Turner, and L. Moses, *The Second Decade,* National Academy Press, Washington, D.C., 1990.
71. National Clearinghouse on AIDS, *Personal Communication,* 1993.
72. Connecticut Department of Health Services, *AIDS in Connecticut: Annual Surveillance Report,* December 31, 1990.
73. R. Hahn, L. Magder, S. Aral, R. Johnson, and S. Larsen, Sandra, Race and the Prevalence of Syphilis Seroactivity in the United States Population: A National Sero-Epidemologic Study, *American Journal of Public Health, 79*:4, pp. 467-470, 1989.
74. Centers for Disease Control, Summary of Notifiable Diseases, United States, 1991, *Morbidity and Mortality Weekly Report, 40*:53, 1992.
75. M. Singer, The Politics of AIDS: An Introduction, *Social Science and Medicine,* 38, pp. 1321-1324, 1994.
76. G. Oppenheimer, Causes, Cases, and Cohorts: The Role of Epidemiology in the Historical Construction of AIDS, in *AIDS: The Making of a Chronic Disease,* E. Fee and D. Fox, (eds.), University of California Press, Berkeley, pp. 49-83, 1992.
77. S. Kane and T. Mason, "IV Drug Users" and "Sex Partners": The Limits of Epidemiological Categories and the Ethnography of Risk, in *The Time of AIDS,* G. Herdt and S. Lindenbaum (eds.), Sage Publications, Newbury Park, California, pp. 199-222, 1992.
78. R. Parker, Acquired Immunodeficiency Syndrome in Urban Brazil, *Medical Anthropology Quarterly, 1*:2, pp. 155-175, 1987.
79. M. Singer, C. Flores, L. Davison, G. Burke, Z. Castillo, K. Scalon, and M. Rivera, SIDA: The Economic, Social, and Cultural Context of AIDS among Latinos, *Medical Anthropology Quarterly, 4*, pp. 73-117, 1990.
80. J. Carrier, Sexual Behavior and Spread of AIDS in Mexico, *Medical Anthropology, 10*, pp. 129-142, 1989.
81. J. Carrier and R. Magaña, 1992 Use of Ethnosexual Data on Men of Mexican Origin for HIV/AIDS Prevention Programs, in *The Time of AIDS,* G. Herdt and S. Lindenbaum (eds.), Sage Publications, Newbury Park, California, pp. 243-258, 1992.
82. M. Levine, The Implications of Constructionist Theory for Social Research on the AIDS Epidemic among Gay Men, in *The Time of AIDS,* G. Herdt and S. Lindenbaum (eds.), Sage Publications, Newbury Park, California, pp. 185-198, 1992.

83. S. Fiddle, *Portraits from a Shooting Gallery*, Harper and Row, New York, 1967.
84. N. Freudenberg, *Preventing AIDS,* American Public Health Association, Washington, D.C., 1989.
85. S. Friedman, D. Des Jarlais, and J. Sotheran, AIDS Health Education for Intravenous Drug Users, *Health Education Quarterly, 13*, pp. 383-393, 1986.
86. R. Rettig, M. Torres, and G. Garrett, *Manny A Criminal-Addict's Story,* Houghton Mifflin Co., Boston, 1977.
87. A. Snyder, Junkie Personality, *Science Digest , 68*, p. 62, 1970.
88. I. Iglehart, Brick' It and Going the Pan: Vernacular in the Black Inner-City Heroin Lifestyle, in *Life With Heroin,* B. Hanson, G. Beschner, J. Walters, and E. Bovelle (eds.), Lexington Books, Lexington, Massachusetts, pp. 111-134, 1985.
89. R. Convisier and J. Rutledge, The Need for Innovation to Halt AIDS among Intravenous Drug Users and Their Sexual Partners, *AIDS and Public Policy Journal, 3*, pp. 43-50, 1988.
90. M. Singer, Confronting the AIDS Epidemic among IV Drug Users: Does Ethnic Culture Matter, *AIDS Education and Prevention, 3*:3, pp. 258-283, 1992.
91. J. Page, Shooting Scenarios and Risk of HIV-1 Infection, *American Behavioral Scientist, 33*:4, pp. 478-490, 1990.
92. M. Singer and Z. Jia, AIDS and Puerto Rican Injection Drug Users in the U.S, in *Handbook on Risk For AIDS: Injection Drug Users and Their Sexual Partners,* B. Brown and G. Beschner, (eds.), Greenwood Press, Westport, Connecticut, pp. 227-255, 1993.
93. N. Glick Schiller, S. Crystal, and L. Denver, Risky Business: An Examination of the Cultural Construction of AIDS Risk Groups, *Social Science and Medicine, 38*, pp. 1337-1346, 1994.
94. E. Bovelle and A. Taylor, Conclusions and Implications, in *Life With Heroin: Voices from the Inner City*, B. Hanson, G. Beschner, J. Walters, and E. Bovelle (eds.), Lexington Books, Lexington, Massachusetts, pp. 175-186, 1985.
95. R. Carlson, R. Falck, and H. Siegal, Ethnography, Epidemiology and Public Policy: Needle Use Practices and Risk Reduction among IV Drug Users in the Midwest, in *Global AIDS Policy,* D. Feldman (ed.), (in press), 1995.
96. D. Waldorf, S. Murphy, D. Lauderback, C. Reinarmon, and T. Marotta, Needle Sharing among Male Prostitutes: Preliminary Findings of the Prospero Project, *Journal of Drug Issues, 20:*2, pp. 309-334, 1990.
97. W. Penk, R. Robinowitz, W. Roberts, M. Dolan, and H. Atkins, MMPI Differences of Male Hispanic-Americans, Black, and White Heroin Addicts, *Journal of Consulting and Clinical Psychology, 49*, pp. 488-490, 1981.
98. M. Anglin, M. Booth, T. Ryan, and Y-I. Hser, Ethnic Differences in Narcotics Addiction, I. Characteristics of Chicano and Anglo Methadone Maintenance Clients, *The International Journal of Addictions, 23*, pp. 125-149, 1988.
99. N. Glick Schiller, What's Wrong with this Picture? The Hegemonic Construction of Culture in AIDS Research in the United States, *Medical Anthropology Quarterly, 6*:3, pp. 237-254, 1992.
100. S. Kane, HIV, Heroin and Heterosexual Relations, *Social Science and Medicine, 32*:9, pp. 1037-1050, 1991.
101. D. Stone, Preventing Chronic Disease: The Dark Side of a Bright Idea, in *Chronic Disease and Disability: Beyond the Acute Medical Model*, Institute of Medicine, Washington, D.C., pp. 83-103, 1990.
102. D. Nelkin, D. Willis, and S. Parris, Introduction, A Disease of Society: Cultural Responses to AIDS, *The Milbank Quarterly, 68* (Supplement 1), pp. 1-9, 1990.

103. P. Treichler, AIDS, HIV, and the Cultural Construction of Reality, in *In the Time of AIDS*, G. Herdt and S. Lindenbaum (eds.), Sage, Newbury Park, California, pp. 65-98, 1992.
104. R. Shilts, *And the Band Played On*, St. Martin's Press, New York, 1987.
105. S. Joseph, Current and Future Trends in AIDS in New York City, *AIDS and Substance Abuse*, L. Siegel (ed.), Harrington Park Press, New York, pp. 159-174, 1988.
106. S. Morsy, Political Economy in Medical Anthropology, in *Medical Anthropology: Contemporary Theory and Method*, T. Johnson and C. Sargent (eds.), Praeger, New York, pp. 26-46, 1990.
107. W. Roseberry, *Anthropologies and Histories*, Rutgers University Press, New Brunswick, 1991.
108. M. Singer, *Farewell to Adaptationism: Unnatural Selection and the Politics of Biology*, presented at Political-Economic Perspectives in Biological Anthropology: Building a Biocultural Synthesis a Wenner-Gren Foundation for Anthropological Research conference, Cabo San Lucas, Mexico, 1992.
109. N. Touchette, Wistar Panel Disputes Polio Vaccine—HIV Link, *The Journal of NIH Research, 4*:12, p. 42, 1992.
110. A. Crosby, *Ecological Imperialism: The Biological Expansion of Europe. 900-1900*, Harvard University Press, Cambridge, Massachusetts, 1986.
111. J. Comaroff and J. Comaroff, *Of Revelation and Revolution*, University of Chicago Press, Chicago, 1991.
112. J. Comaroff and J. Comaroff, *Ethnography and the Historic Imagination*, Westview, Boulder, 1992.
113. M. Baldo and A. Cabral, Low Intensity Wars and Social Determination of the HIV Transmission: The Search for a New Paradigm to Guide Research and Control of the HIV-AIDS Pandemic, in *Action on AIDS in Southern Africa*, Z. Stein and A. Zwi (eds.), CHISA, New York, pp. 34-45, 1990.
114. B. G. Schoepf, Women at Risk: Case Studies from Zaire, in *The Time of AIDS*, G. Herdt and S. Lindenbaum (eds.), Sage Publications, Newbury Park, California, pp. 259-286, 1992.
115. A. Wiley, Adaptation and the Biocultural Paradigm in Medical Anthropology: A Critical Review, *Medical Anthropology Quarterly, 6*:3, pp. 216-236, 1992.
116. D. Worth, Minority Women and AIDS: Culture, Race, and Gender, in *Culture and AIDS*, D. Feldman (ed.), Greenwood Publishing Group, New York, pp. 111-136, 1990.
117. J. Cohen, Why Women Partners of Drug Users Will Continue to be at High Risk for HIV Infection, in *Cocaine, AIDS, and Intravenous Drug Use*, S. Friedman and D. Lipton (eds.), Harrington Park Press, New York, pp. 99-110, 1991.
118. A. Kline, E. Kline, and E. Oken, Minority Women and Sexual Choice in the Age of AIDS, *Social Science and Medicine, 34*:4, pp. 447-457, 1992.
119. B. Sibthorpe, The Social Construction of Sexual Relationships as a Determinant of HIV Risk Perception and Condom Use among Injection Drug Users, *Medical Anthropology Quarterly, 6*:3, pp. 255-270, 1992.
120. M. Connors, Risk Perception, Risk Taking and Risk Management among Intravenous Drug Users: Implications for AIDS Prevention, *Social Science and Medicine, 34*:6, pp. 591-601, 1992.
121. M. C. Bateson and R. Goldsby, *Thinking AIDS*, Addison-Wesley Publishing Co., Reading, Massachusetts, 1988.
122. J. Watters and P. Biernacki, Targeted Sampling Options for the Study of Hidden Populations, *Social Problems, 36*:4, pp. 416-430, 1989.

123. L. Novick, D. Bems, R. Stricof, R. Stevens, K. Pass, and J. Wethers, HIV Seroprevalence in Newborns in New York State, *Journal of the American Medical Association, 261*, pp. 1745-1750, 1989.
124. Y. Davila and J. Rosett, Rambling with Yadira, *Sidahora, 1*, pp. 41-55, 1989.
125. J. Arras, The Fragile Web of Responsibility: AIDS and the Duty to Treat, *Hastings Center Report, 18*:2, pp. 10-20, 1988.
126. S. Lindenbaum, Knowledge and Action in the Shadow of AIDS, in *In the Time of AIDS*, G. Herdt and S. Lindenbaum (eds.), Sage Publications, Newbury Park, California pp. 319-334, 1992.

CHAPTER 8

The Drive for Professionalization in British Osteopathy

The literature on professionalization in the health arena has focused on bourgeois medicine and its allied or auxiliary professions, and little attention has been given to alternative or heterodox practices. Of the various alternative forms of medicine in Western society, such as homeopathy, osteopathy, chiropractic and naturopathy, only chiropractic in the United States has received much attention from social scientists. Wardell refers to chiropractic as a "marginal profession" in that "chiropractors claim to be doctors of a special kind and are so regarded by many people but the society at large does not accord them this status" [1, p. 17]. As late as the 1950s American osteopathy also could be described in this way, but it has since developed a practice acceptable to bourgeois medicine. Philosophical and therapeutic differences remain between osteopathic and regular medicine in the United States, but osteopathic physicians had full rights to medical practice in all fifty states since the early 1970s. They have an elaborate hospital system, and can no longer be labeled a marginal profession, or even an alternative or heterodox one. Conversely, osteopathy in Great Britain occupies a status comparable to chiropractic [2].

THE DIFFUSION OF OSTEOPATHY FROM AMERICA TO BRITAIN

Osteopathy was invented in the 1860s and 1870s as a reaction to what its founder, Andrew Taylor Still, called the excesses of allopathic medicine, along with other nineteenth-century medical sects, including bleeding surgery. Dr. Still believed that many, if not all, diseases were due to the faulty articulation of the musculoskeletal system, particularly the spinal vertebra and their associated musculature. Such dislocations produce disordered nerve connections which impair the proper circulation of blood and other fluids. Still used physical manipulation, and opposed drugs, vaccines, serums and, except in special circumstances, surgery.

Although the connections between bonesetting and osteopathy are obscure, Gevitz suggests that they were historically related [3]. Bonesetting and massage worked in an unrestricted environment in pre-industrial America from the colonial period. Still advertised himself as the "lightening bone setter" during the 1880s, and in essence what he may have done was to add a theoretical rationale to a pre-existing empirical practice. During the early years several British students studied osteopathy at the founder's school in Kirksville, Missouri. Shortly after Still opened the American School of Osteopathy in 1892, he met William Smith, a Scottish physician trained at the University of Edinburgh [4, p. 37]. Smith became so enthralled by Still's theories that he became the first lecturer in anatomy at the new school.

The most important figure linking osteopathy in Britain and America was John Martin Littlejohn (1865-1947). After being cured by osteopathic treatment, Littlejohn, who had attended Glasgow University, and obtained a Ph.D. at Columbia University in 1894, enrolled as a student at the American School. He was soon appointed Dean of the Faculty and Professor of Physiology [5]. In 1898 Littlejohn read a paper entitled "Osteopathy in the Line of Apostolic Succession with Medicine" before the Society of Science and Arts in London [6, p. 31]. After receiving his Doctor of Osteopathy (DO) degree in 1900, Littlejohn, with his brothers, James and John, founded the American College of Osteopathic Medicine and Surgery, the forerunner of the Chicago College of Osteopathic Medicine.

A small but growing number of American-trained osteopaths established practices in Britain after 1900. By the 1920s practitioners trained in American schools, and others trained in osteopathy as apprentices or by self-instruction, were practicing in Britain. In contrast to the United States, where state licensing laws made sectarian practitioners marginal by limiting the scope of their practice, the British system defined their marginality by withholding statutory recognition and by refusing admission to the state-sanctioned register. According to Falder and Munro, the "practice of alternative forms of therapy is a customary right in the U.K. and is part of Common Law. There are no legal restrictions under the law of any kind of treatment per se, although there are certain restrictions relating to certain diseases, appellations, and remedies" [7, p. 4].

This policy provides the British alternative therapist with a freedom that his or her counterpart in America does not enjoy, but it also serves as an impediment in claiming legal control of therapy. Larson maintains that a legal monopoly is an essential component of professional status [8]. Since under Common Law, regardless of the length of nature of the training undertaken, anyone may claim to be an osteopath, chiropractor, homeopath, naturopath, herbalist or any other type of alternative healer, these practices function in a virtually total laissez-faire manner.

STRATEGIES TOWARD PROFESSIONALIZATION ADOPTED BY OSTEOPATHS

Harries-Jenkins asserts that professionalization has escaped definition due to "the concomitant failure to define 'professional' or to delineate 'profession' " [9, p. 57]. Professionals have been defined by a set of traits including specialized skills and training, esoteric knowledge, limited membership associations, codes of ethics, a service orientation, income by fees rather than wages, universalism and recognition of their authority by the larger society [10, p. 322]. Social scientists thus construct an ideal type which is used as a measure of the degree of professionalization achieved by different occupational groups. Critics of this method assert that it "justifies the prerogatives and power of the leading professions" [11, p. 75]. Other scholars view professionalization as the degree to which an occupational group has exclusive access to a particular type of work, and the power to delegate related work to subordinate occupations. Larson used this definition in asserting that professionalization "is aimed at monopoly: monopoly of opportunities in a market of services or labor, and, inseparably, monopoly of status and work privileges in an occupational hierarchy" [12, p. 609]. Since this definition assumes that bourgeois medicine has achieved dominance over subordinate occupations, it obscures the on-going struggle for greater autonomy by these occupations and related marginal professions.

Osteopathic groups in Britain have attempted to obtain a monopoly of manipulative therapy, and a major component of their drive for professionalization has involved what Krause describes as a "process of seeking a wider community and occupational mandate . . . usually through a series of strategies intended to increase the prestige of the occupation" [13, p. 74]. British osteopaths have attempted to obtain legitimacy in the eyes of both the state and the public by claiming to be a complementary system of medicine. At the same time, the osteopathic groups have attempted to eliminate the competition of practitioners who claim to be osteopaths but whom they consider "unqualified."

Wilensky contends that professionalization consists of 1) defining a full-time, specialized activity; 2) establishing a training school, preferably affiliated with a university; 3) forming an association limited to those who have the required training; 4) political agitation to obtain a legal monopoly of work in the area of expertise; and 5) the creation of a formal code of ethics to reduce competition and to claim a service orientation [14, pp. 142-146]. This model by no means exhausts the strategies for professionalization, as will become apparent in our discussion of this process in British osteopathy.

Establishment of Associations and Training Schools

A group of twelve osteopaths convened in 1910 or 1911 in Manchester to establish a society which became the British Osteopathic Association [6, p. 31; 15, p. 44]. This is the premier association of British osteopathy and the only one recognized by the American Osteopathic Association. Most osteopaths in the first few decades of the twentieth century in Britain did not receive their training in American schools. Some of them were trained by osteopaths educated at American osteopathic schools not recognized by the American Osteopathic Association [16, p. 12]. Others learned manipulative therapy in apprenticeships with bone-setters, osteopaths and chiropractors or through self-instruction.

Littlejohn and F. J. Horn established the British School of Osteopathy in London in 1917. Another school, established in 1921 by William Looker, was the Manchester College of Bloodless Surgery [17, p. 173]. The school, which offered a three to six month course, was renamed the Manchester College of Osteopathy and Chiropractic, and eventually relocated in London. Although the "Looker School" taught both osteopathy and chiropractic, the majority of its graduates called themselves osteopaths [18, p. 140]. In 1925 graduates of the Looker School, who were not eligible to join the British Osteopathic Association, founded the Incorporated Association of Osteopaths, Ltd. Sixteen of its members took a course of study at the British School of Osteopathy in 1928 and merged their organization with that institution [18, p. 144]. This same privilege was also extended to graduates of the South-Western School of Osteopathy in 1929 and to a few graduates of the old British College of Chiropractors [16, p. 21; 19, p. 107]. In 1936 the Incorporated Association of Osteopaths also absorbed the National Society of Osteopaths, Ltd. "whose members held diplomas from other training establishments since defunct, or had acquired their proficiency by means of apprenticeship perfected by long practice" and was renamed the Osteopathic Association of Great Britain [16, p. 25]. Since that time, this group has essentially functioned as the alumni association of the British School of Osteopathy.

The 1920s and the 1930s are described by the "old osteopaths" as the heyday of British osteopathy. The profession went into a holding pattern during World War II, and after the war the British Osteopathic Association founded a post-graduate institution called the London College of Osteopathy. The school ceased operations in 1975 and was reestablished in 1978 as the London College of Osteopathic Medicine [20]. The enrollment was always small, and in 1983 consisted of five students who were taking a thirteen month course. Admission to the college was available only to regular medical practitioners, and this widened the rift between the association and osteopaths trained by the British School of Osteopathy. In essence it formalized the distinction between the "medical osteopaths" or osteopathic physicians, and the "lay osteopaths."

Since World War II at least two more lay osteopathic factions have formed. As naturopathy or nature cure lost some of its appeal at the time of the "wonder drugs," naturopaths turned to osteopathy. In 1961 the British Naturopathic Association was renamed the British Naturopathic and Osteopathic Association and its associated training institution, the British College of Naturopathy, was renamed the British College of Naturopathy and Osteopathy. Although a few members of the naturopathic association continue to function as "straight" naturopaths, most members view themselves as naturopathic osteopaths, arguing that the forms of therapy are intertwined so that they cannot be separated.

The Society of Osteopaths emerged in the early 1970s as a result of a schism in the College of Naturopathy and Osteopathy. The director of a part-time course in osteopathy for French and Belgian physiotherapists at the college founded a separate Ecole Europeene d'Osteopathie in Maidstone Kent. A large portion of the faculty and student body at the college joined him to become a full-time section of the Ecole Europeene d'Osteopathie or European School of Osteopathy. The Society of Osteopaths also attracted disgruntled osteopaths from other backgrounds.

Since its beginnings British osteopathy has had freelance practitioners who have not been eligible for membership in the major associations. These osteopaths have over the years formed a number of small associations of their own, many of which are affiliated with part-time schools offering courses in osteopathy and other natural therapies. Among these people one finds associations and schools such as the British and European Osteopathic Association, the College of Osteopaths, the Faculty of Osteopaths, the Natural Therapeutic and Osteopathic Society, the Foster Clinic and Osteopathic Guild and the Northern School of Message, the London School Osteopathy [21, p. 114].

Lobbying for State Recognition

Larkin maintains health occupations have attempted to break through the physician-state alliance by: 1) eschewing contact with the bourgeois medical profession and relying on popular support; 2) petitioning for a royal charter or applying for incorporation under the Companies' Acts; or (3) obtaining some type of state registration through Parliament [22, p. 9-10]. He notes that the first path "was typical of heterodox occupations like osteopathy, and was a reaction to medical rebuttal and failure in other routes" [22, p. 9]. Osteopathic groups have also used the other two strategies.

The British Osteopathic Association in particular pursued an active policy of seeking state recognition. The first attempt occurred at the outbreak of World War I when the Association applied for registration "under the Companies' Act as a Scientific Society but this was opposed by the General Medical Council and the Board of Trade refused the application" [4, p. 37]. In 1931 the Association petitioned the Privy Council for a royal charter, but the Council rejected the request when it ruled that its admission requirements were so restrictive that only three members would qualify as charter members [16, p. 13]. Bills to establish a government-sanctioned register for osteopaths were submitted to the House of Commons in 1931, 1933, and 1934. When the last bill was not read, Viscount Elibank reintroduced it in the House of Lords in December 1934. After the bill received a second reading, it was referred to a Select Committee of the House of Lords. The supporters of the bill, which asserted that "an unqualified and incompetent quack and charlatan would be debarred from practicing osteopathy," included the British Osteopathic Association, the Incorporated Association of Osteopaths, the Osteopathic Defence League and the British School of Osteopathy [quoted in 6, p. 69].

Littlejohn was initially opposed to the bill because of the Minister of Health's admonition that the existence of an acceptable school was a prerequisite for statutory recognition of osteopathy. Due to an eleventh hour appeal, he consented to support the bill. Opponents included the British Medical Association, the General Medical Council, the Royal College of Surgeons of England, a number of universities and medical schools, the Chartered Society of Medical Gymnastics, the Nature Cure Association and British Chiropractors' Association. Wilfred Streeter argued that a state register for osteopaths was needed since of the some two or three thousand practitioners of manipulative therapy, only 170 were "qualified" [6, p. 399].

Due to the opposition, the internal struggles among osteopaths about educational standards, and the ill-prepared testimony by Littlejohn, supporters of the bill decided that it should be withdrawn [23, p. 25]. Instead the Select Committee recommended that the concerned osteopathic bodies establish a voluntary register and a reputable educational system.

The Establishment of an Umbrella Organization

Upon the advice of the Select Committee of the House of Lords, three bodies—the British Osteopathic Association, the Incorporated Association of Osteopaths and the National Society of Osteopaths, Ltd. "whose members held diplomas from other training establishments, since defunct, or had acquired their proficiency by means of apprenticeship perfected by long practice," joined together in 1936 to form the General Council and Register of Osteopaths [16, p. 25]. The Council was designed to be an umbrella organization that would transcend intraprofessional rivalries and present a "united front" while distinguishing "qualified" osteopaths from "unqualified" ones. The Register permits an osteopath to use the letters MRO (Member of the Register of Osteopaths) after the letter DO (Diploma in Osteopathy or Doctor of Osteopathy). Graduates of the London College of Osteopathic Medicine are also eligible and as are members of the Society of Osteopaths and graduates of the European School of Osteopathy.

The Council unified the British Osteopathic Association and the Osteopathic Association of Great Britain, yet the alliance between these rival groups has been an uneasy one. Over the years many members of the British Osteopathic Association have disaffiliated from the Register as the number of other osteopaths came to surpass them. Members of the Osteopathic Association of Great Britain constitute the dominant force in the governing board of the Council. Only one individual belonging to the British Osteopathic Association sits on the twelve-person board; the headquarters of the Council is located at the British School Osteopathy. Members of the British Osteopathic Association consider themselves to be socially and technically superior to the lay osteopaths. According to one member, to gain the respect of regular medical practitioners, "naturally we have to maintain our distance from the lay osteopaths."

The Creation of Additional Voluntary Registers

Osteopathic groups ineligible for membership in the Register of Osteopaths created additional registers. By the 1950s many naturopaths had incorporated osteopathic and chiropractic techniques. The promotion of osteopathy by certain practitioners in the British Naturopathic Association strained the harmonious relationship between the Naturopathic Association and the Osteopathic Association of Great Britain. This relationship was partly a result of the dual memberships of some practitioners. There was even discussion of accepting osteopathic naturopaths into the Register. Many Register osteopaths, however, feared that a rival group was forming in the Naturopathic Association.

When it became clear that most Register osteopaths opposed inclusion of the naturopathic osteopaths in the Register, the Naturopathic Association established its own register [24, p. 100]. In 1971 the Society of Osteopaths also created a register as did many quasi-organized osteopathic bodies. This situation means that the prospective client is confronted with a bewildering assortment of initials that organized osteopaths contend makes it impossible for the public to differentiate between "qualified" and "unqualified" practitioners.

Narrowing the Scope of Practice

The British School of Osteopathy asserts that "the scope of osteopathy is wide and covers the treatment of many common disorders, including not only pain and stiffness in the joints of the vertebral column and extremities, but also such disturbances of function in the organs of the body as do not involve pathology or organic disease" [25, p. 1]. The British Osteopathic Association maintains that "the osteopathic lesion is a principal factor in the cause or aggravation of disease" [26, p. 6]. Despite this broad philosophical base, most British osteopaths are musculoskeletal specialists — a niche which is far less threatening to the medical establishment than if they were to function as heterodox general practitioners. In his study of 5310 random-selected osteopathic patients, Burton found the following order of presenting complaints: low back 52 percent, neck 20 percent, thorax 13 percent, head 7 percent, lower extremity joint 7 percent, upper extremity joint 5 percent, and visceral 2 percent [27, p. 2]. Colin Dove, a former principal of the British School of Osteopathy, states that "our students are still taught a broad osteopathic concept of disease, with the emphasis on the fundamental osteopathic lesion; but general practice as such is an impossibility. Over the years there has been a tendency to adapt and become proficient in various adjustive procedures" [28, p. 1314].

Conversely, as an outgrowth of the holistic health movement, many British osteopaths stress the need to function as general practitioners. Many students at the European School of Osteopathy, the British College of Naturopathy and Osteopathy, and the British School of Osteopathy are interested in a wide range of alternative therapies, including naturopathy, homeopathy, herbalism, acupuncture, Alexander technique and yoga. Unlike most established osteopaths, they minimize the differences between osteopathy and chiropractic. How the British medical establishment will react to this development remains to be seen.

FURTHER DEVELOPMENTS IN THE PROFESSIONALIZATION OF BRITISH OSTEOPATHY

In contrast to American osteopathic medicine, British osteopathy is small. In 1983 the British Osteopathic Association of Great Britain had sixty-nine members, the Osteopathic Association of Great Britain 296, the British Naturopathic and Osteopathic Association 155 and the Society of Osteopaths 115. Some osteopaths maintain dual memberships. No reliable data exist on the number of free-lance and quasi-organized osteopaths. Baer found some 800 osteopaths listed in the Yellow Pages directories of Britain; some osteopaths, however, do not list their office telephone numbers.

British osteopathy shows signs of future growth. Between 1968 and 1983, the British School of Osteopathy increased its enrollment from thirty to over 300. In 1983 the European School of Osteopathy and the British College of Naturopathy and Osteopathy each enrolled over 100 students. Some osteopaths viewed the expansion of the British School of Osteopathy as an economic threat. Others argued that most graduates will establish practices in areas with low osteopath/population ratios, particularly outside of Greater London and the Home Counties, and believed that an enlarged profession would enhance the prospect of obtaining statutory recognition.

According to Denzen, emerging professions resemble social movements in that both avidly seek converts. The organized groups, however, fear competition from free-lance and quasiorganized osteopaths whose credentials detract from the public image of osteopathy [29, p. 3]. As Jackson observes, professionalization involves "increasingly protective measures to define the boundaries between the sacred company of those within the walled garden and those outside" [30, p. 10].

In an effort to upgrade its program, the British School of Osteopathy hired Stanley Bradford, a non-osteopath and former administrator in the polytechnic system. In 1980 Bradford approached the Department of Education and Science about "designation"—a status which would qualify students for mandatory grants. Presently some students receive discretionary grants from local governments. Acting upon the recommendation that the school needed a larger facility, it relocated near Trafalgar Square in the heart of central London. Wilensky maintains that if the training institutions of aspiring occupations "do not begin within universities, . . . they always eventually seek contact with universities, and there is a steady development of standard terms of study, academic degrees, and research programs to expand the base of knowledge" [14, p. 144]. The Council for National Academic Awards suggested that the School of Osteopathy approach a degree-granting institution to be accredited for granting a bachelor of science honors degree in osteopathy. In 1981 the School of Osteopathy and the Polytechnic of Central London applied jointly for accreditation of a degree program in osteopathy. While the Council maintained that it was prepared to accredit the proposed degree program, it refused to do so until the program is designated by the Department of Education and Science. In keeping with its fiscal policies, the Thatcher government had withdrawn its earlier support for designation.

Leslie makes a distinction between "spurious" and "genuine" professionalization [31, p. 52]. A tendency for aspiring occupations to mistake the counterfeit for the authentic is illustrated by a brief liaison between the British School of Osteopathy and Columbia Pacific University, a California-based operation. The liaison resulted from a desire to provide an interim degree-granting program before the anticipated accreditation would take effect. In 1981 a representative of the Columbia Pacific University "emphasized that CPU was not a degree shop but a 'highly respected university whose degrees were accepted by Yale and Harvard and whose courses were taken up by top U. S. businessmen' " [32]. When it was learned that this institution was listed as a "bogus university" at the University of London negotiations terminated. Shortly after the Council for National Academic Awards accredited the Anglo-European College of Chiropractic in 1988 for granting the Bachelor of Science degree, it finally bestowed this recognition upon the British School of Osteopathy [33, p. 1; 34, p. 43]. The European School of Osteopathy subsequently applied for degree status.

Larson maintains that an aspiring occupation group needs to transcend intraprofessional rivalries and close ranks if it is to achieve legitimacy:

> An impressionistic indicator of organizational strength is the emergence of a professional association recognized as representative by the public. Externally, this means that the professional association must be recognized by the state: for, indeed, given the new 'objective' basis on which privileges are claimed, only the state has the appearance of neutrality necessary to guarantee 'objectively' superior competence of a category of professionals. Internally, the emergence of a professional organization as 'representative spokesmen' for the profession is possible only if the organization is not challenged by another of equal credibility [8, p. 70].

Health officials and Members of Parliament often stated that osteopaths would have to be politically unified before they are granted statutory recognition. The first phase toward unification of the three principal lay osteopathic groups occurred in 1982 when the Council extended eligibility to the Register of Osteopaths to members of the Society of Osteopaths and graduates of the European School Osteopathy. During the mid-1980s members of the British Naturopathic and Osteopathic Association and graduates of the British College of Naturopathy and Osteopathy were also extended eligibility.

Even with unification of the four major osteopathic bodies, their leaders recognized that statutory recognition would not immediately follow. Sharma reports that the

> GRCO continues to seek some kind of statutory positions for osteopaths and in 1986 a Private Members' Bill was presented by Roy Galley and a member of the Convervative MPs at the request if the GRCO. This did not succeed, but the GRCO intends to continue to campaign for some kind of acceptable statutory recognition [35, p. 181].

Although many more regular physicians refer patients to osteopaths than in the past, organized bourgeois medicine would oppose recognition of osteopathy as an independent profession. The General Medical Council formerly ruled that "doctors must not refer patients to, or work in conjunction with any medically unqualified practitioners, other than one who was licensed as an auxiliary" [24, p. 33]. In 1974 the Council lifted this ban and permitted regular physicians to refer patients to heterodox practitioners, provided that the physician retains responsibility for the management of the patient. Most osteopaths, however, regard osteopathy as complementary rather than supplementary to medicine, as are physiotherapists and other health occupations under the jurisdiction of the Professions Supplementary to Medicine Act of 1960 [36, pp. 1092-1117]. Ironically, like the osteopaths, many of the professions under this act had hoped to achieve a legal status similar to that of dental surgeons. Although, as Larkin observes, "in a number of important ways para-medical workers have wrested control from doctors in the division of labour," their status remains a subordinate one [22, p. 190].

Despite the neglect of manipulative therapy by most orthopedists, some regular physicians are now trained in this area. Membership in the British Association of Manipulative Medicine reportedly fluctuates between 200 and 300 [24, p. 80]. Over the past two decades graduates of the London College of Osteopathic Medicine have become influential in the manual medicine movement. Since World War II the number of American-trained osteopathic physicians in the British Osteopathic Association has declined whereas the number of London College graduates has increased. Whereas the Osteopathic Association had seventy-nine DO's in 1936, in 1983 it had nineteen DO's and fifty London College graduates. Since the flow of American-trained osteopathic physicians virtually ceased, the Osteopathic Association became isolated from both American osteopathic medicine and the rest of British osteopathy. Although the manual medicine people initially excluded DO's from their ranks, the Association of Manipulative Medicine eventually extended honorary membership to them. Members of the Osteopathic Association are now teaching manipulation to the manual medicine people. While some of the "old osteopaths" in the Osteopathic Association feel uneasy about this arrangement, other members view it as an important avenue for introducing osteopathy into bourgeois medicine.

The implications of this trend are difficult to predict. One possibility is that lay osteopaths will face a formidable rival within bourgeois medicine. Although many osteopaths assert that manipulative therapy cannot be adequately taught in a series of seminars, organized bourgeois medicine may attempt to coopt osteopathy by making it a specialty within its own ranks. Since manipulative therapy generally requires more time than most medical procedures, medical manipulators could train physiotherapists to conduct routine tasks. James Cyriax, a consultant at St. Andrew's Hospital in London, has taught some 1000 physiotherapists in manipulative therapy [37, p. 1].

BRITISH OSTEOPATHY, STRATEGIC ELITES AND PROFESSIONALIZATION

The professionalization of an occupation depends on its appeal to strategic elites in the larger society. Freidson maintains that the professional dominance of regular medicine is "secured by the political and economic influence of the elite which sponsors it—an influence that drives competing occupations out of the same area of work, that discourages others by virtue of the competitive advantages conferred on the chosen occupation, and requires still others to be subordinated to the profession" [38, p. 72]. Although the position of organized bourgeois medicine is preeminent in British society, its power is delegated rather than absolute. If competing health occupations find support among political, economic and social elites, they may be able to make inroads upon the professional dominance of regular physicians. For example, the royal family's utilization of homeopathic physicians gives homeopathy a form of protection that other heterodox health groups do not enjoy.

The ability of osteopathic physicians in the United States to appeal to various corporate and governmental elites permitted them to obtain rights to full practice in all fifty states as well as financial support from the federal government. As Baer argues elsewhere, the organizational rejuvenation of American osteopathic medicine, illustrated by its tripling of osteopathic of osteopathic schools since 1964,

... can only be understood by viewing it within the larger context of the political economy of health care in capitalist America. Its dynamic growth is related to a variety of strategies that are being employed by certain strategic elites to deal with the contradictions of capital intensive medicine. Especially important among these contradictions are the processes that contribute to increased specialization in medicine and the fragmentation as well as the maldistribution of health services [39, p. 710].

In essence American osteopathic physicians succeeded in their drive for professionalization because they filled part of the gap left in primary care by bourgeois medicine.

Although Britain does not face the same acute shortage of primary care physicians as does the United States, it has been experiencing many of the same contradictions in the health arena, including escalating costs. According to Navarro,

> specifically in terms of the NHS, the enormous increase in expenditures in the health sector—from 455 million pounds to approximately 2,500 million pounds within 25 years—had created a good deal of alarm, leading to a demand for slowing down, cutting back, and generally trimming the fat in the NHS, and it was this concern that produced the call for further strengthening the centralized direction of the NHS and its management structure, as well as an exploration of alternatives to the care provided by costly hospital-oriented medicine [40, p. 53].

In addition to keeping labor costs down by increasing productivity and lowering wages among health workers and utilizing nurse practitioners rather than physicians, many administrators at the Department of Health and Social Services and the National Health Service accept the growing critique of high-technology medicine [41, pp. 209-212]. One approach to the fiscal crisis is an emphasis on prevention through healthy living. According to Sharma, "[b]oth Conservative rhetoric and many non-orthodox therapists approve of the principle that people should be encouraged to take more and more responsibility for their own health care" [35, pp. 213-214]. Despite the opposition of organized bourgeois medicine, some health policy decision-makers are considering alternative medicine as a way of cutting health care cost.

In 1973 a committee of the House of Commons invited representatives of natural therapeutic associations, including the Acupuncture Association, the British Chiropractors' Association, the British Naturopathic and Osteopathic Association, the Osteopathic Association of Great Britain, the Society of Osteopaths, the National Institute of Medical Herbalists, the Research Society for Naturopathy and the General Council and Register of Osteopaths, to a meeting on the status of alternative medicine [4]. Although the Council and Register of Osteopaths was not represented at the meetings, it desired to be included in legislation recognizing the natural therapies. In 1976 David Owens, the Minister of Health, announced the formation of a Working Group to examine techniques for back pain [42]. The Back Pain Association was one of the forces leading to the establishment of the Group. It was established by Stanley Grundy, a beneficiary of chiropractic treatment and the Institute of Directors— an assemblage of corporate board directors. Some corporate executives are deeply concerned about financial losses due to back pain and injury. Referring to a report in the *Industrial Relations Services Bulletin,* Lord Ferrier stated in 1979 before the House of Lords that:

> Back pain cost British industry 18 million lost working days last year compared with 9.3 million lost from strikes. It cost more than 900 in lost production and cost the State 90 million in social security payments. Some 50,000 people are estimated to be off work every day because of back pain. It represents one of the major causes of sickness absence in industry [quoted in 43, p. 3].

The Working Group, also known as the Cochrane Committee, included regular physicians, medical researchers and a graduate of the London College of Osteopathic Medicine [42]. It considered whether heterodox techniques, particularly osteopathic and chiropractic, are as effective for back pain as bourgeois medical treatment and requested information from natural therapeutic associations. The Committee recommended that heterodox techniques be considered in comparative studies on the treatment of back pain. At a symposium of the British Association of Manipulative Medicine, Gerald Vaughn, the Minister of Health, stated that medical manipulators, osteopaths and chiropractors meet an important need, and that the Department of Health and Social Services and the Medical Research Council are interested in funding research on the nature and treatment of back pain [44, p. 3]. It seems paradoxical that regular physicians are among the elites who are interested in heterodox medicine as an alternative to high-technology medicine. Larkin observes, however, that medical elites are divided into "conservative monopolists," who wish "to maintain direct rule on the division of labor" and "liberal reformists," who see "adjustments as essential for the continuity of control" [22, p. 18]. Whereas the monopolists, who belong to the British Medical Association and the Royal Colleges, oppose state registration of certain therapists, the reformists, who adhere to the editorial policies of *Lancet,* view it as a mechanism for transforming them into auxiliaries. In the case of the occupations under the Professions Supplementary to Medicine Act, Larkin argues that "state registration is a part of the evolution of medical dominance rather than its alteration" [22, p. 184].

Larson maintains that "professionalization, as a movement for status advancement, must appeal to general values of the dominant ideology if it is to make its own values acceptable" [8, p. 157]. An emerging profession must form organic and ideological ties with the ruling class. According to Sharma,

> Complementary medicine has always had its influential friends, members of the elite and of both sides of the Houses of Parliament who have used it themselves and who have acted as its informal advocates in high places. In February 1989 an all-party alliance of parliamentarians was launched, the Parliamentary Alternative and Complementary Medicine Group, with a membership of 30 MPs, 15 peers and a number of eminent non-orthodox practitioners [35, p. 98].

Since its beginning osteopathy sought patronage among the upper class of British society. Some osteopaths, particularly members of the British Osteopathic Association, maintain practices on Harley Street and other fashionable sections of London, and count influential businesspeople, politicians, and celebrities among their patients. Osteopaths frequently rely upon prominent patients for assistance in their drive for professionalization. Viscount Elibank served as the President of the General Council and Register of Osteopaths from 1936 to 1944. More recently, the British School of Osteopathy hired Sir Norman Lindop, a former director of Hatfield Polytechnic, as its principal. Sir Norman had served on many high-ranking government health bodies, including the General Health Services Council. Between 1974 and 1979 he was the Chairperson of the Council for Professions Supplementary to Medicine. Sir Norman was appointed a lay member of the General Medical Council, which since the nineteenth century has been "practically controlled . . . by the upper class physicians and surgeons" [40, p. 8]. In essence, he functions as a key patron for organized osteopathy in its drive for professionalization.

In contrasting their philosophy to the reductionist one of regular physicians, osteopaths claim that they practice a holistic form of health care which focuses on treatment of the whole person. In reality, like bourgeois medicine, the holism of osteopathy is limited in that in relies heavily on notions such as the machine analogy and the single causation of disease. McQueen discusses the similarities of bourgeois medicine (or allopathy), osteopathy and chiropractic:

> The body is viewed as a machine, in some cases a godgiven perfect machine, in other cases a chemical-physical machine. In both cases the body is seen as normally running without trouble; occasionally, however, it needs repair or adjustment. Chiropractic and osteopathic concern themselves with the structure and function of then machine. Healing occurs by making structural corrections . . . Allopathic doctrines concern themselves with how the machine has been damaged by foreign parts, either injury, tumors, germs, or other invaders. Healing takes place through the active intervention of alternative chemicals which purge the foreign parts and restore correct chemical balance [45, p. 74].

Furthermore, allopathy, osteopathy and chiropractic, at least in their original form, imply that healing involves the removal of a single cause: a pathogen in the case of allopathy, a lesion in the case of osteopathy, and a subluxation in the case of chiropractic. McQueen maintains that "the priority of the belief in a single cause has resulted in the downplaying of social factors in the etiology of disease" [45, p. 74]. All three paradigms are compatible with capitalist ideology in that they depoliticize the sources of disease.

Whether British osteopaths, particularly lay osteopaths, will be absorbed into the medical division of labor as auxiliaries, or whether they will function as independent state-registered practitioners is difficult to determine. Bloomfield suggests that the government desires to incorporate them as auxiliaries:

> Before Mrs. Butler introduced her 1976 Bill she asked Dr. David Owen, then Health Minister, for his advice on the question of legislation for all branches of alternative medicine. Not unexpectedly, being both a doctor and a career politician, Dr. Owen took the orthodox viewpoint and suggested that an approach be made to the Council for Professions Supplementary Medicine . . .
>
> An informal approach was then made to Dr. B. L. Donald, register of the CPSM. It was made clear that it would be statutorily possible to set up a multidisciplined Board within the meaning of the 1960 Act and this could include all the practitioners of alternative medicine thus registered auxiliary to the medical profession . . . [46, pp. 3-4].

CONCLUSION

In contrast to the United States, where osteopathic medicine has joined the medical mainstream therapeutically while retaining organizational separatism, British osteopathy remains a marginal profession. Nevertheless, strategic elites exhibit interest in it as an alternative to high-technology medicine. This interest parallels the retrenchment of the British welfare state initiated by the Labour administration in 1975 and expanded, particularly in the form of an "ideological attack" on the concept of the welfare state, by the Conservative administration [47].

In their effort to obtain statutory recognition during the 1930s, osteopaths relied on Labourite and union support [48, p. 168]. In its present effort, organized osteopathy seeks support wherever it can find it. Although many osteopaths favor inclusion of osteopathic treatment under the National Health Service, most osteopaths are opposed to this arrangement. Since the entrepreneurial orientation of osteopaths is consistent with the fiscal policies of the Conservative government, they see their success as congruent with the continuation of the current administration. Labour politicians sympathetic to osteopathy insist that their support for statutory recognition of osteopaths would be contingent upon inclusion of osteopathic services under the National Health Service.

For the foreseeable future the Conservative government is unlikely to grant statutory recognition to osteopaths or chiropractors, particularly as independent practitioners. Indeed, in the early 1980s the government denied inclusion under the Professions Supplementary to Medicine Act to the British Chiropractors' Association. As Sharma observes,

> [t]he arguments that complementary health care is very cost-effective, that it concentrates on preventive care, that it cures problems that orthodox medicine cannot deal with, are as much arguments for the reform of orthodox medicine as for the incorporation of yet another set of services into the over-stretched NHS. Ultimately, as has already been the case in the United States, the ability of osteopathy in Britain to gain legitimacy depends on it convincing strategic elites, not of its efficacy as an alternative form of therapy, but of its utility in responding to the contradictions of capital intensive medicine [35, p. 210].

REFERENCES

1. W. Wardwell, The Reduction of Strain in a Marginal Social Role, *American Journal of Sociology, 61,* pp. 16-25, 1955.
2. H. A. Baer, The Divergent Evolution of Osteopathy in Two Countries, in *Research in the Sociology of Health Care: International Comparsions in Health Service, Vol. 5,* R. A. Roth (ed.), JAI Press, Greenwich, Connecticut, pp. 63-99, 1987.
3. N. Gervitz, *The D.O.'s: Osteopathic Medicine in America,* Johns Hopkins University Press, 1982.
4. T. Hall and J. Wernham, *The Contribution of John Martin Littlejohn to Osteopathy,* Maidstone Osteopathic Clinic, Maidstone, Kent, 1974.
5. T. Berchtold, *To Teach, To Heal, To Serve: The Story of the Chicago College of Osteopathic Medicine,* Chicago College of Osteopathic Medicine, Chicago, 1975.

6. L. McKeon, *Osteopathic Polemics*, C. W. Daniel, London, 1938.
7. S. Falder and R. Munro, *The Status of Complimentary Medicine in the United Kingdom*, Threshold Foundation, London, 1981.
8. M. Larson, *The Rise of Professionalization: A Sociological Analysis*, University of California Press, Berkeley, 1977.
9. G. Harries-Jenkins, Professions in Organizations, in *Professions and Professionalization*, J. Jackson (ed.), Cambridge University Press, London, 1970.
10. M. Goldstein and P. Donaldson, Exporting Professionalism: A Case Study of Medical Education, *Journal of Health and Social Behavior, 20*, 1979.
11. R. Manning, Shamanism as a Profession, in *The Realm of the Extra-Human: Agents and Audiences*, A. Bharati (ed.), Mouton, The Hague, 1976.
12. M. Larson, Professionalism: Rise and Fall, *International Journal of Health Services, 9*, pp. 607-627, 1979.
13. E. Krause, *Power and Illness: The Political Sociology of Health and Medical Care*, Elsevier, New York, 1977.
14. H. Wilensky, The Professionalization of Everyone?, *American Journal of Sociology, 70*, pp. 137-158, 1964.
15. R. Puttick, *Osteopathy*, Faber & Faber, London, 1956.
16. *The Osteopathic Blue Book: The Origin and Development of Osteopathy in Great Britain*, General Council and Register of Osteopaths, n.d.
17. C. Hill and H. Clegg, *What Is Osteopathy?*, J. M. Denton, London, 1937.
18. L. McKeon, *A Healing Crisis*, Mitchell Health Products, WestonSuper-Marie, England, 1933.
19. M. Beal, London College of Osteopathy, in *1950 Year Book of Selected Osteopathic Papers*, American Academy of Applied Osteopathy, Colorado Springs, Colorado, 1950.
20. *Prospectus of the London College of Osteopathic Medicine*, London College of Osteopathic Medicine, London, n.d.
21. K. Brady and M. Considine, *Holistic London*, Brainwave, London, 1990.
22. G. Larkin, *Occupational Monopoly and Modern Medicine*, Tavistock, London, 1983.
23. J. Darlinson, *The New Art of Healing: Osteopathy*, W. H. Smith, London, 1935.
24. B. Inglis, *The Book of the Back*, Hearst, London, 1978.
25. *Osteopathy as a Career*, British School of Osteopathy, London, n.d.
26. *Osteopathy: The Story of Andrew Still House*, British Osteopathic Association, London, n.d.
27. A. Burton, *A Work Study of the Osteopathic Association of Great Britain*, London, n.d.
28. C. Dove, *A History of the Osteopathic Vertebral Lesion*, Osteopathic Association of Great Britain, London, 1967.
29. N. Denzen, Pharmacy—Incomplete Professionalization, *Social Forces, 46*, 1968.
30. J. Jackson, Professions and Professionalization—Editorial Introduction, in *Professions and Professionalization*, J. Jackson (ed.), Cambridge University Press, London, 1970.
31. C. Leslie, The Professionalization of Ayurvedic and Unani Medicine, in *Medical Men and Their World*, E. Freidson (ed.), Aldine, Chicago, 1972.
32. *Spout, 3*:1, October 20, 1981.
33. *European Journal of Osteopathy*, Summer 1989.
34. H. A. Baer, The Sociopolitical Development of British Chiropractic, *Journal of Manipulative and Physiological Therapeutics, 14*:10, pp. 38-45, 1991.
35. U. Sharma, *Complementary Medicine Today: Practitioners and Patients*, Routledge, London, 1992.
36. *Public General Acts and Measures*, HMSO, London, pp. 1092-1117, 1960.

37. E. Schioetz and J. Cyriax, *Manipulation: Past and Present,* Heinemann Books, London, 1975.
38. E. Friedson, *Profession of Medicine: A Study of the Sociology of the Applied Knowledge,* Harper & Row, New York, 1970.
39. H. A. Baer, The Organizational Rejuvenation of Osteopathy: A Reflection of the Decline of Professional Dominance in Medicine, *Social Science and Medicine, 15A,* pp. 701-711, 1981.
40. V. Navarro, *Class Struggle, the State and Medicine: A Historical and Contemporary Analysis of the Medical Sector in Great Britain,* Prodist, New York, 1978.
41. L. Doyal with I. Pennell, *The Political Economy of Health,* South End Press, Boston, 1979.
42. *Working Group on Back Pain: Report to the Secretary of State for Social Services,* HMSO, London, 1979.
43. *Journal of the Society of Osteopaths,* No. 8, 1980.
44. *Contact: The Newsletter of the British Chiropractors' Association,* No. 4, 1981.
45. D. McQueen, The History of Science and Medicine as Theoretical Sources for the Comparative Study of Contemporary Medical Systems, *Social Science and Medicine, 12,* 1974.
46. R. Bloomfield, *The Time Bomb Under Alternative Medicine,* Information and Study Centre for Alternative Medicine, Maidstone, Kent, n.d.
47. I. Gough, The Crisis of the British Welfare State, *International Journal of Health Services, 13,* pp. 469-477, 1983.
48. F. Honigsbaum, *The Division in British Medicine: A History of the Separation of General Practice for Hospital Care, 1911-1968,* Kogan Paul, London, 1979.

Section D:

The Micro-Social Level

Medical Hegemony, Biomedical Magic, and Folk Medicine: Reproductive Illness among Haitian Women

In 1982, the plantation town of Puerto Tejada, Columbia was home to 30,000 people, most of them agonizingly impoverished migrants from the Pacific coast. One, a pregnant woman named Maura, lived with her one-year-old child in one room of a dirt-floored house. Maura worked occasionally as a field hand on a cane plantation and sometimes as a servant. Michael Taussig, who carried out field work in Puerto Tejada described Maura's wretched plight in his volume *Shamanism, Colonialism and the Wild Man*. He writes:

> I stopped by a few weeks after Maura's baby was born to find both Maura and her one-year-old son sick. She was coughing badly, talking of tuberculosis. The little boy, cast from the breast, ate nothing. He was in an advanced state of starvation, stupefied, as in a trance. Maura had practically no money, just enough for one person to have a consultation at the cheapest health clinic. The new baby's father refused to help, saying the baby was not his. Her mother and sisters across the way were dirt poor and not very concerned at her plight. It was common enough [1, p. 276].

With Taussig's help, both Maura and her son were able to go to the doctor. He was both enthusiastic and experienced.

> He ordered X-rays. But Maura couldn't pay. He prescribed antibiotics and special protein foods for the little boy. But Maura couldn't pay. And if he took the boy into the hospital for a week or two of intravenous feeding, what then? What would he be going back to? [1, pp. 276-278].

Tragically, Maura's case is not unique. It is the norm in Puerto Tejada and it is the norm in many parts of the Third World. Although surrounded by fertile fields, children like Maura's do not get enough to eat and their parents, even if they work in food production, cannot buy enough food to live on. While biomedical physicians are on hand, ready with X-rays and antibiotic prescriptions, the basic problem, the structure of class domination of productive resources, products, and people, cannot be cured with these medical tools, physician ability or commitment notwithstanding.

> Yet amazingly . . . absurd as they are, these services supplied by the official medical system and its university-trained doctors, backed by the multinational corporations of 'science,' agribusiness, and pharmaceuticals, are sought by many. The optimistically desperate search is testimony to magical attraction, in this case to officialdom and to 'science,' no less and probably a great deal greater than that involved in the magic of so-called magical medicine. Existing in the shadow of the economic and scientific might of the United States, this third-world cult of the modern illuminates the magical power inherent in that might and necessary to it [1, p. 278].

"Biomedicine as magic," this is a connection not often made in anthropological analyses. Yet it is an idea worthy of exploration. Underlying the magic of biomedicine, fueling its broad appeal, according to Taussig, is not so much the undeniable healing power of antibiotics or even the remarkable ability with X-rays to see through flesh and find disease. Rather, the magic of biomedicine among the poor of the Third World "is the promise of the power and wealth of the modern world, a promise as yet denied the vast majority . . . without whose labor and talent there would be little wealth" [1, pp. 281-282]. We are talking about a magic, then, that stems from biomedicine's intimate and historic connection with capitalism, that incomparably powerful economic system that has carried its medical system to all corners of the globe and dramatically shaped, indeed in many ways, produced, the lives of people like Maura and her starving son.

How does this magic work? And especially, how does it work among people like Maura raised on a different form of magic, the magic of shaman healers, possession cults, and anthropomorphic spirits? Among people with intact folk healing traditions, how is biomedicine perceived and used, and what is the broader impact over time of its presence among people who benefit so unevenly from its healing power? In these settings, how are biomedicine and its representations of disease and associated treatment fitted to folk understandings, and what impact does biomedicine have on shaping and reshaping those understandings? Answering these questions, from the perspective of critical medical anthropology, is the goal of this chapter. Its aim, is to take critical medical anthropology as described in earlier chapters beyond the boundaries of medical encounters and health problems of the First World into the shanty dwellings of the poor that have been created by capitalism as it has developed in a Third World setting.

Additionally, this chapter is concerned with answering the foregoing questions in a particular time and place with a specific group of people. As Nichter cautions, "the crude application of a political economic analysis leaves one with the sense that it is the same story again and again" [2, p. 142], as if local conditions, cultures, and communities had no influence on the flow of events and direction of popular discourse. For this purpose, we move from Columbia to Haiti, a land whose very name conjures up rites of magic and mysterious powers in the Western imagination. While the spiritist beliefs and practices of Haiti are part-and-parcel of a syncretic Circum-Caribbean tradition that embraces numerous variants from South America to the southern United States, those of Haiti standout as particularly ominous as well as potent. Even the Westernized name of Haiti's religious healing tradition, voodoo, has come to be synonymous with dark and evil powers. With the emergence of the AIDS epidemic, for example, a foreign missionary (of which Haiti has no shortage) was quoted in *Life* magazine offering the following explanation of the origin the disease:

> It is voodoo that is the devil here . . . . It is a demonic religion, a cancer on Haiti. Voodoo is worse than AIDS. And it is one of the reasons for the epidemic [quoted in 3, p. 85].

These significations are of historic importance as they trace to the successful Haitian overthrow of French colonialism in 1804. In the early years of French rule in Haiti, African slaves were allowed to participate in folk religious rites, as the dancing that is so central to Haitian ritual was seen as a healthy outlet that helped keep slaves in good physical condition for their labor on French plantations. Only gradually did the colonists come to realize that "revolutionary leaders used Voodoo meetings to incite slaves to revolt" [4, p. 58], after which voodoo was summarily banned (by Article 3 of the Black Code) and became an underground tradition steeped in secrecy. Yet banning only increased the popularity and sacredness of voodoo, while consolidating its political agenda [5]. Increasingly, slaves and free-living maroons came to believe that the spirits or *loas* supported anti-French rebels and had "agreed not only to increase their force tenfold, but also to cover their enemies with all sorts of curses" [4, p. 61]. In battles with the French, the rebel leaders openly wore talismans signifying their spirit protectors and employed voodoo priests to rally and motivate their troops. In the end, the French too accepted the power of voodoo. How else were they to explain military defeat at the hands of what they perceived to be mere savages except through imbuing the religion of their enemies with frighteningly demonic qualities? In an inversion as magical as it was comical and tragic, Europeans displaced onto voodoo their fear that the unrelenting oppression and untold suffering they had created might be turned against them. As Taussig suggests, "In the colonial mode of production of reality, . . . such mimesis occurs by a colonial mirroring of otherness that reflects back onto the colonialists the barbarity of their own social relations, but as imputed to the savagery they yearn to colonize" [1, p. 134]. So shocked were Europeans by their defeat and the awareness of what it might portend throughout the colonial world, that Haiti and voodoo have been marked in Western ideology ever since, an occurrence that is not without consequence for the climate in which biomedicine encounters Haitian society.

Our concern with Haiti is rooted in field work conducted there by Singer and two of his colleagues (Lani Davison and Gina Gerdes). Recognizing that health, especially among pregnant women, is a precarious state in Haiti, the focus of this research was on reproductive health problems and illness conceptions among women. This examination of reproductive illness among Haitian women began, appropriately enough, among refugees in Miami, Haitian women who had fled the social and economic causes of much illness. Through a set of interviews conducted with Haitian women as they awaited health services in a community clinic, an understanding was developed of the most salient reproductive illness categories and help-seeking strategies. During these interviews, it became evident that a rich corpus of health beliefs among Haitian women were centered on reproductive processes and bodily systems, and on the role of blood in health and reproduction.

This information served as the starting point for further research in Haiti in the southern coastal town of Jacmel. Research in Haiti consisted of several components, including a short door-to-door survey with women in a selected neighborhood to identify common reproductive complaints; in-depth interviews on reproductive history, help-seeking, and etiology beliefs with a set of thirty-one women who lived in this neighborhood or were encountered as outpatients at a nearby hospital; and interviews with the full range of biomedical and folk health-care providers, including doctors, nurses, health department officials, spiritual healers (*houngans, manbos, malfeté*), herbal healers (*dokté féy*), and midwives (*famm saj*), concerning their treatment of reproductive illnesses. Interviews with women focused on recent episodes of reproductive illness and educed what Early has termed "therapeutic narratives"—that is, participants' commentaries on illness, progression, help-seeking resort, and related life events and social relations. As Early has emphasized, such narratives "link the unique, somatic event with shared cultural knowledge about illness" [7, p. 149]. Therapeutic narratives, in other words, constitute a window on sufferers' experience in particular cultural settings. Under changing conditions, as seen in the case of Haiti, therapeutic narratives can reflect historical reconstruction of the very experience suffering. Further, such narratives help us to link the flow of experience in the settings we study to changes in the configuration of social and political life. As Keesing emphasized in his account of narrative collection among Kwaio women, "All talk is contextually situated, social implicated" [8, p. 32].

REPRODUCTIVE ILLNESS IN HAITI

The term "reproductive illness" is used here to refer to indigenously named complaints and conditions that are localized in reproductive organs or are associated with reproductive functions. In some cases, these conditions overlap with biomedically constructed and recognized problems; in other they do not. Frequently mentioned reproductive complaints among Haitian women include *matris deplase* (displace uterus), *lamné tonbé* (fallen uterus), and *grann chalé* (vaginal burning). However, the most commonly cited reproductive illness was found to be a phenomenon we label *pédisyon-fibróm*. While *pédisyon* has been described by Murray as a Haitian culture-bound syndrome, here we are concerned not so much with the place of this illness in traditional Haitian health culture but with its relationship to a larger and changing complex of interrelated reproductive illnesses experienced by women in contemporary Haiti [9]. Examining this complex sheds light on both the underlying Haitian illness model and the wider forces now shaping Haitian society.

Not insignificantly, Murray begins his account of *pédisyon* by stressing the social and historic isolation of Haitian society. He writes,

> In the context of almost total national isolation after 1804, the Haitian peasantry has had to call on its own resources for the development of folk institutions and theories to handle the gamut of problems that confront all human societies [9, p. 59].

This isolation meant that "sickness and healing had to be handled by locally developed practices rather than by modern medical practices" [9, pp. 75-76]. But when it came to certain health issues, such as sterility and subfecundity, the ethnomedical system was handicapped by its rootedness in a particular ideological history. These health conditions, not surprisingly, are common in Haiti, which, like the Colombian example discussed above, is characterized by poor nutrition, underdeveloped hygienic facilities, and numerous unchecked infectious diseases [10, 11]. Elsewhere, indigenous healers intervene openly in the arena of reproduction; for example, Nzoamambu, the Kongo folk therapist from lower Zaire, described so well by Janzen, understands infertility as a consequence of obstructed social relations, leading to obstructed bodily passages, both of which can be treated with herbs and the resolution of interpersonal tensions [12]. Through such intervention, Nzaoamambu has cured almost a thousand barren women, all of whose children must, as advertisement, bear his name. But in Haiti, argues Murray,

> The persistent social dominance of French symbols has shaped the course of rural Haitian theology. The Christian God has been exalted, the African *loua* have been dethroned and weakened ... [O]nly God can place a child in a woman's womb. The *loua* cannot do anything to help a woman conceive .... If a woman is barren, it is God's work [9, pp. 76-77].

This understanding is based on the idea that the fetus must be constructed in stages, like erecting a building or sewing a garment. Indeed, some Haitians literally

> talk about the growth of the fetus during pregnancy in the terminology of house building or the terminology of sewing. In this case, the architect and tailor is *Bon-Dié* (God). (The *loua*, the spirits of the folk-religious pantheon, are not believed to have a role in conception and fetal development. They can only have negative effects on these matters ...). God is viewed as gradually adding pieces to the body until it is finished. The most commonly used verb is "koud"-to-sew. One by one God "sews" on the parts of the body [13, p. 4].

As one of the women interviewed in Jacmel explained, "only God has the power over life and death."

Consequently, the traditional health care providers of Haiti, the *houngans, manbos,* and midwives—curers who are skilled at working the body, spirits, and therapeutic plants—readily admit their helplessness in the treatment of infertility. As a *manbo*, a female voodoo practitioner, explained to Singer and his co-workers:

> Some women God doesn't give them any child. ... I can't do anything .... If God won't give them, I can't tell God to give them.

A *houngan*, a male healer, concurs

> If a person doesn't have children, it's God that didn't give you children. It's God that gives you children. If God doesn't give you children, you can't want to have children.

But culture, is not a fixed or frozen thing. It can be manipulated in response to changing circumstance and to pressing human need. As Mintz has stressed, culture is best conceived as a resource people utilize, *not* a straitjacket that permanently binds them [14]. While traditions may appear to be confining and, not infrequently, maladaptive, upon closer inspection we often find that what has been painted as "blind custom is neither blind nor customary" [14, p. 97]. The culturally constructed pathway out of the infertility dilemma in the case of Haiti, according to Murray, is offered by the folk illness of *pédisyon*.

This Creole term is linked by Murray as a cognate to the French or English word perdition—a state of spiritual liminality and ruin. But in its cultural meaning also lies in its component morphemes as a state of losing blood (*pédi san*). A woman in *pédisyon*, Haitian women say, is pregnant but does not deliver. Initially, as with other pregnancies, the woman's menstrual flow ceases and other indications of pregnancy are evident. However, something goes wrong. Because of a natural or supernatural abnormality, the women suddenly resumes bleeding each month, but heavier and longer than her normal menstruation. The women is not believed to have aborted because she can still feel the child within her. The unborn child who, it is believed, normally would be nourished by this blood, loses its source of nutrition and begins to deteriorate, to shrink. As one women explained to Singer and his colleagues, "When the period doesn't come, the child grows, but when I bleed, the baby goes down." Importantly, a women can remain in this state of encumbered pregnancy for months or even for years—still pregnant but unable to deliver a child that is unable or ready to be born.

Pédisyon is not a rare condition among Haitian women. As one of the women interviewed in Jacmel commented, "It's not something to be ashamed of because a lot of women have it, it's a sickness you see all the time." For example, Gerta, a thirty-one-year-old women interviewed at the hospital in Jacmel, reported that she has lived with her common-law husband for thirteen years and has had no children. But she is not infertile nor is her partner sterile, rather she believes she is in *pédisyon*.

> The baby has been there for more than a year. I know it is still there, because from time to time before I eat, I can feel it moving. My stomach is hard, my lower back hurts, and sometimes I can't sit down. I have bleeding every month since the fourth month of the pregnancy, sometimes three times a month. The herbal doctor told me it was *pédisyon*.

Similar is the case of twenty-two-year-old Marie Rose. She has been in a sexual union for two years, but, like Gerta, has no children. She explained that she has suffered from *pédisyon* for almost two years.

> Before I was with a man, my period was normal. Since I have been with him, it never stops. The *pédisyon* started after we were together for two months. No one

told me; I know because the bleeding isn't the same as before. I saw that my period wasn't normal. I bleed for 8-10 days every month.

At the clinic, the doctor told Marie Rose that he did not want to hear anything about *pédisyon*, a common attitude among physicians. As a prominent doctor in Jacmel, in explaining physicians' response to folk constructions, stated,

> If you're not initiated in the language, you could not understand what they're saying. . . . Now if there's a problem of education, so that the person doesn't understand at all what is going on—they have a false idea of what is going on, you have to first of all educate the person, to say it's not what they think it is. . . . That is, they come with their own ideas on the problems; you have to give them the correct ideas, and you have to prove it too. . . . So as a doctor in this environment, you have this challenge, you have to enhance biomedicine, to challenge traditional medicine, to give a more important place to the education of the people. Even if they don't believe you, sometimes they argue with you, so you have to be aggressive at times to get them away from their belief.

Indeed "educating" the population emerges as central to the physician's self-defined role, not just about clinical issues but about cultural values as well. Discussing the reason even very poor women must pay for medical treatment, a doctor stated:

> We can't do it for free because we can't have people thinking that it is a gift. We have to give them an idea of being responsible for themselves from the point of view of health. The fact that they have to give a little money is important to preserve this feeling of self-responsibility for their health.

In Marie Rose's case, the physician's diagnosis was menorrhagia, or excessive menstrual discharge. But Marie Rose's self-diagnosis was confirmed by an herbal healer from a rural area outside of town who began treating her for *pédisyon*.

Women like Gerta and Marie Rose describe *pédisyon* with graphic images, evoked perhaps in part by their memories of an impoverished childhood, their endless struggles with a harsh, hilly, and denuded environment, and their daily encounter with a social reality that is inherently injurious. Moreover, these women know that those close to them frequently cannot be depended on to provide social support or even to survive. As Prince comments, "Women carry a disproportionate load of the work and suffering endured by the majority of Haitians" [15, p. 62]. Consequently, like their counterparts elsewhere in Haiti studied by Farmer, the women interviewed in Jacmel are "emblematic of the uncounted Haitian women who labor against increasingly dismal odds" [6, p. 66]. Concerning *pédisyon*, these women say, "The child has no nourishment," "It is being sucked dry," "It is trapped, It can't find a place to grow well." Living among these women, watching the toil and pain of their lives, holding their emaciated babies, knowing only too well the infant mortality rate in Haiti and the rates of a host of other preventable health conditions, it is hard not to think the significations attached to *pédisyon* apply as well to the women who speak them. While these women cannot quote health statistics, they have the direct and personal experience of what it means to live in a country in which half of all deaths are among children under five years of age and the majority of these are caused directly or indirectly by malnutrition [16]. These women too have no nourishment, are being sucked dry, are trapped, and can find no place in their difficult world to flourish. In their illness perceptions, these women appear to weave in their own experience of the oppression of daily life [17] and the not so hidden injuries of inequality.

Thus Lucienne, a mother of five small children, linked her *pédisyon* (and an array of other reproductive symptoms, including an earlier miscarriage) to having to work so hard every day as a seamstress.

> I have a pain in my back and cramps in my legs. Sometimes when I am walking, all of a sudden I can't bend. And I feel something like a ball under my stomach on the right side, it hurts. I work too much bent over, it's hard, it opens my back.

Another women in *pédisyon*, a domestic servant who feels the growing burden of supporting her children, expressed this sentiment in the following way:

> Having a child is not a good thing. It hurts, it's hard; you're sick, and the same money you spend you could spend on something else. . . I would agree to have sterilization because I already have four children.

Similarly, a twenty-six-year-old woman whose husband left her to a life of poverty and lack of support after he lost his land, sees her child as the source of her health problems. She complains:

> I can tell you he left me with the child, but he didn't leave anything for me . . . I tell you, not even five cents did he leave me, he left nothing for me. Even the baptism, I had to borrow money for it . . . I feel really sick . . . When I go to the pharmacy, I'll find out how much the medicine costs. But if it's a lot of money, how can I find even five cents? Today I came, but I only have 40 cents. I'm so tired; I haven't had anything to eat all day. . . I have this child and this child is the one who gave me the *maladi dlo-a* (water sickness). It's the child, the child who gave me all these problems . . .

Lack of financial and social support is a regular theme in the women's narratives. One of the women interviewed in Jacmel had just sold her bed because her child was sick and she had no money to take him to the hospital. She spoke of her *pédisyon* in the following words:

> I have been pregnant for a year. Sometimes I bleed for 15 days. Sometimes I bleed two times a month. I suffer a lot. . . Even though I am sick, I have to get up. I have to do my work. There is no one else to do it. I have a child to take care of. But I have no one to help me. I don't tell anyone because they will gossip. I suffer my pain alone. . . And when my husband hits me, I don't do anything. I just take the blows. I don't fight with him. I don't want to make any noise so that people will crowd around. I cry, I don't do anything else. . . If we don't have any money and I am hungry, I don't tell anyone. I don't talk to people about it.

In the Haitian folk division of medical labor, there are illnesses that are for physicians, illnesses for herbal healers and midwives, and illnesses for spiritual healers. Each type of healer is said to have her own "territory." Traditionally, *pédisyon* has not been thought of as a "doctor's illness" (*maladi dokté*). Often herbal healers and midwives are the first to diagnose and treat cases of *pédisyon*. These healers treat those cases of *pédisyon* that are caused either by a fall (*bitaj*) or blow that displaces the internal organs so that the embryo cannot assume its normal place and become properly attached, or by coldness that has entered the woman through an opening in her lower back (*senti louvi*). These folk healers use massage, compresses of medicinal leaves, such as *masketi* (*Ricinus communis*), and herbal potions to shift the baby back into place and allow it to resume normal growth and development. The process is described by Michelle, a twenty-eight-year-old mother of two children.

> I was pregnant and I fell, two times. After the second fall, I was bleeding. I went to the herbal doctor. He had me lie down on a bed and looked at my stomach. He told me I had *fraidi* (coldness) and *gaz*. I said, "that's all you see?" He said, "That's all." He didn't see the pregnancy. The herbal doctor massaged me very hard and gave me a bottle remedy for *fraidi*. He gave me four bottles. It cost $9. Then Anne Marie, my neighbor, told me about Mme Laurent. I went to see her. She examined me to find the reason. She put her ear on my stomach. She said I am pregnant but the child has become weak. She said that she would give me remedies.

Spiritist healers are able to teat these types of "natural" *pédisyon,* but they specialize in "persecution *pédisyon*," cases with a malevolent personalistic etiology such as harmful spirits (*mové zespri*), ancestral gods (*loua*) or were-wolves (*!ougarou*) These beings are believed to "tie up" the child in the womb or to suck its blood. A *manbo* explained:

> I'll tell you what causes *pédisyon*. Sometimes it is *mové zé* (bad air). Sometimes on the mother's side, there is a *lougarou*. It is a family member who died and they are sucking it, sucking the child in the stomach. So that today she has her period and for two months she doesn't have it and as soon as she gets to three months, she has it again. The *lougarou* is working on her.

Folk healers have elaborate procedures for treating *pédisyon*. One *houngan* explained his treatment for persecution *pédisyon* as follows:

> The woman arrives, I see it's a persecution *pédisyon* . . . She doesn't have to tell me. I'm the one that tells her what she has. . . She gives you 51 gourdes so you can buy medicine in the pharmacy. You get the leaves, everything you need. You light three candles . . . You have powder, powder from the pharmacy, *poud dakti,* and you prepare it with a liquid [from the pharmacy] called *vinturin dlo* . . . You make a bottle and give it to her. The bottle is not to drink. You give this bottle to rub on her body at night. And I give her another bottle to drink. In it is *miskad,* a seed. You grind it with bay rum and prepare it with roots. This will bring back the blood that was lost . . . When the child is in place, she is cured, the *pédisyon* stops. When the child is born, they come and pay you.

Another folk healer, a *manbo,* states:

> I do the cards to see what sent the problem. I call the evil spirit, I receive the evil spirit, I remove it. . . I buy a piece of meat from a bull, a goat, a pig, and a chicken. I make the spirit eat the meat. I put in cane syrup, honey, tobacco. I remove the spirit. After I remove it, I massage her stomach and then it's finished.

> One day, one night. It's finished. They are always cured. They gain weight; the
> child gains weight. The child grows. They deliver the baby.

In short, as Murray argues,

> Perdition is in effect a diagnostic redefinition. . . . By virtue of this ingenious
> definitional maneuver, the problem of sterility is made compatible with the
> historically imposed theological constraints within which the population of rural
> Haiti must function. Once an afflicted woman's condition is diagnosed as life
> which already exists but is held back, a series of ritual and folk medicinal
> treatments suddenly become relevant and there is hope for a cure [9, pp. 77-78].

But, it must now be stressed, Murray's study of *pédisyon* was carried out in a rural
village with no locally available biomedical services. Jacmel, by contrast, is a town
that in 1985 had a population of 112,000 people, according to the Haitian Ministry of
Health, and the neighborhood surveyed for this study was only a five-minute walk
from a 100-bed hospital staffed by eleven physicians who represent an array of
medical specialties, including ob-gyn. In addition, the Ministry of Health maintains a
district office in Jacmel that serves as a base for health educators and providers who
do outreach to the local community and surrounding rural areas. It is from this
hinterland that a large proportion of Jacmel's population comes, and many use the
town as a way station on their way to the burgeoning shantytowns of the capital, 60
km to the northeast. The neighborhood studied by Singer and co-workers lies on the
edge of town and serves as the entryway to the local market for the weekly flow of
buyers and sellers from nearby mountain villages. It is thus heavily populated by
impoverished rural migrants.

In this neighborhood and throughout Jacmel, folk health culture rubs shoulders
with biomedicine. As has been reported in similar situations elsewhere in the Third
World, the system most affected by this encounter is the folk culture, which is the
more permeable and absorbing of the two. As Press notes,

> folk healing systems are *open* systems, accepting substantial input from . . .
> economic, familial, ritual, moral and other institutional sectors. Modern, scien-
> tific medicine, on the other hand, is largely a closed system [18, p. 71].

Silverblatt's analysis of the process of transformation of indigenous healing beliefs in
the Andes following contact with the Spanish suggests a pattern that is relevant to the
Haitian case [19]. According to Silverblatt "European cosmology, which split the
moral universe into spheres of good and evil, was grafted onto indigenous religious
beliefs" [19, p. 420], reshaping thereby the meanings of health and healing mobilized
by folk curers. In the case of Haiti, we find peacefully co-existing with *pédisyon*,
what appears to be a newer, culturally grafted illness concept, *fribróm*. Like the folk
concept of *infección*, described for Guatemala by Cosminsky and Schrimshaw [20],
this folk illness with a medical name [21,22] borrowed from the biomedical term
"fibroma" (a tumor composed of fibrous tissue) has been reshaped to meet the
changing needs and experiences of the local population.

To the women of Jacmel, *fibróm* is a "hard ball of spoiled blood," enclosed in
tissue that forms inside the womb and attaches itself to the uterine wall. Some women
say it is like rancid meat but it "jumps like a baby." Others say it is like an animal.

Each month it causes the woman to lose blood. What produces *fibróm*? One women explains,

> A child in *pédisyon* gives a woman *fibróm*. If she doesn't have the child, it will turn into *fibróm*. It's very serious. You can die from it. If it becomes *fibróm*, the child will never come. With *fibróm* the child will never come. With *fibróm*, the child is dead.

According to another woman,

> If you have *pédisyon* and have it for one, two, three years, it will turn into a sack, a pocket, like water, and it becomes *fibróm*. The women's belly becomes big. She has to go to the doctor.

Without treatment, the child ultimately dies because the *fibróm* absorbs all the blood and as it grows larger, the child grows smaller until it is killed. Folk healers add a malevolent twist to this explanation. According to one voodoo practitioner from Jacmel:

> When a man dies, if the husband loved his wife a lot, the husband's spirit will keep bothering her every night. He can break her neck. . . . If the woman is pregnant, the spirit will turn it into a *fibróm* so she won't have the child.

Whether the ultimate cause is spiritual or not, many of the women interviewed in Jacmel expressed the idea that unless *pédisyon* is successfully treated it will, as one woman expressed it, "give" a woman *fibróm*. In other words, these women do not believe that *pédisyon* can continue indefinitely without consequence.

Significantly, however, both women and folk healers agree that *fibróm* can only be treated by a physician. Explained one women,

> A woman with *fibróm*, she had a child but its not the same any more. Something might be eating her inside, in her belly. If she doesn't go to the doctor, it turns into a *boulé* [ball]. It's made of blood. You have to go to the doctor, it's very serious. You have to get an operation. There is nothing else you can do for it.

Another women commented,

> You need an operation for it. . . They clean it to take it out. . . The leaf doctor can't do anything for it. You have to go to a hospital.

Folk healers agree. In the words of a *manbo* who claimed that her treatment for *pédisyon* was always successful, "As soon as I see it's a case of *fibróm*, I send them to the doctor. I don't treat *fibróm*. I can't." Similarly, a *houngan* states, "*fibróm* sickness is not for me because these are sicknesses for doctors in hospitals" *Fibróm* is seen as a "doctor's illness" because it requires surgical removal, a known specialty of biomedicine. Moreover, *fibróm* is progressive and will get worse and threaten the life of the women if she does not have an operation.

> The child has turned into a stone, the stone is what they call *fibróm*. If you don't go to the doctor, it can get more serious and you will have a hard time to cure it. If you go to the doctor, he can stop the sickness right away. You have to go to the doctor to have it removed, they have to take it out.

This belief is maintained, despite the high and, for most women, prohibitive cost of abdominal surgery (approximately $500 in 1985). Defined as a doctor's illness, *fibróm* returns the woman again and again to biomedical treatment, seeking from this undeniably powerful source of therapy a solution to her overpowenng problem.

A related transformation of the Haitian folk health culture that reflects the new social and medical environment is the relabeling and reconceptualizing of the main symptom of *pédisyon*. As described, the central feature of this illness is the abnormal loss of blood during what women and folk healers believe to be pregnancy, a condition that women frequently refer to as *emoraji* (hemorrhage). *Emoraji* is used specifically to refer to loss of blood during pregnancy. Explains one *manbo*:

> It's not her period. It's a little child that's forming. The child isn't well placed; it doesn't sit well. It's a persecution that causes the bleeding. If you're not pregnant, you can't have *emoraji*. If you used to have your period for three days and you have bleeding for seven or eight days, it is an attack of *emoraji*.

While recognizing *emoraji* to be a symptom of *pédisyon*, woman commonly present only the symptom and not their interpretation to physicians, thus adopting a label that is meaningful and powerful in biomedical thinking. A regular biomedical treatment in such cases, dilation and curettage, has come to be seen by some of the women of Jacmel as a means of ending *pédisyon* and thereby allowing them to conceive anew, presumably with a healthier outcome. As one woman with *emoraji* remarked about going to the doctor,

> I won't tell him I'm in *pédisyon*: I'll tell him I'm sick. I have a headache, fever, or I'll say I don't have a normal period. The doctor will consult me and tell me . . . if I should have Cesarean or *kitaj* [curettage]. A *kitaj* is an operation; they cut your side or belly to the *matris* [uterus] where the child is. They take it all out; they clean it, give you medicines, shots. After that the women can have children if they want.

However, some women feel that this medical procedure will permanently inhibit conception and see it only as a final and desperate escape from unending *pédisyon*.

TRANSFORMING FOLK CONCEPTS

We see in the *fibróm* concept and in the relabeling of bleeding as *emoraji* what appears to be a creative reconstruction of Haitian reproductive illness beliefs under changed social circumstances—a reaffirrnation of Frankenberg's reminder that playing with words is serious business [23]. Just as *pédisyon* emerged among rural Haitians as a route to social action under conditions of French cultural hegemony, *fibróm* and *emoraji* developed among urban migrants under conditions of a new, biomedical hegemony. Doctors, who are known to be powerful healers and are said to be God's representatives on earth, are no more interested in *pédisyon* than they are other folk illnesses like *mové san* [6], both of which they dismiss as ignorant superstition, as evidence of backwardness that must be confronted with education and replaced by biomedical concepts. The transformation of *pédisyon* into *fibróm* and its main symptom, loss of blood, into *emoraji*—an alchemy that transpires within the realm of folk health culture—changes an illness that can only be treated by folk healers into one that can only be treated by doctors, and in the process, biomedicine emerges as a source and influence in the folk construction of health and illness.

In this transformation, we see how illness is a world of contradictions. Illness expresses an experience over which we exercise little control, but it does so through a language and a set of meanings that we either create or borrow. Into illness we pour our experience of life, filtered as always through collective representations. In the metaphor of lost or trapped blood there is for Haitian women the link that unites the micro-phenomenological and cultural with the macro-economic.

Blood, the vital force in Haitian health ideology, provides a colorful idiom in which one's life condition finds culturally salient expression. Beliefs about blood are extensive in Haitian health culture, with irregularities in the blood system seen as the most dangerous type of illness [24]. Indeed, as Weidman suggests, based on the statements of Haitians interviewed in the Miami Health Ecology Project, a "blood paradigm" lies at the core of Haitian health beliefs, providing "the central dynamic in Haitian understandings of bodily functioning and pathological process" [25, p. 522]. Within this paradigm lies a typology of blood conditions: "blood can be *cho* ("hot") or *frét* ("cold"); *clé* ("thin"), *fébl* ("weak"), or *épé* ("thick"); *sal* ("dirty"); *noa* ("dark"); or *jó-n* ("yellow") [24, p. 186]. Weak or watery blood is said to cause palor and physical or emotional weakness and is linked by Haitians with their grinding poverty, just as obesity generally is seen as healthy and a sign of wealth while "thin people are believed to be in poor health, wasted by psychological and emotional problems" [24, p. 182]. Farmer illustrates the connection Haitians draw between thin blood and poverty with the words of several of his informants from the village of Do Kay located in Haiti's central plateau [6]. Based on his analysis of women's illness narratives, he maintains that Haitian health ideology sees bodily fluids like blood as being especially sensitive to negative emotions and difficult life experiences, allowing blood-related disorders to be read as "barometers" of social experience. In this light, trapped blood, one of the important anatomical representations of *pédisyon,* would seem to graphically express the seemingly trapped lives of *pédisyon* sufferers.

While women traditionally have sought the help of folk healers to magically free them and their baby from the entrapment of *pédisyon,* in Jacmel and elsewhere in Haiti they now turn as well to physicians, who, by their own comparatively wealthy lifestyle, evidence their powerful and perhaps magical connection to a world most Haitians see but are blocked from entering. However, beyond the financial cost, there is also a linguistic and conceptual price to be paid for entering into relationship with physicians. Women quickly learn that doctors have no interest in folk illnesses like *pédisyon,* and indeed may rebuke them for discussing them. They also learn that doctors are not very interested in the fact that they are not having children. As one physician stated, "for Haiti, which has a problem of overpopulation, we don't see that we have to spend much in studying infertility. We're more interested in investigating nutrition problems, prevention problems." What most interests women as sufferers may be of least interest to physicians as healers and as representatives of a world of wealth and power. The women apparently recognize this and they also seem to understand that

> a doctor wants to hear those words that are consistent with previously defined
> diagnostic categories. Parts of patients' stories that do not fit into these categories
> function as unwanted strangers in medical discouse and tend to be shown the
> door [26, p. 31].

Yet, it is possible to learn the language of doctors and to reconstruct reproductive illness ideas accordingly. Then, women can present problems that are potentially of interest to doctors and gain thereby access to the material and seemingly magical universe of biomedicine.

While women as patients clearly recognize they are not always fully presenting all that they experience and know (a no doubt common practice in clinical encounters everywhere), this is not a simple matter of deception. *Fibróm* and *emoraji* are not merely borrowed facades used to gain access to biomedical attention. They have become meaningful and polyvalent components of women's health culture in Jacmel and probably beyond. Too, they are not solely markers of the impact of biomedicine on that culture, evidence of the "educational" work done by physicians in the process of treatment. In addition to all of these, *fibróm* and *emoraji,* like *pédisyon* before them in an earlier period, are windows for studying the making of culture in historic and social context, which is to say, in the context of contested and unequal social relationship at a particular place and time.

MEDICINE: CULTURE, IDEOLOGY, HEGEMONY

This discussion draws attention to more general theoretical issues in medical anthropology, issues that touch on core concepts of the subdiscipline, in particular the concept of culture. As John and Jean Comaroff say, culture is "the anthropological keyword par excellence" [27, p. 27]. The centrality of the culture concept to the anthropological imagination is undisputed. Indeed, Wagner suggests

> if we should ever want to, we could define an anthropologist as someone who
> uses the word 'culture' habitually. Or else, since the process of coming to depend
> on this concept is generally something of a 'conversion experience,' we might
> want to amend this somewhat and say that an anthropologist is someone who
> uses the word 'culture' with hope—or even faith [28, p. 1].

This faith, or perhaps more aptly, this insight about the nature of the human totality, allows anthropologists to *see* the cultural construction hidden beneath natural, God-given, scientific, or medical veneers. In the terms of a well known fable, through the window of culture, anthropologists see that the emperor is indeed naked, but, in addition, we also see that the garment he supposes himself to be wearing has such an "aura of factuality" [29, p. 108] that it is possible to analyze the pattern of its contours, hues, and textures, and, although we recognize the garment is a product of the emperor's own symbolic construction, we see too that it bends him to its design no less than it adheres to the pattern of his intent, and finally, we see that beyond form the garment has meaning sufficient to allow the emperor not only to wear it but to do so with pride and gloating.

Yet, despite the tremendous understanding offered by the culture concept, it has been "criticized for overstressing the implicit and categorical, for treating signs and symbols as if they were neutral and above history, and for ignoring their empowering and authoritative dimensions" [30, p. 205]. Relative to health culture, raising and exploring the implications of this criticism have been central to the project of critical medical anthropology. For example, it is now widely (although far from universally) accepted that *medical systems are cultural systems.* Even biomedicine, long treated by anthropologists as "*the* reality through the lens of which the rest of the world's cultural versions are seen, compared, and judged," now is analyzed as culture [31, p. 4, italics in original; also 32-34]. And yet, despite a broadly shared acceptance of the cultural nature of medicine, the understanding of culture anthropologists bring to their analyses varies. Consequently, the effort of medical anthropologists to analyze medical systems as cultural systems gives rise to important questions about the understanding of culture appropriated by the subdiscipline. Clarification in this area is vital, for as Scotch remarks, "What comes out of research is not dependent on the *nature* of the problem to be studied but rather on the *way* the problem is studied" [35, p. 32] (emphasis in original). This point is underscored by the observation of Kroeber and Kluckhohn in their classic work on the anthropological conceptualization of culture that "all definitions are constructed from a point of view" [36, p. 79].

In no small measure, anthropological thinking about culture has been shaped by what has been termed the culturalist perspective. Culturalism, in its purest form, sees meaning as "the essential property of the cultural object, as symboling is the specific faculty of man" [37, p. 22]. Culture, in this understanding, is sui generis, a thing unto itself, possessing an inner rhythm that confers structure and meaning on every sphere of human life and activity, however mundane or monumental. Given its degree of autonomy, culture can be explained primarily in terms of itself, in terms of the working out of its own internal and particularist logic; it cannot be reduced to or ultimately explained by material, practical, or relational forces. The result is an immanentist understanding of culture. Immanentism has been defined by Lawner as "a theory according to which no external forces operate on the historical process, the process itself, containing the prime motor, causes, and end of its own development" [38, p. 19]. Thus, Sahlins argues that "different cultural orders have their own modes of historical action, consciousness and *determination*" and require as a result "*distinctive anthropologies*" for their decoding [39, p. 518, emphasis added].

Within medical anthropology, what might be termed "medical culturalism" takes several forms. Illustrative is Fabrega's early call for the development of an "ethnography of illness" [40, p. 566], by which he meant the collection of a body of descriptive accounts of "persons who are judged as being ill or who believe themselves to be ill, with explicit attention given to the role played by cultural influences." Culture to Fabrega is a "system of social symbols and their meanings" or more fully, the "patterns of thinking and feeling including the programs for behaving, that are shared in large part by all members of a particular society" [40, p. 566]. An alternative perspective in medical anthropology that is even closer to the heart of culturalism is the meaning-centered approach advocated by Good and Good [41].

A meaning-centered approach "recognizes all illness realities to be fundamentally semantic" and "all clinical transactions to be fundamentally hermeneutic or interpretive" [41, p. 167]. In short, illness from this perspective represents a distillation of interrelated understandings distributed within a cultural system. For example, meaning-centered medical anthropologists have been involved in developing an *ethnography of chronic pain*, a topic of relevance to Haitian women whose pain, as we have seen, is of an enduring sort. What are the key questions that guide this project? According to Kleinman et al., the goal is to understand the experience of persons afflicted by chronic pain by exploring

> the crucial categories that exert a strong but unseen effect on these people's lives: How does pain feel? What is at stake for the sick person and family? What is learned from the encounter with pain by those who undergo it and those who provide care? How is the meaning of pain created, expressed, and negotiated? How are meanings reflected or constituted in stories people tell? What is the relationship between narratives and lived experience? And how do the meanings of pain and suffering emerge from, and then reciprocally influence, particular worlds of pain? [42, pp. 14-15].

While shedding light on the ways "culture . . . intervenes directly in consciousness and its expression" [30, p. 205], as the foregoing program for the study of chronic pain suggests, meaning-centered approaches in medical anthropology

> have tended to elevate the cultural component into an omnibus explanation. The emphasis is on cultural determinism. Even when social relations receive more than reflexive recognition, medical social scientists restrict the social relations to small 'primary' group settings, such as the family, and factions at the micro unit. . . . Little or no attempt is make to encompass the totality of the larger society's structure [43, p. 22].

The set of questions identified as setting the direction for a meaning-centered ethnography of pain focus attention on the individual sufferer, his/her family, and interactions in the clinical setting. The result is a phenomenology rather than a fully realized anthropology of pain. While meaning-centered researchers recognize that significant growth of a "market" for pain-reduction products, pain-focused health care providers, and pain-centered health institutions suggests the beginnings of a "political economic transformation of pain and its treatment" [42, p. 7], the political economy of pain receives but passing attention in their research. Only by going beyond a meaning-centered approach to a direct consideration of political-economic context [e.g., 44, 45] are the limitations of cultural determinism circumvented.

Keesing identifies three fundamental shortcomings of the meaning-centered approach that are relevant for the development of a critical medical anthropology that neither obscures the importance of symbols and meanings nor overly empowers them [46]. First, he stresses, an understanding of culture as a shared set of symbols and meanings "must be qualified by a view of knowledge as distributed and controlled" [46, p. 167]. Society, even classless society, is never seamless and unified; as Wallace has argued, nonsharing is socially as significant as sharing, and access to meaning is socially regulated [47]. While Wallace stressed the availability of procedures for establishing shared meaning sufficient for carrying out a task of importance to participants (e.g., the ad hoc development of ground rules at the beginning of any social activity), from a critical perspective it must be stressed that such negotiation does not take place on a level playing ground; parties in the negotiation process have different social status and ability to enforce their interests. In the case of a subaltern Haitian woman being examined by a upper middle class or upper class physician, these inequalities are multiple (class, gender, education, Westernization) and mutually reinforcing. They are, in a word, over-determined. This does not mean that in this context the physician is all-powerful and the patient powerless, but rather that the "weapons of the weak" [48] and those of the strong are not of the same caliber. More importantly, as the Haitian data indicate, physicians define part of their mission as changing the beliefs of their patients, while patients, especially in this setting, do not appear to set changing the beliefs of the physician as an achievable objective (and hence they engage in subtler strategies of managed communication).

Second, culture is constituted not solely by "webs of significance," to use Geertz's now classic phrase, but also by "webs of mystification." Cultures, including health cultures, not only generate meaning, they also produce legitimation for inequality, justification of subordination, denials of exploitation, and disguises for oppression. Thus, writing of apartheid and biomedicine in South Africa, de Beer states.

> A sick individual is regarded as a set of physical symptoms, rather than as a person who belongs to a social class in a particular society. This process turns our attention away from the political roots of disease, and conceals these roots by providing us with an alternative explanation. By and large, says this explanation, people are responsible for their own health. If they get sick it is a chance occurrence, no-one is to blame, and it is their own fault. If people get cholera, it is because they do not use 'safe, chlorinated water.' If children are malnourished, their parents do not feed them properly, and they have more children than they can look after properly. Illness is seen as nature's revenge on people who live unhygenically and do not observe proper rules of cleanliness [49, p. 70].

While illness clearly has an important semantic component (symptoms are culturally constructed in meaningful ways) and clinical interaction has an interpretive dimension (e.g., physicians fit self reported patient symptoms into a clinically meaningful diagnosis), it is necessary to analyze these processes in terms of the role of culture in sustaining power and privilege. In the Haitian context, as elsewhere, in the clinical encounter, the emphasis is not on identifying and communicating the political economic causes of poor health, but rather, as the physician quoted earlier stated, on reinforcing patients' "feeling of self-responsibility for their health."

Finally, Keesing cautions that "cultural metaphors may be read too deeply" [46, p. 162]. Colorful metaphoric language of the kind known so well to the ethnography of health culture may be conventional expression lacking rich symbolic content. Is the angry North American who claims to be "seeing red," or whose "blood is boiling," deploying significant tropes, pregnant with cultural meaning, or merely uttering symbolically shallow figures of customary speech.

In sum, a meaning-centered approach that is not thoroughly grounded in an analysis of the structure of relationships in which meaning is generated, sustained, deployed, and changed produces dissatisfaction for several reasons, including its tendency, on the one hand, to assert that "symbolism is structurally determining" [37,

p. 211], and on the other, its failure to fully explore the consequence of what Friedman has called the "social embeddedness of meaning" [50]. With reference to the foregoing discussion of the ethnography of chronic pain, for example, questions about capitalist construction of the individual, individual consciousness, and individual responsibility would seem to be important starting points for the analysis of sufferer experience in capitalist society. Similarly, explanation of the logic of Haitian reproductive illness categories and help-seeking behavior, demands an awareness of much more than the relationship of symbol to symbol (e.g., *pédisyon* to *fibróm*): it requires, in addition, an appreciation of culture as an inventive and creative process that unfolds within particular historic, political-economic, and conflicted relational contexts.

Anthropologists concerned with what Wolf [in 50] has termed the "retreat to culturalism" have embarked on efforts to relate culture to political economy and to conflicted social relationship. Guiding this effort is recognition that culture is produced and reproduced as part of a broader social process and therefore "cannot be explained merely as the formal working out of an internal . . . logic" [51, p. 388]. As Wolf indicates,

> In the rough-and-tumble of social interaction, groups are known to exploit the ambiguities of inherited forms, to impart new evaluations or valences to them, to borrow forms more expressive of their interests, or to create wholly new forms to answer to changed circumstances. Furthermore, if we think of such interaction not as causative in its own terms but as responsive to larger economic and political economic forces, the explanation of cultural forms must take account of that larger context, of that *wider field of force* [51, p. 387, emphasis added].

This approach has special relevance to the Haitian women described in this chapter, women who live under changed circumstance as they come into increasing intimate contact with biomedicine and other institutions and relations borne within the wider field of capitalism. Exploiting ambiguities in their inherited cultural forms, they impart new valences, borrowing and creating alternatives expressive of their contemporary needs, a process similar to the one we described in an earlier analysis of African-American religious development [52]. Within the domain of health issues and concerns, this cultural process has been both directly and indirectly affected by biomedicine and can be read, in part, as an expression of the construction of biomedical hegemony.

The notion of *hegemony* has been said to hold special relevance for medical anthropology because the doctor-patient relationship is a significant point of contact between social classes/genders/ethnicities and provides therefore a critical locus for the transfer of ideas across social strata [53]. The term has its roots in Marx and Engels' recognition that beyond possessing the physical power to enforce their will, dominant groups maintain their position because their ideas are the ruling ideas in society. Introduced by Lenin with an emphasis on the role of political groups and institutions in the maintenance and overthrow of class domination, the current understanding of hegemony was developed, if not fully realized, in the writings of Antonio Gramsci.

Born in Sardinia at the end of the nineteenth century, Gramsci grew up both poor and sickly. As a linguistics student at the University of Turin, he joined the Italian Socialist Party and latter helped to form the Communist Party of Italy. Gramsci first addressed the issue of hegemony in the *Southern Question*, a work motivated by the traditional geographic division of wealth and power in Italian society. However, the fullest articulation of the concept by Gramsci occurred in the voluminous notes (3,000 pages) he recorded while incarcerated under Fascist rule from 1929 to 1935. Unfortunately, these notes, most of which have not been translated into English, are highly fragmentary due both to difficult conditions in prison and to Gramsci's own chronic health problems, including curvature of the spine, stunted growth, Pott's disease, tuberculosis, chronic urinary tract infections, hypertension, angina, and insomnia, all of which were exacerbated by poor diet and living conditions before and especially during his imprisonment [54].

Gramsci approach to hegemony differs from Lenin's in that he was deeply interested in the role non-political institutions and individuals play in establishing and reinforcing dominant ideas. In this, as Frankenberg [53, p. 328] emphasizes, Gramsci "shares with anthropology the insight of seeing the importance of culture" in the making and functioning of society. Specifically, Gramsci analyzed the role of what he termed "civil society" (which he differentiates from "political society" or the government structure) and the intellectuals who function within civil society in creating (and potentially changing) dominant ideas. Civil society, a term borrowed from Hegel but recast by Gramsci, refers to those institutions and social roles that develop and disseminate culture. In Italy, for example, it was clear to Gramsci that the Catholic Church played a fundamental role in sustaining the existing structure of society, not by force of arms but by the force and privileging of ideas.

> Gramsci's Italy was a semi-developed country with deep internal differences between north and south, industrial areas and countryside, modern and ancient. It possessed a labouring mass at widely divergent stages of development in different parts of the country, a proletariat with a broad rural base, a large, essentially conservative peasantry, a preponderance of intellectuals in the working-class leadership, and a style of politics at once bombastic and conspiratorial, conditioned by centuries of fragmentation and foreign domination. *Looming above the bewildering and contradictory set of circumstances was the mass spiritual and social power of the Catholic Church, sustained not only by transcendental premises but also by a vast army of clerics and functionaries* [55, pp. 2-3, emphasis added].

The Church and its functionaries helped to construct a world of experience for the Italian masses by defining reality and establishing, to the degree possible, acceptable standards of behavior, in short, to "create and diffuse modes of thought" throughout society [55, p. 26]. Similar "cultural work" was performed by educational systems, social clubs and professional associations, the media, the arts, sports programs, and related institutions.

Importantly, in Gramsci's understanding, civil society is based upon consensus. Whereas other scholars working in a Marxist tradition had emphasized the oppositional nature of class conflict, Gramsci recognized that oppressed groups often appear to wear their chains willingly. Indeed, they commonly embrace ideas about themselves and society that justify their own subordination to a greater or lesser degree. Because of this acquiescent behavior, the ruling class need not at every turn use brute physical force to achieve its ends. Herein enters the concept of hegemony. As used by Gramsci, although never succinctly defined by him, it refers to the process by which the dominant class exercises control through the nearly universal diffusion of its ideas by the institutions of civil society. Through the multiple and redundant expression of "ruling ideas" by these institutions, a certainty about their unquestionable truthfulness is established and maintained. As Wolf notes

> The development of an overall hegemonic pattern or 'design for living' is not so much the victory of a collective logic or aesthetic impulse as the development of redundancy—the continuous repetition in diverse instrumental domains, of the same basic propositions regarding the nature of constructed reality. . . . There is thus an economic and political side to the formation of ideas [51, pp. 388-390].

Hegemony "performs functions the military and political machinery could never carry out: it mystifies power relations, public issues, and historic events; it encourages fatalism and passivity toward political action; it justifies various types of system-serving deprivation and sacrifice" [56, p. 161]. Additionally, hegemonic control is less costly than raw coercion or even a blatantly imposed ideological dominance, because it does not automatically generate resentment and resistance. There are some maintenance costs however. While civil society has an existence independent of political society, control over civil society is maintained in two ways.

> Governments can often mobilize the support of the mass media and other ideological instruments, partly because the various elites, political and otherwise, share similar worldviews and lifestyles, and partly because the institutions of civil society, whether or not they are directly controlled by the state, must operate within a legal framework of rules and regulations [55, pp. 27-28].

Hegemony, as the Comaroffs stress, offers "a cogent way of speaking about the force of meaning and the meaning of force—the inseparability, that is, of power and culture" [27, p. 28]. Consequently, they have attempted to use hegemony in their health and cultural analyses, and in so doing, have developed the concept in particular ways. Of special note is the way they link hegemony to both culture and ideology. Culture, as they use the term, refers to the field of both symbols and practices used by humans to construct themselves and their social worlds. Culture, in short, is "a historically situated, historically unfolding ensemble of signifiers-in-action, signifiers at once material and symbolic, social and aesthetic" [27, p. 27], a perspective that is similar in many ways to the approach adopted by Roseberry that was discussed in Chapter 7. Only some components of culture are hegemonic in the Comaroffs' view. These are the symbols and practices that

> come to be taken for granted as the natural, universal, and true shape of social being—although [their] infusion into local worlds, always liable to challenge by the logic of prevailing cultural forms, is never automatic. [Hegemony] consists of things that go without saying: things that being axiomatic, are not normally the subject of explication or argument. . . . Indeed, the moment that any set of values,

meanings, and material forms comes to be explicitly negotiable, its hegemony is threatened; at that moment it becomes the subject of ideology or counterideology. . . . Here, then, is the basic difference between hegemony and ideology. Hegemony consists of constructs and conventional practices that have come to permeate a political community; ideology originates in the assertion of a particular social group. . . . Hegemony, then is that part of a dominant ideology that has been naturalized and, having contrived a natural world in its image, does not appear to be ideological at all [27, pp. 28-29].

Thus conceived, we have means of emphasizing the true importance of culture without falling into the culturalist abyss identified by Keesing, Onoge, and Wolf. This is achieved through recognition that there are both *contested* (i.e., ideological) and (at least at any point in time) *consensual* (i.e., hegemonic) aspects of culture, and while all arenas of culture contain spun webs of significance, only hegemonic ones serve well to construct effective webs of mystification. History, in short,"everywhere is actively made in a dialectic of order and disorder, consensus and contest" [27, p.18], while culture, as a result, unfolds as a dynamic unity of opposites. For example, in our analysis of religion among African-Americans, we found that

the multifarious forms of African-American religion juxtapose elements of protest and accommodation to racism and social stratification in various ways. Along with others, we see this dynamic tension as the heart and soul of African-American religion [52, p. 236].

But what then of the making of hegemony? How does ideology—the ideas of one group, the dominant group—achieve consensual acceptance by subordinate groups? The Comaroffs suggest that typically

the making of hegemony involves the assertion of control over various modes of symbolic production: over such things as educational and ritual processes, patterns of socialization, political and legal procedures, canons of style and self-representation, public communication, *health and bodily discipline,* and so on [27, p. 25, emphasis added].

Indeed, the very processes that we have seen in the interactions between doctors and women patients in Jacmel. Writing about the clinical experience for British or American patients, Frankenberg asserts that "we do not consult physicians and have their social and medical views forced upon us. We consult them because we already share their views" [53, p. 328]. But this is not quite so in Jacmel, not fully, not yet. Physicians are consulted and regularly so, if funds can be found, if arrangements can be made. Afterall, they are potent healers whose wealth and stature advertise their power, just as children named Nzoamambu advertise the abilities of their namesake among the Kongo of Zaire. But Haitian patients still hold views that physicians do not share and cannot tolerate. While the "seeds of hegemony" have been scattered on fertile ground, ground well prepared by wrenching need and desperate expectation, the seedlings of consensus (e.g., *fibróm* and *emoraji*), "must establish themselves at the expense of prior forms" [27, p. 25], a process that, while it may never be total, is, for better or worse (or both), certainly under way.

REFERENCES

1. M. Taussig, *Shamanism, Colonialism and the Wild Man,* University of Chicago Press, Chicago, 1987.
2. M. Nichter, Ethnomedicine: Diverse Trends, Common Linkages. Commentary, *Medical Anthropology, 13*, pp. 137-171, 1991.
3. P. Farmer, AIDS and Accusation: Haiti, Haitians, and the Geography of Blame, in *Culture and AIDS,* D. Feldman (ed.), Praeger, New York, pp. 67-91, 1990.
4. M. Laguerre, *Voodoo and Politics in Haiti,* St. Martin's Press, New York, 1989.
5. J. Jahn, *Muntu: An Outline of Neo-African Culture,* Faber and Faber, London, 1958.
6. P. Farmer, Bad Blood, Spoiled Milk: Bodily Fluids as Moral Barometers in Rural Haiti, *American Ethnologist, 15*:1, pp. 63-83, 1988.
7. E. Early, The Logic of Well Being: Therapeutic Narratives in Cairo, Egypt, *Social Science and Medicine, 16*, pp. 1491-1497, 1982.
8. R. Keesing, Kwaio Women Speak: The Micropolitics of Autobiography in a Solomon Island Society, *American Anthropologist, 87*, pp. 27-39, 1985.
9. G. Murray, Women in Perdition: Fertility Control in Haiti, in *Natality and Family Planning,* J. Marshall and S. Polgar (eds.)., Carolina Population Center, Chapel Hill, North Carolina, pp. 59-78, 1976.
10. D. Jelliffee and E. Jelliffee, The Nutritional State of Haitian Children, *Acta Tropica, 18*, pp. 1-45, 1961.
11. A. Pitchenik, Tuberculosis, Atypical Mycobacteria, and AIDS among Haitian and Non-Haitian Patients in South Florida, *Annals of Internal Medicine, 101*, pp. 641-645, 1984.
12. J. Janzen, *The Quest for Therapy,* University of California Press, Berkeley, 1978.
13. M. Alvarez and G. Murray, *Socialization for Scarcity: Child Feeding Beliefs and Practices in a Haitian Village,* USAID, Port-au-Prince, Haiti, 1981.
14. S. Mintz, a Note on the Definition of Peasants, *Journal of Peasant Studies, 1*, pp. 91-106, 1973.
15. R. Prince, *Haiti: Family Business,* Latin American Bureau, London, 1985.
16. UNICEF, *The State of the World's Children,* New York, 1987.
17. B. Good, The Heart of What's the Matter, *Culture, Medicine and Psychiatry, 1*, pp. 25-58, 1977.
18. I. Press, Urban Folk Medicine, *American Anthropologist, 80*, pp. 71-84, 1978.
19. I. Silverblatt, The Evolution of Witchcraft and the Meaning of Healing in Colonial Andean Society, *Culture, Medicine and Psychiatry, 7*, pp. 413-427, 1983.
20. S. Cosminsky and M. Scrimshaw, Medical Pluralism on a Guatemalan Plantation, *Social Science and Medicine, 14B*, pp. 267-278, 1980.
21. D. Blumhagen, Hyper-tension: a Folk Illness with a Medical Name, *Culture, Medicine and Psychiatry, 4*, pp. 197-227, 1980.
22. M. Singer, C. Arnold, M. Fitzgerald, L. Madden, and C. Voight von Legat, Hypoglycemia: A Controversial Illness in U.S. Society, *Medical Anthropology, 8*:1, pp. 1-35, 1984.
23. R. Frankenberg, Sickness as Cultural Performance: Drama, Trajectory, and Pilgrimage. Root Metaphors and the Making Social of Disease, *International Journal of Health Services, 16*, pp. 603-626, 1986.
24. M. Laguerre, Haitian Americans, in *Ethnicity and Medical Care,* A. Harwood (ed.), Harvard University Press, Cambridge, Massachusetts, pp. 170-210, 1981.
25. H. Weidman, *Miami Health Ecology Project Report: A Statement on Ethnicity and Health,* Vol. l, University of Miami, Florida, 1975.
26. Waitzkin, *The Politics of Medical Encounters,* Yale University Press, New Haven, 1991.

27. J. Comaroff and J. Comaroff, *Ethnography and the Historical Imagination,* Westview Press, Boulder, 1992.
28. R. Wagner, *The Invention of Culture,* The University of Chicago Press, Chicago, 1981.
29. C. Geertz, *The Interpretation of Cultures,* Basic Books, New York, 1973.
30. J. Comaroff and J. Comaroff, *Of Revelation and Revolution: Christianity, Colonialism, and Consciousness in South Africa,* University of Chicago Press, Chicago, 1991.
31. A. Gaines and R. Hahn, Among Physicians: Encounter, Exchange and Transformation, in *Physicians of Western Medicine,* R. Hahn and A. Gaines (eds.), Reidel, Dordrecht, pp. 3-22, 1985.
32. E. Mishler, L. Amarasingham, S. Hauser, R. Liem, S. Osherson, and N. Waxler, *Social Contexts of Health, Illness, and Patient Care,* Cambridge University Press, Cambridge, 1981.
33. L. Rhodes, Studying Biomedicine as a Cultural System, in *Medical Anthropology: Contemporary Theory and Method,* T. Johnson and C. Sargent (eds.), Praeger, New York, pp. 159-173, 1990.
34. M. Lock and D. Gordon, *Biomedicine Examined,* Kluwer Academic Publishers, Dordrecht, 1988.
35. N. Scotch, Medical Anthropology, in *Biennial Review of Anthropology,* B. Siegel (ed.), Stanford University Press, Stanford, pp. 30-68, 1963.
36. A. Kroeber and C. Kluckhohn, *Culture: A Critical Review of Concepts and Definitions,* Vintage, New York, 1952.
37. M. Sahlins, *Culture and Practical Reason,* University of Chicago, Chicago, 1976.
38. L. Lawner (transl.), *Letters from Prison by Antonio Gramsci,* Jonathan Cape, London, 1975.
39. M. Sahlins, Other Times, Other Customs: The Anthropology of History, *American Anthropologist. 85*:3, pp. 517-544, 1983.
40. H. Fabrega, The Ethnography of Illness, *Social Science and Medicine, 13A,* pp. 565-575, 1979.
41. B. Good and M-J. Good, The Meaning of Symptoms: A Cultural Hermeneutic Model for Clinical Practice, in *The Relevance of Social Science for Medicine,* L. Eisenberg and A. Kleinman (eds.), Reidel, Dordrecht, pp. 165-196, 1981.
42. A. Kleinman, P. Browdwin, B. Good, and M-J. Good, Pain as Human Experience: An Introduction, in *Pain as Human Experience: An Anthropological Perspective,* M-J. Good, P. Brodwin, B. Good, and A. Kleinman (eds.), University of California Press, Berkeley, pp. 1-28, 1992.
43. O. Onage, Capitalism and Public Health: A Neglected Theme in the Medical Anthropology of Africa, in *Topias and Utopias in Health,* S. Ingman and A. Thomas (eds.), Mouton, The Hague, pp. 219-232, 1975.
44. M-J. Good and B. Good, Ritual, the State, and the Transformation of Emotional Discourse in Iranian Society, *Culture, Medicine, and Psychiatry, 12,* pp. 43-64, 1988.
45. A. Kleinman, *The Social Origins of Distress and Disease: Depression, Neurathenia, and Pain in Modern China,* Yale University Press, New Haven, 1986.
46. R. Keesing, Anthropology as Interpretive Quest, *Current Anthropology, 28*:2, pp. 161-176, 1987.
47. A. Wallace, *Culture and Personality,* Random House, New York, 1970.
48. J. Scott, *Weapons of the Weak,* Yale University Press, New Haven, Connecticut, 1985.
49. C. de Beer, *The South African Disease: Apartheid Health and Health Services,* African World Press, Trenton, New Jersey, 1986.
50. J. Friedman, an Interview with Eric Wolf, *Current Anthropology, 28,* pp. 107-118, 1987.

51. E. Wolf, *Europe and the People Without History*, The University of California Press, Berkeley, 1982.
52. H. Baer and M. Singer, *African American Religion in the Twentieth Century; Varieties of Protest and Accommodation*, University of Tennessee Press, Knoxville, 1992.
53. R. Frankenberg, Grarnsci, Culture, and Medical Anthropology: Kundry and Parsifal? or Rat's Tail to Sea Serpent?, *Medical Anthropological Quarterly*, 2:4, pp. 324-337, 1988.
54. K. Breda, *Politics, Culture and Gramscian Hegemony in the Italian Health Service: A Comparison of USL's*, doctoral dissertation, Department of Anthropology, University of Connecticut, 1992.
55. J. Femia, Review Article: Gramsci's Patrimony, *British Journal of Political Science, 13*, pp. 327-364, 1981.
56. C. Boggs, *The Two Revolutions: Gramsci and the Dilemmas of Western Marxism*, South End Press, Boston, 1984.

CHAPTER 10

Prophets and Advisors in African-American Spiritual Churches: Therapy, Palliative, or Opiate?

In Chapter 6, we saw that complex societies exhibit dominative medical systems that reflect social relations along class, racial/ethnic, and gender lines. Although bourgeois medicine as well as professionalized heterodox medical systems often function in bureaucratic settings, religious healing practices and ethnomedicine generally occurs within more informal settings. Anthropologists in the United States have given considerable attention to not only the traditional healing practices of Native Americans but also ethnomedical systems such as *curanderismo* among Mexican Americans [1-3], *espiritismo* among Puerto Ricans [4-7], *santeria* among Cuban Americans [8], and *vodun* among Haitian Americans [9, 10]. Although folklorists have gathered extensive, however often unsystematic, data on African-American folk medicine and magic, particularly in rural areas, there continues to be a paucity of studies of Black ethnomedicine in urban areas, despite the fact that the majority of Blacks have been located in them for some time [11, 12]. However, a small but growing literature now exists on this topic [13-18]. The work of Snow [19-21], which includes an extensive ethnography of ethnomedicine in a Black neighborhood in Tucson, Arizona, and an interview with a "Voodoo practitioner," has been particularly significant in addressing this problem.

The purpose of this chapter is to explore a variant of African-American ethnomedicine in urban areas, namely the complex which centers upon prophets and advisors in certain highly syncretic sects known as "Spiritual" churches. Particular attention is given to patterns of prophesying in public settings and advising in private settings which Spiritual groups provide both for their adherents and other individuals. The classification and etiology of illness, diagnostic and treatment procedures, and the nature of the practitioner-client relationship will be described. We argue that the complex of folk healers found within the Spiritual movement provides a significant coping mechanism for certain Blacks who are subjected to the social inequities and racism inherent in American society. Structurally speaking, the social function of the prophet or Spiritual advisor is to a large degree comparable to that of the professional psychiatrist, psychologist, or psychiatric social worker. This chapter also examines the double-edged nature of the complex of folk healers by arguing that while, on the one hand, it provides its adherents and clients with a sense of emotional relief, on the other hand, it prevents them from recognizing that many of their personal troubles or "problems of living" derive from the existing social structure of the larger society.

METHODOLOGY

Many of the data presented in this chapter were a product of Baer's observations of Black Spiritual churches in various large and medium-sized cities [22-24]. Between October 1977 and July 1979, he conducted fieldwork among all of the eleven Spiritual churches in Nashville, Tennessee. Baer also visited Spiritual churches in many other cities, including Detroit, New York, North Little Rock, Baltimore, Chicago, Kansas City, New Orleans, Indianapolis, Memphis, Pittsburgh, and Flint. Pseudonyms are used for the names of the religious figures and churches involved in this study.

As Baer became acquainted with Spiritual churches, he realized that Spiritual advisors were serving two categories of people: 1) those who were more or less active members of the local congregations themselves and 2) those who sought the services of specific religious functionaries for a variety of personal problems. While people in the first category also utilize the services provided by prophets in order to deal with personal problems, their rationale for membership in the spiritual congregation involves other dimensions (e.g., sociability, a sense of social achievement, and perhaps a certain sense of respectability). Since this chapter focuses on the ethno-medical aspects of the Black Spiritual religion, it merges these two clienteles in speaking of the advisor-client relationship. It should be noted, however, that on occasion clients who feel that they have been assisted by the advisor or prophet may choose to become members of his or her church.

A number of social scientists have remarked upon the difficulties which they have encountered in attempting to interview Black folk healers [13, p. 97; 14, p. 138; 16]. Although Baer generally was treated in a cordial manner during his visits to Spiritual churches, he also experienced a reluctance on the part of some pastors (who are generally healers) as well as other therapists to speak with him in detail concerning their practices and beliefs. In the case of his work in Nashville, this problem was greatly overcome by the fact that he became a familiar sight in the Spiritual network of the community. Nevertheless, despite some persistence on his part, some advisors repeatedly evaded his attempts to interview them in detail about the manner in which they provided private consultations for their clients.

While the effect of Baer's racial status as a Caucasian was not entirely apparent during his fieldwork in the Black community, he did not feel that overall it was a major handicap. In fact, in some ways it may have been an advantage in that he was probably not regarded as a potential competitor for the clients of the prophets whom he interviewed. Although some advisors would occasionally refuse to divulge information about their practice at certain times because they would be giving away "secrets," he found that on other occasions they might reveal formerly withheld information. Baer suspected that the greatest handicap in his ability to gather data was his refusal to join any of the churches. The pastor of the Temple of Spiritual Truth, for example, repeatedly urged him to affiliate. Needless to say, he was flattered and tempted by the offer, but felt that to do so would be unethical considering his agnosticism. At any rate, the fact that he was identified as a "member" of the congregation to the pastor of a Spiritual church in Indianapolis indicates that he was regarded as sort of an honorary member. Nevertheless, the pastor of another church strongly advised him to join a Spiritual church if he decided to continue fieldwork elsewhere after leaving Nashville.

Baer was able to conduct extensive interviews with eight Spiritual advisors on their counseling activities during the spring and early summer of 1979. While he utilized an interview schedule which touched upon the social background of the healers, client characteristics, the classification and etiology of illness, methods of diagnosis and treatment, and compensation for services, questions regarding these matters were not presented in the same order or manner for each advisor. To have insisted on a standardized interviewing procedure would have stifled the nature of many responses and thereby precluded access to data that he had not thought to inquire about. Of course, the completeness of responses on various items varied greatly from informant to informant.

SPIRITUAL CHURCHES AS A RELIGIOUS CATEGORY

An examination of the Spiritual movement requires placing it within the larger context of Black religion in the United States. As a result of the work that we have done on certain relatively unknown religious movements in the Black community, we came to believe that there was a need for a typology which systematically recognized the diversity of Black religious groups and simultaneously places them into a context that they all share [25, 26]. In constructing such a classificatory scheme, we chose to view African-American sectarianism as a religious response to a stratified and racist society, largely because it appears to be the most overriding factor which is shared by all Black religious groups in the United States. On the basis of two variables—strategies of social action and attitudinal orientation—four types of Black sects were delineated: 1) established sects or mainstream denominations within the context of the African-American community, 2) messianic-nationalist sects, 3) conversionist sects, and 4) thaumaturgical sects.

The established sects or the mainstream denominations within the context of the Black community, particularly those with large, middle-class Baptist and Methodist congregations, have adopted a reformist strategy which attempts to create improvements for Blacks by working within the system and essentially accepts the "American Dream." Perhaps because of their greater sense of powerlessness, lower-class Blacks have been particularly creative in developing strategies which ultimately attempt to instill dignity and meaning in their lives. The messianic-nationalist sects, such as the Black Muslin, Black Hebrew and Black Christian groups, have tended to construct counter-cultures, which tend to reject many of the values and goals of the larger society while at the same time developing utopian communities. Perhaps the majority of lower-class Blacks with a religious orientation have turned to various conversionist sects, such as the multitude of small Baptist, Holiness, and Pentecostal groups, which often tend to seek their salvation in some ill-defined afterlife.

Of the four types in our scheme, the thaumaturgical sect has been the most neglected by scholars, despite their prevalence in the Black community. The largest representative of this type by far are those groups which refer to themselves as "Spiritual" churches. Thaumaturgical sects maintain that the most direct way to achieve socially desired ends, such as financial prosperity, prestige, love, and health, is by engaging in various magico-religious rituals or by acquiring esoteric knowledge which provides an individual with spiritual power over oneself and over others. Such groups generally accept the cultural patterns, values, and beliefs of the larger society, but attempt to change the means for obtaining the "good life." In comparison to other Black sects, one finds a pronounced tendency toward syncretism—the process of combining elements from a number of religious traditions into a new tradition [26].

Since the syncretic nature of spiritual churches has been discussed in detail elsewhere [22, 27], remarks on this dimension will be brief. The Spiritual movement in the Black community essentially combines elements from American Spiritualism, Roman Catholicism, African-American Protestantism (particularly of the Baptist and Pentecostalist varieties), and Voodooism (or at least its diluted version generally known as "hoodoo" in the United States). Furthermore, specific congregations or associations in the Spiritual movement may add elements from other esoteric systems, such as New Thought, Islam, or Judaism, to this common assemblage of religious elements. The historical development of the Spiritual movement remains obscure, but it appears that it emerged in various large cities, particularly Chicago, New Orleans, Detroit, Cleveland, and Kansas City during the 1910s and 1920s [28].

Because of its somewhat close but vague relationship to the Spiritual religion, it is important to mention another thaumaturgical religion, namely *vodun* or Voodoo. *Vodun* emerged among African slaves on the island of Haiti as a syncretism of West African religions and Roman Catholicism [29]. Its most important supernatural figures are the *loa,* many of whom are supernatural beings that were venerated in Africa. The *loa* tend to be identified in some way with various Catholic saints—either as one and the same, as separate but mutually cooperative spirits, or an antagonistic beings [30, p. 65]. Voodoo priests or *houngans,* not only conduct ceremonies in honor of the gods and the dead, but also engage in healing, divination, and evidently, at least on occasion, sorcery. Voodoo appears to have entered the United States in the vicinity of New Orleans around 1809 when French masters escaping the Haitian revolution brought Black slaves with them [31, pp. 135-136]. During the nineteenth century, Voodoo meetings presided over by "queens" and "witch doctors" catered to slaves, free Blacks, and some white women. According to Hurston, Spiritualism which initially took on aspects of Catholicism in New Orleans was often combined with "hoodoo" and provided the hoodoo doctor with a protective screen [32, pp. 318-320]. Apparently, various aspects of Black Protestantism were added to the mixture as the Spiritual movement developed in New Orleans and in other urban areas.

SPIRITUAL ADVISORS AND PROPHETS: EXAMPLES OF FOLK HEALERS

A wide variety of "emic" terms (those used by members of a particular socio-cultural group) are used to refer to the types of healers that are found in the Black community. While various scholars have attempted to create typologies which recognize these therapists, the general shortcomings of these endeavors include the exclusion of certain categories, a tendency to lump categories, and/or restricting the classification to healers in a specific community or neighborhood [14, 16, 17]. Others who have worked on various aspects of Black ethnomedicine may not even make clear-cut distinctions among its variants [15, 20, 21].

In attempting to address these problems, Baer [33] devised a systematic typology of Black folk healers which is illustrated in Figure 1. The typology is constructed on the basis of two axes, namely the institutional affiliation of the healer and the extensiveness of his or her practice. The first axis recognizes that healers may or may not affiliate their healing practice within a religious group or congregation. If a healer operates on an individual basis or is affiliated with some sort of occult supply store, either as the owner, an employee, or someone who rents office space therein, he or she is referred to as an "independent healer." If the healer is affiliated with a religious group, he or she is referred to as a "cultic healer." The second axis recognizes the extensiveness of a healer's practice, that is, whether it tends to be broad or generalized in scope, dealing with a wide variety of illnesses and conditions, or whether it

| | | Scope of Healer's Practice | |
		Generalist	Specialist
Form of Affiliation	Independent	Conjurer, root worker, Spiritualist	Herbalist, granny mid-wife
	Cultic	Spiritual advisor, Voodoo priestess	Faith healer, divine healer

Figure 1. Prophets and Advisors

tends to be limited, focusing on specific disorders or problems. By intersecting these two axes, as can be seen from Figure 1, one obtains a four-cell typology which recognizes the following categories of healers: 1) independent generalists, 2) independent specialists. 3) cultic generalists, and 4) cultic specialists. A wide variety of emic terms are used to refer to the kinds of healers found among African Americans.

Probably the most renowned character in Black ethnomedicine is a type of independent generalist known as the "conjurer," who goes under a wide variety of labels, including "conjure doctor," "hoodoo doctor," "rootworker," "blood doctor," and "hungan." The hoodoo doctor has a detailed knowledge of the use of roots and herbs, and possesses the ability to interpret signs in nature as good or bad omens. He or she claims to solve personal problems, heals incurable ailments, and provides a variety of magico-religious paraphernalia for clients which will provide them with spiritual power. Kuna stresses the importance of making a distinction between "hoodoo" and "Voodoo," noting that the former, "although a system of belief and therapy, is not a cult, nor does it engage in cult or group activities or worship" [34]. Voodoo or *vodun*, by contrast, is supported by a full-blown ceremonial complex and is found in Haiti although it still occurs sporadically or even regularly in various parts of the United States.

Another type of independent generalist, the Spiritualist, may also be referred to as a "reader" or a "prophet." The Spiritualist is an individual who has received a "call" from God to help people with their personal problems [15, 17]. The Spiritualist may be affiliated with an occult supply store (often referred to as a "candle store") or operate on a strictly individual basis. The Spiritualist tends to have little knowledge of the use of roots and herbs, and may advertise in various newspapers, magazines, and radio stations serving the Black community.

Probably the best known independent specialists are herbalists or rootworkers in the strict sense of the word. Herbalists are specialists in the application of various medicinal plants and other remedies for common ailments. Female neighborhood practitioners, who are closely related to herbalists, often are referred to as the "Old Lady," "granny," or "Mrs. Markus." She does not have office hours or dispense medicine per se but merely advises clients on how to treat ordinary ailments. Yet another independent specialist, the magic vendor, often works in conjunction with the Spiritualist, or in some cases both roles may be combined. Magic vendors own or are employees of "candle stores," and while they often are not healers per se, they offer advice as what are the appropriate articles for overcoming various problems or ailments [14].

Unlike independent healers, those affiliated with specific religious groups may engage in healing activities in both public and private settings. The Voodoo priest or priestess perhaps constitutes the cultic generalist *par excellence*. Although southern Louisiana was a renowned center of Voodoo during the nineteenth century, the recent migration of Haitians has shifted the centers of this religion to New York and southern Florida [35]. The best example of the cultic specialist is the evangelistic faith healer who tends to be the pastor or a prominent member of a fundamentalist congregation, generally of the Holiness or Pentecostal variety. He or she resorts to techniques such as praying, laying-on-of-hands, anointing with holy oil, and giving the client blessed handkerchiefs or aprons.

Our discussion of cultic healers brings us to the prophets and advisors who function largely within the context of the Black Spiritual movement. Although the complex of prophets and advisors in the Spiritual movement may be viewed as a variant of Black ethnomedicine, many of the concepts and techniques utilized by its practitioners have much in common with other healing traditions in the Black community. Nevertheless, these prophets and advisors attempt to generally disassociate themselves from many of these other traditions, particularly hoodoo and Voodoo.

Members of Spiritual churches generally recognize two categories of healers: 1) the "Spiritual advisor" or "prophet" and 2) the "divine healer." In addition to teaching, speaking-in-tongues and interpretation of tongues, prophecy and healing are considered to be among the gifts of the Spirit. Some members of Spiritual churches claim to have the gift of healing, but note that they lack the gift of prophecy. On the other hand, Spiritual advisors generally claim to possess both the ability to prophesy and heal. Whereas the divine healer is comparable to the faith healer in many fundamentalist Protestant churches and tends to focus on various physical ailments, the Spiritual advisor or prophet tends to focus upon a wide variety of socioeconomic and psychosocial problems which individuals may encounter in everyday life. The medium is believed to have the ability to "read" people and tell them things about their "past, present, and future." While mediums generally claim that their messages come from the Spirit (which may more specifically refer to God or the Holy Spirit), some admit that on occasion they may receive messages from a saint or a deceased loved one or acquaintance of the recipient.

Most Spiritual pastors appear to have been affiliated with other Spiritual congregations at one time or another. An ambitious individual, who possesses the gifts of prophecy and healing and wishes to assume the role of pastor, may decide that the best way to achieve this is to establish his or her own church. Although most Spiritual congregations are small, often serving thirty or fewer regular members, some may have memberships of several hundred. Pastors of such congregations often establish associations or daughter churches.

A medium also may visit other Spiritual churches in his or her own vicinity, or in other cities. Although the visit of a traveling prophet may be received with great anticipation, Spiritual people often complain about charlatans who take advantage of their short stay by charging exorbitant fees for blessings that they fail to deliver.

PROPHECY SESSIONS IN SPIRITUAL CHURCHES

Although Spiritual churches exhibit a variety of practices, such as testifying, shouting, and anointing with holy oil, that they share with many Black Protestant groups, their great emphasis on public prophecy is one of the characteristics that distinguishes them from the latter. Prophesying generally takes place within the context of a special service, which may be designated a "bless service" or a "prophecy service." It also may occur in some Spiritual churches toward the end of a regular Sunday morning or afternoon service. Prophecy sessions are particularly common on occasions when prophets from other cities visit a Spiritual congregation.

Prophecy sessions may be regularly scheduled on a particular night of the week. In other Spiritual churches, the "bless service" may be scheduled only when the Spirit directs the pastor or prophet to do so. In most cases the "bless service" is essentially similar to the regular Sunday morning service, except the prophecy session will be substituted for the sermon. During the session, the prophet relates various aspects of the "present, past, and future" of selected individuals in the congregation. As few as three or four individuals or as many as ten or more may be chosen by the prophet to be recipients of messages. In most small Spiritual churches, the prophet will generally deliver his or her messages from the pulpit or the front portion of the sanctuary. If the sanctuary of a particular church is relatively large, the prophet may move up and down aisles, selecting various recipients for messages.

Prophets sometimes approach and give certain individuals private messages or tell them that they will receive a private message after the service. In most cases, the recipient of a public message is not expected to make financial donation to a prophet for this particular service. Conversely, on certain occasions, particularly when a traveling prophet is in town, there may be such an expectation.

Recipients of prophecies often are expected to make certain comments to indicate that they understand what they are being told. Bishop G. Jones, the assistant pastor of the Temple of Spiritual Truth in Nashville and the now-deceased wife of the pastor, instructed recipients to say, "Thank you, kind Spirit," in response to various portions of messages. A prophet may ask an individual certain questions about his or her background or circumstances in order to better understand the message which is being received from the Spirit. Prophets occasionally rebuke people for being too passive in the course of receiving a message. The recipient is expected, at least in theory, to correct the prophet if he or she is misinterpreting the message. Although prophets are considered to be instruments of the Spirit, they are not infallible and must rely on the assistance of recipients when the message is symbolic in nature.

PRIVATE CONSULTATIONS IN THE
SPIRITUAL MOVEMENT

This section summarizes the data that Baer gathered in interviews with eight Spiritual advisors, who had some sort of affiliation with the Spiritual movement. Unfortunately, he was unable to observe these Spiritual advisors in situations in which they interacted with their clients in a private setting. Just as the practitioner-client relationship is considered to be sacrosanct in biopsychiatry, the same is true in the Spiritual movement. Since Baer's data were based upon the responses of informants rather than upon direct observation of their behavior in private consultations, they must be viewed somewhat tentatively.

Social Background of Spiritual Advisors

All of the Spiritual advisors whom Baer interviewed concerning their techniques of counseling were individuals of humble social origins. For some of them, their activities in the Spiritual movement had been, to a greater or lesser extent, a source of upward social mobility. For others it provided at least a modest supplement to the income that they derive from secular jobs. Spiritual advisors generally became aware that they possessed the gifts of prophecy and/or healing during childhood or during early adulthood. Many resisted using their gifts, but found that the Spirit insisted that they did so as they became older. Rev. Arnold realized when she was eight years old that she had the gift of prophecy, but was afraid that people would regard her to be a "fortuneteller." Many years later, the Lord "put" her into a coma during which time he told her that her mission was to prophesy and heal. Because she refused to abide by the Spirit's wishes, He had to "put her down" a second time before she began her ministry.

Client Characteristics

Although it appears that the majority of clients who frequent Spiritual advisors are poor Blacks, advisors claimed that they were visited by some individuals of relatively affluent backgrounds. Rev. Arnold, whose congregation consists primarily of lower-class individuals but also includes a fair number of working class and some professional people, boasted that most of her clients are "doctors, lawyers, and people with master's degrees." Many Spiritual pastors are sensitive about the low status of their congregations and often need to inflate the numbers of more affluent members in them. It also appears that a large percentage, perhaps the majority, of people who frequent Spiritual advisors are not members of Spiritual churches. While whites are seldom seen in Black Spiritual churches, except for a few in some of the larger congregations, some whites do seek the assistance of Spiritual advisors. However, one of the healers in Baer's sample claimed that about five of her fifty or so regular clients are white.

Most clients who frequent Spiritual advisors are between twenty and sixty years of age. Some Spiritual advisors said that older people tend not to visit them as frequently because of the difficulties involved in leaving home. Occasionally a Spiritual advisor may be visited by a teenager or a child, often upon the prompting of a parent. It also appears that female clients in most cases outnumber male clients by two to one or more. The number of clients that a Spiritual advisor may see during the course of a typical week is highly variable. Since many Spiritual advisors are regularly employed, they may see an average of only four or five clients during the course of a week. Bishop Gilmore said that during the summer months when she does not work, she may see fifteen to twenty clients a week. While Elder Marcus only saw a few clients a week, at the height of her career during the 1950s she counseled as many as thirty clients a week. Furthermore, Rev. Arnold had an appointment secretary and saw between fifty and 100 clients during the course of a typical week. On Saturdays of the weeks she visited Nashville, ten or more individuals sat in the waiting room in order to see her for a private consultation.

Classification and Etiology of Illness

Spiritual advisors tend to have generalized theories of illness and do not appear to be as interested in the cause of a problem or "disturbance" as much as identifying and alleviating or eliminating it. Nevertheless, a rough system of illness classification and etiology among Spiritual advisors may be delineated. While Spiritual advisors do not generally make a sharp dichotomy between psychological and organic disorders, there is a tendency to refer to the former as "conditions" and the latter as "ailments." Furthermore, most Spiritual advisors noted that some people seek their assistance after medical doctors were unable to effectively diagnose and/or treat their problems.

Spiritual advisors also make a distinction between natural illness and unnatural illness. A natural illness results from factors such as exposure to bad weather, excessive eating or failure to eat proper foods, drinking, running around too much, particularly late at night, and general misuse of one's body. A person may become ill because s/he has transgressed God's will. Illness, however, can be caused by the Devil, an evil spirit, or by a malicious person who performs hoodoo or wishes one ill. God also may permit the Devil to make someone ill in order to test their "faithfulness" to Him. An important distinction between a natural and unnatural illness is that a physician can detect the former, whereas only a Spiritual advisor or "a person of God" can identify the latter.

The Spiritual advisors in Baer's sample stated that most individuals who seek their services have "conditions" rather than "ailments." The two main categories of problems for which people consult a Spiritual advisor are financial and domestic difficulties. Financial problems include unemployment or underemployment, a low-paying job, or lack of money to purchase food, pay the rent, a fine or bills, etc. Domestic problems, which may be intimately related to financial problems, include various conflicts within one's family, (e.g., a husband who drinks excessively or gambles away his paycheck, a son who repeatedly runs into trouble with the law or who is on drugs, a daughter who is disobedient or disrespectful). Other reasons why individuals may visit Spiritual advisors include inability to find a place to live after being evicted from an apartment, alcoholism, trouble at work with one's boss or employer, conflict with a friend or a lover, and a general feeling of hopelessness. Elder Marcus of St. Mark's Spiritual Temple described her clients as "poor people with low income, who got a fine, got sick, lost a job, or got to eat . . . or six and a half dozen other things."

Spiritual advisors estimated that as many as 25 percent or more of their clients believe they have been "hoodooed," "hexed," "crossed," or "fixed." Spiritual advisors tend to regard most clients who believe that they have been hoodooed as suffering from "nervousness" or a general feeling of anxiety.

Diagnosis and Treatment

Spiritual advisors may see their clients in a variety of settings, including the advisor's home or church office and in some cases the client's home. Bishop G. Jones often conducted consultations in her bedroom where she had a small altar. In contrast, Rev. Arnold saw her clients in her spacious church office which conspicuously displayed her success as a pastor and an advisor. While some advisors prefer that their clients see them personally, others are willing to counsel them over the telephone.

According to Baer's subjects, they generally spend from twenty-five minutes to forty-five minutes or sometimes longer with each client when seeing them in private. Conversely, Bishop Rogers claimed that he usually only spends about ten to fifteen minutes with a client, and that sometimes five minutes was sufficient for this purpose. Although some clients may be personal acquaintances of a Spiritual advisor, many of them are not. Some clients visit a particular Spiritual advisor only once, and others may establish a regular visitation pattern with the latter.

Spiritual advisors stated that they prefer that clients not discuss the nature and source of their problems in the initial stages of private consultations. Instead, the advisor generally proceeds to "read" or divine the reason why the client is seeking help. When attempting to diagnose the client's problem, the Spiritual advisor may say a prayer and begin to meditate or "concentrate." Sometimes the Spirit communicates with the advisor almost instantaneously and at other times a few minutes may pass before the advisor receives a message. Bishop F. Jones said that sometimes he turns out the lights in the room and lights a candle when he is attempting to make contact with the Spirit. Spiritual advisors claim that the messages may come to them in a vision, or from a voice, or in one's mind. Furthermore, advisors often note that it is necessary to cultivate one's gift of prophecy by praying and fasting. Advisors often ask various questions of their clients during divination and expect them not to merely agree with everything they say. In addition, the client may be given an opportunity to ask questions of the Spirit.

Some Spiritual advisors use a variety of articles to assist them in determining a client's problem. Beside her bed, Bishop G. Jones had an altar with a votive candle, an incense burner, a white vase for "donations" and an open-faced Bible with six crosses and an oval-shaped jewel. She looked at the crosses or the jewel in order to receive certain "vibrations" which provided her with insights into her client's condition or ailment.

After the Spiritual advisor has diagnosed the client's problem, he or she receives instructions from the Spirit as to what course of action the client should pursue in obtaining a blessing or overcoming a condition or ailment. Such instructions tend to fall into one or more of the following categories: 1) advice from the Spirit, 2) saying prayers or reciting scriptural passages, 3) the ritual use of magico-religious articles, 4) taking a ritual bath, and 5) the use of roots, herbs, teas, or other medicinal substances. If the client has a financial problem, he may be given advice on how to acquire additional funds. Bishop F. Jones noted that in some cases, individuals have sufficient financial resources to maintain themselves or their families, but are given a "program" by the Spirit on how best to spend their money. If the client is seeking a job, he or she may be told where to look or whom to contact. In some cases, the client may be advised not to be too selective at first, but to accept a less desirable position until a better one comes along. The Spirit may note that it is essential that the client exudes an aura of confidence and competence in seeking a job.

In the case of marital problems, the client may be told to be willing to compromise with his or her spouse. Bishop F. Jones noted that in such cases, he prefers to see the couple together. It often is noted that marital conflict is not merely the fault of one person. A husband who leaves his family may leave against his desires but does so perhaps because, his wife nags him about his inadequacies or inability to be a good provider. Clients also often are advised to control feelings of jealousy and envy in their relations with family members or others. A woman who is looking for a husband may be told that she needs to be cautious in doing so and must now allow her romantic impulses to outweigh the pragmatic dimensions of marriage. Mrs. Collins noted that many women who ask her to help them to find a husband are extremely anxious and even desperate in their search. She strongly urges them to wait if necessary, to fast and pray, to take a ritual bath, and "tell God everything."

Although Spiritual advisors admit to the efficacy of witchcraft or sorcery, as noted earlier, they tend to regard clients who believe that they have been "hoodooed" as suffering from "nervousness." Advisors may first try to talk to such persons in order to try to calm them down. In many such cases, Elder Davis said that she is not particularly interested in trying to change the client's self-diagnosis of his or her problem. Instead, she attempts to reassure the client that if indeed he or she has been "hexed," the Spirit easily can remove that condition. She may instruct the client to engage in some type of ritual in order to "get his mind turned in a different direction."

In addition to being instructed to fast and pray, clients often are told to read various scriptural passages, particularly ones in the Book of Psalms. Although the 23rd Psalm is the most popular and is used in a wide array of problems, certain other psalms may be recommended for specific problems. For a $2 "donation," one may receive a cloth book marker with Rev. Arnold's picture and a long list of scriptural passages for a wide variety of problems. Rev. Arnold recommends Psalm 27 for "when you fail," Psalm 91 for "when you are in danger," Psalm 121 for "when leaving home for labor or travel," and Psalm 90 for "when the world seems bigger than God."

Most Spiritual advisors give blessed candles, at least occasionally, to clients in order to assist them. A red candle is generally associated with love or power, a blue candle with hope, a green candle with love or financial success, and a white candle with purity and truth. Although many people view the burning of a black candle as a malevolent act, some Spiritual advisors noted that it may be used for various benign reasons as well, such as breaking a streak of bad luck. Some Spiritual advisors report that burning candles or praying before the statue of a saint are techniques by which a client may focus upon the accomplishment of a particular goal.

Other religious articles that Spiritual advisors may give clients for a small donation include blessed handkerchiefs and aprons, blessed oil (generally olive oil), and blessed water. Blessed handkerchiefs and aprons, which are also commonly used in Holiness and Pentecostal sects, are used for a variety of ailments and are applied by the client to areas where he feels pain. The client also may be told to anoint himself periodically with blessed oil, which is believed not only to have curative powers but also preventive ones. Blessed water, which also has curative and preventive aspects, may be used to bless oneself with the sign of the cross, may be applied to areas of bodily pain, or may be consumed orally.

Some Spiritual advisors also recommend that their clients take a "spirit bath" or "blessed bath." One common pattern involves saying a prayer while one pours Epsom salt or table salt into the bathtub as it fills with water. Blessed water or oil also may be placed into the bath water. The individual then sits in the tub and says various prayers, makes the sign of the cross several times, and anoints himself or herself with olive oil. After bathing, the individual burns one or more candles and recites several more prayers. Although spirit baths may be taken for a variety of reasons, a common purpose for them is the elimination of the influence of evil spirits in one's life. For example, Bishop G. Jones noted that she once administered a series of seven spirit baths for a woman in Kentucky who had been hexed.

While Spiritual advisors appear to make less use of roots, herbs, and other medicinal substances than do rootworkers and Voodoo doctors, some do so on occasion, particularly for physical ailments. Bishop Gilmore, an elderly man reared in Georgia, complained that roots and herbs are not as readily available today as they were in the past. Oak, red ash, and snake root were among his favorite remedies in the earlier years of his practice. Bishop G. Jones said that she did not use roots but did prescribe herbal teas. Dandelion tea or bark tea, for example, may be used to counteract an ailment caused by the consumption of "bad food." She added that food may be poisoned by malicious individuals who put snake powder in it.

Compensation for Services

Perhaps one of the most sensitive topics for Spiritual advisors is the issue of compensation for their services. Most Spiritual advisors vehemently deny they "charge" for their services, but admit that they will accept a "donation" for a "free-will offering." It is often maintained that since the ability to prophesy is a gift from God, it is not proper to charge people for its use. Clients, however, are often aware that a "donation" of a certain amount is expected by a Spiritual advisor when seeking his or her services. Several individuals mentioned that the standard donation for seeking the help from Rev. Arnold in 1979 was $10. While she admitted that this was the usual amount she received for her services, she stated that often she received less or even no money, though on occasion a donation of $50 or $60 was received. Although the more popular Spiritual advisors may receive donations of $10 or more for a session, most apparently receive only a few dollars or in some cases only an expression of gratitude from a client. For the majority of Spiritual advisors, their counseling activities are at best a supplement to other sources of income or financial support.

A common stereotype in the African-American community is that many mediums are charlatans and "phonies." Spiritual people are able to recall seemingly countless numbers of incidents in which a medium swindled a congregation or an individual out of large sums of money. One subject spoke of a prophet who sold rocks which he claimed were from the Holy Land and another prophet who sold an imprint of a "blessed hand" for $50. She also spoke of a Spiritual prophet from Cincinnati who placed a snake underneath one woman's doorstep and told her that someone had hoodooed her, but that he could kill the snake that was sent after her for $500. One Spiritual pastor noted that a lot of "quacks have gotten into the Spiritual work in the last twenty years" and added that they hurt Spiritual people. A woman observed an incident in which a Spiritual prophetess erected a "fortune tree" in her churches. She told the congregation that she had placed 150 "fortunes" on the tree and that for a $7 donation the Spirit would direct people to the fortune that was intended for them. According to Baer's subject, at the appointed time for people to select their fortunes there was a frantic rush to the tree.

According to one renowned scholar of the Black religious experience, "[f]undamentally, then, a Spiritualist cult is a house of religious prostitution where religion is only the means for the end of commercialization" [31, p. 115]. Although this indictment may apply to some Spiritual advisors and prophets, one must be more cautious in characterizing the Black Spiritual movement. Despite the fact that certain questionable practices occur in Spiritual churches, the majority of pastors, prophets, and advisors who Baer interviewed lived in modest surroundings, had a salaried occupation or a legitimate source of income, and seemed to be sincere in their beliefs. Any financial benefits that they may have reaped from their position were not generally commensurate with the time and energy that they invested in it.

DISCUSSION

The acquisition of the "good life," or even more modest improvements of one's condition, are central concerns of both the adherents of Spiritual churches, as well as those who occasionally visit prophecy sessions conducted in them or the Spiritual advisors who are affiliated with them. Glick proposes that the notion of power—"not diffuse unattached power, but power existing as a manifest attribute of persons and of objects in their environment"—is the aspect of the total domain of religion that is crucial to the lesser domain comprising concepts about illness [36, p. 60]. The Black Spiritual movement emphasizes the acquisition of "mysteries" or "secrets"—a set of magico-religious techniques and beliefs that provide an individual with power over his destiny. Since mediums are repositories of knowledge concerning mysteries and secrets, they become important vehicles through which others may acquire power— either the power to overcome a condition or ailment or the power to obtain a blessing. As noted earlier, mediums are believed to have the gift of prophecy—an extraordinary ability to look into the hearts of people and penetrate their deepest concerns and desires. In addition, mediums often have perfected their gift by studying at schools of psychology, mediumship, or the esoteric sciences which are found in the Black community. It is not uncommon for people to fear mediums since it is believed that they are in close contact with the spirit world and are able to discern one's innermost thoughts. The medium may use his or her power to diagnose and treat his clients and/or provide them with various magico-religious techniques or paraphernalia by which they themselves may obtain power.

As is the case in many preliterate societies and in certain ethno-religious systems in American society, such as *espiritismo* and *santeria,* the medium in the Black Spiritual church operates both in a group setting and in a private setting. While his or her style cannot be as intimate and personal in the prophecy session as it can be in the private consultation, the medium sees his or her role to be essentially the same in both. Although coded in religious terms, the ultimate aim of the prophet is psychotherapeutic, that is to alleviate any frustration, anxiety, and pain which the recipient of the message may feel as well as to instill a sense of dignity, confidence, and hope in that person. In many cases, the recipient of a message is a member of the prophet's congregation or at least an acquaintance of the prophet. Consequently the prophet may be intimately familiar with his or her circumstances. On the other hand, when the prophet is not acquainted with the recipient of the message, he or she may be able to determine much about them by observing the individual's age, sex, dress, facial expressions, posture, and temperament. Since mediums see a wide variety of individuals, they have learned to quickly size up a person without specific knowledge of his or her life history or present circumstances.

The recipient of a message also receives the implicit and, in some cases, the explicit support of others in the congregation. If the recipient cries or becomes ecstatic, members of the congregation may offer verbal approval or encouragement. Furthermore, the recipient receives a form of recognition and preferential treatment which in all likelihood he or she does not obtain in the larger society. Apparently it is for these reasons that prophecy sessions often attract a relatively large number of people. There is always the hope that one will be the recipient of a message and a blessing from the Spirit.

In contrast to the professional psychotherapist, the Spiritual advisor is a "poor person's psychiatrist" whose services tend to be congruent with the economic means and the world view of his clients. Whereas the former may charge a hundred dollars for a consultation, the latter tends to provide his or her clients advice for a nominal donation or fee of several dollars. Furthermore, while the professional therapist is likely to be a member of a higher social class and a different ethnic group, the Spiritual advisor tends to have the same humble origins as his or her clients and consequently shares a common etiology of disorder with them. According to Torrey, the act of naming an illness has a therapeutic effect on an individual because he or she lives in the same world as his or her patient [37, p. 16]. He or she has encountered the same experiences of deprivation and prejudice—the stigma of being Black in a racist society, the frustration and humiliation associated with poverty, the concern for seeing one's children being victimized by the conditions of the ghetto. Furthermore, the Spiritual advisor meets his or her clients in familiar surroundings, rather than in an impersonal office complex filled with white middle-class faces. Even when the Spiritual advisor, such as in the case of Rev. Arnold, imitates the trappings of this forbidding environment, the effect on the client is probably not the same. Instead, the client is visiting a charismatic and successful healer "who has arrived," despite the barriers that the system creates for the poor and minority groups in their attempts to obtain economic security.

Spiritual advisors are generally empathetic, warm, and compassionate individuals who are well acquainted with and communicate a genuine concern about the problems of their clients. Although Spiritual advisors view some illnesses as predominantly physiological and others predominantly psychosocial in nature, their approach to healing tends to focus much more on the latter category of problems than the former. Even in instances where an ailment is recognized, one finds a tendency on the part of the Spiritual advisor to resort to psychotherapeutic techniques, such as laying-on-of-hands, anointing with holy oil, or giving the client a blessed handkerchief or apron, rather than using physical treatments, such as the prescription of roots and herbs.

In addition to the actual treatment that the Spiritual advisor conducts for the client, he or she also may prescribe that the client perform certain magico-religious acts which are intended to augment the private consultation. The following remarks by Whitten are particularly relevant to our discussion of this component of the therapy prescribed by mediums in the Black Spiritual movement:

> The proclivity of the American Negro to cope by magical means due to his social, political and economic position in the greater American social structure may well be another crucial factor. Malinowski, among others, has presented evidence for the hypothesis that the greater the uncertainty regarding the means to an end, the greater the tendency to cope by magical means. Due to his suppressed social position a Negro can find little satisfaction by coping directly with his frustrations and dissatisfactions. Misfortunes that befall him may have no real solution, though magical practices or the relegation of problems to magical causes may offer at least partial satisfaction by relieving some anxiety and tensions [38, p. 322].

CONCLUSIONS

In assessing the role of the complex of mediums found in the Black Spiritual movement, we are led to ask the question whether or not this complex is a form of therapy, merely a palliative, or an opiate. This question becomes particularly significant when one takes into consideration the continuing interest in a "therapeutic alliance" between representatives of biomedicine and those of traditional healing systems, both in industrial societies and in Third World nations [39, 40]. Such an alliance is viewed by many social scientists, clinicians, health planners and health policy makers as an important strategy for dealing with a shortage of professional health providers as well as reducing communication barriers due to sociocultural differences that exist between the former and their clients—many of whom constitute the subproletariats of their respective societies. While it is not our specific intention in this chapter to elaborate on the critique of the therapeutic alliance that has been made by others, we wish to add a cautionary note in considering the incorporation of traditional healers, such as those discussed in this chapter, into the institutions of biomedicine.

Various anthropologists have come to regard many aspects of African-American culture to be adaptive mechanisms which have enabled the majority of Blacks to survive against seemingly insurmountable odds in a hostile environment [41, 42]. Mithun cites the extended family, an existential philosophy exhibited in music, dance, religion, folklore, and verbal styles, and cooperative networks as examples of strategies that Blacks have devised in dealing with the uncertainties of their condition [43]. The complex of prophets and advisors affiliated with the Spiritual movement may be included among the various strategies that Blacks have developed in attempting to cope with the social realities of a stratified and racist society. Like many other African-American cults, such as *vodun* in Haiti and in the United States, *shango* in Trinidad, and *batuque* in Brazil, the Spiritual religion with its complex of prophets and advisors provides people with a theology for existence and survival [35, 44, 45].

Although Spiritual people deny any connection between their religion and Voodoo or hoodoo, it, like the later, is a "practical and utilitarian religion which cares more for earthly than heavenly goings-on" in that it emphasizes the acquisition of health, love, economic prosperity, and interpersonal power [29, p. 25].

It often has been noted that healing rituals tend to be public in non-Western societies whereas they tend to be more private in Western societies. Illness in non-Western or traditional societies often is viewed as a reflection of stress or conflict in social relations. Therapy goes beyond restoring the sick person to personal well-being but also involves reintegrating him or her into the social group. In his classic study of a Ndembu doctor, Turner argues that the healer's "main endeavor was to see that individuals were capable of playing their social roles successfully in a traditional structure of social position" [46, p. 262]. In the case of the complex of mediums within the Black Spiritual movement, we also find that healing occurs both in public and private settings. Individuals who attend prophecy sessions are often not members of the congregation where these events occur. Also, the prophets who give messages on such occasions may not be even affiliated with the groups where the prophecy sessions occur, but rather are merely charismatic individuals who are passing through town and provide the opportunity of obtaining a "blessing." Furthermore, many individuals who seek the assistance of a Spiritual advisor in a private consultation are not affiliated with the latter's congregation. Just as a middle-class person may wish to conceal that he is seeing a psychiatrist, the client who visits a Spiritual advisor may be just as secretive about his actions. Consequently, it is not clear to us exactly to what extent the medium serves to reincorporate the recipient of a message or the client into a social network.

In the case of the prophecy session, the prophet may emphasize the need of the recipient of a message to reconcile his differences with significant others. As noted earlier, the content of messages from the Spirit often makes mention of reunion with persons whom the recipient has not seen in some time. It is possible that such a prediction will prompt the recipient to take initiative in actualizing such an event, resulting in a self-fulfilling prophecy. In a somewhat similar vein, the advisor in the private consultation may stress the need for the client to compromise with significant others in situations of strained social relations, thereby reintegrating the latter into his social matrix. On occasion, individuals who seek assistance from Spiritual advisors actually join the congregation to which the latter belongs. Bishop F. Jones, for example, stated that a fair number of the people in his congregation joined the group after he had successfully treated them. A very similar pattern occurs in various religious groups, such as the Yoruba possession cults and the Ethiopian zar cults, whereby patients become members after they have been cured by one of its healers [47]. In situations such as these, the client or patient does not necessarily become reintegrated into his earlier social network but acquires instead a new one.

It is also possible that the techniques utilized by prophets and advisors affiliated with Spiritual churches enable clients, at least to some extent, to overcome a state of "demoralization." According to Frank, all persons seeking psychotherapy are demoralized in some way—that is they have lost confidence in their abilities to cope with the pressures of everyday problems in whatever sociocultural milieu that they might function and consequently are "prey to anxiety and depression . . . as well as to resentment, anger, and other dysphoric emotions" [48, pp. 314-315]. Psychotherapy can restore morale by enabling the patient to change his or her perceptions and behavior which in turn enable him or her to overcome obstacles that at one time seemed insurmountable. A common theme in the Spiritual movement is the notion that one has to think positively and overcome negative modes of thought. It is often noted in some Spiritual groups that "heaven" and "hell" are not places that people go to after this life, but states of the human mind. This emphasis on positive thinking is not only evident in public prophecy sessions and private consultations, but also is present in sermons and testimonies. Prophets and advisors constantly remind their clients that they must believe in themselves, and that if they do not, no one else will.

Based upon observations among Spiritual churches in New Orleans, Jacobs argues,

> The rituals of the Spiritual religion incorporate all of the contributing belief systems (Catholicism, Pentecostalism, Spiritualism, Voodoo/hoodoo), so that the churches constitute a multi-dimensional religious space in which ministers handle people's problems in a variety of ways. This is seen in regularly scheduled services of worship, and emerges from descriptions of what ministers do when they see clients private. . . .
> The Spiritual churches' ritual, including healing and prophecy, are effective for two reasons. First, worshippers have the opportunity to act out the sacred, thereby linking the temporal to the eternal, and second, they participate in religious celebrations that reflect a feature of black culture . . . [49, pp. 364-365].

While Jacobs' phenomenological analysis partially captures the essence of the complex of prophets and advisors in the Spiritual movement, it overlooks its hegemonic components that unwittingly prompt its clients to acquiesce to the status quo in a racist and socially stratified society and over the long run may prevent them from improving their mental health.

For the most part, however, it appears that the nature of therapy provided by prophets and advisors focuses on individualistic concerns. The factors that have contributed to a transition from the sociocentric focus found in traditional societies to a largely egocentric one needs to be further investigated, but we suspect that it is related to the increasing privatization or what Wilson terms "individuation" that characterizes much of modern life, particularly in urban areas. Consequently, the approach used by prophets and advisors has a maladaptive dimension for Blacks in that it tends to deny "political conflict by stressing the importance of individual over society, the insignificance of social arrangements and plans, and the irrelevance of group conflict beside the paramount importance of the individual" [50, p. 356]. In this regard, their approach is similar to that of the conventional psychotherapist who may urge the client to muster the psychic resources necessary to adjust to the demands of society. There is often a tendency for mediums in the Spiritual movement to engage in what amounts to "blaming the victim" in that they often overlook the social and economic roots of many of their clients' problems. Instead, it is common for mediums to promise their clients improvement in their lives if they engage in various magico-religious rituals, develop a positive attitude and overcome negative thoughts. In this regard, the medium often unwittingly contributes to the "cult of private life" which is championed by various agencies of socialization, such as the family, the schools, the media, advertisers, and psychiatrists, and which serves to legitimize the existing social system [51, p. 61]. According to this perspective,

> The source, if not the cause of mental disorders, is invariably traced to the client himself and/or his friends and relations. Society-at-large does not, and cannot, figure significantly in these treatments, although the collective ill-effects of living day-to-day in advanced industrial society have been repeatedly demonstrated. Thus psychology, counseling, and allied techniques further privatize the individual, leading her or him to search for exclusively existential solutions, more sophisticated avoidance mechanisms, and tried and true adjustment techniques. Marcuse's remark about "shrinks" being so-called because they shrink minds to manageable proportions is appropriate as social problems are telescoped into personal ones [51, pp. 61-62].

It must be noted, however, that at least some professional therapists are cognizant of problems that may arise if social variables are not taken into account when evaluating the potential of the patient to cope with his situation. In his discussion of the role of psychotherapy in assisting the demoralized person, Frank cautions that it may be limited in its effectiveness by various political economic factors, such as "poverty, unemployment, and other forms of social oppression" [48, p. 316]. Elsewhere, in their discussion of the potential deleterious effects of psychotherapy, Strupp, Hadley, and Gomes-Schwartz warn that "problems may arise when the therapist entertains assumptions of omniscience" [52, p. 70]. It is argued that a therapist may inadvertently mislead a patient into taking on unrealistic expectations and goals for himself. Given the structural constraints faced by many lower-class Blacks, the message that "therapy can solve everything," be it communicated by a professional psychotherapist or the Spiritual advisor, may serve to frustrate those undergoing treatment even more once they come to the realization that this cannot be the case.

It is for this very reason that we tend to become skeptical of approaches, such as the therapeutic alliance, or improving client/healer communication, that often are viewed as solutions for dealing with the contradictions inherent in the health care systems of both advanced industrial and Third World nations. While we do not wish to dismiss certain potential benefits of the therapeutic alliance, it is all too easy for many to view such arrangements as adequate responses to the multifarious problems experienced by the underclasses of the world. The complex of prophets and advisors existing within the Spiritual movement tends to be compensatory and accommodative rather than corrective. Rather than encouraging lower-class as well as some more affluent Blacks to seek social change or challenge the existing political economy, it serves to control their alienation from society by promising financial success or the restoration of personal conflict in return for carrying out certain magico-religious rituals. While the Spiritual religion and its complex of mediums appears to provide an important coping mechanism for a segment of the Black community, at best it tends to be ameliorative. The problems that its adherents and clients experience in most cases will not be eliminated until there has been a drastic transformation in the social structure of American society. In conclusion, however, let us be reminded of Marx's recognition that religion (and its associated dimensions such as those found in ethnomedicine) is more than an escape, but "at the same time the *expression* of real distress and the *protest* against real distress" [53, p. 42; emphases his].

REFERENCES

1. A. J. Rubel, *Across the Tracks: Mexican-Americans in a Texas City,* University of Texas, Austin, 1966.
2. W. Madsen, *The Mexican-Americans of South Texas,* Holt, Rinehart and Winston, New York, 1964.
3. A. Kiev, *Curanderismo: Mexican-American Folk Psychiatry,* Free Press, New York, 1968.
4. A. Harwood, *RX: Spiritist as Needed,* John Wiley & Sons, New York, 1977.
5. V. Garrison, Doctor, Espirista, or Psychiatrist?: Health-seeking Behavior in a Puerto Rican Neighborhood of New York City, *Medical Anthropology, 1,* pp. 61-191, 1977.
6. M. Singer with M. Borrero, Indigenous Treatment for Alcoholism: The Case for Puerto Rican Spiritism, *Medical Anthropology, 8,* pp. 446-272, 1984.
7. M. Singer, "Becoming a Puerto Rican Espirista: Life History of a Female Healer, in *Women as Healers,* C. Shepherd McClain (ed.), Rutgers University Press, New Brunswick, pp. 157-185, 1989.
8. M. C. Sanoval, Santeria as a Mental Health Care System: An Historical Overview, *Social Science and Medicine, 13B,* pp. 137-151, 1979.
9. M. Laquerre, Haitian Americans, in *Ethnicity and Medical Care,* A. Harwood (ed.), Harvard University Press, Cambridge, Massachusetts, pp. 172-210, 1981.
10. M. Laquerre, *American Odessey: Haitians in New York,* Cornell University Press, 1984.
11. N. N. Puckett, *Folk Beliefs of the Southern Negro,* University of North Carolina, Chapel Hill, 1926.
12. H. M. Hyatt, *Hoodoo, Conjuration, Witchcraft,* 4 volumes, Western Publishing, Hannibal, Missouri, 1970-1974.
13. H. Stewart, Kindling the Hope of the Disadvantaged: A Study of the Afro-American Healer, *Mental Hygiene, 55,* pp. 96-100, 1971.
14. A. L. Hall and P. G. Bourne, Indigenous Therapists in a Southern Black Urban Community, *Archives General Psychiatry, 28,* pp. 137-142, 1973.
15. C. S. Scott, Health and Healing Practices among Five Ethnic Groups in Miami, Florida, *Public Health Reports, 89,* pp. 524-531, 1974.
16. H. Weidman et al., *Miami Health Ecology Project, Volume 1,* Miami University Press, Miami, 1978.
17. W. C. Jordan, 1975, Voodoo Medicine, in *Textbook of Black-related Diseases,* R. A. Williams (ed.), McGraw-Hill, New York, 1975.
18. A. Raboteau, The Afro-American Traditions, in *Caring and Curing: Health and Medicine in the Western Religious Tradition,* R. L. Numbers and D. W. Amundson (eds.), Macmillan, New York, 1986.
19. L. F. Snow, "I was Born Just Exactly with the Gift": An Interview with a Voodoo Practitioner, *Journal of American Folklore, 86,* pp. 272-281, 1973.
20. L. F. Snow, Popular Medicine in a Black Neighborhood, in *Ethnic Medicine in the Southwest,* E. F. Spicer (ed.), University of Arizona Press, Tucson, 1977.

21. L. F. Snow, Sorcerers, Saints and Charlatans: Black Folk Healers in Urban America, *Culture, Medicine and Psychiatry, 2*, pp. 69-106, 1978.
22. H. A. Baer, *The Black Spiritual Movement: A Religious Response to Racism,* University of Tennessee Press, Knoxville, 1984.
23. H. A. Baer, Black Spiritual Israelites in a Small Southern City: Elements of Protest and Accommodation in Belief and Oratory, *Southern Quarterly, 23*:3, pp. 103-124, 1985.
24. H. A. Baer, The Metropolitan Spiritual Churches of Christ: The Largest of the Black Spiritual Associations, *Review of Religious Research, 30,* pp. 140-150, 1988.
25. H. A. Baer and M. Singer, Toward a Typology of Black Sectarianism as a Response to Racial Stratification, *Anthropological Quarterly, 54,* pp. 1-14, 1981.
26. H. A. Baer and M. Singer, *African-American Religion in the Twentieth Century: Varieties of Protest and Accommodation,* University of Tennessee Press, Knoxville, 1992.
27. C. F. Jacobs and A. J. Kaslow, *Spiritual Churches of New Orleans: Origins, Beliefs, and Rituals of an African-American Religion,* University of Tennessee Press, Knoxville, 1991.
28. R. Tallant, *Voodoo in New Orleans,* Macmillan, New York, 1946.
29. A. Metraux, *Voodoo in Haiti,* Schocken, New York, 1972.
30. G. S. Simpson, *Black Religions in the New World,* Columbia University Press, New York, 1978.
31. J. Washington, Jr., *Black Sects and Cults,* Anchor/Doubleday, Garden City, New Jersey, 1973.
32. Z. N. Hurston, Hoodoo in America, *Journal of American Folklore, 44,* 1931.
33. H. A. Baer, Toward a Systematic Typology of Black Folk Healers, *Phylon, 43,* pp. 327-342, 1982.
34. R. R. Kuna, Hoodoo: The Indigenous Medicine and Psychiatry of the Black American, *Ethnomedizin, 3*:3/4, pp. 273-295, 1974-1975.
35. K. McCarthy Brown, *Mama Lola: A Vodu Priestess in Brooklyn,* University of California Press, Berkeley, 1991.
36. L. B. Glick, Medicine as an Ethnographic Category: The Gimi and the New Guinea Highlands, in *Culture, Disease, and Healing,* D. Landy (ed.), Macmillan, New York, 1977.
37. E. F. Torrey, *The Mind Game: Witchdoctors and Psychiatrists,* Bantam, New York, 1972.
38. N. E. Whitten, Jr., Contemporary Patterns of Malign Occultism among Negroes in North Carolina, *Journal of American Folklore, 75,* pp. 311-325, 1978.
39. P. Singer (ed.), *Traditional Healing: New Science or New Colonialism?,* Conch, New York, 1977.
40. P. K. New, Traditional and Modern Health Care: An Appraisal of Complementarity, *International Social Science Journal, 24,* pp. 483-495, 1977.
41. C. A. Valentine, *Black Studies and Anthropology: Scholarly and Political Interests in Afro-American Culture. A McCaleb Module in Anthropology,* Addison-Wesley, Reading, Massachusetts, 1972.
42. C. B. Stack, *All Our Kin: Strategies for Survival in a Black Community,* Harper & Row, New York, 1974.
43. J. S. Mithun, Survival as a Way of Life: Some Adaptive Mechanisms Contributing Toward the Perpetuation of Afro-American Culture, in *Ethnicity in the Americas,* F. Henry (ed.), Mouton, The Hague, 1976.
44. S. Leacock and R. Leacock, *The Spirits of the Deep,* Anchor/Doubleday, Garden City, New York, 1975.
45. J. M. Murphy, *Santeria: An African Religion in America,* Beacon Press, Boston, 1988.
46. V. W. Turner, An Ndembu Doctor in Practice, in *Magic, Faith, and Healing,* Ari Kiev (ed.), Free Press, New York, 1964.

47. S. D. Messing, Group Therapy and Social Status in the Zar Cult of Ethiopia, in *Culture and Mental Health: Cross-Cultural Comparisons,* M. K. Opler (ed.), Macmillan, New York, 1959.
48. J. Frank, *Persuasion and Healing: A Comparative Study of Psychotherapy,* Johns Hopkins University Press, Baltimore, 1973.
49. C. Jacobs, Healing and Prophecy in the Black Spiritual Churches: A Need for Re-examination, *Medical Anthropology, 12,* pp. 349-370, 1990.
50. J. Wilson, *Religion in American Society: The Effective Presence,* Prentice-Hall, Englewood Cliffs, New Jersey, 1978.
51. H. C. Greisman and S. S. Mayers, The Social Construction of Unreality: The Real American Dilemma, *Dialectical Anthropology, 2,* pp. 57-67, 1977.
52. H. H. Strupp, S. W. Hadley, and B. Gomes-Schwartz, *Psychotherapy for Better or Worse,* Jason Aronson, New York, 1977.
53. K. Marx and F. Engels, *On Religion,* Schocken Books, New York, 1967.

Section E:

The Individual Level

CHAPTER 11

Confronting Juan García's Drinking Problem: The Demedicalization of Alcoholism

In this chapter, we examine the health and social issue of problem drinking among Puerto Rican men. Over the years, medical anthropologists have exhibited a growing interest in substance use and abuse, with attention being especially concentrated since the early 1970s. Disciplinary involvement in substance research has produced both the Alcohol and Drug Study Group of the Society for Medical Anthropology and the American Anthropological Association Task Force on Alcohol and Drugs, as well as an increasingly rapid expansion of the anthropological substance literature. The AIDS pandemic and the recognized role of drug use in viral transmission, susceptability to involvement in risk behavior, and immune system dysfunction have intensified anthropological work in the study of substance use, including drinking [1]. Since the beginning of the AIDS crisis in 1981 numerous anthropologists have found work studying substance use behavior as a risk factor in the United States and elsewhere. The resulting reports, papers, and publications have potential of shaping the orientation of medical anthropology into the next century. Already, they have contributed to a newfound respectability for anthropology and its research methods [2].

The sheer volume of anthropological work on substance use now being undertaken suggests the importance of reconsidering the theoretical perspectives that anthropologists bring with them to research. In the arena of drinking behavior, it is clear that anthropologists embrace a range of viewpoints. They achieve a disciplinary unity, a distinctly anthropological frame, however, "by focusing attention on social and cultural variables that otherwise tend to be overlooked or are presumed to be more nearly uniform than is the case" [3, p. 357]. This insight is a notable advance.

However, it is not sufficient. From the viewpoint of critical medical anthropology, we have argued that

> the anthropological examination of drinking has failed to systematically consider the world-transforming effects of a global market and global labor processes associated with the evolution of the capitalist mode of production. Anthropological concentration on the intricacies of individual cases, while a necessary and useful method for appreciating the rich detail of cultural variation and insider understandings, has somewhat blinded researchers to the uniform processes underlying global social change, including changes in drinking patterns. While the literature notes some of the effects of incorporation into the capitalist world-system, rarely does it attempt to comprehend alcoholism in terms of the specific dynamics of this system. Rather, the central thrust has been to locate problem drinking within the context of normative drinking and normative drinking within the context of prevailing local cultural patterns [4, p. 115].

Anthropological contribution to the U.S. Latino drinking literature has grown steadily [5-19]. To date, however, most studies have been concerned with Mexican Americans. Drinking among Puerto Rican men has been a relatively neglected topic, although it has been suggested that this population is particularly at risk for alcohol-related problems [20].

The goal of this chapter is to deepen our understanding of problem drinking among Puerto Rican men by examining this phenomenon from the holistic perspective of critical medical anthropology. Analysis of problem drinking from a critical perspective can be traced to Frederick Engels' nineteenth-century study of the living conditions of the working class of Manchester, England. In Engels' clearly articulated view:

> All possible temptations, all allurements combine to bring workers to drunkeness. Liquor is almost their only source of pleasure, and all things conspire to make it accessible to them. . . . [It provides] the certainty of forgetting for an hour or two the wretchedness and burden of life, and a hundred other circumstances so mighty that the worker can, in truth, hardly be blamed for yielding to such overwhelming pressure. Drunkeness has here ceased to be a vice . . . They who have degraded the working-man to a mere object have the responsibility to bear [21, pp. 133-134].

Our approach to problem drinking among Puerto Rican men, as well as studies of mood-altering substance use by other critical medical anthropologists [e.g., Stebbins 22, 23], is deeply influenced by Engels' insights and point of view [4]. By integrating Engels approach with understandings gained from conventional medical anthropology studies of drinking behavior, a perspective emerges that leads naturally to the examination of such issues as: 1) the political economy of alcohol production, distribution and advertising; 2) the social utility of defining alcoholism as an intrapsychic or micro-social problem; 3) the ideological nature and social control functions of messages communicated to alcohol patients in treatment; 4) the political and economic character of the burgeoning alcoholism treatment industry; 5) the economic motivation for narrowly directing national attention to the health and social costs of illicit drug use and away from the much more costly use of legal drugs like alcohol and tobacco; and 6) the social causes of the limited effectiveness of prevention and treatment programs.

As noted in Chapter 1, beyond research, critical medical anthropology is committed inherently to the development of appropriate practical expression. Thus, the data for this essay were drawn from work that Singer, Freddie Valentin, Roberto Garcia and others have carried out for many years through the Hispanic Health Council, a community action agency dedicated to creating short- and long-term health improvements in the Latino community of Hartford, Connecticut and beyond [e.g., 24, 25]. As noted in further detail in Chapter 15, this work has included the development of applied substance abuse prevention and treatment programs that seek to avoid blaming the victim while raising client consciousness about the social causes of abuse and the importance of social action in overcoming community problems.

We begin our analyses with an examination of the development of the reigning paradigm on problem drinking: the medical/pathology model. We next present the case of Juan Garciá (pseudonym), a Puerto Rican man who in 1971 died with a bottle in his hand and booze in his belly. Following a location of this case in its historic and political-economic contexts, we discuss findings from two community studies[1] of drinking behavior and drinking-related health and social consequences among Puerto Rican men and adolescents to demonstrate the representativeness of the case material. In this chapter, it is argued that the holistic model of critical medical anthropology advances our understanding beyond narrow psychologistic or other approaches commonly employed in social scientific alcohol research. Moreover, it extends medical anthropological insight by situating local examples of drinking behavior in a broader political economic context.

THE MEDICALIZATION OF PROBLEM DRINKING

While now accepted as an established "fact," the conceptualization of problem drinking as a medical issue involved a protracted process that began in 1785 with Benjamin Rush but was only completed relatively recently. As the National Council on Alcoholism stated in an educational pamphlet a number of years ago: "The main task of those working to combat alcoholism . . . is to remove the stigma from this disease and make it as 'respectable' as other major diseases such as cancer and tuberculosis" [quoted in 26, p. 449]. A significant step in this process was a 1944 statement of the American Hospital Association proposing that "the primary attack on alcoholism should be through the general hospital" [quoted in 27, p. 599]. Four years later, the World Health Organization included alcoholism in its International Classification of Diseases. But it was not until 1956 that the American Medical Association declared alcoholism to be an officially recognized disease in U.S. biomedicine. Four years later, E. M. Jellinek published his seminal book, *The Disease Concept of Alcoholism.* Finally, in 1971, the National Institute on Alcohol

[1]These studies were supported by National Institute on Alcohol Abuse and Alcoholism grants R23 AA06057 and R01 AA07161.

Abuse and Alcoholism was established "premised on the belief that alcoholism is a disease and an important health problem" [28, p. 108].

Since then, the disease concept has become "everyone's official dogma, with medical organizations, alcoholics themselves, and well-meaning people speaking on their behalf urging governments and employers to accept and act on its implications" [29, p. 367]. And with notable success! As Schaefer points out, "Alcoholism is a growth industry. Empty hospital beds are turned into alcoholism 'slots.' The disease concept has become . . . integrated into the political and economic consciousness" [30, p. 302]. While ambiguity remains about how much blame to lay at the feet of the drinker for causing his/her own problems, research indicates that the majority of people in the United States accept alcoholism as a real though ambiguous disease [31, 32].

But what is this *disease* called "alcoholism?" Morris Chafetz, a psychiatrist and one of the leading figures in the alcohol field, writes:

> We define alcoholism as a chronic behavioral disorder which is manifested by undue preoccupation with alcohol to the detriment of physical and mental health, by a loss of control when drinking has begun . . . , and by a self-destructive attitude in dealing with personal relationships and life situations. Alcoholism, we believe, is the result of disturbance and deprivation in early infantile experience and the related alterations in basic physio-chemical responsiveness; the iden-tification by the alcoholic with significant figures who deal with life problems through the excessive use of alcohol; and a socio-cultural milieu which causes ambivalence, conflict, and guilt in the use of alcohol [33, p. 4].

Even more more absolute is De Ropp, who asserts:

> The cause of alcoholism lies not in the whiskey bottle but in the psyche of those unfortunates who swallow its contents too freely. The alcoholic is sick, mentally and emotionally. He belongs . . . to that group of disturbed individuals who are labeled 'impulsive neurotics.' He is an insecure, emotionally immature individual who sees in alcohol a crutch to support him in his journey through life [34, pp. 133-134].

While others would add or subtract particular definitional elements, the basic message is the same: like all diseases, alcoholism is a malfunction of the individual, be it at the chemical, genetic, biological or psychological level. Even those who go so far as to view alcoholism as a defect at the microsocial level—a disease of the family system—still tend to speak in psychomedicalistic terms.

From the perspective of critical medical anthropology, the conventional disease model of alcoholism must be understood as an ideological construct comprehensible only in terms of the historic and political-economic contexts of its origin. The appeal of the disease concept is understood, in that its embrace has achieved several things simultaneously, including: 1) offering "a plausible solution to the apparent irrationality of . . . [problem drinking] behavior" [28, p. 87]; 2) guaranteeing social status as well as a livelihood to a wide array of individuals, institutions, and organiza-tions, within and outside of biomedicine; and 3) limiting the growing burden on the criminal justice system produced by public drunkenness, the most common arrest made by police nationally. In the perspective of critical medical anthropology, however, the disease model hinders *exploration of alternative, politically more challenging understandings of destructive drinking*. This point is argued below by presenting the case of Juan García in terms of contrasting conventional psychologistic and critical medical anthropological interpretations.

THE CASE OF JUAN GARCÍA

Juan was born in Puerto Rico in 1909. The offspring of an adulterous relationship, he deeply resented his father. At age eight, Juan's mother died and he went to live with an aunt, and later, after his father died, was raised by his father's wife. As expression of his undying hatred of his father, Juan took his mother's surname, García.

As a young man, he became romantically involved with a cousin named Zoraida, who had been deserted with a small daughter by her husband. They lived together for a number of years in a tiny wooden shack, eking out a meager living farming a small plot of land. Then one day, Zoraida's ex-husband came and took his daughter away. Because of his wealth and social standing, there was little Juan and Zoraida could do. In resigning themselves to the loss, they began a new family of their own.

Over the years, Zoraida bore nineteen children with Juan, although most did not survive infancy. According to Juan's daughter, who was the source of our information about Juan:

> My mother went to a spiritual healer in Puerto Rico and they told her witchcraft had been done on her, and that all her children born in Puerto Rico would die; her children would only survive if she crossed water.

Given their intensely spiritual perspective, the couple decided to leave Puerto Rico and migrate "across water" to the United States. It was to New York, to the burgeoning Puerto Rican community in Brooklyn, that Juan and Zoraida moved in 1946.

New to U.S. society and to urban life, Juan had great difficulty finding employment. Unskilled and uneducated, and monolingual in Spanish, he was only able to find manual labor at low wages. Eventually, he began working as a janitor in an appliance factory. Here, a fellow worker taught him to draft blueprints, enabling him to move up to the position of draftsman.

Juan's daughter remembers her parents as strict disciplinarians with a strong bent for privacy. Still, family life was stable and reasonably comfortable until Juan lost his job when the appliance factory where he worked moved out of state. At the time, he was in his mid-fifties and despite his efforts was never again able to locate steady employment. At first he received unemployment benefits, but when these ran out, the García family was forced to go on welfare. This greatly embarrassed Juan. Always a heavy drinker, he now began to drink and act abusively. According to his daughter:

> A big cloud came over us and everything kept getting worse and worse in the house. This was 1964, 1965, 1966. . . . The pressure would work on him and he used to drink and then beat my mother. But my mother wouldn't hit him back. . . . I went a year

and a half without speaking to my father. He would say that I wasn't his daughter. We respected our father, but he lost our respect cause of the way he used to treat us. He would beat me and I would curse at him. . . . When my mother couldn't take the pressure any more, she would drink too. . . . My parents would get into fights and we had to get in between. Once they had a fight and my father moved out.

By the time Juan died of alcohol-related causes in 1971, he was a broken man, impoverished, friendless, and isolated from his family.

If we think of problem drinking as an individual problem, then it makes sense to say that Juan suffered from a behavioral disorder characterized by a preoccupation with alcohol to the detriment of physical and mental health, by a loss of control over drinking, and by a self-destructive attitude in dealing with personal relationships and life situations. Moreover, there is evidence that he was an insecure, emotionally immature individual who used alcohol as a crutch to support himself in the face of adversity. Finally, without probing too deeply we even can find, in Juan's troubled relationship with his father, a basis in infantile experience for the development of these destructive patterns. In short, in professional alcohol treatment circles, among many recovered alcoholics, and in society generally, Juan could be diagnosed as having suffered from the disease of alcoholism.

In so labeling him, however, do we hide more than we reveal? By remaining at the level of the individual actor, that is, by locating Juan's problem *within* Juan, do we not pretend that the events of his life and the nature of his drinking make sense separate from their wider historic and political-economic contexts? As Wolf reminds us, approaches that disassemble interconnected social processes and fail to reassemble them falsify reality. Only by placing the subjects of our investigation "back into the field from which they were abstracted," he argues, "can we hope to avoid misleading inferences and increase our share of understanding" [35, p. 3]. To really make sense of Juan's drinking, to move beyond individualized and privatized formulations, to avoid artificial and unsatisfying psychologistic labeling, the critical perspective moves to the wider field, to an historic and political-economic appraisal of Puerto Ricans and alcohol.

HISTORIC AND POLITICAL ECONOMIC CONTEXT

When Columbus first set foot on Puerto Rico on November 19, 1493, he found a horticultural tribal society possessed of alcohol but devoid of alcoholism. While there is limited information on this period, based on the wider ethnographic record, it is almost certain that the consumption of fermented beverages by the indigenous Taino (Arawak) and Carib peoples of Puerto Rico was socially sanctioned and controlled, and produced little in the way of health or social problems. As Davila writes, the available literature suggests that "the Taino made beer from a fermentable root crop called manioc, and . . . they might also have been fermenting some of the fruits they grew. However, the existing evidence suggests that alcohol was used more in a ritual context than in a social one" [36, p. 10]. Heath notes that among many indigenous peoples of what was to become Latin America periodic fiestas in which most of the adults drank until intoxicated was a common pattern. However, "both drinking and drunkenness were socially approved in the context of veneration of major deities, as an integral part of significant agricultural ceremonies, or in celebration of important events in the lives of local leaders" [37, p. 9]. At times other than these special occasions, alcohol consumption was limited and nondisruptive, controlled by rather than a threat to the social group.

These and other features of Arawak life greatly impressed Columbus. He also was quick to notice the limited military capacity of the Indians, given their lack of metal weapons. Setting the tone for what was to follow, in one of his first log entries describing the Arawak, Columbus noted: "With fifty men we could subjugate them all and make them do whatever we want" [recorded in 38, p. 1]. In effect, this was soon to happen, prompted by the discovery of gold on the Island. Under the Spanish *encomienda* system, ostensibly set up to 'protect' the Indians and assimilate them to Spanish culture, indigenous men, women and children were forced to work long hours in Spanish mines. Within 100 years of the arrival of the Columbus, most of the indigenous people were gone, victims of the first phase of 'primitive accumulation' by the emergent capitalist economy of Europe.

Once the gold mines were exhausted, the island of Puerto Rico, like its neighbors, became a center of sugar production for export to the European market. Almost unknown in Europe before the thirteenth century, 300 years later sugar was a staple of the European diet. Along with its derivatives, molasses and rum, it became one of the substances Mintz has termed the "proletarian hunger-killers" during the take-off phase of the Industrial Revolution [39]. In time, rum became an essential component of the diet of the rural laboring classes of Puerto Rico.

This process was facilitated by two factors. First, alcohol consumption among Spanish settlers was a normal part of everyday life. Prior to colonial contact, in fact, the Spanish had little access to mood-altering substances other than alcohol. As Heath indicates, among the Spanish, alcoholic beverages were consumed "to relieve thirst, with meals, and as a regular refreshment, in all of the ways that coffee, tea, water, or soft drinks are now used . . ." [37, p.14]. Alcohol "thus permeated every aspect of . . . life" among the settlers [36, p. 11]. Second, there was a daily distribution of rum to workers and slaves on the sugar plantations [39]. Not until 1609 did King Felipe III of Spain forbid the use of alcohol as a medium for the payment of Indian laborers. Rum distilleries, in fact, were one of the few industrial enterprises launched by the Spanish during their several hundred year reign in Puerto Rico. Commercial production was supplemented by a home brew called *ron cañita* (little cane rum) that was widely consumed among poor and working people [40].

While the exact ethnohistorical pathway has yet to be reconstructed, it is evident that by the end of Spanish colonial rule, heavy alcohol consumption had become part and parcel of Puerto Rican cultural tradition and national identity. In his comprehensive history of Puerto Rico, published in 1788, for example, Fray Iñugo Abbad y Lasierra, notes that the favorite recreational activity of rural-dwelling *criollos* (native-born Puerto Ricans) was dancing. Dances lasting as long as a week were held on various occasions, including the celebration of Easter and Ash Wednesday, weddings, and the birth or death of a child. At these events, he notes, the hosts "serve bowls of breadstuffs with milk and honey, bottles of *aguardiente* [cane alcohol], and cigars" [quoted in [41, p. 46]. So popular was drinking that in 1826 the Spanish governor, Miguel de la Torre, instituted restrictions on alcohol consumption by slaves [42].

The U.S. acquisition of Puerto Rico in 1898, as war booty from the Spanish-American War—an event marking the beginning of "a major political realignment of world capitalism" [43, p. 152]—ushered in a new phase in Puerto Rican history and Puerto Rican drinking. At the moment of the U.S. invasion of Puerto Rico, 91 percent of the land under cultivation was owned by its occupants and an equal percentage of the existing farms were possessed by locally resident farmers [44]. Intervention, as Mintz [45] has shown, produced a radical increase in the concentration of agricultural lands, the extension of areas devoted to commercial cultivation for export, and the mechanization of agricultural production processes. Indeed, it was through gaining control over sugar and related production "that the United States consolidated its economic hegemony over the Island" [46, p. 95]. Shortly after assuming office, Guy V. Henry, the U.S. appointed Military Govenor of Puerto Rico, issued three rulings that facilitated this process: a freeze on credit, a devaluation of the peso, and a fix on land prices. Devaluation and the credit freeze made it impossible for farmers to meet their business expenses. As a result, they were forced to sell their property to pay their debts and thousands of small proprietors went out of business. The fix on land prices ensured that farm lands would be available at artificially low prices for interested buyers. At the time, the principle buyers in the market were either North American corporations or Puerto Rican companies directly linked to U.S. commerce. As a result, within "the short span of four years, four North American corporations . . . dedicated to sugar production came to control directly [275,030 square meters] of agricultural land" [47, p. 56]. As contrasted with the rural situation prior to U.S. intervention, by 1926 four out of five Puerto Ricans were landless. The inevitable sequel to the consolidation of coastal flat lands for sugar cane plantations was a large migration out of mountains to the coast, and the formation of "a vast rural proletariat, whose existence was determined by seasonal employment" [48, p. 44].

In the newly expanded labor force of sugar cane workers, a group that formed a large percentage of the Puerto Rican population until well into the twentieth century, drinking was a regular social activity. Mintz, who spent several years studying this population, notes the importance of drinking in men's social interaction. During the harvest season, the day followed a regular cycle. Work began early, with the men getting to the fields at sunrise and working until three or four in the afternoon, while women stayed at home caring for children, cleaning, doing the laundry, and preparing the hot lunches they would bring to their husbands in the fields.

> It is in the late afternoon that the social life of the day begins. . . . After dinner the street becomes the setting for conversation and flirting. Loafing groups gather in front of the small stores or in the yards of older men, where they squat and gossip; marriageable boys and girls promenade along the highway. Small groups form and dissolve into the bars. The women remain home. . . . The bachelors stand at the bar drinking their rum neat—each drink downed in a swallow from a tiny paper cup. The more affluent buy half pints of rum . . . and finish them sitting at the tables [49, pp. 16-17].

In the off season, known as *el tiempo muerto* (the dead time), life was harder and money scarcer, but drinking still provided an important outlet. Short on cash, the "drinkers of bottled rum turn[ed] back to canita," [50, p. 21], the traditional home brewed drink of the Puerto Rican *jibaro* (rural dweller).

During this period, a deeply rooted belief, reflecting the alienated character of work under capitalism, began to be established. This is the culturally constituted idea that *alcohol is a man's reward for labor:* "I worked hard, so I deserve a drink" [36, p. 11]. Gilbert, who notes a similar belief based on her research among Mexican-American men, describes the widespread practice of "respite drinking," "that is to say, drinking as a respite from labor or after a hard day's work" [9, pp. 265-266]. As Marx asserts, under capitalism

> labor is external to the worker, i.e., it does not belong to his essential being; . . . in his work, therefore, he does not affirm himself but denies himself. . . . The worker therefore only feels himself outside his work, and in his work feels outside himself. He is at home when he is not working, and when he is working he is not at home. His labor is not voluntary, but coerced; it is forced labor. It is therefore not satisfying a need; it is merely a means to satisfy needs external to it. Its alien character emerges clearly in the fact that as soon as no physical or other compulsion exists, labor is shunned like the plague [51, pp. 110-111].

Because labor for cane workers was not intrinsically rewarding, its performance required external motivation, a role which alcohol in part—probably because of its ability in many contexts to produce euphoria, reduce anxiety and tension, and enhance self-confidence, as well as having a low cost and ready availability—filled. Serving as a valued recompense for the difficult and self-mortifying work undertaken by men, alcohol consumption became culturally entrenched as an emotionally charged symbol of manhood itself. Vital to the power of this symbolism was the emergent reconceptualization of what it meant to be a man in terms of sole responsibility for the economic well being of one's family. Although there existed a sexual division of labor prior to the U.S. domination of Puerto Rico, in rural agricultural life work was a domestic affair that required family interdependence and close proximity. Proletarianization produced a devaluation of female labor as homemaking, while relegating it to an unpaid status. Additionally, it "led to Puerto Rican masculinity being defined in terms of being paid laborers and *buenos proveedores'* (good providers)" [52, pp. 42-43]. In this context, drinking came to be seen as a privilege "earned by masculine self-sufficiency and assumption of the provider role" [9, p. 266]. In the words of one of Gilbert's informants: " 'Yo soy el hombre de la casa, si quiero tomar, tomo cuando me de la gana' (I am the man of the house, and if I want to drink, I drink when I feel like it)."

The 1930s marked a significant turning point in the lives of the sugar cane workers as well as most other Puerto Ricans. Prior to the Depression, sugar cane provided one-sixth of Puerto Rico's total income, one-fourth of its jobs, and two-thirds of the dollars it earned from the export of goods. One out of every three factories on the Island was a sugar mill, a sugar refinery, a rum distillery, or molasses plant. The Depression nearly destroyed this economic base. Sugar prices fell drastically, while two hurricanes (1928 and 1932) all but demolished what remained of the damaged economy.

In response, control of Puerto Rico was transferred from the U.S. War Department to the Department of the Interior and federal taxes on Puerto Rican rum sold in the United States were remitted to the Puerto Rican treasury, providing the Island's Commonwealth government with $160 million in working capital. This money was used to build a number of government-owned manufacturing plants. However, concern in the U.S. Congress with "the crazy socialistic experiment going on down in Puerto Rico" [quoted in 41, p. 108] led to the sale of these factories to local capitalists. The Commonwealth government also launched Operation Bootstrap at this time "to promote industry, tourism and rum" [41, p. 108]. Operation Bootstrap was an ambitious initiative designed to reduce the high unemployment rate caused by the stagnation of a rural economy that had been heavily dependent on the production of a small number of cash crops for export. The program offered foreign investors, 90 percent of whom came from the United States, tax holidays of over ten years, the installation of infrastructural features such as plants, roads, running water and electricity, and most importantly, an abundant supply of cheap labor.

Significantly, however, as Maldonado-Denis points out, "What is altered in the change from the sugar economy based on the plantation to the new industrialization is merely the form of dependency, not its substance" [53, pp. 31-32]. In line with the unplanned nature of capitalist economy—at the world level, displaced agricultural workers quickly came to be defined as both an undesired "surplus population" and a *cause* of Puerto Rico's economic underdevelopment. As Day indicates, in a capitalist economy "if there is some cost to maintain [a] . . . surplus, it is likely to be 'pushed out' " [54, p. 441]. This is precisely what occurred. Between 1952 and 1971, the total number of agricultural workers in Puerto Rico declined from 120,000 to 75,000. So extensive was the exodus from rural areas that it threatened "to convert many towns in the interior of the Island into ghost-towns" [53, p. 33]. Male workers, in particular, were affected by industrialization, because over half of the new jobs created by Operation Bootstrap went to women.

Although Juan and Zoraida understood their decision to leave Puerto Rico as part of an effort to protect their children from witchcraft, the folk healer's message and its interpretation by Juan and Zoraida must be located in this broader political-economic context. As Maldonado-Denis cogently observes, the "dislocation of Puerto Rican agriculture—and the ensuing uprooting of its rural population—is the result of profound changes in the structure of the Puerto Rican economy and not the result of mere individual decisions arrived at because of fortuitous events" [48, p. 33]. However, "migrants do not usually see the larger structural forces that create [their] personal situation" and channel their personal decisions [55, p. 13].

The first significant labor migration of Puerto Ricans to the United States began in the 1920s, with the biggest push coming after World War Two. The focus for most migrants until the 1970s was New York City. As noted, it was to New York that Juan and Zoraida, along with 70,000 other Puerto Ricans, migrated in 1946. As many as 60 percent of these migrants came from the rural zones of the Island. They arrived during a post-war boom in the New York economy that created an urgent demand for new labor [56]. Employment was the primary motivation for migration and many found blue collar jobs, although often at wages lower than those of Euro-American and even African American workers performing similar toil.

By the time of the post-war migrations, heavy alcohol consumption among men was woven deeply into the cultural fabric of Puerto Rico. However, as Coombs and Globetti conclude in their review of the literature on drinking in Latin America generally, "Until recently, most studies, conducted mainly in small communities or rural areas, found relatively few visible ill effects. Little guilt or moral significance was attached to alcohol use or even drunkenness" [57, p. 7]. This description appears to hold true for Puerto Ricans as well. According to Marilyn Aguirre-Molina,

> If we look at the Puerto Rican experience, we can clearly see how alcohol use and the alcohol industry are entrenched within the population. . . . [D]istilled spirit is very available (at low cost), and part of the national pride for production of the world's finest rum. . . . Alcohol consumption has an important role in social settings—consumption is an integral part of many or most Hispanic functions. . . . At parties, or similar gatherings, a child observes that there's a great deal of tolerance for drinking, and it is encouraged by and for the men. A non-drinking male is considered anti-social. . . . Tolerance for drinking is further evidenced in the attitude that there is no disgrace or dishonor for a man to be drunk. . . . [I]t becomes evident that alcohol use is part of the sociocultural system of the Hispanic, used within the contexts of recreation, hospitality [and] festivity [58, pp. 3-6].

Adds Davila, "In our culture, weakness in drinking ability is always humiliating to a man because a true man drinks frequently and in quantity. Therefore, for a Puerto Rican man not to maintain dignity when drinking would be an absolute proof of his weakness, as would be his refusal to accept a drink" [36, p. 17]. Refusal to drink among Puerto Rican men, in fact, can be interpreted as an expression of homosexuality because drinking is defined as a diacritical male activity [16]. In Puerto Rico, these attitudes are supported by an extensive advertising effort by the rum industry, few restrictions on sales, ready availability of distilled spirits at food stores, and low cost for alcoholic beverages.

Most aspects of Puerto Rican life were transformed by the migration, drinking patterns included. According to Gordon,

> Puerto Ricans have . . . adopted U.S. drinking customs and *added* them to their traditional drinking customs. . . . They follow the pattern of weekday drinking typical of the American workingman. . . . Weekday drinking among Puerto Ricans does not affect the importance of their traditional weekend fiesta drinking more commonly seen in a rural society [8, p. 308, emphasis added].

Our ethnographic study of drinking in Hartford reveals that working class bars are quite common in the Puerto Rican community. Beyond being a place to drink, many bars sponsor baseball teams that play against each other in local park leagues. These games often culminate in the consumption of beer by the players. Bars, as well as social clubs, also are significant centers of domino playing, a widely enjoyed game in Puerto Rican culture. In short, barrooms tend to be centers of social and recreational life for Puerto Rican men, and drinking is a pivotal component of social interaction. But drinking is by no means limited to bar-related activities. In fact, outdoor consumption by small groups of men while talking, working on cars, or escaping from the heat in the shade of a tree, is a common pattern in the *barrio*. Public consumption of alcohol reflects community acceptance of drinking as a normal and appropriate activity. Lacking is the middle class American ambiguity concerning the propriety of drinking in many settings or in mixed aged groups.

While it is evident from Mintz's account of sugar cane workers that many Puerto Rican men had adopted working class drinking patterns even prior to migration, these behaviors were generalized and amplified following movement to the United States [49]. As a consequence of cultural pressure to maintain traditional drinking patterns as well as adopt U.S. working class norms, many Puerto Rican men have adopted a heavy drinking pattern. The development of this pattern was facilitated by the high density of businesses in poor, inner city neighborhoods that dispense alcohol, especially beer, for on and off premise consumption; multiple encouragements to drink in the media, including advertisements, films, and television programs; and structural factors that have contributed first to a redefinition and ultimately to the marginalization of the Puerto Rican man. This last factor was especially important in transforming heavy drinking into problem drinking in this population.

As suggested above, the transition from yeoman farmer to rural proletariat began a process of reconceptualizing the meaning of masculinity among Puerto Ricans. This transition was completed with the migration. Work-related definitions of manliness and provider-based evaluations of self-worth became dominant. To be *un hombre hecho y derecho* (a complete man) now meant demonstrating an ability to be successful as an income earner in the public sphere. This is "the great American dream of dignity through upward mobility" analyzed so effectively by Sennett and Cobb [59, p. 169], a dream that threatens always to turn into a nightmare for the working man. And the name of this nightmare, as every worker knows so well, is unemployment. The fear of unemployment is not solely an economic worry, it is equally a dread of being blamed and of blaming oneself for inadequacy, for letting down one's family, for failing while others succeed. The "plea ... to be relieved of having to prove oneself this way, to gain a hold instead on the innate meaningfulness of actions" is a central theme in the lives of working people [59, p. 246].

Juan's hard work, enabling his movement from janitor to draftsman, achieved without formal education or training, is the embodiment of the dream and the fear of the working man. During the period that Juan was successful at realizing the dream, his daughter remembers her family life as stable and happy. These golden years provided a stark contrast with what was to follow. Throughout this period Juan drank heavily, and yet he had no drinking problem. Alcohol was his culturally validated reward for living up to the stringent requirements of the male role in capitalist society. The swift turn around in Juan life following the loss of his job suggests that Puerto Rican male drinking problems should be considered in relationship to the problem of unemployment.

Several studies, in fact, indicate a direct association between unemployment and problem drinking. In his study of alcohol-related problems in Toronto, for example,

Smart reports that 21 percent of unemployed respondents suffer from three or more alcohol-related problems compared to only 6 percent of employed workers [60]. While an increase in consumption levels following unemployment has not been found in all studies of small groups of workers in particular settings, a national study by McCornac and Filante's of distilled spirit consumption and employment in the United States at the time of Juan's death supports this linkage. Their study concludes

> The unemployment rate had a positive and significant impact on the consumption of distilled spirits in both the cross-sectional and pooled analyses. During a recessionary period, rising unemployment stimulates consumption while decreasing real per capita income decreases consumption. However, the two effects are not equal. From 1972-1973 to 1974-1975, the rate of unemployment rose by 37% ... while real per capita income declined by less than 1%. Thus, the net effect of simultaneous changes in these two variables was to increase consumption by approximately 8%. The important implication of this finding is that the negative consequences of higher rates of unemployment can be extended to include the increased social and economic costs of an increase in the use of distilled spirits [50, pp. 177-178].

Similarly, analysis of national data on long and short term trends in alcohol consumption and mortality by Brenner shows an increase in alcohol consumption and alcohol-related health and social problems during periods of economic recession and rising unemployment [61]. His study, covering the years during Juan's period of heaviest drinking and subsequent death, finds that "[n]ational recessions in personal income and employment are consistently followed, within two to three years, by increases in cirrhosis mortality rates" [61, p. 1282]. Economic disruptions, he argues, create conditions of social stress, which in turn stimulate increased anxiety-avoidance drinking and consequent health problems. Research by Pearlin and Radabaugh indicates that anxiety is "especially likely to result in the use of alcohol as a tranquilizer if a sense of control is lacking and self-esteem is low" [62, p. 661]. The key variable in this equation, as Seeman and Anderson stress, is powerlessness [63]. Based on their study of drinking among men in Los Angeles, they argue, "The conclusion is inescapable that the sense of powerlessness is related to the experience of drinking problems quite apart from the sheer quantity of alcohol consumed" [63, p. 71]. Increased alcohol consumption and alcohol-related problems and mortality have been found to be associated in several studies [64, 65].

The major economic factor of concern here, of course, was the flight of the appliance factory where Juan was employed to a cheap labor market outside of the industrial Northeast. Juan was not alone in losing his job to the corporate transfer of production. About the same time, thousands of U.S. workers were being laid off by the "runaway shop;" 900,000 U.S. production jobs were lost, for example, between 1967 and 1971 alone [66]. In New York City, during this period, 25 percent of the largest companies relocated, reflecting a shift away from a production-centered economy. This transition has intensified the problem of Puerto Rican unemployment [53]. Mills and his coworkers, in their study of Puerto Rican migrants in New York, found that lacking specialized job skills Puerto Rican workers are at the mercy of economic forces. During periods of economic upturn they are welcomed, but when the business cycle "is on the way down, or in the middle of one of its periodic breakdowns, there is a savage struggle for even the low wage jobs . . ." [67, p. 82].

Consequently, at the time that Juan died in 1971, Puerto Ricans had the one of the highest unemployment rates of all ethnic groups in the country. While 6 percent of all men in the United States were jobless, for Puerto Rican men the rate of unemployment was 8.8 percent. Significantly, the actual rate of unemployment for Puerto Rican men was even higher than these figures suggest because, as measured by the Department of Labor, the unemployment rate does not include numerous individuals who have given up on the possibility of ever locating employment. If discouraged workers were included, the "unemployment among Puerto Rican men would be more accurately depicted—not at the 'official' rate of 8.8 percent—but at the 'adjusted' (and more realistic) level of 18.7 percent" [53, pp. 79-80].

For many older workers like Juan, whose age made them dispensable, and many younger Puerto Rican workers as well, whose ethnicity and lack of recognized skills made them equally discardable, the changing economic scene in New York meant permanent unemployment. Increased drinking and rising rates of problem drinking were products of the consequent sense of worthlessness and failure in men geared to defining masculinity in terms of being *un buen proveedor* [68, pp. 537-538]. As De La Cancela asserts, "living with limited options, uncertainty, and violence breeds fertile ground for ego-exalting substance use among Latinos" [69, p. 140]. Pappas identifies the general reasons in his ethnography of the effects of factory closing on rubber workers in Barberton, Ohio. Beyond a salary, a job provides workers with a feeling of purpose and means of participation in the surrounding social world. In addition to contributing to the expenence of uselessness, loss of work fragments social networks and produces increased isolation, placing increased strain on domestic relations. Restriction of the quantity of outside social interaction "narrows the psychic space in which the unemployed maneuver" [70, p. 86].

Importantly, Pappas reports that "Drinking and divorce were commonly mentioned by the people in Barberton as problems they saw among the unemployed they knew" [70, p. 89]. Problem drinking in this context, in part, expresses the refusal of the individual to conform to the reigning mechanistic ideology of capitalist society, namely the "view of people as machines and . . . society as a gigantic machine" [71, p. 228]. In accord with this machine model of humanity—the same model that conditions thinking in biomedicine, workers are treated like mechanical parts, used, relocated, and discarded as dictated by the changing needs of profitable production. The deepest concern of capitalism, in the words of one of its advocates, lies not in meeting human needs or realizing human dreams, but "in increasing the efficiency of the human machine" [quoted in 72, p. 179]. Osherson and AmaraSingham identify three dimensions of this machine metaphor: 1) *a mind-body split* predicated on the assumption that thought is "a separate faculty independent of the machine-like body;" 2) *an exclusion of emotion* because "[m]achines, as merely the expression of the interaction of observable physical forces, do not feel;" and 3) *inattention to value* in that "[e]fficiency . . . is . . . emphasized over considerations of meaning and purpose. . ." [71, pp. 238-239]. Problem drinking in the working class, whatever its tragic effect on the health and social life of drinkers, expresses the rejection of all of these severings. It affirms the drinker as a flesh and blood creature with ideas, emotions, and purpose. Drinking spirits, somewhat like praying to them, is "at the same time the expression of real distress and the protest against real distress" [73, p. 42].

Within the context of Puerto Rican culture, these general processes take on a particular slant. Drinking among Latino males is commonly linked both in the alcohol literature and in popular thinking with the concept of *machismo,* or the notable Latino emphasis on appearing manly at all times, particularly in public. Some have gone so far as see *machismo* as the golden key to understanding the high rates of drinking found among Latino males on *machismo.* However, while it is certainly the case that drinking is culturally defined as a male thing to do, as a culturally approved means of expressing prowess as a male, this does not lead directly to alcoholism. Rather, it is the combination of a cultural emphasis on drinking as a proper, appropriate, and manly activity, with considerable availabilty of alcohol and constant encouragement to drink, with political and economic subordination in a system in which most alternative expressions of manliness are barred to Puerto Rican access that is of real significance. This interpretation underscores De La Cancela's argument that "just as capitalism obscures the necessity of institutionalized un-employment by defining the unemployed as somehow lacking in the required skills to succeed, machismo obscures the alienation effects of capitalism on individuals by embodying the alienation in malefemale sex-role terms . . . " [74, p. 292].

Unemployment blocked Juan, as it has so many other Puerto Rican men, from the major socially sanctioned route to success as a man. It did not, however, exterminate the ever present and powerful need to achieve the cultural values of *machismo* (mastery), *dignidad* (honor and dignity of the family), and *respeto* (respect of one's peers). In a sense, however counterproductive, drinking was all that was left for Juan that was manly in his understanding. Hard drinking replaced hard work, and alcohol, as a medium of cultural expression, was transformed from compensation for the sacrifices of achieving success into salve for the tortures of failure.

JUAN IS NOT ALONE

The "personal problems" of the unemployed workers of Barberton, like the problems experienced by Juan Garciá [53, pp. 31-32], constitute part of the human fallout of so-called economic development. Although often portrayed as natural and inevitable, changes in the nature and location of production exact enormous human costs, costs that tend to be borne disproportionately by the poor and working classes. The extent of the agony for Puerto Rican men is captured by Davila.

> I have a father who is an alcoholic and a brother who died of cirrhosis of the liver
> a year ago at the age of 42. I have a young son who is having alcohol problems
> of his own. I have cousins and uncles who have died of alcoholism. I have friends
> who likewise have died of alcoholism or are currently alcoholic. And I am a
> recovering alcoholic. . . . All the persons I have listed are Puerto Rican and . . .
> they are all men [36, pp. 17-18].

A study comparing mortality differentials among various Latino subgroups residing in the United States during the years 1979-1981, found that Puerto Rican population had a distinct pattern of mortality from chronic liver disease and cirrhosis. The age-adjusted death rate among Puerto Ricans from liver-related problems, which are common among heavy drinkers, is about twice that among Mexicans and almost three times the rate among Cubans. Further, the rate among Puerto Ricans is over two times the African American rate and triple the Euro-American rate [75]. In fact, New York Board of Health data for 1979-81 indicate that cirrhosis was the second leading cause of death among Island-born Puerto Ricans age fifteen to forty-five [cited in 8].

These data suggest that Juan's case, while having special features peculiar to his individual life course, is not, on the whole, unique. His life and his death, in fact, are emblematic of the broad experience of working class Puerto Rican men in the United States, a conclusion supported by findings from our studies of drinking patterns and experiences among Puerto Rican men and adolescents in Hartford, Connecticut. For both studies, the sampling frame consisted of all Puerto Rican households in high-density Puerto Rican neighborhoods as defined by census reports (25% Latino surnames). In the first of these studies, interviews were conducted with a randomly selected sample of Puerto Rican adolescents aged fourteen to seventeen years. The sampling unit consisted of 210 adolescents (1 adolescent subject per participating household), of which eighty-eight were boys.

A series of national household surveys of drinking among adolescents indicates that over half of the adolescents in the United States report using alcohol during the past year, compared to 31 percent of the Puerto Rican adolescents in our sample [76, 77]. In the national samples, about one-third of participants report drinking within the month prior to the survey, compared to 14 percent in our sample. Similarly, Rachal et al., in a national sample of over 13,000 adolescents in grades seven to twelve, found that 55 percent reported usually drink at least once a month, compared to 10 percent in our sample [78]. Regarding the quantity of alcohol consumed per drinking episode, these researchers found that 55 percent of their sample reported more than one drink per drinking occasion, compared to only 19 percent in our sample. In short, as have other researchers, we found a lower drinking prevalence among Puerto Rican adolescents than tends to be found for the general U.S. adolescent population [79].

We also found lower levels of problem drinking in our adolescent sample. In their studies of middle-class Anglo high school students (aged 16-18 years) in Colorado, Jessor and co-workers classified problem drinkers as adolescents that had been drunk six or more times in the past year, or had experienced at least two different negative consequences due to drinking two or more times in the past year [80]. They found that one out of four of the boys and one out of six of the girls in their sample qualified as problem drinkers, and that the drunkenness component of the joint criterion was most significant in contributing to the problem drinking rates. The mean frequency for drunkenness in their sample for a one year period was 23.9, or about twice a month for the male problem drinkers and 17.8 for the female problem drinkers. Using similar criteria, Rachal et al. found a problem drinking rate of 27.8 percent in a national study of adolescents in grades seven to twelve. Although we did not collect full year data for many of the variables used to construct the problem drinking definition used in the studies cited above, we did collect one month data that allow some comparison with the conclusions of these studies. During the month prior to being interviewed, eight individuals in our sample reported getting drunk (5 on a single occasion, 2 on two different occasions, and 1 on more than 6 occasions). Using this as an indicator of problem drinking, we have a problem drinking rate in our sample of about 4 percent. With an even more liberal definition of problem drinking—two or more drinking occasions during the last month—the problem drinking rate in our sample would be 6 percent. This rate is significantly lower than for (somewhat older) Anglo samples, but fits the trend for generally lower rates of drinking among Latino adolescents.

The existing literature suggests that family controls are a major factor limiting alcohol consumption among Latino youth to levels below those of their white counterparts. This was found to be a primary reason given for not drinking by the adolescents in our study. Based on his research among Mexican-Americans in Texas, Trotter states: "Unmarried children who smoke or drink in front of parents are often thought to be extremely disrespectful, and to shame their family" [18, p. 286]. This explanation fits with the cultural understanding that drinking is an earned reward for assuming the responsibilities of employment and family support, roles not open to dependent children.

Our second study examined drinking patterns in 398 Puerto Rican men, eighteen to forty-eight years of age, recruited to a research sample structured by type of residence (private home, rented apartment, housing project). These primary sampling units were chosen because of expected differences in socio-economic status and the sense from prior research that residents in rented apartments in low income neighborhoods often are under greater economic pressure than households in rent controlled housing projects or owners of private homes or condominiums. The housing project included in this study is located at some distance from the central city area and tends to be in better repair than other Hartford housing projects. Respondents living in targeted neighborhoods (selected because of census data indicating a high density Spanish surname population) were randomly recruited and interviewed in their place of residence.

Among the men in the sample, 84 percent were born in Puerto Rico and half had been living in the United States for under ten years. Most of the other men were born in the United States, 37 percent in Hartford. Fifty-four percent were married or living with a partner, and 83 percent had a high school education or less. Data on these respondents indicate the economic difficulties faced by Puerto Rican men generally. Thirty-three percent reported that they were unemployed and looking for work and another 17 percent worked only part-time at the time of the interview. More than half of the men (55%) reported annual household incomes of under $8,000; 85 percent reported incomes under $15,000. Rates of unemployment for men across the three residential subgroups was as follows: private home: 3 percent; rented apartment: 44.3 percent; housing project: 68.5 percent Additionally, rates of part-time employment across these three residence types was 12 percent, 19.8 percent, and 10.8 percent respectively. These data are consistent with other research in Hartford indicating "that whites . . . on average have a higher socioeconomic level than the Black and

Hispanic samples, and *the Hispanic group is consistently ranked lowest* . . . in socioeconomic indicators in Hartford" [81, p. 9; emphasis in original].

About 80 percent of the men in our study reported that they have consumed alcohol. Of these, 31 percent indicated that they drink at least once a week. Regarding quantities normally consumed when drinking, we found that 53 percent of the drinkers reported having at least three drinks per drinking occasion. Ten percent indicated that they normally drink until "high" or drunk, although drinking for these effects was reported as a motivation for consumption by 41 percent. The frequency of heavy drinking among these men is reflected in the Total Sample column of Table 1. Almost 20 percent of the men reported having eight drinks per drinking occasion at least ont to three times per month during the last year. Another 7.5 percent reported this level of drinking three to eleven times during the last year. The majority of the men, however, reported lower levels of drinking.

As seen in the Total Sample column of Table 2, approximately 10 percent of the men in the study reported they felt that their drinking was not completely under control during the last year. If a longer time period is included (since a man's first drink), approximately 20 percent reported having felt out of control.

Additionally, 34 percent of the men stated that drinking as a means of forgetting about problems was a very to somewhat important motivation for them to drink, while almost a quarter reported they drink because they have nothing else to do.

Data reported in Table 3 show that between 7 to 28 percent of the men reported at least one drinking-related problem. Notably, 28.4 percent of the men indicated that drinking has had a harmful effect on their homelife or marriage.

Table 1. Frequency of Heavy Drinking by Residence Type (%) During the Last 12 Months

Drinking Frequency	Total Sample	Rented Apartment	Housing Project	Private Home	$p <$
At least 1-3 times/month drank 8 drinks at a time	19.4	20.9	19.0	10.0	.026
3-11 times/year drank 8 drinks at a time	7.5	7.4	10.3	0	.026
1-2 times/year drank 8 drinks at a time	14.1	18.2	6.9	0	.026
Never drank 8 drinks during last year	59.0	53.4	63.8	90.0	.026

Table 2. Distribution of Lack of Control Over Drinking Across Residence Types (%)
During the Last 12 Months

Reported Lack of Control	Total Sample	Rented Apartment	Housing Project	Private Home	$p <$
Sometimes keep on drinking after wanting to stop	12.1	68.8	31.3	0	.01
Difficult to stop drinking before becoming intoxicated	6.5	69.2	30.8	0	.04
Tried but was unable to quit or cut down on drinking	10.3	73.2	26.8	0	.04

Table 4 compares negative drinking consequences among Puerto Rican men (21 and older) with finding among men from a national probability sample of the general population aged twenty-one or older [82]. The problem drinking scales displayed on this table were constructed by combining responses from several related questions following Cahalan [82]. In most cases, quite similar questions (pertinent to these scales) appear on both the national and Hartford instruments. Symptomatic drinking refers to signs of physical dependence and loss of control suggestive of Jellinek's gamma alcoholism (e.g., drinking to relieve a hangover, blackouts, having difficulty stopping drinking). Three variables used to construct this scale (tossing down drinks quickly, sneaking drinks, drinking before a party to ensuring having enough alcohol) were not included in our survey, possibly resulting in a lower score for Puerto Rican men. Half of the variables used to construct an additional scale on psychological dependence for the national study were not included in our instrument and consequently this item is not included in the table.

In the national sample, 25 percent of the respondents were abstainers compared to 20 percent in our study. Additionally, it is evident from Table 4 that the prevalence of drinking-related problems is higher for the Hartford sample on most of the scales, supporting the epidemiological data suggesting higher problem drinking rates among Puerto Rican men. These differences are especially notable on the two scales (complaints about drinking by friends or spouses) that involve the impact of drinking on personal relationships. The final column on this table reports problem frequencies just for drinkers in the Hartford study (i.e., abstainers are not included). Positive responses on two of the scales, belligerence (getting into heated agruments while drinking) and binge drinking (being intoxicated for several days at a time), were reported by approximately half of the Puerto Rican drinkers.

Table 3. Distribution of Problem Drinking Experiences Across
Residence Types (%)

Problem Drinking Experience	Total Sample	Rented Apartment	Housing Project	Private Home	p <
Skipped a number of regular meals while drinking because of hangover	14.6	75.9	22.4	1.7	.61
Taken a strong drink in the morning	11.8	66.0	25.5	8.5	.25
Awakened not able to remember some things done while drinking	14.6	67.2	27.6	5.2	.12
Drinking has interfered with spare time activities	7.3	69.0	31.0	0	.16
Sometimes awakened sweating after drinking	13.3	67.9	22.6	9.4	.61
Gotten into a heated argument while drinking	8.5	70.6	29.4	0	.05
Gotten into a fight while drinking	7.5	66.7	33.3	0	.01
Drinking has had harmful effect on health	9.0	72.2	27.8	0	.04
Drinking has had harmful effect on marriage/home life	28.4	74.3	16.8	8.8	.001
Spouse or loved one threaten to leave because of respondent's drinking	7.0	75.0	25.0	0	.05

Table 4. Prevalence of Drinking-related Problems among Men (21 Years and Older) Over Last 12 Months

Drinking Related Problems	Probability Sample $N = 751$	Puerto Rican Sample $N = 352*$	Puerto Rican drinkers $N = 180*$
Health problems associated with drinking	4.0	9.4	31.7
Acting belligerently under the influence	8.0	9.1	48.5
Friends complain about drinking	3.0	30.7	35.9
Symptomatic drinking	20.0	19.9	36.5
Job-related drinking problems	7.0	6.8	19.7
Problems with law, police, accidents	2.0	4.8	38.6
Engaging in binge drinking	1.0	4.5	50.0
Spouse complains about drinking	2.0	7.7	13.0

*Excludes participants under 21 years of age.

Importantly, Tables 1-3 also reveal that drinking and drinking-related problems are unevenly distributed by residential category. As seen in Table 1, men who live in rented apartments or in housing projects are much more likely to engage in frequent heavy drinking (i.e., at least 1 to 3 times a month having at least 8 drinks at a time). Men who own their own home or condominium are the least likely to ever consume this many drinks per drinking occasion. While 46 percent and 36 percent of rental apartment and housing project dwellers reported having consumed eight or more drinks at least once during the last year, this is true for only 10 percent of the men who live in private homes. Additionally, of the men who reported drinking on ten or more days during the previous month, 64 percent live in rented apartments, 29 percent live in a housing project, and 7 percent live in a privately owned dwelling. This same pattern also appears in respondent answers concerning control over drinking, as seen in Table 2. Men who live in rented apartments were significantly more likely to have reported that they have difficulties stopping drinking when they want to, stopping drinking before they are intoxicated, and giving up or cutting down on drinking. Men who own their own home were the least likely to report loss of control over drinking. Finally, Table 3 shows that problem drinking experiences are consistently and significantly more likely among men who live in rented apartments and least likely in men who own private homes. Statistically significant levels of association were reached for almost all of the variables recorded in these tables.

Overall, we found high rates of heavy and problem drinking in our study of Puerto Rican men, with the heaviest and most problematic drinking occurring among men who lived in rented apartments in high density, low income inner city neighborhoods. The correlation coefficients between employment and the problem drinking scales reported in Table 4 are displayed in Table 5. As this table indicates, there is a negative correlation between being employed and all eight problem drinking scales. Unemployment, in sum, is a clear correlate of problem drinking in Puerto Rican men.

Our research suggests that the onset of drinking problems among Puerto Rican males is associated with a *post-adolescent transition* into the world of adult responsibilities and sociocultural expectations. Specifically, findings from our second study indicate this transition occurs in the mid-twenties. After that point, rates of problem drinking continue to rise until Puerto Rican men are well into their forties [see 83-84]. Confronted repeatedly with setbacks in attaining regular and rewarding employment, and unable to support their families, many Puerto Rican men in Hartford drink to forget their problems and their boredom, while seeking through heavy and often problem drinking what they cannot achieve otherwise in society: respect, dignity, and validation of their masculine identity. While 38.5 percent of the men in our sample who reported two or more drinking related health or social problems indicated that they drink to forget about their personal worries, the figure was 7.1 percent for

Table 5. Zero-order Correlation Coefficents between Employment and Drinking-related Problems among Puerto Rican Men

Drinking Related Problems	Correlation Coefficient (r)
Health problems associated with drinking	-.1805
Acting belligerently under the influence	-.0634
Friends complain about drinking	-.0069
Symptomatic drinking	-.1165
Job-related drinking problems	-.0573
Problems with law, police, accidents	-.2171
Engaging in binge drinking	-.3371
Spouse complains about drinking	-.1530

problem-free drinkers. Similarly, 30.8 percent of problem drinkers reported drinking to release tension compared to 6.5 percent of problem-free drinkers. As our data show, not all Puerto Rican men become involved in problem drinking (or the use of other mind-altering drugs). Indeed, the majority do not. That so many do however reveals the folly of remaining at the micro-level in developing an explanation of this phenomenon.

CONCLUSION

In this examination of the broader context of Juan's drinking, we see the intersection of biography and history, that critical link uniting "the innermost acts of the individual with the widest kinds of social-historical phenomena," [85, p. xvi]. In reviewing the social environment of "Juan's disease," we have not, we believe, "depersonalize[d] the subject matter and the content of medical anthropology" [86, p. 137]. The goal of critical medical anthropology is not to obliterate the individual nor the poignant and personal expressions produced by the loss and struggle to regain well-being. Nor does our perspective seek to eliminate psychology, culture, the environment, or biology from a holistic medical anthropology. Instead, by taking "cognizance of processes that transcend separable cases" [35, p. 17], we attempt to unmask the ways in which suffering, as well as curing, illness behavior, provider/patient interactions, etc., have levels of meaning and cause beyond the narrow confines of immediate experience. As Mintz suggests, "When we can accurately specify the effects of policies readily imposed by external authority, the relationships between outside and inside, and between the living of life events and the weight of the world system, are clear" [87, p. 791]. Situated in relationship to relevant history and political economy, Juan's drinking loses the bewildering quality commonly attached to destructive behavior. This is achieved by an exploration of the macro-micro nexus which includes and requires an examination of symbolic, environmental, and psychological factors, but does not reduce analysis to any of these factors.

On the one hand, by "refocussing upstream," to use John McKinlay's [88] apt phrase, we recognize the degree to which alcoholism is not merely "Juan's disease" but a disease of the capitalist world economic system, and at the same time, an expression of human suffering and coping, as well as resistance to the forces and pressures of that system. Writing of his key informant among the Puerto Rican sugarcane workers, Taso Zayas, Mintz confirms

> Many of the events that Taso describes were the specific consequences of external interventions in local life. These interventions affected ecology, housing, diet, labor, and the whole tempo of daily experience, powerfully and directly. It might not be too much to say that the condition of Taso's teeth, for example, can be fairly viewed as the direct consequence of external influences upon local life. Much of what Taso did, and what he recounts, was in reaction to the effects of such external intervention [87, p. 791].

In this, we see the distortion inherent in separating problem drinking, decaying teeth, or any other health condition from its wider political-economic environment, as is routine in the medicalization of health problems. Moreover, in the analysis of Puerto Rican drinking practices and understandings we find validation of Keesing's insight that not only behavior but cultural symbols and beliefs as well "must be situated historically, [and] viewed in a theoretical framework that critically examines their embeddedness in social, economic, and political structures" [89, p. 166].

On the other hand, as Juan's case reveals, however misdirected and self-destructive, problem drinking is a dramatic and nagging reminder that medical anthropology must be more than the study of health systems and political-economic structures, it must be sensitive also to the symbolically expressed experiential and meaning frames of struggling human beings reacting to and attempting to shape their world, although never "under circumstances chosen by themselves" [90, p. 15]. In its disruptiveness, problem drinking, in any type of society or social system, brings to light the dynamic tensions between structure and agency, society and the individual, general processes and particular human responses. Addressing these issues is the special contribution of critical medical anthropology to the wider arena of the political economy of health and to anthropology itself.

REFERENCES

1. R. Stall, Alcohol, Drug Use and AIDS: An Anthropological Research Agenda, *Newsletter of the Alcohol and Drug Study Group, 23*, pp. 12-22, 1989.
2. C. Turner, H. Miller, and M. Lincoln, *AIDS: Sexual: Behavior and Intravenous Drug Use,* National Academy Press, Washington, D.C., 1989.
3. D. Heath, Emerging Anthropological Theory and Models of Alcohol Use and Alcoholism, in *Theories on Alcoholism,* C. D. Chaudron and D. A. Wilkinson (eds.), Addiction Research Foundation, Toronto, 1988.
4. M. Singer, Toward a Political-Economy of Alcoholism: The Missing Link in the Anthropology of Drinking, *Social Science and Medicine, 23,* pp. 113-130, 1986.
5. G. Ames and J. Mora, Alcohol Problem Prevention in Mexican American Populations, in *Alcohol Consumption among Mexicans and Mexican Americans,* M. J. Gilbert (ed.), Plenum, New York, pp. 253-280, 1988.
6. A. Gordon, Hispanic Drinking after Migration: The Case of Dominicans, *Medical Anthropology, 10,* pp. 154-171, 1978.
7. A. Gordon, The Cultural Context of Drinking and Indigenous Therapy for Alcohol Problems in Three Migrant Hispanic Cultures; An Ethnographic Report, in Cultural Factors in Alcohol Research and Treatment of Drinking Problems, *Journal of Studies on Alcohol (Special Supplement No. 9),* D. Health, J. Waddell, and J. Topper (eds.), pp. 217-240, 1981.
8. A. Gordon, Alcohol and Hispanics in the Northeast, in *The American Experience with Alcohol,* L. Bennett and G. Ames (eds.), Plenum, New York, pp. 297-314, 1985.
9. M. J. Gilbert, Mexican-Americans in California: Intracultural Variation in Attitudes and Behavior Related to Alcohol, in *The American Experience with Alcohol,* L. Bennett and G. Ames (eds.), Plenum, New York, pp. 255-278, 1985.
10. M. J. Gilbert, Alcohol Consumption Patterns in Immigrant and Later Generation Mexican American Women, *Hispanic Journal of the Behavioral Sciences, 9,* pp. 299-314, 1987.
11. M. J. Gilbert, *Alcohol Consumption among Mexicans and Mexican Amerians: A Binational Perspective,* Spanish Speaking Mental Health Research Center, University of California, Los Angeles, 1988.

12. M. J. Gilbert and R. Cervantes, *Mexican Americans and Alcohol,* Monograph No. 11, Spanish Speaking Mental Health Research Center, University of California, Los Angeles, 1987.
13. D. Heath, *Sociocultural Perspectives on Hispanic Drinking,* presented at the North American Congress on Alcohol and Drug Problems, Boston, 1986.
14. J. B. Page, L. Rio, J. Sweeney, and C. McKay, Alcohol and Adaptation to Exile in Miami's Cuban Population, in *The American Experience with Alcohol,* L. Bennett and G. Ames (eds.), Plenum, New York, pp. 315-332, 1985.
15. M. Singer and M. Borrero, Indigenous Treatment for Alcoholism: The Case of Puerto Rican Spiritualism, *Medical Anthropology, 8,* pp. 246-273, 1984.
16. M. Singer, L. Davison, and F. Yalin, (eds.), *Alcohol Use and Abuse among Hispanic Adolescents,* Hispanic Health Council, Hartford, 1987.
17. R. Trotter, Ethnic and Sexual Patterns of Alcohol Use: Anglo and Mexican American College Students, *Adolescence, 17,* pp. 305-325, 1982.
18. R. Trotter, Mexican-American Experience with Alcohol: South Texas Examples, in *The American Experience with Alcohol,* L. Bennett and G. Ames (eds.), Plenum, New York, pp. 279-296, 1985.
19. R. Trotter, and J. Chavira, Discovering New Models for Alcohol Counseling in Minority Groups, in *Modern Medicine and Medical Anthropology in the United States-Mexico Border Population,* B. Velimirov (ed.), Pan American Health Organization, Washington, D.C., pp. 164-171, 1978.
20. V. Abad and J. Suares, *Cross Cultural Aspects of Alcoholism among Puerto Ricans,* in Proceedings, Fourth Annual Alcoholism Conference of the National Institute on Alcohol Abuse and Alcoholism, Washington, D.C., 1974.
21. F. Engels, *The Condition of the Working Class in England,* Granada, London, 1969.
22. K. Stebbins, Tobacco or Health in the Third World? A Political-Economic Analysis with Special Reference to Mexico, *International Journal of Health Services, 17,* pp. 523-538, 1987.
23. K. Stebbins, Transnational Tobacco Companies and Health in Underdeveloped Countries: Recommendations for Avoiding a Smoking Epidemic, *Social Science and Medicine, 30*:2, pp. 227-236, 1990.
24. M. Singer, R. Irizarry, and J. Schensul, Needle Access as an AIDS Prevention Strategy for IV Drug Users: A Research Perspective, *Human Organization, 50*:2, pp. 142-153, 1991.
25. M. Singer, C. Flores, L. Davison, G. Burke, and Z. Castillo, Puerto Rican Community Mobilizing in Response to the AIDS Crisis, *Human Organization, 50*:1, pp. 73-81, 1991.
26. P. Davies, Motivation, Responsibility and Sickness in the Psychiatric Treatment of Alcoholism, *British Journal of Psychiatry, 134,* pp. 449-458, 1979.
27. M. Chafetz and R. Yoerg, Public Health Treatment Programs in Alcoholism, in *Treatment and Rehabilitation of the Chronic Alcoholic,* B. Kissin and H. Begleiter (eds.), Plenum Press, New York, pp. 593-614, 1977.
28. P. Conrad and J. Schneider, *Deviance and Medicalization: From Badness to Sickness,* The C. V. Mosby Company, St. Louis, 1980.
29. R. Kendell, Alcoholism: A Medical or Political Problem?, *British Medical Journal, 1*:6160, pp. 367-371, 1979.
30. J. Schaefer, Ethnic and Racial Variation in Alcohol Use and Abuse, in *Special Population Issues,* U.S. Department of Health and Human Services, Washington, D.C., pp. 239-311, 1982.
31. H. Mulford and D. Miller, Measuring Public Acceptance of the Alcoholic as a Sick Person, *Quarterly Journal of Studies on Alcohol, 25,* pp. 314-323, 1964.

32. N. Chrisman, Alcoholism: Illness or Disease?, in *The American Experience with Alcohol,* L. Bennett and G. Ames (eds.), Plenum, New York, pp. 7-22, 1985.

33. M. Chafetz and H. Demone, *Alcoholism and Society,* Oxford University Press, New York, 1962.

34. R. De Ropp, *Drugs and the Mind,* Delta, New York, 1976.

35. E. Wolf, E., *Europe and the People without History,* University of California Press, Berkeley, 1982.

36. R. Davila, The History of Puerto Rican Drinking Patterns, in *Alcohol Use and Abuse among Hispanic Adolescents,* M. Singer, L. Davison, and F. Yalin (eds.), Hispanic Health Council, Hartford, pp. 7-18, 1987.

37. D. Heath, Historical and Cultural Factors Affecting Alcohol Availability and Consumption in Latin America, in *Research Papers in Anthropology, No. 2,* Department of Anthropology, Brown University, Providence, Rhode Island, 1984.

38. H. Zinn, *A People's History of the United States,* Harper & Row, New York, 1980.

39. S. Mintz, The Caribbean as a Socio-cultural Area, in *Peoples and Cultures of the Caribbean,* M. Horowitz (ed.), Natural History Press, Garden City, New York, pp. 17-46, 1971.

40. A. Carrion, *Puerto Rico: A Political and Cultural History,* Aldine, Chicago, 1983.

41. K. Wagenheim, *The Puerto Ricans,* Anchor Books, New York, 1973.

42. C. Coll y Toste, *Historia de la Esclavitud en Puerto Rico,* Sociedad de Autores Puertorriquenos, San Juan, 1969.

43. F. Bonilla, Ethnic Orbits: The Circulation of Capitals and Peoples, *Contemporary Marxism, 10,* pp. 148-167, 1985.

44. B. Diffie and J. Diffie, *Porto Rico: A Broken Pledge,* Vanguard Press, New York, 1931.

45. S. Mintz, *Caribbean Transformation,* Aldine, Chicago, 1974.

46. History Task Force, *Labor Migration Under Capitalism: The Puerto Rican Experience,* Monthly Review Press, New York, 1979.

47. J. Herrero, V. Sanchez Cardona, and E. Gutierrez, La Politicia monetaria del '98, *El Nuevo Dia,* July 30, 1975.

48. R. Maldonado, Why Puerto Ricans Migrated to the United States in 1947-73, *Monthly Labor Review,* pp. 7-18, September 1976.

49. S. Mintz, *Worker in the Cane,* Yale University Press, New Haven, 1960.

50. D. McCornac and R. Filante, The Demand for Distilled Spirits: An Empirical Investigation, *Journal of Studies on Alcohol, 45,* pp. 176-178, 1984.

51. K. Marx, *The Economic and Philosophic Manuscripts of 1844,* International Publishers, New York, 1964.

52. V. De La Cancela, Labor Pains. Puerto Rican Males in Transition, *Centro Bulletin, 2,* pp. 41-55, 1988.

53. M. Maldonado-Denis, *The Emigration Dialectic: Puerto Rico and the USA.,* International Publishers, New York, 1980.

54. R. Day, The Economics of Technological Change and the Demise of the Share Cropper, *American Economic Review, 47,* pp. 427-449, 1967.

55. C. Rodríguez, *Puerto Ricans: Born in the U.S.A.,* Unwin Hyman, Boston, 1989.

56. M. Maldonado-Denis, *Puerto Rico: A Socio-Historic Interpretation,* Vintage Books, New York, 1972.

57. D. Coombs and G. Globetti, Alcohol Use and Alcoholism in Latin America: Changing Patterns and Sociocultural Explanations, *The International Journal of the Addictions, 21,* pp. 59-81, 1986.

58. M. Aguirre-Molina, *Alcohol and the Hispanic Woman,* paper presented at the Conference on Women in Crisis, New York, 1979.

59. R. Sennett and J. Cobb, *The Hidden Injuries of Class,* Vintage Books, New York, 1973.
60. R. Smart, Drinking Problems among Employed, Unemployed and Shiftworkers, *Journal of Occupational Medicine, 21,* pp. 731-735, 1979.
61. H. Brenner, Trends in Alcohol Consumption and Associated Illnesses, *American Journal of Public Health, 65,* pp. 1279-1292, 1975.
62. L. Pearlin and C. Radabaugh, Economic Strains and the Coping Functions of Alcohol, *American Journal of Sociology, 82,* pp. 652-663, 1976.
63. M. Seeman and C. Anderson, Alienation and Alcohol: The Role of Work, Mastery, and Community in Drinking Behavior, *American Sociological Review, 48,* pp. 60-77, 1983.
64. K. Makela et al., *Alcohol, Society and the State,* Addiction Research Foundation, Toronto, 1981.
65. R. Wilson, Changing Validity of the Cirrhosis Mortality-Alcoholic Beverage Sales Construct: U.S. Trends, 1970-1977, *Journal of Studies on Alcohol, 45,* pp. 53-58, 1984.
66. R. Barnet and R. Muller, *Global Reach,* Simon and Schuster, New York, 1974.
67. C. W. Mills, et al., *The Puerto Rican Journal,* Russell and Russell, New York, 1967.
68. I. Canino and G. Canino, Impact of Stress on the Puerto Rican Family: Treatment Considerations, *American Journal of Orthopsychiatry, 50,* pp. 535-541, 1980.
69. V. De La Cancela, Minority AIDS Prevention: Moving Beyond Cultural Perspectives Toward Sociopolitical Empowerment, *AIDS Education and Prevention, 1,* pp. 141-153, 1989.
70. G. Pappas, *The Magic City: Unemployment in a Working Class Community,* Cornell University Press, Ithaca, New York, 1989.
71. S. Osherson and L. AmaraSingham, The Machine Metaphor in Medicine, in *Social Contexts of Health, Illness, and Patient Care,* E. Mishler et al. (eds.), Cambridge University Press, Cambridge, pp. 218-249, 1981.
72. D. Noble, *America by Design: Science, Technology, and the Rise of Corporate Capitalism,* Alfred A. Knopf, New York, 1979.
73. K. Marx and F. Engels, *On Religion,* Schocken Books, New York, 1967.
74. V. De La Cancela, A Critical Analysis of Puerto Rican Machismo: Implications for Clinical Practice, *Psychotherapy, 23:*2, pp. 291-296, 1986.
75. I. Rosenwaike, Mortality Differentials among Persons Born in Cuba, Mexico, and Puerto Rico Residing in the United States, 1979-1981, *American Journal of Public Health, 77,* pp. 603-606, 1987.
76. H. Abelson and R. Atkinson, *Public Experience with Psychoactive Substances,* Response Analysis Corporation, Princeton, 1975.
77. H. Abelson and P. Fishburne, *Nonmedical Use of Psychoactive Substances,* Response Analysis Corporation, Princeton, 1976.
78. J. Rachal et al., *Final Report: A National Study of Adolescent Drinking Behavior, Attitudes, and Correlates,* Research Triangle Institute, Research Triangle Park, North Carolina, 1975.
79. J. Welte and G. Barnes, Alcohol Use among Adolescent Minority Groups, *Journal of Studies on Alcohol, 48:*4, pp. 329-346, 1987.
80. R. Jessor, Adolescent Problem Drinking: Psychosocial Aspects and Developmental Outcomes, in *Proceedings: NIAAA-WHO Collaborating Center Designation Meeting & Alcohol Research Seminar,* U.S. Department of Health and Human Services, Rockville, Maryland, pp. 104-143, 1984.
81. AIDS Community Research Group, *AIDS: Knowledge. Attitudes and Behavior in an Ethnically Mixed Urban Neighborhood,* Special Report to the Connecticut State Department of Health Services, Hartford, Connecticut, 1988.

82. D. Cahalan, Epidemiology: Alcohol Use in American Society, in *Alcohol, Science and Society Revisited,* E. Gomberg, H. White, and J. Carpenter (eds.), University of Michigan Press, Ann Arbor, pp. 96-118, 1982.
83. R. Caetano, *Drinking Patterns and Alcohol Problems in a National Study of U.S. Hispanics,* paper presented at the National Institute on Alcohol Abuse and Alcoholism Conference, Epidemiology of Alcohol Use among U.S. Ethnic Minorities, Bethesda, Maryland, 1986.
84. C. Mendenhall, P. Gartside, G. Roselle, C. Grossman, R. Weesner, and A. Chedid, Longevity among Ethnic Groups in Alcoholic Liver Disease, *Alcohol and Alcoholism, 24,* pp. 11-19, 1989.
85. H. Gerth and C. W. Mills, *Character and Social Structure,* Harbinger Books, New York, 1964.
86. N. Scheper-Hughes and M. Lock, 'Speaking Truth' to Illness: Metaphors, Reification, and a Pedagogy for Patients, *Medical Anthropology Quarterly, 17,* pp. 137-140, 1986.
87. S. Mintz, The Sensation of Moving, While Standing Still, *American Ethnologist, 16*:4, pp. 786-796, 1989.
88. J. McKinlay, A Case for Refocusing Upstream: The Political Economy of Illness, in *The Sociology of Health and Illness: Critical Perspectives,* P. Conrad and R. Kern (eds.), St. Martin's Press, New York, pp. 484-498, 1986.
89. R. Keesing, Anthropology as Interpretive Quest, *Current Anthropology, 28,* pp. 161-176, 1987.
90. K. Marx, *The 18th Brumaire of Louis Bonaparte,* International Publishers, New York, 1963.

CHAPTER 12

Cure, Care, and Control: Agency and Structure in the Clinical Encounter

In its effort to understand health and human behavior in terms of a political economic perspective, critical medical anthropology confronts a urgent issue: how does this perspective view the role and impact of individual actors in relationship to influential macro-level forces and inegalitarian social structures. The relative importance placed on the behaviors of goal-oriented, decision-making actors (a phenomenon often referred to as "agency") versus the emphasis placed on the weight of macro-level relationships and institutions (i.e., structure) in determining the development of events in any situation has been an issue of controversy and debate in the social sciences. Pappas, a physician and critical medical anthropologist has written, we are "caught in [a] dualism of structure and agency, with competing theoretical perspectives leading to opposing reductionist interpretations" [1, p. 199]. He elaborates on this problem, noting:

> Functionalist and structuralist authors alike have given priority to structure over action. For functionalism, a social reality exists that is not only separate from the lives of individual members of a society but is also dominant over them. The characterization, found in both functionalism and structuralism, of the social whole as separate from the individual presumes various senses in which a society is in some ways external to its members. . . . On the other hand, theories of action have found no way of dealing with or have focused little attention on structural explanations or social causality. In anthropology a number of approaches, including symbolic interactionism, correctly view social life as action accomplished by purposive, knowledgeable actors, but deal with structure as a vague context. The context may be presented formally in ethnographic detail but is not meaningfully integrated with an analysis of action [1, p. 199].

In other words, studies that seek to explain social events while limiting their focus to actions at the local level and to the ability of identifiable actors to make a difference in the immediate flow of occurrences in which they directly participate, fail "to leave sufficient play for the operation of [the] autonomous social forces" often described as the macro-level [2, p. 5]. Conversely, narrow concentration on macro-level processes and relations, such as the impact of market forces, national systems of labor control, or institutional hierarchies, "cannot adequately grasp the level of control which agents are characteristically able to sustain reflexively [i.e., through conscious self-monitoring] over their conduct" [2, p. 5]. Within the broad field of health social sciences (e.g., epidemilogy, health sociology, health psychology, medical anthropology), different disciplines and trends within disciplines have been seduced by either the agential or the structural approaches to understanding. Thus, conventional medical anthropology has a preponderant number of studies in which attention is restricted largely to the micro-level and to what anthropologists claim is the firm ground of directly observable ethnographic reality, while the political economy of health literature has been faulted often for ignoring "the active role played by subjugated peoples, or how those people shape medical systems over time" [3, p. 142].

Because of its emphasis on the importance of structure, the response of actor-oriented researchers has been to assume that critical medical anthropology represents yet another expression of structuralist reductionism. Missed in this interpretation is the consistent emphasis critical medical anthropologists have placed on the analysis of action and actors in political economic context, as seen, for example, in Chapter 5, in our discussion of the nuclear regulatory system in the United States and the challenge to that structure launched by grassroots activists, or in Chapter 10, in our examination of a single life and death in terms of the link between powerful social forces and historic trends on the one hand and personal decisions and local actions on the other. We elaborate on the CMA perspective on the relationship between structure and agency in this chapter with an analysis of patient experience and doctor-patient interactions, topics of enduring concern in medical anthropology.

The frame for our discussion is the contemporary discourse in the medical social sciences about relations in the clinical encounter. One party to this discussion consists of physicians and physician-helpers concerned about "problem patients." Thus, a literature has developed directed at assisting physicians to better understand so as to better control difficult patients. For example, a popular medical school and allied health textbook by Alvin Burstein analyzes the varieties of the clinical role known as the "angry patient." One variant of angry patient, of relevance to several ethnographic cases to be discussed below, which Burstein calls the "controlling patient,'"is typified . . . by his struggle to stay in charge of his own treatment. Hence he may attempt to anticipate his doctor's diagnosis, press for his physician's working hypothesis and then challenge it, quarrel about the appropriateness of the treatment regimen, etc." [4, p. 54]. Why would a patient act, or, to stay within the idiom, "act out" in such a fashion? Burstein tells us, or more precisely tells future physicians, nurses and other health care professionals: "this form of antagonism often reflects a lifelong characteristic pattern of relating to potential helpers, and it springs from a basic distrust of parental figures and their surrogates" [4, p. 54].

In allegiance with this perspective, a major sector of the medical social sciences including parts of medical anthropology, what might be called the biomedical "service sector," has taken as its mission the understanding of patients of diverse cultural, ethnic, or class backgrounds so as to arm physicians with a culturally informed bedside manner. As discussed further in Chapter 14, proponents of this approach argue that to be socially relevant the health social sciences must be clinically useful. While in most cases the service literature consists of simple solicitations for greater sympathy and sensitivity on the part of physicians for the meaning systems and illness behavior patterns of particular populations [e.g., 5-6], there also exist calls for the utilization of cultural information to facilitate patient management and increase compliance [e.g., 7].

Counterpoised to this stance and as such another party to the clinical encounter discussion are those who bemoan the medical monopolization of modern life. In the perspective of this group, which was alluded to in Chapter 1, biomedicine functions as a crippler of personal autonomy and initiative, rendering people impotent to handle their affairs without the aid of a medical crutch. In the words of Ivan Illich, a leading exponent of this view, biomedicine

> creates ill-health by increasing stress, by multiplying disabling dependence, by generating new painful needs, by lowering the levels of tolerance for discomfort or pain, by reducing the leeway that people are wont to concede to an individual when he suffers, and by absolving even the right to self-care [8, p. 41].

Within medical anthropology, this view finds expression in a call for "the development of an anthropological discourse on problematic, non-biological forms of healing in terms of their own meaning-centered and emic frames of reference, and as possible, indeed valid, alternatives to biomedical hegemony . . ." [9, p. 193].

In short, while one set of observers of the clinical encounter, what might be termed the "pro-physician group," is concerned about the dominating patient, the other, the "pro-patient group," focuses its attention on the dominating physician and the dominance of biomedicine generally. Each side recognizes that a key determinant of the clinical episode is power, but who has it and more significantly who *should* have it, are contested. Moreover, neither side has a well developed theory or model of power.

Finally, there is a third position in this debate. It too views power as a key, if not the key, issue, but not just power relations in the microcosm of the clinical encounter or even within the broader boundaries of the medical institution. Adherents of this perspective seek to locate the clinical relationship and the whole medical complex within its encompassing political-economic framework so as to remind us that physicians and patients alike are but two sets of players in a larger social dynamic, a dynamic that can only be understood by incorporating both structure and agency through the examination of, to use Cardoso's phrase, the "internalization of the external" [10, p. 13]. This perspective is the one embraced within critical medical anthropology. It recognizes structure simultaneously as the product of agency and the context that conditions action. Its project is to map the tension-filled intersection of structure and agency in space and time within the health domain. And it seeks to carry out this kind of analysis without retreating in the face of postmodern attacks on approaches that suggest the importance of identifying and understanding social causation [11].

In the contemporary period, the clinical encounter is not merely an arena for the enfeeblement of people as patients, it is, at the same time, a "combat zone of disputes over power and over definitions" [12, p. 9]. These disputes are not best explained, as the pro-physician group would have it, by limiting attention to patient (or even physician) psychology. To restrict analysis of social dynamics to the examination of individual psyches is the social scientific equivalent of executing foot soldiers for major war crimes as if foot soldiers begin, direct, or even fully understand the wars they fight and die in. Similarly, doctor-patient disputes are not insignificant, not mere epiphenomena relative to the real (i.e., structural) business that gets done inside the clinic, as the position of the pro-patient group might imply, just because, as cannot and should not be denied, the physician has the upper hand. To attend solely to the power of the most powerful and thereby loose sight of resistance and struggle by the oppressed is itself an act of unintended expropriation and enfeeblement, and an act of social distortion as well.

THE CLINICAL ENCOUNTER: TWO CASES

We explore these issues by reviewing two cases. The first is situated in the medical domain of obstetrics, which, no pun intended, is a fertile arena for the investigation of the issues discussed above because of the sweeping changes that have occurred in this speciality over the past several years [13]. As Wertz and Wertz have shown, early in its history obstetrics adopted a mechanical model of childbirth, viewing the process as a dangerous procedure regularly necessitating medical intervention [14]. This perspective gained widespread acceptance as male obstetricians came to be the dominant caretakers during maternity and delivery and female midwives were relegated to ever more subordinate and marginal roles. This displacement was achieved, in part, through overt bigotry.

> In the process of creating birth as a medical event, class and race joined gender and economics and contributed to the consolidation of male medical power. Existing midwives, who were predominantly women of the lower classes, many of whom were immigrants and black women, were described as ignorant and dirty and all women were discredited as unsafe. To seal their fate, women were told that if they knew their place, they would not want to compete with physicians, who were mainly men of the upper classes, for to do so would unsex them [15, p. 138].

Although at first obstetricians practiced in patient's home, increasingly the hospital came to be seen as the appropriate site for delivery and, because of the prevalence of hospital infection, "[d]octors had to regard each woman as diseased" [14, p. 128]. By the 1930s, delivery routines were fixed in accordance with the needs of doctors and hospitals. Women were automatically placed in the lithotomy position and their arms strapped down. Anesthetics and analgesics were administered to control women's experience. Episiotomies were standard and forceps were employed in 50 percent of all deliveries. Further, the decision-making input of the mother was increasingly restricted.

> When physicians began defining their own terms for decision making, they continued informing and getting consent from the woman and her family, but by responding decreasingly to the woman's point of view, they began to see the parturient as the antagonist of the fetus. She could not be viewed as objective in such a decision; therefore she should be excluded from it [16, p. 245].

In short order, birth became "the processing of a machine by machines and skilled technicians" [14, p. 165].

In recent years, however, the mechanization of obstetric practice has faced widening challenges. As summarized by DeVries

> It appears as if the trend toward the 'medicalization' of birth, marked by increasing numbers of surgical deliveries and new technological capabilities for intervening and controlling the birth process, has been slowed—if not halted—by a desire on the part of both consumers and professionals to 'humanize' the care given to childbearing women and their families. There has been a flurry of professional and consumer activity based on a concern for "humanized" or 'family centered' care in birthing. . . . The changes made in the medical treatment of childbirth . . . [include] the creation of alternative birth centers which provide 'homey' birthing environments and the establishment of programs to limit the separation of families during birth [17, p. 89].

Has the purported "humanization" of obstetrics pacified the so-called controlling patient? Or, conversely, has it cured the structural iatrogenesis of doctor/patient interactions? In short, has it harmonized "the conflicting paradigms of pregnancy" [18]? Consider the following case.

Case 1

Elaine is a thirty-one-year old, college-educated Caucasian woman who in July 1983 sought medical attention for what she feared might be an ectopic pregnancy. Ectopic pregnancy—the development of a fertilized ovum outside of the uterus, most commonly in a fallopian tube—is a major health problem for women. Although it accounts for one fourth of maternal deaths in the United States [19], and several studies indicate that the frequency of ectopic pregnancy is increasing, recognition of this life-threatening condition is commonly missed by physicians [20-22]. Elaine, was interviewed by Singer for a total of eight hours over the course of five sessions spread throughout the full course of her prenatal care in a prepaid health maintenance organization (HMO) with a recently expanded OB/GYN department.

Five years prior to the events described here, Elaine had suffered a tubal pregnancy and rupture. At the time, she was newly wed and unaware of being pregnant. One evening, after experiencing acute abdominal discomfort, she suddenly collapsed and was rushed by ambulance to a local hospital. During emergency surgery, her right fallopian tube was removed. As she was recuperating, Elaine was told by her physician that she was at-risk for a second ectopic pregnancy, and that the chances this would occur increased with time because of the postoperative internal scarring common patients who have had abdominal surgery. In Elaine's view, the most traumatic aspect of this entire episode was not the immediate threat to her life but the realization that up until that point she had taken her fertility for granted and suddenly it was in question. As a result, and gaining momentum over time, Elaine's self-concept and her view of medicine began to change.

Needing a fuller understanding of her situation, Elaine began to explore the popular women's literature on tubal pregnancy. Contacting the Boston Women's Health Book Collective, the feminist organization that produced a widely read women's health manual [23], she learned that "IUD-associated infection may cause tubal blockage resulting in tubal pregnancy." This particularly angered her because for seven years prior to her tubal rupture she had worn a Lippe's Loop IUD. As she indignantly commented, "When they gave me the IUD, that was a form of butchery. They knew damn well that I'd never had kids before. They knew that my generation of women was a bunch of guinea pigs. . . . They . . . put this device in me that they knew nothing about and for seven years never took the thing out of me. I asked them about taking it out, but they never did. As far as I'm concerned, they didn't even care whether I could have kids."

A vague desire to one day have children now took on new urgency. But Elaine's husband was not ready to have children and continued to refuse for the next three years. As a result of this and other conflicts, their marriage deteriorated and finally dissolved in 1981. Elaine's efforts to conceive resumed two years later, shortly after she was remarried. Not wanting to have children after age thirty-five because she believed there was an increased risk for birth defects or still birth, Elaine felt that her "biological clock" was running out. Her second husband concurred and they began trying to conceive. At about the same time, through his work, her husband joined an HMO that operated its own health center near his work site.

Elaine's first interaction with the OB/GYN department of this health center initiated a string of frustrating encounters that might be best characterized its as an *ectopic* experience. The incongruity between patient and provider attitudes, expectations, and behaviors activated in these encounters can be organized in terms of three issues: *cure* (i.e., adherence to the safest and most effective procedures to ensure the health of the patient), *care* (i.e., sympathetic treatment of the patient), and *control* (i.e., not allowing the patient to participate in and understand her treatment). Elaine's expectations in these encounters were shaped by a variety of factors, including: 1) her socialization into the lay biomedical worldview and her familiarity with the technology and procedures of bourgeois medicine: 2) her exposure the feminist critique of male-dominated medical practice; 3) her fears generated by the previous ectopic pregnancy; 4) her strong desire to have children; and 5) her sense that as a client in a prepaid program she had a contractual right to satisfying health care.

When she first contacted the OB/GYN department, Elaine (correctly) suspected that she was pregnant. Consequently, she expected to be given an appointment to meet with the medical staff, discuss her obstetric and general medical history, receive answers to her numerous questions about her condition, and be given a preliminary examination and routine blood workup. She also recognized that she had certain responsibilities in this situation and had arranged for her medical records to be forwarded to the HMO (although as it turned out, a complete record of her salpingectomy were not sent). She also stopped drinking coffee and alcoholic beverages.

Elaine's initial call to the OB/GYN department was handled by an "advice nurse," an RN whose job is to "answer questions, provide advice and arrange appropriate care of urgent OB/GYN problems" [24, p. 2]. To her surprise, "they wouldn't let me talk to a doctor. They didn't ask me to come in for an appointment. They said, our policy is prevention and unless there is something wrong with you, there is no need for you to see the doctor. As if there was nothing wrong with me!" Elaine was particularly upset by the advice nurse's instruction to come in for a pregnancy blood test two weeks after missing her period, to be followed, if necessary, three weeks latter by an ultrasound evaluation of the location of the developing gestational sac. Adherence to this schedule, she quickly realized, would not have allowed detection of tubal pregnancy until the seventh week, a full week later than the rupture she had experienced during her previous near-fatal ectopic episode.

Consequently, Elaine rejected the nurse's counsel and pressed to speak with a doctor. Instead her call was returned by an OB/GYN nurse practitioner, the occupier of the next rung in the institutional hierarchy, who, after reviewing the medical records that had been forwarded, instructed her to come in for a blood test as soon as she missed her period. Elaine reported that after this telephone conversation she felt "satisfied with what they said, but I still didn't understand why they didn't ask me to come in for an appointment to do a check-up and meet me face-to-face."

One day after missing her period, Elaine went to the health center's lab for an HCG (human chorionic gonadotrophin) blood test. The next day she called the advice nurse and learned that her score was 55, a borderline reading on a scale on which figures under 10 are considered negative for pregnancy and those above 100 are positive. A second blood test was scheduled for three days later. When Elaine called back at the appointed time to receive her second score, it was not available. Several hours later she was told that her first score had been misread and was actually 95 and that her second score was over 200. The misreading of the score reinforced her apprehension about the HMO while, learning that they still did not want her to come in for an examination even though her pregnancy was now confirmed, magnified her uneasiness. The subsequent ultrasound was unable to locate the gestational sac and the radiologist informed her that it was still too early in the pregnancy for successful sonographic visualization. He instructed her to return in a week to ten days. Then to Elaine's surprise, he quickly departed, leaving her with an array of unanswered questions about sonographic efficacy and side effects.

At this juncture, Elaine began to feel quite distressed. She had banked on the ultrasound providing her with a definitive answer and instead she went home empty handed. She stated, "I didn't feel that they knew what they were doing. . . . It was a complete bureaucracy. I go into the lab for a blood test and . . . the guy in the lab doesn't even know when the results will be back . . . this place doesn't know its arm from its leg. Not only do they not know what they are doing, they don't care about me as a patient. I wanted the doctor to give me a full plan of what he intended to do to monitor me. He also should give me his point of view of what should be done . . . but these people didn't even want to talk to me about it."

In response to her dissatisfaction with the medical treatment she was receiving and the mounting anguish she was experiencing as a result, Elaine activated her social support network. Although she did not know any health care professionals personally, she had friends and relatives who did. Her sister's boyfriend was a medical student, a close friend was engaged in a pregnancy research project, and another friend shared an apartment with a nurse. All were called on and supplied Elaine with information about the signs and symptoms of ectopic pregnancy. Additionally, her sister conducted a computer search in the Harvard Medical School library and provided her with a number of articles from medical journals on the subject. Armed with this information, she called the HMO and insisted on an appointment with the obstetrician. At the same time, she suggested that they begin regular HCG monitoring, a recommended procedure because in intrauterine pregnancy HCG levels double every few days while in extrauterine pregnancy scores begin to fall off. The nurse practitioner agreed with this suggestion and scheduled the appropriate tests.

At her appointment with the obstetrician, Elaine was handled by a new nurse practitioner, who wanted a full account of why she had come. Elaine objected because she already had detailed her history to the first nurse practitioner and expected momentarily to retell her tale to the obstetrician. In fact, the obstetrician did not arrive until forty-five minutes after the scheduled appointment (a replication of the radiologist's tardiness) and then, according to Elaine, walked into the examining room and said, "So what's your traumatic story, why are you here?" Elaine reported, "I felt like punching him. He had a very smart alecky attitude, as if there was nothing wrong with me and why should I be so concerned. He sat down in a chair and didn't examine me, didn't examine me the whole time. He said, I don't know why you're so upset and think you are going to have an ectopic." As it eventually became clear, the obstetrician did not know that Elaine had suffered a previous tubal rupture because he had only been sent a brief and somewhat inaccurate summary of her medical records. Even after she told him about her full obstetric history, however, Elaine felt that the doctor still seemed unconcerned and retained a condescending tone.

Elaine's next HCG score was lost, but a subsequent test revealed that her plasma HCG levels were rising rapidly. Finally, during the fifth week of her pregnancy, a second ultrasound showed normal intrauterine implantation, and her first internal examination was scheduled. This encounter, in Elaine's view, continued the previous pattern. She commented, "This physician hardly talked to me. He came in and didn't introduce himself. I was feeling lousy because of morning sickness and he never even asked me how I was. I was treated like an object. He rushed through it. When he did the exam, he didn't tell me why he was doing what he was doing, he just did it. I had to push him to tell me. Every piece of information I got out of him, I had to push for."

At the end of this examination, Elaine was instructed to return for check-ups once a month. By approximately the thirtieth week of her pregnancy, she began to be concerned because she recorded no weight gain in between two clinical visits. She explained, "I read that I should be gaining but nobody said anything to me about the fact that I wasn't gaining. So I asked and the nurses said I should be gaining. So I asked why they didn't seem concerned that I wasn't gaining weight. They decided I should come back in two weeks so they could check my weight again. This time I put on some weight but my uterus didn't grow. So they said come back in a week. That time my uterus had grown, but I hadn't gained any weight. The next time I gained weight, but my uterus didn't grow. When I pressed and asked the obstetrician who examined me that time, she casually said, "Oh, you might have interuterine growth retardation" and she began to leave the examining room. Alarmed, I asked what that was and she said, "I'm sorry, we only have seven minutes per patient." Then she paused a moment and left. I was shocked. I thought she was saying my baby might be retarded because of insufficient nutrition and she wouldn't stay to explain. I went back to work in tears. I called my childbirth educator from the Lamaze classes and she explained what interuterine growth retardation meant."

After several additional examinations, it was determined that the fetus was developing normally, although Elaine was told that she probably would have a small baby. In fact, she delivered a full-term, healthy baby with above average length and weight.

Asked to evaluate her experience with the HMO not long after her baby was born, Elaine replied, I've had to push and push and push for every single response I've gotten out of the health care system. If it hadn't been that I told them I was concerned, that I wanted to be monitored, they would never have done anything. I don't trust the health care system at all. I feel I have to constantly be on top of the situation, reading as much as I can, pushing them to see me. I feel I can't stop for a single moment being on top of the situation. It occurred to me that the word patient must come from the word patience, because that's what patients are expected to have."

Case 2

While the details of the case reported above are particular, and have special reference to patients who share Elaine's social class and educational background, there is sufficient literature on the subject of doctor-patient interaction to suggested that the general pattern described here is not unique. Millman, for example, based on a two year study of daily life in several private, university affiliated hospitals, reports the following case that includes features that are notably similar to the one described above [25]. The case involves a thirty-five-year-old female patient, a biochemist by profession, told by several doctors that her recurrent and sometimes excruciating abdominal pains were not serious and did not require treatment. Only when she appeared at her doctor's office with signs of jaundice were her complaints "no longer . . . passed off as the fabrications of what doctors imagined to be a hysterical women" [25, p. 138]. Diagnostic x-rays suggested a problem in her hepato-biliary system and her doctor decided that a liver biopsy was called for. When the patient suggested further tests to be sure, "Her doctor responded . . . by informing her that *he* was the doctor and *she* the patient, and that he was practically certain that she suffered from chronic active hepatitis, a very serious disease, and that she had better not delay the procedure since only a liver biopsy could confirm the diagnosis" [25, p. 139]. As Millman reports, the biopsy was performed "with the customary joking of her physician" [25, p. 139].

Over the course of the next several days, the patient was unable to reach her doctor to learn about her test results. Looking up chronic hepatitis in a medical book, she was startled to learn that the disease had no cure and usually led to death within a few years after diagnosis. Continued efforts to learn her test results proved futile, as her doctor had gone on a long week-end holiday. Upon his return, however, her doctor proved vague about the biopsy results although he informed her that her most recent blood tests indicated that her liver function had returned to normal, suggesting a stone in the bile duct rather than hepatitis. The woman pressed again to learn the results of her biopsy and the doctor promised that he would call with the results that evening. He did not call and his answering service repeatedly told the woman he was unavailable.

After surgery, the woman asked her physician if she could see her chart to learn what the biopsy had discovered. Although her doctor agreed to let her see the chart, she was rebuffed when she attempted to review it at the nurse's station:

> Obviously annoyed with the patient's assertiveness, the nurse smugly informed her that even though her medical physician had agreed, when her surgeon had been informed of her request to see the chart he had left word that she was not to be allowed to look at it [25, p. 142].

When she queried her surgeon about his objection, he insisted that it was against hospital policy. She then stressed that she would like to know all of the facts pertinent to her condition. The surgeon responded,

> Well, I'm sorry, but it is not a good idea and it wouldn't mean anything to you anyway. You wouldn't understand anything you were reading and then you'd have a million questions [25, p. 143].

When she sternly retorted that she would not ask him any questions, the surgeon finally relented.

> Hurriedly, she searched through the record for the report of her biopsy. She discovered that it was only a single line written on an otherwise blank sheet of paper. It merely read: 'no analysis, Specimen Insufficient For Diagnosis'. . . . The evasiveness of the doctors was finally explained to the patient. No one had wanted her to learn that the procedure had been a total waste [25, p. 144].

THE MEDICAL ENCOUNTER IN
CRITICAL PERSPECTIVE

From the pro-physician perspective presented earlier, the two women whose cases have been presented would probably be seen as typical "controlling patients," and apparently were seen as such by their respective physicians judging by their reported comments to the women. As Elaine's case suggests, the starting assumption of her physician was that she presumed to know too much, challenging thereby the medical premise that assigns the authority to speak about birth to the medical profession. Jordan, who has studied birthing practices in several societies, notes with reference to the United States, obstetrics is organized around the idea that

> what the woman knows and displays, by virtue of her bodily experience, has no status. Within the official scheme of things, she has nothing to say that matters in the actual management of her birth. Worse, her knowledge is nothing but a problem for her and the [medical] staff. What she knows emerges not as a

contribution to the store of data relevant for making decisions, but rather as something to be cognitively suppressed and behaviorally managed . . . [because] authoritative knowledge is privileged, the prerogative of the physician, without whose official certification of the woman's state the birth cannot proceed [26, p. 157].

Among other things, this situation reflects bourgeois medicine's disregard for women's ability to diagnose their own pregnancies [26]. Consequently, in established medical practice, the variety of signs and symptoms of pregnancy that are open to women's immediate experience, so-called presumptive indications such as breast changes, headaches, nausea, alteration of the mucous membranes, are assigned a low ranking as medical diagnostic criteria. As summarized in the *Handbook of Obstetrics and Gynecology,* "there is no subjective evidence of pregnancy which can be accepted as diagnostic" [27, p. 45]. Evidence that requires the utilization of medical instruments, and is therefore accessible to the physician but outside the patient's awareness, by contrast, is accorded a high ranking. In a telephone survey of obstetricians and gynecologists, while posing as a patient seeking an abortion, Jordan found that

> The policy of each and every physician was to require a positive pregnancy test before any further action would be considered. Moreover, the test turned out to be a nonnegotiable requirement, even if I insisted that I knew I was pregnant, citing the classic (presumptive) symptoms and pointing to my experience with previous pregnancies [26, p. 8].

Empirical investigation by Jordan, however, found that women's competence in diagnosing their own pregnancy is quite good [28]. This research finding not-withstanding, physicians respond very strongly to self-diagnosis because "it threatens the very foundation of their authority. This dimension of of the doctor-patient relationship is, for most physicians, an absolutely 'nonnegotiable' item" [29, p. 1401].

Physicians report having their greatest difficulty in this area with women patients. In one survey, over 450 general practitioners described their most troubling and time consuming patients as distrustful and demanding women [30]. One approach doctors take with these patients is simply to ignore what they have to say. Graham and Oakley report that of the 677 statements made by women patients during prenatal care visits to a London clinic, 12 percent concerned the experience of pain or discomfort which the doctor ignored or dismissed as medically insignificant [31]. Prenatal patients interviewed in the latter study [31, p. 65] reported the following negative experiences in their encounters with obstetricians:

1. not feeling like they are allowed to ask questions;
2. not receiving a sufficient explanation of the medical treatment they are receiving or the progress of their pregnancy;
3. feeling like they are seen as ignorant by physicians;
4. feeling like they have to see too many different doctors;
5. feeling rushed as if they were on an assembly line.

That physicians are taught during their medical school training to view women's health problems as uninteresting, their medical history relating skills as underdeveloped, their personalities as highly emotional, and their symptoms as commonly reflecting nondisease has been suggested by several health care researchers and medical school textbook evaluators as we noted in Chapter 1 [13, 32-35].

In the liberal critique of bourgeois medicine formulated by the pro-patient group, we have in the cases presented above clear-cut examples of a "high-tech," irrationally bureaucratic, objectifying, infantilizing, expert-controlling medical system acting insensitively to the care-needs of a oppressed women patients. This control is described as having "reached the proportions of an epidemic" and as having itself become "a major threat to health" [8, p. 3]. The most socially pernicious consequence of professional dominance is that patients become addicted to dependency and are transformed thereby from independent actors and decision-makers into passive medical consumers. Especially affected by the onerous aspects of the bourgeois medical system are women. In the homocentric understanding of health and health care developed by adherents of the pro-patient view "men act while women suffer" [36, p. 448].

Yet the words and actions of the two women whose cases have been described in this chapter reveal that the image of an active, aggressive male physician in control of health care, and a female patient that is a passive victim, manipulated and dominated, is faulty. Martin presents additional support for this view, describing incidents of women in delivery unstrapping external fetal monitors when doctors and nurses leave the labor room or ignoring doctor's orders and taking showers during labor [34]. On the one hand, it is clear that whatever their criticisms of medicine, a central concern of these women is a demand for more and better expert attention and not for emancipation from medical enslavement. Like most of us, these women are caught up in the medicalization of modern life. No less than physicians and nurses, they are swayed by the power and hegemony of bourgeois medicine. Thus, there is a protest over "what physicians do [or fail to do], not what medicine is" [36, p. 426].

But this clearly does not mean that these women are passive or impotent. Rather, they are both active and resourceful in addition to being willing and able to confront physicians and to defend their rightful interests. Thus, theirs are not one-sided tales of powerless pawns, pushed, probed, and prodded by domineering physicians. Instead, we have accounts of the gathering of intelligence, the mobilizing of allies, the formulating of strategies, and the pressing of demands; in short, narratives of struggle and combat in the very heart of physician-controlled territory. Indeed, Martin, in her discussion of women's resistence to the biomedicalization of birth, notes that "Childbirth activist literature can be seen (and sometimes describes itself) as guides to 'self-defense in the hospital,' and the methods women have developed are strikingly similar to those that workers have tried in the workplace" [34, p. 140]. In other words, as these cases reported here suggest, social process in the medical arena is not narrowly determined by the unrestrained will and might of potent oppressors or by indomitable institutional structures. Rather, it is a *product* of an ongoing clash between those best served and those least served by the prevailing medical system, and between those most in control of and those least in control of medical knowledge, procedures, locations, and technology.

Giddens stresses that the concept of "agency" should not be used to label the mere fact that people carrying out behaviors with intentions; that is, that they are guided as they do things by the wish to achieve particular ends. Rather, he uses the term to refer to "their capacity of doing those things in the first place" [2, p. 9]. He writes,

Agency concerns events of which an individual is the perpetrator, in the sense that the individual could, at any phase in a given sequence of conduct, have acted differently. Whatever happened would not have happened if that individual had not intervened [2, p. 9].

Additionally, he urges that we "not conceive of the structures of domination built into social institutions as in some way grinding out 'docile bodies' who behave like the automata suggested by objectivist social science" [12, p. 16].

Through her pressing for closer monitoring, Elaine was able to receive medical services that could have detected an ectopic pregnancy early in its course and as a result have saved her life. Similarly, in the case described by Millman, a patient was able to overcome institutional policy and gain access to medical information that could have proved important to her health. Neither woman acted as a pre-determined "docile body." In both cases, the course of events in the clinical encounter was influenced by agency and contested action within a given conditioning structure. It is for this reason that in our analyses the starting point for many questions must be the structurally conditioned activity and ideas of real individuals and groups [37].

But what of this structure? For truly neither woman got quite what she wanted in the way that she wanted it. Both felt the counterpress of a resistant force, one that incorporated but was far larger than the immediate setting of the events described, one that crosscut and united both cases even though they occurred in different times and places. The behavior of all of the participants, including patients, doctors, nurses, and others, was in no small way shaped by what McKinlay has labeled the changing political and economic context of the patient-physician encounter [38]. Seen in this light, everything from the seemingly indifferent attitude of the physicians, the bureaucratic and assembly line character of treatment, the resistance to patient acquisition of adequate information, the increasingly complex medical division of labor, the labeling of concerned and questioning patients as demanding or controlling, the use of the telephone or closed files as protective barriers, the transformation of prevention into a cost-cutting gimmick, the revolt of the patient, the demystification of medical knowledge, and the blossoming of the health maintenance organization are all products of the expansion of the logic and structure of corporate capitalism into the medical domain. As aptly summarized by Navarro

We find that the major conflict in the health sector replicates the conflict in the overall system. And that conflict is primarily not between the providers and the consumers, but between those that have the dominant influence in the health system (the corporate class and upper middle class) who represent less than 20 percent of our population and control most of the health institutions, and the majority of our population (lower-middle class and working class) . . . who have no control whatsoever over either the production or consumption of those health services [39, p. 119].

The HMO as a type of medical institution provides an illustration of the way in which the health care industry, to use Navarro's phrase "is administered but not controlled by the medical profession" [39, p. 118]. The HMO is a product of the often-described but still unresolved financial crisis in health care, created as a market-oriented approach to self-regulation and cost-cutting, and designed with the hope of forestalling a government imposed national health care system. In the words of the leading physician advocate of HMOs:

> The emergence of a free-market economy could stimulate a course of change in the health industry that would have some of the classical aspects of the industrial revolution—conversion to larger units of production, technological innovation, division of labor, substitution of capital for labor, vigorous competition, and profitability as the mandatory condition of survival [40, p. 350].

An added rationale for the prepaid health maintenance strategy was the emergence of an alleged alliance of interests between providers and consumers. Explained Ellwood, "Since the economic incentive of the contracting parties are identical [i.e., cutting costs], both would have an interest in maintaining health" [40, p. 351]. Seemingly, the HMO then is not only a solution to skyrocketing health costs (based on the understanding that maintaining "health" is cheaper than restoring it), but also a corrective to professional dominance and patient pacification. Both are said to be joined by the dollar in a prevention-partnership.

But things have not worked out quite as harmoniously as intended, for, human agency notwithstanding, many of the consequences of action are neither planned or expected. Patient complaints about HMOs are legion: physicians are inaccessible, waiting periods for appointments are protracted, and treatment is rushed, impersonal, and fragmented [41]. In the evaluation of the Health Policy Advisory Center, HMOs take the profit motivation of fee-for-service medicine and and turn it on its head: "Whereas fee-for-service doctors and hospitals make more money by seeing more patients, performing more operations and hospitalizing people longer, HMOs increase their net income by doing less" [41, p. 361]. What fee-for-service and HMO medicine have in common, however, is that service provision is driven by profit-seeking rather than patient need.

Importantly, HMO doctors and other care takers have their complaints too, and these are not just about the increasingly demanding patients. At Kaiser-Permanente, a growing HMO program founded and largely controlled by a multinational industrial corporation, physicians lament management's emphasis on the quantity of subscribers over the quality of treatment: "Some doctors feel their schedules are so rushed and inflexible as to preclude delivering adequate, humane care" [41, p. 379]. Thus one of the nurse practitioners involved in Elaine's case confirmed that providers are instructed to limit routine clinical encounters to seven minutes per patient. This caregiver complained that the seven minute rule is unfair for patients and stressful for doctors and nurses.

In sum, the physician-patient encounter/confrontation is played out on a stage increasingly owned and operated by a medical industrial complex of profit-seeking corporations [42-44]. As Lazarus emphasizes, "Decisions concerning procedures that physicians once controlled are now dictated by private insurers, federal programs, and hospital administrations" [35, p. 4]. Of the nine individual sitting on the Advisory Council of the HMO referred to in Elaine's case, for example, at least six represented industrial corporations, retail conglomerates, insurance companies, and banks. As the logic of business and commodity production become dominant, patients and physicians are left to squabble like grocery clerks and customers over a mispriced can of corn. Here is the classic example of health and healing succumbing to the idiom of business, reaffirming Taussig's observation that "Ours is the culture of business which put business as the goal of culture" [12, p. 11]. In this sense, the key ideological issue for medical social science research is not the cultural construction of clinical reality" as Kleinman [7] suggests, nor even, "the clinical construction of culture" as Taussig [12] asserts, but the *hegemonic capitalist construction of medical and non-medical reality*. It is this social constructed reality, forged in the larger arena of capitalist production, reproduction, and bureaucratic control, that multiplies the conditions for ectopic encounters in the biomedical setting.

Contradictions in this constructed reality, and in the structures created directly and indirectly by capital, set the parameters and define the issues of clinical combat in bourgeois medicine. Structure, in this sense, sets the context for the expression of agency by participating actors. In and through their actions actors make their world and their history, but, as Marx reminds us, "they do not make it just as they please, they do not make it under circumstances chosen by themselves" [45, p. 15]. This is true in two senses. First, much of the world, as actors know it, is the conventional reality of their society. Anthropology commonly employs the term culture to label this established and shared set of understandings. However, traditional anthropological definitions have overplayed the shared dimension of culture while underplaying the ways in which the constant reinforcement of official, naturalized truths by central social institutions (i.e., hegemony) helps to reproduce established social inequalities. Second, social structures tend to constrain choice and action, by delimiting the range of thinkable ideas and conceivable behaviors.

Here lies an important distinction between the pro-patient critique of medicine and the broader critique of critical medical anthropology. While the former is concerned with the *de-medicalization* of social life and experience, the latter takes as its objective the *re-socialization* of medical ideology and practice. The social importance of the doctor-patient relationship lies in the inherent asymmetry of the interaction. Inavoidably, the medical encounter reproduces, while revealing contradictions in, the wider structure of class, ethnic, and gender stratification. Through the encounter, and the expression given thereby to underlying contradictions, medicine is established as both an arena of social conflict and a structure of social control. Control work is achieved, in part, through value legitimation.

> [A] feature of the authority-subordination relationship that characterizes doctor-patient interaction is the tendency for doctors to impose their values on patients. . . .
> The outright imposition of the doctor's values on the patient can easily extend to non-medical areas as well [46, p. 31].

But control in whose interest? Whose values does medicine reinforce? Waitzkin comments:

> From a position of relative dominance, doctors can make ideological statements
> that convey the symbolic trappings of science. These messages reinforce the
> hegemonic ideology that emanates from other institutions—the family, educa-
> tional system, mass media, and so forth—and that pervade society. The same
> messages tend to direct a client's behavior into safe, acceptable, and nondisrup-
> tive channels . . . [and] . . . thus may help legitimate and reproduce class structure
> and current relations of economic production. . . . What can be done tends to
> encourage coping and accommodation. Conscious recognition of . . . choices and
> possible alternatives seldom occurs. Thus in sincerely seeking to help patients,
> the health professional becomes a 'helping agent' for the very structures
> which produce the social conditions responsible for much patient distress [47,
> pp. 342-343].

When the patient is a woman, as in the two cases presented in this chapter, the
social control functions of medicine involve reinforcing ideologies concerning
women's ability to handle their emotions and to make rationale decisions, as well as
"ideologies of women's appropriate role in work and the family" [48, p. 120]. As a
result, the "ideological impact of the medical encounter tends to be conservative"
[48, p. 142]. So too, much health social science including medical anthropology. By
seeking to limit analysis to the medical arena and thereby interpreting the medical
bureaucracy or some other institutional defect as the ultimate cause of most of the
failures and contradictions of health care, the health social science professional
becomes a helping agent for the very structures that help produce the problems they
seek to eliminate from the health care system. For example, the obstetric reforms of
recent years, reforms designed to "humanize" or "debureaucratize" childbirth, have
maintained, and possibly even furthered professional (and through them, corporate)
dominance over the birthing process [49]. Argues DeVries

> Although the alternative birth center provides a home-like environment for birth,
> its location in the hospital reduces client control. In the hospital the client is a
> guest of the practitioner and is less able to control or direct her care. . . . Patterns
> of interaction between hospital medical personnel and their clients remain essen-
> tially unchanged in the alternative birth center [17, p. 99].

As Davis-Floyd emphasizes, the humanistic approach in obstetrics now "is part of the
technological model" rather than an opposition to it [50, p. 309]. Further, Sargent and
Stark, in their Texas study of childbirth education classes, found that even this lay
movement, initiated to further humanize modern birthing, encourages participants
"to accept interventions at delivery without challenge and in general to accept
hospital policy" [51, p. 49].

A deeper message transmitted in childbirth classes, in clinical encounters, in
medical schools, and elsewhere in society is acceptance of the beneficence of the
existing structure and thus the beneficence of power as constituted in society. While
contradictions within structures (e.g., the contradiction between profit-making and
sensitive, effective health care) generate challenges to those structures, resistance is
constrained by redundant hegemonic messages confirming the givenness, indeed the
naturalness, of the existing social order. These messages are expressions of the

"dominant system of meanings and values, which are not merely abstract but which are organized and lived" [52, p. 38]. Consequently, calls for health care reform that are concerned only with rising medical costs, unequal distribution of treatment access, the impersonal character of care, or even the extension of medicine into new realms of social and bodily experience, that do not consider as well the role of medicine in social control and social reproduction, overlook fundamental issues, perhaps the most fundamental issues, in the health domain.

Herein, lies the shortcoming of Good's assertions about the nature of medical practice. He writes

> Surely there are occasions when physicians, some even knowingly, 'wage war' on the poor, acting as agents of the state and corporate interests, duping the poor with scientific labels and placebo drugs which only serve to mystify, or even worse carrying out medical experimentation disguised by lies or silience. But equally sure am I that these occasions serve badly as the analytic prototype for understanding medical practice [53, p. 60]

Why are repeated reports of discriminatory treatment of the poor across medical specialties and medical conditions not seen as normative in biomedicine? How is it that physicians act as agents of the state or corporate interests only on occasion? Why are physician consistent attempts to dominate medical knowledge not seen as prototypical? The answer to all of these questions lies in a failure to look beyond biomedicine's areas of clinical efficacy to its larger contribution to social control and social reproduction.

One final question is raised. Thus far, the argument has been made that what transpires in the medical encounter (and thus the nature of medicine itself) is not determined, so to speak, from above, but rather is a product of interaction (including both conflict and accommodation) between structure and agency under a given set of historic and cultural conditions. But what of fundamental social change (i.e., structural change), how does agency figure into that? Stephen Jay Gould, whose theory of punctuated equilibrium in biology has helped to throw open to question Charles Darwin's assumption that natural selection acts slowly through the accumulation of slight, successive variations and without sudden or sweeping modifications, has summarized a punctuated model of society in the following words:

> modern punctuationalism—especially in its application to the vagaries of human history—emphasizes the concept of contingency: the unpredictability of the nature of future stability, and the power of contemporary events and personalities to shape and direct the actual path taken among myriad possibilities. Contingency may provoke more anxiety in its failure to specify an outcome, but it surely embodies more hope in the power granted to people over their own futures. We are not pawns in a grand chess game played by inexorable natural (and social) laws, but effective rooks, knights, bishops, kings, and queens on a revolving board of alterable history with no set outcome [54, p. 21].

In his effort to be hopeful, Gould may overstate somewhat our effectiveness as actors to create a desirable history. It may be more accurate, if less inspiring, to say that history, like a game of chess, is the unintended outcome of the mix and clash of opposed and unequally empowered intentions and interests within a given frame of historic potential. History is contingent, but it is hardly the outcome of willed intentions.

REFERENCES

1. G. Pappas, Some Implications for the Study of the Doctor-Patient Interaction: Power, Structure, and Agency in the Works of Howard Waitzkin and Arthur Kleinman, *Social Science and Medicine, 30*:20, pp. 199-205, 1990.
2. A. Giddens, *The Constitution of Society,* University of California Press, Berkeley, 1984.
3. L. Morgan, Dependency Theory in the Political Economy of Health: An Anthropological Critique, *Medical Anthropology, 1*:2, pp. 131-154, 1987.
4. A. Burstein, The Angry Patient, in *Psychosocial Basis Of Medical Practice*, G. Bowden and A. Burstein (eds.), Williams and Williams, Baltimore, 1979.
5. A. Harwood, *Ethnicity and Medical Care,* Harvard, Cambridge, Massachusetts, 1981.
6. D. Davis, Medical Misinformation: Communication between Outport Newfoundland Women and their Physicians, *Social Science and Medicine, 18*:3, pp. 273-278, 1984.
7. A. Kleinman, Concepts and a Model for the Comparison of Medical Systems as Cultural Systems, *Social Science and Medicine, 12*, pp. 85-93, 1978.
8. I. Illich, *Medical Nemesis: The Expropriation of Health,* Calder and Boyars, London, 1975.
9. N. Scheper-Hughes, Three Propositions for a Critically Applied Medical Anthropology, *Social Science and Medicine, 30*:2, pp. 189-197.
10. F. Cardoso, Dependency and Development in Latin America, University of California Press, Berkeley, 1979.
11. A. Southhall, On Perilous Ideas, *Current Anthropology, 35*:2, pp. 174-175, 1994.
12. M. Taussig, Reification and the Consciousness of the Patient, *Social Science and Medicine, 14B*, pp. 3-13, 1980.
13. R. Hahn, Divisions of Labor: Obstetrician, Woman, and Society in Williams Obstetrics, 1903-1985, *Medical Anthropology Quarterly. 1*:3, pp. 256-282, 1987.
14. R. Wertz and D. Wertz, *Lying In: A Natural History of Childbirth in America,* Schocken Books, New York, 1979.
15. S. Fisher, *In the Patient's Best Interest: Women and the Politics of Medical Decisions,* Rutgers University Press, New Brunswick, New Jersey, 1988.
16. J. Leavitt, The Growth of Medical Authority: Technology and Morals in Turn-of the-Century Obstetrics, *Medical Anthropology Quarterly, 1*:3, pp. 230-255, 1987.
17. R. DeVries, "Humanizing" Childbirth: The Discovery and Implementation of Bonding Theory, *International Journal of Health Services, 14*:1, pp. 89-104, 1984.
18. J. Comaroff, Conflicting Paradigms of Pregnancy: Managing Ambiguity in Antenatal Encounters, in *Medical Encounters: Experience of Illness and Treatment,* A. Davis and G. Horobin (eds.),Goom Helm, London, 1977.
19. F. Laing and R. Jeffrey, Ultrasound Evaluation of Ectopic Pregnancy, *Radiologic Clinics of North America, 20*:2, pp. 383-396, 1982.
20. A. Helvacioglu, E. Long, and S. Yang, Ectopic Pregnancy: An Eight-Year Review, *Journal of Reproductive Medicine, 22*, pp. 87-92, 1982.
21. J. Hallat, Repeat Ectopic Pregnancy: a Study of 123 Consecutive Cases, *Annual of Obstetrics and Gynecology, 122*, pp. 520-524, 1974.

22. J. Breen, A 21 Year Survey of 654 Ectopic Pregnancies, *American Journal of Obstetrics and Gynecology, 106,* pp. 1004-1018, 1970.
23. Boston Women's Health Collective, *The New Our Bodies, Ourselves,* Touchstone, New York, 1984.
24. B. Snyder, BB/GYN Department Provides Growing Number of Services, *Planning for Health, 3:*1, p. 2, 1984.
25. M. Millman, *The Unkindest Cut: Life in the Backrooms of Medicine,* Morrow Quill, New York, 1977.
26. B. Jordan, *Birth in Four Cultures,* Waveland Press, Prospect Heights, Illinois, 1993.
27. R. Benson, *Handbook of Obstetrics and Gynecology,* Lange Medical Publications, Los Altos, 1971.
28. B. Jordan, The Self-Diagnosis of Early Pregnancy: An Investigation of Lay Competence, *Medical Anthropology, 1:*2, pp. 1-38, 1977.
29. D. Stewart and T. Sullivan, Illness Behavior and the Sick Role in Chronic Illness, *Social Science and Medicine, 61,* pp. 1401-1414, 1982.
30. G. Stimpson, General Practitioners, "Trouble" and Types of Patients, in *Sociology of National Health Service,* M. Stacy (ed.), University of Keele, Keele, Great Britain, 1982.
31. H. Graham and A. Oakley, Competing Ideologies of Reproduction: Medical and Maternal Perspectives on Pregnancy, in *Women, Health and Reproduction,* H. Roberts (ed.), London, Routledge, pp. 50-75, 1981.
32. J. Weaver and S. Garrett, Sexism and Racism in the American Health Care Industry: a Comparative Analysis, *International Journal of Health Service, 8:*4, pp. 677-703, 1978.
33. M. Singer, A. Arnold, M. Fitzgerald, L. Madden, and C. Von Legat, Hypoglycemia: A Controversial Illness in U.S. Society, *Medical Anthropology, 8:*1, pp. 1-35, 1984.
34. E. Martin, *The Woman in the Body,* Beacon Press, Boston, 1987.
35. E. Lazarus, What Do Women Want?: Issues of Choice, Control, and Class in Pregnancy and Childbirth, *Medical Anthropology Quarterly, B:*l, pp. 25-46, 1994.
36. E. Stark, Doctors in Spite of Themselves: The Limits of Radical Health Criticism, *International Journal of Health Services, 12:*3, pp. 419-457, 1982.
37. W. Roseberry, *Anthropologies and Histories,* Rutgers University Press, New Brunswick, New Jersey, 1989.
38. J. McKinlay, The Changing Political and Economic Context of the Physician-Patient Encounter, in *The Doctor-Patient Relationship in the Changing Health Scene,* E. Gallagher (ed.), U.S. Department of Health, Education and Welfare, Washington, D.C., pp. 155-188, 1976.
39. V. Navarro, *Medicine Under Capitalism,* Prodist, New York, 1976.
40. P. Ellwood, N. Anderson, J. Billings, R. Carlson, E. Hoagberg, and W. McClure, Health Maintenance Strategy, in *Prognosis Negative,* Vintage, New York, pp. 347-352, 1976.
41. J. Carnoy, L. Coffee, and L. Koos, Corporate Medicine: The Kaiser Health Plan, in *Prognosis Negative,* D. Kotelchuck (ed.), Vintage, New York, pp. 363-386, 1976.
42. P. Starr, *The Social Transformation of American Medicine,* Basic Books, New York, 1981.
43. S. Wohl, *The Medical Industrial Complex,* Harmony, New York, 1984.
44. H. Waitzkin, *The Second Sickness,* Free Press, New York, 1983.
45. K. Marx, *The 18th Brumaire of Louis Bonaparte,* International Publishers, New York, 1963 (original 1869).
46. M. Glasser and G. Pelto, *The Medical Merry-Go-Round,* Redgrave, Pleasantville, New York, 1980.
47. H. Waitzkin, The Micropolitics of Medicine: A Contextual Analysis, *International Journal of Health Service, 14:*3, pp. 339-378, 1984.

48. H. Waitzkin, *The Politics of Medical Encounters,* Yale University Press, New Haven, 1991.
49. B. Rothman, Awake and Aware, or False Consciousness: The Cooptation of Childbirth Reform in America, in *Alternatives to Medical Control of Childbirth,* S. Momalis (ed.), University of Texas Press, Austin, pp. 150-180, 1981.
50. R. Davis-Floyd, Obstetric Training as a Rite of Passage, *Medical Anthropology Quarterly, 1*:3, pp. 288-318, 1987.
51. C. Sargent and N. Stark, Childbirth Education and Childbirth Models: Parental Perspectives on Control, Anesthesia, and Technological Intervention in Birth Process, *Medical Anthropology Quarterly, 3*:1, pp. 36-5, 1989.
52. R. Williams, *Problems in Materialism and Culture,* Verso, London, 1980.
53. B. Good, *Medicine, Rationality, and Experience: An Anthropological Experience,* Cambirdge University Press, Cambridge, 1994.
54. S. Gould, Life in a Punctuation, *Natural History, 101*:10, pp. 10-21, 1992.

Section F:

Directions

CHAPTER 13

How Critical Can Clinical Anthropology Be?

Despite the fact that some believe that critical medical anthropology has split into two contending camps, the so-called political economy/world systems theorists and the Foucaultian post structuralists (or radical phenomenonologists) [1], both approaches recognize the need to examine the impact of power relations on health status, health care, and human distress in a broad range of social settings. In keeping with critical medical anthropology's attempt to establish macro-micro connections, most clinical anthropologists recognize that patients' and physicians' explanatory models (EMs) are shaped by "large-scale external factors" [2, p. 27]. Yet, in reality, they generally eschew detailed analyses of such connections and focus their attention upon aspects of the physician-patient relationship. Nonetheless, some clinical anthropologists are attempting to incorporate the critical perspective in their analyses of the social, psychological, and cognitive dynamics of the clinical setting. The most notable effort along these lines is a 1990 symposium of "Social Science and Medicine," guest edited by Anne L. Wright and Thomas M. Johnson titled "Critical Perspectives in Clinically Applied Medical Anthropology." Earlier drafts of most of the papers in this symposium were presented in a session at the 1987 American Anthropological Association Meeting. In both their session and symposium, Wright and Johnson attempted to synthesize critical medical anthropology and clinical anthropology. They argue:

> Our goal was to explore how work in clinical settings could promote our understanding of the larger political and economic forces in health, illness, and critical care and to begin to define how a focus on macro-level phenomena can be made clinically relevant. Rather than merely asking those colleagues of the 'critical' persuasion to make their work 'clinically relevant,' and in so doing implicitly criticize their perspectives, we hoped that our analyses might assist in the development of theory regarding the political economy of health by using live clinical data to explore the relationships between practice and theory, ideology and politics [3, p. V].

While some of the contributors to both the session and the symposium strived to demonstrate connections between political-economic structures and clinical encounters, as Baer pointed out in his role as a discussant at the former and in the latter, others operated with a considerably more restricted conception of the critical perspective within medical anthropology [4].

Nevertheless, as Wright and Johnson recognize, ultimately a truly critical medical anthropology will need to combine theory and social action into a unified endeavor that aims to liberate human beings in all societies from political-economic structures that exploit and oppress them. Given its applied orientation, clinical anthropology contains the potential to contribute to this endeavor. Yet, most clinical anthropologists find themselves in the dilemma of being expected by the biomedical profession and medical institutions to serve as cultural interpreters rather than critics of existing health care arrangements and the larger political-economic structures within which they are embedded. Given these constraints, we explore the question as to how critical can clinical anthropology or applied clinically medical anthropology be.

In the first section of this chapter, we discuss various conceptions of clinical anthropology that have developed since the initial appearance of this subfield of medical anthropology. We then argue that the expectations that physcans and health administrators impose upon medical anthropologists have contributed to the development of a conservative orientation within clinical anthropology. We must ask how easily will health policy makers, hospital administrators, and physicians take to a critical clinical anthropology that challenges the hierarchical and sexist nature of bourgois medicine, the non-clinical functions of medicine, the economic organization, the role of medicine as moral regulation, and the reductionist bourgeouis medical model. We also examine barriers to the development of a critical clinical anthropology. Finally, we suggest some potential strategies that critical medical anthropologists, whether they are employed in academic or applied positions, may pursue in merging theory and social action.

CONCEPTIONS OF CLINICAL ANTHROPOLOGY

While medical anthropologists such as Otto Von Mering have been working in clinical settings since the early 1950s, Johnson maintains that the term "clinical anthropology" was coined around 1979 [5]. Prior to this, however, various overviews of what emerged by the late 1960s into a distinct subdiscipline called "medical anthropology" referred to the work of anthropologists in clinical settings [6, 7]. Physician-anthropologist Arthur Kleinman presented perhaps the earliest systematic delineation of the scope of clinical anthropology when he urged medical anthropologists to engage in clinically relevant research that seeks "applied strategies that could be used in patient management or incorporated into research and teaching by medical, psychiatric, and nursing practitioners" [8, p. 14]. Since then, various other anthropologists have attempted to define the scope and orientation of clinical anthropology.

Ailon Shiloh, one of the participants in the Open Forum on clinical anthropology in the *Medical Anthropology Newsletter*, coined the term "therapeutic anthropology" to refer to a sub-type of "clinical medical anthropology" or "applied medical anthropology" (as opposed to "ethnographic medical anthropology") [9]. Therapeutic anthropology refers to a private or independent profession which "integrates applicable knowledge, attitudes, and practices of the medical system pertinent to the specific patient to help resolve that patient's therapeutic problems" [9, p. 14]. Most clinical anthropologists, however, do not regard themselves to be anthropologist clinicians in this vein because they are not certified or practising therapists [10, p. 16].

Various other participants in the Open Forum regarded clinical anthropology to encompass anthropological activities in a variety of medical settings, including private and community health clinics, voluntary and teaching hospitals, medical, nursing, and public health schools, and health planning agencies [10-12]. More recently, Kleinman stated that

> the field of clinically applied medical anthropology consists of a variety of different research and teaching interests including: mental illness, chronic disease, disability, birthing, indigenous healers and healing, practitioner-patient communication and relationships, self care and lay help seeking, biomedical institutions, training of different types of health professionals—nurses, family physicians, psychiatrists, pediatricians, osteopaths, public health practitioners, etc.—to mention the more prominent ones [13, p. 273].

Anthropologists working in health care settings continue to disagree on the best designation for their endeavors. Some prefer the term "clinical anthropology" [14] whereas others prefer the term "clinically applied anthropology" [15]. In a recent overview article, while admitting that the former term is "shorter and snappier," Chrisman and Johnson prefer the latter because it "does not carry the connotation of clinical practice and its implicit threat to the many more traditional clinicians who constitute the medical care system." They also preclude applied anthropology in public health from the scope of clinically applied anthropology because most clinical anthropologists restrict the "application of anthropological data, research methods, and theory to clinical matters" [16, p. 97].

As our discussion thus far indicates, anthropologists for the most part tend to operate with a more restricted conception of the domain of clinical activities than do sociologists. Gondolf defines clinical sociology as the application of sociological perspectives to programs of intervention and social change which not only assist individuals in adjusting to social changes but also assists them in altering harmful aspects of their social environment [17, p. 144]. In many ways, the goals and objectives of the Clinical Sociology Association, which was established in 1978, converge with those of the Society for Applied Anthropology.

THE CONSERVATIVE ORIENTATION WITHIN
CLINICAL ANTHROPOLOGY

Clinical anthropology emerged in the wake of the development of "biopsychosocial medicine" [18] as well as various changes in medical education designed to humanize bourgeois medical treatment. As stated by its principal proponent, George Engel, biopsychosocial medicine constitutes a new medical model which not so much transcends the bourgeois medical model but adds to it by taking into account the psychosocial dimensions that accompany illness and the physician-patient relationship. As Phillips observes [19, p. 31], many clinical anthropologists explicitly pay an intellectual debt to Engel. Katon and Kleinman, for example, note, "we hope to contribute to the development of a 'biopsychological' approach to patients, one which integrates biomedical, psychiatric, and social science frameworks [20, p. 253]. More recently, Howard Stein, a well-known clinical anthropologist, states that Engel's position comes the closest of the many critiques of bourgeois medicine to his own [21, p. 15].

In a critique of Engel's concept of biopsychosocial medicine, David Armstrong contends that its original formulation is "grossly medicocentric and sociologically naive" in that the "core of disease was still the lesion but its precursors could be psychosocial, though not exclusively" [22, pp. 1213-1214]. Like the old "biomedical" model, biopsychosocial medicine continues to subordinate the patient to the physician. Despite their differing views of biopsychosocial medicine, Katon and Kleinman [20] and Armstrong [22] regard the new medical model as a response by bourgeois medicine to its recent crisis of legitimacy. This crisis has taken various forms, ranging from the outcry against the bureaucratization and profit-making in bourgeois medicine, increasing rates of malpractice suits against physicians, a growing interest in alternative therapies under the loose rubric of the holistic health movement, and a renewed public demand for national health insurance, particularly along the lines of the Canadian system. Katon and Kleinman suggest that, although "structural power differentials basic to the doctor-patient relationship are unlikely to be significantly altered in the forseeable future," the concept of biopsychosocial medicine paves the way for "clinical negotiation" which in turn could greatly diminish many of the barriers to effective communication between physician and patient [20, p. 264]. In the context of an ever-deeping medical crisis in American society, the approach that Katon and Kleinman call for seems timid at best. As Lyng so aptly notes,

> In Engel's view, the biopsychological model should serve as a template for transforming the medical practice system at the micro-level but not at the macro-level. . . . The more holistic approach he advocates will simply build on 'what is already there' in current medical practice, subjecting aspects of existing practice to rational, scientific organization and updating the skills that most physicians currently employ. Most importantly, his model does not threaten one of the chief pillars of the existing health care system medical profession's control over medical knowledge [23, p. 234].

In addition to serving as response to efforts to reform, but certainly not revolutionize, bourgois medicine, the emergence of clinical anthropology has been tied up with the search for alternative careers in anthropology. As Morgan demonstrates in detail, the tight academic job market prompted many anthropology students to seek careers in medical anthropology because it held out of the hope of finding employment in nonacademic settings, including clinical ones [24]. Some time earlier, Stein, who has worked in clinical settings for many years conjectured that despite the "high idealism and social purpose" of clinical anthropology, much of the motivation of its practitioners "has to do with a wish to gain a sense of legitimacy in the eyes of medicine, the public, and ourselves: to obtain a certain sweet revenge upon our medical 'bad parents'; to assure for ourselves a cut in the pie if not a corner on the market ('turf') by usurping the place of those whose jobs we are certain we could do better" [21, p. 18]. In 1980 Golde estimated that about 500 persons where involved nationwide in clinical anthropology [25]. Shimkin and Golde estimated that perhaps 1,000 people, including graduate students, were involved in clinical anthropology. In all probability, the number of clinical anthropologists, part-time or full-time, has increased in number since the early 1980s [14, p. 384].

As Alexander so aptly observes, the role of the clinical anthropologist is an ambiquous and even a lonely one [26]. While its ambiguity may have certain advantages, such as providing "access to information which might not be available to others whose roles are stereotyped or who threaten by their status some informants," she notes that it is tempting to succumb to the expectations of the medical establishment and to become a "pseudophysician" or "ersatz-therapist" [26, p. 75]. Indeed, one clinical anthropologist who worked at the time in a department of psychiatry told Baer that she felt that she had been "coopted" by virtue of being the sole anthropologist in the department. Her status forced her to increasingly engage in the discourse of psychiatry while at the same time dropping much of the anthropological insights that she initially brought to her position. Despite her concerns, Alexander advises clinical anthropologists to function as "important adjuncts and resources" to health professionals in their work [26, p. 103]. Most clinical anthropologists probably do not wish to view themselves in this particular manner. Nevertheless, their status in clinical settings is tenuous. As Phillips observes, in contrast to social workers and psychologists, anthropologists "are not successful participants in the 'politics of legitimation' (that enables disciplines entering the health arena to establish their status and turf" [19, p. 34].

In their roles as cultural interpreters and clinical negotiators, clinical anthropologists may be forced to downplay the social origins and reification of illness, the increasing medicalization of social problems, and inequities in the availability and quality of health care. Efforts to call attention to these issues may be seen by many health providers as an inappropriate intrusion of political ideology into the sanitized corridors of "scientific medicine." Indeed, Stein asserts that

> [t]he anthropologist or any social/behavioral scientist working in clinical settings must become aware that he or she might be asked to function in a way that deflects attention away from medical culture toward a more suitable, emotionally acceptable topic for which the anthropologist is employed to use his or her 'expertise' [27, p. 4].

The process by which the restricted role of the clinical anthropologist evolves is perhaps generally a subtle one, particularly in academic medical settings, rather than one resulting from direct censorship. Much of it emanates simply from the reductionist orientation of the bourgeois medical model that is inculcated into medical students and physicians in numerous ways. Andre Gorz summarizes the hegemony of the bourgeois medical model which is internalized by most physicians and patients as follows:

> Unlike ancient medicine, bourgeois medicine knows only individuals, not populations. This is appropriate, of course, to the relationship the doctors have with 'their' patients. They are private individuals, customers, and they ask that the doctors relieve their pain, cure them, advise them here and now, as they are, in the world as it it. The doctors conform to this demand. That is their trade. No one [or hardly anyone] asks the doctor to see beyond individual cases to the social, economic, and ecological causes of the disease. In this way medicine is turning into a bizarre 'science' that studies partial structures minutely without taking into consideration the whole structure to which they belong.
>
> Only a few pioneers, missionaries, and crazies are interested in the epidemiology and the biology of whole populations, or in *anthropology* (italics mine), or in work-related diseases. These true researchers and theoreticians, while they preserve the honor of the medical profession, have no influence on the practice and function of medicine [28, p. 172].

While Gorz overstates his case, medical anthropologists should pay careful heed to his remarks. Some progressive physicians have recognized the social origins of disease. For the most part, social medicine in the Virchowian tradition has at best been a marginal element of American bourgeois medicine, even in schools of public health. A single clinical anthropologist or even a team of clinical anthropologists with a critical perspective can probably at best receive a polite hearing to their insights within the corridors of bourgeois medicine.

In reality, clinical anthropologists along with other social and behavioral scientists are expected to legitimize the traditional dominance of physicians in the health care system. As Riska and Vintin-Johnansen assert, the medical profession has employed behavioral scientists to

> depoliticize issues in health politics. Political conflicts actually reflecting different structural interests in the health care system are turned into 'social problems' to be solved apolitically by the intervention of experts [29, p. 574].

Given this structural dilemma, it should not be surprising that certain prominent clinical anthropologists have advised their colleagues to assume an allegedly neutral posture toward both patients and the medical establishment and to resign themselves to the hierarchical structure of the clinical setting. Chrisman and Maretzki caution that " [a]nthropologists, who are accustomed to the more egalitarian style of interaction and debate of an academic department, need to quickly learn now to work within the frequently rigid hierarchy of a health science school" [15, p. 21]. Barnett chastises anthropologists for becoming patient advocates and admonishes them not to act as social critics [30, p. 59]. Press advises anthropologists to "avoid being critical" because "generally, hospital administration is interested in results of immediate, mainstream relevance, not theory, 'studies,' or exotica" that reveal backstage scenarios and agendas [31, p. 68]. Although he participated in the session on "Towards a Critical Clinical Anthropology" and contributed to the subsequent symposium on the theme, Press maintains that "some perspectives of the parent 'critical medical anthropology' may be inappropriate to understanding clinical phenomena, . . . [particularly] "at the so-called micro level, the locus of the clinical encounter between patient and professional within our own society" [32, p. 100]. Even Johnson, one of the organizers of the session and symposium, counsels against "taking sides" with one group or other in the health care system, particularly patients [33, p. 333].

Some, if not many, clinical anthropologists might argue that these admonitions are of a methodological rather than doctrinal nature which recognize that confronting health professionals, particularly physicians, and affecting change from within depends upon success at building relationships. Indeed, clinical anthropologists often try to maneuver into a positions in which their critique of biomedical practices will not be seen as frontal attacks on biomedicine as a whole. Kleinman's disclaimer in *Rethinking Psychiatry* in part illustrates this strategy:

> There is also the danger that this review, because I have tried to engage so many aspects of psychiatry, will be read as a program for a radical reform of all psychiatric education and practice, an evangelical vision of a utopian future. That is definitely not my intent. While I do believe the key questions raised in these chapters should challenge the way we think of psychiatric categories, diagnosis, and the influence of the profession's values on the work of the practitioner, I do not believe anthropology or social science at large can specify a program of major reform, or that such reform would necessarily be desirable [34, p. 164].

To be sure, clinical anthropologists must walk a tight rope in conducting their work in clinical settings, but they are not the only ones who face this situation. Even critical anthropologists teaching within the "ivory towers" of social science departments often face similar dilemmas, but perhaps in more subtle ways. Howard Waitzkin, a physician and a critical medical sociologist, notes that health care personnel concerned about social change face difficult dilemmas in their work, including the issue of how to care for patients who need immediate medical assistance [35, p. 230]. In facing the latter situation, he cautions health workers not to engage in "patching"— that is simply tending to the patient's problem on the individual level and thereby permitting him or her to continue functioning in a sociocultural system that is often the root of the problem. According to Waitzkin,

> The contradictions of patching have no simple resolution. Clearly health workers cannot deny services to clients, even when these services permit clients' participation in illness-generating social structures and do not attack the deeper roots of their problems. On the other hand, it is important to draw this connection between social issues and personal troubles [following C. Wright Mills' advice]. Although the contradictions of patching are difficult for practitioners who want progressive social change, their recognition leads to certain conclusions about health praxis. The most basic conclusion is that health work in itself is not sufficient. Instead, health workers should try to link their clinical activities to efforts aimed directly at basic sociopolitical change [35, p. 230].

Unfortunately, the structural inequality that exists between social scientists, on the one hand, and physicians and health administrators, on the other hand, often contributes to what Roth terms a "management bias" on the part of the former [36].

Katon and Kleinman explicitly admit their acceptance of heirarchical arrangements within bourgeois medicine by arguing that

> some degree of structural inequality, regulated and monitored to be sure, is not only inevitable but potentially desirable, as long as it is neither extreme nor abused to exploit patients, but rather allows the physician to maximize the clinical efficacy of his therapeutic mandate to act [20, pp. 264-265].

While Kleinman argues that clinical anthropologists need to see themselves as "advocates of patients and practitioners in the interest of improved, culturally-approved care" [13, p. 285], his acceptance of a hierarchical relationship between physician and patient precludes the possibity of serving as a co-equal advocate for both of them. In a similar vein, Chrisman and Johnson argue that clinical anthropologists should function as " system advocates: helping to resolve the problems of patient and practitioner alike" [16, p. 99]. The question is which system do they wish to advocate: the traditional physician-patient relationship, the clinical system, the bourgeois medical system, the capitalist world-system. System advocacy ultimately translates into system maintenance and support for old-fashioned structural-functionalism, a theoretical perspective that stands in diametric opposition to critical anthropology. In sum, the conservative orientation in clinical anthropology stems from a perceived need to avoid rocking the boat so as not to be tossed overboard. As a consequence, in their effort to appear neutral, many clinical anthropologists unwittingly become upholders of the status quo, a far from neutral position.

Unfortunately, some medical anthropologists have come to equate certain critiques of bourgeois medicine with "doctorbashing." Physician-anthropologist Melvin Konner in particular feels that he must come to the defense of physicians against critical medical anthropology (he places quotation marks around the adjective "critical") for allegedly analyzing bourgeois medicine as a "capitalist plot" [37, p. 81]. We know of no critical medical anthropologist who has ever analyzed biomedicine in this manner. Conversely, bourgeois medicine by virtue of its integration in capitalist societies functions as 1) an arena for profit-making; 2) a mechanism for maintaining and reproducing the working class; 3) an arena for social control and the reproduction of class, racial/ethnic, and gender relations; and 4) and a mechanism of imperialist expansion and bourgeois cultural hegemony [38, p. 102]. Konner indirectly recognizes the global hegemony of biomedicine by sarcastically noting, "It is fascinating how similar Soviet medicine at its best is to American 'bourgeois' medicine." Indeed, Vicente Navarro, a progressive physician with extensive training in the social sciences, argues that "medicine in today's Soviet Union represents clear signs of alienation, undemocratic control and inequitable distribution of resources, a *bourgeois* (italics ours) and individualist interpretation, and hierarchicalization and discrimination in the health sector" [39, p. xvii].

Critical medical anthropology strives to present a critique of bourgeois medicine not only in capitalist societies, but also in socialist-oriented societies [40]. Regardless of the society, critical medical anthropologists do seek, in Konner's words, to "understand the forces that make physicians ignore psychocultural factors in illness in some settings, practice legally defensive medicine in others, and rely excessively on technology in still others" [37, p. 81].

BARRIERS TO DEVELOPING A
CRITICAL CLINICAL ANTHROPOLOGY

While Taussig [41], Young [42], and Baer [43] allude to the tendency of clinical anthropology to depoliticize clinical encounters, some of its practitioners have begun recently to engage in a reflexive scrutiny of their endeavors. Phillips maintains that clinical anthropologists face three major dilemmas: (1) They have not been able to make their theoretical concepts relevant to the practical needs of clinicians. (2) The participant-observation role in clinical settings forces them to accept the physical reductionism and Cartesianism of biomedicine. (3) They lack a clearly-defined role in the clinical setting [19, p. 31].

As Phillips observes,

> The current financial retrenchment of the medical institution and the more con-
> servative atmosphere of the nation are making social science teaching
> progresssively less important in clinical departments. The demand for more
> humanistic standards of medical care is no longer a *cause celebre* for the public
> [19, p. 34].

Despite his astute assessment of the dilemmas that clinical anthropologists currently face, Phillips recommends essentially that they "adapt" to it rather than struggle for its transformation. In doing so, he maintains that clinical anthropologists must adopt a seemingly contradictory posture—one which provisionally accepts the "rules and ideology of the medical culture" and yet transcends the limitations of medicine by developing "epistemologically sound theories that address general anthropological principles and challenge the existing assumptions of the medical institution" [19, p. 35].

In contrast to this accommodative stance vis-a-vis bourgeois medicine recommended by Phillips, in recent years a small number of clinical anthropologists have called for a synthesis of clinical anthropology and critical medical anthropology. In a paper presented in the session on "Toward a Critical Clinically Applied Anthropology," by drawing upon upon their teaching and research experience on psychiatry consultation-liason, Padgett and and Johnson presented a succinct effort toward the development of a critical clinical anthropology [44]. Given the generally micro-analytic approach of the psychiatric consultation process in hospitals, they suggest that anthropologists make their analyses of clinical situations more critical by informing physicians, nurses, and other health providers of macro-level factors, including class, racial, and ethnic stratification, that add to patient distress. Padgett and Johnson feel at somewhat of a loss in going beyond this individualistic strategy within the context of the hospital or medical center. Their inability to suggest other ways of incorporating a critical perspective in clinical settings, including informing both health providers and clients of the impact of the hierarchical nature of medical settings on health care, pinpoints the basic dilemma of clinical anthropology.

Despite an admirable effort on the part of some clinical anthropologists to incorporate critical perspectives, we are left with the question as to how critical anthropologists working in biomedical clinical settings can be. As Phillips argues, the medical hierarchy may object to certain theoretical insights on the part of clinical anthropologists "because they may point to structural deficiencies in the health care system" [19, p. 85]. Stein, for example, demonstrates this basic dilemma by describing the suppression he encountered when he attempted over a period of five years to find departmental forums to present and discuss the clinical/political implications of his model of alcoholism and drug addiction [45]. In their efforts to "study up," anthropologists generally eneounter the problem of access if they wish to utilize ethnographic methods. As opposed to the relatively easy access that anthropologists have had to the "little peoples of the world" (e.g., foragers, horticulturalists, peasants, ethnic minorities, subproletariats, religious sects), they generally find that entree into the medical arena for research purposes tends to be more problematic "due to the predominance of elites in the setting" [46, p. 514]. In her efforts to gain entree into a university hospital, Joan Matthews [47] relates how she repressed the antidoctor bias that she had acquired during her twenty-year stint as a nursing educator and administrator in order to adopt a posture of "affective neutrality" that she feels was essential in her study of information exchange processes among physicians, nurses, and patients. In reality, the "value-free" approach that Matthews aspires to is an elusive one. As Riska and Vinten-Johansen argue, "By using a clinical model, the medical leadership has managed to force behavioral scientists into limited roles as social engineers providing technical expertise within the parameters largely defined by the medical profession alone" [29, p. 595]. Baer encountered difficulty with access when as a post-doctoral fellow in a medical anthropology program when he sought to compare the interactional styles in two family medicine clinics, one affiliated with the biomedical school and the other with the osteopathic medical school, at the Michigan State University. Although the physicians in the osteopathic clinic had allowed him to conduct observations on an informal basis, his research proposal was summarily denied by a committee of physicians affiliated with the bourgeois medical clinic. It seems very likely that the bourgeois medical physicians felt threatened by a systematic comparsion that may have shown them to be deficient in any way as opposed to the osteopathic physicians, members of a rival "medical sect" that has undergone increasing legitimation over the past decade.

How easily will health policy makers, hospital administrators, and physicians take to a critical clinical anthropology given the reductionist model which they use in treating illness and disease? In addition to the incidents related above, the social structure of the hospital and its place in the political economy of health care in American society strongly suggest that they will resist efforts to apply such a perspective.

While no data have been compiled on the various settings where clinical anthropologists work, many, if not most, of them conduct their clinical work in hospitals, particularly university and teaching hospitals. In addition to their activities in clinical settings, many of them teach in medical and nursing schools or in departments of anthropology. At any rate, Navarro [48], Krause [49], Waitzkin [35], Riska [50] and others maintain that the modern hospital reflects the current require-ments of capital accumulation and the political struggle within the American capitalist system. The hospital has become the locus of industrial or technologi-cal medicine, the major element within the medical-industrial complex, and a fac-tory-like enterprise. According to Turner "the hospital resembles a bureaucratic collective of workshops" which deliver a "labour-intensive system of medical care" [51, pp. 158-159]. Like the factory, the hospital has an elaborate division of labor which replicates and reinforces the class, racial/ethnic, and gender relations in the larger society [48]. Most studies of the social structure of the hospital focus upon its dual system of authority or system of multiple subordination headed up by the hospital administration and the medical staff. While in small and even in many intermediate-sized hospitals a rough balance of power exists between these two authority structures, the hospital administration in large hospitals and medical centers has achieved dominance over the physician group in the process of organizing new health occupations and technology. Despite an on-going power struggle between administrators and physicians, "government intervention is putting more and more weapons into the hands of the administrator, as new laws require review teams composed of more than just physicians" [49, p. 67].

Regardless of how much power administrators and physicians exert over each other, ultimately their power over other health workers and other hospital staff is delegated rather than absolute. Hospital boards generally do not involve themselves in the day-to-day operations of the hospitals, but ultimately their members control hospital governing policy. Hospital boards tend to recruit members from local private elites.

> Analyzing the boards of trustees of these [voluntary community] hospitals, one sees less predominance of the representatives of financial and corporate capi-tal, and more of the upper-middle class, and primarily of the professionals—espe-cially physicians—and representatives of the business middle class. Even here, the other strata and classes, the working class and lower-middle class, which constitute the majority of the U.S. population, are not represented. Not one trade union leader (even a token one), for instance, sits on any board in the hospitals in the region of Baltimore [48, p. 154].

The corporate class does not exert the same degree of direct input into the policies of hospital boards as it does into those of private health foundations, private medical schools, and even state medical schools. Nevertheless, its interests are more than adequately represented by middle-level managers and other social actors who are in basic agreement with premises of a capitalist economy. American hospitals fall into one of three categories: 1) private community hospitals, 2) government hospitals, and 3) proprietary hospitals. Despite their purported "non-profit" status, the first two types support capital accumulation by acting as "ideal conduits for the profits of drug companies, equipment manufacturers, construction and real estate firms, and finan-cial institutions" [52, p. 18]. Furthermore, private community hospitals frequently share overlapping directors with profit-making health industries [53, p. 109]. These hospitals also provide an arena within which physicians may charge high fees to their patients or third-party payers while at the same they have free access to sophisticated medical equipment.

Regardless of whether clinical anthropologists work in university hospitals, voluntary community hospitals, or other clinical settings, they generally find themselves as either employees or consultants for highly hierarchical organizations committed to what Berliner terms a "monopoly-capitalist mode of production in which the production of the commodity health is controlled by the producers of the commodity and in which production is both centralised and concentrated" [54, p. 163]. Conventional clinical anthropologists functioning in such settings are politically naive when they assert that they maintain a neutral stance by simply not becoming patient advocates. As Stavenhagen correctly observes,

> The moment a social scientist either sells his labor to the highest bidder on the professional market or puts his knowledge at the service of a government, a bureaucracy, a political party, a labor union, an international organization or a revolutionary movement, then he can hardly claim to be simply a neutral observer. He becomes directly involved in the value systems and ideologies of the groups or organizations he works with, for, or against [55, p. 339].

BEYOND CONVENTIONAL CLINICAL ANTHROPOLOGY: THE CASE FOR ADVOCACY

To date most clinical anthropologists have restricted their role to that of cultural intrepeters for physicians, other health practitioners, and even, although probably less frequently, individual patients. Chrisman and Johnson state that clinically applied anthropologists use two "general bundles of information" in their work with clinicians: (1) data about various ethnic groups and (2) general anthropological and medical anthropological concepts, such culture, custom, value, beliefs, cultural relativism, the illness-disease distinction, and the explanatory model [16, p. 105]. The role of cultural interpretation or brokerage is a needed one in the clinical setting and should be part of even the most progressive health care system. However, clinical anthropology functions as a conservative endeavor when its practitioners feel comfortable to enlightening health providers with information about the cultural patterns of patient populations, including their EMs, with the hope of somehow helping to humanize bourgeois medicine. Yet, as Marcus and Fischer assert, such a simple juxtaposition of alien customs to familiar ones denies the promise of anthropology as a cultural critique [56].

Fortunately, some clinical anthropologists have come to recognize the potential for clinical anthropology to subsume a wider purview of activities. Stein, who seeks to integrate applied medical anthropology, critical medical anthropology of the radical phenomenological genre, and clinical anthropology, urges anthropologists to move beyond the mere teaching about "ethnic, religious, familial, social class, and other features of the patient population" [57, p. 238]. He urges medical anthropologists to inform clinical teachers, researchers, and practitioners about the world in which they move, namely the culture of bourgeois medicine, including its financial and social control dimensions. Some time ago, Maretzki called for a broader conception of clinical anthropology by defining it as "anthropology in clinical medical settings, or anthropology related to clinical medical activities, including the preventive orientation of public health and the primary public health and the primary care orientation of community" [12, p. 19]. The latter part of this definition is congruent with Rudolf Virchow's famous assertion that "medicine is a social science." Some clinical anthropologists, such as Padgett and Johnson, recognize that the ultimate solution to many patients' problems lies outside the realm of bourgeois medicine and depends on changes in social policies [58].

Even if anthropologists can enlighten physicians and other health providers to the impact of macro-structures on the social production of illness, the development of a critical clinical anthropology requires a shift from the individualistic approach to a collective one which forms an alliance with other progressive medical social scientists, physicians, patients, and even administrators who seek to create a health care system which places human needs above profit-making and medical empire-building. Critical clinical anthropologists will need to inform patients that their health problems are not unique but are shared by others of their class, race, ethnicity, and gender and that social action can serve as a form of therapy. In short, clinical anthropologists who wish to adopt a critical perspective will need to discard their eschewal of patient advocacy. Indeed, some clinical anthropologists reportedly actively support national health insurance and other needed health programs and seek to empower individual patients by encouraging them to work in support groups and community action organizations. After all, as Heggenhougen observes, "Isn't advocacy part of the therapeutic process? Advocacy for its own sake and championing of a minority against a so-called pervasively evil society at large is not part of the process; an attempt to rectify inequities that deteriorate the 'health' of a society and its people is" [59, p. 649]. In a similar vein, Frankenberg maintains that "adopting a posture of alliance with patients is already a revolutionary step" [60, p. 35].

Critical clinical anthropologists along with other critical medical anthropologists will need to consider alternative outlets for their energies, no easy task in an era of limited employment opportunities. As Scheper-Hughes observes, critical medical anthropologists should work "at the margins, questioning premises, and subjecting epistemologies that represent powerful, political interests to oppositional thinking" [61, p. 196]. She identifies three possible projects by which to develop a "critically applied medical anthropology." The first of these calls for a reduction rather than expansion of the parameters of medical efficacy or a process of demedicalization which recognizes that experts other than physicians are more qualified to address issues such as the social origins of illness. The second of these proposes anthropological collaboration with alternative healers who emphasize non-biological modes of therapy. Some alternative healers manifest counterhegemonic values that question the reductionist perspective of the biomedical model of disease and hierarchical relationships both within biomedicine and the larger society. Conversely, many members of other alternative medical systems, such as chiropractic, while giving lip service to the notion of holistic health, often subscribe to reductionist etiologies of disease and illness and often exhibit strong entrepreneurial tendencies similar to those of biomedical physicians. The last of Scheper-Hughes' proposals calls for "the radicalization of medical knowledge and practice, taking (and using) the hospital and the clinic—in Foucault's enlarged sense of the terms—as the locus of social revolution" [61, p. 194].

In addition to these, critical medical anthropologists will need to place their expertise at the disposal of labor unions, women's health collectives, ethnic community organizations, gays and others victimized by the stigma of having AIDs, health consumer groups, self-help and self-care groups. Despite the fact that some of these movements, including the holistic health movement [62], exhibit conservative tendencies of their own, they also may act as counterhegmonic forces against biomedicine and the larger political economy within which it is embedded. We may draw inspiration from progressive scholars such as Vicente Navarro who for years has been supporting the efforts on the part of unionists to improve occupational health conditions in the Baltimore area and assisted Jesse Jackson in defining the health policies, including a national health program, of the Rainbow Coalition [63].

Critical medical anthropologists should consider establishing linkages with environmental groups, many of which have been in the process of forming coalitions with working class people, people of color, and peace groups [64]. In essence, critical medical anthropologists, regardless of whether their primary work occurs in academia or in a clinical setting, need to become proponents of "patient power" [65]. Ultimately, as Bolough contends, "the problem of alienated patient cannot be overcome until medical knowledge becomes social property in practice" [66, p. 202]. Such a transformation will entail "patient class" ownership and control over the means of medical production [66, p. 204].

The national toxic victims movement offers another locus for conducting critical clinical anthropology or simply applying critical medical anthropology. John O'Connor, director of the National Campaign Against Toxic Hazards, contends that there is more activity in the United States on the toxic waste issue than on any other single issue [67]. This movement is a highly decentralized one and generally consists of lower-middle and working-class people, including an increasing number of minorities, whose health and lives are being disrupted by toxic wastes located near or below their homes. Initially many of the participants in the toxic victims movement have been ordinary citizens who accept the American political economy and its culture of consumption. In dealing with chemical and nuclear corporations and regulatory agencies, such as the Environmental Protection Association, the Nuclear Regulatory Agency, and the Center for Disease Control, they come to recognize the unstated cooperative relationships between industry and government that they never learned about in high school civics classes [68].

Some participants in the toxic victims movement have begun to gather epidemiological data, sometimes in collaboration with sympathetic scientists, concerning their health problems. Phil Brown, a critical medical sociologist who rejects the widely held belief that epidemiology is a value-free scientific activity, coined the term "popular epidemiology" to describe such an effort on the part of Love Canal residents:

> Popular epidemiology is important for medicine and society because people often
> have access to data about themselves and their environment that are inaccessible

to scientists. In fact, public knowledge of community toxic hazards in the last two decades has largely stemmed from the observations of ordinary people. Similarly, most cancer clusters in the workplace are detected by employees [69, p. 127].

According to Brown and Mikkelsen, Woburn, a town of some 37,000 people lying twelve miles north of Boston and the site of a large chemical industry, is the most significant instance to date of the popular epidemiological approach [69, p. 125]. In addition to toxic waste contamination, popular epidemiology can be applied to other phenomena, including nuclear plants, pesticide spraying, and occupational hazards. Given that many clinical anthropologists are interested in conveying patient's explanatory models (EMs) to health care providers, it is interesting to note that in part Brown and Mikkelsen refer to popular epidemiology as a "system of folk beliefs" that "deserve attention from professionals" [69, p. 126].

Many medical scientists, including medical anthropologists and social epidemiologists, may dismiss popular epidemiology for its lack of scientific rigor. In countering this objection, Brown and Mikkelsen contend that

> In practice science is limited by such factors as finances and personnel. Without popular participation it would be impossible to carry out much of the research needed to document health hazards. Science is also limited in its conceptualization of what problems are legitimate and how they should be addressed. As we have pointed out, physicians are largely untrained in environmental and occupational health matters, and even when they observe environmentally cause disease, they are unlikely to blame the disease on the environment [69, pp. 132-133].

In addition to exploring strategies for creating a more healthly work place and environment, providing for more equitable and humane health services, and empowering patients, critical medical anthropologists need to explore alternative medical paradigms. Lyng, a critical medical sociologist, provides one possible beginning for such an endeavor [23]. His utopian countersystem incorporates elements from the holistic health movement and the public health and psychiatric/biopsychosocial medical models. Although it contains various individualistic and narcasssistic features, Lyng adovocates a praxis approach which regards the new health consciousness as "a resource to be shaped and mobilized for the purpose of advancing the interests of the patient population within the health care system" [23, p. 240].

Critical medical anthropologists have to date only begun to explore the issue of praxis, even though they espouse the merger of theory and social action. Until recently, little direct communication occurred between critical medical anthropologists and clinical anthropologists. Various sessions at American Anthropological Association and Society for Applied Anthropology meetings hold out the promise of a provocative and stimulating dialogue that will be part of the larger process of merging theory and social action in medical anthopology and the medical social sciences in general (after all, medicine is a social science). Anthropologists interested in the critical perspective need to communicate even more about the application of critical medical anthropology in a number of settings, not only the clinic but also the workplace and the environment.

Howard Waitzkin speaks of the need for blending long-range and short-range goals in the creation of a new health care system. Ultimately, the achievement of such a system lies beyond the boundaries of bourgeois medicine and involves "nothing short of revolutionary restructuring of social institutions that now create suffering and unhappiness" [70, p. 261]. Waitzkin maintains that short-range goals can contribute to the development of a humane and equitable society [70, p. 261]. These include the creation of a national health care program in the United States, the only developed industrial country along with South Africa that does not have one, and modifications in medical discourse, a strategy that clinical anthropogists advocate in one form or another. In the following remarks, however, Waitzkin points out the limitations of the latter strategy:

> [I]t is foolish to think that changing the doctor-patient relationship in itself would lead to wider social change. Although medical encounters may reinforce structural patterns of domination and oppression, a transition toward a nondominating, nonoppressive doctor-patient relationships will not create social revolution (despite ardent claims by alternative health movements of various persuasions). Modification of doctor-patient relationships need to accompany change in the larger contextual conditions that impede a decent and humane health-care system [70, p. 262].

The Critical Anthropology of Health Interest Group of the Society for Medical Anthropology holds the potential for providing one forum for developing long-range and short-range goals for the creation of a new health care system. In addition to exploring strategies by which clinical anthropologists can promote progressive medical encounters in which health professionals and patients "overcome the domination, mystification, and distorted communication that result from asymmetric technical knowledge" [70, p. 275], critical medical anthropologists can work in cooperation with other members of the Society for Medical Anthropology for the creation of a comprehensive national health program. At the same time, critical medical anthropologists need to establish contacts with other critical medical scientists and health providers, such as the some 1,000 members of the Socialist Caucus of the American Public Health Association [71, p. 270], who are advocating this short-term goal. Critical medical anthropologists should also consider organizing sessions at the Socialist Scholars Conference, a gathering of several thousand radical academicians and social activists. Vicente Navarro, Barbara Ehrenreich, and Peter Townsend spoke in a session on "The Politics of Health Care" at the tenth annual conference in April 1992. While only a few of the some 130 sessions at the conference focused on health issues, the conference organizers are quite open to the inclusion of such sessions. The growing interest of the American public in the Canadian health care system, despite its limitations, indicates that the time is ripe for medical anthropologists, critical or otherwise, to become part of a nation-wide drive for the implementation of a national health program, preferably one that minimizes and ultimately eradicates the profit-making interests of medical-industrial complex. Such reforms would further facilitate the development of a truly critical clinical anthropology.

REFERENCES

1. L. M. Morgan, Dependency Theory in the Political Economy of Health, *Medical Anthropology Quarterly, 1*, pp. 131-154, 1987.

2. A. Kleinman, *Patients and Healers in the Context of Culture,* University of California Press, Berkeley, 1980.
3. A. L. Wright and T. M. Johnson, Preface to Symposium on Critical Perspectives in Clinically Applied Medical Anthropology, *Social Science and Medicine, 30*:9, p. v, 1990.
4. H. A. Baer, The Possibilities and Dilemmas of Building Bridges between Critical Medical Anthropology and Clinical Anthropology: A Discussion, *Social Science and Medicine, 30,* pp. 1011-1013, 1990.
5. T. M. Johnson, Practicing Medical Anthropology: Clinical Strategies for the Work in the Hospital, in *Applied Anthropology in America* (2nd Edition), E. M. Eddy and W. L. Patridge (eds.), Columbia University Press, New York, pp. 316-339, 1987.
6. W. Caudill, Applied Anthropology in Medicine, in *Anthropology Today,* A.L. Kroeber (ed.), University of Chicago Press, Chicago, pp. 771-801, 1953.
7. N. A. Scotch, Medical Anthropology, in *Biennial Review of Anthropology,* B. J. Siegal (ed.), Stanford University Press, Stanford, California, pp. 30-68, 1963.
8. A. Kleinman, Lessons from a Clinical Approach to Medical Anthropological Research, *Medical Anthropology Newsletter, 8,* pp. 5-8, 1977.
9. A. Shiloh, Therapeutic Anthropology, *Medical Anthropology Newsletter, 12*:1, pp. 14-15, 1980.
10. H. H. Weidman, Comments on Clinical Anthropology, *Medical Anthropology Newsletter, 12*:1, pp. 16-17, 1980.
11. L. Kaufman, Thoughts on Clinical Anthropology, *Medical Anthropology Newsletter, 12*:1, pp. 17-18, 1980.
12. T. W. Maretzki, Reflections on Clinical Anthropology, *Medical Anthropology Newsletter, 12*:1, pp. 19-21, 1980.
13. A. Kleinman, Clinically Applied Medical Anthropology: The View from the Clinic, in *Advances in Medical Social Science,* Vol. 2, J. Ruffini (ed.), Gordon and Breach, Science Publishers, New York, pp. 269-288, 1984.
14. D. B. Shimkin and P. Golde, Clinical Anthropology: Contributions, Problems, and Wider Perspectives, in *Clinical Anthropology: A New Approach to American Health Problems,* D. B. Shimkin and P. Golde (eds.), University Press of America, Lanhan, Maryland, pp. 369-387, 1983.
15. N. J. Chrisman and T.W. Maretzki, Anthropology in Health Science Settings, in *Clinically Applied Anthropology,* N. J. Chrisman and T. W. Maretzki (eds.), Reidel, Dordrecht, Netherlands, pp. 1-27, 1982.
16. N. J. Chrisman and T. M. Johnson, Clinically Applied Anthropology, in *Medical Anthropology, Contemporary Theory and Methods,* T. M. Johnson and C. F. Sargent (eds.), Praeger, New York, pp. 93-113, 1990.
17. E. W. Gondolf, Teaching Clinical Sociology: The Introductory Course, *Clinical Sociology Review, 2,* pp. 143-149, 1985.
18. G. L. Engel, The Need for a New Medical Model: A Challenge for Biomedicine, *Science, 196,* pp. 129-136, 1977.
19. M. R. Phillips, Can "Clinically Applied Anthropology" Survive in Medical Settings?, *Medical Anthropology Quarterly, 16*:2, pp. 31-36, 1985.
20. W. Katon and A. Kleinman, Doctor-Patient Negotiation and Other Social Science Strategies in Patient Care, in *The Relevance of Social Science for Medicine,* L. Eisenberg and A. Kleinman (eds.), Reidel, Dordrecht, Netherlands, pp. 253-279, 1981.
21. H. F. Stein, Clinical Anthropology and Medical Anthropology, *Medical Anthropology Newsletter, 12*:1, pp. 18-19, 1980.
22. D. Armstrong, Theoretical Tensions in Biopsychological Medicine, *Social Science and Medicine, 25,* pp. 1213-1218, 1987.

23. S. Lyng, *Holistic Health and Biomedical Medicine,* State University of New York Press, Albany, 1990.
24. L. M. Morgan, The Medicalization of Anthropology: A Critical Perspective on the Critical-Clinical Debate, *Social Science and Medicine, 30,* pp. 945-959, 1990.
25. P. Golde, Clinical Anthropology—An Emerging Health Profession? *Medical Anthropology Newsletter, 12:*10, pp. 15-16, 1980.
26. L. Alexander, Clinical Anthropology: Morals and Methods, *Medical Anthropology, 3,* pp. 61-107, 1979.
27. H. F. Stein, The Culture of the Patient as a Red Herring in Clinical Decision Making: A Case Study, *Medical Anthropology Quarterly, 17:*1, pp. 2-5, 1985.
28. A. Gorz, *Ecology as Politics,* South End Press, Boston, 1980.
29. E. Riska and P. Vinten-Johansen, The Involvement of the Behavioral Sciences in American Medicine: A Historical Perspective, *International Journal of Health Services, 11,* pp. 583-596, 1981.
30. C. Barnett, Anthropological Research in Clinical Settings: Role Requirements and Adaptations, *Medical Anthropology Quarterly, 16:*2, pp. 59-61, 1985.
31. I. Press, Speaking Hospital Administration's Language: Strategies for Anthropological Entree in the Clinical Setting, *Medical Anthropology Quarterly, 16:*30, pp. 67-69, 1985.
32. I. Press, Levels of Explanation and Cautions for a Critical Clinical Anthropology, *Social Science and Medicine, 30,* pp. 1001-1009, 1990.
33. T. M. Johnson, Practicing Medical Anthopology: Clinical Strategies for the Work in the Hospital, in *Applied Anthropology in America,* (2nd Edition), E. M. Eddy and W. L. Partridge (eds.), Columbia University Press, New York, pp. 316-339, 1987.
34. A. Kleinman, *Patients and Healers in the Context of Culture,* University of California Press, Berkeley, 1980.
35. H. Waitzkin, *The Second Sickness: Contradictions of Capitalist Health Care,* Free Press, New York, 1983.
36. J. A. Roth, Management Bias in Social Science Research, *Human Organization, 21,* pp. 47-50, 1962.
37. M. Konner, The Promise of Medical Anthropology: An Invited Commentary, *Medical Anthropology Quarterly, 5,* pp. 78-82, 1991.
38. M. Singer and H. A. Baer, Toward an Understanding of Capitalist and Socialist Health, *Medical Anthropology, 11,* pp. 97-107, 1989.
39. V. Navarro, *Social Security and Medicine in the U.S.S.R.,* Lexington, Masschusetts, 1977.
40. H. A. Baer, Towards a Critical Medical Anthropology of Health-Related Issues in Socialist-Oriented Societies, *Medical Anthropology, 11,* pp. 181-194, 1989.
41. M. Taussig, Reification and the Consciousness of the Patient, *Social Science and Medicine, 14B,* pp. 3-13, 1980.
42. A. Young, The Anthropologies of Illness and Sickness, *Annual Review in Anthropology, 11,* pp. 257-285. 1982.
43. H. A. Baer, The Replication of the Medical Division of Labor in Medical Anthropology, *Medical Anthropology Quarterly, 17:*3, pp. 63-65, 1986.
44. D. Padgett and T. M. Johnson, *Patients and Physicians in Distress: The Role of Critical Perspectives in Clinically Applied Medical Anthropology,* paper presented at the American Anthropological Association Meeting, Chicago, November 18-21, 1987.
45. H. Stein, In What Systems Do Alcohol/Chemical Addictions Make Sense? Clinical Ideologies and Practices as Cultural Metaphors, *Social Science and Medicine, 30,* pp. 987-1000, 1990.
46. S. Danziger, On Doctor-Watching: Fieldwork in Medical Settings, *Urban Life, 7,* pp. 513-532, 1979.

47. J. Mathews, Fieldwork in a Clinical Setting: Negotiating Entree, the Investigator's Role and Problems of Data Collection, in *Encounters with Biomedicine: Case Studies in Medical Anthropology*, H. A. Baer (ed.), Gordon and Breach, Science Publishers, New York, pp. 295-314, 1987.
48. V. Navarro, *Medicine Under Capitalism*, Prodist, New York, 1976.
49. E. Krause, *Power and Illness: The Political Sociology of Health and Medical Care*, Elvesier, New York, 1977.
50. E. Riska, *Power, Politics, and Health: Forces Shaping American Medicine*, Finnish Society of Sciences and Letters, Helsinki, 1985.
51. B. S. Turner, *Medical Power and Social Knowledge*, Sage, London, 1987.
52. D. U. Himmelstein and S. Woolhandler, Medicine as Industry: The Health-Care Sector in the United States, *Monthly Review, 35:*11, pp. 13-25, 1984.
53. H. Waitzkin and B. Waterman, *The Exploitation of Illness in Capitalist Society*, Bobbs-Merrill, Indianapolis, 1974.
54. H. Berliner, Medical Modes of Production, in *The Problem of Medical Knowledge*, A. Treachers and P. Wright (eds.), University of Edinburgh, Edinburgh, pp. 163-173, 1983.
55. R. Stavenhagen, Decolonizing Applied Social Sciences, *Human Organization, 30*, pp. 333-344, 1971.
56. G. E. Marcus and M. M. J. Fischer, *Anthropology as Cultural Critique, An Experimental Movement in the Human Sciences*, University of Chicago Press, Chicago, 1986.
57. H. Stein, *American Medicine as Culture*, Westview Press, Boulder, Colorado, 1990.
58. D. Padgett and T. M. Johnson, Somatizing Distress: Hospital Treatment of Psychiatric Co-Morbidity and the Limitations of Biomedicine, *Social Science and Medicine, 30*, pp. 205-209, 1990.
59. H. K. Heggenhougen, Therapeutic Anthropology: Response to Shiloh's Proposal, *American Anthropologist, 81*, pp. 647-651, 1979.
60. R. Frankenberg, Functionalism and After? Theory and Developments in Social Science Applied to the Health Field, in *Health Care in the U.S.: A Critical Analysis*, V. Navarro (ed.), Baywood, New York, pp. 21-37, 1977.
61. N. Scheper-Hughes, Three Propositions for a Critically Applied Medical Anthropology, *Social Science and Medicine, 30*, pp. 189-197, 1990.
62. H. S. Berliner and J. W. Salmon, The Holistic Health Movement and Scientific Medicine: The Naked and the Dead, *Socialist Review, 43*, pp. 31-52, 1979.
63. V. Navarro, The Rediscovery of the National Health Program by the Democratic Party of the United States: A Chronicle of the Jesse Jackson 1988 Campaign, *International Journal of Health Services, 19*, pp. 1-18, 1989.
64. N. Freudenberg, *Not in Our Backyards: Community Action for Health and the Environment*, Monthly Review Press, New York, 1984.
65. C. Wiener, S. Fagenhaugh, and B. Suczek, Patient Power: Complex Issues Need Complex Answers, *Social Policy, 11:*2, pp. 30-38, 1980.
66. R. W. Bolough, Grounding the Alienation of Self and Body: A Critical, Phenomenological Analysis of the Patient in Western Medicine, *Sociology of Health and Illness, 3*, pp. 188-206, 1981.
67. M. R. Edelstein, *Contaminated Communities: The Social and Psychological Impacts of Residential Toxic Exposure*, Westview Press, Boulder, Colorado, 1988.
68. H. A. Baer, Kerr-McKee and the NRC: From Indian Country to Silkwood to Gore, *Social Science and Medicine, 30*, pp. 237-248, 1990.
69. P. Brown and E. J. Mikkelsen, *No Safe Place: Toxic Waste, Leukemia, and Community Action*, University of California Press, Berkeley, 1990.

70. H. Waitzkin, *The Politics of Medical Encounters: How Patients and Doctors Deal with Social Problems,* Yale University Press, New Haven, Connecticut, 1991.
71. M. Turshen, *The Politics of Public Health,* Rutgers University Press, New Brunswick, New Jersey, 1989.

CHAPTER 14

Critical Praxis in Medical Anthropology

In what might be called the first phase of its development, critical medical anthropology struggled with issues of self-definition and acceptance within academic medical anthropology. The primary objectives of this phase were to develop a critique of and alternatives to the concepts, theories, scope, alignments, and self-image of conventional medical anthropology, and to bring these alternative ideas into the usual forums of scholarly exchange. While this first phase is far from over—there is both much to be resolved among those who have found common cause behind the label critical medical anthropology, much to be clarified with colleagues who do not recognize or are undecided about the advantage of a critical approach, and much to be countered in the recent postmodernist suspension of interest in so-called totalizing paradigms, there is a concern with moving beyond the academy, the scholarly conference, and the academic journal, into the applied field of clinics, health education and development projects, federal health research institutes, international health bodies, private voluntary organizations, health movements, and community based agencies. Simply put, we believe the time has come to ask whether there is life beyond the ivory tower for critical medical anthropology. And, if so, what factors and forces will determine its entry, position, and program within the professional health world.

It is fairly evident why this question is being raised. As Pelto has affirmed, "medical anthropology is, on the whole, an applied field, in which researchers ask the question, 'How can this situation be improved?'" [1, p. 436]. Yet, it is recognized that the answers medical anthropologists develop often are not welcomed by decision-makers and power wielders. Too often, as Kendall found in his work in diarrheal disease control in Honduras, "when anthropological evidence clash[es] with the viewpoint of medical authorities and with evidence collected from other sources, the former [is] not considered to be of sufficient weight to change the implementation strategy" [2, pp. 289-290]. Consequently, Wulff and Fiske observe: "Much of the

371

literature in applied anthropology is neutral or negative reporting of the frustration of ignored or underutilized anthropological data—what 'might have been' if we could only get policymakers' attention" [3, p. 1]. If conventional medical anthropology has had to struggle to gain a shaky foothold in the health field [4], what does this portend for an approach that seeks not to serve neutrally but to challenge directly the underlying political structures and relations that it sees as responsible for much ill health and poor treatment? In this light, those who discount critical medical anthropology have questioned its relevance to the health field and its viability beyond the cloistered environs of the university campus. Writing of the clinic, Eisenberg and Kleinman assert:

> the patient who seeks help from the doctor is today's victim, not salvageable by tomorrow's hoped-for reform. His or her distress will not be put aright by injunctions for political action . . . [5, p. 18].

In this vein, Wiley accuses CMA of callous disregard of contemporary misery because of its assessment that significant social restructuring is needed to achieve a fundamental reduction in the level of human suffering [6, p. 232].

These and similar statements appear to assume that critical praxis begins and ends with the advocacy of global transformation, since anything less would seem to amount to little more than system-maintaining reformism, a notion shared by some critical thinkers. Following a review of the critical social science literature, for example, Morgan notes that "one begins to anticipate the concluding paragraphs of each article: socialist revolution is the only path to a more humane, equitable, and healthy society" [7, p. 138]. By implication, in the view of these articles there can be no applied critical medical anthropology, because, as one critical colleague in an applied setting expressed it, "political economy leads you to put on macrostructural glasses but the applied setting forces you to be myopic" [8].

Additional questions confront critical medical anthropologists who seek to work in applied settings. Pflanz asks what would happen to the applied medical social scientist "who even tried to show how far the values set up by medicine are deliberately fostered in order to strengthen an unholy alliance between physicians and an elite bourgeoisie" [9, p. 8]. Others have wondered whether projects with a critical component can be approved by review panels dominated by health professionals. Note Pelto and Pelto, "Proposals for research in any of [the] national and international agencies are judged by interdisciplinary review panels, often (but not always) dominated by biomedical scientists" [10, p. 270]. Given the "considerable influence" [10] of biomedicine on proposal review, applied research generated by critical theory gain funding? Indeed, are self-identifed critical medical anthropologists even employable in applied work? In short, while it has been possible to develop a critical anthropology *of* health, there is concern that there may be insurmountable political barriers to the creation of a critical anthropology *in* health.

In this final chapter, we present our response to these criticisms and questions by addressing two apparent dilemmas confronting critical praxis: 1) if, as we have suggested in this book, powerful social classes ultimately control the health care system, is the whole notion of critical praxis in health an exercise in futility? and 2) if, as we also have asserted, the health care system both reflects and reproduces the wider system of social inequality and social control, is critical praxis a contradiction in terms? The perspective developed in this chapter is based on a recognition that there are both openings for critical praxis in the health domain and that such work can avoid cooptation into system-maintaining liberal reform. In short, we show that the practice of CMA need not be restricted to injunctions for radical political action in the closing paragraphs of journal articles and that there is much that can be achieved on the long and winding road to apogean goals. We support this argument by presenting two case examples of critical praxis.

Our approach to practice is predicated on a recognition of the dialectical unity of thought and action. As Sahlins notes, theory and practice often are construed as phenomenal alternatives, an "objectified distinction . . . that is . . . untrue in practice and absurd as theory" [11, p. 154]. All praxis is theoretical, it is driven and shaped by propositions about the world and the people who inhabit it, while all theorical work, has practical implications and real life consequences. Practice is the fundamental arena—and perhaps the only arena—for building theory, just as theory provides the confidence that enables action. In responding to postmodern critique of the production of knowledge and legitimacy of theory in anthropology, the Comaroffs have stressed, "If the discipline can unmask anything unique about the nature of the human condition—of colonialism and consciousness, of domination and resistance, of oppression and liberation—it is both possible and worthwhile" [12, p. xiv]. Better yet, if we can put that knowledge to active use in raising consciousness, bolstering resistance, and furthering liberation.

> Our practice may not make perfect, and it demands of us a deep awareness of its inevitable dangers and entanglements. Still, it can make something in the cause of praxis [12, p. xiv].

SOCIAL RELATIONS AND SOCIAL ACTION: THE STARTING POINTS OF SOCIAL SCIENCE

Questions about the relevance and viability of critical medical anthropology in the applied domain must be addressed, in part, in terms of an analysis of social relations and social action within the larger health field. These topics warrant renewed attention for two reasons. First, the failure to squarely confront the issue of power continues to diminish the significance of work within medical anthropology. Second, it has been suggested that anthropologists lack social power in medicine and hence are blocked from effective action, except with the approval, and in the face of censure by, institutional gatekeepers.

As Wolf indicates, the very term power leaves many anthropologists feeling uncomfortable [13]. While Bloch sees "extraordinary theoretical cowardice" [14, p. 121], in this trait of the discipline, we are inclined to see one core element of anthropological culture: the potent desire to stay as close as possible to the ethnographic ground of experience, or, in Ortner's words, to describe "real peole doing real things" [15, p. 144], things that matter. While our inclination to remain connected to the immediate worlds of observable behavior is clearly a strength of anthropology, as Wolf emphasizes, "we must take the futher step of understanding the consequences of the exercise of power" [13, p. 594].

Limitations in medical anthropology's effort to integrate a conception of power have been discussed at some length with reference especially to studies guided by the perspective of medical ecology [16, 17]. Recently, it has been asserted, attempts have been made to redress this shortcoming. For example, Carey, argues that

> Medical anthropologists seeking to study health from an integrated biocultural perspective . . . need to add another layer of analysis to current adaptation models. In addition to understanding the biological health consequences of local social relations and the efficacy of individual adaptive coping responses, the model should more thoroughly examine how broader macrolevel social forces affect the local system by shaping social structure and/or access patterns to critical material and social resources [18, p. 268].

In light of this concern, Carey proceeds to show how the exercize of power (expressed through such acts as land expropriation) contributes to enhanced psycho-biological stress and resulting deterioration of health in the rural Peruvian Andes. "Far from being in the 'natural' order of things," he emphasizes, "these social stressors are created by social relations at the local level which are shaped in turn by larger scale political-economic and sociocultural forces generated by the rest of Peru and beyond" [18, p. 272]. The truly secondary character of "natural" stressors is clarified through a presentation of field data on morbidity collected from three local sites situated in varying ecological zones characterized by differing altitudes and resulting differences in subsistence strategies. While the suggestion is made that subsistence options are wider at lower elevations and ease of breathing greater,

> there appears to be an inverse relationship with altitude and morbidity. This is directly opposite to what one would expect if physical stressors associated with altitude were the primary factor leading to poor health . . . in the population [18, p. 285].

In his effort to incorporate the macrolevel into his analysis, Carey is led away from a central pillar of the medical ecology model (the assumption that health is a measure of how well a population has adapted to its environment). Indeed, his work shows the fundamental importance of making social relations the starting point of health social science.

Unfortunately, the tendency within medical anthropology has been to treat the concept of social relations as the pattern of interpersonal bonds maintained among individuals or small groups with face-to-face interaction. For example, Schoepf points out that the doctor-patient relationship is often described as if it were "an internally balanced and self-maintained dyadic social system" [19, p. 112]. Thus Katon and Kleinman tell us:

> In contemporary American culture, it is appropriate for doctor and patient to meet as equals, with the former rendering expert advice and the latter bearing ultimate responsibility for deciding whether or not to follow that advice. Moreover, we

believe . . . [it is] feasible to routinely structure clinical relationships in this way [20, p. 263].

In Kleinman's influential explanatory model approach, the route to achieving equality between doctors and patients and the proper role for medical anthropology is the mediation of the differing cognitive models doctors, patients, and others bring to the clinical encounter [21, 22]. Ultimately rooted in a understanding of society as comprising a set of somewhat like-minded individuals with a generally shared cultural framework, complementary interpersonal relations, and an integrated, inter-related social system, this perspective has been disinclined to recognize the doctor-patient and other relationships in the health field as unavoidably conflictual meeting points between parties with fundamentally different and objectively opposed sociopolitical and political-economic interests. As Pappas indicates,

> While a consideration of power in the doctor-patient interaction is implicit in Kleinman's work, the potentially exploitative character of the power imbalance in this relationship is not developed. His theoretical work does not identify asymmetry in the doctor-patient interaction as a problem, primarily, it seems because the manifest purpose of the profession is to help. Power is seen as exterior (and negative) [23, p. 202].

This exteriority finds expression in Kleinman's suggestion that "the absence of real structural equality need not prevent negotiation from occurring, if both parties to the clinical transaction desire it" [20, p. 264]. In other words, the clinical relationship is primarily a product of interpersonal interaction, an expression of the needs and desires of two parties who may meet on somewhat unlevel ground but have the capacity through honest negotiation to "diminish the discrepancy in power actually constituted in particular doctor-patient relationships" [20, p. 264].

However, as suggested in Chapter 8, much of the tension in the clinical encounter does not derive from the existence of diverse health subcultures nor is it due to a failure in medical education to instill an appreciation of folk models of health and illness, but rather is a reproduction of larger class, racial, and gender conflicts in the broader society. As Habermas has shown, these structural factors prohibit the type of open communication and collective decision-making which the Kleinman model posits [24]. Notes Lazarus

> To develop a theory with the capability of studying and analyzing more accurately any doctor-patient relationship, the focus must embrace all major factors that contribute to the relationship. Above all, these should include the social relationship between the doctor and the patient, with its unequal distribution of power and knowledge. The explanatory model approach has been instrumental in drawing attention both to the importance of incorporating people's knowledge of illness into therapeutics and to the biomedical model that permeates Western medicine. To move beyond the explanatory model approach, however, we must focus on negotiation between patients' and physicians' models within the context of their differential power in social relations [25, p. 54].

Unfortunately, laments Waitzkin "few studies have linked doctor-patient interaction to a broader structural framework" [26, p. 602]. While in more recent writings,

Kleinman [27] has drawn attention to the role of oppression in the social origins of distress and disease, "power remains outside of the doctor-patient interaction as in his original scheme" [23, p. 202].

Lacking in much work done in medical anthropology is a full appreciation of social structure as a configuration of power alignments embodied in all personal relationships and social institutions, including the various sectors of the health system. Power, in fact, can be defined as the determining capacity of social relations [28]. From this perspective the clinical encounter, indeed the whole health system, emerges as an arena and a product of an ongoing social struggle among groups with historically opposed interests and marked differences in their capacity to mobilize institutional power. This expanded understanding allows recognition of the underlying dynamic of the health field, namely that "medicine . . . is a social relation in contradiction" [29, p. 531].

Revealed therein is the limitation in the line of thinking that asserts that medical anthropologists are naive to believe they can have much critical influence on medicine and hence their proper role is to play a mildly critical, mildly influential role as cultural mediators and facilitators in health care provision and decision-making [30]. Such a view reifies medicine, treating it and the wider health field as static entities created and ruled from above, rather than as dynamic, contradictory expressions of overt and covert struggle between dominant groups who promote a system that enhances control on the one hand and subordinate groups who demand care on the other. While there are an array of structural and situational variables influencing the character of a health system or any of its local expressions, the ultimate determinant of the legitimacy accorded critical approaches is the balance of power among contending social groups.

Although analyses dating from before the time of Marx and Engels have attempted to describe the class structure of the capitalist social formation generally or for particular capitalist societies, there has been less attention given to the uneven distribution of power within the various institutions and subparts of a social system. Regarding variability in the distribution of power at the level of the nation-state, Wolf points out that

> While all capitalists share a common interest in class domination, individual groups of capitalists are in fact often at loggerheads, driven by divergent short-term interests. . . . Different segments of the capitalist class will . . . enter into alliances with segments of other classes, including segments of the . . . working class [31, p. 308].

As a result of such conflicts and alliances, the class interests of nonhegemonic social segments find expression and realization in particular policies, institutions, programs, and services. For example, Doyal [32] refers to the creation of the National Health Service (NHS) in Britain as "an important part of the post-war settlement between capital and labour," a partial fulfillment of labor's demand that commitment to the war effort would mean an end to "the heartbreak conditions of the thirties" [33, p. 21].

Consequently, there exist "institutional and situational openings" for influence and activity at many points in health care systems. Community based organizations, community health and mental health centers, women's clinics, union-run health programs, and similar entities—because they must address the concerns of poor, working class, and oppressed groups—are local-level examples of struggle-generated openings for critical intention [34-40]. Progressive social movements concerned with improving the health and well-being of oppressed populations or with limiting the control over health wielded by physicians, the pharmaceutical and medical technology industries, or hospitals have also been instrumental in creating openings for critical involvement in the health field. The network of alternative health programs and practices created by the women's health movement, the gay and lesbian health crisis movement, self-care organizations, occupational health and safety efforts, environmental protection campaigns, and community controlled hospitals are examples of health care settings and activities in which critical medical anthropologists have found opportunities to make useful contributions [41-46]. Even state-run programs brought into existence because of popular pressure, such as those designed to address problems like AIDS, homelessness and hunger, can become important arenas of critical medical anthropology praxis [47-52]. At the international level, the health systems of a number of socialist-oriented countries have provided opportunities for critical medical anthropology practice in recent years [53, 54].

In short, while structural barriers to critical application are both real and impinging, in a class divided social formation riddled by contradiction and enlivened by diverse expressions of class and related struggle, various opportunities exist for critical medical anthropology to affect health. These diverse niches within the health system provide space for the formulation, testing, evaluation, and reformulation of critical praxis. Despite clear difficulties, what we have called "institutional and situational openings" offer room for optimism. As Fresia has argued,

> We have been told all our lives that we can't change anything, that you can't fight city hall. At every meeting there is someone who always makes a case why we should not be radical—it will alienate someone, we are not ready, we need to educate a little more, read a little more, get more numbers. Well, you can always make the case not to be radical. But don't. It's a lie. The doubt is false [55, p. 198].

PRAXIS SHORT OF TRANSFORMATION

Beyond the issue of access lies the question of critical medical anthropology's ability to be something other than a system-maintaining approach to tinkering and patching in health. Unfortunately, like the sundry good intentions paving the road to hell, the evolutionary pathway of capitalist society is lined with the remnants of progressive initiatives co-opted to serve oppressive ends (usually by providing cushioning for the roughest edges of inherently exploitative social relations, e.g., many components of the welfare state). As Waitzkin notes,

> When oppressive social conditions exist, reforms to improve them seem reasonable. However, the history of reform in capitalist countries has shown that reforms most often follow social protest, make incremental improvements that do not change overall patterns of oppression, and face cutbacks when protest recedes [56, p. 359].

Thus, Piven and Cloward have effectively chronicled the history of public welfare in the United States in relation to public protest and the demand for relief from structurally imposed destitution [57]. Health reforms share a common history. Hyman, for example, concluded from his evaluation of the long-term effects of nine reform projects designed to improve the health of poor and working people in New York that "regardless of the nature of the program, support or service, they were underfinanced and thus hardly able to meet the overwhelming needs for health services in the ... community" [58, p. 188]. In addition to financial problems, most of the programs faced "organizational inhibiting constraints, or poor commitment as factors that prevented their achievement" [58, p. 195]. In a somewhat similar vein, Morgen documents the process of state co-optation of a feminist health clinic, a process involving an erosion of democratic decision-making, a narrowing of the organizational mission to service delivery and away from social organizing and community education, and a loss of autonomy [37].

The conclusion sometimes drawn from such cases is that reform *by nature* is suspect because it only leads to further control. This is said to be especially true of medical reform because of the vital regulatory functions performed by biomedicine concomitant with the secularization of society. Echoing Foucault, Turner argues that "the rise of preventive medicine, social medicine and community medicine has extended ... agencies of regulation deeper and deeper into social life" [59, p. 38]. All of these socially oriented medical disciplines, it is asserted, are but new-fangled "power techniques" deployed to more closely observe, know, regulate, and utilize individuals through the manipulation of their bodies [60]. Using a dialectical approach, however, Navarro correctly identifies a weakness of this argument with reference to the popular demand for a national health service.

> To see medicine only as control ... is to fail to see the dialectical nature of medicine in which there is also a useful needed function. To believe otherwise is to think that when the majority of Americans demand a national health program, they are asking for more control. ... The working class demands medical services because, in large degree, it gets benefits from the utilization of these services. ... But as long as these services exist under capitalism, they will be under the influence of the dominant class, which will try to use these medical services ... to optimize its own interests. In the same degree that the capitalist and working classes are intrinsically in conflict ..., these two functions—the dominating and the useful in medicine—are also in contradiction [29, p. 531].

While the provision of medical care as a welfare function can serve to disarm social protest, it is nonetheless true that "by placing pressure on the 'system' real gains can be achieved—such as improved levels of access to care" [61, p. 131]. Following this line of reasoning, a distinction must be drawn between two fundamentally different categories of social and health reform. Gorz accomplished this task in his differentiation between "reformist and non-reformist reform" [62] Gorz used the term reformist reform to designate the conscious implementation of minor material improvements that avoid any alteration of the basic structure of social relations in a social system. In his incisive critique of applied medical anthropology in Latin America, Bonfil Batalla aptly portrayed the underlying character of this type of reform.

Sometimes it looks as if those who work along the road of slow evolution intend to achieve only minimal changes, so that the situation continues to be substantially the same; this is, in other words, to change what is necessary so that things remain the same. Those who act according to such a point of view may honestly believe that their work is useful and transforming; however, they have in fact aligned themselves with the conservative elements who oppose the structural transformations that cannot be postponed . . . [63, p. 92].

Characteristic of reformist reform is its vulnerability to co-optation by dominant forces in a social system. Exemplary is the work of medical social scientists in the health field in Britain. As Susser showed, the history of British medical social science can be divided into three phases [64]. In the first, medical social scientists "struggled for a place, any place" in the health system [64, p. 407]. The second phase was marked by the acceptance of social scientists into the system because they were seen as serving a useful function by those with power over health policy. In the last phase, "social science can be said to have been co-opted by those at the administrative center of power" [64, p. 408].

Between the poles of reformist reform and complete structural transformation, Gorz identified a category of applied work that he labeled *non-reformist reform*. Here he referred to efforts aimed at making permanent changes in the social alignment of power. While reformist reform tends to obscure the causes of suffering and sources of exploitation, non-reformist reform is concerned with unmasking the origins of social inequity. Moreover, this type of praxis strives to heighten rather than dissipate social action. Sanders suggested two principles to guide such work: enhancing democratization and eliminating mystification [65]. According to Sanders, critical health workers

should show themselves to be in solidarity with the people by putting their skills at the disposal of those acting with the poorest and most powerless. Encouraging democratic control over the provision of health care and showing oneself to be willing to submit to the will of the majority, rather than asserting one's professional autonomy, is crucially important. And its accompaniment, constantly attempting to demystify medical knowledge and practice, is the second principle [65, p. 219].

A third principle is suggested by the long struggle to improve living and working conditions expressed in Virchow's famous assertion that "Medicine is a social science and politics is nothing else but medicine on a large scale." It has been well established that the major gains in health status and longevity that separate the United States and Europe from much of the rest of the world were in large part a product of improved social conditions [66, 67]. In short, disease cannot simply be reduced to a pathological entity in nature, but must be understood as the product of historically located sociopolitical processes. Consequently, medicine "ought to be . . . a form of applied sociology, since to understand the illness of a patient it is important (indeed necessary) to locate the patient in a social and personal environment" [59, p. 5]. To cite one example:

an insulin reaction in a diabetic postal worker might be ascribed (in a reductionist mode) to an excessive dose of insulin causing an outpouring of adrenaline, a failure of the pancreas to respond with appropriate glucagon secretion etc. Alternatively, the cause might be sought in his having skipped breakfast because he was late for work; unaccustomed physical exertion demanded by a foreman; inability to break for a snack; or, at a deeper level, the constellation of class forces in U.S. society which assures capitalist domination of production and the moment to moment working lives of the proletariate [68, p. 1208; also see 69, 70].

The larger lesson is that "disease . . . [all disease] must be put to the test of political practice's rather than be accepted routinely as natural, inevitable, or best responded to through clinical intervention [71, p. 454] . To evoke McKnight's axiom for critical health action: "To convert a medical problem into a political issue is central to health improvement" [45, p. 415].

Such conversion, which constitutes a reversal of the standard medical tendency to individualize and privatize sickness, is the first step in critical practice. Praxis, therefore, can never be reduced to an "anthropology for medicine" [cf. 73] but must be guided by the recognition that the key determinants of health are social relations. Consequently, the non-reformist reforms that comprise the day-to-day work of critical practice must "be regarded as a means and not an end, as dynamic phases in a progressive struggle, not as stopping places" [62, p. 84].

As this discussion implies, critical medical anthropology praxis must emerge from a recognition of a significant limitation in contemporary globalist approaches to social change [see 72]. In world system, dependency, and related globalist theories, there is "a tendency to assign all causality to the world capitalist system, and, in the process, to ignore the impact of local-level actors" [73, pp. 123-124]. The corrective for this form of "global functionalism" [72] is a restoration of a dialectical understanding of social process and organization. Such an approach directs attention toward opportunities for critical action, such as the two examples that follow.

THE STRUGGLE FOR NON-REFORMIST REFORM: TWO CASE EXAMPLES

Case 1: The Hispanic Health Council

In 1978, a community based health institute called the Hispanic Health Council was formally organized in the Puerto Rican community of Hartford, Connecticut. The Council began as a partnership between several university-based applied medical anthropologists and a small group of health activists from the local Puerto Rican community. While various factors contributed to the birth of this community based organization, a tragic incident in the local community played a pivotal role in unleashing the energy needed to launch the organization. The incident began when the eight month old child of a young Puerto Rican mother who was monolingual in Spanish took ill. The baby developed a fever, became increasingly irritable, and started to vomit. Lacking a family physician or health insurance program, the mother hurried her child to the emergency room of one of the three hospitals in Hartford. The medical staff of the ER instructed the mother (in English) to give the baby liquids and aspirin. The mother found the treatment she received at the hands of the medical providers to be harsh and alienating. They, in turn, experienced the mother as 'hysterical' and 'overreactive.' Nonetheless, when the child's condition continued to deteriorate, the mother responded by going the next day to a second ER. The experience was not very different from the first clinical encounter. Then, on the evening of the second day, the child's condition became critical and the police were called. The baby died of dehydration in the police car on the way to the last of the city's ERs. This incident, which crystallized many of the problems Puerto Ricans faced in receiving adequate and appropriate treatment and care from dominant health care institutions, sparked a series of angry community demonstrations and produced a heightened awareness of health as a pressing political issue in the Puerto Rican community. Local activists came to the conclusion that an organized and sustained effort was needed to achieve meaningful change in this domain [75].

Despite a sizeable increase in Hartford's Puerto Rican population since 1960, it was felt that health care providers and institutions had made only a very limited effort to respond to the linguistic, cultural, social, and health needs of the Puerto Rican community. The initial goal of the Council, as a result, was to ascertain the nature and contours of these needs. Specifically, in its first efforts the Council attempted to determine the range of health and living conditions in the Puerto Rican community, assess popular health beliefs and illness behaviors, discern unmet needs for specific types of health care and services, and evaluate the organization, ethnic composition, attitudes, and behaviors of prominent health care institutions. This agenda contributed to the centrality of community research in the Council's approach to health change, a development that has helped to sustain an opening for critical medical anthropology in the organization.

As data were collected, a primary organizational concern at the Council became the translation of research findings into effective, empirically grounded, culturally appropriate interventions. Based on its various research projects the Council began to organize specific programs designed to impact the health scene in Hartford as it relates to Puerto Ricans and other groups suffering from poverty, discrimination, poor health, and linguistic and cultural differences with dominant institutions [76].

For example, one of the interventions begun by the Council was called Project Apoyo. The project trained and placed a bicultural/bilingual case coordinator in a local neonatal intensive care unit (NICU) to assist Hispanic families during and after their infant's hospitalization and to facilitate the transition from hospital to home and community.

> A key element in this case coordination approach was that of assuring adequate parent-professional communication, a function which goes well beyond the translation of information from one language to another. Rather, the goal was to help families understand, from their own perspective, the meaning and implications of professionals' communications about infants' medical problems, to help families deal with their own reactions to medically-related events, and to promote parent advocacy on behalf of their children. . . . The coordination function also included helping professionals to understand families' concerns and reactions and to appreciate cultural and social influences on parental perceptions and behaviors [77, p. 1].

This project was developed in response to growing recognition of the lack of culturally sensitive services and training for service providers. Consequently, major discrepancies were found between the experience of Hispanic mothers and staff in the NICU. Before placement of the project's case coordinator, nurses at the NICU reported that most Hispanic mothers did not visit their hospitalized infant even once per day and that only about 7 percent called to check on the condition of their child. Moreover, nurses indicated that Hispanic mothers asked fewer questions, were less realistic about the nature of their baby's problems, participated less in discharge planning, had a poorer understanding of their child's condition, and maintained poorer relations with unit staff than non-Hispanic mothers. Mothers in the Council's research sample reported visiting the unit much more often than indicated in nurses' reports, and generally saw themselves as being more involved in the care of their child than did the nurses. However, with the placement of the case coordinator, staff perceptions began to change.

> Nurses reported that the intervention caused noticeable behavioral changes in the Puerto Rican mothers. When a mother saw the coordinator in the unit, she was much more likely to feed, bath, and interact with her baby. Nurses reported that prior to the intervention, mothers were intimidated by the unit (as most people are when they first see all the sick and small babies attached to machines), but throughout the intervention they came in and touched their babies, asked more questions, and generally appeared more involved [77, p. 53].

In short, the Apoyo Project was able to demonstrate the importance of cultural differences in health care and the need for culturally appropriate treatment. Whatever the initial perceptions of nurses or mothers, both groups agreed that the intervention facilitated communication and participation in care-giving.

However, this knowledge fell on deaf ears! At the project's conclusion, the Council was unable to convince the local hospital to institutionalize the case coordinator role. Administrator perceptions of the appropriate investment of hospital resources, into new high-tech treatment procedures and equipment, new structures, and new parking lots (which nibble constantly at the housing stock in the surrounding Puerto Rican neighborhood), have slowed appreciation of the importance of culturally sensitive treatment and communication.

Experiences like the one described above have shown the Council that good research and innovative projects are not sufficient to make changes in the health care system. *Political action is also a necessary component of the Council's repertoire.* Factors other than explanatory models influence the organization of health care and health-related living and working conditions. Consequently, the Council has been actively involved in various health and social struggles in the Puerto Rican community and has lent support and resources to most progressive initiatives launched by Puerto Rican and other activists concerned with changing oppressive social relations. For example, the Council played important roles in fighting the effort to consecrate English as the official language of Connecticut, organizing the local community in response to a hit-and-run death of a Puerto Rican girl by a prominent attorney, and defending several Puerto Rican nationalists on trial in a local court. Research findings from Council studies of the health and social status of Puerto Ricans in the city, the nature of the health care system, and illness beliefs and behaviors in the community provide vital information for exposing health problems, countering official stereotypes, questioning institutional and governmental policies, empowering local activists, and training community members in the sources of their pressing health problems. Exemplary, is the recent Council study of hunger among children in the city. A carefully structured community survey carried out by the Council found that 41 percent of low-income families with school-aged children under twelve experience hunger each year [78]. Rather than urging a stop-gap response to this growing problem, the Council launched a media and community drive to make fundamental and long-lasting changes in local, regional, and federal programs, policies, and institutional practices that contribute to hunger, as well as seeking ways to empower the local community to respond directly to the threat of hunger.

Indeed, empowerment and community education have been central to the Council's mission. For example, in response to the AIDS crisis the Council launched a variety of initiatives designed to counter both the homophobic portrayal of AIDS as a disease caused by gay people and the religious construction of the epidemic as divine retribution. Council research helped to determine the actual character of community beliefs and attitudes about AIDS, the nature and extent of AIDS-related risk behavior in the community, and the range of social, economic, and health problems faced by injection drug users attempting to avoid HIV infection. Based on this research, the Council developed several AIDS initiatives. The Comunidad y Responsibilidad Project, for example, was designed to serve as a community-centered, primary AIDS prevention, education, and support model for the Puerto Rican population. In particular, the aim of the project was to reach and mobilize Puerto Rican women, a group not only suffering increasingly from HIV infection but one having the capacity to offer education to all layers of the community — children, family, friends, neighborhood, church, etc. The project actively addressed and attempted to creatively mobilize features of Puerto Rican culture to overcome existing linguistic, cultural, and socioeconomic barriers and develop for the Puerto Rican community the type of culturally congruent community empowerment model that has appeared in recent years in the gay community in response to the AIDS crisis. In the project, a cadre of community members were trained as AIDS activists and provided with the resources and support to organize community discussions about the nature of the AIDS crisis in the Puerto Rican community, the need for collective community response to the epidemic, and the health and social support needs of Puerto Rican PWAs [79]. Despite opposition from various corners, the Council also played a leading role in advocating for the implementation of sterile needle exchange as an AIDS prevention strategy for injection drug users. Because of broad support from community AIDS activists, Connecticut became the first state to sponsor a needle exchange program [80]. In 1992, Connecticut extended government supported needle exchange beyond the initial pilot project in New Haven. AIDS activists in Hartford, including medical anthropologists at the Hispanic Health Council and the Institute for Community Research, who helped to push this change at both the state and local levels, then participated in the effort to develop, implement, and evaluate the Hartford needle exchange program.

Activities like these have provided an important critical edge to the Council's work, while opening opportunities for the efforts of several critical medical anthropologists and political activists on the Council's staff. Like many community agencies, the Council strives to please several audiences, including its Board of Directors, the professional Hispanic sector in Hartford, the poor and working class Puerto Rican community, funders, and the health care institutions it is attempting to influence. As a result, contradictions exist in the Council's work. Nonetheless, organizations like the Council, which must remain close to the struggles, overt and covert, of local communities, are important arenas for the advancement of non-reformist reforms and for testing alternative strategies for praxis in critical medical anthropology.

Case 2: The U.S. Farm Labor Movement

As succinctly summarized by Friedland and Nelkin:

> For too many farmworkers life is poor, nasty, brutish, and short. Too many farmworkers are present-day slaves, subservient to and dependent upon the fluctuations of economies, the whims of growers, the vargaries of weather, the march of technology, and the decisions of government. This condition is the predictable consequence of economic and political powerlessness [81, p. ix].

The contribution of the oppressive life conditions experienced by farm laborers to adverse health outcomes through specific physiological mechanisms has been examined by Scheder [69]. While numerous anthropologists over the years have provided support to farmworker efforts to improve their living and working conditions, Ken Barger's contribution (in collaboration with Ernesto Reza) is notable because it has involved a sustained and systematic attempt to bring anthropological concepts and methods to this endeavor [82]. Over the last decade, Barger and Reza have collaborated in a number of applied research and action projects in conjunction with farmworker organizations in the midwest and in California. They describe the development of their collaboration as follows:

> Ernesto Reza was a FLOC [Farm Labor Organizing Committee] staff member working with the boycott campaign and a doctoral student in organizational psychology at the University of Michigan. Ken Barger was an associate professor of anthropology at Indiana University at Indianapolis and coordinator of the Indianapolis Farm Worker Support Committee, a citizen's group involved in social action and advocacy on behalf of FLOC. We met in 1980 on a bus of FLOC farmworkers going to a UFW [United Farm Workers] convention in Texas, and on that trip we actively discussed ways in which FLOC and academics could cooperate. Contributing to our relationship were the personal values and views we shared that led us both to become involved in the farm labor cause. We also shared common academic interests in applied change [83, p. 64].

Two of the projects they have worked on together, the Campbells Labels Project and the California farmworker's survey, will be discussed.

Because of a radical imbalance of power at the site of production between farmworkers on the one hand and growers, law enforcement, and politicians on the other, since the 1960s the farmworkers movement in the United States has focused much of its energies on mobilizing popular support for consumer boycotts of selected goods produced by agricultural corporations. As Barger and Reza indicate: "The rationale of [the] boycott . . . is that the combined social and economic power of millions of individual Americans who are concerned with justice can counterbalance the relative political powerlessness of farmworkers" [83, p. 271]. In this regard, Barger and Reza helped to organize the Campbells Labels Project in Indiana in 1981. The critical praxis of the project had two notable features. First, it was oriented toward changing the social context (the surrounding dominant society) of a targeted population (farmworkers) rather than the targeted population itself. Second, "the project included active involvement and commitment in advocating change, rather than a detached role of providing ideas and information but not assuming responsibility, which is more common to many applied academics" [82, p. 269]. The project was organized in response to the Campbells Soup Company's "Labels for Education" program in which schools and churches were encouraged to collect labels from soup cans and to send these to the company in exchange for educational and athletic equipment. This promotional program—which was predicated on the inadequate funding of public schools—benefited the company by providing increased sales, tax deductions, advertisement, and improved public relations. The latter helped to counter some of the "bad press" Campbells received in response to its staunch refusal to negotiate with FLOC when its members launched a strike at the company's tomato field operations in 1978.

The action project was designed to encourage schools to review their involvement in the labels program with the intention of undercutting the company's promotional efforts. The project focused on providing education about the social issues involved directly to parents' organizations affiliated with local schools. The educational materials developed and widely distributed by the project did not specifically ask schools to drop involvement in the labels program but rather emphasized that school parents had an opportunity to "set a positive example of citizenship for their children by openly and responsibly examining the issues" [82, p. 271]. The effort was supported by the involvement of teachers organizations, church committees, and other community groups and through an active mass media campaign. In conjunction with the project, pre- and post-test telephone surveys of all local schools were conducted to test the impact of the campaign on involvement in the labels program. The post-test survey, implemented about six months after the project began, found that participation in the labels program had dropped by 43 percent while school awareness of the farmworkers struggle had risen from 9 percent to 82 percent. Feedback from parents indicated that the education campaign was a major (although not the only) factor in school decisions to terminate involvement in the campaign. One additional indicator of the project's success was that Campbells was forced to launch its own public relations effort to explain its refusal to negotiate with FLOC.

Based on the success of the labels project, Barger and Reza were contacted by the UFW to conduct a scientifically valid survey of farmworker attitudes in California. The purpose of the survey was to determine farmworkers views of the farm labor movement as a vehicle for improving their living and working conditions. The study was a joint project with the National Farm Workers Ministry, an ecumenical group with a long history of involvement in farm labor issues. As expressed by Barger and Reza, the survey "was an example of a community action model of applied change, where our role as professionals was to support democratic self-determination of farmworkers" [83, p. 261].

The study targeted a random sample of 137 local farmworkers employed by Kern and Tulare country table grape growers (based on employment lists prepared for another purpose by employers) and a stratified random sample of fifty-seven migrant farmworkers housed at local labor camps. The majority of the farmworkers (72%) were employed on farms not covered by UFW contracts. Interviews were conducted with a 200-item standardized, pretested questionnaire, which included both open and closed questions as well as built-in validity checks. Completed interviews were coded and recoded for accuracy, entered into a computer file, and then rechecked against the original for accuracy. As Barger and Reza emphasize,

> we used the highest scientific standards possible in the research . . . because the study . . . focus[ed] on a major social issue . . . [W]e wanted to be absolutely sure of the concepts and methods used in collecting and analyzing the data for two reasons. First, the results of applied work can impact directly on people's lives, and we therefore have a moral obligation to be sure that findings are both accurate and predictive. . . .And second, just because we are committed to our social convictions, we want to be sure our understandings are as accurate and predictive as possible, so we can make effective changes [83, p. 262] .

Findings from the study show that farmworkers in California overwhelmingly supported the UFW as their collective bargaining agent (78%) and that the UFW offers the best alternative for improving their lives (83%). Endorsement of the union was as strong among those not already affiliated with the UFW as those who were current UFW members. Moreover, it was found that farmworkers that are covered by UFW contracts reported significantly better living and working conditions, factors that, as Scheder's shows, have direct and significant impact on farmworker health [69]. Workers protected by UFW contracts expressed much higher job satisfaction, greater employment benefits (including paid sick leave), far greater access to health care, and significantly better social stability (e.g., residential and marital stability). As concisely summarized by one of the respondents: "Look at it. Things are much better off now than before the Union. We have better wages, more benefits, and bathrooms in the fields" [quoted in 83, pp. 266-267]. In short, the study scientifically validated the UFW's claim to represent farmworkers, a claim that growers and politicians with vested political interests have attempted to discredit during the entire history of the farm workers movement. In addition to refuting allegations that the UFW lacks broad support among workers, findings of the study have been used by the union to expand services to members, lobby legislators on behalf of farmworkers needs, improve contract clauses to better reflect farmworkers' concerns, and publicize the dismal state of farmwork living and working conditions.

In explaining their work, Barger and Reza specifically address a question raised by some critics of critical medical anthropology, namely: is there not a contradiction between social commitment and valid anthropological research? According to Barger and Reza:

> We would like to make clear ... that taking value positions does not mean that professional standards are compromised.... Since applied work inherently involves social changes and can therefore make direct impacts on peoples lives, we need to be very sure of where we are valid in our understandings and also of where we are limited... *Valid scientific research is ... based on the control of biases and limitations (rather than their absence),* and such controls must be consciously included in the conceptualization of the issue, in the collection of data, in the analysis of data, and in making grounded interpretations of findings. We argue that it is because of the very value positions involved that the highest scientific standards are needed ... , because we have to have valid understandings if our contributions are to be effective and constructive [83, pp. 276-277, emphasis added].

Neither the commitment of Barger and Reza to democratic self-determination among farmworkers nor their conclusion that the poor health, noxious working conditions, poverty-level wages, and substandard housing and sanitation facilities experienced by this population are the product of economic exploitation by their employers, precluded these researchers from conducting valid research [84]. By extension, it is evident that all researchers (whatever their political orientation) are influenced in their choice of research areas, adoption of theoretical perspectives, and design of research methods, by the values and commitments they hold near and dear.

CONCLUSION

Nutrition and health activists, Lappe, Collins and Kinley, have written

> It's hard to work toward a vision of something better without believing that change is possible. That seems obvious. But what allows us to believe that change is possible? Certainly part of the answer is discovering that much of the suffering we see today is not due to geographic or other physical givens but is the result of the actions of people. What people create, people can change [85, p. 153].

This insight raises questions about responsibility. Critical medical anthropology is predicated on the conviction that "no anthropologist can escape involvement" [86, p. 302]. In light of this realization, critical medical anthropology is characterized by its abiding concern with the question: involvement in whose interest? Ultimately, critical medical anthropology cannot achieve its goals without serious consideration of the appropriate application of critical knowledge to the practical domain of health because "the exercise of critical thought implies a discrimination between what is merely given and what ought to exist" [87, p. 127]. As the Comaroffs note, "the social sicentist has in the end to suspend disbelief and *act*" [12, p. xiv]. Unfortunately, an enduring effect of the the 1960s anti-war movement—which grew out of and was sustained by campus activism—has been the tendency to assume that critical ideas have no natural home in the so-called "real world" outside the protective walls of the academy. There is a good deal of anti-working class sentiment embedded in such thinking, as well as a distorted sense of the origin of many counter-hegemonic insights. Recognition that in complex stratified societies counter-hegemonic struggles ensue on various levels across multiple axes of oppression (e.g., struggles against racism, sexism, heterosexism, classism, ageism, discrimination against the physically challenged, environmental destruction) helps bring into focus the numerous opportunities for critical intervention. In this light, it is appropriate to ask what special attributes critical medical anthropology has to offer movements to create and sustain nonreformist reform of health care. Several are identifiable:

1. The anthropological tradition of cultural relativism (whatever its limitations) and the discipline's enduring concern with insider understanding arm critical medical anthropology with an appreciation of and commitment to the principle of self-determination. Support of self-determination is further supported by the anthropological obligation to counter Western, colonial ethnocentrism and to create opportunities for the voices of so-called "people without history" (i.e., oppressed Third Word populations) to be heard on the contemporary world stage. Critical medical anthropology practice, as a consequence, brings recognition of the folly inherent in the act of imposing externally generated "solutions" to externally determined health problems and seeks instead to work in conjunction with struggling communities and groups in responding to their felt needs. To this collaboration, critical medical anthropology brings several attributes including an understanding of research as potentially potent weapon in social struggle.

2. Critical medical anthropology is empowered by its understanding of local contexts in relationship to their location in the encompassing world or national systems [31]. As opposed to the earlier tendency within the discipline to isolate social dynamics within artificially boundable cultures, as exemplified by the labels program boycott, the holistic orientation of critical medical anthropology guides attention to the optimum level for effective praxis.

3. Recognition, on the one hand, of the historic role of culture in the shaping of human behavior and social configuration and, on the other, of the contribution of social relations to the generation of culture, establishes the ground for an awareness of the social origin and ideological function of concepts like disease, medicine, and social development. This awareness limits (but does not eliminate) the ever present threat of co-optation of community initiatives [37].

4. Acknowledgment of the contested nature of culture and the inherent contradictions of social relations directs the gaze of critical medical anthropologists toward opportunities for expanding the focus of health-related struggles from immediate to ultimate causes of illness and disease. In other words, critical medical anthropology is oriented toward consciousness-raising and empowerment through the unmasking of the structural roots of suffering and ill health.

5. Concern with social relations as a determinant force in social life directs critical attention to the alignment of forces in practical work. In an effort to offset the imbalance in social power across class, race or other social division, critical praxis emphasizes collaboration and coalition building. Central to critical praxis is the forging of collaborative relations across social segments that heretofore have been subject to divide and conquer tactics.

Providing a theoretical framework for the emergence of a critical anthropological praxis in health, based on a dialectical understanding of social relationship and social action, has been the major intent of this chapter. Convening discussions of the "dynamic phases" to be passed through in bringing to fruition what "ought to exist," as well as developing analyses of the obstacles to and strategies for accomplishing this goal, remain important tasks for critical medical anthropology.

REFERENCES

1. P. Pelto, A Note on Critical Medical Anthropology, *Medical Anthropology Quarterly, 2*:4, pp. 435-437, 1988.
2. C. Kendall, The Use and Non-Use of Anthropology: The Diarrheal Disease Control Program in Honduras, in *Making our Research Useful*, J. van Willigen, B. RyLko-Bauer, and A. McEkoy (eds.), Westview Press, Boulder, pp. 283-303, 1989.
3. R. Wulff and S. Fiske, Introduction, in *Anthropological Praxis*, R. Wulff and S. Fiske (eds.), Westview Press, Boulder, pp. 1-11, 1987.
4. N. Chrisman and T. Maretzki, *Clinically Applied Anthropology: Anthropologists in Health Science Settings*, Reidel, Dordrecht, 1982.
5. L. Eisenberg and A. Kleinman, Clinical Social Science, in *The Relevance of Social Science for Medicine*, L. Eisenberg and A. Kleinman, (eds.), D. Reidel, Dordrecht, pp. 1-23, 1981.
6. A. Wiley, Adaptation and the Biocultural Paradigm in Medical Anthropology: A Critical Review, *Medical Anthropology Quarterly, 6*:3, pp. 216-236, 1992.
7. L. Morgan, Dependency Theory in the Political Economy of Health: An Anthropological Critique, *Medical Anthropology Quarterly, 1*:2, pp. 131-154, 1987.
8. Personal communication with Rick Jacobsen, 1990.
9. M. Pflanz, Relations Between Social Scientists, Physicians and Medical Organizations in Health Research, *Social Science and Medicine, 9*, pp. 7-13, 1975.
10. P. Pelto and G. Pelto, Methods in Medical Anthropology, in *Medical Anthropology: Contemporary Theory and Method*, T. Johnson and C. Sargent (eds.), Praeger, New York, pp. 269-297, 1990.
11. M. Sahlins, *Islands of History*, University of Chicago Press, Chicago, 1985.
12. J. Comaroff and J. Comaroff, *Of Revelation and Revolution: Christianity, Colonialism, and Consciousness in South Africa*, University of Chicago Press, Chicago, 1991.
13. E. Wolf, Distinguished Lecture: Facing Power—Old Insights, New Questions, *American Anthropologist, 92*:3, pp. 586-596, 1990.
14. M. Bloch, *Marxism and Anthropology*, Oxford University Press, Oxford, 1983.
15. S. Ortner, Theory in Anthropology Since the Sixties, *Comparative Studies in Society and History, 26*:1, pp. 126-166, 1984.
16. M. Singer, The Limitations of Medical Ecology: The Concept of Adaptation in the Context of Social Stratification and Social Transformation, *Medical Anthropology, 10*, pp. 223-234, 1989.
17. M. Singer, *Farewell to Adaptationism: Unnatural Selection and the Politics of Biology*, presented at the International Symposium Program: Political-Economic Perspectives in Biological Anthropology: Building a Biocultural Synthesis, Wenner-Gren Foundation for Anthropological Research, Cabo San Lucas, Mexico, 1992
18. J. Carey, Social System Effects on Local Level Morbidity and Adaptation in the Rural Peruvian Andes, *Medical Anthropology Quarterly, 4*:3, pp. 266-295, 1990.
19. B. Schoepf, Human Relations Versus Social Relations in Medical Care, in *Topias and Utopias in Health*, S. Ingman and A. Thomas, (eds.), Mouton, The Hague, pp. 99-120, 1975.

20. W. Katon and A. Kleinman, Doctor-Patient Negotiation and Other Social Science Strategies in Patient Care, in *The Relevance of Social Science for Medicine,* L. Eisenberg and A. Kleinman, (eds), D. Reidel, Dordrecht, pp. 253-279, 1981.
21. A. Kleinman, Concepts and a Model for the Comparison of Medical Systems as Cultural Systems, *Social Science and Medicine, 12,* pp. 85-93, 1978.
22. A. Kleinman, *Patients and Healers in the Context of Culture,* University of California Press, Berkeley, 1980.
23. G. Pappas, Some Implications for the Study of the Doctor-Patient Interaction: Power, Structure, and Agency in the Work of Howard Waitzkin and Arthur Kleinman, *Social Science and Medicine, 30*:2, pp. 199-204, 1990.
24. J. Habermas, *The Theory of Communicative Action,* Beacon Press, Boston, 1984.
25. E. Lazarus, Theoretical Considerations for the Study of the Doctor-patient Relationship: Implications of a Perinatal Study, *Medical Anthropology Quarterly, 2*:1, pp. 34-58, 1988.
26. H. Waitzkin, Medicine, Superstructure and Micropolitics, *Social Science and Medicine, 13A,* pp. 601-609, 1979.
27. A. Kleinman, *Social Origins of Distress and Disease,* Yale University Press, New Haven, 1986.
28. W. Roseberry, *Anthropologies and Histories,* Rutgers University Press, New Brunswick, 1991,
29. V. Navarro, U.S. Marxist Scholarship in the Analysis of Health and Medicine, *International Journal of Health Services, 15,* pp. 525-545, 1985.
30. N. Scheper-Hughes, Three Proposition for a Critically Applied Medical Anthropology, *Social Science and Medicine, 30*:2, pp. 189-198, 1990.
31. E. Wolf, *Europe and the People Without History,* University of California Press, Berkeley, 1982.
32. L. Doyal, *The Political Economy of Health,* South End Press, Boston, 1979.
33. G. Forsyth, *Doctors and State Medicine: A Study of the British Health Service,* Pitman Medical Publishers, London, 1966.
34. M. Borrero, J. Schensul, and R. Garcia, Research Based Training for Organizational Change, *Urban Anthropology, 11*:1, pp. 129-153, 1982.
35. R. Chamberlin and J. Radebaugh, Delivery of Primary Care—Union Style, *New England Journal of Medicine, 29*:4, pp. 641-645, 1976.
36. P. Rudd, The United Farm Workers Clinic in Delano, Calif: A Study of the Rural Poor, *Public Health Reports, 90,* pp. 331-339, 1975.
37. S. Morgen, The Dynamics of Cooptation in a Feminist Health Clinic, *Social Science and Medicine, 23*:2, pp. 201-210, 1986.
38. J. Nashand M. Kirsch, The Discourse of Medical Science in the Construction of Consensus Between Corporation and Community, *Medical Anthrogology Quarterly, 2*:2, pp. 158-171, 1986.
39. S. Schensul and J. Schensul, Advocacy and Applied Anthropology, in *Social Scientists as Advocates,* G. Weber and G. McCall (eds.), Sage, Beverly Hills, pp. 121-165, 1982.
40. M. Singer, C. Flores, L. Davison, G. Burke, and Z. Castillo Puerto Rican Community Mobilizing in Response to the AIDS Crisis, *Human Organization, 50*:1, pp. 73-81, 1991.
41. H. Baer, Kerr McKee and the NRC: From Indian Country to Silkwood to Gore, *Social Science and Medicine, 30*:2, pp. 237-248, 1990.
42. C. Douglas and J. Scott, Alternative Health Care in a Rural Community, *Win Magazine, 14,* pp. 20-24, 1978.
43. L. Levin, Self-care: An International Perspective, *Social Policy, 7*:2, pp. 70-75, 1976.
44. H. Marieskind and B. Ehenreich, Toward Socialist Medicine: The Women's Health Movement, *Social Policy, 6*:2, pp. 34-42, 1975.

45. J. McKnight, Politicizing Health Care, in *The Sociology of Health and Illness,* P. Conrad and R. Kern, (eds.), St. Martins Press, New York, pp. 10-23, 1986.
46. N. Scheper-Hughes and A. Lovell, Breaking the Circuit of Social Control: Lessons in Public Psychiatry from Italy and Franco Basaglia, *Social Science and* Medicine, 23:2, pp. 159-178, 1986.
47. M. Singer, Community Centered Praxis: Toward an Alternative Nondominative Applied Anthropology, *Human Organization* (in press), 1995.
48. K. Hopper, More Than Passing Strange: Homelessness and Mental Illness in New York City, *American Ethnologist, 15*:1, pp. 155-167, 1986.
49. E. Susser and S. Conover, The Epidemiology of Homelessness and Mental Illness, in *Psychiatric Epidemiology: Progress and Prospects,* Brian Cooper (ed.), Croom Helm, London, 1987.
50. E. Susser, E. Struening, and S. Connover, Psychiatric Problems in Homeless Men, *Archives of General Psychiatry, 46,* pp. 845-850, 1989.
51. I. Susser, and M. Alfredo Gonzalez, Sex, Drugs and Videotape: The Prevention of AIDS in a New York City Shelter for Homeless Men, *Medical Anthropology, 14*, pp. 307-322, 1991.
52. M. Singer, Knowledge for Use: Anthropology and Community-Centered Substance Abuse Research, *Social Science and Medicine , 37*, pp. 15-25, 1993.
53. J. Donahue, International Organizations, Health Services, and Nation Building in Nicaragua, *Medical Anthropology Quarterly, 3*:3, pp. 258-269, 1989.
54. S. Guttmacher, Minimizing Health Risks in Cuba, *Medical Anthropology, 11*:2, pp. 167-180, 1989.
55. J. Fresia, *Toward an American Revolution,* South End Press, Boston, 1988.
56. H. Waitzkin A Marxist Analysis of the Health Care Systems of Advanced Capitalist Societies, in *The Relevance of Social Science for Medicine,* L. Eisenberg and A. Kleinman (eds.) D. Reider, Dordrecht, pp. 333-339, 1981.
57. F. F. Piven, and R. Cloward, *Regulating the Poor: The Functions of Public Welfare*, Vintage, New York, 1971.
58. H. H. Hyman, *The Politics of Health Care: Nine Case Studies of Innovative Planning in New York*, Praeger, New York, 1973.
59. B. Turner, *Medical Power and Social Knowledge,* Sage, London, 1987.
60. M. Foucault, *Discipline and Punish: The Birth of the Prison,* Pantheon Books, New York, 1977.
61. R. Jacobsen, Using Organizations to Pursue Political Economic Analysis: The Case of Primary Health Care for the Poor, *Medical Anthropology Quarterly, 17*:5, pp. 131-132, 1986.
62. A. Gorz, *Socialism and Revolution,* Basic Books, Garden City, New York, 1973.
63. G. Bonfil Batalla, Conservative Thought in Applied Anthropology: A Critique, *Human Organization, 25*:2, pp. 89-92, 1966.
64. M. Susser, Introduction to the Theme: A Critical Review of Sociology in Health, *International Journal of Health Services 4,* pp. 407-409, 1974.
65. D. Sanders, *The Struggle for Health,* MacMillan, London, 1985.
66. T. McKeown, *The Role of Medicine,* Nuffield Provincial Hospital Trust, London, 1976.
67. J. McKinlay and S. McKinlay The Questionable Contribution of Medical Measures to the Decline Motality in the United States in the 20th Century, *Milbank Memorial Fund Quarterly, 55*, pp. 405-428, 1977.
68. S. Woolhandler and D. Himmelstein Ideology in Medical Science: Class in the Clinic, *Social Science and Medicine, 28*:11, pp. 1205-1209, 1989.

69. J. Scheder, A Sickly-Sweet Harvest: Farmworker Diabetes and Social Equality, *Medical Anthropology Quarterly, 2*:3, pp. 251-277, 1988.
70. M. Singer, C. Arnold, M. Fitzgerald, L. Madden, and C.Voight von Legat Hypoglycemia-A Controversial Illness in U.S. Society, *Medical Anthropology, 8*:1, pp. 1-35, 1984.
71. E. Stark, Doctors in Spite of Themselves: The Limits of Radical Health Criticism, *International Journal of Health Services 12*:3, pp. 419-455, 1982.
72. C. Smith, Local History in Global Context: Social and Economic Transitions in Western Guatemala, in *Micro and Macro Levels of Analysis in Anthropology,* B. DeWalt and P. Pelto, (eds.), Westview Press, Boulder, pp. 147-164, 1985.
73. B. Schroder, Ethnic Identity and Non-capitalist Relations of Production in Chimborazo, Ecuador, in *Perspectives in U.S. Marxist Anthropology,* D. Hakken and H. Lessinger (eds.), Westview Press, Boulder, pp. 123-139, 1987.
74. M. Singer, Organizational Culture in A Community-based Health Organization: The Hispanic Health Council, *Anthropology of Work Review, 11*:3, pp. 7-12, 1990.
75. S. Schensul, and M. Borrero, Introduction: The Hispanic Health Council, *Urban Anthropology, 11*:1, pp. 1-8, 1982.
76. J. Schensul et al., Urban Comadronas: Maternal and Child Health Research and Policy Formulation in a Puerto Rican Community, in *Collaborative Research and Social Change,* D. Stull and J. Schensul, (eds.), Westview Press, Boulder, pp. 9-32, 1987.
77. L. Allen et al., *Coping with Neonatal Intensive Care: The Puerto Rican Experience,* Hispanic Health Council, Hartford, 1988.
78. G. Damio and L. Cohen, *Policy Report of the Hartford Community Childhood Hunger Identification Project,* Hispanic Health Council, Hartford, 1990.
79. M. Singer et. al., Implementing a Community Based AIDS Prevention Program for Puerto Ricans: The Comunidad y Responsibilidad Project, in *Community Based Research and AIDS Prevention,* J. P. Van Vugt, (ed.), Bergin and Garvey Press, 1993.
80. M. Singer, R. Irizarry, and J. Schensul, Needle Access as an AIDS Prevention Strategy for IV Drug Users: A Research Perspective, *Human Organization,* 1991.
81. W. Freidland and D. Nelkin, *Migrant Agricultural Workers in America's Northeast,* Holt, Rinehart and Winston, New York, 1971.
82. W. K. Barger and E. Reza, Processes in Applied Sociocultural Change and the Farmworker Movement in the Midwest, *Human Organization, 44:*3, pp. 268-283, 1985.
83. W. K. Barger and E. Reza, Policy and Community-Action Research: The Farm Labor Movement in California, in *Making our Research Useful,* J. van Willigen, B. Rylko-Bauer and A. McElroy, (eds.), Westview Press, Boulder, pp. 258-282, 1989.
84. W. K. Barger and E. Reza, Community Action and Social Adaptation: The Farmworker Movement in the Midwest, in *Collaborative Research and Social Change,* D. Stull and J. Schensul, (eds.), Westview Press, Boulder, pp. 55-76, 1987.
85. F. M. Lappe, J. Collins, and D. Kinley, *AIDS as Obstacle,* Institute for Food and Development Policy, San Francisco, 1981.
86. K. Hastrup and P. Elsass, Anthropological Advocacy, *Current Anthropology, 31*:3, pp. 301-311, 1990.
87. G. Lichtheim, *Marxism in Modern France*, Columbia University Press, New York, 1966.

Topic Index

Adaptationism, 45, 46, 47

Advocacy, 362-366

African Americans, 70, 72, 89, 183, 188,
190, 196, 203, 208-213, 219,
273, 277-298

Agency versus structure, 101-102, 329-348

American Medical Association, 184, 187,
188, 189

Anthropology of medicine/health, 74, 372

Anthropology in medicine/health, 74, 372

Asiatic mode of production, 140

Biology and culture, 223

Blaming the victim, 77, 209, 225, 294

Biopsychosocial medicine, 353-354

Bourgeois/Biomedicine

coronary care/cardiovascular disease,
67, 72, 80, 209

class structure of, 69-70, 104, 190-192,
259, 364

defined, 37, 68

depoliticalization, 13, 21, 83, 359

doctor/patient relationship, 71, 72, 73,
83, 84, 86, 87-88, 100-102, 329-
348, 374-376

dominative status, 68, 69, 181-202

features, 3, 12, 17, 27, 30, 31, 59, 65-66,
81, 83, 86-87, 91, 99, 143-144,
196-198, 264-265, 339-346, 351-
370

emergence, 187-192

hospitals, 66, 67, 69, 72, 82, 359-362

iatrogenesis, 19, 32

magical characteristics, 254

medical-industrial complex, 65, 68

[Bourgeois/Biomedicine]

nursing, 70-71, 75

psychiatry, 43, 75-76, 80, 83-84, 88,
304, 357, 359

Capitalism, 23, 48, 49, 61, 64, 96, 157,
172, 182, 183, 308-310,
361-362

Clinically Applied Medical Anthropology,
26-27, 28, 351-370

Colonialism, 98-99, 225, 255, 373

Commitment, 123, 158

Critical Anthropology of Health Interest
Group, 44, 366

Critical medical anthropology defined, 5

Diagnostic and Statistical Manual, 4, 81

Displacement of social etiology, 77

Doctor bashing, 35, 358

Ethnocentrism, 17, 124

Ethnomedicine, 18, 23, 31, 41, 71, 100,
125, 183, 253-276, 277-298

culture bound syndromes, 4, 256-273

Ethnography, 14, 25, 65, 85, 117-120, 125-
128, 205-206, 267, 269-270,
311-312, 373-374

Explanatory models, 82, 362, 365, 375

Flexner report, 144, 188, 189, 192

Former Soviet Union, 37, 139, 140, 141,
142-145, 149, 358

German Revolution of 1848, 19-20

Health
  alcoholism, 94, 209-210, 301-328
  asbestosis, 94-95
  black lung disease, 93-94
  children's health, 78-79, 93, 149, 208,
      209, 210, 221, 226-227, 253-
      254, 380-383
  chlorosis, 93
  disease causation, 13, 78, 79, 91
  disease/illness distinction, 32, 97
  drug use, 210-212, 214, 216-219
  epidemics, 19, 78, 206-207, 226
  farm workers health, 384-387
  HIV/AIDS, 81, 92-93, 102, 203-234,
      255, 301, 377, 383
  hypoglycemia, 74
  injection drug use, 212, 214, 216-219,
      221, 226, 383
  malnutrition/hunger, 25, 96-97, 98, 208-
      209, 253-254, 259-260, 377
  malaria, 224
  privitization of health, 76, 95, 380
  reproductive health, 256-273, 332-342
  sexually transmitted diseases, 212-213
  social origins of health, 92, 95, 161,
      221, 224-225, 226
  somatization, 88, 89-90
  syndemic, 207-213, 227-228
  women's health, 35, 72, 75, 81, 89-90,
      93, 212, 213, 225-226, 256-273,
      332-348
Health maintenance organizations, 80, 342-
      343
Healthism, 79, 80
Hegemony, 27, 37, 61, 62, 81, 82, 83, 98,
      104, 123, 187, 189, 198, 253-
      276, 358, 387-388
Heterodox and alternative medical systems
  Anglo-American spiritualism, 195-196
  Ayurvedic medicine, 68, 181-182
  Chinese medicine, 68
  chiropractic, 181-182, 183, 186, 189,
      193-194, 197-198, 235, 236,
      242, 247, 363
  Christian Science healing, 182, 183,
      185, 195, 197
  eclecticism, 185, 186, 188, 189, 190
  Espiritismo/Santeria, 196, 277, 290
  homeopathy, 68, 184, 186, 188, 189,
      190, 236

[Heterodox and alternative medical
      systems]
  naturopathy, 181, 192, 194-195, 236,
      240, 241, 242, 243
  osteopathy, 182, 183, 186, 187, 189,
      190, 192-193, 196-198, 235-
      250, 360
  Thomsonianism, 184-185
  Uani medicine, 68
Hispanic Health Council, 7, 209, 215, 225,
      303, 380-384
Homophobia, 80-81, 213-214, 215
Homosexuality, 80-81, 214-216

Ideology, 62, 63, 82, 87, 127, 141, 187,
      248

Latinos/Hispanics, 70, 196, 203, 208-213,
      214-215, 219, 302-328, 380-383
Meaning and power, 38, 222, 266-273
Medical ecology, 45
Medical pluralism, 99, 181, 264-266
Medicalization, 31, 32, 33, 71, 80, 81, 303-
      305, 343
Mystification, 126

Native Americans/Indians, 70, 71, 160-
      161, 165, 166, 167, 171, 183,
      306-307
Nature, 45, 46, 48, 223
Nuclear industry, 157-178

Peoples Republic of China, 139, 146-147
Pharmaceutical industry, 66, 67, 78, 86, 99
Phenomenology, 5, 33, 44-45, 121, 362
  sufferer experience, 5, 73, 74, 83, 101,
      258-260, 265-266
Pollution, 24, 49, 150-151, 163-165, 167-
      168, 170, 364-365
Popular health movements, 165-178, 184,
      185
  gay health movement, 90-91
  holistic health movement, 195, 198,
      241, 364
  woman's health movement, 90, 377
Postmodernism, 113-131
Power, 206, 376, 378

Praxis, 104, 158-159, 228, 363-366, 371-389

Professionalization, 191-192, 236-237, 242-243, 244, 247

Puerto Rico, 204, 305-310

Racism, 16, 213, 322

Reification, 31, 75-76

Sick role, 84

Slavery, 16, 77, 94, 280

Social class and health, 61, 62, 77, 86, 93, 95, 99-101, 103, 190, 196, 204-205, 208-213, 226-227, 312-315, 374, 376, 379-380

Social control, 5, 83, 85

Socialist-oriented societies, 64, 135-155
  socialism defined, 136-137
  Stalinism, 141

Struggle, 89, 104, 376, 380

Tobacco industry, 78-79

Total institutions, 77

World economic system, 37, 64, 65, 71, 149-150

World medical system, 68

Name Index

Abad, V., 325
Abbotts, J., 177
Abdul-Quader, B., 230
Abelson, H., 327
Abercrombie, N., 62, 105
Ackerknecht, E., 22, 23, 52
Adorno, T., 119, 120
Aguirre-Molina, M., 311, 326
Aidoo, T., 111, 130
Albright, G., 199
Alexander, L., 355, 368
Allen, L., 392
Alvarez, M., 274
Ames, G., 324
Amin, S., 140, 153
Anastos, K., 92, 110
Anderson, B., 18, 51, 107
Anderson, N., 230
Anderson, R., 22
Anglin, M., 231
Appadurai, A., 205, 228
Aral, S., 231
Aries, N., 107
Armstrong, D., 354, 367
Aronson, B., 110
Arnold, C., 57, 107, 274, 347, 392
Arras, J., 227, 234

Baer, H., 7, 8, 9, 39, 41, 42, 55, 56, 57,
        105, 141, 152, 153, 158, 200,
        201, 228, 230, 244, 248, 249,
        250, 276, 278-279, 281, 284,
        297, 359, 360, 367, 368, 369,
        390

Bahro, R., 46, 58, 140, 153
Baldo, M., 224-225, 233
Bale, A., 108
Banerji, D., 130
Barger, K., 384-387, 392
Barker, D., 209, 228
Barnes, G., 327
Barnet, R., 48, 58, 327
Barnett, C., 356, 368
Bart, P., 56
Basaglia, F., 56
Bass, M., 109
Bassuck, E., 110
Bates, M., 57, 67, 106
Bateson, M., 233
Battjes, R., 230
Baudrillard, J., 119, 129
Bauman, Z., 125, 130
Beatty, W., 207, 229
Becker, H., 84
Benson, R., 347
Berliner, H., 183, 188, 198, 199, 200, 362,
        369
Beschner, G., 230
Best, S., 128
Bell, R., 177
Bellah, R., 61, 105
Benkert, K., 80
Berchtold, T., 248
Bergler, E., 108
Bettelheim, 140, 153
Biernacki, P., 233
Biggs, L., 201
Birenbaum, A., 106
Black, D., 127, 131

Blakey, M., 58
Bloch, M., 373, 389
Bloomfield, R., 247, 250
Blumhagen, D., 274
Bochner, S., 109
Bodley, J., 48, 58
Boggs, C., 276
Bolough, R., 364, 369
Bonfil Batalla, G., 130
Bonilla, F., 326, 378-379, 391
Borrero, M., 111, 200, 296, 390, 392
Bourne, P., 296
Bovelle, E., 218, 230, 232
Bowden, C., 97, 111
Bradley, W., 52
Brady, K., 249
Brandt, 207, 229
Breda, K., 276
Breen, J., 347
Brenner, H., 313, 327
Browdwin, P., 55, 275
Brown, E., 25, 34, 50, 187, 199
Brown, P., 364-365, 369
Browner, C., 4, 9
Bullough, V., 108
Bures, A., 106
Burke, G., 231, 325, 390
Burrow, J., 199
Burstein, A., 97, 111, 330, 346

Cabral, A., 224-225, 233
Caetano, R., 229, 328
Cahalan, D., 319, 328
Callinicos, A., 113, 128
Cameron, K., 153
Camilleri, J., 172, 177
Canino, G., 327
Canino, I., 327
Carey, J., 47, 48, 58, 374, 389
Carlson, R., 231
Carnoy, J., 347
Carrier, J., 214-215, 231
Carrion, A., 326
Cartwright, E., 78, 108
Cassell, E., 112
Caster, J., 54
Castillo, Z., 231, 325, 390
Caudill, W., 14, 51, 367
Caufield, M., 177
Cavanagh, J., 48, 58

Cereseto, S., 155
Cervantes, R., 325
Chafetz, M., 304, 325, 326
Chamberlin, R., 390
Chase-Dunn, C., 152
Chein, I., 230
Chomsky, N., 143, 154
Chrisman, N., 50, 54, 326, 353, 356, 358,
    362, 367, 389
Churchill, W., 177
Clark, M., 53
Clatts, M., 91-92, 110
Clawson, P., 152
Clemens, F., 52
Cliff, T., 153
Clifford, J., 116, 117, 118, 119, 120, 128,
    129, 131
Cloward, R., 378, 391
Cobb, J., 109, 312, 327
Coburn, D., 201
Cohen, C., 130
Cohen, J., 233
Cohen, M., 154, 199
Colby, B., 55
Coll, C., 326
Collins, J., 53, 387, 392
Comaroff, J., 131, 233, 266, 272-273, 275,
    346, 373, 387, 389
Commoner, B., 155
Connors, M., 233
Conrad, P., 55, 83, 107, 112, 325
Conover, S., 391
Conviser, R., 217, 232
Coombs, D., 311, 326
Cooper, R., 151, 155
Cosminsky, S., 262, 274
Coulter, H., 199
Coulter, I., 201
Cox, R., 142, 154
Craddock, D., 35, 56
Crandon-Malamud, L., 53, 85, 109, 199
Crapanzano, V., 115, 118, 129, 130
Crawford, R., 76, 79, 107, 209, 229
Crosby, A., 58, 223-224, 233
Crozier, R., 146, 154
Crutcher, J., 109
Csordas, T., 33, 34, 54
Cyriax, J., 250

Damio, G., 229, 392
Daniels, A., 94, 109

Danziger, S., 368
Darlingson, J., 249
Davies, P., 325
Davies, R., 155
Davila, R., 311, 315, 326
Davila, Y., 233
Davis, C., 154
Davis, D., 346
Davis-Floyd, R., 54, 344, 348
Davison, L., 96, 105, 231, 255, 325, 390
Day, R., 310, 326
Denny, J., 56, 108
de Beer, C., 54, 269, 275
de Cavallo, J., 111
De L Cancela, V., 326, 327
De Ropp, R., 304, 326
de Swaan, A., 55, 84, 109
Des Jarlais, D., 230, 232
Denzen, N., 240
Derber, C., 69, 106
Derrida, J., 105, 113
De Vries, R., 333, 344, 346
Dewalt, K., 53
DiGiacomo, S., 82-83, 85-86, 108
Diamond, M., 108
Diamond, S., 177
Discoll, L., 56
Domhoff, G., 153
Donahue, J., 43, 53, 57, 148, 155, 391
Donaldson, P., 249
Douglas, C., 390
Dove, C., 249
Doyal, L., 41, 106, 144, 152, 250, 376, 390
Dressler, W., 229
Dross, D., 108
Du Bois, W. E. B., 205, 228
Duden, B., 46, 58
Dwyer, K., 118

Early, E., 256, 274
Ebbin, S., 174, 175, 177
Eckberg, D., 200
Edelman, M., 229
Edelstein, M., 369
Ehrenreich, B., 89-90, 110, 200, 366, 390
Eisenberg, L., 102, 112, 372, 389
El-Sadr, W., 230
Elling, R., 37, 38, 39, 41, 53, 57, 108, 110,
    111, 141, 153, 200
Elsass, P., 392

Engel, G., 354, 367
English, D., 89-90, 110
Epstein, E., 72, 107
Epstein, P., 110
Erwin, D., 55
Escudero, J., 155
Estroff, S., 22, 52
Evans-Pritchard, E. E., 14, 22, 50
Eyer, J., 129
Ezell, J., 177

Fabrega, H., 267, 275
Falck, R., 231
Falder, S., 236, 249
Faris, J., 14, 51
Farmer, P., 97, 109, 110, 265, 274
Featherstone, M., 128
Fee, E., 228
Femia, L., 276
Ferguson, A., 105, 199
Ferris, J., 80
Feshbach, M., 154
Fiddle, S., 216, 232
Fife, W., 127, 131
Figlio, K., 34, 56, 93, 110
Filante, R., 313, 326
Firth, R., 3, 8, 15, 50
Fischer, M., 121, 128, 362, 369
Fisher, S., 56, 346
Fishman, R., 201
Fiske, S., 50, 371-372, 389
Fitchen, J., 208, 229
Fitzgerald, M., 57, 107, 274, 347, 392
Flexner, A., 200
Flitcraft, A., 50
Flores, C., 105, 231, 325, 390
Forsyth, G., 390
Foster, G., 18, 51, 52, 74, 107
Foucault, M., 44, 59, 92, 104, 364, 391
Fox, D., 228
Frank, A. G., 65
Frank, J., 293, 298
Frankenberg, R., 39, 40, 57, 99, 105, 111,
    130, 199, 271, 273, 274, 276,
    363, 369
Frazier, W., 50
Freed, R., 52
Freed, S., 52
Freedman, H., 207, 229
Freidland, W., 392

Freidson, E., 11, 50, 69, 84, 106, 244, 250
Freitag, P., 177
Fresia, J., 377, 391
Freudenberg, N., 216, 232, 369
Friedman, J., 275
Friedman, S., 216, 230, 232
Friendly, A., 154
Fuchs, V., 78, 108
Fuller, R., 199

Gaines, A., 9, 30, 51, 230, 275
Gallo, R., 81
Galston, I., 15, 50
Garcia, R., 390
Garret, G., 231
Garret, S., 107
Garrison, V., 296
Genovese, E., 61-62, 105
Gerdes, G., 255
Geertz, C., 82, 121, 130, 269, 275
Gerth, H., 328
Gervitz, N., 193, 200, 248
Giddens, A., 341, 346
Gilbert, M., 309, 324, 325
Gillies, E., 51
Gillum, R., 107
Ginsburg, F., 129
Glasser, M., 347
Glick, R., 230, 297
Glick Schiller, N., 219, 220, 232
Goffman, I., 77, 93, 107, 110
Golde, P., 355, 367, 368
Goldsby, R., 233
Goldsmith, D., 230
Goldstein, M., 202, 249
Gondolf, E., 353, 367
Gonzalez, A., 391
Good, B., 54, 58, 274, 275, 345, 348
Good, M-J., 54, 275
Gordon, A., 311, 324
Gordon, D., 50, 58, 200, 275
Gorz, A., 46, 58, 141, 153, 355-356, 368,
      378, 379, 391
Gough, I., 250
Gould, R., 155
Gould, S., 61, 105, 124, 130, 345, 348
Gouldner, A., 141, 153
Goulet, D., 53
Graff, S., 42
Graham, H., 347

Gramsci, A., 5, 35, 56, 187, 192, 270-272
Gray, B., 68, 106
Greenwood, D., 54
Greisman, H., 298
Griffith, J., 107
Gruenbaum, E., 111
Gudeman, S., 121, 130
Guttmacher, S., 391

Habermas, J., 115, 126, 130, 375,
      390
Haddon, A., 16, 50
Haddon, A., 51
Hahn, R., 9, 30, 35, 51, 56, 200, 231, 275,
      346
Hakken, D., 129
Hall, A., 296
Hall, O., 201
Hall, T., 248
Hallat, J., 346
Haller, J., 199
Hamilton, V., 85, 109
Hannerz, U., 230
Hanson, B., 211, 230
Haraway, D., 129
Harries-Jenkins, G., 236, 249
Harris, M., 18, 50, 143, 154
Harrison, I., 100, 112
Harwood, A., 296, 346
Hastrup, K., 392
Haug, M., 145, 152
Haynes, R., 109
Heath, D., 324, 325, 326
Heggenhougen, K., 12, 32, 50, 363, 369
Helvacioglu, E., 346
Henderson, G., 154
Henriquez, J., 155
Henry, J., 83, 109
Herskovits, M., 11-12, 50, 54
Herd, D., 210, 230
Herdt, G., 219, 228
Herrero, J., 326
Hertsgaard, M., 177
Hill, C., 249
Hills, S., 62, 86, 105, 109
Hiltgartner, S., 177
Himmelstein, D., 105, 131, 369, 391
Hochschild, A., 88, 109
Holmes, K., 231
Honigsbaum, F., 250

Hope, K., 229
Hopper, K., 391
House, J., 109
Hrdlicka, A., 52
Hu, T., 154
Huang, S., 154
Hudson, M., 53
Hughes, C., 4, 9, 51
Hunt, J., 15-16, 51
Hunter, S., 24, 26, 51
Hurston, Z., 297
Huyssen, A., 116, 129
Hyman, H., 391
Hyatt, H., 296

Iglehart, I., 216, 218, 232
Illich, I., 32, 55, 331, 346
Illsley, R., 154
Inciardi, J., 217, 230, 231
Ingman, S., 38, 57
Inglis, B., 249
Inkels, C., 155
Irizarry, R., 325, 393
Irvine, J., 123, 130

Jackson, D., 229
Jackson, J., 242, 249
Jacobs, C., 294, 297, 298
Jacobson, M., 111
Jacobson, R., 391
Jahn, J., 274
Jameson, E., 118, 129
Janzen, J., 39, 41, 57, 199, 257, 274
Jelliffee, D., 274
Jellinek, E., 303
Jencks, C., 117, 129
Jessor, R., 316, 327
Jia, Z., 230, 232
Johnsen, J., 9, 42, 57, 105, 141, 152, 153
Johnson, T., 43, 54, 58, 67, 106, 351-352,
        353, 357, 358, 359, 362, 363,
        367, 368, 369
Jones, Y., 228
Jordan, B., 25, 53, 347
Jordan, W., 296
Joseph, S., 233

Kane, S., 213, 214, 219, 232

Kantor, D., 201
Kapferer, B., 4, 9, 33, 54
Kaser, M., 52
Kaslow, A., 297
Kasper, R., 174, 175, 177
Katon, W., 354, 358, 367, 374, 389, 390
Katz, P., 107
Kaufman, L., 367
Kaufman, M., 188, 200
Keesing, R., 105, 136, 153, 256, 268, 269,
        274, 275, 324, 328
Kellner, D., 128
Kelman, S., 110
Kelner, M., 201
Kemper, V., 56, 108
Kendall, C., 25, 53, 371, 389
Kendell, R., 325
Kennedy, L., 107
Kessler, R., 109
Kiev, A., 52, 296
Kinley, D., 53, 387, 392
Kirmayer, L., 55, 83, 109
Kirsch, M., 110, 390
Kleinman, A., 26, 52, 53, 54, 82, 88, 108,
        109, 200, 268, 275, 343, 346,
        352, 353, 354, 357, 358, 368,
        372, 374, 375, 376, 389, 390
Kline, A., 233
Kluckhohn, C., 267, 275
Knox, R., 229
Konner, M., 12, 35, 37, 50, 77-78, 95,
        108, 110, 358, 368
Koos, E., 201
Kopstein, A., 210, 211, 230
Kotarba, J., 121, 130, 200
Krause, E., 69, 71, 100, 105, 135, 152,
        191, 200, 237, 249, 361,
        369
Kroeber, A., 267, 275
Kuhn, T., 104
Kuna, R., 297
Kundstadler, P., 53
Kuper, A., 14, 51

La Barre, W., 52
LaDuke, W., 177
Laguerre, M., 274, 296
Laing, F., 346
Landaur, G., 38
Landy, D., 28, 29, 30, 51, 53

Lane, D., 141, 152, 153, 154
Lappe, F., 387, 392
Larkin, G., 197, 201, 239, 243, 246, 249
Larson, M., 191, 200, 236-237, 243, 249
Lasker, J., 98-99, 111
Lawson, J., 151, 155
Lazarus, E., 62, 72, 105, 107, 152, 342-
    343, 347, 375, 390
Leacock, E., 122
Leacock, R., 297
Leacock, S., 297
Leatherman, T., 48
Leavitt, J., 346
Leeson, J., 111
Leighton, A., 52
Leighton, D., 52
Leslie, C., 39, 42, 50, 199, 242,
    249
Lesser, A., 19, 52
Lessinger, H., 129
Lett, J., 131
Levine, M., 231
Levin, L., 390
Levine, R., 177
Levins, R., 46, 58
Levy, J., 199
Lewellen, T., 112
Lewonton, R., 46, 58
Lichtheim, G., 392
Lieban, R., 50
Liem, J., 109
Liem, R., 109
Light, D., 154
Lin, V., 151, 155
Lincoln, M., 324
Lindenbaum, S., 54, 234
Linder, R., 91
Lipton, D., 231
Lock, M., 9, 31, 44, 54, 55, 108, 200, 275,
    328
Long, T., 152
Lorau, R., 36, 57
Lorber, J., 109
Lovell, A., 9, 43, 55, 391
Lukac, G., 76
Lyng, S., 354, 365, 368
Lyotard, J-F., 113, 127, 129

Madden, L., 57, 107, 274, 347, 392
Madsen, W., 296

Magaña, R., 231
Magubane, B., 14, 51
Makela, K., 327
Maldonado-Denis, M., 310, 326
Marlin, J., 230
Mandel, E., 139, 153
Manners, R., 228
Mannheim, K., 38
Manning, R., 249
Marcus, G., 119, 121, 128, 129, 143, 152,
    362, 369
Maretski, T., 50, 356, 362-363, 367, 389
Margolese, M., 108
Marieskind, H., 390
Marks, G., 207, 229
Marte, C., 92, 110
Martin, E., 31, 55, 104, 105, 228, 340, 347
Marx, K. and Engels, F., 5, 16, 20, 21, 41,
    42, 46, 59, 60, 62, 76, 88, 94,
    95, 110, 127, 136, 137, 157,
    177, 270, 296, 298, 302, 309,
    325, 326, 327, 328, 343, 347,
    376
Mascia-Lees, F., 126, 130
Maslansky, R., 230
Mason, T., 214, 231
Matthews, J., 360, 369
Mauge, C., 230
Maxwell, B., 111
Mayers, S., 298
McCarthy, K., 297
McClain, C., 201
McCombie, S., 206, 228
McCord, C., 207, 229
McCorkle, T., 199
McCornac, D., 313, 326
McDermott, K., 99, 111
McGowan, D., 131
McGurie, M., 111, 201
McKeon, L., 249
McKeowan, T., 51
McKinlay, J., 111, 157, 177, 323, 328,
    341, 347
McKnight, J., 391
McLean, A., 42
McNeill, W., 97, 111
McQueen, D., 240, 247
Mechanic, D., 69, 106
Mendenhall, C., 328
Mensentseva, E., 155
Merrick, T., 111

Messing, S., 298
Metraux, A., 297
Meyers, F., 116, 129
Mikkelsen, E., 365, 369
Miliband, R., 153
Mill, J., 16
Millard, A., 54
Millard, F., 154
Miller, D., 325
Miller, H., 229, 231, 324
Millman, M., 86, 109, 337, 347
Mills, C. W., 42, 88, 109, 313-314, 327, 328
Minton, L., 112
Mintz, S., 122, 222, 228, 258, 274, 307, 312, 323, 326, 328
Mishler, E., 32, 55, 275
Mithun, J., 292, 297
Moerman, D., 55
Montagnier, L., 81
Moore, J., 53
Mora, J., 324
More, T., 38
Morgan, L., 43, 56, 58, 346, 354, 366, 368, 372, 389
Morgen, S., 90, 110, 390
Morsy, S., 41, 55, 57, 62, 63, 104, 105, 130, 233
Moses, L., 229, 231
Muchler, K., 91-92, 110
Mulford, H., 325
Mull, D., 36, 56
Mull, J., 36, 53, 56
Muller, R., 327
Munro, R., 236, 249
Muramoto, N., 108
Murphy, J., 297
Murphy, R., 125, 130
Murray, S., 9, 112, 256-258, 262, 274

Nadar, L., 157, 177, 159
Nadar, R., 177
Nash, J., 110, 122, 390
Navarro, V., 41, 50, 57, 69, 106, 136, 137, 141, 152, 153, 154, 181, 182, 187-188, 190, 199, 200, 229, 245, 250, 341-342, 347, 358, 361, 366, 368, 369, 378, 390
Nelkin, D., 231, 392

Nersesian, W., 229
New, P., 43, 57, 192, 200, 297
Newman, M., 96, 111
Nichter, M., 50, 78, 108, 254, 274
Nobel, D., 327
Norwood, C., 110
Novak, V., 56, 108
Novick, L., 226-227, 233

Oakley, A., 347
O'Conner, J., 58
O'Conner, R., 177
O'Neil, J., 53, 71, 72, 107
O'Reilly, B., 106
Onoge, O., 41, 123, 130, 273, 275
Opler, M., 52
Oppenheimer, G., 213-214, 231
Ortiz De Monellano, B., 4, 9
Ortner, S., 205, 228, 373, 389
Osherson, S., 314, 327
Overby, P., 56, 108
Owens, C., 130

Packard, R., 27, 53
Padgett, D., 359, 363, 368, 369
Padilla, E., 228
Page, J. B., 217, 232, 325
Panitch, L., 153
Pappas, G., 85, 109, 314, 327, 329, 346, 375, 390
Parenti, M., 153
Parker, G., 110
Parker, R., 231
Parmeless, D., 154
Parson, H., 58
Parsons, T., 83-84, 109
Patton, C., 110, 112
Paul, B., 24, 52
Paul, J., 65, 106
Payne, K., 9, 22, 112
Pearlin, L., 313, 327
Pelto, G., 53, 347, 372, 389
Pelto, P., 371, 372, 389
Pendleton, D., 109
Penk, W., 231
Pfifferling, J., 54
Pflanz, M., 74, 107, 372, 389

Phillips, M., 354, 355, 359-360, 367
Pickens, R., 230
Pitchenik, A., 274
Piven, F., 378, 391
Podhorzer, M., 56
Poirier-Bures, S., 106
Polgar, S., 14, 26, 51
Pollner, M., 105
Press, I., 17, 51, 262, 274, 356, 368
Price, J., 177
Primm, B., 230
Prince, R., 259, 274
Puckett, N., 296
Puttick, R., 249

Quan, R., 201

Rabinow, P., 52, 59, 104, 129
Raboteau, A., 296
Rachal, J., 316, 327
Radabaugh, C., 313, 327
Radebaugh, J., 390
Radnitzky, G., 60, 105
Raffel, N., 154
Rapp, R., 55
Raskhe, R., 177
Rebel, H., 130
Reed, L., 195, 201
Relman, A., 67-68, 106
Rettig, R., 232
Reverby, S., 71, 107
Rey, I., 105
Reza, E., 384-387, 392
Rhodes (AmaraSingham), L., 11, 50, 104, 275, 314, 327
Ricoeur, P., 117
Rimachevskaya, N., 155
Riska, E., 28, 54, 356, 360, 361, 368, 369
Rivera, A., 121, 130
Rivera, M., 105, 231
Rivers, W. H. R., 16-17, 18, 21, 50
Roberts, H., 34-35, 56, 107
Rodriquez, C., 326
Rodriquez-Trias, H., 106
Roebuck, J., 201
Rogers, E., 230
Rolph, E., 177

Roseberry, W., 130, 204, 222, 228, 233, 272, 347, 390
Rosengren, W., 70, 106
Rosenwaike, I., 327
Rosett, J., 233
Ross, W., 110
Roth, J., 112, 200, 357, 367
Roth, P., 210, 211, 230
Rothchild, E., 56
Rothman, B., 348
Rothstein, W., 184, 185, 186, 199
Rubel, A., 4, 9, 296
Rudd, P., 390
Rutledge, R., 217, 232
Ryan, W., 77, 107
Rychards, A., 145, 152

Sackett, D., 109
Sahlins, M., 64, 105, 267, 275, 373, 389
Salmon, J., 198, 199, 201, 369
Salzman, P., 129
Sanders, D., 155, 379, 391
Sangren, P., 126, 129
Sanoval, M., 296
Sargent, C., 58, 348
Saville, J., 153
Sayer, D., 84, 109
Scalon, K., 231
Schaefer, J., 304, 325
Schatzkin, A., 151, 155
Scheder, J., 384, 391
Scheele, R., 228
Scheider, J., 55, 83, 107, 325
Schell, L., 54
Schensul, J., 325, 390, 392
Schensul, S., 390, 392
Scheper-Hughes, N., 9, 26, 31, 43, 44, 45, 53, 55, 57, 96-97, 103-104, 111, 112, 328, 346, 363, 369, 390, 391
Schioetz, E., 250
Schmitt, M., 201
Schroder, B., 392
Schoepf, B., 100, 112, 225, 233, 374, 389
Scholte, B., 105
Schrimshaw, N., 262, 274
Schwartz, J., 141, 153

Scotch, N., 28, 50, 275, 367
Scott, C., 296
Scott, J., 390
Scully, D., 56, 109
Seeman, M., 313, 327
Segal, D., 107
Segall, M., 43, 57, 135, 152
Selwyn, P., 231
Sennett, R., 109, 312, 327
Serrano, M., 105
Sharma, S., 200
Sharma, U., 245, 248, 249
Sharpe, P., 130
Shaw, J., 80
Sherman, H., 141, 152, 153
Shiloh, A., 352-353, 367
Shilts, R., 233
Shimkin, D., 355, 367
Shostack, M., 118
Sibthrope, B., 226, 233
Sidel, R. and V. Sidel, 57, 69, 106, 144,
        146-147, 154
Siegal, H., 231
Sigerist, N., 52, 93, 154
Silkwood, K., 161-163, 169
Silver, G., 153
Silverblatt, I., 262, 274
Simons, R., 4, 9
Simpson, G., 297
Singer, M., 6, 7-8, 9, 34, 55, 56, 57,
        58, 73, 105, 107, 108, 111,
        141, 152, 153, 158, 177,
        199, 201, 207, 208, 215, 228,
        229, 230, 231, 232, 233, 255,
        257, 258, 274, 276, 296, 324,
        325, 347, 368, 389, 390, 391,
        392
Singer, P., 297
Skipper, J., 200
Smart, R., 327
Smith, B., 110
Smith, C., 392
Smith, H., 106
Snipes, C., 229
Snow, L., 201, 277, 296, 297
Snyder, A., 231
Sokolowska, M., 145, 152
Sorenson, J., 231
Sothern, J., 230, 232
Southall, A., 346
Spaulding, H., 58

Stack, C., 297
Stall, R., 324
Stark, A., 54
Stark, E., 50, 80, 81, 95, 108, 347, 392
Stark, N., 348
Starn, O., 58
Starr, P., 347
Stavenhagen, R., 362, 369
Stebbins, K., 34, 56, 108, 111, 325
Stein, H., 354, 355, 360, 362, 367, 368,
        369
Stein, L., 106
Stepherson, B., 230
Sternberg, D., 200
Steward, D., 347
Steward, H., 296
Steward, J., 228
Steward, K., 129
Stimson, G., 231
Stimpson, G., 347
Stocking, G., 51
Stone, D., 219-220, 232
Strang, J., 231
Strathern, M., 114, 128
Straus, R., 74, 112
Strelnick, H., 106
Struik, D., 51
Stubbs, J., 155
Strupp, H., 298
Sullivan, T., 347
Susser, I., 105, 379, 391
Sweezy, P., 140-141, 153
Swendenburg, T., 131
Szymanski, 138, 153, 158, 175, 177
Szasz, T., 80-81, 108

Tabb, W., 153
Tallant, R., 297
Tarpinian, G., 153
Taussig, M., 25, 27, 53, 75-76, 82, 96,
        103, 105, 111, 115, 118, 120,
        125, 129, 253-254, 255, 274,
        343, 346, 359, 368
Taylor, A., 218, 232
Taylor, R., 109
Teal, D., 108
Tedeschi, P., 107
Tess, D., 126, 131
Thomas, A., 38, 43, 57
Thomas, B., 48

Todd, H., 53
Tomas, D., 130
Topley, M., 111
Torres, M., 231
Torrey, E., 197, 291
Trachenberg, S., 129
Treichler, P., 92, 110, 221, 223, 232
Trostle, J., 87, 109
Trotter, R., 317, 325
Tucker, R., 152
Turner, B., 53, 62, 105, 107, 361, 369,
    391
Turner, C., 229, 231, 324
Turner, J., 109
Turner, V., 293, 297
Turshen, M., 58, 98, 111, 370
Tyler, S., 115, 118, 119, 129, 130

Ulbright, P., 109
Ungar, S., 106

Valdes-Brito, J., 155
Valentin, F., 230
Valentine, C., 297
Vallette, J., 58
van der Geest, S., 55, 106
von Legat, C., 57, 107, 274, 347, 391
Von Mering, O., 352
Vickery, D., 15
Virchow, R., 19-21, 62, 356, 379
Viten-Johansen, P., 28, 54, 256, 360,
    368

Wagenheim, K., 326
Wagner, R., 266, 275
Wagoner, J., 110
Waitzkin, H., 20, 27, 36, 41, 50, 52, 54,
    56, 67, 85, 105, 106, 108, 109,
    110, 130, 152, 187, 200, 274,
    343-344, 347, 348, 357, 361,
    365-366, 368, 369, 370, 375,
    377, 390, 391
Waldorf, D., 211, 218, 230, 232
Wallace, A., 268, 275
Wallace, R., 227, 228, 229

Wallerstein, I., 64, 65, 105, 139, 153
Ward, T., 230
Wardwell, W., 199, 201, 248
Warheit, G., 109
Washington, J., 297
Waterman, B., 108, 369
Watters, J., 233
Weaver, J., 107, 347
Weber, M., 61, 82
Weidman, H., 54, 265, 274, 296,
    367
Weise, G., 199
Wellin, E., 17, 23, 51
Welte, J., 327
Wenneker, M., 72, 107
Wertz, D., 346
Wertz, R., 346
Westbrooks, B., 200
Weyler, R., 177
White, M., 200
Whiteford, L., 53, 111
Whitehead, T., 43
Whitten, N., 297
Whorton, J., 201
Whyte, S., 55, 106
Wild, P., 201
Wilensky, H., 236, 242, 249
Wiley, A., 124, 130, 233, 372, 389
Williams, R., 45, 58
Williamson, L., 52
Willis, E., 191, 200
Wilson, B., 201
Wilson, J., 298
Wilson, P. 107
Wilson, R., 327
Wnuk-Lipinski, E., 154
Wohl, S., 347
Wolf, E., 17, 51, 57, 59, 65, 82, 104,
    106, 122, 206, 228, 270,
    272-273, 276, 373-374, 376,
    389, 390
Wolpe, P., 202
Wood, C., 111
Wood, J., 141, 153, 230
Woolgar, S., 105
Woolhandler, S., 105, 131, 369, 391
Worth, D., 233
Wright, A., 351, 352, 367
Wright, E., 152, 155
Wright, R., 35, 56
Wulff, R., 50, 371-372, 389

Yang, P., 151, 155
Yih, K., 48, 58
Young, A., 30, 40, 41, 54, 57, 108, 359, 368
Younge, R., 106

Zaidi, S., 111
Zimbardo, P., 36, 56
Zimmerman, R., 109
Zola, I., 76-77, 80, 84, 107, 108
Zorbaugh, H., 230